Active Server Pages Bible

Active Server Pages Bible

Eric Smith

IDG Books Worldwide, Inc.
An International Data Group Company

Foster City, CA ✦ Chicago, IL ✦ Indianapolis, IN ✦ New York, NY

Active Server Pages Bible

Published by
IDG Books Worldwide, Inc.
An International Data Group Company
919 E. Hillsdale Blvd., Suite 400
Foster City, CA 94404
www.idgbooks.com (IDG Books Worldwide
Web site)

ISBN: 0-7645-4599-X

Printed in the United States of America

10 9 8 7 6 5 4 3 2 1

1O/QX/RS/ZZ/FC

Distributed in the United States by IDG Books
Worldwide, Inc.

Distributed by CDG Books Canada Inc. for Canada; by
Transworld Publishers Limited in the United
Kingdom; by IDG Norge Books for Norway; by IDG
Sweden Books for Sweden; by IDG Books Australia
Publishing Corporation Pty. Ltd. for Australia and
New Zealand; by TransQuest Publishers Pte Ltd. for
Singapore, Malaysia, Thailand, Indonesia, and Hong
Kong; by Gotop Information Inc. for Taiwan; by ICG
Muse, Inc. for Japan; by Intersoft for South Africa; by
Eyrolles for France; by International Thomson
Publishing for Germany, Austria and Switzerland; by
Distribuidora Cuspide for Argentina; by LR
International for Brazil; by Galileo Libros for Chile; by
Ediciones ZETA S.C.R. Ltda. for Peru; by WS
Computer Publishing Corporation, Inc., for the
Philippines; by Contemporanea de Ediciones for
Venezuela; by Express Computer Distributors for the
Caribbean and West Indies; by Micronesia Media
Distributor, Inc. for Micronesia; by Chips
Computadoras S.A. de C.V. for Mexico; by Editorial
Norma de Panama S.A. for Panama; by American
Bookshops for Finland.

For general information on IDG Books Worldwide's
books in the U.S., please call our Consumer Customer
Service department at 800-762-2974. For reseller
information, including discounts and premium sales,
please call our Reseller Customer Service
department at 800-434-3422.

For information on where to purchase IDG Books
Worldwide's books outside the U.S., please contact
our International Sales department at 317-596-5530 or
fax 317-596-5692.

For consumer information on foreign language
translations, please contact our Customer Service
department at 800-434-3422, fax 317-596-5692, or
e-mail rights@idgbooks.com.

For information on licensing foreign or domestic
rights, please phone +1-650-655-3109.

For sales inquiries and special prices for bulk
quantities, please contact our Sales department at
650-655-3200 or write to the address above.

For information on using IDG Books Worldwide's
books in the classroom or for ordering examination
copies, please contact our Educational Sales
department at 800-434-2086 or fax 317-596-5499.

For press review copies, author interviews, or other
publicity information, please contact our Public
Relations department at 650-655-3000 or fax
650-655-3299.

For authorization to photocopy items for corporate,
personal, or educational use, please contact
Copyright Clearance Center, 222 Rosewood Drive,
Danvers, MA 01923, or fax 978-750-4470.

Library of Congress Cataloging-in-Publication Data
Smith, Eric A., 1970-
    Active server pages bible / Eric A. Smith.
      p. cm.
    ISBN 0-7645-4599-X
    1. Active server pages. 2. Web sites. 3. Web
servers–Computer programs. I.Title.
TK5105.8885.A26 S64   1999
005.2'76–dc21   99-052736
                                   CIP

ABOUT IDG BOOKS WORLDWIDE

Welcome to the world of IDG Books Worldwide.

IDG Books Worldwide, Inc., is a subsidiary of International Data Group, the world's largest publisher of computer-related information and the leading global provider of information services on information technology. IDG was founded more than 30 years ago by Patrick J. McGovern and now employs more than 9,000 people worldwide. IDG publishes more than 290 computer publications in over 75 countries. More than 90 million people read one or more IDG publications each month.

Launched in 1990, IDG Books Worldwide is today the #1 publisher of best-selling computer books in the United States. We are proud to have received eight awards from the Computer Press Association in recognition of editorial excellence and three from Computer Currents' First Annual Readers' Choice Awards. Our best-selling ...For Dummies® series has more than 50 million copies in print with translations in 31 languages. IDG Books Worldwide, through a joint venture with IDG's Hi-Tech Beijing, became the first U.S. publisher to publish a computer book in the People's Republic of China. In record time, IDG Books Worldwide has become the first choice for millions of readers around the world who want to learn how to better manage their businesses.

Our mission is simple: Every one of our books is designed to bring extra value and skill-building instructions to the reader. Our books are written by experts who understand and care about our readers. The knowledge base of our editorial staff comes from years of experience in publishing, education, and journalism — experience we use to produce books to carry us into the new millennium. In short, we care about books, so we attract the best people. We devote special attention to details such as audience, interior design, use of icons, and illustrations. And because we use an efficient process of authoring, editing, and desktop publishing our books electronically, we can spend more time ensuring superior content and less time on the technicalities of making books.

You can count on our commitment to deliver high-quality books at competitive prices on topics you want to read about. At IDG Books Worldwide, we continue in the IDG tradition of delivering quality for more than 30 years. You'll find no better book on a subject than one from IDG Books Worldwide.

John Kilcullen
Chairman and CEO
IDG Books Worldwide, Inc.

Steven Berkowitz
President and Publisher
IDG Books Worldwide, Inc.

WINNER

*Eighth Annual
Computer Press
Awards ≥1992*

WINNER

*Ninth Annual
Computer Press
Awards ≥1993*

WINNER

*Tenth Annual
Computer Press
Awards ≥1994*

WINNER

*Eleventh Annual
Computer Press
Awards ≥1995*

IDG is the world's leading IT media, research and exposition company. Founded in 1964, IDG had 1997 revenues of $2.05 billion and has more than 9,000 employees worldwide. IDG offers the widest range of media options that reach IT buyers in 75 countries representing 95% of worldwide IT spending. IDG's diverse product and services portfolio spans six key areas including print publishing, online publishing, expositions and conferences, market research, education and training, and global marketing services. More than 90 million people read one or more of IDG's 290 magazines and newspapers, including IDG's leading global brands — Computerworld, PC World, Network World, Macworld and the Channel World family of publications. IDG Books Worldwide is one of the fastest-growing computer book publishers in the world, with more than 700 titles in 36 languages. The "...For Dummies®" series alone has more than 50 million copies in print. IDG offers online users the largest network of technology-specific Web sites around the world through IDG.net (http://www.idg.net), which comprises more than 225 targeted Web sites in 55 countries worldwide. International Data Corporation (IDC) is the world's largest provider of information technology data, analysis and consulting, with research centers in over 41 countries and more than 400 research analysts worldwide. IDG World Expo is a leading producer of more than 168 globally branded conferences and expositions in 35 countries including E3 (Electronic Entertainment Expo), Macworld Expo, ComNet, Windows World Expo, ICE (Internet Commerce Expo), Agenda, DEMO, and Spotlight. IDG's training subsidiary, ExecuTrain, is the world's largest computer training company, with more than 230 locations worldwide and 785 training courses. IDG Marketing Services helps industry-leading IT companies build international brand recognition by developing global integrated marketing programs via IDG's print, online and exposition products worldwide. Further information about the company can be found at www.idg.com.   1/24/99

Credits

Acquisitions Editor
John Osborn

Development Editors
Barbra Guerra
Matthew E. Lusher

Technical Editor
Tom Hsieh

Copy Editors
Eric Hahn
Amy Eoff

Project Coordinators
Linda Marousek
Joe Shines

Graphics and Production Specialists
Mario Amador
Stephanie Hollier
Jude Levinson
Dina Quan
Ramses Ramirez

Quality Control Specialist
Chris Weisbart

Book Designer
Drew Moore

Proofreading and Indexing
York Production Services

Cover Illustration
Andreas Schueller

About the Author

Eric A. Smith is an independent consultant who lives in the Washington, D.C. area. He is a Microsoft Certified Solution Developer and works extensively in both Web and traditional client/server environments. He has written, edited, or contributed to eight books in the Visual Basic and Web markets.

Mr. Smith is also the owner of both the VB Techniques Web site (http://vbtechniques.com) and the ASP Techniques Web site (http://asptechniques.com). These sites are used to provide "service after the sale" to his readers. You can get updated code and related articles for all of his books at these sites. He is also the creator of inquiry.com's Ask the VB Pro site, now part of Fawcette Technical Publications.

Mr. Smith is active at his church and is a volunteer Emergency Medical Technician for the Fairfax County Fire and Rescue Department. If you'd like to contact him with questions about the book, you can reach him via e-mail at aspbible@asptechniques.com.

To my wife, Jodi

Preface

Building Web applications has certainly evolved since the advent of graphical browsers. Sites have evolved from plain, gray backgrounds with static content to highly adaptable, personalized content. Some sites have even gone so far as to create predictive content; that is, content based on your past selections. Sites feature everything from complex e-commerce stores to threaded discussion forums capable of handling thousands or millions of messages.

All of these features are great; however, someone has to program them. Very few Web-based applications are shrink-wrapped and distributed as complete packages. In most cases, you have to combine these applications into a coherent application yourself. That's what you'll use this book for. This book is designed to give you the tools and some useful techniques for building robust, complex applications that take advantage of performance improvements in a number of different ways.

All of these applications can be built using the technology known as Active Server Pages. Active Server Pages is a platform originally designed for use with Microsoft's Internet Information Server. Other tools enable the use of ASP on other platforms now, but we won't be covering those tools. ASP provides some programming objects and can be used with Javascript or VBScript. Javascript is a popular language for client-side scripting, because it is supported on both Netscape's and Microsoft's Web browsers. For server-side programming (which this book focuses on almost exclusively), we'll be using VBScript. VBScript is a derivative of Visual Basic's language but doesn't have as many features as VB itself. The language is easy to learn and is well suited for working in the ASP environment.

How to Get Started

If you're like me, you learn by doing. Almost all of the chapters have examples that you can build as you read. This is really the best way to learn, since you'll learn from any mistakes you might make along the way. To make it easier for you to see the examples in action, all of the examples are running live at my Web site, ASP Techniques (http://www.asptechniques.com). Instead of just looking at dull screen shots, you can see the applications working. This lets you experiment with the behavior of the application and see how data is moving from one section to another.

Besides working examples, you can also download the code from the ASP Techniques Web site. Because my readers often suggest improvements, Web distribution seemed like a better way to make the code available. You can also get any updates to the code since the book was written.

You'll also find other resources at ASP Techniques, as well as my site for Visual Basic, VB Techniques (http://www.vbtechniques.com). You'll see how much ASP and VB work together (especially in large applications), and you'll get good information, articles, reviews, and tips at both sites.

Assembling Your Tools

You'll need some software tools to build the applications in this book. Depending on your desktop environment, you will need different tools. Here is the minimum set of software tools you'll need for each environment:

Windows 95/98

✦ Personal Web Server

✦ A Web browser

✦ A text editor

✦ A database system, such as Microsoft Access

The database is optional; however, most applications need a permanent data storage area to be useful. Since ASP pages are just plain text files, any text editor (including Notepad) will do. You might want to look into getting a copy of Visual InterDev from Microsoft or HomeSite 4.0 from Allaire, since both tools can help you develop your ASP code. HomeSite does a good job of managing multiple files on remote servers, but InterDev provides IntelliSense which gives you drop-down lists of objects, properties, methods, and keywords. I personally have both and use them interchangeably.

Another thing you'll learn is that ASP pages eventually evaluate out to plain HTML. For this reason, you can use either browser to view your ASP pages. I'm partial to Internet Explorer, but I keep both installed on my machine so I can check how pages load in different browsers. Again, it's a personal preference and both will work fine.

Windows NT 4.0 Workstation

✦ Peer Web Services

✦ A text editor

✦ A database system (SQL Server, Access, etc.)

Windows NT 4.0 Server

✦ Internet Information Server

✦ A text editor

✦ A database system (SQL Server, Access, etc.)

Windows 2000

The best part about ASP is that very few things are changing with the introduction of Windows 2000 and Internet Information Server 5.0. All of the code in this book will work in IIS 5 and W2K. Depending on the version of Windows 2000 you get, you'll need to install the appropriate Web services. Refer to the ASP Techniques Web site for updates on Windows 2000 as they are made available.

Parts of the Book

To make it easier to use, the book is divided into several parts. These parts are described here for you.

Part 1: Language Tools (Chapters 1-3)

Because ASP works with HTML, the first part of the book will give you the HTML essentials you need to work in this book. These chapters will also cover the concepts of the VBScript language.

Part 2: ASP Concepts (Chapters 4-9)

Web programming is done quite differently from traditional client/server computing. This section will show you how to use Web programming concepts and integrate those concepts with the use of the ASP engine. You'll learn about all of the built-in objects and how to make the most of each one.

Part 3: Integrating with Databases (Chapters 10-14)

Because ASP was originally designed to make it easier to publish data from a database, we spend quite a bit of time on building applications that publish database tables and queries. You'll build several commonly used applications in these chapters, and the core code from each of these applications will be used in nearly every application you build.

Part 4: Integrating with Other Tools (Chapters 15-18)

ASP has the benefit of being able to use other components, libraries, and tools. These chapters show you how to work with Index Server, Visual Basic, and Microsoft Transaction Server.

Part 5: Building a Real-World Application (Chapter 19)

The final chapter in the book is a start-to-finish application design and development session. The concepts introduced here are not difficult, but the chapter is designed to show you how to go from idea to finished application.

Conventions Used in This Book

There are a number of typographic conventions in this book used to identify certain types of information. You'll find that words or characters you're instructed to type or enter will be in **bold**. Elements of program code, as well as URLs and email addresses, appear in monospace font: for example, `http://msdn.microsoft.com` or the `Variant` data type.

Monospace font is also used to format code listings — one or more lines of program code. Here's an example:

```
Function OpenDatabase()

    Dim dcnDB        ' As ADODB.Connection
    Set dcnDB = Server.CreateObject("ADODB.Connection")
    dcnDB.ConnectionString = _
        "Provider=Microsoft.Jet.OLEDB.3.51;" _
          & "Persist Security Info=False;Data Source=" _
          & DBLOCATION
    dcnDB.Open
        Set OpenDatabase = dcnDB

    End Function
```

Not all lines of code in a code editor will fit on a single line in a book; therefore, this book follows the Visual Basic convention of identifying line breaks with the underscore (_) character. When you see a line end with this character, you know the following line is a continuation of it.

You'll also find a number of icons throughout the text that point out special information:

A Note icon identifies an interesting piece of information for you to remember.

A Tip icon marks a recommendation about best practices, useful techniques, and things to make you more productive.

A Caution icon flags a warning to you of potential dangers to your code or your system.

A Cross-Reference icons points you to other places with information related to the topic you are reading about.

Support

You'll find all the code examples, as well as other useful information, at the ASP Techniques Web site (http://asptechniques.com). If you'd like to contact me with questions about the book, you can reach me via e-mail at aspbible@asptechniques.com. Good luck!

Acknowledgments

First and foremost, I thank God for giving the talent and strength to do this and everything else in my life. All of my efforts on this book and everything else are for his glory and not my own.

I also want to thank my wife, Jodi, for putting up with me as I raced to get this book done. Without her support, I never would have continued my writing career. A cruise to the Caribbean should help in making it up to her. Max, our dog, had to stay in the kitchen a lot as I wrote, but he can't read or go on the cruise, so I'll just have to go play ball with him to thank him instead.

Tom Hsieh and Bryan Kim deserve a lot of credit for creating the three extensive appendices that appear at the end of this book. Writing appendices is a lot of work, especially when you're dealing with spotty and incorrect Microsoft documentation. Thanks for the hard work, guys.

I also want to thank Margot Maley, my agent, and the other staff at Waterside Productions for their help with some of the administrative details of this project (like getting paid).

Finally, a big thank you goes to the folks at IDG Books Worldwide for getting this book to market. John Osborn, Matt Lusher, Barbra Guerra, Amy Eoff, and Eric Hahn, my editors, deserve all the credit for getting this book out to you. It's a big job and they did it well.

Contents at a Glance

Preface ix
Acknowledgments xv

Part I: Language Tools 1
Chapter 1: HTML Essentials 3
Chapter 2: VBScript Language Elements 29
Chapter 3: VBScript Functions and Objects..67

Part II: ASP Concepts 95
Chapter 4: Using Server-Side Includes 97
Chapter 5: Using the Request Object 113
Chapter 6: Using the Response Object 149
Chapter 7: Using Cookies 159
Chapter 8: Using the Application, Session, and Server Objects 183
Chapter 9: Error Handling...197

Part III: Integrating with Databases..207
Chapter 10: Active Data Objects Essentials 209
Chapter 11: Creating a Data Browser 231
Chapter 12: Adding Data Entry Features 263
Chapter 13: Enhancing the Data Browser..303
Chapter 14: Advanced Database Integration 333

Part IV: Integrating with Other Tools 363
Chapter 15: Integrating with Index Server 365
Chapter 16: Using Classes in Visual Basic 389
Chapter 17: Using WebClasses 433
Chapter 18: Integrating with Microsoft Transaction Server....................463

Part V: Building a Real-World Application 479
Chapter 19: Creating a Discussion Forum 481

Appendix A: Setting Up your Development Environment 521
Appendix B: HTML Reference 533
Appendix C: VBScript Reference 587
Appendix D: Object Reference 647
Appendix E: What's New in ASP 3.0...727
Index 735

Contents

Preface ix

Acknowledgments...xv

Part I: Language Tools   1

Chapter 1: HTML Essentials 3
Document Structure Elements 3
    HTML Tag 4
    HEAD Tag 4
    TITLE Tag..4
    BODY Tag 4
Text Formatting...5
    Headings...5
    BLOCKQUOTE Tag 8
    PRE Tag...8
    CODE Tag 10
    FONT Tag 11
    Miscellaneous Formatting Tags 12
Positioning Tags 12
    CENTER Tag 12
    Paragraph Tag..13
    BR Tag...13
    HR Tag...13
List Tags 15
    Unordered List...15
    Ordered List 17
Table Formatting Tags 20
    TABLE Tag 20
    TR Tag...21
    TH 22
    TD 22
    Table Example..23
Other Tags...25
    Anchor Tag 25
    Image Tag...26
Learning More about HTML..26

Chapter 2: VBScript Language Elements 29
Constants 29
Variables and Data Types...31

Creating a Variable 31
Using Arrays...32
Variable-Checking Functions...33
Array Functions 36
Conversion Functions 40
Mathematical Operations 40
Addition and Subtraction Symbols 40
Multiplication Symbol 41
Division Symbols 41
Modulus/Remainder Function 41
Exponentiation Operator 42
Grouping Expressions 42
Comparison Operators 44
Logical Operators 44
Not Operator...44
And Operator...45
Or Operator..46
Xor Operator..46
Eqv Operator...47
Imp Operator..47
Implicit Type Conversion 48
Looping and Decision Structures...48
If/Then/Else Structure..49
For/Next Structure 53
Select/Case Structure..56
Do/Loop Structure...59
While/Wend Structure..63
Unsupported Looping Structures 64

Chapter 3: VBScript Functions and Objects 67

Data Conversion Functions...67
Type Conversion Functions 67
Character to Number Functions..71
Base Conversion Functions...72
Integer Conversion Functions..72
Mathematical Functions 72
Abs Function 73
Atn Function 73
Cos Function 73
Exp Function 74
Log Function 74
Rnd Function, Randomize Statement...................................74
Round Function 75
Sin Function 76
Sqr Function 76
Sgn Function 76

Tan Function 76
Data Formatting Functions 77
FormatCurrency Function 77
FormatDateTime 78
FormatNumber Function 79
FormatPercent Function..79
Text Manipulation Functions 80
Filter Function..80
InStr Function 81
InStrRev Function 81
Join Function..82
LCase Function 83
Left Function 83
Len Function 83
LTrim Function 83
Mid Function 83
Replace Function 84
RTrim Function 84
Space Function 85
Split Function 85
StrReverse Function 85
String Function 86
Trim Function 86
UCase Function 86
Date and Time Functions 86
Date Function 86
DateAdd Function 87
DateDiff Function..87
DatePart Function 88
DateSerial Function 88
DateValue Function 88
Day Function 88
Hour Function 88
Minute Function 88
Month Function 89
MonthName Function 89
Now Function 89
Second Function 89
Weekday Function 89
WeekdayName Function 89
Year Function 89
Built-in Objects..89
Dictionary Object 90
Err Object 90
FileSystemObject..90

Part II: ASP Concepts   95

Chapter 4: Using Server-Side Includes 97

Learning the SSI Directives 98
#config Directive...98
#echo Directive..103
#exec Directive 105
#flastmod Directive..106
#fsize Directive 107
#include Directive 109
Creating Modular ASP Code...109

Chapter 5: Using the Request Object...113

Using Form Information 114
Creating a Single Box Form 114
Working with Radio Buttons 119
Working with Check Boxes...121
Working with Select Lists 127
Working with Hidden Input Fields 133
Using Query String Information 133
Using Server Variables..140
ALL_HTTP Variable 144
PATH_INFO Variable 146

Chapter 6: Using the Response Object 149

Introduction to the Response Object 149
Creating Output...150
Using Response.Write...150
Using Equal Sign with Delimiter Characters 151
Using HTML Outside of Delimiter Characters 151
Managing Output...153
Redirecting the Browser..153
Buffering Output...153
Caching and Expiration Dates 154
Changing Content Types 155
Rating Your Content...156
Managing the Connection 156
IsClientConnected Property..157
End Method..157

Chapter 7: Using Cookies 159

Introduction to Cookies 159
Cookies and Your Browser...162
Configuring Internet Explorer 4 and 5 162
Configuring Netscape 4.61...162

Creating a Cookie 163
Modifying and Removing Cookies...166
Tracking Preferences with Cookies 168
    Creating the Form...168
    Adding the Size Cookie 170
    Adding the Toppings Cookie 171
    Building the Back-end Code 175

Chapter 8: Using the Application, Session, and Server Objects 183

The Application Object 183
    Contents Collection..184
    StaticObjects Collection 185
    Lock and Unlock Methods..186
    Application Events 186
The Session Object 186
    Contents Collection..187
    StaticObjects Collection 188
    Session Control 188
    Miscellaneous Properties..189
    Session Events 189
The Server Object 189
    ScriptTimeout Property...190
    CreateObject Method..190
    Execute Method 190
    GetLastError Method 191
    HTMLEncode Method 191
    MapPath Method 191
    Transfer Method 192
    URLEncode Method 192
Using the global.asa File...192
    Creating Application Event Code 193
    Creating Session Event Code 194
    Declaring Objects 195
    Referencing Type Libraries 195

Chapter 9: Error Handling..197

Part III: Integrating with Databases   207

Chapter 10: Active Data Objects Essentials 209

Microsoft's Universal Data Access Strategy 209
    OLE DB..210
    ODBC...210
    Remote Data Service..211
    Active Data Objects...211

The Connection Object 212
    Making a Connection 212
    Using a Data Link File 214
    Closing a Connection 216
The Recordset and Field Objects 217
    Executing a Query 217
    Opening a Recordset 218
    Navigating in a Recordset 220
    Editing Records in a Recordset 221
    Adding New Records to a Table 222
The Command and Parameter Objects 223
    Creating a Recordset with a Command Object 223
    Running a Query with Parameters 224
Using the Errors Collection 228

Chapter 11: Creating a Data Browser **231**
    Getting Started 231
    Retrieving Table Data 233
    Publishing the Recordset 234
    Cleaning Up 235
    Trying It Out 236
Adding a Drilldown Feature 237
    Modifying the Category Viewer 237
    Creating the Product List Page 239
    Enhancing the Product List 242
Adding Product Information 247
    Changing the Product Listing Page 247
    Creating the Product Information Page 249
Creating a Search Utility 252
    Building the Search Form 252
    Creating the Search Results Page 254

Chapter 12: Adding Data Entry Features **263**
Creating a Data Entry Form 263
    Adding Structure to the Page 267
    Creating the ViewRecord Subroutine 271
    Creating the AddRecord Subroutine 275
    Creating the EditRecord Subroutine 277
    Creating the DeleteRecord Subroutine 278
    Creating the ShowPage Subroutine 280
    Linking to the Other Pages 287
Summary 301

Chapter 13: Enhancing the Data Browser **303**
    Creating the Basic Browser 303
    Adding Paging Capabilities 307

Adding Sorting Features 312
Wrapping Up 318
Creating Application Security..318
The Target: Our Order Status Application 319
Garden Gate Security 326
Adding Session-level Security..329
Wrapping Up 332

Chapter 14: Advanced Database Integration 333

What Are We Building? 333
Designing the Invoice Query..339
Designing the Order Details Query 342
Executing the Invoice Info Query 342
Executing the Invoice Details Query..348
Tracking User Activity...351
Determining What to Track...353
Creating the Database Tables 354
Modifying the Code..355
Wrapping Up 362

Part IV: Integrating with Other Tools   363

Chapter 15: Integrating with Index Server 365

Introduction to Index Server 365
Configuring Index Server 365
Creating a Simple Search Page 370
Index Server Object Model 374
Query Object Properties and Methods 374
Utility Object Methods 381
Index Server Query Language 383
Basic Query Rules 383
Boolean and Proximity Operators 384
Wildcards...385
Free-Text Queries 386
Property Value Queries..386
Relational Operators...387
Final Notes...387

Chapter 16: Using Classes in Visual Basic 389

The Business Model..390
Creating the Classes 393
Adding Data Access Code 400
Adding to the Employee Class..401
Adding to the Store Class 405
Compiling and Deploying the Objects...424

Compiling the Component 424
Testing the Component in VB 425
Creating a Deployment Package 426
Testing on the Web 430
Summary 431

Chapter 17: Using WebClasses 433

What Is a WebClass? 433
Building Your First WebClass 434
The "Hello World" WebClass 434
Using HTML Templates 440
Creating the Template 441
Using Custom WebItems and Events 444
Using ADO with WebClasses 450
Advanced Techniques 454
Summary 461

Chapter 18: Integrating with Microsoft Transaction Server 463

What Is Microsoft Transaction Server? 464
Creating an MTS Component 465
Building an Ad Tracking System 469
Design Tips for MTS 469
Building the Database 470
Creating the AdMgr Class 471
Testing the Impression Code 474
Adding the Clickthrough Code 475
Enhancements You Can Make 476
Summary 477

Part V: Building a Real-World Application   479

Chapter 19: Creating a Discussion Forum 481

Designing a Discussion Forum 481
The Object Model 481
System Functions 482
Designing the Forum Database 483
Building the Object Library 485
Creating the Group Object 485
Building the Member Object 487
Creating the Message Object 489
Creating the Subscription Class 492
Generating the Library 495

Building the ASP Code 495
  Creating the Login Page 496
  Creating the User Profile Editor 502
  Creating the Group Listing Page..508
  Creating the Group Viewer...509
  Creating the Message Viewing Page...511
  Creating the Message Editor Page..514

Appendix A: Setting Up your Development Environment **521**

Appendix B: HTML Reference **533**

Appendix C: VBScript Reference **587**

Appendix D: Object Reference **647**

Appendix E: What's New in ASP 3.0...**727**

Index **735**

Language Tools

Because ASP works with HTML, the first part of the book will give you the HTML essentials you need to work in this book. You'll also learn about the concepts of the VBScript language in these chapters.

Chapter 1
HTML Essentials

Chapter 2
VBScript Language
Elements

Chapter 3
VBScript Functions
and Objects

HTML Essentials

As mentioned in the introduction, HTML works hand in hand with Active Server Page (ASP) technology. ASP code can be used to generate HTML, which is what eventually finds its way to the user's browser. As a result, this chapter is devoted to HTML. While the chapter doesn't cover all the tags used in HTML, it does cover some of the tags used throughout the rest of the book. At the end of the chapter, there is a list of good books that can serve as HTML reference guides.

Document Structure Elements

Because ASP files normally have output, they need to generate standard HTML. Let's start with the standard HTML page structure, as follows:

```
<html>
    <head>
        <title>Page Title</title>
    </head>

    <body>

    </body>
</html>
```

Note

While some browsers still show the contents of the page if you are missing these standard tags, you should provide all the tags in every page that generates output. In following chapters, you see how you can use these tags to provide additional information to the user. For instance, you can dynamically generate an appropriate TITLE tag for the page you are creating.

In This Chapter

Learn how to create a basic HTML page

Learn how to create commonly used Web page effects

Learn about extra parameters that can be used in HTML tags

HTML Tag

The HTML tag is used to mark the beginning of a page. This tag should be the first tag sent to the user's browser. As discussed in following chapters, this rule doesn't mean that the HTML tag is the first tag in the file. In some cases a lot of code is required before a single piece of HTML is sent to the browser. The end /HTML tag should be the last tag sent to the user's browser. Again, you may have ASP code that follows the last HTML tag, but /HTML should be the last tag sent to the browser.

HEAD Tag

The HEAD tag is the second level of tags in a page. This tag is used to contain page header information, such as the title of the page. Other tags, like the META tag, can also go into the heading section. The heading needs to be closed before using the BODY tag, as covered in the following "BODY Tag" section. The heading is treated as a separate section of the document and should not be enclosed by the BODY tag.

TITLE Tag

The TITLE tag provides the title of the page. This title shows up in numerous places in the user's browser, such as the title bar of the browser window and in the user's browsing history list. The title can be printed on as many lines as you wish, and the end of the title is marked by /TITLE.

BODY Tag

The BODY tag marks the beginning of the content of the page. All of the remaining HTML in the page follows this tag. At the end of the file, the /BODY tag ends the content for the page. The BODY tag has a number of optional parameters that can be used to customize the look of the page. The most commonly used parameters are shown in Table 1-1.

Table 1-1 Common BODY Tag Parameters	
Parameter Name	**Description**
BACKGROUND	Specifies an image to repeat as the background of the page
BGCOLOR	Specifies a color to use as the background for the page
TEXT	Specifies the color to use as the default color for text
ALINK	Specifies the color to use for a link being clicked (Netscape only)
LINK	Specifies the color to use for a link that has not been clicked
VLINK	Specifies the color to use for a link that has been clicked

Text Formatting

Since HTML has become a standard language, both Microsoft and Netscape have introduced many extra tags that were not in the official specification for HTML. Unfortunately, neither company implemented all of these extra tags. As a result, if you want your text to be formatted in a similar manner in both browsers, you have to avoid both sets of extra tags.

Fortunately, most HTML authors take this approach, and many of the tags in the specification have been forgotten. This section shows you the most commonly used text formatting tags and introduces a few extras that might be unfamiliar. If the tag is not available in both Microsoft and Netscape's browser, it is not listed here.

Note For those using other browsers, be aware that the tags covered in this section are part of the official HTML specification and should be supported in your browser. However, because Microsoft and Netscape control an overwhelming majority of the browser market, we won't be spending our time with the other browsers that are still available.

Headings

One of the earliest additions to HTML was the ability to have different levels of headings, just as you would have in an outline. The heading tags are used for this purpose. There are six levels of headings and each level has its own tag pair. Each tag pair is the letter *H* followed by a number from 1 to 6. Figure 1-1 demonstrates all six sizes for easy comparison. The source code for the picture is in Listing 1-1, which follows the figure.

Listing 1-1: Source code for Figure 1-1

```
<html>
<head>
    <title>Heading Tag Demonstration</title>
</head>
<body>
<h1>This is Heading 1 (H1) Font</h1>
<h2>This is Heading 2 (H2) Font</h2>
<h3>This is Heading 3 (H3) Font</h3>
<h4>This is Heading 4 (H4) Font</h4>
<h5>This is Heading 5 (H5) Font</h5>
<h6>This is Heading 6 (H6) Font</h6>
</body>
</html>
```

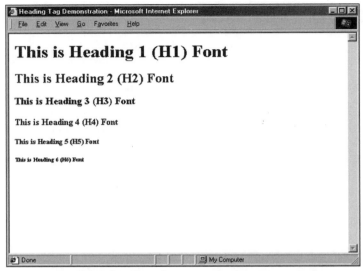

Figure 1-1: Six levels of headings, as seen in Internet Explorer

Notice that when the closing heading tag is used, it automatically adds a line break and adds some extra space between the lines.

One of the basic problems with the heading tags is that you have little control over the appearance of your text in the user's browser. For instance, the browser in Figure 1-1 defaults to Times New Roman font and there is no way to change it using just the heading tags. In addition, the sizes of the fonts are all relative and can be changed by the user. In Internet Explorer, the base font size can be changed by selecting View ⇨ Fonts and then picking the base size. Netscape has a similar function in its Preference window.

For comparison, Figure 1-1 shows the fonts in Medium mode. Figure 1-2 shows the text in Largest mode, and Figure 1-3 shows the text in Smallest mode.

Don't despair, however. A technology called Cascading Style Sheets (CSS) makes it possible to redefine these heading styles to include font names, sizes, colors, and so forth. Check the list of books at the end of this chapter for more information on CSS.

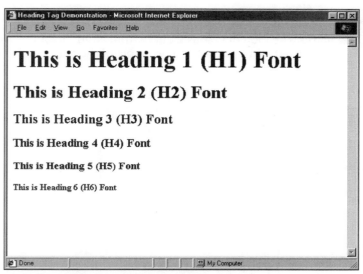

Figure 1-2: Text shown in Largest font size in IE

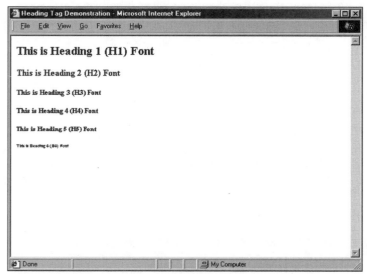

Figure 1-3: Text shown in Smallest font size in IE

BLOCKQUOTE Tag

The BLOCKQUOTE tag marks a section of text as a quote from another source. The text is indented on both the left and right side. An example of the tag is shown in Figure 1-4.

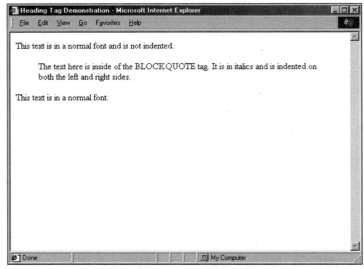

Figure 1-4: Text within the BLOCKQUOTE tag is indented on both sides.

PRE Tag

The PRE tag shows text in a monospace font. PRE is short for preformatted. Any text surrounded with the PRE tag pair will be shown exactly as it appears in the source file. Figure 1-5 shows an example of preformatted text as rendered by the browser. Listing 1-2 shows the source code for this example.

Listing 1-2: **Preformatted text example in Figure 1-5**

```
<html>
<head>
   <title>Preformatted Text Example</title>
```

```
</head>

<body>

This text is on
multiple lines
in the file but will
be automatically wrapped
in the browser.

<pre>
Text inside of the PRE
tags will show exactly
as it is in the file.
</pre>
</body>
</html>
```

Figure 1-5: Preformatted text, as shown in the browser

One problem with the PRE tag, as shown in Figure 1-5, is that it automatically adds a line break and extra space. If you need to include code in the same line, use the CODE tag, which is covered in the following section.

CODE Tag

Like the PRE tag, the CODE tag shows text in a monospace font. However, it does not add a line break before and after the text. Figure 1-6 shows a comparison between the two methods, and Listing 1-3 shows the source code for the window.

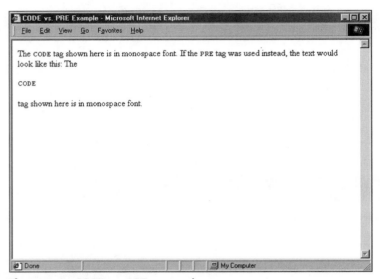

Figure 1-6: CODE vs. PRE comparison

Listing 1-3: Source code for CODE vs. PRE comparison in Figure 1-6

```
<html>
<head>
   <title>CODE vs. PRE Example</title>
</head>

<body>
The <code>CODE</code> tag shown here is in monospace font.

If the <code>PRE</code> tag was used instead, the text would
look like this:

The <pre>CODE</pre> tag shown here is in monospace font.

</body>
</html>
```

In short, if you want to show a block of text, use the PRE tag. If you need to emphasize a term in the same sentence, use the CODE tag.

FONT Tag

One of the more flexible text-formatting tags is the FONT tag. A number of parameters can be supplied to change the look of the text. The most commonly used parameters are listed in Table 1-2.

Table 1-2	
FONT Tag Parameters	
Parameter	*Description*
COLOR	Specifies the color in which the text should be displayed
FACE	Specifies the font name to use
SIZE	Specifies the relative size to use for the text

The FACE parameter can list multiple fonts, separated by commas. If you are using a font specific to a particular machine, be sure you specify a similar font as the second font in the tag. For instance, Tahoma is a font normally available with Windows. However, Tahoma is not normally available on other platforms. A good use of the FACE parameter follows:

```
<font face="Tahoma, Arial, Helvetica">
```

If the Tahoma font is not available, the browser looks for Arial. If Arial isn't available, it looks for Helvetica. If Helvetica is also missing, the browser reverts to the default font for the browser.

The SIZE parameter does not allow exact pixel or point sizes; rather, it uses relative values. You can specify values using two different methods. The first uses an absolute value of 1 through 7, as follows:

```
<font face="Arial" size=3>
```

You can also specify a change in font size using the values –4, –3, –2, –1, +1, +2, and +3.

Miscellaneous Formatting Tags

Several other tags can provide quick formatting for your HTML. These tags are shown in Table 1-3.

Table 1-3	
Formatting Tags	
Tag	**Description**
B	Boldface text
I	Italic text
S	Strikethrough text
U	Underlined text

A quick example of boldfacing text follows:

```
<b>This text will be shown in boldface text.</b>
```

You can follow this model for all of the tags shown in Table 1-3. Remember to close the tag pair or you could get unexpected formatting results.

Positioning Tags

A number of tags position text and graphics on Web pages. These tags can be used within any of the tags covered in this chapter. Depending on the browser you're using, these tags can produce different results.

CENTER Tag

This tag is used to center text between the sides of the browser window — if the text is not within another tag, such as a table. If the text is within another tag, the text will be centered within the relevant area. Any text that is centered should be between the CENTER tag pair, as follows:

```
<center>This text is centered.</center>
This text will not be centered.
```

Paragraph Tag

The P tag is one of the most commonly used tags, but it isn't normally used as shown in the HTML specification. Many users simply add a P tag to add a break between paragraphs, as follows:

```
This text is in paragraph 1.
<P>
This text is in paragraph 2.
```

The specification uses an ending paragraph tag, as follows:

```
<P>
This text is in paragraph 1.
</P>
<P>
This text is in paragraph 2.
</P>
```

Because the second example follows the specification, you should use that format instead of the first example. While browsers will probably always support the first method, the second format has an extra option unavailable in the first. You can add the ALIGN parameter and specify LEFT, RIGHT, or CENTER. An example of the ALIGN parameter follows:

```
<CENTER>
This text is centered.
</CENTER>

<P ALIGN=CENTER>
This text is also centered.
</P>
```

BR Tag

The BR tag puts a line break between two lines of text. The tag behaves the same as hitting your Enter key. BR won't put extra space between the lines, however, as with the paragraph tag. The BR tag does not need a closing tag. Simply use it as follows:

```
This is line 1.<br>
This is line 2.<br>
```

HR Tag

HR stands for horizontal rule, which is a horizontal bar that can appear on a page. A simple use of this tag is shown in Figure 1-7, and the code is shown in Listing 1-4.

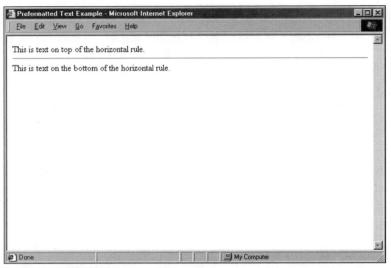

Figure 1-7: Use of horizontal rule on a page

Listing 1-4: Code for what is shown in Figure 1-7

```
<html>
<head>
   <title>Preformatted Text Example</title>
</head>

<body>

This is text on top of the horizontal rule.
<hr>
This is text on the bottom of the horizontal rule.

</body>
</html>
```

This tag has a number of additional parameters that can be used to change the appearance of the bar. Table 1-4 lists these parameters.

Table 1-4
HR Tag Parameters

Parameter	Description
SIZE	Specifies the thickness of the bar
WIDTH	Specifies the width of the bar in either pixels or as a percentage
ALIGN	Indicates how the bar should be placed on the page (left, center, right)
NOSHADE	Removes the shadow that normally appears below the bar
COLOR	Specifies the color of the bar; if omitted, the default is a dark gray

List Tags

You can create three different lists in HTML. Each of the lists has a slightly different format and can be used for different purposes. This section shows how these lists are created.

Unordered List

Unordered lists will probably be the list you use most often. This type of list is also known as a bulleted list, because all of the items are shown following some sort of dot or other bullet. An unordered list uses the UL tag, as shown in the following example:

```
<html>
<head>
    <title>List Sample</title>
</head>

<body>

<ul>
<li>This is item 1.
<li>This is item 2.
<li>This is item 3.
</ul>

</body>
</html>
```

When loaded into the browser, this code produces the page shown in Figure 1-8.

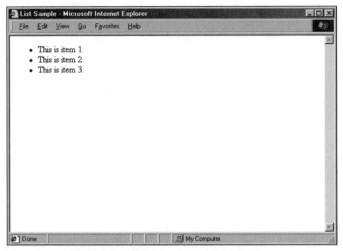

Figure 1-8: Unordered lists display with bullets

You can also have a list within a list. As shown in Figure 1-9, the sublist uses a different bullet than the primary list.

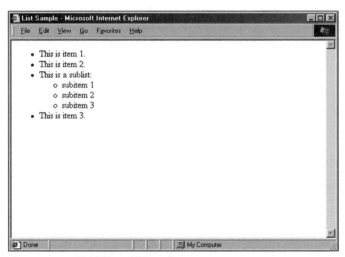

Figure 1-9: A sublist within a list

The code for the previous figure is shown in Listing 1-5. No special tags are needed, because the browser determines that the list is within another list.

> **Listing 1-5: Source code that has a list within another list (Figure 1-9)**

```
<html>
<head>
    <title>List Sample</title>
</head>

<body>

<ul>
<li>This is item 1.
<li>This is item 2.
<li>This is a sublist:
    <ul>
    <li>subitem 1
    <li>subitem 2
    <li>subitem 3
    </ul>
<li>This is item 3.
</ul>

</body>
</html>
```

You can nest any of the lists covered in this section, and you can also mix and match list types.

Ordered List

The ordered list uses cardinal numbers instead of bullets. Listing 1-6 would be rendered as Figure 1-10 if the ordered list tag (OL) was used instead.

> **Listing 1-6: Source code for ordered lists example (Figure 1-10)**

```
<html>
<head>
```

Continued

Listing 1-6 *(continued)*

```
    <title>List Sample</title>
</head>

<body>

<ol>
<li>This is item 1.
<li>This is item 2.
<li>This is a sublist:
    <ol>
    <li>subitem 1
    <li>subitem 2
    <li>subitem 3
    </ol>
<li>This is item 3.
</ol>

</body>
</html>
```

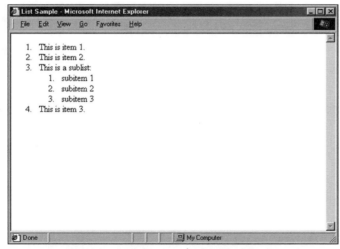

Figure 1-10: Nested lists using ordered list tags

The code for Figure 1-10 is shown in Listing 1-6.

As you can see from Figure 1-10, using only Arabic numerals makes the view of the page confusing. However, both Netscape and Internet Explorer support the use of the TYPE and START tags. If you change the code marked in Listing 1-7, the result is easier to read.

Listing 1-7: The START and TYPE tags alter the look of ordered lists

```
<html>
<head>
    <title>List Sample</title>
</head>

<body>

<ol type=I start=1>
<li>This is item 1.
<li>This is item 2.
<li>This is a sublist:
    <ol>
    <li>subitem 1
    <li>subitem 2
    <li>subitem 3
    </ol>
<li>This is item 3.
</ol>

</body>
</html>
```

The result is shown in Figure 1-11.

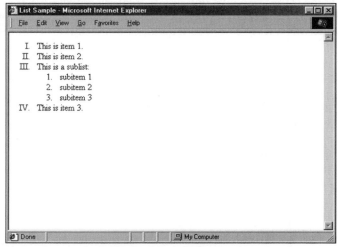

Figure 1-11: The lists are shown in a mix of Roman and Arabic numerals

The START parameter specifies the value with which to start the list. The TYPE parameter specifies the format in which the numbers should be displayed. Table 1-5 lists the valid parameter values.

Note   The value used for the TYPE parameter is case-sensitive.

Table 1-5 START Parameter Values	
Value	*Result*
A	Capital letters (A, B, C, ...)
a	Lowercase letters (a, b, c, ...)
I	Large Roman numerals (I, II, III, ...)
ii	Small Roman numerals (i, ii, iii, ...)
1	Arabic numerals (1, 2, 3, ...)

Table Formatting Tags

Tables are probably the most flexible of all the tags due to the unique way in which they can be combined. As you've probably seen by now, HTML evaluates from top to bottom and you don't have a lot of control over how the text is displayed. However, using tables can give you much greater control over how your text is displayed. While this section doesn't give you all of the ins and outs of using tables in unique ways, it teaches you enough to build the basic tables used throughout this book.

TABLE Tag

The TABLE tag marks the beginning of a table. It can take a number of optional parameters, the most common of which are shown in Table 1-6.

The end of this section has a sample table using all the tags covered in the section. As with all table tags, be sure that you match the TABLE tag with a /TABLE tag, or the browser may not interpret the code properly.

Table 1-6 **TABLE Tag Parameters**	
Parameter Name	**Description**
ALIGN	Specifies whether the table should be aligned to the left or right side of the page
BACKGROUND	Specifies an image to use as the background of the table
BGCOLOR	Specifies the color to be used as the background for the table
BORDER	Specifies the width of the border around the table cells; if you use zero, no border will be shown
CELLPADDING	Specifies the number of pixels between the border of each cell and the contents of the cell
CELLSPACING	Specifies the number of pixels between the cells in the table
COLS	Specifies the number of columns in the table; this value is not required as the table will count the number of columns you create
HEIGHT	Specifies, in pixels or a percentage, the height of the table
WIDTH	Specifies, in pixels or a percentage, the width of the table

TR Tag

The TR tag marks the beginning of a table row. The tag can take several optional parameters, some of which are shown in Table 1-7.

Table 1-7 **TR Tag Parameters**	
Parameter Name	**Description**
ALIGN	Specifies whether the contents of the cells in the row should be aligned to the left, center, or right side of the page
BACKGROUND	Specifies an image to use as the background of the cells in the row
BGCOLOR	Specifies the color to be used as the background for the cells in the row

The end of this section has a sample table using all of the tags covered in the section. As with all table tags, be sure that you match the TR tag with a /TR tag, or the browser may not interpret the code properly.

TH

The TH tag marks a table heading. A table heading can be used at the top of each column. The tag can take several optional parameters, some of which are shown in Table 1-8.

	Table 1-8 **TH Tag Parameters**
Parameter Name	**Description**
ALIGN	Specifies whether the contents of the cells in the row should be aligned to the left, center, or right side of the page
BACKGROUND	Specifies an image to use as the background of the cells in the row
BGCOLOR	Specifies the color to be used as the background for the cells in the row
COLSPAN	Specifies how many columns the heading should span
ROWSPAN	Specifies how many rows the heading should span
VALIGN	Specifies whether the contents should be aligned vertically to the top, middle, bottom, or to the text baseline of the cell
WIDTH	Specifies the width of the cell; the largest width that is used for the column will be used for all cells in the column

Any text within the table heading will be shown in boldface. You can add other tags such as italics and underline, if you wish. The end of this section has a sample table using all of the tags covered in the section. As with all table tags, be sure that you match the TH tag with a /TH tag, or the browser may not interpret the code properly.

TD

The TD tag stands for table definition and marks the contents of a cell. The tag can take several optional parameters, some of which are shown in Table 1-9.

Any text within the table heading will be shown in boldface. You can add other tags such as italics and underline, if you wish. The end of this section has a sample table using all of the tags covered in the section. As with all table tags, be sure that you match the TD tag with a /TD tag, or the browser may not interpret the code properly.

Table 1-9
TD Tag Parameters

Parameter Name	Description
ALIGN	Specifies whether the contents of the cells in the row should be aligned to the left, center, or right side of the page
BACKGROUND	Specifies an image to use as the background of the cells in the row
BGCOLOR	Specifies the color to be used as the background for the cells in the row
COLSPAN	Specifies how many columns the heading should span
ROWSPAN	Specifies how many rows the heading should span
VALIGN	Specifies whether the contents should be aligned vertically to the top, middle, bottom, or to the text baseline of the cell
WIDTH	Specifies the width of the cell; the largest width that is used for the column will be used for all cells in the column

Table Example

The code shown in Listing 1-8 shows a complete table, complete with table headings and examples of the most common properties. Figure 1-12 shows how the table appears in Internet Explorer.

Listing 1-8: **Table example code**

```
<html>
<head>
    <title>Table Example</title>
</head>

<body>
<h2>Product List</h2>

<table cellpadding=3>
    <tr>
        <th colspan=2>Item</th>
        <th>Quantity</th>
        <th>Price</th>
        <th>Extended</th>
```

Continued

Listing 1-8 *(continued)*

```
      </tr>
      <tr>
         <td>127250</td>
         <td>PC Hard Drive</td>
         <td align=center>3</td>
         <td align=right>$150.00</td>
         <td align=right>$450.00</td>
      </tr>
      <tr>
         <td>199240</td>
         <td>Modem</td>
         <td align=center>1</td>
         <td align=right>$75.00</td>
         <td align=right>$75.00</td>
      </tr>
      <tr>
         <td colspan=4 align=right><b>Total:</b></td>
         <td align=right>$525.00</td>
      </tr>

   </table>
   </body>
   </html>
```

Figure 1-12: Table example, as seen in Internet Explorer

If you want to see how the cell structure is built, you can add `border=1` to the `TABLE` tag. The result looks like Figure 1-13.

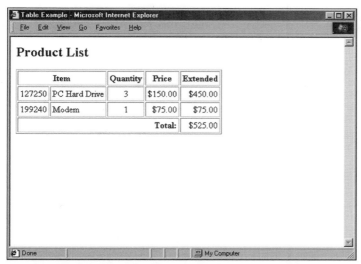

Figure 1-13: Table example shown with borders around the cells and table

Other Tags

One set of tags not covered in this chapter deals with the creation of data input forms. Because forms are not particularly useful without code behind them, forms are discussed in a later chapter. This section demonstrates a few other tags used in the rest of the book.

Anchor Tag

The anchor tag marks a link to another document or object. Anchor tags can also be used as relative links within a document. To add a link to another document, you can use the following code:

```
<a href="http://www.idgbooks.com">IDG Books Worldwide</a>
```

The text in the `HREF` parameter specifies the actual link. Any text that precedes the `</A>` tag will be shown as a link; that is, colored and underlined. If you want to use a link within a document, you first mark the destination location with the following tag:

```
<a name="destination">
```

Replace the word `destination` with the name of the location you wish to use. To provide a link in the document to the destination, use the following code:

```
<a href="#destination">
```

Using the pound sign indicates that the browser should go to a relative location in the page.

Image Tag

The image tag is used to show a graphic within a page. Typical graphic formats supported by most browsers include CompuServe Graphics Interchange Format (GIF) and Joint Photographic Experts Group (JPEG) format. To specify an image, use the following code:

```
<img src="/pics/icon.gif">
```

The `src` parameter specifies the filename to use. Depending on the Web server you are using, the source will either be a relative link or an absolute link. A relative link begins with a slash and does not include a hostname. An absolute link includes the hostname where the file is located.

The image tag can include the `WIDTH` and `HEIGHT` parameters that specify the size of the graphic. If you use a height and width that are not the same size as the graphic, the graphic will be stretched or shrunken to fit the size specified.

Learning More about HTML

There's no way that this chapter can teach you everything about HTML. Instead, you learned the most commonly used tags and how tags are structured in a page. With that knowledge, you can add some of the optional tags and parameters to your HTML to make pages look better for your users. Check out the following books for more information on HTML.

DHTML: The Definitive Reference by Danny Goodman (O'Reilly and Associates; ISBN 1565924940)

This book covers all the basic HTML tags and their parameters. It also covers Cascading Style Sheets and Dynamic HTML, which is available within Internet Explorer and Netscape Navigator. DHTML has slightly different flavors between browsers and these differences are covered in this book.

HTML 4 Bible by Bryan Pfaffenberger and Alexis D. Gutzman (IDG Books Worldwide, Inc.; ISBN: 0764532200)

This book has a comprehensive definition of what is considered state of the art in Web-publishing languages. The book explains HTML tags and Cascading Style Sheets thoroughly, with some attention to JavaScript as well.

HTML 4 Visual Quickstart Guide by Elizabeth Castro (Peachpit Press; ISBN: 0201696967)

This book presumes no prior knowledge of HTML or even the Internet. It uses clear, concise instructions for creating each element of the Web page, from titles and headers to creating links and adding tables, frames, forms, and multimedia.

Summary

This chapter illustrates the basics of HTML used throughout the rest of the book. HTML will be used in combination with Active Server Pages code in the following chapters, so you need to have a grasp of the fundamentals.

✦　　✦　　✦

VBScript Language Elements

✦   ✦   ✦   ✦

In This Chapter

Learn about VBScript
constants, variables,
and data types

Learn about looping
and decision
structures in VBScript

Learn about creating
your own functions
and subroutines

✦   ✦   ✦   ✦

Constants

As its name suggests, a *constant* maintains the same value
while a program is running. Constants are used in Visual Basic
and in VBScript to hold values such as the name of the current
month or the name of your Web site. Regardless of its content,
the value does not change.

Besides the constants you might define, VBScript has a
number of built-in constants that have been predefined. If
you are familiar with Visual Basic, it is interesting to note that
VBScript does not have the enormous number of built-in
constants available in Visual Basic. However, VBScript does
have several important and frequently used constants.

The following constants are always available to your VBScript
code without additional definitions. The documentation for
each constant is available here for reference.

- ✦ Empty. The Empty keyword is used to indicate an
  uninitialized variable value. Empty is not the same
  thing as Null.

- ✦ Nothing. The Nothing keyword in VBScript is used to
  disassociate an object variable from any actual object.
  Use the Set statement to assign Nothing to an object
  variable, as shown in the following example:

  ```
  Set MyObject = Nothing
  ```

By setting a variable to Nothing, you indicate to VBScript that
you have finished using the object to which the variable
refers. VBScript frees up the memory and other system

resources that were assigned to that object. However, if you have several variables that refer to the same object, VBScript does not free up the system resources until all the variables referring to an object are set to Nothing.

✦ `Null`. The Null keyword is used to indicate that a variable contains no valid data. Null is not the same thing as Empty.

✦ `True`. The True keyword has a value equal to –1.

✦ `False`. The False keyword has a value equal to 0.

The difference between Null and Empty may be confusing, so here is a real-world example of how to use these two constants. Think of a variable as a box or container where data may be placed. If the variable is set to Empty, the container is empty. The container is ready to hold data, but it isn't holding any data at this point. If your variable is set to Null, the box is holding invalid data. Null values are common when you are accepting user input. If the user did not enter data for a particular field, the value for the field is Null.

If you need to define your own constants, you can use the `Const` keyword to define all types of constants. VBScript has several restrictions on the numbers at which you can set your variables. You can neither use exponent-based real numbers (6.02E+23) nor trailing data type characters (256&). A few examples of using the Const keyword follow:

```
Const DirectoryName = "C:\Windows"
Const ExchangeRate = 5.224
Const Year2000Start = #01/01/2000#
```

You could define all the constants that Visual Basic provides and add them to your HTML document; however, remember that the user has to download that page over the Internet. On a 28.8k baud modem, a page downloads at 2.5K per second on a perfect connection. All the unused constants you have put into your page are just wasting the user's time without providing any benefit.

However, if you are using these constants in an ASP page, the constants and the rest of the code will be evaluated before being sent to the user's browser. As a result, unless the code you're writing is specifically for client-side scripting, the constants won't be downloaded to the browser.

One other point: any constants defined on a page are restricted for use on that page only. You can't see constant values on a second page unless you specifically define the constant there. You can include your constants within include files (as discussed in Chapter 4) so that the constants are included automatically. However, you should remember that each constant takes server memory and you should keep your constant declarations to a minimum.

Variables and Data Types

In other programming languages, the data that you use in your code is stored in variables. Variables can be described as boxes into which you put data. In most languages, a variable can only hold one type of data—text, integers, decimal numbers, or dates. In VBScript, there are no specific data types. Instead, VBScript uses a special type of variable called a Variant. A variant is "smart" enough to handle any type of data. If you want to put in a piece of text (or string), you can. If you then want to put in a number, you can. However, programming with variants can be somewhat difficult if you're not careful.

Because all variables are of the same data type, many of Visual Basic's data type conversion functions (such as the Int and Fix functions) are neither available nor necessary with VBScript. You cannot create custom data types by using the Type keyword, as you can with Visual Basic.

Creating a Variable

To declare a variable (which will automatically be of the Variant type), use the Dim keyword, as in the following example:

```
Dim X
```

As you may guess, the name X is not particularly descriptive. You can also declare a variable as follows:

```
Dim strDirectoryPath
```

In this case, the variable will store the directory path to something, and the data is a string. Granted, the variable is able to store integers, dates, or any other data type; however, the programmer has decided to designate this variable as a string variable. As in other languages, the prefix on the variable can be used to indicate the data type.

You can also declare multiple variables in one shot using the following format:

```
Dim strDirectory, intValue, strFilename
```

This single line will create three separate variables, all of which are variants.

Variables declared with Dim outside of a subroutine or function are available globally to all subroutines and functions. Any variables declared within a subroutine or function are only available to that subroutine or function.

You can also use the Dim statement with empty parentheses to create a dynamic array. After declaring a dynamic array, use the ReDim statement within a procedure to define the number of dimensions and elements in the array. If you redeclare a dimension for an array variable whose size is explicitly specified in a Dim statement, an error occurs.

When variables are initialized, a numeric variable is initialized to 0, and a string is initialized to a zero-length string. To store a zero-length (empty) string in a variable, use the following method:

```
Dim A
A = ""
```

When using the Dim statement in a procedure or function, you should put the Dim statement at the beginning of the procedure or function.

While declaring variables is optional, you can run into all sorts of problems when, for instance, you misspell a variable name later in your code. Upon a variable's first use, VBScript will create the variable. This arrangement can be a problem if you misspell a variable's name. To avoid this problem, add the following statement at the top of your file:

```
Option Explicit
```

This statement forces you to declare every variable you use, thereby eliminating the problems caused by a misspelled variable. VBScript will flag an undeclared variable as an error when the page is run.

Using Arrays

In addition to using single variables, you can also create and use arrays of Variant variables. To do so, use the Dim keyword and add a number of dimensions to the variable declaration, as follows:

```
Dim arrInputData(4, 3)
```

These dimensions create an array that has 12 cells. You can think of a two-dimensional array as a grid, where the first number is the width and the second number is the height, or vice versa. To access a particular cell, add the index values to the variable name in the following manner:

```
Document.Write arrInputData(0, 2)
```

For this example, the first dimension can have values from 0 to 3, and the second dimension can range from 0 to 2. Unlike Visual Basic, all VBScript array indexes begin at 0. Visual Basic enables you to specify the lower bound on any array.

Note You can create an array with up to 60 dimensions. However, because most people think in only three dimensions, using more than three dimensions makes your data storage routine hard to visualize.

Variable-Checking Functions

Because you cannot determine a data type by the type of variable, VBScript provides the following functions designed to deal with Variant data variables:

✦ IsArray

✦ IsDate

✦ IsEmpty

✦ IsNull

✦ IsNumeric

✦ IsObject

✦ VarType

These functions enable you to determine what type of data is stored in a Variant.

IsArray

IsArray returns a Boolean value that indicates whether a variable is an array. The syntax for IsArray is as follows:

```
IsArray(varname)
```

The `varname` argument can be any variable. IsArray returns True if the variable is an array; otherwise, it returns False. IsArray is especially useful with variants containing arrays.

IsDate

IsDate returns a Boolean value that indicates whether an expression can be converted to a date. The syntax for IsDate is as follows:

```
IsDate(expression)
```

The `expression` argument can be any date or string expression recognizable as a date or time. IsDate returns True if the expression is a date or can be converted to a valid date. If the expression is not a date or a valid date, a False value returns. In Microsoft Windows, the range of valid dates is January 1, 100 A.D. through December 31, 9999 A.D.; the ranges vary among operating systems.

IsEmpty

IsEmpty returns a Boolean value that indicates whether a variable has been initialized. The syntax for IsEmpty is as follows:

```
IsEmpty(expression)
```

The `expression` argument can be any expression. However, because IsEmpty determines whether individual variables are initialized, the `expression` argument is most often a single variable name. IsEmpty returns True if the variable is uninitialized or set to Empty. Otherwise, the IsEmpty function returns False. In addition, False is always returned if the expression contains more than one variable.

IsNull

IsNull returns a Boolean value that indicates whether an expression contains no valid data (Null). The syntax for IsNull is as follows:

```
IsNull(expression)
```

The `expression` argument can be any expression. IsNull returns True if the expression contains no valid data. If the expression is not Null, IsNull returns False. If you are using an expression with more than one operand, IsNull will return False if any one of the operands is Null.

The Null value indicates that the variable contains no valid data. Remember that Null is not the same as Empty, which indicates that a variable has not yet been initialized. Null is also not the same as a zero-length string, which is sometimes referred to as a null string.

Note   Use the IsNull function to determine whether an expression contains a Null value. Expressions that you expect to evaluate to True under some circumstances, such as `If Var = Null` and `If Var <> Null`, are always False because any expression containing a Null is itself Null and, therefore, False.

IsNumeric

IsNumeric returns a Boolean value that indicates whether an expression can be evaluated as a number. IsNumeric's syntax is as follows:

```
IsNumeric(expression)
```

The `expression` argument can be any expression. IsNumeric returns True if the entire expression is recognized as a number. If the expression is not a number, IsNumeric returns False. IsNumeric returns False if the expression is a date expression.

IsObject

IsObject returns a Boolean value that indicates whether an expression references a valid OLE Automation object. The syntax for IsObject is the following:

```
IsObject(expression)
```

The `expression` argument can be any expression. IsObject returns True if the expression is a variable of an Object subtype or a user-defined object; otherwise, it returns False.

VarType

VarType returns a value indicating the subtype of a variable. VarType's syntax is as follows:

```
VarType(varname)
```

The `varname` argument can be any variable. Values returned by VarType represent the variable subtypes in Table 2-1.

<table>
<tr><td colspan="2" align="center">Table 2-1
VarType Return Values</td></tr>
<tr><td>*Value*</td><td>*Variable type description*</td></tr>
<tr><td>0</td><td>Empty (uninitialized)</td></tr>
<tr><td>1</td><td>Null (no valid data)</td></tr>
<tr><td>2</td><td>Integer</td></tr>
<tr><td>3</td><td>Long integer</td></tr>
<tr><td>4</td><td>Single-precision floating-point number</td></tr>
<tr><td>5</td><td>Double-precision floating-point number</td></tr>
<tr><td>6</td><td>Currency</td></tr>
<tr><td>7</td><td>Date</td></tr>
<tr><td>8</td><td>String</td></tr>
<tr><td>9</td><td>Automation object</td></tr>
<tr><td>10</td><td>Error</td></tr>
<tr><td>11</td><td>Boolean</td></tr>
<tr><td>12</td><td>Variant (used only with arrays of Variants)</td></tr>
<tr><td>13</td><td>Non-Automation object</td></tr>
<tr><td>17</td><td>Byte</td></tr>
<tr><td>8192</td><td>Array</td></tr>
</table>

The VarType function never returns the value for Array by itself. The function is always added to some other value to indicate an array of a particular type. For example, the value returned for an array of integers is calculated as 2 + 8192, or 8194. If an object has a default property, VarType (object) returns the type of its default property.

Array Functions

VBScript has the following useful functions that help your code handle arrays:

- ✦ Redim
- ✦ LBound
- ✦ UBound
- ✦ Erase

The first useful function is the ReDim statement. In many cases, you may be adding an indeterminate amount of data and need a place to store the data. Because you cannot use user-defined types, a multidimensional array often works well. However, you need to be able to enlarge and reduce the size of your array as data is entered or deleted. The ReDim statement is used to adjust the size of the array. In the following example, the array arrInputData is enlarged from 10 elements to 20:

```
Dim arrInputData(10)
'
' More code
'
ReDim Preserve arrInputData(20)
```

Tip

If you are defining your variable and do not know the size of the array, define the array with a single item. You can use ReDim later to enlarge the array to the correct size.

One restriction on the ReDim statement is that it can change only the final dimension of a multidimensional array. For example, if arrInputData in the preceding example was defined as (10, 20), the array would always have to remain 10 cells wide, but you could enlarge or reduce the height of the array from 20 cells high by using the ReDim statement.

Another important note about the preceding example: the ReDim statement, by default, automatically erases all the data in your array when you use it. To prevent this behavior, add the Preserve keyword. Any existing data is left alone, and new blank cells are added. Obviously, if you reduce the size of your array, any data in the cells that were downsized is lost.

Caution

Always use the Preserve keyword with the ReDim statement to prevent the loss of data in your array.

Because the array is aware of its upper and lower bounds, you can use these values within your code and avoid having to use a separate counter. The LBound and UBound functions return the lower and upper bounds of an array. You can then use this information, for example, to add a new row to an existing array. Both of these functions can take an optional argument to specify which dimension you want to retrieve. If no dimension is given, the first dimension is assumed.

Finally, the Erase statement is a simple way to erase an array that you have been using. Just give the Erase statement the name of your array, and Erase empties the array of all data.

All the array-handling functions are documented in the following section for reference.

ReDim Statement

The ReDim statement is used to enlarge and reduce dynamic array variables previously created with the Dim statement. The syntax for this statement is as follows:

```
ReDim [Preserve] varname(subscripts) [,varname(subscripts)] ...
```

Table 2-2 contains an explanation for the parts of the ReDim statement.

Table 2-2 ReDim Statement Parameters	
Part	*Description*
Preserve	This keyword saves the data in the array when the array is resized. The default behavior (when this keyword is missing) is to erase the array when it is resized.
Varname	This is the name of the variable you want to create. The name cannot contain spaces or other punctuation characters. It can contain numbers and uppercase or lowercase letters; however, the first letter of the variable name must be a letter.
Subscripts	The subscripts for the variable are used when you are declaring arrays. Each dimension of the array should be separated by a comma from the previous dimension, as in the following examples: ReDim A(5) ReDim Preserve B(5, 6) ReDim C(5, 2, 1) The lower bound of an array is always zero.

You can use the ReDim statement repeatedly to change the number of elements and dimensions in an array.

The ReDim statement can only resize one dimension of an array. If you have an array of one dimension, that dimension can be resized. However, for arrays with multiple dimensions, only the last dimension can be resized. Look at the following example:

```
ReDim X(1, 2, 3)
```

In this case, only the last dimension can be changed from its current size of 3. If you reduce the size of your array, any data stored in the eliminated rows will be lost. The data will be lost even if you use the Preserve keyword.

When you resize your array and omit the Preserve keyword, all the cells of the array are cleared. If you look at the value as a number, it will be zero. If you look at the string value of the cell, it will equal the empty string, represented by double quotes ("").

Erase Statement

The Erase statement reinitializes the elements of fixed-size arrays and frees dynamic array storage space. The syntax for the Erase statement follows:

```
Erase array
```

The array argument is the name of the array variable to be erased. All the cells in the array will be cleared. If you view the contents of a cell after it has been cleared, it will be 0 (if printed as a numeric) or " " (if printed as a string).

Erase frees the memory used by dynamic arrays originally created by the Dim statement and modified by the ReDim statement. If you want to reuse a dynamic array variable, you must use the ReDim statement to set the array's size.

LBound Function

The LBound function returns the smallest available subscript for the indicated dimension of an array. The syntax for the LBound function is as follows:

```
LBound(arrayname[, dimension])
```

Table 2-3 contains an explanation for the parameters of the LBound function.

The LBound function is used with the UBound function to determine the size of an array. Use the UBound function to find the upper limit of an array dimension. The default lower bound for any dimension is always 0.

Table 2-3 **LBound Parameters**	
Part	**Description**
arrayname	Name of the array variable.
dimension	This parameter is a whole number indicating which dimension you want. Use 1 for the first dimension, 2 for the second, and so forth. If you omit this parameter, dimension 1 is returned.

UBound Function

The UBound function returns the largest available subscript for the indicated dimension of an array. The syntax for the UBound function appears as follows:

```
UBound(arrayname[, dimension])
```

Table 2-4 contains an explanation for the parameters of the UBound function.

Table 2-4 **UBound Parameter List**	
Part	**Description**
arrayname	Name of the array variable.
dimension	This parameter is a whole number indicating which dimension you want. Use 1 for the first dimension, 2 for the second, and so forth. If you omit this parameter, dimension 1 is returned.

The UBound function is used with the LBound function to determine the size of an array. Use the LBound function to find the lower limit of an array dimension.

The default lower bound for any dimension is always 0. Here are some sample results of using the UBound function on the array named B.

```
Dim B(5,3,4)

UBound(B, 1) equals 4
UBound(B, 2) equals 2
UBound(B, 3) equals 3
```

Conversion Functions

Because all variables in VBScript classify as type Variant, conversion functions become less important for data storage and more important for formatting output data either for display or input to other functions. VBScript provides a conversion function for each subtype of data. Each function accepts a Variant as an argument and displays a value in the subtype named by the function.

- ✦ `CBool`   Converts to subtype Boolean
- ✦ `CByte`   Converts to subtype Byte
- ✦ `CDate`   Converts to subtype Date
- ✦ `CDbl`   Converts to subtype Double
- ✦ `CInt`   Converts to subtype Integer
- ✦ `CLng`   Converts to subtype Long Integer
- ✦ `CSng`   Converts to subtype Single
- ✦ `CStr`   Converts to subtype String

Although the variable's type will always be Variant, these functions enable you to change the subtype of data stored in that variable. After you have converted the subtype, you can use the appropriate group of functions for that data. If a function is not assigned the correct subtype of data, you will get a `Type Mismatch Error`.

Mathematical Operations

VBScript includes many features for performing mathematical operations on both numeric and logical values. This section describes the operations you can perform and covers the functions that can be used to perform mathematical and logical calculations.

Addition and Subtraction Symbols

As with mathematics, VBScript uses the plus (+) sign for the addition operation; the minus (–) sign represents subtraction. Both symbols can represent positive and negative numbers and can be used with all types of numeric data.

```
Document.Write 1 + 2
```

The previous example prints a result of 3, and the following example prints 1.

```
Document.Write 2 - 1
```

Multiplication Symbol

VBScript uses the asterisk (*) to represent the multiplication operation. This operator can be used with all types of numeric data.

The following example prints a result of 18.

```
Document.Write 6 * 3
```

Division Symbols

Note   *Integer division* — This type of division rounds the two numbers to integer values and produces an integer result. Any remaining decimal values are discarded.

VBScript provides two different division operators. For normal division, use the forward slash (/) character between the operands. VBScript also provides *integer division*. Integer division rounds the two numbers (which need not be integers) to integer values and produces the result as an integer. Decimal values are truncated. Standard decimal division does not round or truncate the operands or the result. An example of the difference follows:

```
Document.Write 5.6 / 2
```

The preceding example uses standard decimal division and its expected result is 2.8.

```
Document.Write 5.6 \ 2
```

In the preceding example, integer division (with the back slash (\) character) produces a result of 3. The process rounds 5.6 to 6, and division produces the result of 3.

With integer division, you can calculate the number of pages filled by a certain number of lines. Use integer division to divide the number of lines by the number of lines per page. The result is the number of full pages produced.

In general, integer division should only be used when you are dividing other integers. Using integer division with non-integers can produce unexpected results, as seen in the preceding examples.

Modulus/Remainder Function

Keeping the preceding example in mind, imagine that you need to know how many lines the last page of the document holds. The *modulus function* calculates this value by producing the remainder left when dividing the two integers. Because the modulus function deals with remainders not logically associated with point numbers, you should avoid using the function with non-integer values. When used with non-integers, the function rounds both operands before processing the result.

The following is an example of the modulus function:

```
Document.Write 8 Mod 3
```

This statement produces the value 2, which is the remainder of dividing 8 by 3.

```
Document.Write 8 Mod 2
```

This statement produces the value 0, which is the remainder of dividing 8 by 2.

Exponentiation Operator

VBScript provides a function equivalent to assigning an exponent to a number. The caret (^), placed between two operands, raises the first number to the power specified by the second. This operator can be used with all valid numeric operands.

The following are some examples:

```
Document.Write 8 ^ 2
```

This statement produces the value 64, which is 8 squared.

```
Document.Write 4 ^ 0.5
```

This statement produces the value 2, which is the square root of 4. The square root is symbolized by taking a number to the $1/2$ power.

```
Document.Write 4 ^ -0.5
```

This statement displays the value 0.5, which is 4 to the –0.5 power.

Grouping Expressions

As in mathematics, the left and right parenthesis characters [(,)] can be used to group expressions that should be evaluated out of their normal order. For reference, the following list displays the correct order for operators. When operators from more than one of the groups listed below come together in the same expression, arithmetic operators are always evaluated first. Comparison operators follow, and logical operators are evaluated last. When in doubt about the order that an expression will actually be evaluated, use parentheses to group the expression in the correct manner. For example, the following expression will be evaluated by the system as 4 + (3 * 5):

```
4 + 3 * 5
```

However, you may require this expression to be evaluated as (4 + 3) * 5. The first, and correct, evaluation yields 19, but the alternate interpretation produces 60 as the answer. Grouping symbols are especially important when you are creating complex expressions, as in the following example that calculates the hypotenuse of a right triangle:

```
c = a * a + b * b
```

In this case, it is not immediately obvious which parts of the expression should be calculated first. VBScript, according to the rules of operator precedence, multiplies a * a first, b * b next, and then adds the results. However, if this order is not carried out, the result would be incorrect.

✦ Arithmetic Operator Precedence

Exponentiation (^)

Negation (–)

Multiplication and division (*, /)

Integer division

Modulo arithmetic (Mod)

Addition and subtraction

String concatenation

✦ Comparison Operator Precedence

Equality (=)

Inequality (<>)

Less than (<)

Greater than (>)

Less than or equal to (<=)

Greater than or equal to (>=)

Is operator

✦ Logical Operator Precedence

Not

And

Or

Xor

Eqv

Imp

&

Comparison Operators

Six operators are used when comparing numeric expressions:

✦ Equal to (=)

✦ Not equal to (<>)

✦ Less than (<)

✦ Less than or equal to (<=)

✦ Greater than (>)

✦ Greater than or equal to (>=)

These operators are valid for numeric, string, and date expressions. Unlike Visual Basic, which generates the words *True* and *False,* VBScript displays a 0 for False or a –1 for True when printing a logical expression.

Logical Operators

Logical operators are used to compare expressions and numbers. They can be used to create Boolean expressions.

Note   A Boolean expression is a mathematical expression that consists exclusively of True or False conditions. By evaluating each part of a Boolean expression, you get a result of True or False.

Not Operator

The Not operator is useful for simple negation. If the argument for this function is originally True, it will become False, and vice versa (see Table 2-5). The Not operator typically precedes an expression, as in the following example:

```
If Not (A < 4) Then ...
```

Because the expression generated by the Not operator can be confusing to read, many logical expressions can be reversed. For example, the code could be rewritten as follows:

```
If A >= 4 Then ...
```

In this case, the opposite of "less than" is "greater than or equal to." The reversal creates an expression that is easier to read and debug, if necessary.

Table 2-5 Result Table for Not Operator	
Expression1	**Result**
True	False
False	True

And Operator

The And operator is used to evaluate two Boolean expressions together. When you link the two expressions with And, the resulting expression is only True if both operands are True. Otherwise, the expression displays a result of False. Refer to Table 2-6 for the range of results for the And operator.

Table 2-6 Result Table for And Operator		
Expression1	**Expression2**	**Result**
True	True	True
True	False	False
False	True	False
False	False	False

The following examples illustrate the And operator:

```
If (3 < 5) And (5 > 6) Then ...    ' Because 5 is less than 6,
this expression is False.
If True And (3 < 5) Then ...       ' Both operands are True, so
the expression is True.
```

Or Operator

As with the And operator, the Or operator joins two Boolean expressions. The operator returns True if either expression is True, as shown in Table 2-7.

	Table 2-7	
	Result Table for Or Operator	
Expression1	**Expression2**	**Result**
True	True	True
True	False	True
False	True	True
False	False	False

The following examples illustrate the Or operator:

```
If (3 < 5) Or (5 > 6) Then      ' The first expression is True,
                                ' as is the entire expression.
If True Or (3 < 5) Then         ' Both operands are True, so the
                                ' expression is True.
```

Xor Operator

The Xor, or Exclusive Or, operator is also used to join two expressions. This operator displays True if one of the two expressions is true. However, if both expressions are true or both false, this operator displays False. Refer to Table 2-8 for the range of results for the Xor operator. Although the Xor operator is not as common as the And and Or operators, VBScript supports it to enable other more complex binary logic calculations.

	Table 2-8	
	Result Table for Xor Operator	
Expression1	**Expression2**	**Result**
True	True	False
True	False	True
False	True	True
False	False	False

Eqv Operator

The Eqv operator performs a logical equivalence on two Boolean expressions. If the two expressions are either both true or both false, the Eqv operator displays True. Otherwise, it displays False, as shown in Table 2-9.

Table 2-9 Result Table for Eqv Operator		
Expression1	*Expression2*	*Result*
True	True	True
True	False	False
False	True	False
False	False	True

Imp Operator

The Imp operator performs a logical implication on two Boolean expressions. A logical implication can be defined as follows: if A is True AND B is False, then (A Imp B) is False; otherwise A Imp B is True. The results of the operator, based on the operands, are shown in Table 2-10.

Table 2-10 Result Table for Imp Operator		
Expression1	*Expression2*	*Result*
True	True	True
True	False	False
True	Null	Null
False	True	True
False	False	True
False	Null	True
Null	True	True
Null	False	Null
Null	Null	Null

Implicit Type Conversion

When VBScript adds an integer to a floating-point number, the *implicit type conversion* process changes the precision of one or more of the values in the calculation so that all operands are of the same precision. For example, if you add an integer to a single precision number, the result would be a single precision number, as illustrated in the following example:

> In the expression 1 + 1.52 = 2.52, the implicit conversion would make the equation look like this: 1.00 + 1.52 = 2.52.

Although this concept usually does not rank as a crucial one to remember, ignoring it can introduce errors into your calculations. For instance, if you calculate numbers and round them before you add them, you may gain a different result than if you add the original values before you round them. The following is an example of this error-producing behavior:

```
<SCRIPT LANGUAGE=VBScript>
Dim IntegerValueA, FloatValueA
Dim IntegerValueB, FloatValueB

IntegerValueA = 6
FloatValueA = 0.3

IntegerValueB = 8
FloatValueB = .6

Document.Write CInt(IntegerValueA * FloatValueA) _
    + CInt(IntegerValueB * FloatValueB)

Document.Write (IntegerValueA * FloatValueA) _
    + (IntegerValueB * FloatValueB)
</SCRIPT>
```

In this example, the values 7 and 6.6 are generated for the two calculations. Although these results are not the expected ones, this behavior is easy to regulate with the appropriate type conversion functions. In most cases, you will know the type of data before you store it in a variable. Naming your variables to reflect the type of data that is stored makes it easier to track down this kind of error when you are debugging your VBScript code.

Looping and Decision Structures

Now that you have learned the functions and expressions in VBScript, let's use them in some more complex structures. VBScript supports five looping and decision structures:

✦ If/Then/Else

✦ For/Next

✦ Select/Case

✦ Do/Loop

✦ While/Wend

If/Then/Else Structure

If you have ever done any programming, you are probably familiar with the If/Then/Else decision structure, which is one of the most common programming constructs. Even if you are not a programmer, you are already familiar with the concept as it is used in language. For example, the following sentence uses the If/Then/Else structure:

If your car's gas tank is empty, you need to get gas. Otherwise, you do not have to stop at the gas station.

Three separate pieces make up this sentence:

"If your car's gas tank is empty,"

"You need to get gas."

"Otherwise, you do not have to stop at the gas station."

The first clause is known as the *conditional expression*. If this condition is true, the second clause occurs. If the condition in the first clause is false, the third clause occurs. These three pieces of the statement correspond directly to the three keywords of the If/Then/Else construct. The conditional expression in the first clause follows the If keyword. The second clause follows the Then keyword. Finally, the third clause follows the Else keyword. If this sentence was formatted in a computer program, it would appear as follows:

```
If (Your car's gas tank is empty) Then
    You need to get gas
Else
    You do not have to stop at the gas station.
End If
```

The sentence structure converts easily to code, as shown in the preceding example. For this reason, and because it is used so often in the real world, the If/Then/Else structure is the most understandable of the structures discussed in this chapter.

The basic syntax of the If/Then/Else construct follows:

```
If logical-expression Then statement1 Else statement2
```

You can use any valid logical expression in the If/Then/Else statement. Logical expressions are covered in the preceding section.

If the `logical-expression` is True, `statement1` is executed. If the `logical-expression` is False, `statement2` is executed. A simple example of this expression follows:

```
If A > B Then Document.Write "Variable A is greater" Else
Document.Write "Variable B is greater"
```

In some cases, you may not have an Else condition that requires code. In the cases where you do not need to use the Else condition, you can simplify the statement and omit the Else condition. You may, for instance, want to check a condition and do something only if the condition is True. An example of omitting the Else clause looks like the following:

```
If A > B Then Document.Write "Variable A is greater and we
don't care about variable B."
```

Using the End If Statement

What if `statement1` actually needs to be multiple statements? VBScript provides a way to format the If/Then/Else condition to enable multiple statements in a more readable format. An example of the multiple-line format follows:

```
If A > B Then
    Document.Write "Variable A is greater." & "<P>"
    Document.Write "Variable B is less than or equal to variable
A."
Else
    Document.Write "Variable B is greater." & "<P>"
    Document.Write "Variable A is less than or equal to variable
B."
End If
```

In the preceding example, you see the addition of the End If statement. End If is used at the end of the final section of the If/Then/Else structure. If you are using the Else clause, End If follows the end of the Else code block. If the Else clause has been omitted, as in the following example, the End If statement follows the Then code block.

```
If A > B Then
    Document.Write "Variable A is greater." & "<P>"
    Document.Write "Variable B is less than or equal to variable
A."
End If
```

Enhancing Readability in If/Then/Else Code

Notice that the code within the If/Then/Else block is indented in the preceding example. Typically, the code should be indented three or four spaces. The indents help readability by showing which code is associated with which conditions. When you learn about nested If/Then/Else structures, you see the need for this type of formatting.

As you learned in the preceding section, logical expressions can be quite complex. Any valid logical expression can be used in the If/Then/Else statement, as in the following example that verifies a character is an uppercase letter:

```
Dim strCharacter
strCharacter = "E"
If Asc(strCharacter) >= Asc("A") And Asc(strCharacter) <=
Asc("Z") Then
    Document.Write "The letter is an uppercase letter."
Else
    Document.Write "The letter is not an uppercase letter."
End If
```

In some cases, the condition may be so long that it scrolls past the right edge of your window. Lengthy conditions are common, but not being able to see the entire condition makes it prone to errors. When you have a lengthy condition, you can use the *continuation character* to split the line into multiple lines. The continuation character is the underscore character (_). The following example (with the continuation character in bold) shows how this character can be used:

```
Dim strCharacter
strCharacter = "E"
If (Asc(strCharacter) >= Asc("A") And Asc(strCharacter) <=
Asc("Z")) _
    Or (Asc(strCharacter) >= Asc("a") And Asc(strCharacter) <=
Asc("z")) Then
    ·Document.Write "The character is a letter."
Else
    Document.Write "The character is not a letter."
End If
```

Tip   Use the underscore continuation character to split a long line of code into multiple lines that are easier to read. You can split any line between any space as long as you are not splitting a string enclosed in quotes.

Nested If/Then/Else Structures

Within an If/Then/Else structure, you can have other If/Then/Else structures. These structures are called *nested* structures. In the preceding example, you may need to determine whether the character is actually a number. The following example shows how to nest an additional If/Then/Else condition to determine whether the character is a number:

```
Dim strCharacter
strCharacter = "E"
If (Asc(strCharacter) >= Asc("A") And Asc(strCharacter) <=
Asc("Z")) _
    Or (Asc(strCharacter) >= Asc("a") And Asc(strCharacter) <=
Asc("z")) Then
    Document.Write "The character is a letter."
Else
    If Asc(strCharacter) >= Asc("0") And Asc(strCharacter) <=
Asc("9") Then
        Document.Write "The character is a number."
    Else
        Document.Write "The character is not a letter or a
number."
    End If
End If
```

Note the placement of the two End If statements. One follows the outside If/Then/Else construct at the end of the sample. This End If closes the structure that began at the top of the sample. The second End If closes the structure within the Else clause of the first If/Then/Else structure. Formatting your code consistently makes reading the code much easier. Imagine trying to decode the following piece of code that lacks any formatting:

```
Dim strCharacter
strCharacter = "E"
If (Asc(strCharacter) >= Asc("A") And Asc(strCharacter) <=
Asc("Z")) _
Or (Asc(strCharacter) >= Asc("a") And Asc(strCharacter) <=
Asc("z")) Then
Document.Write "The character is a letter."
Else
If Asc(strCharacter) >= Asc("0") And Asc(strCharacter) <=
Asc("9") Then
Document.Write "The character is a number."
Else
Document.Write "The character is not a letter or a number."
End If
End If
```

Even in this simple example, quickly finding the decision blocks is difficult. As your code becomes more complex, reading code formatted in this manner becomes impossible.

Using the ElseIf Keyword

The preceding example brings up a good question: What happens when the nesting goes too deep? The following example illustrates this question:

```
If condition Then
    If condition2 Then
        If condition3 Then
```

In some cases, the structure can be flattened by using the ElseIf keyword. If you are using mutually exclusive possibilities, as in the example that checked a character against several ranges, you can use ElseIf to create a less complex structure. The structure in the preceding example changes as follows when you add the ElseIf keyword:

```
Dim strCharacter
strCharacter = "E"
If (Asc(strCharacter) >= Asc("A") And Asc(strCharacter) <=
Asc("Z")) _
    Or (Asc(strCharacter) >= Asc("a") And Asc(strCharacter) <=
Asc("z")) Then
    Document.Write "The character is a letter."
ElseIf Asc(strCharacter) >= Asc("0") And Asc(strCharacter) <=
Asc("9") Then
    Document.Write "The character is a number."
Else
    Document.Write "The character is not a letter or a number."
End If
```

This type of structure is similar to a series of filters designed to trap smaller and smaller particles. The first If clause traps certain cases, the ElseIf clause traps others that didn't match the first, and so forth. Finally, cases that didn't match any of the first conditions are handled by the final Else clause. In the preceding example, the code traps letters and numbers. All other cases are handled by the final condition.

For/Next Structure

The computer excels at performing repetitive tasks. For coding these structures, VBScript provides the For/Next structure to perform loops where the beginning and ending values are known. For loops where a logical condition should be evaluated to determine the end of the loop, you can use the While/Wend or Do/Loop structures, which are discussed in following sections of this chapter.

The basic format of this structure follows:

```
For loopvariable = startvalue To endvalue
    <statements that should be repeated>
Next
```

The statements within the For and Next statements execute once for each value between `startvalue` and `endvalue`. While the loop is executing, the variable `loopvariable` increments by 1 after each iteration. In the following example, all the values between 1 and 5 print on-screen.

```
Dim loopVar
For loopVar = 1 To 5
    Document.Write loopVar & "<P>"
Next
```

The starting and ending values must be numbers; however, they are not restricted to being simple numbers. You can use expressions that evaluate to numbers, as in the following example, which prints all the letters from A to Z by looping through the ASCII values of the letters:

```
Dim loopVar
For loopVar = Asc("A") To Asc("Z")
    Document.Write Chr(loopVar) & "<P>"
Next
```

The `loopvar` function is assigned the ASCII (numeric) values of the letters from A to Z. The `Chr` function returns the actual character assigned to an ASCII value.

The For/Next structure enables negative numbers to be used as starting or ending values, as in the following example:

```
Dim loopVar
For loopVar = -5 To 5
    Document.Write loopVar & "<P>"
Next
```

Using the Step Keyword

In cases where you need to increment by a value other than 1, you can use the Step keyword to indicate how much each iteration should increment the counter. The following example counts by two to 20:

```
Dim loopVar
For loopVar = 0 To 20 Step 2
    Document.Write loopVar & "<P>"
Next
```

The Step value can also be negative to make a loop iterate backwards. To step backwards by one, for example, you would use a step value of –1.

The For loop keeps iterating as long as the counter variable is less than or equal to the ending value given in the loop. In the preceding example, the value 20 is the last value printed because the next value in the sequence, 22, is greater than 20.

You don't have to end exactly on the ending value. For instance, in this example, the counter is never given the value 21, but will be given 22. Because 22 is greater than 21, the loop will terminate when it passes the ending value.

```
Dim loopVar
For loopVar = 0 To 21 Step 2
    Document.Write loopVar & "<P>"

Next
```

Exiting For/Next Loops Prematurely

In certain cases, it may be necessary to exit the For/Next loop before reaching the ending value. In these cases, you can use the Exit For statement to exit the loop and continue at the first line following the Next keyword. Although exiting a loop in this manner is considered by some to be poor programming style, it often simplifies the logic for the reader of your code. In the following example, the For loop exits when it matches the first letter of the string held in the stringVar variable:

```
Dim loopVar
Dim stringVar
stringVar = "Components"

For loopVar = Asc("A") to Asc("Z")

    <statements>

    If Left$(stringVar, 1) = Chr(loopVar) Then Exit For

    <statements>
Next
```

Nested Loops

For/Next structures, like all other programming structures, can be nested. For instance, to generate a grid, you can create code, as in the following example:

```
Dim xVar, yVar

For xVar = Asc("A") to Asc("Z")
    For yVar = 1 to 10
        Document.Write Chr(xVar) & yVar & Space(1)
    Next   ' yVar
    Document.Write "<P>"
Next   ' xVar
```

Several characteristics of the preceding example are worth mentioning. For each time that the outer loop is executed, the inner loop is completely executed; that is, it iterates through all the values from 1 through 10 before the next iteration of the outer loop. The resulting output appears as follows:

```
A1 A2 A3 A4 A5 A6 A7 A8 A9 A10

B1 B2 B3 B4 B5 B6 B7 B8 B9 B10

C1 C2 C3 C4 C5 C6 C7 C8 C9 C10

D1 D2 D3 D4 D5 D6 D7 D8 D9 D10

E1 E2 E3 E4 E5 E6 E7 E8 E9 E10

F1 F2 F3 F4 F5 F6 F7 F8 F9 F10

G1 G2 G3 G4 G5 G6 G7 G8 G9 G10

H1 H2 H3 H4 H5 H6 H7 H8 H9 H10

I1 I2 I3 I4 I5 I6 I7 I8 I9 I10

J1 J2 J3 J4 J5 J6 J7 J8 J9 J10
```

To move to a new line after the inner loop finishes executing, a paragraph tag is printed right after the inner loop finishes. Because the Document.Write function prints characters without any formatting, insert the <BR> tag and force a line break at the end of each logical row.

Tip   In nested loops, you can become confused about which Next keyword matches with the appropriate For keyword. In Visual Basic, the variable name is normally placed with the Next keyword; however, VBScript does not support this placement. Therefore, you should place a comment next to the Next keyword to indicate the loop it matches. This comment is a handy trick that you can use to help you debug your code. By placing the comments consistently, your nested loops will become much easier to read.

Select/Case Structure

In cases where you have a number of items against which you want to match a variable, you can code it as an If/Then/Else or an If/ElseIf/Else structure. However, if some of the items have the same action to be performed, you end up with a lot of duplicated code. To eliminate the duplication, the Select/Case structure enables you to create a list of values against which to test and perform various actions based on the results. An example of Select/Case structure follows:

```
Dim stringVar
stringVar = "B"
```

```
Select Case stringVar
    Case "A":
    Document.Write "Letter is A"
    Case "B", "C":
    Document.Write "Letter is B or C"
    Case Else:
    Document.Write "I don't know what letter it is"
End Select
```

Tip   The colon after the Case value is optional.

The equivalent code, using If/ElseIf/Else statements, appears as follows:

```
Dim stringVar
stringVar = "B"

If stringVar = "A" Then
    Document.Write "Letter is A"
ElseIf stringVar = "B" Or stringVar = "C" Then
    Document.Write "Letter is B or C"
Else
    Document.Write "I don't know what letter it is"
End If
```

For short lists, either structure can be used. However, in the cases where you are testing for multiple items to perform the same action (as in the preceding example for B or C), the Select/Case is much easier to use and change later. You can separate each of the items in the acceptable list with commas (as in the first example), and any matching value causes the statements below it to be executed. You can add items to any of the Case statements more easily than you can add additional ElseIf clauses to an already large If/ElseIf block.

Using the Case Else Keyword

In cases where you are evaluating a user's input, you should assume that the user may type invalid characters. The Case Else keyword enables you to have a generic case that catches all values not handled in a previous case. Note that only one Case can be matched for any given value. In the following example, the first Case is matched and "Letter is A or B" is printed on-screen. This event occurs even though the letter *B* can be matched by either of the first two Case statements.

```
Dim stringVar
stringVar = "B"

Select Case stringVar
    Case "A", "B":
    Document.Write "Letter is A or B"
```

```
    Case "B", "C":
    Document.Write "Letter is B or C"
    Case Else:
    Document.Write "I don't know what letter it is"
End Select
```

Besides string values, you can use the Select/Case structure to match any valid values.

Performing Blank Actions

In cases where you do not want to perform any statements when a value is matched, you can leave the statement section blank, as in the following example. If the letter is *A*, no action is taken. This method is used when a large number of values is checked. In these cases, you can add a blank action to show that you did consider the value, but no action was required.

```
Dim stringVar
stringVar = "B"

Select Case stringVar
    Case "A":
    ' No action is required
    Case "B", "C":
    Document.Write "Letter is B or C"
    Case Else:
    Document.Write "I don't know what letter it is"
End Select
```

In cases where you use a placeholder, a comment is usually used to explain your actions to later users of the code. Otherwise, users may think that you introduced an error into your code.

Using the Underscore Character

If you are writing a Case condition for a large number of choices, you can use the underscore character to format your lines, as in the following example:

```
Dim stringVar
stringVar = "B"

Select Case stringVar
    Case "A":
    ' No action is required
    Case "B", "C", _
         "D", "E", _
         "F", "G":
    Document.Write "Letter betwen B and G"
    Case Else:
    Document.Write "I don't know what letter it is"
End Select
```

The underscore character enables you to combine the conditions into more logical groups and save yourself from having to write multiple conditions that have the same actions. As always, the fewer times that you use the same code translates into fewer possibilities for errors.

Do/Loop Structure

As mentioned in the preceding section, every For/Next loop can be written as a Do/Loop structure. However, the Do/Loop structure offers more possibilities than the For/Next loop. For instance, you can exit the loop based on a logical condition instead of just when the counter reaches an ending value that you previously specified. In the following example, which emulates the behavior of the For/Next structure, the loop iterates as long as the loop variable is less than a given value:

```
Dim loopVar
loopVar = 1
Do
    <statements>
    loopVar = loopVar + 1
Loop While loopVar <= 5
```

Just as the For/Next loop initializes the counter variable to the starting value, the value of `loopVar` is set to the starting value before entering the loop. At some point within the loop, `loopVar` increments. Finally, at the end of the loop, the counter is checked to determine whether the loop should continue.

The Do/Loop structure can be written by using the Until keyword. The Until keyword essentially reverses the logic in the condition. For example, the preceding example can be rewritten using the Until keyword as follows:

```
Dim loopVar
loopVar = 1
Do
    <statements>
    loopVar = loopVar + 1
Loop Until loopVar > 5
```

Using this keyword is similar to reversing the logic when you have a complex If/Then/Else condition. As mentioned before, your syntax is clearer when you use fewer symbols and keywords. In this case, the condition `Until loopVar > 5` is clearer than `While loopVar <= 5` because you only have to determine whether the number is larger than 5 and not larger or equal to 5. You have fewer possibilities for confusion about how large the counter can become before exiting the loop.

Reversing Operators

In several of the preceding examples, you needed to reverse the logic of a condition. All logical operators can be reversed and used in an alternative manner. Table 2-11 contains several examples of operator reversals.

Table 2-11 Converting Logical Expressions	
Original Condition	*Converted Condition*
If X < 5	If Not(X >= 5)
If X = 5	If Not(X <> 5)
If X > 5	If Not(X <= 5)
If X >= 5	If Not(X < 5)
If X <= 5	If Not(X > 5)
If X <> 5	If Not(X = 5)

In these conversions, the original logic stays the same, but the condition can be used with a different keyword. If, for example, you want to change a While condition to an Until condition, you first follow the rules given previously. Then, because the Until keyword uses the opposite condition of the While keyword, you would use the reversed condition without the Not keyword. Look at the following steps to see how a condition can be reversed:

1. The original code statement is as follows:

```
Do
    <statements>
    loopVar = loopVar + 1
Loop While loopVar <= 5
```

2. You can reverse the condition by using the information in Table 2-11. The condition now becomes the following:

```
Loop While Not(loopVar > 5)
```

3. Finally, you replace the While Not keywords with Until, as follows:

```
Loop Until loopVar > 5
```

Following these rules, you can reverse any condition to make it easier to read. In cases where you have a compound condition that uses the And or Or keyword, the conversion is slightly more difficult. However, you still follow the same steps. Look at the following examples to see how the conversion is accomplished for the keywords:

```
Do While (Asc(stringVar) >= Asc("A")) And (Asc(stringVar) <=
Asc("Z"))
```

To reverse this condition, follow these steps:

1. Change the And keyword to Or, or vice versa, as follows:

   ```
   (Asc(stringVar) >= Asc("A")) Or (Asc(stringVar) <= Asc("Z"))
   ```

2. Reverse the conditions on either side of the And/Or operator, as follows:

   ```
   Not(Asc(stringVar) >= Asc("A")) Or Not(Asc(stringVar) <=
   Asc("Z"))
   ```

3. Using the rules about reversing operators, simplify the condition. Each Not operator reverses the conditions on either side of the Or keyword. After the simplification has occurred, the condition becomes the following:

   ```
   (Asc(stringVar) < Asc("A")) Or (Asc(stringVar) > Asc("Z"))
   ```

At this point, you can use this condition in the Do Until clause, as follows:

```
   Do Until (Asc(stringVar) < Asc("A")) Or (Asc(stringVar) >
Asc("Z"))
```

If you look at this condition logically, it still uses the same logic. The loop should continue until the ASCII value of `stringVar` is outside the range bounded by the letters *A* and *Z*. In the unreversed condition, the character has to be between the letters. In the reversed condition, the letter has to be outside the range. Either way, the same effect is achieved.

The preceding examples are designed to provide good models for converting and simplifying your logic. Boolean math has many other complex rules for converting expressions, but the preceding examples covered the most common conversion rules.

Exiting the Loop

When the condition is checked at the end, use the Do/Loop structure so that the program enters the loop immediately without checking conditions first. Checking the condition at the end of the loop guarantees that the statements within the Do/Loop structure are executed at least once. However, sometimes you will have statements that should not execute at all. In these cases, the logical expression following the Loop keyword can be repositioned to follow the Do keyword. By checking the exit condition first, the entire block of statements can be skipped when dictated by conditions in the program. In the following example, the preceding structure has been rewritten with the alternative method just described:

```
Dim loopVar
loopVar = 1
Do Until loopVar > 5
   <statements>
   loopVar = loopVar + 1
Loop
```

If `loopVar` is set initially to 6, the statements within the Do/Loop structure do not execute. The exit condition is met when the program flow reaches the Do Until statement. This example can be written by using the While keyword in place of the Until keyword. Again, when you make the replacement, you have to reverse the logic of the exit condition, as in the following example:

```
Dim loopVar
loopVar = 1
Do While loopVar <= 5
    <statements>
    loopVar = loopVar + 1
Loop
```

Both of the preceding examples are programmatically identical. They both stop iterating when the counter reaches 6.

Nesting the Do/Loop Structure

As with all the other looping structures, you can also nest the Do/Loop structure. In the following example, the For/Next example has been rewritten to use two Do Until loops instead of the For/Next loops used previously:

```
Dim xVar, yVar

xVar = Asc("A")
Do Until xVar > Asc("Z")
    yVar = 1
    Do Until yVar > 10
        Document.Write Chr(xVar) & yVar & Space(1)
        yVar = yVar + 1
    Loop ' yVar loop
    Document.Write "<P>"
    xVar = xVar + 1
Loop ' xVar loop
```

The Loop keywords are commented to indicate which loop they match. The statements within each loop are also indented so that you can tell to which loop they belong. If you do not indent and comment this code, it will look something like the following:

```
Dim xVar, yVar

xVar = Asc("A")
Do Until xVar > Asc("Z")
yVar = 1
Do Until yVar > 10
Document.Write Chr(xVar) & yVar & Space(1)
yVar = yVar + 1
Loop
```

```
Document.Write "<P>"
xVar = xVar + 1
Loop
```

As you can see, several more lines are needed to perform the same functions that the For/Next structure performs automatically. You have to initialize your counters manually to their starting values, increment them manually, and reset them manually (for the inner loop) each time you want to use them again.

Exiting the Do/Loop Prematurely

Finally, as with the For/Next statement, you will have some cases where it is easier to exit the loop when a condition is met. For instance, you may be using a For loop and have multiple exit conditions. If one of the optional exit conditions is met, you can use Exit For to exit immediately instead of waiting until the end of the loop. In these cases, the Exit Do statement can be used to exit the current Do/Loop structure. The Exit Do statement exits the current loop. If you have nested loops, you must use one Exit Do statement for each Do/Loop structure you have to exit.

While/Wend Structure

The final looping structure supported by Visual Basic is the While/Wend structure. This structure is identical to the Do While <condition>/Loop structure variation. The Wend stands for End While and takes the place of the Loop keyword in the preceding examples. The following example uses the Do While keywords:

```
Dim loopVar
loopVar = 1
Do While loopVar <= 5
    <statements>
    loopVar = loopVar + 1
Loop
```

The preceding example can be rewritten by using the While/Wend structure as follows:

```
Dim loopVar
loopVar = 1
While loopVar <= 5
    <statements>
    loopVar = loopVar + 1
Wend
```

Unlike the Do/Loop structure, the While/Wend structure does not have an Exit keyword that enables you immediately to exit the currently iterating loop. For this and several other reasons, you should use the Do/Loop structure instead of the While/Wend structure. The While/Wend structure is included primarily for compatibility and consistency with Visual Basic.

Unsupported Looping Structures

Visual Basic programmers are probably familiar with many structures that are not supported in VBScript. These unsupported structures include the following:

✦ DoEvents. This keyword forces the Visual Basic event queue to be processed. Using this keyword helps to control the visual interface to your Visual Basic program.

✦ For Each/Next. This structure is used to iterate through a collection of objects in much the same way that the For/Next structure is used to iterate through a list of values. Because the Collection object is not supported by VBScript, the For Each/Next structure cannot be used either.

✦ GoSub/Return. This structure is similar to the subroutines and functions that are used in Visual Basic. GoSub is similar to a subroutine, but it works based on line numbers that were formerly used in BASIC coding. Because line numbers and line labels are unsupported, GoSub cannot be used.

✦ GoTo. For the same reason that the GoSub keyword does not work, GoTo requires a line number or a label to function.

✦ On Error GoTo. This common error-handling construct is unsupported in VBScript because it requires a line label to work correctly. VBScript, as you learn in Chapter 9, "Programming with Events," supports the On Error Resume Next statement, which enables the program to continue even after a runtime error occurs. Any error handling has to be handled inline.

✦ With/End With. The With/End With structure is used in combination with user-defined types and objects. It is used to execute a series of statements on an object or variable declared with a user-defined type. Because user-defined types are not supported in VBScript, this operator is not needed.

The five structures introduced in this chapter are identical to those used in Visual Basic. However, several key constructs are missing: GoTo, On Error GoTo, GoSub/Return, For Each/Next, With/End With, and DoEvents. However, these omissions can be supplemented by other similar structures that are supported in VBScript. Some of these omissions, such as the For Each/Next and With/End With, are omitted because they are not needed. Both of these structures deal with the Collection object, which is not supported in VBScript.

Summary

This chapter introduced the basic code elements of VBScript. You learned about constants, variables, and data types, and how they can be used to manage data in your ASP pages. Subsequent chapters show how to use these elements as part of your code.

This chapter also introduced you to the basic flow control structures used in VBScript. Using the If/Then/Else, Do/Loop, While/Wend, For/Next, and Select/Case structures and the examples from this chapter, you will be able to use these structures in your own pages to control how code is executed. In addition, understanding these structures is important because this book's examples use them extensively.

✦   ✦   ✦

VBScript Functions and Objects

◆ ◆ ◆ ◆

In This Chapter

Learn about the
VBScript data
conversion functions

Use text-formatting
functions to control
data output

Use mathematical,
date, and time
functions to do
complex calculations

Learn about the
objects built into the
VBScript language

◆ ◆ ◆ ◆

Data Conversion Functions

Even though all the variables with which you work in VBScript
are Variants, you still have many (if not more) data conversion
issues. For instance, when a user enters data into a form, you
may put it in a Variant in VBScript, but the data probably will
go into a database that doesn't recognize Variants. Similarly,
you have to take data out of a database and put it into a form,
and often you need to change the format in which the data is
displayed. The VBScript Data Conversion functions covered in
this section will help you handle these conversions easily.

Type Conversion Functions

VBScript includes nine functions that convert a Variant into a
particular data type. While a Variant can hold any type of data,
it is aware of the type of data it is holding. This characteristic is
helpful when dealing with databases, which are quite particular
about the data being given to them. In some cases, you will
need to use one of these functions to change input data to the
proper format before putting it into the database.

Cross-Reference   You'll learn more about database interaction starting in
Chapter 11.

CBool Function

This function takes a value and converts it to a `True` or `False`
value. However, the conversion is accomplished in a slightly
unexpected manner. If you run the code shown in Listing 3-1,
you get the results displayed after the code.

Listing 3-1: **CBool Test Code**

```
<%
    For i = -5 To 5
        Response.Write i & ": " & CBool(i) & "<br>" & vbCrLf
    Next
%>

-5: True
-4: True
-3: True
-2: True
-1: True
 0: False
 1: True
 2: True
 3: True
 4: True
 5: True
```

This example shows that any value other than zero converts to a True Boolean value. While many people use zero for false and one for true, this arrangement is not a universal standard, so be careful when using this function on numbers — the results may surprise you.

CByte Function

This function takes a value and converts it to a Byte data type. A Byte can hold a positive number from zero to 255. If you put in a number that falls outside of that range, you will get an Overflow runtime error from VBScript. Here are a few examples:

```
Response.Write CByte(98.6)    ' converted value is 99
Response.Write CByte(32.1)    ' converted value is 32
Response.Write CByte(-1)      ' Overflow error
```

CCur Function

This function takes a numeric value and converts it to a Currency data type. The Currency data type does not have as many decimal digits of precision as other data types. Data types with high precision (Single, Double) do not work as well for currency calculations, because most currency calculations only need to deal with two decimal digits. The Currency data type can handle, at most, four digits to the right of the decimal point. The overall range is −922,337,203,685,477.5808 to 922,337,203,685,477.5807. Here are a few examples:

```
Response.Write CCur(54.12236)     ' prints 54.1224
Response.Write CCur(-54.12236)    ' prints -54.1224
```

CDate Function

This function converts a piece of text or a number into a date. The function is pretty forgiving on format and deals with four-digit years correctly. You learn about the `FormatDateTime` function in a subsequent section of this chapter, but to illustrate the point, we will examine the function now. Look at the code in Listing 3-2. It shows how VBScript deals with two-digit years when it needs to convert them to four digits.

Listing 3-2: **CDate Test Code**

```
For i = 0 To 99
    Response.Write CDate("4/12/" & i) _
        & " is " _
        & FormatDateTime(CDate("4/12/" & i), 1) & "<br>"

Next ' i
```

The 1 in the `FormatDateTime` call specifies that the long date format is to be used, which shows the day and a four-digit year. The results of this code follow:

```
4/12/00 is Wednesday, April 12, 2000
4/12/01 is Thursday, April 12, 2001
4/12/02 is Friday, April 12, 2002
4/12/03 is Saturday, April 12, 2003
.
.
.
4/12/28 is Wednesday, April 12, 2028
4/12/29 is Thursday, April 12, 2029
4/12/30 is Saturday, April 12, 1930
4/12/31 is Sunday, April 12, 1931
4/12/32 is Tuesday, April 12, 1932
4/12/33 is Wednesday, April 12, 1933
.
.
.4/12/97 is Saturday, April 12, 1997
4/12/98 is Sunday, April 12, 1998
4/12/99 is Monday, April 12, 1999
```

This preceding code demonstrates what VBScript assumes if you use only a two-digit year. For values of *i* that are 0–29, VBScript place 20 in front of the value. All values 30 and higher are preceded by 19.

CDbl Function

This function converts a value (numeric or text) to a Double data type. The Double is the largest capacity data type in VBScript, and can hold values –1.79769313486232E308 to –4.94065645841247E-324 for negative values and from 4.94065645841247E-324 to 1.79769313486232E308 for positive values. If you have any doubt whether your variable is large enough to hold a number, use a Double, unless you're planning to do monetary calculations, in which case you should use a Currency data type. Of course, Double has a significantly larger range than a Currency, but you rarely need to perform currency calculations of values bigger than 922 trillion.

CInt Function

This function converts a value (numeric or text) to an Integer data type. The Integer data type can hold values from –32768 to 32767. For larger numbers, use a Long. Also, remember that giving this function an empty string will not return zero; rather, an empty string causes an error. Check your string against the empty string ("") before feeding it to this function.

CLng Function

This function converts a value (numeric or text) to a Long data type. The Long data type can hold values from –2,147,483,648 to 2,147,483,647. For larger numbers, use a Single, Currency, or Double. Also, remember that giving this function an empty string will not return zero; rather, it causes an error. Check your string against the empty string ("") before feeding it to this function.

CSng Function

This function converts a value (numeric or text) to a Single data type. The Single data type can hold values from –3.402823E38 to –1.401298E-45 for negative values and 1.401298E-45 to 3.402823E38 for positive values. For larger numbers, use a Double. Also, remember that giving this function an empty string will not return zero; rather, it causes an error. Check your string against the empty string ("") before feeding it to this function.

CStr Function

This function takes any expression and converts it to a string. As a result, this function can be helpful when dealing with databases that won't always allow a number in a text field. You can use CStr to convert the value to a string before using it in another function.

Character to Number Functions

Every character that can be used as part of a text string is assigned a number. This code is known as the ASCII value of the character. ASCII, or American Standard Code for Information Interchange, is a standard used in all computers in the United States. Every character in this set is given a number from 0 to 127. This number makes it easier to determine if a letter is within a certain range, such as from A to C. VBScript provides two functions to convert back and forth between a character and a number: Asc and Chr. The Asc function returns the ASCII value for a character, and Chr returns the character for an ASCII value. Here are some examples:

```
Response.Write Asc("A")     ' prints 65
Response.Write Asc("a")     ' prints 97
Response.Write Chr(66)      ' prints "B"
Response.Write Chr(126)     ' prints "~"
```

The ranges of codes are as follows:

   0–31 are non-printable control characters

   32 is a space

   33–47 are punctuation

   48–57 are numbers from zero to nine

   58–64 are punctuation

   65–90 are uppercase letters

   91–96 are punctuation

   97–122 are lowercase letters

   123–126 are punctuation

   127 is the DEL character, which is non-printable

Online help for any Visual Studio product has a complete list of all ASCII character codes, but you can always use the function to find a particular letter. In addition, if you want to check a range, you can simply compound the functions so you don't have to know the number, as follows:

```
If Asc(strLetter) >= Asc("A") _
   And Asc(strLetter) <= Asc("Z") Then
      Response.Write "Letter is uppercase."
End If
```

This method is actually more reliable and readable, because the reader may not remember that 65 is an uppercase A. However, by putting the letters in the function, the purpose of the code is easier to ascertain.

Base Conversion Functions

VBScript provides several convenient functions for converting numbers to octal or hexadecimal representations. These functions produce strings that display the results of the conversion. Hexidecimal and octal numbers are used frequently when dealing with the operating system. Specifying colors is one common example of hexadecimal numbers. Because every color can be represented by three numbers that specify the red, green, and blue components of the color, the resulting value is often written in hexadecimal. For instance, FFFFFF is the same as 255, 255, 255, which is white. These hex numbers are used frequently in HTML tags to specify colors for text and HTML elements. The following examples illustrate the functions:

```
Response.Write Hex(65536)    ' Prints 10000
Response.Write Oct(400)      ' Prints 620
```

If you need to specify an octal or hexadecimal number in your code, prefix the number with &0 or &H, respectively, as in these examples:

```
Response.Write &H10000    ' Prints 65536
Response.Write &0620      ' Prints 400
```

Integer Conversion Functions

Besides the CInt function, VBScript also provides the Int and Fix functions. Each of these functions truncates the number given and produces an integer result. However, the functions differ when dealing with negative numbers. Int removes the decimal portion and displays the first negative integer that is less than the input number. Fix removes the decimal portion and displays the first negative integer that is greater than the input number. The following examples illustrate this difference:

```
Response.Write Int(65.3)    ' Prints 65
Response.Write Fix(65.3)    ' Prints 65

Response.Write Int(65.6)    ' Prints 65 - does not round number
Response.Write Fix(65.6)    ' Prints 65 - does not round number

Response.Write Int(-10.5)   ' Prints -11
Response.Write Fix(-10.5)   ' Prints -10
```

Mathematical Functions

VBScript has many built-in functions designed to make it easier to work with mathematical values. While you probably won't use many of these functions, some applications will be able to take advantage of the rich function library.

✦ Absolute Value function

✦ Sine function

- ✦ Cosine function
- ✦ Tangent function
- ✦ Arctangent function
- ✦ Exponent function
- ✦ Logarithm function
- ✦ Square Root function
- ✦ Sign function
- ✦ Random Number function
- ✦ Base Conversion function
- ✦ Integer Conversion functions

Abs Function

This function produces the absolute value of a number, which is the number without a positive or negative sign. The following examples illustrate the absolute value function:

```
Response.Write Abs(-50)    ' Prints 50
Response.Write Abs(100)    ' Prints 100
Response.Write Abs(0)      ' Prints 0
```

Atn Function

The arctangent function evaluates an angle and displays the inverse tangent of the angle. Both the input argument and the return value must be in radians.

```
Response.Write Atn(3.1415926535/4)
```

This statement produces the value 0.66577375001447, which is the arctangent of pi/4 radians.

Cos Function

The cosine function evaluates an angle and displays the ratio of the side adjoining the angle to the hypotenuse of the triangle. Both the input argument and the return value must be in radians. The returned radian value will fall between −1 and 1, inclusive.

```
Response.Write Cos(3.1415926535/3)
```

This statement produces the value 0.5, which is the cosine of pi/3 radians, or 60 degrees.

Exp Function

This function accepts any number as an argument and displays the value produced by raising *e* to that exponent. *e* represents the base of natural logarithms and equals approximately 2.71828182845905.

```
Response.Write Exp(1)
```

This statement produces the value 2.71828182845905, which is *e* raised to the power of one.

Log Function

This function produces the natural logarithm of a number. The logarithm function is the inverse of the exponent function. By calculating the logarithm of the exponent function of a number, you produce the original number, as the following example illustrates:

```
Response.Write Exp(Log(15))
```

This statement generates the value 15. To determine a logarithm for a base other than *e,* use the following conversion:

```
Logn(x) = Log(x) / Log(n)
```

For example, to determine the base 10 logarithm of 100, use the following code:

```
Response.Write Log(100) / Log(10)
```

This produces the value 2, which is the exponent to which you raise 10 to obtain 100.

Rnd Function, Randomize Statement

To obtain a random number for your program, use the Rnd function. This function returns a value greater than or equal to zero, but less than one. However, if you enter the following code in a page, you see that the Rnd function is not necessarily random.

```
Response.Write Rnd()
```

Each time you reload the page, you expect to see a different number on the screen. Without any arguments, the Rnd function always displays the same initial number. Further calls to the Rnd function in the same code returns each successive number in the random number sequence.

Sometimes you want a truly random number. In this case, follow the `Randomize` statement that uses the system timer to generate a sequence of random numbers. Under this process, reloading the page results in a different number each time.

```
Randomize
Response.Write Rnd()
```

In addition to random number generation feature of the `Rnd` function, specifying a number for the function's argument can help you predict that function's behavior. Table 3-1 displays the function's behavior with each type of input:

Table 3-1 Rnd Function Parameter Options	
If number is	**Rnd generates**
Less than zero	The same number every time, using the number as the seed
Greater than zero	The next random number in the sequence
Equal to zero	The last random number retrieved from the sequence
Not supplied	The next random number in the sequence

To generate a number from one to ten, use the following formula:

Int((upperbound – lowerbound + 1) * Rnd + lowerbound)

In this example, the formula looks as follows:

```
Response.Write Int((10 - 1 + 1) * Rnd + 1)
```

Round Function

This function, as its name suggests, rounds a number to a specified number of decimal places, as follows:

```
Response.Write Round(1.21125, 2)    ' prints 1.21
Response.Write Round(1.5624, 0)     ' prints 2
```

The only restriction is that the number of digits has to be greater than zero. If you use a number less than zero, you get a message that may make you think the Round function doesn't exist: the message says, "Invalid procedure call or argument, 'round'."

Sin Function

The sine function evaluates an angle and displays the ratio of the side opposite the angle to the hypotenuse of the triangle. Both the input argument and the return value must be expressed in radians. The returned radian value will fall between –1 and 1, inclusive.

Note   To convert radians to degrees, multiply the value by 180/pi. Similarly, multiply by pi/180 to convert degrees to radians. For reference, pi is approximately equal to 3.141592654.

```
Response.Write Sin(3.1415926 / 2)
```

This statement produces the value 1, which is the sine of pi/2 radians, or 90 degrees.

Sqr Function

This function produces the square root of a number, which is identical to raising a number to the 0.5 power. The square root function is included primarily for convenience and readability.

```
Response.Write Sqr(100)
```

This statement generates the value 10, which is the square root of 100.

Sgn Function

This function returns the sign of a number. The sign indicates whether the number is positive, negative, or zero. Positive numbers return 1, negative numbers return –1, and zero returns 0, as in the following examples:

```
Response.Write Sgn(-50)     ' Prints -1
Response.Write Sgn(100)     ' Prints 1
Response.Write Sgn(0)       ' Prints 0
```

Tan Function

The tangent function evaluates an angle and displays the ratio of the side opposite the angle to the side adjoining the angle. Both the input argument and the return value must be in radians.

```
Response.Write Tan(3.1415926535/4)
```

This statement produces the value 1.0, which is the tangent of pi/4 radians, or 45 degrees.

Data Formatting Functions

This section teaches you about the limited capabilities in VBScript for formatting output data. You don't have the same capabilities as in Visual Basic, but the built-in functions work adequately. For more complex formatting of data coming from a database, you may want to rely on the database to do the formatting. Most databases have extensive data formatting functions, all of which can be used in creating your output recordset to your specifications. Also, because VBScript i s an interpreted language, the database formats text more quickly; the database, especially when you use stored procedures, is in a compiled format and runs much faster.

FormatCurrency Function

This function, as its name suggests, formats variables that contain `Currency` data. This function, along with the other Format functions, is highly localized to your country. Any settings that you have changed in the Regional Settings applet of your Control Panel will be picked up automatically by this and other Format functions.

The `FormatCurrency` function's syntax is as follows:

```
FormatCurrency(Expression[,NumDigitsAfterDecimal
[,IncludeLeadingDigit [,UseParensForNegativeNumbers
[,GroupDigits]]]])
```

The first argument is the value you want to format. The next argument specifies the number of digits that you want to follow the decimal point. Remember that a `Currency` value can only hold up to four decimal digits, so anything more than four digits will give you four as a result.

The next argument is used only if a zero is to the left of the decimal point. This flag indicates whether to show a zero for numbers between –1 and 1. The values for this argument are shown in Table 3-1. This argument is an optional parameter and can be omitted, as shown in the examples that follow.

The third argument specifies whether to use parentheses around negative numbers, which is a common practice in accounting. This parameter takes the same values as the previous parameter, which are shown in Table 3-1. This argument is an optional parameter and can be omitted, as shown in the examples that follow.

The final argument specifies whether the digits should be grouped using the regional number grouping symbol. For large numbers, the United States uses commas between groups of three numbers, as follows:

```
1,002,045
```

This parameter also takes the values shown in Table 3-2. This argument is an optional parameter and can be omitted, as shown in the examples that follow.

	Table 3-2 **Parameter Values**
Value	**Meaning**
−1	Yes
0	No
2	Use the computer's regional settings (default)

Here are few examples of how to use this function. Remember that the local currency and grouping symbols will be displayed instead of what is shown here if you are using a regional setting other than United States.

```
Response.Write FormatCurrency(1.231)                   ' $1.23
Response.Write FormatCurrency(1.231, 3)                ' $1.231
Response.Write FormatCurrency(0.523, 2)                ' $.52
Response.Write FormatCurrency(0.523, 2, -1)            ' $0.52
Response.Write FormatCurrency(-23520.523, 2, , -1, -1)
    ' ($23,520.52)
```

FormatDateTime

This function is used to format variables and values that represent times or dates. Because this function is quite limited, it can only show five formats: two date, two time, and one with both. The function's syntax is as follows:

```
FormatDateTime(Date[, NamedFormat])
```

The NamedFormat parameter is a number from zero to four, with each value being a different format. The format values are shown in Table 3-3.

	Table 3-3 **NamedFormat Parameter Values**
Value	**Meaning**
0	Displays a date and/or time, if either part is present.
1	Displays a date using the long format specified in your regional settings.
2	Displays a date using the short format specified in your regional settings.

Value	Meaning
3	Displays a time using the format specified in your regional settings.
4	Displays a time using the 24-hour format (hh:mm).

If you haven't changed your regional settings from the defaults for the United States, these formats look as follows:

```
Response.Write FormatDateTime(#6/19/2000 11:59 AM#, 0)
' 6/19/00 11:59:00 AM

Response.Write FormatDateTime(#6/19/2000 11:59 AM#, 1)
' Monday, June 19, 2000

Response.Write FormatDateTime(#6/19/2000 11:59 AM#, 2)
' 6/19/00

Response.Write FormatDateTime(#6/19/2000 11:59 AM#, 3)
' 11:59:00 AM

Response.Write FormatDateTime(#6/19/2000 11:59 AM#, 4)
' 11:59
```

As mentioned in the introduction to this section, if you want a date or time in a different format, use your database's formatting functions to do the work for you.

FormatNumber Function

This function works in the same way as the `FormatCurrency` function, except that no currency symbol will be displayed. You can refer to the preceding section for the arguments for this function.

FormatPercent Function

This function works in the same way as the `FormatCurrency` and `FormatNumber` function, except for the fact that no currency symbol will be displayed. However, a percent sign will be displayed at the end of whatever value you use. In addition, the value you provide will be multiplied by 100 to create a percentage. If you get a percentage in the thousands and aren't expecting one, you are probably doing the function's work beforehand. You can refer to the preceding section for the arguments for this function.

Text Manipulation Functions

Of the many functions in VBScript, you will use the data-formatting functions most often. The latest version of the VBScript language included some bonus functions that many programmers had built countless times, such as a find and replace function that works on strings. This section of the chapter shows you these functions and how to use them in your code.

Filter Function

This function looks at an array of strings and returns another array with only the strings matching your criteria. The code in Listing 3-3 demonstrates how this function works.

Listing 3-3: **Filter Function Test**

```
Option Explicit

Dim a_strURLs(5)    ' As Array of Strings
Dim a_strResult     ' As Array of Strings
Dim i               ' As Integer

a_strURLs(1) = "http://search.microsoft.com"
a_strURLs(2) = "http://www.rational.com"
a_strURLs(3) = "http://www.vbtechniques.com"
a_strURLs(4) = "http://www.inquiry.com"
a_strURLs(5) = "http://www.microsoft.com"

a_strResult = Filter(a_strURLs, ".com", -1, 1)

For i = 0 To UBound(a_strResult)
    Response.Write a_strResult(i) & "<br>"
Next ' i
```

In this case, we want to filter the array for any strings that include ".com". The third argument, –1, specifies that we should look for strings that have the search string. You can specify a zero here to do the reverse and look for all the strings that don't contain the search string. The final argument specifies that this should be a text-based search and not a binary search. If you want to match case, use the value zero here.

When you run this code, all of the strings will be returned and printed as follows:

```
http://search.microsoft.com
http://www.rational.com
http://www.vbtechniques.com
```

```
http://www.inquiry.com
http://www.microsoft.com
```

If you were to change ".com" to "microsoft", the results would be as follows:

```
http://search.microsoft.com
http://www.microsoft.com
```

InStr Function

This function looks for a string within another string. You can specify where to start looking from the front of the string and whether to match case. Here is the simplest use of the function:

```
intResult = InStr("Little Miss Muffet", "Muffet")
    ' intResult = 13
```

If we wanted to start looking in the middle of the string, the code would look like the following:

```
intResult = InStr(13, "Little Miss Muffet", "Miss")
    ' intResult = 0
```

We get a zero result because we started looking after the substring. If we don't need to match case, adding 1 as the final argument forces the function to ignore case, as shown here:

```
intResult = InStr(1, "Little Miss Muffet", "mISS", 1)
    ' intResult = 8
```

To specify a case-sensitive search manually, use a zero (instead of a one) as the final argument.

InStrRev Function

This function works the same way as InStr except for the fact that it starts at the end of the string and works backwards from there. However, all character positions are given using the front of the string as a reference point. For instance:

```
strSearch = "She sells sea shells by the seashore"
intResult = InStrRev(strSearch, "se")
```

After this code runs, intResult contains the value 29, which is where the word seashore starts if you count from the beginning of the string. Let's say, for instance, we don't want to check the word "seashore". In this case, we can specify a different starting point, again counting from the beginning of the string.

```
intResult = InStrRev(strSearch, "se", 28)
```

Now intResult has the result of 11, which is the next occurrence of "se" working from the back to the front of the string.

If you need to do a case-insensitive search, add 1 as the final argument to the function. A binary search, which is the default, can be specified manually by using a zero as the final argument to the function. Also note that the position of the starting point argument is different than the InStr function, so be sure to check the position if you get an error in your code that you cannot figure out.

Join Function

The Join function is the opposite of the Split function, because it takes the strings from an array and combines them into a single string. Besides the array you have to give the function as an argument, you can also specify a delimiting character or string to use between each of the strings as they are reassembled. For instance, the following code puts a favorite cartoon family together with a comma followed by a space.

```
Dim a_strSource(4)
a_strSource(1) = "Dilbert"
a_strSource(2) = "Dogbert"
a_strSource(3) = "Catbert"
a_strSource(4) = "Ratbert"

Response.Write Join(a_strSource, ", ")
```

This code generates the following output:

```
, Dilbert, Dogbert, Catbert, Ratbert
```

Note that the delimiter is added before the string. You need to adjust your code to compensate. On the other hand, you could conpensate manually with the following code:

```
Dim i
Dim strResult
strResult = a_strSource(1)
For i = 2 To UBound(a_strSource)
    strResult = strResult & ", " & a_strSource(i)
Next  ' i
Response.Write strResult
```

This code produces the corrected result of:

```
Dilbert, Dogbert, Catbert, Ratbert
```

This is our desired result.

LCase Function

This function converts all the letters in a string to their lowercase equivalents. Non-letter characters are left alone. Here is a quick example:

```
Response.Write LCase("this Is a Test!")  ' this is a test!
```

Left Function

This function returns a specified number of characters from the left, or beginning, of a string. Here are some examples:

```
Response.Write Left("This is a test", 4)
    ' prints This

Response.Write Left("This is a test", 99)
    ' prints entire string, since 99 is longer than string
```

Len Function

This function returns the length of a string. This result includes all characters, including both printable and non-printable control characters. You can then use this value to loop through the string to process it for whatever you need.

LTrim Function

This function removes spaces from the left, or beginning, of a string. It stops removing spaces when it finds a non-space character. This function is similar to RTrim and Trim. Here's a quick example:

```
strNew = LTrim(" this is a test ")
    ' strNew contains "this is a test "
```

Mid Function

This function returns a specified number of characters from a string beginning at a given point. Here is a quick example:

```
strNew = Mid("Humpty Dumpty sat on a wall", 8, 6)
    ' strNew contains "Dumpty"
```

This function also enables you to pick a starting point and get everything to the right of that point as the result. For instance:

```
strNew = Mid("Humpty Dumpty sat on a wall", 19)
    ' strNew contains "on a wall"
```

Replace Function

This is one of those functions that every programmer has built and no longer needs. This function enables you to replace every occurrence of a substring in another string with a replacement string. The function also has some extra options so you can specify how many times to replace, where to start replacing, and whether to look at each letter's case. Here is a basic example:

```
strNew = Replace("this is a test", "test", "drill")
   ' strNew becomes "this is a drill"
```

If you wanted to start looking at the fifth letter, for instance, you would add a 5 as the final argument, as shown here:

```
strNew = Replace("this is a test", "test", "drill", 5)
   ' strNew becomes "this is a drill"
```

In this case, the result is the same; however, the word "this" is not being checked because it is located before the fifth character.

For a large string, you may only want to do a single replacement. In this case, you add a fifth argument after the starting point, which would be required when using the count argument, as shown here:

```
strOriginal = "She sells sea shells by the seashore"
strNew = Replace(strOriginal, "she", "ZZZ", 1, 1)
   ' strNew is "She sells sea ZZZlls by the seashore"
```

Why didn't the function match the first "She"? By default, the function does a binary comparison, which matches the case of the letters. To do a case-insensitive search, change the preceding code to the following:

```
strOriginal = "She sells sea shells by the seashore"
strNew = Replace(strOriginal, "she", "ZZZ", 1, 1, 1)
   ' strNew is "ZZZ sells sea shells by the seashore"
```

To specify a binary/case-sensitive search, use a zero as the final argument to the Replace function.

RTrim Function

This function removes spaces from the right, or end, of a string. It stops removing spaces when it finds a non-space character. This function is similar to LTrim and Trim. Here's a quick example:

```
strNew = RTrim(" this is a test ")
   ' strNew contains " this is a test"
```

Space Function

This function has a single purpose: to create a string of spaces of the length you specify. Give it a positive number and it returns a string of spaces that many spaces long. This function can be used to help format text, especially when used with fixed width fonts like Courier. Here's an example:

```
StrSpacer = Space(50)   ' creates a string of 50 spaces
```

Split Function

This function is designed to break apart a string into an array based on a delimiter character you specify. This functionality can be helpful when parsing user input. For instance, if you ask for a person's name, first then last name, you could use the Split function as follows:

```
Dim strInput
Dim a_strResult
Dim i

strInput = "Charlie Brown"
a_strResult = Split(strInput, " ")

For i = 0 To UBound(a_strResult)
    Response.Write "Word #" & i+1 & ": " & a_strResult(i)
Next    ' i
```

This code would print the following:

```
Charlie
Brown
```

You can use any delimiter character; however, you cannot specify a list of characters to use. For instance, if you were parsing a sentence, a word can be ended by either a space or a piece of punctuation. You would first need to replace all of these characters with spaces and then run the Split function. That way, the Split function only has to worry about a single delimiter character.

This function can also take a third argument to specify the maximum number of strings to remove, as well as a fourth argument to specify whether to compare case when checking for delimiter characters (use 0 for binary, 1 for text).

StrReverse Function

Here's a handy function that may also be in your programmer's box of tricks. This function only reverses a string. No other options and parameters other than the string are reversed. Here's an example:

```
strNew = StrReverse("Able was I ere I saw Elba.")
   ' strNew contains ".ablE was I ere I saw elbA"
```

All characters are reversed using this function, including any punctuation.

String Function

This function is a bit more generic than the Space function, but it essentially performs the same task. If you give this function a character and a number, it returns a string of that many of that character. For instance, here's how you emulate the Space function:

```
strSpacer = String(" ", 50) ' creates a string of 50 spaces
strLine = String("-", 50)   ' creates a line of 50 dashes
```

Trim Function

This function removes all leading and trailing spaces from a string. It is the equivalent of doing an LTrim followed by an RTrim, or vice versa. The function stops removing spaces when it finds a non-space character. Here's an example:

```
strNew = Trim(" this is a test ")
   ' strNew contains "this is a test"
```

UCase Function

This function takes all the letters in a string and changes them to their uppercase equivalents. Non-letter characters are left alone and returned as is. Here is a quick example:

```
Response.Write UCase("this Is a Test!")  ' THIS IS A TEST!
```

Date and Time Functions

Visual Basic has a number of helpful functions that work with date and time values. You can add, subtract, and manipulate date and time values easily with the functions covered in this section. In addition, Microsoft databases like SQL Server and Access also have the functions described (or variations of them, in some cases), so you may already be familiar with these functions.

Date Function

This function returns the current date. For pages running on a server, the date is the date on the server at the time. If you are running this function in a client-side script, the date will be the date on the local machine. The return value of this function can also be put into a variable and manipulated as a date.

DateAdd Function

This function adds dates together. It can also be used to increment (or decrement) a date by an amount in any time or date unit. For instance, if you want to know the date 30 days from the current date, the DateAdd function can be used as follows:

```
Dim datCurrent
Dim datFuture

datCurrent = Date()
datFuture = DateAdd("d", 30, datCurrent)
Response.Write datFuture
```

This code prints the date that is 30 days from the current date. The DateAdd function's first argument specifies the unit of time to use. The following strings are valid for this argument:

✦ yyyy – year

✦ q – quarter year

✦ m – month

✦ y – day of year

✦ d – day

✦ w – weekday

✦ ww – week of year

✦ h – hour

✦ m – minute

✦ s – second

You can also use the DateAdd function to decrement a date/time value. Just use a negative number for the number of intervals you want, and the date/time will decrease accordingly.

DateDiff Function

The DateDiff function gives the difference between two dates in the unit that you specify. Here is a simple example:

```
Response.Write DateDiff("yyyy", #1/1/1999#, #1/1/2000#)
```

This code, as you may guess, gives a result of one. If you reversed the date values, the result would be –1 instead. The constants used here are the same as in the preceding DateAdd function. Also, the DateDiff function cannot be used to decrement a date; rather, this function simply tells you the difference between two dates.

DatePart Function

This function extracts a part of a date/time value. The part can be any of the constants used for the `DateAdd` function, and the function is used as follows:

```
Response.Write DatePart("ww", Date)
```

This code gives the week number of the year to date. This function is similar to the `Hour`, `Month`, `Second`, and similar functions that return a particular part of a date. This function is more generic and can handle all parts, including a few (like `Quarter`) with which the individual functions can't deal.

DateSerial Function

This function creates a date value based on an integer year, month, and day values. Here is an example:

```
datCurrent = DateSerial(2000, 2, 3)
```

The variable holds the date February 3rd, 2000 after this code executes. This function is an alternative to creating a date by concatenating values together and then feeding it through the `CDate` function. The end result is the same, but this method takes less code.

DateValue Function

This function converts a string to a date, similar to the `CDate` function. This function makes certain assumptions that the `CDate` function does not. For instance, if you provide a date without a year, the `DateValue` function assumes the date to be in the current year. It will also accept time values and simply not include them in the returned date.

Day Function

This function returns the day of the month when given a valid date variable.

Hour Function

This function returns the hour of the day when given a valid date/time variable.

Minute Function

This function returns the minute of the hour when given a valid date/time variable.

Month Function

This function returns the month of the year when given a valid date/time variable.

MonthName Function

This function returns the regional name of the month number provided to it, where January is given the value 1 and December is given the value 12.

Now Function

This function returns both the date and time in a valid date/time variable. It is the equivalent of concatenating the results of the Date and Time functions together.

Second Function

This function returns the second of the minute when given a valid date/ time variable.

Weekday Function

This function returns the weekday number (1 is Sunday, 7 is Saturday) when given a valid date/time variable.

WeekdayName Function

This function returns the regional name of the weekday number provided to it, where Sunday is given the value 1 and Saturday is given the value 7.

Year Function

This function returns the year of a date when given a valid date/time variable.

Built-in Objects

The VBScript language includes a wide variety of functions, but it also includes some handy objects. This section covers the objectives and uses of the objects.

Dictionary Object

A Dictionary object is essentially a lookup table. Each "row" in a Dictionary object has two values: a key and a value. By using the key, you can rapidly look up data in the Dictionary object. The only downside is that you have to load the Dictionary object every time you want to use it. However, the object is quite fast and efficient for local caching of frequently used data. Listing 3-4 shows an example of how to use the Dictionary object.

Listing 3-4: **Dictionary Object Test**

```
Dim objDictionary    ' As Object
Set objDictionary = Server.CreateObject("Scripting.Dictionary")
objDictionary.Add "MSFT", "Microsoft"
objDictionary.Add "INTC", "Intel"
objDictionary.Add "RATL", "Rational Software"
objDictionary.Add "SEG", "Seagate"
objDictionary.Add "DELL", "Dell Computer"

Response.Write objDictionary("DELL")
```

This code generates the response of "Dell Computer". When you learn about database programming, you may want to combine database table reads with Dictionary objects. While creating lots of objects will take more memory, it will be much quicker than having to search a recordset every time you need a piece of data. However, Dictionary objects are destroyed after the page loads, so don't put in anything that is not stored permanently somewhere else.

Err Object

The Err object is used for error handling in the ASP environment. However, there are several other objects that are also involved in error handling. Chapter 10 covers error handling in depth.

FileSystemObject

This object (and its relatives) have made file operations a breeze under VBScript. Unlike the older versions of Visual Basic, VBScript no longer uses file numbers and antiquated methods for accessing files. The FileSystemObject (FSO) is the key to the whole operation. It has full access to the file system on the server through a series of programmable objects. All of the objects related to the FSO are covered in Appendix E, but here are a few examples of how to use this object in some common situations.

The following are objects of interest:

✦ Drive – Represents a single storage device, including floppy disk, hard drive, CD-ROM, and more.

✦ Drives – A collection of all the drives in the system.

✦ File – Represents a single disk file somewhere on the system.

✦ Files – A collection of disk files, typically located in a particular directory.

✦ FileSystemObject – An object to represent the entire file system on your computer, including all drives, directories, and files.

✦ Folder – Represents a single directory, whether local or network.

✦ Folders – A collection of directories, which can be located at either the root level or in another directory.

✦ TextStream – Represents a file that has been opened for reading or writing of data.

To get information on all the drives on your system, you could use the following code:

```
Sub Main()
    Dim objFSO ' As Scripting.FileSystemObject
    Dim drvLoop ' As Scripting.Drive

    Set objFSO =
Server.CreateObject("Scripting.FileSystemObject")
    For Each drvLoop In objFSO.Drives
        Response.Write drvLoop.DriveLetter & ":\"
        If drvLoop.DriveType = Fixed _
            Or drvLoop.IsReady Then
            Response.Write "   Total size:    " _
            & Format$(drvLoop.TotalSize / (1024 ^ 2), "#0.00 Mb")
            Response.Write "   Free space:    " _
            & Format$(drvLoop.FreeSpace / (1024 ^ 2), "#0.00 Mb")
            Response.Write "   Volume Label: " &
            drvLoop.VolumeName
        Else
            Response.Write "   Disk information unavailable"
        End If

    Next ' drvLoop

    Set objFSO = Nothing

End Sub
```

Besides looping through drives, you can also loop through files in folders. This feature is especially helpful when you need to search your entire drive for a particular file. Recursion is also very helpful in these cases, because you need to keep performing the same action as you work your way down the tree. The following code counts the number of files that have the .GIF extension. This code can obviously be adapted to list the files, do something to each file, and so forth. The main point is the actual traversal of the directory tree.

```
Option Explicit
Dim m_lngFileCount ' As Long
Dim m_objFSO ' As Scripting.FileSystemObject

Sub Main()
    Set m_objFSO =
Server.CreateObject("Scripting.FileSystemObject")
    m_lngFileCount = 0
    CheckFolder "C:\"
    Response.Write "Total files: " & m_lngFileCount
End Sub

Sub CheckFolder(strPath)
    Dim objFolder ' As Scripting.Folder
    Dim objFile ' As Scripting.File
    Dim objSubdirs ' As Scripting.Folders
    Dim objLoopFolder ' As Scripting.Folder

    Response.Write "Checking directory " & strPath
    Set objFolder = m_objFSO.GetFolder(strPath)

    '
    ' Check files in this directory
    '
    For Each objFile In objFolder.Files
        If UCase(Right(objFile.ShortPath, 4)) = ".GIF" Then
            m_lngFileCount = m_lngFileCount + 1
        End If
    Next ' objFile

    '
    ' Loop through all subdirectories and
    ' do the same thing.
    '
    Set objSubdirs = objFolder.SubFolders
    For Each objLoopFolder In objSubdirs
        CheckFolder objLoopFolder.Path
    Next ' objLoopFolder

    Set objSubdirs = Nothing
    Set objFolder = Nothing

End Sub
```

To simplify the code, the `FileSystemObject` and the file counter are made global to this page (hence the m_ prefix). The `CheckFolder` routine is first called with `C:\` as the starting point. This routine first goes through all the files in the selected directory. If any match, the counter is incremented. After all the files have been checked, each subdirectory is fed into the `CheckFolder` routine. This is the recursive part of the code—a routine is calling itself. Eventually, there are no more subdirectories and all the `CheckFolder` calls end. The total is then printed by `Sub Main`.

Summary

As you can tell from the content in this chapter, VBScript has benefited from years of work on the Visual Basic language. While all of VB's functions didn't make it into VBScript, most of the useful ones did. Also, some extra features make Web development easier. Between the math, text, and date functions, you have quite a development arsenal at your command. In following chapters, you put that arsenal to work in various applications.

✦   ✦   ✦

ASP Concepts

Web programming is done quite differently from traditional client/server computing. The chapters in this section will show you how to use Web programming concepts and integrate those concepts with the use of the ASP engine. You'll learn about all of the built-in objects and how to make the most of each one.

✦ ✦ ✦ ✦

Chapter 4
Using Server-Side Includes

Chapter 5
Using the Request Object

Chapter 6
Using the Response Object

Chapter 7
Using Cookies

Chapter 8
Using the Application, Session, and Server Objects

Chapter 9
Error Handling

✦ ✦ ✦ ✦

Using Server-Side Includes

In This Chapter

Learn about server-side includes (SSI)

Learn how to bypass the features not available with SSI inside ASP pages

Learn to create modular ASP code files

Introduction to Server-side Includes

◆　◆　◆　◆

As you learned in Chapter 1, the key difference between Active Server Pages code and HTML is that ASP code is always kept on the server. The code is evaluated before it is sent to the user's browser. *Server-side includes* (SSI) provide another way to build the ASP page before it is sent to the user. These special commands are inserted into ASP and HTML files that are evaluated before the actual ASP code is evaluated.

These SSI commands can do the following in your pages:

+ Insert the value of an environment variable into a page
+ Run an application or command and insert the results into a page
+ Insert the time a file was last modified into a page
+ Insert the size of a file into a page
+ Include a file into another file

Because these commands are run before the ASP commands are run, you can use server-side include directives to create modular code. For instance, in subsequent chapters, you'll need to include a constants file into your pages so that you can use named constants instead of numbers. This process uses the `include` directive available in server-side includes. By the time the ASP code is evaluated, the constants have already been added to the file and the code works properly. You can design a hierarchy of files for common subroutines, error-handling features, and so forth. You can also have one file include other files, making it even easier to create well-structured code. No longer does everything have to be in every single file. You can simply create a file with your subroutines and include it anywhere you need it, just as you might do with other programming languages.

Learning the SSI Directives

This section covers each of the directives that are available to you. If you're familiar with SSI from other Web servers, please note that the directives work somewhat differently under Microsoft's Web server. Any known problems or differences will be covered in the text for each directive. One bonus is that even if a server-side include directive doesn't work as expected, you can always write ASP code to do the same work. When possible, the following sections show you how to work around some of the limitations.

One other point to note is that none of these directives except for #include will work within ASP files. The directives will only work within files that have extensions configured to be processed through the SSI DLL. .

#config Directive

This directive configures a number of SSI options on a page-by-page basis. You can provide a different error message for SSI errors, as well as specify how dates and times are displayed when they are created through SSI directives.

The first configuration option you can set is the error message to be displayed when an SSI-related error occurs. These errors can include file not found errors (for includes), failed commands (for execs), and so forth. The default behavior is to display the actual error; however, if you're running a site, you may not want visitors to see the actual error text. To make this change, use the following code:

```
<!--#config errmsg="A server error has occurred." -->
```

Unfortunately, this directive can't be used to include another file. However, you can reconfigure your Web server to display customized error messages when you hit file not found (404) or server error (500) messages. Refer to your server documentation for more information on these settings.

The second configuration option deals with how dates and times are displayed. SSI directives can generate time and date results, and the options you set control how they are displayed. Here is an example of how to use this feature:

```
<!--#config timefmt="%H:%M:%S" -->
```

This directive specifies that any date/time entries are to be displayed in 24-hour clock format without any date portion. If you're familiar with the C language, the formatting specification should look familiar. If you know VB's Format function, the codes are a bit different but do the same thing. Table 4-1 shows a list of all the available formatting codes and their meanings.

Table 4-1
Time/Date Formatting Codes

Code	Meaning
%a	Abbreviated name for day of the week (for example, Mon).
%A	Complete name for day of the week (for example, Monday).
%b	Abbreviated month name (for example, Feb).
%B	Complete month name (for example, February).
%c	Date and time representation that is appropriate for the locale (for example, 05/06/91 12:51:32).
%d	Day of the month as a decimal number (01–31).
%H	Hour in 24-hour format (00–23).
%I	Hour in 12-hour format (01–12).
%j	Day of the year as a decimal number (001–366).
%m	Month as a decimal number (01–12).
%M	Minute as a decimal number (00–59).
%p	Current locale's A.M. or P.M. indicator for 12-hour format (for example, PM).
%S	Second as a decimal number (00–59).
%U	Week of the year as a decimal number, with Sunday as the first day of the week (00–51).
%w	Day of the week as a decimal number, with Sunday as the first day (0–6).
%W	Week of the year as a decimal number, with Monday as the first day of the week (00–51).
%x	Date representation for the current locale (for example, 05/06/91).
%X	Time representation for the current locale (for example, 12:51:32).
%y	Year without the century as a decimal number (for example, 69).
%Y	Year with the century as a decimal number (for example, 1969).
%z, %Z	Time-zone name or abbreviation; no characters if time zone is unknown.
%%	Percent sign.

If you want to refine your date and time values, you can stretch the #config line, but it should be on the same line to work properly. Some Web servers handle multiple line SSI directives; however, most do not. Here is an extreme example.

```
<!--#config timefmt="The %dth day of %B in the year of our Lord %Y" -->
```

Note   All of the code shown here should be put on one line.

The only problem is that you can't deal with cases like 1 and 2, which should be 1st and 2nd, respectively. If you need that type of detail, you could use the code in Listing 4-1 in place of the SSI directive. You will need to use this code in every situation where you want to show the date in this format, however.

Listing 4-1: Creating a fancy date with VBScript

```
<%
    Dim datCurrent     ' As Date
    Dim intDay, intMonth, intYear  ' As Integer
    Dim strDate        ' As String
    Dim strTemp        ' As String

    datCurrent = Date ' use your own date here
                      ' or use a function parameter

    '
    ' Pull off the parts of the date for use
    '
    intDay = Day(datCurrent)
    intMonth = Month(datCurrent)
    intYear = Year(datCurrent)

    strDate = "the " & intDay
    '
    ' Determine the ending for the day number
    '
    Select Case intDay
    Case 1, 21, 31
        strTemp = "st"
    Case 2, 22
        strTemp = "nd"
    Case 3, 23
        strTemp = "rd"
    Case Else
        strTemp = "th"
    End Select
    strDate = strDate & strTemp & " day of "
    strDate = strDate & MonthName(intMonth) & " "
    strDate = strDate & " in the year "

    '
    ' Determine the century. This code can easily be
    ' expanded in case you need it for earlier or later
    ' dates than these.
    '
```

```
Select Case intYear \ 100
Case 18
   strTemp = "eighteen hundred"
Case 19
   strTemp = "nineteen hundred"
Case 20
   strTemp = "two thousand"
End Select
strDate = strDate & strTemp

intYear = intYear Mod 100

'
' Determine the tens digit
'
If intYear >= 10 And intYear < 20 Then
   strDate = strDate & " "
   Select Case intYear
   Case 11
      strTemp = "eleven"
   Case 12
      strTemp = "twelve"
   Case 13
      strTemp = "thirteen"
   Case 14
      strTemp = "fourteen"
   Case 15
      strTemp = "fifteen"
   Case 16
      strTemp = "sixteen"
   Case 17
      strTemp = "seventeen"
   Case 18
      strTemp = "eighteen"
   Case 19
      strTemp = "nineteen"
   End Select
   strDate = strDate & strTemp
ElseIf intYear >= 20 Then
   strDate = strDate & " "
   Select Case intYear \ 10
   Case 2
      strTemp = "twenty"
   Case 3
      strTemp = "thirty"
   Case 4
      strTemp = "forty"
   Case 5
      strTemp = "fifty"
```

Continued

Listing 4-1 *(continued)*

```
      Case 6
         strTemp = "sixty"
      Case 7
         strTemp = "seventy"
      Case 8
         strTemp = "eighty"
      Case 9
         strTemp = "ninety"
      End Select
      strDate = strDate & strTemp
      If intYear Mod 10 > 0 Then
         strDate = strDate & "-"
      End If
   End If
   intYear = intYear Mod 10

   '
   ' Add on the ones digit
   '
   If intYear > 0 Then
      Select Case intYear
      Case 1
         strTemp = "one"
      Case 2
         strTemp = "two"
      Case 3
         strTemp = "three"
      Case 4
         strTemp = "four"
      Case 5
         strTemp = "five"
      Case 6
         strTemp = "six"
      Case 7
         strTemp = "seven"
      Case 8
         strTemp = "eight"
      Case 9
         strTemp = "nine"
      End Select
      strDate = strDate & strTemp
   End If
   Response.Write "Today is " & strDate & "."

   '
```

```
' You could also return the string as the result of
' a function at this point.
'
%>
```

For tax season in the year 2000, the result of this code would be:

```
Today is the 15th day of April in the year two thousand.
```

The final option you can configure is whether file sizes (returned with the #fsize directive) are returned in bytes or kilobytes. This code will cause file sizes to be returned in bytes:

```
<!--#config sizefmt="BYTE" -->
```

This code will return sizes in kilobytes, which is the default:

```
<!--#config sizefmt="ABBREV" -->
```

The discussion of the #fsize directive provides some more useful information about this feature.

#echo Directive

This SSI directive displays the value of an HTTP environment variable. Whenever you visit a Web page, there are a number of pieces of information that are made available about you, your browser, and any current session information. These pieces of information are available to the Web programmer through the HTTP environment variables. You learn more about retrieving these values in Chapter 5 by using the Request.ServerVariables method. However, if you just need to display the information in the Web page, you can use the #echo directive, as shown here:

```
You are visiting the host
named <!--#echo var="SERVER_NAME" -->.
```

To do the same thing in an ASP page, you would use the following code:

```
You are the host named
<% = Request.ServerVariables("SERVER_NAME") %>.<p>
```

Both of these examples will print the name of the server where the page is hosted. Table 4-2 contains the complete list of variables.

Table 4-2
HTTP Environment Variables

Variable Name	Description
ALL_HTTP	All HTTP headers that were not already parsed into one of the other variables described in this table. These variables are of the form HTTP_*header field name*. The headers consist of a null-terminated string with the individual headers separated by line feeds. Note that this won't return all the variables shown here. It will only return the header information.
AUTH_TYPE	This contains the type of authentication used. For example, the string will be "Basic" if Basic authentication is used, and it will be "Integrated Windows NT Authentication" for integrated authentication. Other authentication schemes will have other strings. Because new authentication types can be added to the Web server, it is not possible to list all the string possibilities. If the string is empty, then no authentication is used.
AUTH_PASSWORD	The value entered in the client's authentication dialog box. This variable is only available if Basic authentication is used.
AUTH_USER	The value entered in the client's authentication dialog box.
CONTENT_LENGTH	The number of bytes that the script can expect to receive from the client.
CONTENT_TYPE	The content type of the information supplied in the body of a POST request.
DOCUMENT_NAME	The current file name.
DOCUMENT_URI	The virtual path to the current document.
DATE_GMT	The current date in Greenwich Mean Time (GMT).
DATE_LOCAL	The current date in the local time zone.
GATEWAY_INTERFACE	The revision of the CGI specification used by the Web server.
LAST_MODIFIED	The date when the current document was last modified. The date will be displayed in the format specified by the #config directive, if applicable.
PATH_INFO	Additional path information, as given by the client. This consists of the trailing part of the URL after the script name, but before the query string, if available.
PATH_TRANSLATED	This is the value of PATH_INFO, but with any virtual path expanded into a directory specification.
QUERY_STRING	The information that follows the question mark (?) in the URL that referenced this script.

Variable Name	Description
QUERY_STRING_ UNESCAPED	Unescaped version of the query string; that is, a version that is not URL-encoded.
REMOTE_ADDR	The IP address of the client or agent of the client (for example, gateway or firewall) that sent the request.
REMOTE_HOST	The host name of the client or agent of the client (for example, gateway or firewall) that sent the request.
REMOTE_USER	This contains the user name supplied by the client and authenticated by the server. This comes back as an empty string when the user is anonymous (but authenticated).
REQUEST_METHOD	The HTTP request method. (GET and POST are most common).
SCRIPT_NAME	The name of the script program being executed. For ASP pages, this will be the pathname to the ASP file.
SERVER_NAME	The server's host name or IP address.
SERVER_PORT	The TCP/IP port on which the request was received. By default, the port is 80.
SERVER_PORT _SECURE	A string of either 0 or 1. If the request is being handled on the secure port, this will be 1. Otherwise, it will be 0.
SERVER_PROTOCOL	The name and version of the information retrieval protocol relating to this request. This is usually HTTP/1.0.
SERVER_SOFTWARE	The name and version of the Web server answering the request. This will vary, but IIS 4.0 returns "Microsoft-IIS/4.0".
URL	Gives the base portion of the URL. Parameter values will not be included. The value is determined when the Web server parses the URL from the header.

Note   Using the Request.ServerVariables method takes quite a bit of system time to process. If you need to retrieve this information, use a Session variable to store it for later use. With this strategy, you don't spend a lot of time constantly retrieving the same information from the Web server.

#exec Directive

This directive enables you to execute a command on the server. The results will be displayed in the Web page containing the directive. Most Web servers have this option turned off because it is a HUGE security hole. Imagine a Web page that had a box for a user to type in a command to execute. Using this directive, the command would execute on the server. If someone was being malicious, the page could be given administrator privileges and a rmdir C:\ could wipe out a hard drive.

If you are working on a system where this command is allowed, here is an example of getting a directory listing:

```
Results of "dir" Command:
<p>

<!--#exec cmd="dir" -->
```

You can also specify a CGI script to run by using the parameter cgi instead of cmd. This directive, like most of the others, is not allowed in ASP pages. In addition, there is no equivalent command in the VBScript language or ASP objects to do this function.

#flastmod Directive

This directive returns the last date/time a file was modified. This is helpful to put at the bottom of your pages so that the user can see when the Web page was last modified. For instance, you can use this code to generate a nice message on your HTML pages:

```
<!--#config timefmt="%B %d, %Y" -->
Last Modified: <!--#flastmod file="test.shtml" -->
```

You would need to replace the file name shown here with your own file name, of course. This code will generate the following result:

```
Last Modified: September 15, 1999
```

You can also specify a virtual Web path to your file by using the virtual parameter instead of the file parameter, as shown in this example:

```
<!--#config timefmt="%B %d, %Y" -->
Last Modified: <!--#flastmod virtual="/index.shtml" -->
```

This code would display the last date/time that index.shtml in the Web server's root directory was updated.

Because this feature is not available in ASP pages, you need to use different code to make this work. Listing 4-2 shows a replacement function that uses the FileSystemObject to return the appropriate information.

Listing 4-2: **FileDateTime Function and Usage**

```
<%
Function FileDateTime()
```

```
' The assumption made here
' is that this function is
' included in another file.
' This lets the server variables
' resolve correctly within this
' function.
'

Dim objFSO      ' As FileSystemObject
Dim objFile     ' As Scripting.File

Set objFSO = _
   Server.CreateObject("Scripting.FileSystemObject")
Set objFile = _
   objFSO.GetFile(Request.ServerVariables("PATH_TRANSLATED"))

FileDateTime = objFile.DateLastModified
Set objFile = Nothing
Set objFSO = Nothing
End Function

Dim datModified      ' As Date
datModified = FileDateTime()
Response.Write "Last Modified: " _
   & MonthName(Month(datModified)) _
   & " " & Day(datModified) & ", " _
   & Year(datModified)

%>
```

This code produces exactly the same result as the #flastmod directive. The function makes the assumption that it is in the file being checked, which would always be correct under ASP. If you wanted to modify the function, you could simply have it print the date using the code at the bottom of the listing. You could also switch it into a subroutine and not worry about a return value. It just depends how you think you would use the function.

#fsize Directive

This directive returns the size of a file. This feature is especially handy if you are providing a list of links to files but don't want to update the listing manually when the file sizes change. Here's an example of how to use this directive:

```
File Size: <!--#fsize file="data.zip" -->
```

This code prints the size of the file in kilobytes. The #config directive will change whether the file size is printed in bytes or kilobytes.

Once again, this directive doesn't work in ASP pages. Instead, you have to use the FileSystemObject to get this information. Listing 4-3 shows code that will return the size of a file whose name is specified as a virtual file name; that is, using the Web directory structure and not the file system structure.

Listing 4-3: **FileSize Function and Usage**

```
<%
Function FileSize(strFilename)

    '
    ' The filename being supplied is
    ' assumed to be a virtual path
    ' to the file. The path can either
    ' have or omit the directory names.
    ' If the directory names are omitted,
    ' Server.MapPath makes the assumption
    ' that the file is in the current
    ' directory.
    '

    Dim objFSO      ' As FileSystemObject
    Dim objFile     ' As Scripting.File
    Dim lngSize     ' As Long

    Set objFSO = _
        Server.CreateObject("Scripting.FileSystemObject")

    Set objFile = _
        objFSO.GetFile(Server.MapPath(strFilename))

    lngSize = objFile.Size

    If lngSize >= 1024^3 Then
        FileSize = FormatNumber(lngSize / 1024^3, 2, True) _
            & " Gb"
    ElseIf lngSize >= 1024^2 Then
        FileSize = FormatNumber(lngSize / 1024^2, 2, True) _
            & " Mb"
    ElseIf lngSize >= 1024 Then
        FileSize = FormatNumber(lngSize / 1024, 2, True) & " Kb"
    Else
        FileSize = lngSize & " bytes"
    End If

    Set objFile = Nothing
    Set objFSO = Nothing
End Function
```

```
Response.Write FileSize("/db/adtrack.mdb")

%>
```

This function will determine the appropriate unit for displaying the file size, do a conversion, and return the textual size of the file in question. You can use either a file name without directory names in front of it, or you can use a virtual path as shown in the example.

#include Directive

This directive is used to include one file's contents into another. This is the only directive that works in both ASP and HTML pages. Here's an example that will include a file in the same directory:

```
<!--#include file="adovbs.inc" -->
```

When the page finishes loading, the contents of adovbs.inc will replace the #include directive. Using the file parameter will cause the directive to look for a file in the same directory. If you need to load a file in another directory, you can use the virtual parameter instead, as shown here:

```
<!--#include virtual="/includes/adovbs.inc" -->
```

In this case, the file being included is suffixed with inc, which is a common extension for files included into other files. You can include any text file into your ASP code files, regardless of extension.

One limitation of this directive is that you cannot dynamically generate the file name you want to include. For instance, you can't have a list of files in a database table and include them each through a code loop. The reason: All #include directives are processed before the ASP code.

Creating Modular ASP Code

As mentioned in the preceding section, you can use any extension for your code files. However, the problem with using extensions other than ASP for your include files is that they can't be processed for further #include directives.

Let's say you want to use a single #include directive in your file, but you don't want all your functions in one file. This arrangement means that you have multiple files with functions in them, all of which need to be included into a file, which is then included into each of the other files. In order for the #include directives to be processed in all the levels of include files, the files all need to be suffixed with ASP. Listing 4-4 shows sample files and how you need to create the files to include each of the function files.

Listing 4-4: Include File Samples

```
<%
'
' Function1.asp
'
' This file includes one function or a group of functions.
'

' code goes here

%>


<%
'
' Function2.asp
'
' This file includes more functions.
'

' code goes here
%>
<%
'
' Function3.asp
'
' This file includes even more functions.
'

' code goes here
%>


<%
'
' FunctionLibrary.asp
'
' This file is included in all other pages and
' includes the three function pages.
'
%>
<!--#include file="function1.asp" -->
<!--#include file="function2.asp" -->
<!--#include file="function3.asp" -->
```

The end result is that you only have to include `FunctionLibrary.asp` into each of your files where you want to use the functions you wrote. In addition, if you ever add new functions or new function files, you simply make the new files and then add the appropriate `#include` directives to `FunctionLibrary.asp`.

A final note would be to keep all your include files in a common directory, named something like `includes` or `scripts`. You can then use the virtual parameter in the `#include` directive. This arrangement enables you to use the ASP library files from anywhere on your Web site without encountering problems in finding the proper directories. Listing 4-5 shows a different version of `FunctionLibrary.asp` from the preceding listing.

Listing 4-5: **FunctionLibrary.asp using virtual paths**

```
<%
'
'  FunctionLibrary.asp
'
'  This file is included in all other pages and
'  includes the three function pages.
'
%>
<!--#include virtual="/includes/function1.asp" -->
<!--#include virtual="/includes/function2.asp" -->
<!--#include virtual="/includes/function3.asp" -->
```

If you think that having all these files will slow down the rendering of the file to the end user, remember that none of the code will ever be sent to the user's browser. Instead, it will all be evaluated on the server, which means you can essentially create any level of file hierarchy that you want. There is a minimal cost to include a file into another; however, the benefits of building modular ASP code far outweigh the extra processing cost.

Summary

Server-side include technology has been available in other Web servers for a number of years, and the features that were available are still useful in the newer ASP technology. While many of the directives won't work directly in ASP pages, there are workarounds for each of the directives that are actually more flexible.

You also learned about creating modular ASP code files. These code files are easier to manage, especially in a team development environment. You can make changes to your function library without updating every page for minor changes. A little bit of planning along with some good file layouts will make your tasks much easier to complete.

✦   ✦   ✦

Using the Request Object

◆ ◆ ◆ ◆

In This Chapter

Learn the basic functions of the Request object

Understand the meanings of each of the object's properties

Use the methods of the Request object

Learn to use the server variables available to your program

See the Request object in action with some practical examples

Introduction to the Request Object

◆ ◆ ◆ ◆

This chapter introduces the first of the built-in objects provided in Active Server Pages: the Request object. This object makes available all of the information provided to the server by a user's browser. This information may be provided through an input form, a URL's parameters, or there may be other types of information provided to your page. The Request object can also give you access to binary files sent to the server as file uploads. Some of this information, such as browser type and operating system, can be used to help customize your site to a particular user's needs. For instance, some older browsers can't support certain HTML features. By looking at such information, you can omit features that may not work for that browser. You'll learn how to program this functionality and more in this chapter.

The Request object provides information from five different sources:

+ Client Certificate — If the user is using a security certificate, this information will be available from the Request object. Security is covered in Chapter 13.

+ Cookies — Any cookies related to the site are passed to the server through the Request object. Cookies are covered in Chapter 7.

+ Form — Any forms on the requesting page may have data in their controls. This data will be available through the Request object.

+ QueryString — The URL of a page can include a great deal of information, such as ID values and other numeric and text data. This information is parsed automatically and made available through the Request object.

✦ ServerVariables — Each time a user connects to a Web server, the server collects a number of key pieces of information about the user and the browser. This information is made available through the ServerVariables collection of the Request object.

The Request object also provides a property that gives the total number of bytes that the client sent as part of the request. This property is used in combination with the Request object's BinaryRead method, which is used to retrieve uploaded files sent from the client as part of a posted request. This capability is a relatively new feature that was made available in the latest edition of the HTTP protocol. Several sites, including Microsoft's HotMail site, enable users to upload files through their Web browsers to Web sites.

The rest of this chapter shows you how to use all these types of information when you are building your Web applications.

Using Form Information

Forms are one of the most common ways for users to submit information to Web pages. Forms can be as simple as a text box for doing a search or as complex as a series of forms to enter your federal tax information. Regardless of the form's complexity or the number of controls, you still get this information through the Request object's Form collection of information. Each control or input field is given an ID in the form, and those IDs are used to retrieve information after the form has been submitted. This section shows you how to make use of this information by building a simple form that echoes a user's input back to her. In subsequent chapters, you see how to build more complex form applications; however, they still use this method for retrieving information.

Creating a Single Box Form

On many Web sites, one of the most prominent features is the search box. As shown in Figure 5-1, the search box is in a key location on the home page. A user simply needs to enter a keyword or two and hit the Enter key to start the search.

The HTML required to create this form is quite simple:

```
<form method="GET" action="/cgi-bin/search.asp">
   <input name="keywords" size=20 maxlength=512>
</form>
```

By default, hitting the Enter key in a form with no Submit button causes the data to be submitted. This default is helpful if you are trying to save screen space for content or other graphical elements. You don't have to always provide a Submit button if you just have the single box.

Figure 5-1: The search box is in the upper-left corner of the screen.

To show how to make this search box work in ASP, we're going to create a simple form that has a text box and a Submit button. This form will submit data to a second page that will return the submitted information. You'll never build such a simple application in real life; however, it does help to show how the Request object works.

To get started, follow these steps:

1. Create the form in a new file, which we have called basicform.html. There won't be any ASP code in this file, so you can use HTM or HTML as the extension. The code for basicform.html follows:

```
<html>
<head>
    <title>Chapter 5: Basic Form</title>
</head>

<body>
<h1>Basic Input Form</h1>

<form action="basicform_process.asp" method=POST>
```

```
      Keywords:
      <input type="Text" name="txtKeywords" size="20"><p>
      <input type="Submit" name="cmdSubmit" value="Submit">
</form>
</body>
</html>
```

2. The second part of the form is the "back-end," which processes the input data. The name of this file should be basicform_process.asp; its code follows:

```
<html>
<head>
    <title>Chapter 5: Basic Form Response</title>
</head>
<body>
<h1>Basic Form - Response</h1>

You entered these keywords:
<% = Request.Form("txtKeywords") %>
<p>
</body>
</html>
```

3. With the two files created, use your Web browser to load the first Web page.

4. Enter in a keyword in the text box, and then press the Submit button.

The processing page will return your keywords back to you. As you can see in the code, the text box in the first file is given a name of txtKeywords. Be sure to remember this name, because the back-end file uses that name to retrieve the submitted data. The name of the control is used as a key into the Form collection of the Request object. In this case, any text in the box is printed out to the Web page.

You may have also noticed that the Submit button was given a name: cmdSubmit. Even though there is no information in the button, you pressed it. If there were several Submit buttons, what if you needed to determine which Submit button was pressed? The answer: the caption on the button is passed to the Request.Form collection. You can see this process in action by modifying the second file to have the code in Listing 5-1.

Listing 5-1: **Code for basicform_process.asp**

```
<html>
<head>
   <title>Chapter 5: Basic Form Response</title>
</head>
<body>
<h1>Basic Form - Response</h1>
```

```
You entered these keywords:
<% = Request.Form("txtKeywords") %>
<p>
The cmdSubmit button's value is:
<%= Request.Form("cmdSubmit") %>
</body>
</html>
```

When you press this button, the value printed is the caption on the button; in this case, Submit. One important thing to note is that if you don't press the Submit button but instead press the Enter key, the cmdSubmit variable will be empty. In most cases, when you have a single submit button, you won't need to worry about checking its value. If, however, you have multiple submit buttons for the same form, it's especially helpful to know what button was pressed. To see this process in action, do the following:

1. In a new file called twobuttonform.html, add the following code:

```
<html>
<head>
    <title>Chapter 5: Two Button Form</title>
</head>
<body>
<h1>Basic Input Form</h1>

<form action="twobuttonform_process.asp" method=POST>
Keywords: <input type="Text" name="txtKeywords" size="20"><p>
<input type="Submit"
    name="cmdProgramOne"
    value="Submit to Program One"><br>

<input type="Submit"
    name="cmdProgramTwo"
    value="Submit to Program Two">
</form>
</body>
</html>
```

2. In another new file called twobuttonform_process.asp, add the following code:

```
<html>
<head>
    <title>Chapter 5: Two Button Form Response</title>
</head>
<body>
<h1>Two Button Form - Response</h1>

You entered these keywords:
```

```
<% = Request.Form("txtKeywords") %>
<p>
The cmdProgramOne button's value is:
<%= Request.Form("cmdProgramOne") %>
<p>
The cmdProgramTwo button's value is:
<%= Request.Form("cmdProgramTwo") %>
</body>
</html>
```

When you run the new twobuttonform.html page, you will be presented with two command buttons instead of one. Both of them will submit the keywords, but the button names are different. The back-end code prints the values of both command button variables. The pressed button will actually have a value, and that value will be the caption on the pressed button. If you press the "Submit to Program One" button, its caption will be printed.

To make the back-end form a bit smarter, use the following code in twobuttonform _process.asp instead of the code in Step 2. This code checks the values and tells the user which button was pressed.

```
<html>
<head>
    <title>Chapter 5: Two Button Form Response</title>
</head>
<body>
<h1>Two Button Form - Response</h1>

You entered these keywords:
<% = Request.Form("txtKeywords") %>
<p>
<%
    If Request.Form("cmdProgramOne") <> "" Then
%>
The cmdProgramOne button was pressed.
<%
    Else
%>
The cmdProgramTwo button was pressed.
<%
    End If
%>
</body>
</html>
```

This code checks to see if the first button was pressed by simply checking its variable value against an empty string. If the first button wasn't pressed, the assumption is made that the second one was pressed. Because this form won't be run without one of the buttons being pressed, this is a pretty good assumption for now. There is always the chance that someone could load this page ahead of the other; however, you'll learn later in this chapter how to deal with that situation.

With standard text input boxes and command buttons under your belt, you are ready to move on to some of the other controls. The TEXTAREA tag works in the same way as the text box, by the way. Your form doesn't have to worry about which format was used to accept text input.

Working with Radio Buttons

Radio buttons — or OptionButtons as they are called in Visual Basic — are designed to let the user pick one option from a group of mutually exclusive options. This arrangement is often used with gender so that the user can pick male or female. Radio buttons are normally used with lists of six or less items, but this is not a requirement — merely a guideline. To try your hand at radio buttons in ASP, do the following:

1. Create a new file named pizzaform.html with the following code:

```
<html>
<head>
   <title>Chapter 5: Pizza Delivery Form</title>
</head>
<body>
<h1>Eric's Pizza Parlor</h1>
What size pizza would you like?

<form action="pizzaorder_process.asp" method=POST>
<input type="radio" name="optSize" value="S">
Small<br>
<input type="radio" name="optSize" value="M">
Medium<br>
<input type="radio" name="optSize" value="L" CHECKED>
Large<br>
<input type="radio" name="optSize" value="XL">
Extra Large<br>
<input type="radio" name="optSize" value="XXL">
Call the Doctor in the Morning<br>

<p>
<input type="Submit" name="cmdSubmit" value="Deliver It!">
</p>

</form>
</body>
</html>
```

2. Create the response page named pizzaorder_process.asp with the following code:

```
<html>
<head>
   <title>Chapter 5: Pizza Delivery Confirmation</title>
```

```
</head>
<body>
<h1>Eric's Pizza Parlor</h1>
<p>Here is what you ordered:
</p>

1
<%
   Select Case Request.Form("optSize")
   Case "S"
      Response.Write "Small"
   Case "M"
      Response.Write "Medium"
   Case "L"
      Response.Write "Large"
   Case "XL"
      Response.Write "Extra Large"
   Case "XXL"
      Response.Write "Extra-Extra Large (with Cardiologist)"
   End Select
%>
Pizza<p>

</body>
</html>
```

When you load the first page, you'll see the form shown in Figure 5-2. After making your selection, clicking the button will show an appropriate response, as seen in Figure 5-3.

Figure 5-2: PizzaOrder.html in action

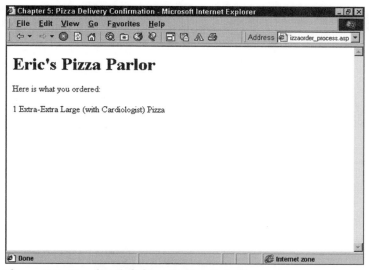

Figure 5-3: Results of clicking the form's button

As the source code for the form shows, all five radio button controls all have the same name. This is how radio buttons are grouped together in HTML. However, each had a different value. This is not required, but you should give them all different values. You should also notice that we checked the "Large" item by default, because radio buttons should never be shown without a value already selected. This arrangement also prevents errors, such as the user not selecting any of the items before clicking the button.

When the form's data gets to the back-end page, retrieving the radio button's value is exactly the same as retrieving the value for the text box control. That value is compared against a list of known values, and then an appropriate response is generated.

If you have more than one group of radio buttons on your form, each group must be given a different name. This requirement enables you to distinguish between groups in the back-end and lets them work properly in the user's browser.

Working with Check Boxes

Check boxes are used for independent yes/no choices. For our example, the check box control will be used to select toppings that you want on your pizza. Each control is given a different name and operates independently of the others. To try this out, either create a new form or edit `pizzaform.html` to contain the code shown in Listing 5-2.

Listing 5-2: **Code for pizzaform.html to add toppings**

```html
<html>
<head>
   <title>Chapter 5: Pizza Delivery Form</title>
</head>
<body>
<h1>Eric's Pizza Parlor</h1>
What size pizza would you like?

<form action="pizzaorder_process.asp" method=POST>
<input type="radio" name="optSize" value="S">
Small<br>
<input type="radio" name="optSize" value="M">
Medium<br>
<input type="radio" name="optSize" value="L" CHECKED>
Large<br>
<input type="radio" name="optSize" value="XL">
Extra Large<br>
<input type="radio" name="optSize" value="XXL">
Call the Doctor in the Morning<br>

<p>
What toppings would you like on your pizza?
</p>

<table cellpadding=4>
<tr>
   <td>
      <input type="checkbox" name="chkTopping1"
             value="Y" checked>Cheese<br>
      <input type="checkbox" name="chkTopping2"
             value="Y" checked>Tomato Sauce<br>
      <input type="checkbox" name="chkTopping3"
             value="Y">Olive Oil<br>
      <input type="checkbox" name="chkTopping4"
             value="Y">Barbecue Sauce<br>
   </td>
   <td>
      <input type="checkbox" name="chkTopping5"
             value="Y">Pepperoni<br>
      <input type="checkbox" name="chkTopping6"
             value="Y">Sausage<br>
      <input type="checkbox" name="chkTopping7"
             value="Y">Mushrooms<br>
      <input type="checkbox" name="chkTopping8"
             value="Y">Onions<br>
   </td>
   <td>
      <input type="checkbox" name="chkTopping9"
             value="Y">Ham<br>
      <input type="checkbox" name="chkTopping10"
             value="Y">Pineapple<br>
```

```
        <input type="checkbox" name="chkTopping11"
            value="Y">Green Peppers<br>
        <input type="checkbox" name="chkTopping12"
            value="Y">Anchovies<br>
    </td>
</tr>
</table>
<p>
<input type="Submit" name="cmdSubmit" value="Deliver It!">
</p>

</form>
</body>
</html>
```

This form generates the result shown in Figure 5-4.

Figure 5-4: New and improved delivery form

We've checked a few options by default, but no options need to be checked for the form to work properly. In addition, the options are named with only numbers used to distinguish them, because the back-end already knows what numbers map to the names of the toppings. In addition, this arrangement enables us to loop through the options instead of writing code for each by hand.

The back-end page is a bit longer, because there are many options to check. In addition, we have added some code to determine the cost of the pizza. The new code for `pizzaform_process.asp` is shown in Listing 5-3.

Listing 5-3: **New code for pizzaform_process.asp**

```asp
<%
    Option Explicit
    Dim curCost      ' As Currency
    Dim curToppingCost ' As Currency
    Dim intToppingCount ' As Integer
    Dim intLoop      ' As Variant
    Dim a_strToppings(12) ' As Array of Strings

    a_strToppings(1) = "Cheese"
    a_strToppings(2) = "Tomato Sauce"
    a_strToppings(3) = "Olive Oil"
    a_strToppings(4) = "Barbecue Sauce"
    a_strToppings(5) = "Pepperoni"
    a_strToppings(6) = "Sausage"
    a_strToppings(7) = "Mushrooms"
    a_strToppings(8) = "Onions"
    a_strToppings(9) = "Ham"
    a_strToppings(10) = "Pineapple"
    a_strToppings(11) = "Green Peppers"
    a_strToppings(12) = "Anchovies"
%>
<html>
<head>
    <title>Chapter 5: Pizza Delivery Confirmation</title>
</head>
<body>
<h1>Eric's Pizza Parlor</h1>
<p>Here is what you ordered:
</p>

<table width=100%>
<tr>
<td align=left>
1
<%
    Select Case Request.Form("optSize")
    Case "S"
        Response.Write "Small"
        curCost = 8.00
    Case "M"
        Response.Write "Medium"
        curCost = 9.50
    Case "L"
        Response.Write "Large"
        curCost = 11.00
    Case "XL"
        Response.Write "Extra Large"
```

```
            curCost = 12.50
        Case "XXL"
            Response.Write "Extra-Extra Large (with Cardiologist)"
            curCost = 14.00
        End Select
        curToppingCost = curCost / 10
        intToppingCount = -2      ' give 2 toppings for free
%>
Pizza<p>
</td>
<td align=right>
<% = FormatCurrency(curCost) %>
</td>
</tr>
<%
    For intLoop = 1 To 12
        If Request.Form("chkTopping" & intLoop) = "Y" Then
            intToppingCount = intToppingCount + 1
%>
<tr>
<td><% = a_strToppings(intLoop) %></td>
<td align=right>
<%          If intToppingCount <= 0 Then
                Response.Write "N/C"
            Else
                Response.Write FormatCurrency(curToppingCost)
            End If
%>
</td>
</tr>
<%
        End If
    Next
    If intToppingCount < 0 Then intToppingCount = 0
%>

<tr>
<td align=right><b>Order Total:</b></td>
<td align=right><b>
<% = FormatCurrency(curCost _
        + (intToppingCount * curToppingCost)) %>
</b></td>
</tr>
</table>


</body>
</html>
```

In the first few lines, we declare some variables that will be used to figure the pizza's cost.

✦ curCost — Currency variable that holds the cost of pizza.

✦ curToppingCost — Currency variable that holds the cost of each topping, which is ten percent of the pizza price. (The bigger pizzas need more amounts of toppings.)

✦ intToppingCount — Integer that holds the number of toppings that the user selected.

✦ intLoop — An Integer used for looping through the topping check boxes.

✦ a_strToppings — An array of strings that holds the names of the toppings. The numbers match with the previous form's control names.

We then load up the array with the appropriate topping names. The loading of topping names could also be done with a database; because we don't have a database yet, we do it by hand.

The next section sets up the response page, and then we determine the type of pizza. Note that the results are now being put into a table, and the cost is stored in the appropriate variable and then printed. We need to hold the cost of the pizza to figure the total cost later.

We then determine the toppings that the user selected. In my pizzeria, we give out the first two toppings for free. Because most people have cheese and tomato sauce, this arrangement allows those toppings to be free. However, you may only want to allow the sauces and cheese to be free. If this is the case, you'll need to modify the loop code a bit to charge if the first two toppings are not toppings that you allow.

We look at each of the 12 topping check boxes and increment the counter if a topping was selected. We also print the cost of the topping in the table. For the first two toppings, N/C, or No Charge, is printed on the resulting page.

The last task after the loop is to figure out the total cost. If the user only wanted a cheese pizza with nothing else, including sauce, the total number of toppings would be negative, which doesn't make sense. We set the number of toppings to zero if it is still negative by the end of the page. The total is then printed using the FormatCurrency function, so that the local currency symbol is printed automatically. Figure 5-5 shows the result of this page.

You could make this form even more extensive by allowing the user to select the number of pizzas, allow for double cheese, and so forth. However, this example gives you a good start in understanding how to use all the basic form controls.

Figure 5-5: Result of sending in an order to the form

Working with Select Lists

Select lists, or drop-down lists, work in a similar manner to text boxes. The control is given an appropriate name, which can be retrieved through the Request.Form object. However, the select list can also be used in a multiple select role. For instance, you may have the option to select multiple states from a list. You use the appropriate key to indicate a multiple selection (Shift or Ctrl on the PC) and then pick all the options you want. All of the items you select will be stored in the same control in the Request object. Look at the code in Listing 5-4, which shows a simplified version of the pizza request form.

Listing 5-4: **Short version of the pizza delivery form**

```
<html>
<head>
   <title>Chapter 5: Pizza Delivery Form</title>
</head>
<body>
<h1>Eric's Pizza Parlor</h1>
What size pizza would you like?

<form action="selectlist_process.asp" method=POST>
<select name="cboPizzaSize" size="5" multiple>
```

Continued

Listing 5-4 *(continued)*

```
<option>Small
<option>Medium
<option>Large
<option>Extra Large
<option>Extra-Extra Large
</select>

<p>
<input type="Submit" name="cmdSubmit" value="Deliver It!">
</p>

</form>
</body>
</html>
```

To see the response, create the response page named selectlist_process.asp with the following code:

```
<% Response.Write Request.Form("cboPizzaSize") %>
```

When you run the HTML page and select the Medium and Extra Large sizes, you will see this output:

```
Medium, Extra Large
```

ASP automatically comma-separates all the items and puts them in the same place for you. Your task is to separate these items out. Luckily, VB provides some handy functions for that job. To see this process in action, we're going to rebuild the pizza form using a select list instead of a series of check boxes. The code for the new version is shown in Listing 5-5.

Listing 5-5: New pizzaform.html with Select List

```
<html>
<head>
    <title>Chapter 5: Pizza Delivery Form</title>
</head>
<body>
<h1>Eric's Pizza Parlor</h1>
What size pizza would you like?
```

```
<form action="pizzaorder2_process.asp" method=POST>
<input type="radio" name="optSize" value="S">
Small<br>
<input type="radio" name="optSize" value="M">
Medium<br>
<input type="radio" name="optSize" value="L" CHECKED>
Large<br>
<input type="radio" name="optSize" value="XL">
Extra Large<br>
<input type="radio" name="optSize" value="XXL">
Call the Doctor in the Morning<br>

<p>
What toppings would you like on your pizza?
</p>

<select name="cboToppings" size="4" multiple>
<option SELECTED>Cheese
<option SELECTED>Tomato Sauce
<option>Olive Oil
<option>Barbecue Sauce
<option>Pepperoni
<option>Sausage
<option>Mushrooms
<option>Onions
<option>Ham
<option>Pineapple
<option>Green Peppers
<option>Anchovies
</select>

<p>
<input type="Submit" name="cmdSubmit" value="Deliver It!">
</p>

</form>
</body>
</html>
```

Figure 5-6 displays this version of the form.

The back-end gets a bit easier using this method, because we can use a number of string-processing functions to simplify our lives. Listing 5-6 displays the code for pizzaform2_process.asp.

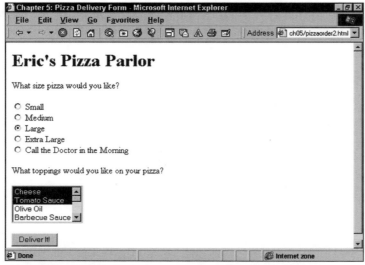

Figure 5-6: Pizza delivery form using a select list instead of check boxes

Listing 5-6: **Code for pizzaform2_process.asp**

```
<%
    Option Explicit
    Dim curCost      ' As Currency
    Dim curToppingCost ' As Currency
    Dim intToppingCount ' As Integer
    Dim intLoop      ' As Variant
    Dim a_strSelectedToppings  ' As Array of Strings

%>
<html>
<head>
    <title>Chapter 5: Pizza Delivery Confirmation</title>
</head>
<body>
<h1>Eric's Pizza Parlor</h1>
<p>Here is what you ordered:
</p>

<table width=100%>
<tr>
<td align=left>
1
```

```asp
<%
    Select Case Request.Form("optSize")
    Case "S"
        Response.Write "Small"
        curCost = 8.00
    Case "M"
        Response.Write "Medium"
        curCost = 9.50
    Case "L"
        Response.Write "Large"
        curCost = 11.00
    Case "XL"
        Response.Write "Extra Large"
        curCost = 12.50
    Case "XXL"
        Response.Write "Extra-Extra Large (with Cardiologist)"
        curCost = 14.00
    End Select
    curToppingCost = curCost / 10
%>
Pizza<p>
</td>
<td align=right>
<% = FormatCurrency(curCost) %>
</td>
</tr>
<%
    a_strSelectedToppings = _
        Split(Request.Form("cboToppings"), ", ")

    '
    ' The resulting array from the Split function
    ' is a base zero array instead of a base one.
    '
    For intLoop = 0 To UBound(a_strSelectedToppings)
%>
<tr>
<td><% = a_strSelectedToppings(intLoop) %></td>
<td align=right>
<%
        If intLoop <= 1 Then
            Response.Write "N/C"
        Else
            Response.Write FormatCurrency(curToppingCost)
        End If
%>
</td>
</tr>
<%
    Next
```

Continued

Listing 5-6 *(continued)*

```
    intToppingCount = UBound(a_strSelectedToppings) - 1
    If intToppingCount < 0 Then intToppingCount = 0
%>

<tr>
<td align=right><b>Order Total:</b></td>
<td align=right><b>
<% = FormatCurrency(curCost _
        + (intToppingCount * curToppingCost)) %>
</b></td>
</tr>
</table>


</body>
</html>
```

Because the toppings are coming back separated by a comma, we can use the Split function to break that big string into an array of strings. Then, we can easily determine how many toppings were selected and loop through them without needing to keep another copy of the array in the page. The key thing to remember about the Split function is that the first element's index is zero and not one, which can screw up your results if you're not careful. As Figure 5-7 shows, the results of submitting this form are identical to the previous examples.

Figure 5-7: Results of submitting an order

The only drawback to this method is that the select list doesn't show all the options, as with a table of check boxes. However, you may not have enough room for all the check boxes. In that case, the select list will do the same job for you.

Working with Hidden Input Fields

Besides all the visible types of controls you can put on your forms, you can also add a hidden input field. This type of field is used for information that needs to be given to the back-end processing form, but doesn't need to be entered by the user. These fields are created in HTML with code like the following:

```
<input type=hidden name="txtHidden" value="Hidden Text">
```

You can use the Request.Form collection to retrieve this information as you would with a text box. This type of input box will be used in subsequent chapters to pass status information to and from the processing pages; for now, know that hidden input fields work exactly the same as other controls.

Using Query String Information

Now that you've got the hang of using the information provided to your code from HTML forms, you can use another source of information: the query string. The query string is the entire URL that the user sees in the browser's address area. For the preceding examples in this chapter, the URL was simply the name of the page. However, that arrangement is just the beginning of what you can do with the query string. The query string can be used to provide a wide variety of information about how to process data, what data to process, and so forth. The only problem with the query string is that the user sees all the information that is passed back and forth. While this is not normally a problem, the information is stored if the user bookmarks a page, whereas the data in forms is not stored on the user's computer. If the information stored in the URL is dynamic, the user may encounter errors when selecting that bookmark later.

With those caveats out of the way, let's take a look at a simple example of how the query string is used. In Listing 5-7, we have the simple form (previously called `basicform.html`) from earlier in the chapter. However, the ACTION parameter is different: it contains extra information on the end of the file name. This information will be parsed and stored in the QueryString collection.

Listing 5-7: **Code for basicqs.html**

```
<html>
<head>
    <title>Chapter 5: Basic QueryString Usage</title>
</head>
<body>
<h1>Basic QueryString Usage</h1>

<form action="basicqs_process.asp?action=validate" method=POST>
Keywords: <input type="Text" name="txtKeywords" size="20"><p>
<input type="Submit" name="cmdSubmit" value="Submit">
</form>
</body>
</html>
```

Listing 5-8 shows the response page.

Listing 5-8: **Code for basicqs_process.asp**

```
<html>
<head>
    <title>Chapter 5: Basic QueryString Usage</title>
</head>
<body>
<h1>Basic QueryString Usage</h1>

You entered these keywords:
<% = Request.Form("txtKeywords") %>
<p>
The query string contained an ACTION parameter,
value = <% = Request.QueryString("action") %>
<p>
The cmdSubmit button's value is:
<%= Request.Form("cmdSubmit") %>
</body>
</html>
```

The results of running the HTML form will look something like Figure 5-8.

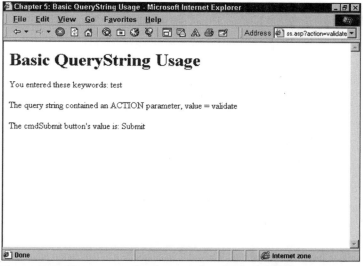

Figure 5-8: The query string is parsed and printed in the output

Now that we know how to get the information in the query string, we have to figure out what to do with it. The first and most useful task is to combine the two pages we've been using into a single page. The page will be smart enough to determine whether it is being used to gather or print data. How will we do this? The query string. Look at the code in Listing 5-9, which combines the two pages into a single page.

Listing 5-9: **Code for SingleForm.asp**

```
<html>
<head>
    <title>Chapter 5: Single Form for Gathering
           and Processing Data</title>
</head>
<body>
<h2>Single Form for Gathering and Processing Data</h2>

<%
    If Request.QueryString("action") = "" Then
    '
    ' Deal with case where form is being
    ' used to gather information.
    '
%>
<form action="SingleForm.asp?action=validate" method=POST>
Keywords: <input type="Text" name="txtKeywords" size="20"><p>
```

Continued

Listing 5-9 *(continued)*

```
<input type="Submit" name="cmdSubmit" value="Submit">
</form>
<%
    Else
    '
    ' Deal with case where form is being
    ' used to display information.
    '
%>
You entered these keywords:
<% = Request.Form("txtKeywords") %>
<p>
The query string contained an ACTION parameter,
value = <% = Request.QueryString("action") %>
<p>
The cmdSubmit button's value is:
<%= Request.Form("cmdSubmit") %>

<%
    End If
%>
</body>
</html>
```

When you load this page, it first resembles Figure 5-9.

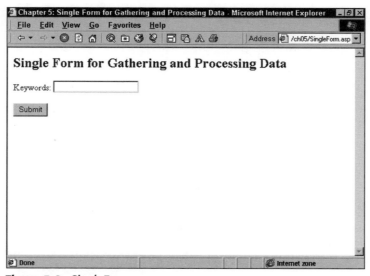

Figure 5-9: SingleForm.asp

After you enter data and press the Submit button, the results resemble Figure 5-10.

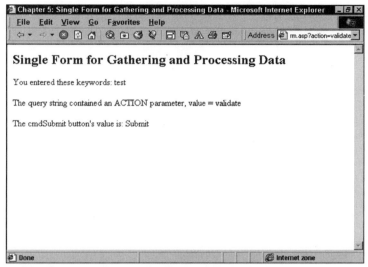

Figure 5-10: Results of pressing the Submit button

As you may have noticed, the address in your browser barely changed from one step to the next. When you started, the end of the URL looked like the following:

```
SingleForm.asp
```

After the results were generated, the URL looked like the following:

```
SingleForm.asp?action=validate
```

This example shows you that all the page's processing is being done in one place. Using this method has a number of advantages over the two-file system:

✦ Half as many files to maintain

✦ Ability to share common code, such as constants and HTML

✦ Keeps gathering and processing logic together, so that you always know where the data from a form is being processed.

You can further refine your pages to follow an even more structured programming path. In Listing 5-10, each "path" is broken into a separate subroutine. The common code is also handled in separate subroutines. ASP will read all the way through a file looking for code that is not within a subroutine or function block and start executing there. With the code in Listing 5-10, the ASP engine will have to read the entire file and then start running at the end.

Listing 5-10: **Code for StructuredForm.asp**

```
<%
Option Explicit

'..................................................
'
' Sub Main()
'
' This routine is the main processing path for this page.
' The name does not hold any special meaning, except that
' it is a carryover from Visual Basic. You can name this
' routine whatever you want.
'
'..................................................
Sub Main()
    Call PrintHeader()
    If Request.QueryString("action") = "" Then
        Call GatherData
    Else
        Call ProcessData
    End If
    Call PrintFooter()
End Sub

'..................................................
'
' Sub PrintHeader()
'
' This routine prints the common HTML content at
' the top of the page.
'
'..................................................
Sub PrintHeader()
%>
<html>
<head>
    <title>Chapter 5: Single Form for
            Gathering and Processing Data</title>
</head>
<body>
<h2>Single Form for Gathering and Processing Data</h2>
<%
End Sub


'..................................................
'
' Sub GatherData()
'
```

```asp
' This routine creates the data entry form.
'
'''''''''''''''''''''''''''''''''''''''''''''''''''''''''
Sub GatherData()
%>
<form action="StructuredForm.asp?action=validate" method=POST>
Keywords: <input type="Text" name="txtKeywords" size="20"><p>
<input type="Submit" name="cmdSubmit" value="Submit">
</form>
<%
End Sub

'''''''''''''''''''''''''''''''''''''''''''''''''''''''''
'
' Sub ProcessData()
'
' This routine generates output based on the
' form input that was received.
'
'''''''''''''''''''''''''''''''''''''''''''''''''''''''''
Sub ProcessData()
%>
You entered these keywords:
<% = Request.Form("txtKeywords") %>
<p>
The query string contained an ACTION parameter,
value = <% = Request.QueryString("action") %>
<p>
The cmdSubmit button's value is:
<%= Request.Form("cmdSubmit") %>
<%
End Sub

'''''''''''''''''''''''''''''''''''''''''''''''''''''''''
'
' Sub PrintFooter()
'
' This routine prints the common HTML content at
' the bottom of the page.
'
'''''''''''''''''''''''''''''''''''''''''''''''''''''''''
Sub PrintFooter()
%>
</body>
</html>
<%
End Sub
'
```

Continued

Listing 5-10 *(continued)*

```
' This code is the last to be read by the
' ASP engine, and it kicks off all the
' processing in this page. This code has
' to be outside of any subroutines or
' functions or it won't be run.
'

Call Main()

%>
```

This amount of structure may seem excessive for a simple form; however, this code is significantly easier to read because there is a defined flow for the program. Instead of creating "stream-of-consciousness" ASP code, this method enables you to be able to see exactly how routines are being called and in what order. It can also enable you to find places where you are sharing code.

Also, note that the action parameter requires a value, but not any value in particular. You can use a single letter, a number, or anything else that has meaning to you. You can also shorten the name of the parameter, as long as you keep track of the name.

The query string will be used extensively in subsequent chapters to help control the processing of data in various forms. Think of it as another way to get data to the ASP code for processing.

Using Server Variables

As mentioned in the introduction, each time someone requests data from your server, a number of key pieces of information are gathered about that user. Items like the person's hostname and/or IP address, browser type, operating system, and more are stored for possible use by your Web pages. These pieces of information are known as server environment variables and are exposed for use through the ServerVariables collection of the Request object. This section shows you what these variables hold and how they can be used.

Table 5-1 displays the variables available for use in ASP. This table also appeared in the preceding chapter, which covered server-side includes. The information will be the same, regardless of how you obtain it.

Table 5-1
HTTP Environment Variables

Variable Name	Definition
ALL_HTTP	All HTTP headers that were not already parsed into one of the other variables described in this table. These variables are of the form HTTP_*header field name*. The headers consist of a null-terminated string with the individual headers separated by line feeds. Note that this won't return all the variables shown here. It will only return the header information.
AUTH_TYPE	This variable contains the type of authentication used. For example, the string will be "Basic" if Basic authentication is used, and it will be "Integrated Windows NT Authentication" for integrated authentication. Other authentication schemes will have other strings. Because new authentication types can be added to the Web server, it is not possible to list all the string possibilities. If the string is empty, then no authentication is used.
AUTH_PASSWORD	The value entered in the client's authentication dialog box. This variable is only available if Basic authentication is used.
AUTH_USER	The value entered in the client's authentication dialog box.
CONTENT_LENGTH	The number of bytes that the script can expect to receive from the client.
CONTENT_TYPE	The content type of the information supplied in the body of a POST request.
DOCUMENT_NAME	The current file name.
DOCUMENT_URI	The virtual path to the current document.
DATE_GMT	The current date in Greenwich Mean Time (GMT).
DATE_LOCAL	The current date in the local time zone.
GATEWAY_INTERFACE	The revision of the CGI specification used by the Web server.
LAST_MODIFIED	The date that the current document was last modified. The date will be displayed in the format specified by the #config directive, if applicable.

Continued

Table 5-1 *(continued)*

Variable Name	Definition
PATH_INFO	Additional path infnormation, as given by the client. This information consists of the trailing part of the URL after the script name, but before the query string, if any.
PATH_TRANSLATED	This variable is the value of PATH_INFO, but with any virtual path expanded into a directory specification.
QUERY_STRING	The information that follows the question mark (?) in the URL that referenced this script.
QUERY_STRING_UNESCAPED	Unescaped version of the query string; that is, a version that is not URL-encoded.
REMOTE_ADDR	The IP address of the client or agent of the client (for example, gateway or firewall) that sent the request.
REMOTE_HOST	The host name of the client or agent of the client (for example, gateway or firewall) that sent the request.
REMOTE_USER	This variable contains the user name supplied by the client and authenticated by the server. This comes back as an empty string when the user is anonymous (but authenticated).
REQUEST_METHOD	The HTTP request method. (GET and POST are most common.)
SCRIPT_NAME	The name of the script program being executed. For ASP pages, this will be the pathname to the ASP file.
SERVER_NAME	The server's host name or IP address.
SERVER_PORT	The TCP/IP port on which the request was received. By default, the port is 80.
SERVER_PORT_SECURE	A string of either 0 or 1. If the request is being handled on the secure port, this will be 1. Otherwise, it will be 0.
SERVER_PROTOCOL	The name and version of the information retrieval protocol relating to this request. This is usually HTTP/1.0.
SERVER_SOFTWARE	The name and version of the Web server answering the request. This will vary, but IIS 4.0 returns "Microsoft-IIS/4.0."
URL	Gives the base portion of the URL. Parameter values will not be included. The value is determined when the Web server parses the URL from the header.

To see the values of all of these variables, you can create a simple variable dump page, as shown in Listing 5-11.

Listing 5-11: Code for envdump.asp

```
<%
Option Explicit
Dim a_strVarNames       ' As Array of Strings
Dim strAllVarNames      ' As String
Dim intLoop             ' As Integer
strAllVarNames = "ALL_HTTP, AUTH_TYPE, AUTH_PASSWORD, " _
    & "AUTH_USER, CONTENT_LENGTH, CONTENT_TYPE, " _
    & "DOCUMENT_NAME, DOCUMENT_URI, DATE_GMT, " _
    & "DATE_LOCAL, GATEWAY_INTERFACE, LAST_MODIFIED, " _
    & "PATH_INFO, PATH_TRANSLATED, QUERY_STRING, " _
    & "QUERY_STRING_UNESCAPED, REMOTE_ADDR, REMOTE_HOST, " _
    & "REMOTE_USER, REQUEST_METHOD, SCRIPT_NAME, " _
    & "SERVER_NAME, SERVER_PORT, SERVER_PORT_SECURE, " _
    & "SERVER_PROTOCOL, SERVER_SOFTWARE, URL"

a_strVarNames = Split(strAllVarNames, ", ")
%>

<html>
<head>
    <title>Server Variables Display Page</title>
</head>
<body>
<table cellpadding=2 border=1>
<%
For intLoop = 0 To UBound(a_strVarNames)
%>
<tr>
    <td><% = a_strVarNames(intLoop) %></td>
    <td>
    <% = Request.ServerVariables(a_strVarNames(intLoop)) %>
    </td>
</tr>
<%
Next ' intLoop
%>
</table>
</body>
</html>
```

This code creates an array of all the available variables and then prints the value of each in a table. When you run this page, the results will vary and many of the variables will be empty. In particular, two variables can be quite helpful in your programming: ALL_HTTP and PATH_INFO. The rest of the variables can be used at times to provide tracking information for various purposes.

Cross-Reference You learn more about tracking user activity in Chapter 14.

ALL_HTTP Variable

This variable contains information about the actual request put into the IIS server. ALL_HTTP contains a lot of key information that your page may need. All of the text is returned with linefeed characters separating each part.

Note A linefeed character can be generated using Chr(10), which is the same as the vbLF constant.

To print this information in a more useful fashion, try the code shown in Listing 5-12.

Listing 5-12: **Code for AllHTTPDump.asp**

```
<%
Option Explicit
Dim a_strContent        ' As Array of Strings
Dim intLoop             ' As Integer
a_strContent = _
    Split(Request.ServerVariables("ALL_HTTP"), Chr(10))
%>

<html>
<head>
    <title>ALL_HTTP Display Page</title>
</head>
<body>
<h1>ALL_HTTP Variable Contents</h1>
<table cellpadding=2 border=1 width=640>
<%
For intLoop = 0 To UBound(a_strContent) - 1
%>
<tr>
<td><% Response.Write Left(a_strContent(intLoop), _
```

```
        Instr(a_strContent(intLoop), ":") - 1) %>
</td>
<td><% Response.Write Mid(a_strContent(intLoop), _
    Instr(a_strContent(intLoop), ":") + 1) %>
</td>
</tr>
<%
Next ' intLoop
%>
</table>
</body>
</html>
```

Your results will vary when you run this page, but you will get output that looks similar to Figure 5-11.

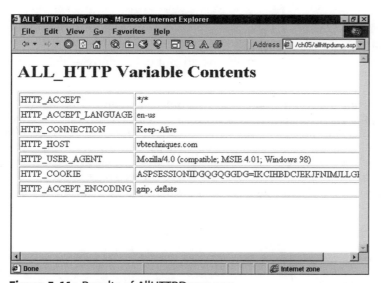

Figure 5-11: Results of AllHTTPDump.asp

Each of these pieces has a purpose:

HTTP_ACCEPT	Indicates the types of content that the user's browser will accept.
HTTP_ACCEPT_LANGUAGE	Specifies the user's native language; in this case, US English.

HTTP_CONNECTION	Keep-Alive is a type of Web connection that runs quicker because the network connection is kept active between page loads.
HTTP_HOST	This is the name of the machine where the ASP page is hosted.
HTTP_USER_AGENT	This is the name of the user's browser. Mozilla was the original name for Netscape's browser. The additional information here indicates that the browser is actually MS IE 4.01 running on Windows 98.
HTTP_COOKIE	ASP makes extensive use of cookies to enable many functions to work properly. The value here is the cookie used to track this particular session.
HTTP_ACCEPT_ENCODING	This specifies the methods by which data can be compressed to be sent.

The helpful variables for your purposes will be HTTP_USER_AGENT and HTTP_HOST. The rest are used internally and are not particularly useful. HTTP_HOST is also available in the SERVER_NAME variable.

One example of using the HTTP_USER_AGENT is browser sniffing. This task is particularly helpful when you are creating browser-specific HTML code. By checking this server variable, you can determine the browser type of the user and send the appropriate HTML code. Unfortunately, no complete list of browsers exists, but you can look for a few keywords, such as "MSIE 4." The best way to learn these keywords is through experience. You can also look in your Web server's logs, assuming the browser information is being tracked. You can reconfigure your logs to store the user's browser information, if necessary.

Cross-Reference   Check your Web server documentation for the process to store the user's browser information.

PATH_INFO Variable

This variable can be helpful when determining a query string for the next step in processing data, for instance. In preceding examples, the pathname to the validation step was hard-coded into the form's code, as shown in an excerpt from Listing 5-10:

```
Sub GatherData()
%>
<form action="StructuredForm.asp?action=validate" method=POST>
Keywords: <input type="Text" name="txtKeywords" size="20"><p>
<input type="Submit" name="cmdSubmit" value="Submit">
</form>
<%
End Sub
```

Using PATH_INFO, we can make this form more flexible and easier to move by changing the code to the following:

```
Sub GatherData()
    Response.Write "<form action="""  _
        & Request.ServerVariables("PATH_INFO") _
        & "?action=validate"" method=POST>"
%>
Keywords: <input type="Text" name="txtKeywords" size="20"><p>
<input type="Submit" name="cmdSubmit" value="Submit">
</form>
<%
End Sub
```

The file can now be moved or renamed without fear of breaking its code.

Summary

The Request object is filled with information that can make ASP programming easier. All of the information the user sends will always be in this object, which makes your life much easier. You don't have to create your own mechanisms for passing data—IIS takes care of it all for you. The examples in this chapter were designed to get you started, and the following chapters make extensive use of the Request object to build lots of cool applications.

✦　　✦　　✦

Using the Response Object

Introduction to the Response Object

In the preceding chapter, you learned how to get all the information that a user submitted through the browser. This chapter shows you how to create result pages to be sent back to the user. While you've already used one of the Response object's methods, Write, you can have even more control over how your page is used by the browser, its disk cache, and even proxy servers that you may encounter along the way.

This chapter covers the following methods of the Response object:

+ Clear

+ End

+ Flush

+ Redirect

+ Write

The Response object also has the following properties that are also discussed in this chapter:

+ Buffer

+ Cache Control

+ ContentType

+ Expires

+ ExpiresAbsolute

+ IsClientConnected

+ Pics

In This Chapter

Learn about controlling output to the user's browser

Learn how to redirect a user's browser

Learn how to add extra information to the Web logs

Learn about other features of the Response object

Finally, the Response object also has a Cookies collection, which will be covered in more depth in the following chapter, because cookies are related to both the Request and Response objects. This chapter shows you how and why to use each of the properties and methods.

Creating Output

Thus far, you've created output in three different ways:

✦ By using Response.Write.

✦ By using an equal sign immediately after an ASP delimiter character to show the value of an expression.

✦ By adding HTML to your ASP pages outside of the ASP delimiter characters.

This section gives you a few more tips about using these methods in your ASP pages.

Using Response.Write

Response.Write is an easy way to generate HTML output in your ASP pages. This method needs to be called from within ASP delimiter characters, and everything that is printed must be enclosed in double-quote characters, just as with any other string function. This requirement often makes it tricky to print content that contains double quotes such as URLs, as follows:

```
Response.Write "<a href=""http://www.microsoft.com"">"
```

That's a lot of double quotes. The pair on the outside marks the beginning and end of the string. The double set within the string is used to indicate where the double-quote character is to be printed. When the line is done running, the following HTML will be generated:

```
<a href="http://www.microsoft.com">
```

Normally, if you've left out the double double-quotes, you get a syntax error, because the double-quote characters must pair up.

You can also run into a problem when printing percent signs, as in the following HTML example:

```
<table width=100%>
```

The problem is not obvious until you create the ASP code to create the following line:

```
Response.Write "<table width=100%>"
```

The ASP engine sees the %> within the string and assumes you are ending the code block, which of course you're not. The solution: Use the backslash to "escape" the angle bracket, as follows:

```
Response.Write "<table width=100%\>"
```

The backslash is not printed when this code runs, and you get the original, desired result.

One final thing to note is that Response.Write does not automatically add line breaks in the resulting HTML. If you want to add a break, you have to append a BR or P tag to your Response.Write statement. Also, depending on the length of the line, you may want to put the text on multiple lines in the file. For this functionality, you can append `Chr(13) & Chr(10)` to create a carriage return/line feed combination. Because you will often have to debug your HTML after it has been generated, remember to add these line breaks to break up your code for readability.

Using Equal Sign with Delimiter Characters

This method of generating output to the browser has its place but is somewhat limited. An example of this method follows:

```
<table>
<tr>
<td><% = intLoop %>
```

This code will print the value of `intLoop` immediately after the TD tag. This method enables you to construct all the HTML without having to use Response.Write to print each line. However, this method using the equal sign cannot span more than one line. If your code is too long and you want to break it using a continuation character, you have to use Response.Write or create a variable with your output before getting to the point where you want to print the output.

Using HTML Outside of Delimiter Characters

This method is the easiest way to create large blocks of HTML. You don't have to worry about lots of double sets of double quotes, as you do with the Response.Write method. With this method, you can also use indenting to lay out your HTML page. This practice, which has been displayed in many preceding examples through this book, makes it much easier to look at code, especially when dealing with tables. Look at the following code and try to figure out which table goes where:

```
<table>
<tr>
<td>
<table>
<tr>
<td colspan=3>
Text
<table>
<tr>
<td>Text 1</td>
<td>Text 2</td>
</tr>
</table>
</td>
</tr>
</table>
</table>
```

It's a little tough, especially because some of the closing table tags are missing. It would be difficult to find the exact location of the missing tags unless you indented, as follows:

```
<table>
<tr>
   <td>
      <table>
      <tr>
         <td colspan=3>
            Text
            <table>
            <tr>
               <td>Text 1</td>
               <td>Text 2</td>
            </tr>
            </table>
         </td>
      </tr>
      </table>
   </td> (missing)
</tr> (missing)
</table>
```

The exact spacing of tables, rows, and cells is up to you, but code is often hard to read without the indentation. It's also difficult to print indentation in your code using Response.Write, because you would have to keep track of how many spaces to indent.

Managing Output

The Response object provides a number of properties and methods that control how your page is used by browsers and servers along the way to your user. This section covers these properties and methods and how they can be used in your applications.

Redirecting the Browser

In some cases, such as with pages that validate, you are going to want to send the user to the next page in the sequence after your validation is done. The Response.Redirect method is used for this function. You simply specify the next URL to go to, whether that URL is a local path or a remote path, and the browser goes to that path. An example follows:

```
Response.Redirect "http://www.microsoft.com"
```

This code will cause the user's browser to go to Microsoft's site. Sites that have "We've Moved" signs and then send you to the new site are basically doing the same thing as the preceding code. The redirect action is part of the HTTP protocol, and this code is the method for doing it under ASP.

The one restriction is that you can't have sent any content to the browser when you call the Redirect method. However, if you are using content buffering (see the following section), you can perform a redirection any time before the buffer is dumped to the user's browser. However, remember that buffering causes the user to see nothing until you have finished processing the page, which can cause the impression that the site is not responding.

Buffering Output

Buffering enables you to build an ASP page in memory. If you need to redirect the user, simply throw out the buffered text and redirect with no problems at all, because no output has been sent to the user. There are two methods and one property used for buffering:

✦ Buffer — A True/False property that indicates whether buffering is turned on. By default, buffering is off.

✦ Clear — A method empties the buffer of any text.

✦ Flush — A method forces all the text in the buffer down to the user's browser window.

If you want to use buffering, you first have to set the Response.Buffer property to True. After that, you can use the normal printing methods to generate output, but none of that output is sent to the user's browser. When you're done building the page, the Flush method will send the text to the browser. If you start building a page and need to erase the content, the Clear method will empty the buffer. In addition, if you clear the buffer, you can use the Redirect method to move to another page, because you never actually sent any content to the user.

The one problem with buffering is that it causes the user to see a blank page while the page is running. This can give the false impression that your server has erred or crashed, which is obviously not the impression you want to give.

Caching and Expiration Dates

Depending on a user's network configuration, there are several places where content can be cached. Caching content is simply the process of storing content for future use. In some cases, such as for static pages, caching content increases performance. America Online makes extensive use of caching to cut down on the amount of bandwidth wasted on repeated downloads of files. Many proxy servers have the ability to cache content, as well, for the same reasons. However, there are many cases with ASP files in which caching is counterproductive. In most cases, ASP documents are dynamically generated each time they are loaded. Even if the entire page is not dynamic, there are normally pieces of content that are dynamic. Take, for instance, a page showing stock quotes. Stock quotes change almost constantly during the trading day. If a server were to cache the quote results and keep showing the cached results to the user, the user would mistakenly think that the stocks were no longer trading or that the prices were constant.

A second place where content can be cached is locally on the user's machine. If you're using Internet Explorer, you'll find a folder called Temporary Internet Files somewhere on your hard drive. This folder is IE's cache of graphics and other text files that it thinks are important enough to retain for future use. Caching graphics, which change less frequently, is a good idea. This practice lets the text on the page, which normally changes more often, download in less time. The graphics are loaded from disk and display almost instantly. However, the same problem that occurs with a network-level cache can also happen with a local cache — content gets out of date.

For this reason, the Response object has a number of properties that enable you to control if and when your content is cached. The first property is CacheControl. This True/False value indicates whether content should be cached by servers along the way. While proxy servers and cache software packages are not required to follow these directives, most do. To indicate that content should not be cached by proxy servers and shared caches, use the following code:

```
Response.CacheControl = "Private"
```

Private, local caches will still cache the content, but proxy servers, for the most part, will not.

For content that can be cached, use the following line of code:

```
Response.CacheControl = "Public"
```

This code needs to go into each page where content can be cached, because the default is not to cache content. Setting this setting to Public can, in some cases, improve your performance. However, if the bulk of your page is created dynamically, setting the CacheControl to Public won't help, because the page is rebuilt every time anyway.

The second property enables you to indicate how long a page is valid before it should be expired from the cache. This property only applies to the local browser cache — not a shared proxy server cache. The value is specified in minutes, as follows:

```
Response.Expires = 10
```

This code will cause the page to expire in 10 minutes. To expire the page immediately, you can use a negative number like –1. This trick enables you to force content to always be retrieved from the network.

In some cases, you may want the content to expire on a certain date and/or time. This strategy is helpful if you are doing a page update each day. If a user hits your page on Monday, that content will be good until you do an update on Tuesday. The ExpiresAbsolute property is a Date/Time value that provides a day and/or time for the content to expire. Here's an example:

```
Response.ExpiresAbsolute = #9/15/99 11:30 AM#
```

This page will expire and be deleted from the browser cache on September 15, 1999 at 11:30 in the morning. Of course, if the user's browser is not active, the page will be deleted the next time the system is run.

Changing Content Types

The ContentType property enables you to tell the browser this information so that the browser knows what to do with the content. A few examples follow:

```
Response.ContentType = "application/x-cdf"
Response.ContentType = "image/GIF"
Response.ContentType = "text/plain"
Response.ContentType = "application/vnd.ms-excel"
```

These content types specify, in order:

✦ Channel Definition File (CDF)

✦ A CompuServe GIF format graphics file

✦ A plain text file

✦ An Excel spreadsheet

In most cases, you won't need to change the content type, because you'll be sending HTML (text/html, by the way). However, for those cases where you are sending a different type of file, the content type is a handy concept to remember.

Rating Your Content

With the massive amount of objectionable content on the Web, many schools, organizations, public terminals, and even companies have turned to net-monitoring software to restrict certain user behavior on the Web. The content rating system known as PICS, or Platform for Internet Content Selection, plays a big role in monitoring content. PICS is a voluntary rating system that the Recreational Software Advisory Council on the Internet (RSACi) helps to maintain. You can visit their Web site at `http://www.rsac.org` for specific information about how ratings work and are assigned.

The PICS property of the Response object enables you to specify your full PICS rating tag assigned by RSAC after you answer a questionnaire on the content of your Web site. Because many monitoring packages will not allow content to be viewed from pages that aren't rated, you should add ratings to your pages. An example of a full ratings tag and how it goes into the PICS variable follows:

```
Response.PICS("(PICS-1.1 <http://www.rsac.org/ratingv01.html> " _
    & "labels on ""1997.01.05T08:15-0500"" until " _
    & """1999.12.31T23:59-0000"" ratings (v 0 s 0 l 0 n 0))")
```

The preceding code adds the rating tag to the appropriate place in the header so that the monitoring software will pick up the tag properly and enable the page to pass (or not pass, as the case may be).

Managing the Connection

Besides the ability to manage both the content you are generating and the generation of the content, the Response object also has the ability to manage the connection to the user. As discussed in this section, several methods and properties are used to handle various details related to the connection.

IsClientConnected Property

In some cases, especially when dealing with complex reports, you may have a long period of inactivity. Unfortunately, people on the Web have short attention spans and tend to leave after a short while if nothing appears to be happening. Because you don't want to waste system resources for a report that no one is going to see, the IsClientConnected property can be used to tell if the user is still connected to your site. By checking this True/False property, you can tell if you should bail out of your current process. This property could be checked in combination with page buffering so that if the user leaves, the buffer gets dumped.

End Method

If the user has left your page, there is no need to run the page any longer. Similarly, if you get to a point on the page where no further processing needs to be done, you can simply exit the execution of the page by calling the End method of the Response object. As with the End statement in Visual Basic, execution immediately halts. The problem, however, is that any open objects don't get closed and any cleanup routines you may have don't trigger. If you're using the code format shown in the preceding chapter where all code is in subroutines, a better way is simply to exit the subroutine and let the code terminate normally. With this strategy, any cleanup code you may have had will still run, and you won't leave a dirty connection open.

Summary

While there's not much to the Response object, some of its functions are absolutely vital to the correct operation of Active Server Pages files. If you're not able to print output or direct traffic flow on your Web site, building Web pages is not very useful. However, you may not use many of the properties and methods available on the Response object during your projects. These methods are covered just in case you may need to use them at some point. We cover some of these features in subsequent chapters so you can see real-world examples of their use.

✦　　✦　　✦

Using Cookies

Introduction to Cookies

In this Chapter

Learn how cookies
help maintain state

Learn to create
cookies

Learn how to modify
and remove cookies

Use cookies to track
user actions between
pages

One of the major differences between Web programming and traditional application programming is that there is no concept of state in Web programming. *State* refers to a variety of methods of keeping track of what the user's identity and actions. For instance, when a user logs into your application, you have their user ID and can get other pieces of information (such as their name) that are keyed to the user ID. In addition, you can open data connections with that user's ID and keep them open for the life of the application. You also know how the user got to a particular form, whether through a menu choice, another form, or a toolbar.

The Web does not provide any of these functions. You can go to any page at any time. There are no "front doors" to applications where a user must first log into a database before continuing. In addition, when a user connects to a page, you have no way of knowing the identity of that person, unless the appropriate information is provided again so that the page can continue where the previous page left off, for instance. You also cannot simply open a connection to one user's ID, because you don't know if that user will be the next one to access a page.

Luckily, one of the early additions to the HTTP protocol was *cookies*. The term cookie has been used over the years in the computer industry. X-Windows uses the term "magic cookie" to represent a unique ID assigned to a particular user's session on the server. For the Web, a cookie is a plain text file that can contain no more than 4K of text. The file sits on your hard drive and is accessed by your Web browser when the remote site requests it. You can open the file and look at it if you suspect a government or business conspiracy to read your whole hard drive. Here are some example cookie files from my own hard drive:

As you can see from Figures 7-1 and 7-2, the cookies do not contain information that is immediately understandable. My personal financial records are not in the Motley Fool cookie. The DoubleClick cookie doesn't contain a list of all the sites that I've visited since the Net was born. These cookies have numbers that mean something different to each of the sites. For instance, the DoubleClick cookie is used to track which ads have been shown to me on different DoubleClick affiliate sites. This cookie prevents the same ad from being shown constantly to the same user. The Motley Fool cookie is used, like many others, to track my preferences on that site. They may have assigned me a unique ID in their database, and the cookie holds that ID for when I revisit the site. Again, nothing insidious is at work here.

Figure 7-1: DoubleClick.Net cookie file

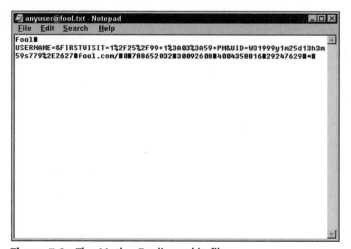

Figure 7-2: The Motley Fool's cookie file

For people who don't want companies to know what they like or what they do in their free time, let me offer this analogy. Unless you're living in the middle of nowhere with no communication to the outside world, people are collecting information on you. Your credit report is available to legitimate companies who bombard you with credit card and other offers. In addition, most companies routinely sell their customer lists to other companies, some of which aren't covering quite the same subject. For instance, I'm a model railroader and subscribe to a railroading magazine. That company sells its lists to other companies dealing with related hobbies, such as collecting train memorabilia. That company in turn sells its lists to companies in similar topics, such as military collectibles. Pretty soon you're getting military surplus catalogs selling NATO camouflage battle gear from an obscure company, just because you subscribed to a magazine covering plastic train models.

The difference between traditional and Web direct marketing is very slight. Both are trying to sell you products, and both are gathering information about you and your preferences. The difference is that you see the remnants of these efforts in your cookie files. You may not ever visit DoubleClick.net, but because they provide advertising to their clients, they have to make sure they are delivering valuable ad impressions. As a result, they can't keep sending the same ad to you over and over again. To make sure, they put a cookie on your computer, which lets them check the next time you hit one of their affiliates.

Besides selling the banner ads, many companies use demographic information about their subscribers. For instance, a company that sells some sort of computer product decides they are going to sell banner advertising. The interested advertisers need to know to whom they are going to be showing ads. If the company selling the space doesn't know, the ads are worth less. However, if the company selling the ads knows that their users always go to certain sections of the site, the ads can be better targeted. In addition, if the user decided to provide profile information about their company and position, the company can track that information with the user's viewing habits and the banner impressions are worth even more to the potential advertiser. However, the only way that this company can track who you are and where you go is through the use of cookies. Because many sites are supported exclusively through banner ads, they rely on selling general demographics about their users to stay in business.

Regardless of their original design, a number of vocal groups oppose cookies because of privacy concerns. These groups advocate blocking every cookie that any Web server sends you because the company that owns the Web server may gain some insight as to who you are and what you want to do. The problem with this view is that technologies such as Active Server Pages, among others, rely on cookies to work properly. Each time you open a session with an ASP server, you get a cookie. This cookie is used strictly for linking your browser with the server memory set aside for your session. Blocking cookies from an ASP-based server will cause most of the ASP functions to fail. Instead of getting a full-featured Web server, you're left with static HTML pages that know nothing about how you want them configured or what you've done with them in the past. Personally, I'd rather allow the little text file onto my machine if it's going to make my life easier when I go out to my favorite Web sites. However, not everyone feels this way, and a number of Web sites cover this somewhat controversial topic.

Cookies and Your Browser

As mentioned in the preceding section, your browser must to accept cookies for ASP to work properly. By default, most browsers are configured to accept cookies when you install them. However, if you need to change the settings, this section will cover the configuration steps for Internet Explorer 4 and 5, as well as Netscape Communicator 4.61. Other browsers will obviously have different instructions and may or may not let you control whether cookies are accepted.

Configuring Internet Explorer 4 and 5

The instructions for IE 4 and 5 are identical and quite simple:

1. Select Settings ➪ Control Panel from your Start Menu.
2. Double-click the Internet Settings icon.
3. Select the Security tab.
4. Click the Internet icon and then click the Custom Level button to bring up the settings for the Internet zone.
5. Scroll down the window and you will see the option to enable, disable, or prompt you for each cookie received by the browser. Make sure this option is set to Enable, or at least set to Prompt.

Configuring Netscape 4.61

For the most part, Netscape has kept its settings in the same place since the browser was released. If you have a newer version of Netscape by the time you buy this book, these steps help you get close to where the settings are changed.

1. Select Edit ➪ Preferences.
2. Click Advanced in the left-hand tree of options.
3. On the right-hand side, you can select whether you want to accept all, accept only cookies that go back to the same server, or not accept any cookies. You can also have Netscape warn you about incoming cookies.

Creating a Cookie

The first task you learn is how to create a cookie on a visitor's system. For this example, we're going to build a cookie that has the last date and time a visitor came to the page. To get started, add the code in Listing 7-1 to a new ASP file.

Listing 7-1: **Code for CreateCookie.asp**

```
<%
   Response.Cookies("LastVisit") = Date & " " & Time
%>
<html>
<head>
   <title>Chapter 7 - Creating a Cookie</title>
</head>
<body>
Cookie has been created.
</body>
</html>
```

To see that code works, modify this file to look like Listing 7-2.

Listing 7-2: **New code for CreateCookie.asp to verify cookie values**

```
<html>
<head>
   <title>Chapter 7 - Creating a Cookie</title>
</head>
<body>
Cookie has been created.
Value: <% Response.Write Request.Cookies("LastVisit") %>
</body>
</html>
```

This code prints the date and time of when the cookie was created, because that information is the value you put into the cookie in Listing 7-1.

Shut down your browser and navigate to `CreateCookie.asp` again. The value for the cookie will be blank and no data will be printed. This is because the cookie you created was not given an expiration date/time. By default, cookies without expiration dates or times are not permanent and do not have a cookie file created for them. To verify this, find your cookies on your hard drive. If you're using Internet Explorer, they will either be in `\Windows\Cookies` or in `\Windows\Profiles\ username\Cookies`. Netscape users should look for a file called `cookies.txt`. If you look in the directory or the file, you won't see any entries for the Web site where you are running the `CreateCookie.asp` page.

To make the cookie semi-permanent, use the code in Listing 7-3.

Listing 7-3: **New code for CreateCookie.asp to create permanent cookie**

```
<%
   Response.Cookies("LastVisit") = Date & " " & Time
   Response.Cookies("LastVisit").Expires = DateAdd("d", 1, Date)
%>
<html>
<head>
   <title>Chapter 7 - Creating a Cookie</title>
</head>
<body>
Cookie has been created.
</body>
</html>
```

This code creates the cookie with the same value, but also adds a value to the `Expires` property. This value is one day after the current date. The cookie will expire at midnight on the day specified, according to the time zone of the server. If your server is in a different time zone, the time will be adjusted for your time zone. For instance, the development server I used to write this book was in the Central time zone, but I live in the Eastern time zone. The cookie sent back to me from the server will expire at 1:00 A.M. instead of midnight on the day after it was created. You can also include a time for expiration as part of the `Expires` property.

In Internet Explorer, you can look at the Temporary Internet Files directory (normally under the Windows directory), which will show you the expiration date and time of cookie files. You'll also see this information:

✦ The Internet address to which it applies

✦ Size of the cookie

✦ Expiration date and time

✦ Last modified date and time

✦ Last accessed date and time

✦ Last read date and time

If you do a lot of surfing, you can use the Last Checked column to see which cookies are out of date and need to be deleted. The little files add up in size, so you should purge old cookies periodically.

To test that the permanent cookie is working, shut down your browser. This action clears all temporary cookies. Change CreateCookie.asp to use this code:

```
<html>
<head>
    <title>Chapter 7 - Creating a Cookie</title>
</head>
<body>
Cookie has been created.
Value: <% Response.Write Request.Cookies("LastVisit") %><br>
</body>
</html>
```

Because we're not setting the cookie at the beginning of the file, if the time and date show up, the cookie is working properly.

If you open the cookie file (for Internet Explorer), you will see text that looks something like Figure 7-3.

Figure 7-3: Cookie file generated by CreateCookie.asp

While the numbers at the end aren't particularly meaningful, the text at the beginning is important and deserves a look. This text is shown here:

```
LastVisit
5%2F5%2F99+3%3A22%3A57+PM
```

The black box in the picture is a newline character. If you copy the text, it will add a new line into your new file. The first line is clearly the name of the cookie that `CreateCookie.asp` created. The second line is a bit confusing, but it shows the value that we stored. The problem here is that the punctuation and other special characters have been translated to their hexadecimal equivalents (similar to the `Server.URLEncode` function). In this case, `%2F` is the slash between the date parts, a `+` is a space, and `%3A` is a colon between the parts of the time. If you were to translate this line, it would look like the following:

```
5/25/99 3:22:57 PM
```

Any information you put into the Cookies collection will be included in the cookie file, just as with this value.

Tip   If you're building a site that uses cookies, you can explain the cookie file to your users by explaining each line in the file. That process will go a long way to quelling any paranoid delusions your users may have about what you are doing with the information.

Modifying and Removing Cookies

Once the cookie has been created, modifying the value is simple. You simply use the same code as you used to create the cookie. In Listing 7-4, each time you load the page, the cookie is updated with the latest date and time.

Listing 7-4: Code to create or update cookie

```
<%
    Dim blnNewCookie     ' As Boolean

    blnNewCookie = (Request.Cookies("LastVisit") = "")
    Response.Cookies("LastVisit") = Date & " " & Time
    Response.Cookies("LastVisit").Expires = _
        DateAdd("d", 1, Date)
%>
<html>
<head>
    <title>Chapter 7 - Creating a Cookie</title>
</head>
```

```
<body>
<%
    If blnNewCookie Then
%>
Cookie has been created.
<%
    Else
%>
Cookie has been updated.
<%
    End If
%>
Value: <% Response.Write Request.Cookies("LastVisit") %><br>
</body>
</html>
```

This code checks the incoming cookie collection in the Request object and determines if the cookie has been created. Note that this code is for information only, but later in the chapter, the code will behave differently if there are no values in the cookie. In this case, we're simply going to print a different message at the end. We then use the same code to create the cookie as we do to update the value. The code is identical for both processes.

Removing cookies is easy as well. Just update the value to an empty string, and the cookie will go away. Listing 7-5 shows the code required to remove the cookie.

Listing 7-5: **Code for RemoveCookie.asp**

```
<%
    Response.Cookies("LastVisit") = ""
%>
<html>
<head>
    <title>Chapter 7 - Removing a Cookie</title>
</head>
<body>
Cookie has been removed.<br>
Value: <% Response.Write Request.Cookies("LastVisit") %><br>
</body>
</html>
```

Setting the cookie's value to an empty string causes the browser to remove the cookie. The removal is checked by attempting to print the value, which is not there. You can also check your cookies directory or file; the entry will be gone.

While cookies do have expiration dates, cookies don't seem to get removed when they should. In my own cookie directory, there are quite a few cookies whose expiration dates have passed, but the cookies have not been removed. They don't go away even if you purge your Temporary Internet Files directory.

If you are using temporary cookies or even cookies for a particular session, remove them yourself if you have the option. For permanent cookies, be sure to provide realistic expiration dates, such as 30 or 60 days, because most people will either visit a site often or not at all. Setting cookie expiration dates 30 years into the future is ridiculous, especially because we will probably have a new scheme within 30 years. (At least we would hope so, that is.)

Tracking Preferences with Cookies

As mentioned in the beginning of this chapter, one of the primary ways cookies are used is to track user preferences. Regardless of the actual preferences, you should have a scheme to do this tracking in a logical way. This section shows you how to create a preference tracking cookie for Eric's Pizza Parlor delivery service, the example used earlier in the book.

Creating the Form

To get started, add the code from Listing 7-6 to a new file.

Listing 7-6: **Code for PizzaDeliveryForm.asp**

```
<html>
<head>
    <title>Chapter 7: Pizza Delivery Form</title>
</head>
<body>
<h1>Eric's Pizza Parlor</h1>
What size pizza would you like?

<form action="PizzaDeliveryForm.asp?action=V" method=POST>
<input type="radio" name="optSize" value="S">
Small<br>
<input type="radio" name="optSize" value="M">
Medium<br>
<input type="radio" name="optSize" value="L" CHECKED>
Large<br>
<input type="radio" name="optSize" value="XL">
Extra Large<br>
<input type="radio" name="optSize" value="XXL">
```

```
Call the Doctor in the Morning<br>

<p>
What toppings would you like on your pizza?
</p>

<table cellpadding=4>
<tr>
    <td>
        <input type="checkbox" name="chkTopping1"
            value="Y" checked>Cheese<br>
        <input type="checkbox" name="chkTopping2"
            value="Y" checked>Tomato Sauce<br>
        <input type="checkbox" name="chkTopping3"
            value="Y">Olive Oil<br>
        <input type="checkbox" name="chkTopping4"
            value="Y">Barbecue Sauce<br>
    </td>
    <td>
        <input type="checkbox" name="chkTopping5"
            value="Y">Pepperoni<br>
        <input type="checkbox" name="chkTopping6"
            value="Y">Sausage<br>
        <input type="checkbox" name="chkTopping7"
            value="Y">Mushrooms<br>
        <input type="checkbox" name="chkTopping8"
            value="Y">Onions<br>
    </td>
    <td>
        <input type="checkbox" name="chkTopping9"
            value="Y">Ham<br>
        <input type="checkbox" name="chkTopping10"
            value="Y">Pineapple<br>
        <input type="checkbox" name="chkTopping11"
            value="Y">Green Peppers<br>
        <input type="checkbox" name="chkTopping12"
            value="Y">Anchovies<br>
    </td>
</tr>
</table>
<p>
<input type="Submit" name="cmdSubmit" value="Deliver It!">
</p>

</form>
</body>
</html>
```

Because we've covered the form in a preceding chapter, we won't dwell on the HTML here. For this form, here's the information we're going to track:

✦ Last size selected

✦ Which toppings were selected

If you added to the form, you could also track the person's name, phone number, address, and so forth. While much of this information would probably work better in a database, cookies are simply another way to store this information without needing the database architecture in place.

Adding the Size Cookie

The first cookie we will add is the pizza size that the user last requested. We will name this cookie "Size" and store it in the back-end code that will be covered later in this section. To use the cookie, modify your code to look like Listing 7-7.

Listing 7-7: New code for PizzaDeliveryForm.asp

```
<%
   Dim strSizeCookie      ' As String
   strSizeCookie = Request.Cookies("Size")
%>
<html>
<head>
   <title>Chapter 7: Pizza Delivery Form</title>
</head>
<body>
<h1>Eric's Pizza Parlor</h1>
What size pizza would you like?

<form action="PizzaDeliveryForm.asp?action=V" method=POST>
<input type="radio" name="optSize" value="S"
<% If strSizeCookie = "S" Then Response.Write " CHECKED" %>
Small<br>
<input type="radio" name="optSize" value="M"
<% If strSizeCookie = "M" Then Response.Write " CHECKED" %>
Medium<br>
<input type="radio" name="optSize" value="L"
<% If strSizeCookie = "L" Or strSizeCookie = "" Then
      Response.Write " CHECKED"
   End If
%>
Large<br>
<input type="radio" name="optSize" value="XL"
<% If strSizeCookie = "XL" Then Response.Write " CHECKED" %>
Extra Large<br>
<input type="radio" name="optSize" value="XXL"
<% If strSizeCookie = "XXL" Then Response.Write " CHECKED" %>
```

```
Call the Doctor in the Morning<br>

<p>
What toppings would you like on your pizza?
</p>
```

The rest of the code following the last line in Listing 7-7 is the same as Listing 7-6. We first declare a temporary variable to hold the value of the cookie. This value is checked several times; it's easier to use the variable name instead of the Request object syntax.

The form radio buttons have been modified to check the value of the cookie. If the value of the cookie matches the radio button, the word CHECKED is printed so that the option button is checked. Because large is the default, we also check the cookie against an empty value for that option to be marked.

Adding the Toppings Cookie

The Toppings cookie is a little trickier. We could create a cookie for each topping, but that leads to problems when the pizzeria decides to add new toppings. Each new topping requires another cookie value, which will tend to get unwieldy after a while.

Instead, we're going to create a cookie that represents all twelve toppings and can be expanded later with more toppings. This cookie's value will look something like the following:

```
YYNNNNYYNNYN
```

If you haven't guessed already, each position in the string indicates whether that topping was selected the previous time. We'll create this string in the back-end, but the form also needs to change to use this string, which will be broken into an array of Boolean values for simplicity. The next step is to add the code marked in Listing 7-8 to your file.

Listing 7-8: **New code for PizzaDeliveryForm.asp**

```
<%
    Dim strSizeCookie      ' As String
    Dim strToppings        ' As String
    Dim a_blnToppings(12)  ' As Array of Booleans
    Dim i                  ' As Integer

    strSizeCookie = Request.Cookies("Size")
```

Continued

Listing 7-8 *(continued)*

```
    strToppings = Request.Cookies("Toppings")
    For i = 1 To 12
        If strToppings = "" Then
            a_blnToppings(i) = False
        Else
            a_blnToppings(i) = _
                CBool(Mid(strToppings, i, 1) = "Y")
        End If
    Next  ' i

    '
    ' Add default values if none are
    ' selected in the cookie
    '
    If strToppings = "" Then
        a_blnToppings(1) = True
        a_blnToppings(2) = True
    End If
%>
<html>
<head>
    <title>Chapter 7: Pizza Delivery Form</title>
</head>
<body>
<h1>Eric's Pizza Parlor</h1>
What size pizza would you like?

<form action="PizzaDeliveryForm.asp?action=V" method=POST>
<input type="radio" name="optSize" value="S"
<% If strSizeCookie = "S" Then Response.Write " CHECKED" %>
Small<br>
<input type="radio" name="optSize" value="M"
<% If strSizeCookie = "M" Then Response.Write " CHECKED" %>
Medium<br>
<input type="radio" name="optSize" value="L"
<% If strSizeCookie = "L" Or strSizeCookie = "" Then
        Response.Write " CHECKED"
    End If
%>
Large<br>
<input type="radio" name="optSize" value="XL"
<% If strSizeCookie = "XL" Then Response.Write " CHECKED" %>
Extra Large<br>
<input type="radio" name="optSize" value="XXL"
<% If strSizeCookie = "XXL" Then Response.Write " CHECKED" %>
Call the Doctor in the Morning<br>
```

```
<p>
What toppings would you like on your pizza?
</p>

<table cellpadding=4>
<tr>
   <td>
      <input type="checkbox" name="chkTopping1"
             <% If a_blnToppings(1) Then
                   Response.Write "CHECKED"
                End If
             %>
             value="Y">Cheese<br>
      <input type="checkbox" name="chkTopping2"
             <% If a_blnToppings(2) Then
                   Response.Write "CHECKED"
                End If
             %>
             value="Y">Tomato Sauce<br>
      <input type="checkbox" name="chkTopping3"
             <% If a_blnToppings(3) Then
                   Response.Write "CHECKED"
                End If
             %>
             value="Y">Olive Oil<br>
      <input type="checkbox" name="chkTopping4"
             <% If a_blnToppings(4) Then
                   Response.Write "CHECKED"
                End If
             %>
             value="Y">Barbecue Sauce<br>
   </td>
   <td>
      <input type="checkbox" name="chkTopping5"
             <% If a_blnToppings(5) Then
                   Response.Write "CHECKED"
                End If
             %>
             value="Y">Pepperoni<br>
      <input type="checkbox" name="chkTopping6"
             <% If a_blnToppings(6) Then
                   Response.Write "CHECKED"
                End If
             %>
             value="Y">Sausage<br>
      <input type="checkbox" name="chkTopping7"
             <% If a_blnToppings(7) Then
                   Response.Write "CHECKED"
                End If
```

Continued

Listing 7-8 *(continued)*

```
            %>
            value="Y">Mushrooms<br>
    <input type="checkbox" name="chkTopping8"
            <% If a_blnToppings(8) Then
                Response.Write "CHECKED"
            End If
            %>
            value="Y">Onions<br>
</td>
<td>
    <input type="checkbox" name="chkTopping9"
            <% If a_blnToppings(9) Then
                Response.Write "CHECKED"
            End If
            %>
            value="Y">Ham<br>
    <input type="checkbox" name="chkTopping10"
            <% If a_blnToppings(10) Then
                Response.Write "CHECKED"
            End If
            %>
            value="Y">Pineapple<br>
    <input type="checkbox" name="chkTopping11"
            <% If a_blnToppings(11) Then
                Response.Write "CHECKED"
            End If
            %>
            value="Y">Green Peppers<br>
    <input type="checkbox" name="chkTopping12"
            <% If a_blnToppings(12) Then
                Response.Write "CHECKED"
            End If
            %>
            value="Y">Anchovies<br>
    </td>
</tr>
</table>
<p>
<input type="Submit" name="cmdSubmit" value="Deliver It!">
</p>

</form>
</body>
</html>
```

We break the long Toppings cookie into an array of twelve (the number could be increased, if necessary) elements of True or False. In the part where the options are shown, we check the appropriate element to see if the user had selected it the last time. If so, the word "CHECKED" is printed within the INPUT tag. If the user doesn't have the cookie, we still want to show the default toppings of cheese and tomato sauce. The few lines of code right before the beginning of the HTML mark the two elements (1 and 2) as True so that they come up correctly without a lot of extra trapping code.

At this point, you can run the form and get the same result as before. However, the meat of this form is in the back-end, which is covered in the next section.

Building the Back-end Code

In Chapter 5, we covered how to combine all the code into a single file. We use the same method for this file as well. The completed back-end code is shown in Listing 7-9.

Listing 7-9: **Completed code for PizzaDeliveryForm.asp**

```
<%
Option Explicit

Sub GatherData()

    Dim strSizeCookie      ' As String
    Dim strToppings        ' As String
    Dim a_blnToppings(12)  ' As Array of Booleans
    Dim i                  ' As Integer

    strSizeCookie = Request.Cookies("Size")
    strToppings = Request.Cookies("Toppings")
    For i = 1 To 12
       If strToppings = "" Then
          a_blnToppings(i) = False
       Else
          a_blnToppings(i) = _
             CBool(Mid(strToppings, i, 1) = "Y")
       End If
    Next ' i


    ' Add default values if none are
    ' selected in the cookie
    '
```

Continued

Listing 7-9 *(continued)*

```
        If strToppings = "" Then
            a_blnToppings(1) = True
            a_blnToppings(2) = True
        End If

%>
<html>
<head>
    <title>Chapter 7: Pizza Delivery Form</title>
</head>
<body>
<h1>Eric's Pizza Parlor</h1>
What size pizza would you like?

<form action="PizzaDeliveryForm.asp?action=V" method=POST>
<input type="radio" name="optSize" value="S"
<% If strSizeCookie = "S" Then Response.Write " CHECKED" %>
Small<br>
<input type="radio" name="optSize" value="M"
<% If strSizeCookie = "M" Then Response.Write " CHECKED" %>
Medium<br>
<input type="radio" name="optSize" value="L"
<% If strSizeCookie = "L" Or strSizeCookie = "" Then
        Response.Write " CHECKED"
    End If
%>
Large<br>
<input type="radio" name="optSize" value="XL"
<% If strSizeCookie = "XL" Then Response.Write " CHECKED" %>
Extra Large<br>
<input type="radio" name="optSize" value="XXL"
<% If strSizeCookie = "XXL" Then Response.Write " CHECKED" %>
Call the Doctor in the Morning<br>

<p>
What toppings would you like on your pizza?
</p>

<table cellpadding=4>
<tr>
    <td>
        <input type="checkbox" name="chkTopping1"
            <% If a_blnToppings(1) Then
                    Response.Write "CHECKED"
                End If
            %>
            value="Y">Cheese<br>
        <input type="checkbox" name="chkTopping2"
```

```
                <% If a_blnToppings(2) Then
                        Response.Write "CHECKED"
                    End If
                %>
                value="Y">Tomato Sauce<br>
        <input type="checkbox" name="chkTopping3"
                <% If a_blnToppings(3) Then
                        Response.Write "CHECKED"
                    End If
                %>
                value="Y">Olive Oil<br>
        <input type="checkbox" name="chkTopping4"
                <% If a_blnToppings(4) Then
                        Response.Write "CHECKED"
                    End If
                %>
                value="Y">Barbecue Sauce<br>
    </td>
    <td>
        <input type="checkbox" name="chkTopping5"
                <% If a_blnToppings(5) Then
                        Response.Write "CHECKED"
                    End If
                %>
                value="Y">Pepperoni<br>
        <input type="checkbox" name="chkTopping6"
                <% If a_blnToppings(6) Then
                        Response.Write "CHECKED"
                    End If
                %>
                value="Y">Sausage<br>
        <input type="checkbox" name="chkTopping7"
                <% If a_blnToppings(7) Then
                        Response.Write "CHECKED"
                    End If
                %>
                value="Y">Mushrooms<br>
        <input type="checkbox" name="chkTopping8"
                <% If a_blnToppings(8) Then
                        Response.Write "CHECKED"
                    End If
                %>
                value="Y">Onions<br>
    </td>
    <td>
        <input type="checkbox" name="chkTopping9"
                <% If a_blnToppings(9) Then
                        Response.Write "CHECKED"
                    End If
```

Continued

Listing 7-9 *(continued)*

```
            %>
            value="Y">Ham<br>
     <input type="checkbox" name="chkTopping10"
            <% If a_blnToppings(10) Then
                  Response.Write "CHECKED"
               End If
            %>
            value="Y">Pineapple<br>
     <input type="checkbox" name="chkTopping11"
            <% If a_blnToppings(11) Then
                  Response.Write "CHECKED"
               End If
            %>
            value="Y">Green Peppers<br>
     <input type="checkbox" name="chkTopping12"
            <% If a_blnToppings(12) Then
                  Response.Write "CHECKED"
               End If
            %>
            value="Y">Anchovies<br>
    </td>
</tr>
</table>
<p>
<input type="Submit" name="cmdSubmit" value="Deliver It!">
</p>

</form>
</body>
</html>

<%
End Sub

Sub ProcessData

    Dim curCost       ' As Currency
    Dim curToppingCost ' As Currency
    Dim intToppingCount ' As Integer
    Dim i     ' As Variant
    Dim a_strToppings(12) ' As Array of Strings
    Dim strToppingCookie ' As String

    a_strToppings(1) = "Cheese"
    a_strToppings(2) = "Tomato Sauce"
    a_strToppings(3) = "Olive Oil"
    a_strToppings(4) = "Barbecue Sauce"
    a_strToppings(5) = "Pepperoni"
```

```
    a_strToppings(6) = "Sausage"
    a_strToppings(7) = "Mushrooms"
    a_strToppings(8) = "Onions"
    a_strToppings(9) = "Ham"
    a_strToppings(10) = "Pineapple"
    a_strToppings(11) = "Green Peppers"
    a_strToppings(12) = "Anchovies"

    Response.Cookies("Size") = Request.Form("optSize")
    Response.Cookies("Size").Expires = _
        DateAdd("m", 2, Date)

    For i = 1 To 12
        If Request.Form("chkTopping" & i) = "Y" Then
            strToppingCookie = strToppingCookie & "Y"
        Else
            strToppingCookie = strToppingCookie & "N"
        End If
    Next ' i
    Response.Cookies("Toppings") = strToppingCookie
    Response.Cookies("Toppings").Expires = _
        DateAdd("m", 2, Date)


%>
<html>
<head>
    <title>Chapter 7: Pizza Delivery Confirmation</title>
</head>
<body>
<h1>Eric's Pizza Parlor</h1>
<p>Here is what you ordered:
</p>

<table width=100%>
<tr>
<td align=left>
1
<%
    Select Case Request.Form("optSize")
    Case "S"
        Response.Write "Small"
        curCost = 8.00
    Case "M"
        Response.Write "Medium"
        curCost = 9.50
    Case "L"
        Response.Write "Large"
        curCost = 11.00
```

Continued

Listing 7-9 *(continued)*

```
    Case "XL"
        Response.Write "Extra Large"
        curCost = 12.50
    Case "XXL"
        Response.Write "Extra-Extra Large (with Cardiologist)"
        curCost = 14.00
    End Select
    curToppingCost = curCost / 10
    intToppingCount = -2      ' give 2 toppings for free
%>
Pizza<p>
</td>
<td align=right>
<% = FormatCurrency(curCost) %>
</td>
</tr>
<%
    For i = 1 To 12
        If Request.Form("chkTopping" & i) = "Y" Then
            intToppingCount = intToppingCount + 1
%>
<tr>
<td><% = a_strToppings(i) %></td>
<td align=right>
<%      If intToppingCount <= 0 Then
            Response.Write "N/C"
        Else
            Response.Write FormatCurrency(curToppingCost)
        End If
%>
</td>
</tr>
<%
        End If
    Next
    If intToppingCount < 0 Then intToppingCount = 0
%>

<tr>
<td align=right><b>Order Total:</b></td>
<td align=right><b>
<% = FormatCurrency(curCost _
        + (intToppingCount * curToppingCost)) %>
</b></td>
</tr>
</table>
```

```
</body>
</html>

<%
End Sub

Sub Main
    If Request.QueryString("action") = "" Then
        Call GatherData
    Else
        Call ProcessData
    End If
End Sub

Call Main
%>
```

If you have read Chapter 5, the processing code should look familiar. The main change is that in the `ProcessData` subroutine, we have to create the cookies for later use. The first cookie is the Size cookie, which gets the value of the `Request.Form("optSize")` variable: S, M, L, XL, or XXL. The second cookie is the Toppings cookie, which is a series of Ys and Ns based on the toppings selected. By looping through the topping check box controls, we store either a Y or N into the temporary string, which is then stored into the cookie.

To test the form, do the following:

1. When you run this page initially, you see the form in its default format, which shows the large pizza with cheese and tomato sauce. Make your selections and then submit the form data.

2. The results show up just as before. Close your browser window.

3. Go to your cookies directory and find the cookie from the site where your form lives. Open it and take a look at the values. A sample cookie file is shown in Figure 7-4.

   Because we loaded the cookie in WordPad, the black boxes in Notepad are turned into line breaks. You can see both the Size and Topping cookie names, immediately followed by the values. In this case, I selected a large pizza with toppings 1–4, 8, and 11.

4. Load the `PizzaDeliveryForm.asp` file again and watch your last selections get repopulated into the form. That's all there is to it!

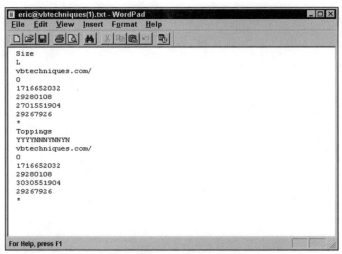

Figure 7-4: Cookie file from PizzaDeliveryForm.asp

Summary

While cookies are surrounded by concerns about privacy and corporate conspiracies, they are a quick and easy way to store user-specific data without having to get into database architectures. For simple forms, you don't always want to mess with a database table that can grow out of control on a busy site. Use the power of cookies to simplify your work and store relevant information on the user's machine. However, if you do use cookies, be aware that people can refuse them. You should always have a backup plan in case a user doesn't accept cookies. You should also make an effort to explain what you're doing with cookies. This explanation will also help alleviate any fears about the use of personal preferences and information.

✦   ✦   ✦

Using the Application, Session, and Server Objects

◆ ◆ ◆ ◆

In this Chapter

Learn about the
Application object
and its function

Learn what the
Session object does

Learn what the Server
object can do

Learn to use the
global.asa file in
your ASP
applications

Introduction to
Service Objects

◆ ◆ ◆ ◆

Up until now, we've been talking about the Request and
Response objects, which have "local" functionality.
They operate for a particular instance of a page and then go
away. However, most applications need information stored
about the entire process or user session for things to make
sense. For this reason, ASP includes three "service" objects:

+ Application object
+ Session object
+ Server object

These three objects, like the Request and Response objects,
are always available to your application and provide some
helpful services not available elsewhere. This chapter shows
you what these three objects can do and how they can simplify
your work with ASP. Subsequent chapters also study these
objects for use in applications.

The Application Object

In other languages, an application is often a single executable
file that may have many different functions. Several executable
files may be grouped together into an application or an
application suite. In ASP-speak, an Application is a group of
ASP files within a single directory, including any

subdirectories. If you have five ASP files in a directory, those files are considered an Application. In many cases, sharing data between these files is critical for proper operation of the application.

The Application object is designed primarily as a storage device for variable contents and objects. The available methods and properties help manage the contents of the Application object. Adding a piece of information to the Application object is quite easy and requires the following code:

```
Application("UserID") = 52
```

This code will create an entry in the Application object that can be accessed by any ASP page in the same directory or any subdirectory. You can also add objects to the Application object. For instance, let's say you only wanted to keep one copy of the FileSystemObject for your application. Here's how you would add it to the Application object:

```
Set Application("objFSO") = _
    Server.CreateObject("Scripting.FileSystemObject)
```

At this point, Application("objFSO") has access to everything that the FileSystemObject can do, and the object is shared across all the ASP pages in the directory.

You can also use the Application object to cache commonly used information for a large application. For instance, if you have several pages that include a list of states or countries, storing a disconnected ADO Recordset object in the Application object enables you to reuse that object whenever you need it.

The remaining properties and methods of the object are designed to help manage the object's contents.

Contents Collection

Any non-object information that you add to the Application object is accessible through the Contents collection. By using code like the following, you are implicitly using the Contents collection to retrieve information:

```
Response.Write Application("UserID")
```

The preceding code is the same as the following code:

```
Response.Write Application.Contents("UserID")
```

You can also loop through the Contents collection using the For Each/Next statement, as shown in the following example, which prints out all the contents of the Contents collection:

```
Dim varItem          ' As Variant

For Each varItem In Application.Contents
    Response.Write varItem & ": " _
        & Application.Contents(varItem) _
        & "<br>"
Next   ' varItem
```

This code will print the name of the contents item followed by its value. While you probably won't need to do this operation regularly, it's a handy way to debug your code and Application collection.

The Contents collection also has two methods of its own: Remove and RemoveAll. The Remove method takes the name of an entry and removes it. Here's an example:

```
Application.Contents.Remove "UserID"
```

The preceding code removes the item named "UserID" from the collection. RemoveAll wipes out everything in the collection and is the same as the following code that uses the Remove method:

```
Dim varItem          ' As Variant

For Each varItem In Application.Contents
    Application.Contents.Remove varItem
Next   ' varItem
```

This example may be a good method to call when the application is shutting down, because it will clear up the memory for later use. The ASP engine normally takes care of this for you, but doing some of your own cleanup never hurts.

StaticObjects Collection

This collection holds all of the objects placed into the Application object. Unlike the Contents collection, StaticObjects does not have the Remove or RemoveAll methods. When you create an object, Microsoft assumed, you'd want to keep it around for the life of the application. This reasoning isn't valid in some cases, but that's how it is.

To see all the objects in your collection, you can loop through the StaticObjects collection and print the names of the objects, just as before, using the following code:

```
Dim objItem          ' As Object

For Each objItem In Application.StaticObjects
    Response.Write objItem & ": object<br>"
Next  ' objItem
```

In this case, we can't look at the contents because each item is an object.

Lock and Unlock Methods

Because Web applications are inherently multiuser, you may need to restrict use of objects to a single user. For instance, you may only want one person to update the counter values for a banner ad at a time. The Application.Lock and Application.Unlock methods are added for that purpose. Before modifying an object to be touched by only one person at a time, you call Application.Lock. You then make the change, and then call Application.Unlock. Any other instances of your page that call Application.Lock will have to wait until the lock is released. Transaction-based systems, such as the ones covered at the end of the book, make extensive use of these methods in combination with other techniques.

Application Events

The Application object also has two events: OnStart and OnEnd. These two events are triggered when the application starts and when it ends, respectively. Because OnStart and OnEnd are defined and used in the global.asa file, these events are covered later in this chapter in the discussion about the file.

The Session Object

While the Application object takes care of all the pages for every user during the life of the application, other pieces of data are specific to one user on the system. Some of the information is transitory and only exists within the context of a single ASP page. However, other information needs to be kept around until the user has left the site. This information is stored in the Session object. A session represents one user's visit to the site during one interval of time. The session may be one page view or 100 page views.

The Session object works in a similar manner to the Application object, with a slightly different set of methods and properties. Adding information to the Session object uses the same syntax:

```
Application("UserID") = 52
```

The preceding code will create an entry in the Session object that can be accessed by any ASP page in the same application during the user's stay at your site. You can also add objects to the Session object. For instance, let's say you only wanted to keep one copy of the FileSystemObject for your Session. Here's how you would add it to the Session object:

```
Set Session("objFSO") = _
    Server.CreateObject("Scripting.FileSystemObject)
```

At this point, `Session("objFSO")` has access to everything that the FileSystemObject can do, and the object is shared across all the ASP pages in the directory.

The rest of the properties and methods of the object are designed to help manage the contents of the object.

Contents Collection

Any non-object information you add to the Session object is accessible through the Contents collection. By using code like the following, you are implicitly using the Contents collection to retrieve information:

```
Response.Write Session("UserID")
```

The preceding code is the same as the following code:

```
Response.Write Session.Contents("UserID")
```

You can also loop through the Contents collection using the For Each/Next statement, as shown in the following example, which prints out all the contents of the Contents collection.

```
Dim varItem          ' As Variant

For Each varItem In Session.Contents
   Response.Write varItem & ": " _
       & Session.Contents(varItem) _
       & "<br>"
Next  ' varItem
```

This code will print the name of the Contents item followed by its value. While you probably won't need to do this operation regularly, it's a handy way to debug your code and Session collection.

The Contents collection also has two methods of its own: Remove and RemoveAll. The Remove method takes the name of an entry and removes it. Here's an example of how to use this method:

```
Session.Contents.Remove "UserID"
```

This code removes the item named "UserID" from the collection. RemoveAll wipes out everything in the collection and is the same as the following code that uses the Remove method:

```
Dim varItem          ' As Variant

For Each varItem In Session.Contents
    Session.Contents.Remove varItem
Next  ' varItem
```

This example may be a good method to call when the Session is shutting down, because it will clear up the memory for later use. The ASP engine normally takes care of this for you, but doing some of your own cleanup never hurts.

StaticObjects Collection

This collection holds all of the objects placed into the Session object. Unlike the Contents collection, StaticObjects does not have the Remove or RemoveAll methods. When you create an object, Microsoft assumed, you'd want to keep it around for the life of the Session. This reasoning isn't valid in some cases, but that's how it is.

To see all the objects in your collection, you can loop through the StaticObjects collection and print the names of the objects, just as before, using the following code:

```
Dim objItem          ' As Object

For Each objItem In Session.StaticObjects
    Response.Write objItem & ": object<br>"
Next  ' objItem
```

In this case, we can't look at the contents because each item is an object.

Session Control

The Session object has a property and a method that controls the session. The Timeout property specifies how many minutes of inactivity constitute the end of a session. The default value is 20 minutes for the session to timeout, but you can check your own system's values with the following code:

```
Response.Write Session.Timeout
```

The result is expressed in minutes.

In addition, you can call the Abandon method to terminate a session immediately. You should use this method when the user has clicked a Quit or Exit button, similar to those found in applications (like HotMail) that have a Log Out button. Abandon releases any system resources that were devoted to that particular session. The contents of the Session object are erased and would be re-created if the user started using the system again. This method is called as follows:

```
Session.Abandon
```

You can also use Abandon if the user wants to connect as a different user ID, for instance.

Miscellaneous Properties

Three other properties of the Session object are primarily for information and are not covered thoroughly in this book:

CodePage	Identifies the character set that will be used for displaying special characters. American English uses a particular code page, Japanese Kanji uses another, and so forth.
LCID	This property identifies the locale for the page. The locale is similar to the code page in that it specifies how certain regional settings are shown. For instance, the locale ID specifies how currency symbols are to be shown.
SessionID	This Long data type value is a unique value for the particular session. This value is passed back and forth by means of a cookie so that the ASP engine can determine whose session is whose.

Session Events

The Session object also has two events: OnStart and OnEnd. These two events are triggered when the session starts and when it ends, respectively. Because OnStart and OnEnd are defined and used in the global.asa file, these events are covered later in this chapter in the discussion about the file.

The Server Object

The final service object is the Server object. This object is designed to provide services available from the Web server. Unlike the Application and Session objects, this object does not store information. In addition, this object has no events in the global.asa file. The Server object simply offers various services to your ASP applications.

ScriptTimeout Property

This property, as its name suggests, enables you to set how long a page can run before timing out. For long-running processes, this value should be set to a higher value, specified in seconds. The default value is 90 seconds before timing out. Setting the property occurs as follows:

```
Server.ScriptTimeout = 180    ' timeout in 3 minutes
```

No single recommendation can be made for the correct timeout value for a page. The best way is to determine the maximum length of time for a long-running page and make sure the timeout covers the bulk of the instances, if not all of them. You may also want to combine your long-running code with the IsClientConnected property discussed in the preceding chapter. This combination enables you to check if someone is still connected while you run your process.

CreateObject Method

You've already used this method a few times to instantiate objects in ASP. You can't use the New keyword as in Visual Basic. Instead, you use this method to create all your objects. Also note that built-in objects, such as Server and Application, can never be instantiated via this method because they are always available. Here's another example of using this method:

```
Dim objFSO          ' As Object
Set objFSO = Server.CreateObject("Scripting.FileSystemObject")
```

You have to specify the library where the object lives as well as the object name to instantiate the object successfully.

Execute Method

Unlike the Redirect method, which causes control to pass to another page, the Execute method can be used like a subroutine or stored procedure. After calling the Execute method on a page, that page is executed as part of the calling ASP page. This process enables you to build a series of other pages that are not necessarily included in the page through a server-side include. Because the code is not included, the speed of execution can be increased; the ASP engine doesn't have to read the entire file before running. However, the file that you call has to be structured in one of two ways: only one function is included in the file, or you pass parameters to the file so that it knows which function you wish to run. Here's an example of using this method:

```
Server.Execute "/library/StringFunctions.asp?name=Parse"
```

The `StringFunctions.asp` file will run and be given the name parameter, just as if it had been called by the browser. The results will be shown in the current page, if any. The only problem with this method is returning data. You can't get a return value from the Execute method, so any data to be returned would have to be put in either the Session or Application objects.

GetLastError Method

This method retrieves the last ASP error that occurred. This method will be covered in Chapter 9, which covers the details of error handling.

HTMLEncode Method

As you saw in a preceding chapter, certain characters, such as angle brackets, quotes, and other HTML delimiters, can receive special meanings when not printed correctly. For this reason, the HTMLEncode method is used to convert any suspicious characters into equivalent but non-functional characters. If you were to run the following statement:

```
Response.Write Server.HTMLEncode("<HTML>")
```

You would get the following result:

```
<HTML>
```

If you looked at the source of this page, you would see:

```
&lt;HTML&gt;
```

The left-angle bracket is turned into the `&lt;` character, and the right-angle bracket is turned into `&rt;`. These characters look the same, but they don't carry the same meaning to the HTML/ASP interpreter. If you ever need to print out HTML code for display in your page, be sure to run it through this method first. HTMLEncode will take care of "neutralizing" the HTML so that it doesn't interfere with your page.

MapPath Method

The MapPath method takes a virtual file name and turns it into a real directory path. For instance, if you used the following code:

```
Response.Write Server.MapPath("test.asp")
```

You would see the complete directory path pointing to this file, assuming that `test.asp` was in the same directory as the file where this code was located. The preceding code was used in Chapter 4 to do some server-side include equivalent code. You can specify a file name with no directories or a virtual path with directories relative to the Web root, and the function will find the file in either case. If the file doesn't exist, you'll get an error.

Transfer Method

Unlike the Redirect method of the Response object, the Transfer method doesn't make you start over when you get to the new page. Instead, the Transfer method transfers all the values of all the built-in objects, as well as the states of those objects, to the new page you selected. Transfer is another method that you can use to break up your processing into logical file chunks without having to rebuild the query string or the form every time. You can call this method like as follows:

```
Server.Transfer "part2.asp"
```

You don't have to worry about the rest of the query string, because it will be transferred along with the other contents of the Request object.

URLEncode Method

The URLEncode method performs a similar service to the HTMLEncode method, except that this method translates all the special characters in a URL into their non-functional equivalents. This method is most often used when passing a URL as part of a query string. If you were to use the following code:

```
Response.Write Server.URLEncode("http://www.idgbooks.com")
```

you would get the following result:

```
http%3A%2F%2Fwww%2Eidgbooks%2Ecom20
```

Breaking this down, the %3A is the colon, the %2F are the forward slashes, the %2Es are the periods, and the 20 at the end is a space. It's not much to look at, but that's what URLs need to be if they are to be passed properly.

Using the global.asa File

As with other applications, tasks that must be performed before an ASP application can start. You may need to open a log file, connect to a database, or start some service objects. Because an application in ASP-speak can span multiple pages, there is no set place to start. In addition, the Session and Application objects both have events that are used for startup and shutdown. All of these tasks are handled in the global.asa file. This file is located in the root directory for your ASP application. IIS will find the file if it is there—you don't need to specify its pathname anywhere.

The global.asa file is used for the following purposes:

✦ Holding Application event code

✦ Holding Session event code

✦ Declaring objects with either Session or Application scope

✦ Referencing type libraries to be used for the application.

This section shows you how to code each part and how each part can be used. These concepts will be used in later applications covered in the book.

Creating Application Event Code

As mentioned previously, the Application object has two events: Application_OnStart and Application_OnEnd. If you're familiar with Visual Basic, the event declarations will look the same as in VB. The OnStart event will only be called once by the first session to use one of the pages. The OnEnd event fires when the last Session terminates. The code template for these two events is shown in Listing 8-1.

Listing 8-1: **Template for Application event code**

```
<SCRIPT Language=VBScript RUNAT=Server>
Sub Application_OnStart
    '
    ' Code goes here
    '
End Sub

Sub Application_OnEnd
    '
    ' Code goes here
    '
End Sub

</SCRIPT>
```

You can't have code outside of these event handlers in this particular file. Besides the four items listed previously, this file cannot contain any other code. In addition, only the Application and Server built-in objects are available to the code in these two events, but the MapPath method is not available. This limitation exists because the application has not started and the MapPath method makes use of some information made available after the application starts.

If you're thinking about declaring objects within these two events, hold off just a second; there is a better way to declare those global objects using the OBJECT tag. However, you can set up other information in the Application object, such as strings and integers that have particular meanings to your applications.

Creating Session Event Code

The events for the Session object look the same as those used for the Application object. Listing 8-2 shows templates for each event.

Listing 8-2: **Template for Session event code**

```
<SCRIPT Language=VBScript RUNAT=Server>
Sub Session_OnStart
    '
    ' Code goes here
    '
End Sub

Sub Session_OnEnd
    '
    ' Code goes here
    '
End Sub

</SCRIPT>
```

In these events, the Application, Session, and Server objects are available, but the MapPath method of the Server is unavailable.

As before, if you're thinking about declaring objects within these two events, hold off just a second longer; there is a better way to declare those global objects using the OBJECT tag. However, you can set up other information in the Application object, such as strings and integers that have particular meanings to your applications.

Declaring Objects

In this file, ASP provides a more efficient way to declare your objects that will be part of the Application and Session objects. The OBJECT tag declares objects of either Application or Session scope. Here's an example of declaring an ADO Connection object that will be available at the Session level:

```
<OBJECT RUNAT=Server
        SCOPE=Session
        ID=conDB
        PROGID="ADODB.Connection">
</OBJECT>
```

This example will store the conDB variable in the Session object for later use. You'll need to make the connection to the database, but the object is already created. The object will be destroyed automatically when the Session terminates; however, the Session_OnEnd event should close the object before destruction.

 Cross-Reference   You'll learn more about ADO objects in Chapter 10.

You can also declare objects with Application scope. Simply substitute the word "Application" in place of "Session" in the preceding code snippet. Any objects declared in this way will become part of the Application object and be available to any file in the root directory or its subdirectories.

The best part about this method is that the objects are not actually created until they are referenced through code. Because only the necessary objects are created, you save resources. You also don't have the hassle of creating and destroying objects constantly, which takes time and system resources. Use this feature sparingly — every object eats more memory — but this feature can really simplify your code when used properly.

Referencing Type Libraries

Just as Visual Basic can reference type libraries to gain access to information about other objects, ASP files can reference these same type libraries. This access is especially critical when you are using your own (or someone else's) object libraries. Referencing the library gives you access to all the objects with their properties and methods, which can help solve problems (such as miscopying constant values, leaving out constants, and so forth) before they start in your code.

The shortest method for referencing a type library is by file name, as follows:

```
<!--METADATA TYPE="TypeLib" FILE="Component.TLB" -->
```

This code will make the `Component.TLB` type library file available to the ASP application. The Microsoft documentation suggests that you locate the type library references at the top of the global.asa file for best results.

Cross-Reference Like the other service objects described in this chapter, you'll be using this feature when you start integrating your Web pages with COM components starting in Chapter 16.

Summary

This chapter introduced three critical objects: Application, Session, and Server. Each object has different features that you will be using as your applications grow larger. For small applications, you may never even use these objects. However, complex applications must use them to make all the necessary components work properly together. The applications that appear in subsequent chapters make extensive use of these objects to simplify the applications being built.

✦   ✦   ✦

Error Handling

Error handling in VBScript is one of the weakest features
in the language. While tools like Visual Basic and Visual
C++ have extensive capabilities for managing errors, VBScript
only has one. This section will show you how error handling
can be done in spite of these limitations.

VBScript has two options for error handling. The first is not to
handle errors, which isn't a particularly good choice. The
second is `On Error Resume Next`. If you're familiar with this
option from Visual Basic, it does the same thing in ASP. In case
of error, control passes to the next line following the error. As a
result, you have to check for an error any place that you think
an error could occur. This is a major pain, and because it is
such a pain, many programmers omit this important step. Look
at the following code, which is an excerpt from a fictional page.

```
Dim intNumber, intDivisor

On Error Resume Next
intNumber = 15
intDivisor = 0

Response.Write intNumber / intDivisor
If Err.Number <> 0 Then
    Response.Write "Error #" & Err.Number _
        & ", " _
        & Err.Description & ", occurred."
End If

' more code would follow
```

In this small example, you see how error handling is done in
VBScript. You first initiate error handling with the `On Error
Resume Next` line. You then write your code as usual.
Wherever you think an error might occur (in this case, after a
divide by zero line), you add error handling. Checking the `Err`
object's `Number` property will tell you if an error occurred. If
so, you have to deal with the error and either bail out or
continue, depending on the error.

◆   ◆   ◆   ◆

In This Chapter

Learn how to work
within ASP's limited
error handling
capabilities

Learn how to create a
global, reusable error
handler for your
applications

Learn about the
objects available for
debugging your
applications

Creating a Reliable
Error Handler

◆   ◆   ◆   ◆

After detecting an error, you have to figure out what to do with it. The error itself will, in most cases, determine what you can do next. Syntax-related errors are pretty rare once you've gotten the page up and running, but they do happen occasionally. Run-time errors are more common, such as invalid parameter values and illegal function calls. In many cases, these errors can be avoided with some extra data checking. The best way to determine what to do in case of an error is to look at the possible errors and group them. Table 9-1 shows a list of all the VBScript errors you can receive along with their numbers.

Table 9-1
VBScript Error Messages

Number	Message
5	Invalid procedure call or argument
6	Overflow
7	Out of memory
9	Subscript out of range
10	Array fixed or temporarily locked
11	Division by zero
13	Type mismatch
14	Out of string space
28	Out of stack space
35	Sub or Function not defined
48	Error in loading DLL
51	Internal error
53	File not found
57	Device I/O error
58	File already exists
61	Disk full
67	Too many files
70	Permission denied
75	Path/File access error
76	Path not found
91	Object variable or With block variable not set

Number	Message
92	For loop not initialized
94	Invalid use of Null
322	Can't create necessary temporary file
424	Object required
429	ActiveX component can't create object
430	Class doesn't support Automation
432	File name or class name not found during Automation operation
438	Object doesn't support this property or method
440	Automation error
445	Object doesn't support this action
446	Object doesn't support named arguments
447	Object doesn't support current locale setting
448	Named argument not found
449	Argument not optional
450	Wrong number of arguments or invalid property assignment
451	Object not a collection
453	Specified DLL function not found
455	Code resource lock error
457	This key already associated with an element of this collection
458	Variable uses an Automation type not supported in VBScript
500	Variable is undefined
501	Illegal assignment
502	Object not safe for scripting
503	Object not safe for initializing
1001	Out of memory
1002	Syntax error
1003	Expected ':'
1004	Expected ';'
1005	Expected '('
1006	Expected ')'
1007	Expected ']'

Continued

	Table 9-1 *(continued)*
Number	**Message**
1008	Expected '{'
1009	Expected '}'
1010	Expected identifier
1011	Expected '='
1012	Expected 'If'
1013	Expected 'To'
1014	Expected 'End'
1015	Expected 'Function'
1016	Expected 'Sub'
1017	Expected 'Then'
1018	Expected 'Wend'
1019	Expected 'Loop'
1020	Expected 'Next'
1021	Expected 'Case'
1022	Expected 'Select'
1023	Expected expression
1024	Expected statement
1025	Expected end of statement
1026	Expected integer constant
1027	Expected 'While' or 'Until'
1028	Expected 'While', 'Until', or end of statement
1029	Too many locals or arguments
1030	Identifier too long
1031	Invalid number
1032	Invalid character
1033	Unterminated string constant
1034	Unterminated comment
1035	Nested comment
1037	Invalid use of 'Me' keyword

Number	Message
1038	'Loop' without 'Do'
1039	Invalid 'Exit' statement
1040	Invalid 'For' loop control variable
1041	Name redefined
1042	Must be first statement on the line
1043	Can't assign to non-ByVal argument
1044	Can't use parens when calling a Sub
1045	Expected literal constant
1046	Expected 'In'
32766	True
32767	False
32811	Element not found

Many of these error messages are syntax-related and will cause your application to fail. These errors should result in the page being exited immediately, because VBScript often won't let you continue with these errors.

An easy way to embed this logic is to create an error handler as a subroutine in a file you can include. Listing 9-1 shows the beginnings of an error handler that you can create:

Listing 9-1: **Code for BasicErrorHandler.asp**

```
<%
Sub HandleError()

If Err.Number = 0 Then Exit Sub

%>
<h2>Error <% = Err.Number %>: <% = Err.Description %></h2>

Source: <% = Err.Source %><br>
</body>
</html>
<%
    Response.End
End Sub
%>
```

To try out this error handler, you have to force an error. Use the code in Listing 9-2 to cause an error to occur so you can see the error handler pick up the ball.

Listing 9-2: **Code for ErrorSource.asp**

```
<!--#include file="BasicErrorHandler.asp" -->
<html>
<head>
    <title>Error Forcing Page</title>
</head>

<body>
<%
    On Error Resume Next
    Response.Write 15 / 0
    HandleError()
%>
```

When you run the ErrorSource.asp file, you will see the results shown in Figure 9-1.

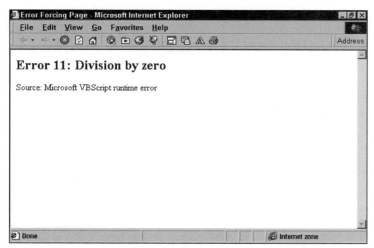

Figure 9-1: Results of an error being trapped by error handler

This code is just the minimum you could do for error handling. However, even this code is preferable to an untrapped error that ends up tripping the server's 500 error page. With all the language tools at our disposal, we can do better.

We have used some properties of the Err object, but we have missed a few. For reference, here are all the properties and methods of the object and how they are used.

✦ **Description Property** contains the text of the error message.

✦ **Number Property** contains the error number that occurred.

✦ **Source Property** specifies the name of the component where the error occurred. In VBScript, most errors will show as "Microsoft VBScript runtime error" for the source.

✦ **Clear Method** clears the last error that was received. This method resets the error handlers so that execution can continue.

✦ **Raise Method** causes an error to occur. You can either use the built-in numbers or make up your own errors. You encounter more of this method when we discuss connecting to COM components.

While we have the error number and error text, we don't have a good description of where the error occurred. For debugging purposes, this information is vital and a major timesaver. If we add a bit more information to the error message using the server environment variables and an extra parameter, the error handler becomes much more useful. Look at the code in Listing 9-3, which has enhanced information about the error that occurred.

Listing 9-3: **Code for EnhancedErrorHandler.asp**

```
<%
Sub HandleError(strLocation)

If Err.Number = 0 Then Exit Sub

%>
<h2>Error <% = Err.Number %>: <% = Err.Description %></h2>

<table cellpadding=5>
<tr>
    <td>Source:</td>
    <td>
    <% = Err.Source %>
    </td>
</tr>
<tr>
    <td>URL:</td>
    <td>
    <% = Request.ServerVariables("URL") %>
```

Continued

Listing 9-3 *(continued)*

```
    </td>
</tr>
<tr>
    <td>Filename:</td>
    <td>
    <% = Request.ServerVariables("PATH_TRANSLATED") %>
    </td>
</tr>
<tr>
    <td>Location:</td>
    <td><% = strLocation %></td>
</tr>
</table>

</body>
</html>
<%
    Response.End
End Sub
%>
```

We take advantage of the fact that the error handler is included in the same file where the problem code happens to reside. This arrangement allows the Request.ServerVariables collection to be populated correctly.

We also add a new parameter: strLocation. This parameter enables the developer to tag errors with a location that makes more sense than a line number. Look at the new code for ErrorSource.asp to see how this parameter is used:

```
<!--#include file="BasicErrorHandler.asp" -->
<html>
<head>
    <title>Error Forcing Page</title>
</head>

<body>
<%
    On Error Resume Next
    Response.Write 15 / 0
    HandleError("After divide by zero")
%>
```

The string passed to HandleError is arbitrary but vital to tracking down this error. When the error happens, you see the result as shown in Figure 9-2.

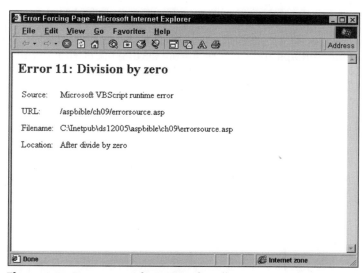

Figure 9-2: New output from error handler

Using this information, the developer can pinpoint exactly which call to Handle Error reported the error. If the location given is accurate, the programmer won't have to waste time identifying where the error occurred.

You may have noticed that all errors are treated as fatal in the error handler and processing halts immediately. Because of the limited capabilities of VBScript when it comes to error handling, you can't do things like retry the line (VB: Resume command) or any other common remedies. The best thing to do is to fix the error so it doesn't return.

A final feature you could add to your error handler would be a log file. The log file could be opened when the application starts and kept open until the application shuts down, at which point it would close. You can record all the information about each error and refer to it later. While the Web log does track errors, it won't have nearly the amount of information that you can add to your own log.

Summary

Error handling is the mark of any good application. Although VBScript doesn't have a lot of capabilities in this area, there are enough functions available to keep the user from seeing nasty, untrapped errors. Even if you think your code can't fail, some user somewhere will figure out how to break it. Always use an error handler to prevent users — and perhaps supervisors — from getting upset about unreliable software. Even if you must terminate gracefully, at least the process is graceful.

✦   ✦   ✦

Integrating with Databases

Because ASP was originally designed to make it easier to publish data from a database, we spend quite a bit of time on building applications that publish database tables and queries. You'll build several commonly used applications in these chapters, and the core code from each of these applications will be used in nearly every application you build.

P A R T

✦   ✦   ✦   ✦

Chapter 10
Active Data Objects
Essentials

Chapter 11
Creating a Data
Browser

Chapter 12
Adding Data Entry
Features

Chapter 13
Enhancing the Data
Browser

Chapter 14
Advanced Database
Integration

✦   ✦   ✦   ✦

Active Data Objects Essentials

In This Chapter

Learn about Microsoft's Universal Data Access strategy

Learn the differences between ADO, OLE DB, and ODBC

Learn how to make a connection to a database with ADO

Learn how to retrieve data from a database with ADO

Learn about the advanced features available in ADO

Microsoft's Universal Data Access Strategy

One of the major complaints from developers using Microsoft products is the confusing array of choices for getting to databases. Early on, you could only use the Open Database Connectivity (ODBC) Application Programming Interface (API), which was not particularly easy to implement, especially in the VB environment. Visual Basic started including a variety of objects to connect to databases, including Data Access Objects (DAO), designed for the Microsoft Access database, and Remote Data Objects (RDO), designed for enterprise databases like Oracle and SQL Server.

While both technologies worked fine, you couldn't take your understanding of one technology to work with the other. The object models were different enough to require you to relearn what you had learned in one model. There were also the ongoing confusions as to when to use one instead of the other. In addition, some of the older methods were still available (such as talking directly to the ODBC API), as were some variations like ODBCDirect.

Something had to change to simplify the whole landscape, and that change was the introduction of Active Data Objects (ADO). ADO is a key component of Microsoft's Universal Data Access strategy. The idea is to give programmers a single set of objects that can be used in any Microsoft environment and for any platform. If you are using VB with SQL Server, you can use ADO. If you are using VB with Oracle, you can use ADO. If you're using Windows CE or Active Server Pages, you can use ADO. See the point?

This section introduces the four major components of the UDA strategy:

✦ OLE DB

✦ ODBC

✦ Remote Data Service

✦ Active Data Objects

OLE DB

OLE DB is a technology designed by Microsoft to make it easier to access all types of data through a single set of interfaces. Most programmers know how to access some type of database, such as Access, Oracle, SQL Server, or dBase. However, each one of these databases has a slightly different query language. Some are similar to standard SQL, but dBase has a different language structure than SQL.

Besides traditional databases, there are other sources of data that may interest your users. If you're working on a Web server, you may want to access data that Microsoft Index Server has produced from your Web site. Index Server is designed to make searchable indexes of your Web data. You may also want to access information in plain text files or in other known document types, such as Microsoft Word or Adobe Acrobat. You may also have a need to do some data mining using Online Analytical Processing (OLAP) tools.

All of these sources of data are now accessible through OLE DB. OLE DB uses a driver called a *provider*. A provider knows how a particular type of data is arranged, regardless of the type of data. The provider translates the given request into a request it can process against its particular type of data. The programmer only has to worry about submitting a request that resembles standard SQL language, and the provider takes care of the rest.

OLE DB emphasizes the break between the components involved in an application. The application submits a request to the provider, which then translates the request to the data source so that the data can be sent to the application. If the data source driver changes, it won't necessarily affect the application's function-ality. Just as with object-oriented applications, encapsulation is helpful here to protect your applications from the whims of your product vendors, who tend to change their interfaces just as you've gotten used to one version.

ODBC

Open Database Connectivity (ODBC) is a specification for a database API. The API is an independent standard supported by a variety of product vendors, including Oracle, Informix, Sybase, and Microsoft. Drivers for these databases are provided by both the vendors and third-party companies, such as Intersolv.

While OLE DB is able to talk directly to several different types of databases, some databases do not yet have OLE DB providers available. In these cases, you can use the ODBC driver for the database in combination with the OLE DB provider for ODBC. Using this method creates an extra layer of interface between your code and the database; that is, ADO talks to OLE DB, which talks to ODBC, which talks to the database. This method would be recommended if you are planning to upgrade the application or the database at some point. Because more and more product vendors are releasing OLE DB providers, new applications should be built using ADO and OLE DB, even if that means using the extra layer of ODBC for the present. This method will require the least code to change to OLE DB/ADO when your database releases an OLE DB provider.

Remote Data Service

Part of Microsoft's strategy is to make data available everywhere on every platform. Besides traditional applications, the Web is gaining ground as a popular way to publish corporate data. The use of this method will only gain ground as the Internet grows and the use of corporate extranets becomes more popular. A feature introduced in Internet Explorer 3.0 and higher is the use of the Remote Data Service (RDS). RDS enables applications to access OLE DB providers running on remote machines or in separate processes on the same machine.

This feature makes it easier to create dynamic Web pages. Instead of bringing down all the possible data a page could use, you get data as you need it. A good example is a tree-based interface. You load the tree with the top-level data when the page loads. As the user clicks on a node, you request the data for the node. Microsoft makes use of this strategy on their MSDN Online site, and it makes the page opera-tion quicker than it would be otherwise. The only downside to this technology is the requirement that only Microsoft Internet Explorer will work with RDS. If you can't guarantee that all your users are using IE, you will have to look at doing more server-side database operations or use another language such as Java to make your components work properly.

Active Data Objects

Regardless of the driver combinations you are using, you will be using Active Data Objects to manipulate the data. ADO provides a number of objects used to traverse all types of data. If you're familiar with DAO or RDO, using ADO should be a fairly easy transition. There are a few differences, as indicated in the following section of this chapter. ADO defines seven objects:

- Connection
- Command
- Recordset

✦ Parameter

✦ Field

✦ Property

✦ Error

In addition, there are four collections used in ADO:

✦ Fields

✦ Parameters

✦ Properties

✦ Errors

The rest of the chapter helps you understand how these objects are used to manipulate your data sources.

The Connection Object

A Connection object represents a single session with a data source. In ADO, you can have multiple Connection objects with each one pointing to a different data source. This can be helpful if you are accessing multiple data sources and combining the results on a Web page of some sort. In the case of a client/server database system, it may be equivalent to an actual network connection to the server. Depending on the functionality supported by the OLE DB provider, some collections, methods, or properties of a Connection object may not be available. This section describes the Connection object and how it is used to access data sources.

Making a Connection

To get started with any other ADO object, you first have to have a Connection object. A Connection object is given information about how to connect to the data source. The code shown in Listing 10-1 is one example of how to connect to the BIBLIO database included with Visual Basic.

Listing 10-1: **Connection code**

```
Dim dcnDB    ' As ADODB.Connection

Set dcnDB = Server.CreateObject("ADODB.Connection")
```

```
dcnDB.ConnectionString = _
    & "Provider=Microsoft.Jet.OLEDB.3.51;" _
    & "Data Source=C:\Visual Studio\VB98\Biblio.mdb"
dcnDB.Open
```

Note You can substitute any Access 97 database following the `Data Source` parameter in the third line of code. For Access 2000, change "3.51" to "4.0" and use the Data Source parameter in the same way.

As mentioned in preceding chapters, the `Dim` statement will help document your code by specifying what the variable is designed to hold. In this case, we are using the prefix `dcn` to specify a variable used to hold a `Connection` object. The next line uses the `Server.CreateObject` method to instantiate a `Connection` object. However, the data connection is still not open. The third line specifies how to connect to the database. The `Provider` parameter specifies the OLE DB Provider to use; in this case, we are using the Jet 3.51 Provider, which corresponds to Access 97. We also have to specify the pathname to the database in the `Data Source` parameter. Finally, the `Open` method activates the connection to the database.

Depending on the data source you are using, the `ConnectionString` property will be different. Listing 10-2 shows a sample of code that can be used to connect to a SQL Server 6.5 database. Notice the extra parameters in the `ConnectionString` property.

Listing 10-2: **Connection code for SQL Server 6.5 database**

```
Dim dcnDB     ' As ADODB.Connection

Set dcnDB = Server.CreateObject("ADODB.Connection")
dcnDB.ConnectionString = _
    & "Provider=SQLOLEDB.1;" _
    & "User ID=myuser;Password=mypassword;" _
    & "Initial Catalog=PUBS;" _
    & "Data Source=db.server.com"
dcnDB.Open
```

To begin, the `Provider` property is different for SQL Server. Next, SQL Server requires a user ID and password, so both of these parameters are provided in the `ConnectionString` property. We then need to specify both the database server and the database name we want to use. The `Data Source` can be either a LAN server name, an Internet-style address as shown in the example, or a numerical IP address, such as 252.100.100.0.

Using a Data Link File

While the previous examples show how to "hard-code" the database information into your application, putting the user ID and password directly in a Web page can be dangerous. While most Web servers are secure, it is best to assume that anything on the Web server is vulnerable. However, Microsoft provides another way to specify the database connection information: the Data Link file. Data Link files can be used to specify all the same information about a database connection that you did in the preceding two examples. However, that information is kept outside of the ASP page, which makes it somewhat more secure, especially if the file is located in a directory not accessible via the Web.

If you have any part of Visual Studio 6.0 installed, you can follow these steps to create a Data Link file.

1. Start Windows Explorer (or Windows NT Explorer).

2. Navigate to the directory in which you wish to create the Data Link file.

3. Select File ➪ New ➪ Microsoft Data Link. Enter a name for the Data Link file and then press the Enter key.

4. Right-click the file and select Open from the popup menu. The dialog shown in Figure 10-1 will be displayed.

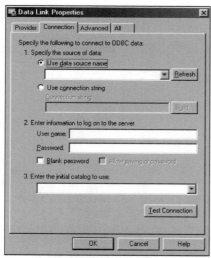

Figure 10-1: Data Link Connection dialog

5. By default, the Data Link is created using the ODBC OLE DB provider. For this example, we will use an Access database on your machine. To select the Jet provider, click on the Provider tab at the top. The dialog shown in Figure 10-2 will display.

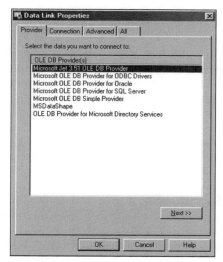

Figure 10-2: Data Link Provider dialog

6. Click on the Jet OLE DB Provider and then click the Next button. The dialog shown in Figure 10-3 will appear to prompt you for parameters specific to Access databases.

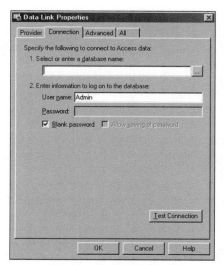

Figure 10-3: Data Link Connection dialog with space for Access parameters

7. Select a database to use and then click the Test Connection button to verify that the Data Link is set up correctly. If the connection test succeeds, click the OK button to save the Data Link file.

At this point, you can use the code shown in Listing 10-3 to select and open the database. You need to supply the full pathname for the Data Link file for it to work properly, so be sure the pathname is correct before using the code.

Listing 10-3: **Connection code using a Data Link**

```
Dim dcnDB    ' As ADODB.Connection

Set dcnDB = Server.CreateObject("ADODB.Connection")
dcnDB.ConnectionString = "File Name=C:\Windows\Sample.udl"
dcnDB.Open
```

The advantage of this method is that if the database location or connection method changes, you can make a single change to the Data Link file (which could be shared between many ASP pages), and all of the connections will be changed. Data Link files can be used for any and all types of connections.

Closing a Connection

When you are at the end of your ASP page, you should always close any open data connections. This practice enables the data source server to release the system resources associated with that connection. Too many connections left open will, over time, cause the system to run out of resources eventually and grind to a halt. Closing a connection is easy. Simply use the `Close` method:

```
dcnDB.Close
```

Before closing the connection, you should also make sure that any other objects using the connection have been closed. Otherwise, you could possibly use an object that was no longer valid, which would cause an error.

In addition, you should clear your object references with a statement as follows:

```
Set dcnDB = Nothing
```

At several conferences, Microsoft staff has said that ASP takes care of releasing its own objects, but no one can verify that clearing actually occurs. If you see slow memory leaks on your Web server, this could be one of the reasons.

The Recordset and Field Objects

A recordset is just what its name says: a set of records. A record is a row from the result of a query. If the query accesses a single table, a record is one row out of the table. If the query joins more than one table, a record is a row from the result. The ADO Recordset object is fairly intelligent and knows how to manage the results to minimize the amount of delay. For instance, if you run a query that returns a large number of rows, the Recordset object knows to only bring back a small batch at a time. While this can cause problems when you are trying to determine the number of records, this management will help the performance of your application in most cases. This section covers the ways in which you can use the Recordset object to access your database.

Executing a Query

The easiest way to create a recordset is to execute a query against your database. The results will be returned in a Recordset object. The following code will determine the number of customers in the Customers table in the Northwind Traders database, and return that value as a single row in a Recordset. The code assumes that a data connection, stored in the dcnDB variable, has already been defined and opened.

```
Dim rsCount       ' As ADODB.Recordset

Set rsCount = dcnDB.Execute("SELECT COUNT(*) FROM Customers")
Response.Write "There are " & rsCount(0) & " customers."
```

Note that we don't use Server.CreateObject to instantiate the Recordset object before using it; rather, we let the Execute method do its thing and return a Recordset for us. When we are printing the number of records, using a zero subscript in the rsCount variable will return the first field of the first record; in this case, the count of records will be there.

Note   The first Field object in the Fields collection is assigned index 0, not 1. If you're using a For/Next loop and not a For/Each, you can get errors if you forget this fact.

While the Execute method can be used to run SQL commands entered directly into your ASP code, it can also execute stored procedures (as they are known in Oracle and SQL Server) and predefined queries (as they are known in Access). In the following example, we want to run a stored procedure named spCountRecords. As you can see, the code is even shorter.

```
Dim rsCount   ' As ADODB.Recordset

Set rsCount = dcnDB.Execute("spCountRecords")
Response.Write "There are " & rsCount(0) & " customers."
```

The method by which you create a stored procedure or query will vary with the database that you are using. Refer to your database documentation for help on creating queries and stored procedures.

Using the `Execute` method uses the least code to retrieve a read-only recordset for use in ASP.

Besides creating recordsets, the `Execute` method can be used to execute all the other types of queries, such as updates and deletes. Because these queries don't return recordsets, you can call the `Execute` method as follows:

```
dcnDB.Execute "DELETE FROM Customers " _
    & "WHERE CustomerID = 'ALFKI'"
```

For updates, you may want to look a bit further in the chapter to see how to edit records in a recordset. This process is less complicated than building an update query in SQL.

One last thing you can do with the `Execute` method is to call stored procedures in Access, SQL Server, or any other database that has similar functionality. In this example, let's say that there is a stored procedure called `sp_UpdateCounter`. We're passing the procedure a string and using the `Execute` method to call it:

```
dcnDB.Execute "sp_UpdateCounter 'testcounter'"
```

This is a shortcut for executing stored procedures that doesn't involve creating `Command` and `Parameter` objects, which are discussed in a following section. Make sure that any string arguments are enclosed in single quotes. Numbers don't need single quotes around them, but date variables should be surrounded with pound signs (#) and/or single quotes, depending on your database.

Opening a Recordset

This method is much more flexible and provides many more options for getting to data. However, this method requires that you define and instantiate your `Recordset` variable before using it. If you don't remember to do this task, you'll end up with errors when you initially attempt to use the object.

The following code opens a `Recordset` object using the same query used in the `Execute` example. This code assumes that you have already opened a connection with the `dcnDB` variable.

```
Dim rsQuery   ' As ADODB.Recordset

Set rsQuery = Server.CreateObject("ADODB.Recordset")
rsQuery.Open "SELECT * FROM Customers", dcnDB
```

This code opens a read-only, forward-only recordset of the Customers table. Forward-only is used for cases in which you are dumping data to a page, such as in a report or as part of a data entry form. This type of recordset is more efficient because it doesn't need to store as much navigation information. Once you have passed a record, the recordset can get rid of the record, thus saving your system resources.

The preceding code takes advantage of the default parameter values used in the Open method. The following code lists all of the arguments with their proper values. For this code to work, be sure you include the adovbs.inc file into your ASP page. Otherwise, the constants used here (prefixed with ad) won't resolve.

```
Dim rsQuery   ' As ADODB.Recordset

Set rsQuery = Server.CreateObject("ADODB.Recordset")
rsQuery.Open "SELECT * FROM Customers", dcnDB, _
    adOpenForwardOnly, adLockReadOnly
```

The adOpenForwardOnly constant, which is the default value, specifies the cursor type. In this context, a cursor is a pointer into a recordset, and not the icon that marks where you type. The valid values for this parameter are shown in Table 10-1.

Table 10-1
CursorType Parameter Values

Constant	Value	Description
adOpenForwardOnly	0	Creates a read-only recordset that can only scroll forward.
adOpenKeyset	1	Cursor enables you to add, modify, and delete records, but you won't see changes made by other users while your recordset is open.
adOpenDynamic	2	Cursor enables you to add, modify, and delete records, and you will see any changes made by other users.
adOpenStatic	3	Creates a read-only recordset that has all capabilities for positioning; that is, forward and backward, as well as bookmarking.

The adLockReadOnly constant, which is also the default value, specifies the method by which the records should be locked. In this case, we don't want to change the records, so the read-only constant is the appropriate choice. The other available values are shown in Table 10-2.

Table 10-2
LockType Parameter Values

Constant	Value	Description
adLockReadOnly	1	Records are read-only and cannot be changed.
adLockPessimistic	2	Records are locked when you start editing them.
adLockOptimistic	3	Records are locked when you call the Update method to commit your changes.
adLockBatchOptimistic	4	Required if you are performing batch updates to a set of records.

As you probably figured out already, some of the possible constant combinations don't really make sense. For instance, using any type of lock with a static recordset will be ineffective, because you can't edit the records anyway. When you are editing records, however, having these options available will make your programming easier to predict. If you are in a high-traffic environment, pessimistic locking of records will prevent two users from changing the same record simultaneously. In a lighter traffic environment, optimistic locking may be more appropriate because it only locks the records for the occasional update you may need to make.

Navigating in a Recordset

Once the recordset is open, you need to be able to navigate through the records. You can display or process them as you loop. The following code can be used for any type of recordset to loop through the records.

```
Dim rsQuery            ' As ADODB.Recordset

Set rsQuery = Server.CreateObject("ADODB.Recordset")
rsQuery.Open "SELECT * FROM Customers", dcnDB

Do While Not rsQuery.EOF
   Response.Write rsQuery("CustomerName")
   rsQuery.MoveNext
Loop

rsQuery.Close
```

This code assumes that the Customers table has a field called CustomerName. (If you don't have that field in your table, use the correct field name.) After opening the recordset as a read-only, forward-only recordset (remember the default values), a Do loop continues until the end-of-file (EOF) flag is true. The EOF flag is true after the last record has been passed by the cursor. As a result, you can look at the last record, do another MoveNext, and then the EOF flag will be True. After the loop exits, the Recordset is closed using the Close method. Like the Connection object, you should close all your Recordsets to help conserve system resources.

All of the following methods are available for navigating in a recordset. If you are in a forward-only recordset, only MoveNext is available from this list.

- ✦ MoveFirst
- ✦ MoveLast
- ✦ MoveNext
- ✦ MovePrevious

Remember to check for EOF before performing a MoveNext, and check for beginning of file (BOF) before performing a MovePrevious while moving backwards. This process will prevent errors from occurring.

Editing Records in a Recordset

Once you've opened the Recordset properly, you can edit the records in that Recordset. As an example, the code in Listing 10-4 will update the name of a customer (stored in the ContactName field) in the Customers table of the Northwind Traders database. This example includes the code to make a connection, because you'll be using this code frequently.

Listing 10-4: **Editing a Record**

```
Dim dcnDB          ' As ADODB.Connection
Dim rsQuery        ' As ADODB.Recordset

Set dcnDB = Server.CreateObject("ADODB.Connection")
dcnDB.ConnectionString = "Provider=Microsoft.Jet.OLEDB.3.51;" _
    & "Data Source=c:\db\nwind.mdb"
dcnDB.Open

Set rsQuery = Server.CreateObject("ADODB.Recordset")
rsQuery.Open "SELECT * FROM Customers " _
    & "WHERE CustomerID = 'ALFKI'", _
    dcnDB, adOpenKeyset, adLockOptimistic

rsQuery("ContactName") = "The New Name Goes Here"
rsQuery.Update
rsQuery.Close
dcnDB.Close
```

Be sure to point the database path to your own database, or you'll get an error. In this example, we select the record we want to edit by using a simple SELECT query. The recordset is created as a keyset with optimistic updates. We assume that we don't need to see other people's changes to this one record in this recordset, which will be closed after the update has been made. Optimistic locking doesn't make the record lock until the Update method has been called. Note that, unlike DAO, we don't have to call an Edit method explicitly. As soon as you make a change to a field, as we do to the ContactName field, the record is considered "edited." The Update method is still necessary to commit the changes at the end.

One bonus with this method is that you don't have to worry whether the values you are storing in the fields have single quotes. Single quotes, if placed into a SQL UPDATE statement, will cause the statement to have errors unless each single quote is replaced with two single quotes. If you are putting data into a field in this manner, you can put all the single quotes you want without errors.

Adding New Records to a Table

Adding records is similar to editing, except for a few small details. The code shown in Listing 10-5 will add a new record to the Shippers table in the Northwind Traders database. Remember to change the pathname to your database for the code to work properly.

Listing 10-5: **Adding a record via ADO**

```
Dim dcnDB          ' As ADODB.Connection
Dim rsQuery        ' As ADODB.Recordset

Set dcnDB = Server.CreateObject("ADODB.Connection")
dcnDB.ConnectionString = "Provider=Microsoft.Jet.OLEDB.3.51;" _
    & "Data Source=c:\nwind.mdb"
dcnDB.Open

Set rsQuery = Server.CreateObject("ADODB.Recordset")
rsQuery.Open "SELECT * FROM Shippers", _
    dcnDB, adOpenKeyset, adLockOptimistic

rsQuery.AddNew
rsQuery("CompanyName") = "Joe and Larry's Shipping Company"
rsQuery("Phone") = "800-BREAK-IT"
rsQuery.Update
rsQuery.Close
dcnDB.Close
```

The addition of the new record is started with the AddNew method. After that, each of the required fields is supplied with a value, and the Update method finishes the job. You can check the Shippers table in the database to see the new record.

Also, if you look at the table design for this table, you should notice that there are actually three fields in the table. The unspecified field is an AutoNumber field that automatically supplies a unique ID for the shippers you add. Because the table has a default value, we don't need to specify it when we add the record.

Note that we opened the recordset without using the Execute method. This strategy takes a few more resources than just using the Execute statement or calling a stored procedure to add the record. Both methods will accomplish the same task, but if you need to optimize your application for a high number of users, stick to a stored procedure to add records — it will run faster.

The Command and Parameter Objects

The Command object is at the heart of ADO. This object is the primary mechanism for instructing the database about the results you want. It contains all the information needed to use a connection, process a query, and return a recordset. This section will cover the most common uses of the Command object in ASP.

Creating a Recordset with a Command Object

Let's begin by creating a Recordset using the Command object, as shown in Listing 10-6.

Listing 10-6: **Creating a Recordset with a Command object**

```
Dim dcnDB      ' As ADODB.Connection
Dim cmdQuery   ' As ADODB.Command
Dim rsQuery    ' As ADODB.Recordset

Set dcnDB = Server.CreateObject("ADODB.Connection")
dcnDB.ConnectionString = "Provider=Microsoft.Jet.OLEDB.3.51;" _
    & "Data Source=c:\nwind.mdb"
dcnDB.Open

Set cmdQuery = Server.CreateObject("ADODB.Command")
cmdQuery.CommandText = "SELECT * FROM Shippers"
Set cmdQuery.ActiveConnection = dcnDB
```

Continued

Listing 10-6 *(continued)*

```
Set rsQuery = cmdQuery.Execute

Do While Not rsQuery.EOF
    Response.Write rsQuery("CompanyName") & "<br>"
    rsQuery.MoveNext
Loop

rsQuery.Close
dcnDB.Close
```

In this example, we are performing the same type of query but using the Command object to do it. We first set the CommandText parameter, which holds the text of the query we want to run. The active database connection, which is an object, is stored in the ActiveConnection parameter. Because you are dealing with objects, you have to use the Set statement. Finally, the Execute method runs the query and creates the resulting Recordset object.

While this method adds yet another object and a few more lines of code, you won't be using this method for simple queries like the preceding example — use the Execute method of the Connection object for this type of action. Rather, this method is appropriate when you need to perform more advanced operations with your query. Some of the instances in which a Command object is more appropriate include:

✦ Creating queries that use parameters

✦ Allowing the query to be prepared on the fly to make subsequent executions quicker

✦ Change the timeout of your query

Running a Query with Parameters

One of the benefits of stored procedures (or queries stored with the database) is that the database has already determined the quickest way to execute the query. Because this precompilation is done when the developer created the query, the user doesn't have to wait around for that extra time while plain SQL is interpreted by the database. However, many queries will require input data in order to function properly. Each piece of data given to a stored procedure or query is called a *parameter*.

Parameters each have a name, a data type, a direction, and a size. If a parameter is text-based, the size (or length) of the parameter will need to be supplied as part of the Parameter object. The direction refers to whether the parameter is passing data into the stored procedure, getting data from the stored procedure, or both.

For this example, let's create a simple lookup query. The query accepts one parameter named `paramShipperID`, which corresponds to a particular shipper's ID number. The query selects all the rows from the Shippers table where that ID is found. In Access, the query is set up as shown in Figure 10-4.

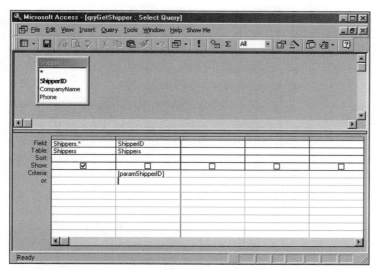

Figure 10-4: Design for Shipper Lookup query

The query has been saved as `qryGetShipper`, but feel free to use your own names. In SQL Server and Oracle, common practice is to prefix stored procedures with `sp`.

The code required to use this query looks a little messy, but the approach is straightforward once you understand how parameters are created for `Command` objects. The code is shown in Listing 10-7.

Listing 10-7: **Code to use qryGetShipper query**

```
Dim dcnDB      ' As ADODB.Connection
Dim cmdQuery   ' As ADODB.Command
Dim rsQuery    ' As ADODB.Recordset
Dim parID      ' As ADODB.Parameter

Set dcnDB = Server.CreateObject("ADODB.Connection")
```

Continued

Listing 10-7 *(continued)*

```
dcnDB.ConnectionString = "Provider=Microsoft.Jet.OLEDB.3.51;" _
    & "Data Source=c:\nwind.mdb"
dcnDB.Open

Set cmdQuery = Server.CreateObject("ADODB.Command")
cmdQuery.CommandText = "qryGetShipper"
Set cmdQuery.ActiveConnection = dcnDB

Set parID = cmdQuery.CreateParameter("paramShipperID", _
    adInteger, adParamInput, ,1)
cmdQuery.Parameters.Append parID
Set rsQuery = cmdQuery.Execute

Do While Not rsQuery.EOF
    Response.Write rsQuery("CompanyName") & "<br>"
    rsQuery.MoveNext
Loop

rsQuery.Close
dcnDB.Close
```

The result of this query is the name of shipper #1, Speedy Express, printed on the Web page. You can print any or all of the fields in the recordset after the query has been executed.

The interesting lines of this example follow immediately after the active connection is stored in the Command object. The first line calls the CreateParameter method of the Command object. This method takes a number of arguments, each of which corresponds to a property of the Parameter object:

✦ paramShipperID represents the name of the parameter created in Access.

✦ adInteger represents the data type of the parameter. The integer data type in ADO can be used for any integer up to four bytes; that is, a Long in Visual Basic. All the valid data types are listed following this example in Table 10-3.

✦ adParamInput represents the direction of the parameter; in this case, an input parameter. The values for this parameter are listed after this example in Table 10-4.

✦ The missing parameter is for the size of the parameter, which only applies if you are using strings.

✦ The last parameter, 1, is the value that we want to give to this parameter so that shipper #1 is retrieved from the database.

The resulting `Parameter` object is stored in the `parID` variable and then appended to the `Parameters` collection of the `Command` object. The query is then executed, as before, but only the matching record is returned.

You can add as many parameters to your `Command` object as necessary. Of course, the limit also depends on your database and how many parameters it allows to be part of a query or stored procedure.

Table 10-3 Commonly Used Data Type Constants		
Constant	**Value**	**Description**
adBigInt	20	An eight-byte signed integer
adBoolean	11	A Boolean value
adChar	129	A String value
adCurrency	6	A Currency value
adDate	7	A Date value
adDouble	5	A double-precision floating point value
adInteger	3	A four-byte signed integer
adSingle	4	A single-precision floating point value
adSmallInt	2	A two-byte signed integer (Integer type)
adTinyInt	16	A one-byte signed integer (Byte type)
adVarChar	200	A String value

Table 10-4 Direction Constants		
Constant	**Value**	**Description**
adParamInput	1	Input parameter
adParamOutput	2	Output parameter
adParamInputOutput	3	Input/output parameter
adParamReturnValue	4	Return value

Using the Errors Collection

The last object you need to learn is the Error object and the Errors collection, which is a property of the Connection object. This collection holds all the database errors that occur as you run your application. Forcing errors is the easiest way to try this collection, as shown in Listing 10-8, which uses an incorrect table name to force an error.

Listing 10-8: **Code to test database error handling**

```
Dim dcnDB      ' As ADODB.Connection
Dim cmdQuery   ' As ADODB.Command
Dim rsQuery    ' As ADODB.Recordset
Dim parID      ' As ADODB.Parameter
Dim intLoop    ' As Integer

On Error Resume Next

Set dcnDB = Server.CreateObject("ADODB.Connection")
dcnDB.ConnectionString = "Provider=Microsoft.Jet.OLEDB.3.51;" _
    & "Data Source=c:\nwind.mdb"
dcnDB.Open

Set cmdQuery = Server.CreateObject("ADODB.Command")
cmdQuery.CommandText = "SELECT * FROM Shipppers"
Set cmdQuery.ActiveConnection = dcnDB

If dcnDB.Errors.Count > 0 then
    For intLoop = 0 to dcnDB.Errors.Count - 1
        Response.Write dcnDB.Errors(intLoop).Description
    Next 'intLoop
Else
    Set rsQuery = cmdQuery.Execute
    Do While Not rsQuery.EOF
        Response.Write rsQuery("CompanyName") & "<br>"
        rsQuery.MoveNext
    Loop
    rsQuery.Close
End If

dcnDB.Close
```

In case you didn't notice, the table name is spelled wrong in the query placed in the CommandText property. The key to making this work is the addition of the On Error Resume Next code at the top of the routine. As you learned in Chapter 9, VBScript has minimal error handling. The best you can do is to tell VBScript to continue to the next line, where you can check for any errors. In this example, we're adopting that strategy. We first open the database connection and then set up the `Command` object. We then check to see if any errors had occurred up to that point by checking the number of items in the `Errors` collection. If the number isn't zero, something went wrong, and we print out the error description and then bail out. If no errors occurred, we go ahead by executing the query and display the data.

As you might have surmised, errors could have occurred in a number of other places besides the location we checked. If you wanted to be thorough, you would need to check for errors in all the places marked in Listing 10-9, which shows the code with absolutely no error handling in place already.

Listing 10-9: **Where to add your error handling**

```
Dim dcnDB        ' As ADODB.Connection
Dim cmdQuery     ' As ADODB.Command
Dim rsQuery      ' As ADODB.Recordset
Dim parID        ' As ADODB.Parameter

On Error Resume Next

Set dcnDB = Server.CreateObject("ADODB.Connection")
dcnDB.ConnectionString = "Provider=Microsoft.Jet.OLEDB.3.51;" _
    & "Data Source=c:\nwind.mdb"
dcnDB.Open

'
' Check to see if connection actually opened
'

Set cmdQuery = Server.CreateObject("ADODB.Command")
cmdQuery.CommandText = "SELECT * FROM Shipppers"
Set cmdQuery.ActiveConnection = dcnDB

'
' Check to see if Command object was created successfully
'

Set rsQuery = cmdQuery.Execute

'
' Check to see if Command object was executed successfully
'

Do While Not rsQuery.EOF
    Response.Write rsQuery("CompanyName") & "<br>"
    rsQuery.MoveNext
Loop

rsQuery.Close
dcnDB.Close
```

This example would be a good use of an error-handling subroutine or function that returns a value for your code to evaluate. In case of fatal errors (which compose most errors), you should terminate gracefully and close up any objects. You may also want to write to a text-based log file using the `FileSystemObject` covered earlier in the book. Because you may have a database error, you need to put your error log in a place other than a database.

Summary

This chapter was designed to provide the essentials of Active Data Objects as used in ASP applications. The `Connection` object represents a single session of communication with the database. The `Recordset` represents the results of a query against the database and can be used in both read-only and read-write modes. A `Command` object provides flexibility for how you manipulate the database, and the `Errors` collection can be used to provide more robust error handling for your ASP applications.

✦   ✦   ✦

Creating a
Data Browser

◆ ◆ ◆ ◆

In This Chapter

Connecting to an
Access database

Reading data and
displaying it with
HTML

Creating links to
other pages

Building a search
page

Handling variable
search criteria

Creating the
Northwind Traders
Data Viewer

◆ ◆ ◆ ◆

The driving force behind Active Server Pages was to create a way to publish databases to the Web easily. Prior to ASP, complex scripts written in Perl, C, and other languages were needed to do what we take for granted in ASP. Using Active Data Objects, ASP can publish nearly every type of data without a lot of custom code. In general, the code you write in this chapter will be used in nearly every ASP application you write in some fashion. You will always need to connect to a database, retrieve data, and then loop through that data in some manner. In short, the topics covered in this chapter are at the heart of ASP.

To help you see how ASP can be used to publish databases on the Web, you will build a series of pages that enable data from the Northwind Traders database (which is included on the CD-ROM) to be published and viewed in a Web browser. You can use any Web browser to view the data, but the figures in this chapter will show the examples in Internet Explorer.

Getting Started

To start building these pages, you need to connect to the database (after creating a new, blank HTML page on your Web server). The Northwind Traders database on the CD-ROM has been stripped of all the non-essential items, such as forms and reports. For best results, you should use that database with these examples. However, reports and forms do not interfere in any way with ASP, so don't remove them from databases you plan to make available over the Web. The developers who built them may get a bit upset with you. Add the code from Listing 11-1 to your HTML page first.

Listing 11-1: **Database Connection Code**

```
<%
    Option Explicit
%>
<html>
<head>
    <title>Northwind Traders: Category Viewer</title>
</head>

<%

    Dim dcnDB                       ' As ADODB.Connection
    Dim strDatabaseLocation         ' As String

    strDatabaseLocation = _
        "C:\NorthwindTraders.mdb"
    Set dcnDB = Server.CreateObject("ADODB.Connection")
    dcnDB.ConnectionString = _
        "Provider=Microsoft.Jet.OLEDB.3.51;" _
        & "Persist Security Info=False;Data Source=" _
        & strDatabaseLocation
    dcnDB.Open
%>
```

While you don't have a complete HTML page yet, this is the first step. After setting the title of the page, we set `Option Explicit` on so that all variables need to be declared. This setting saves a lot of time in debugging — a misspelled variable name will create a new variable in VBScript automatically. Note that the `Option Explicit` must be at the very top of the page or you will get an error when your page runs.

To start, you need two variables: an ADO `Connection` object and a string to store the database location. As followed throughout the book, the variables are prefixed with `dcn` and `str`, respectively, and the data type is added next to the variable in a comment. Because there are no data types in VBScript, there is no way to force the variables to be the proper type. However, if you're a Visual Basic programmer like me, this convention makes it much easier to read the code, because you always know what data types are in use.

We then specify the database location. Remember that this location is the actual pathname **on the server**. Don't make the mistake of putting the network share's pathname here — the server won't understand it.

Note   The database location is specified in a variable name here to make it easier for you to change the samples included on the CD-ROM.

After storing the database name in the variable, we use the `Server.CreateObject` method to create the ADO Connection object. For VB programmers, note that you cannot use the New keyword to create the object. All objects must be created using `Server.CreateObject`.

The next line is a bit messy. The `ConnectionString` specifies how to connect to the database. The first clause specifies the ADO provider to use; in this case, we specify the Jet 3.51 provider because we are using Access 97. If you are using SQL Server, you need to use the code in Listing 11-2 instead.

Listing 11-2: **SQL Server Connection Code**

```
dcnDB.ConnectionString = _
    "Provider=SQLOLEDB.1;" _
    & "Persist Security Info=False;Data Source=" _
    & "User ID=MyUser;Password=MyPassword;" _
    & "Initial Catalog=MyDBName;Data Source=MyServer"
```

The main difference with Listing 11-2 is that you need to specify the database server and database name instead of the filename being used. Unlike Access, you also need to specify a user ID and password.

The last line in this snippet of code opens the database connection. The connection is now available to retrieve data from the database, which is the subject of the next section.

Retrieving Table Data

With the ADO `Connection` open, you can now add code to run a query against the database. For simplicity, we use plain SQL to do the query. Add the code marked in Listing 11-3 to your page.

Listing 11-3: **Creating a recordset from the database**

```
<%

    Dim dcnDB                    ' As ADODB.Connection
    Dim strDatabaseLocation      ' As String
    Dim rsCat                    ' As ADODB.Recordset
    Dim strSQL                   ' As String
```

Continued

Listing 11-3 *(continued)*

```
strDatabaseLocation = _
   "C:\NorthwindTraders.mdb"
Set dcnDB = Server.CreateObject("ADODB.Connection")
dcnDB.ConnectionString = _
   "Provider=Microsoft.Jet.OLEDB.3.51;" _
   & "Persist Security Info=False;Data Source=" _
   & strDatabaseLocation
dcnDB.Open
strSQL = "SELECT * FROM Categories " _
   & "ORDER BY CategoryName"
Set rsCat = dcnDB.Execute(strSQL)
%>
```

The new code adds two new variables: an ADO Recordset object and a string to hold the SQL. You can put the SQL directly in the Execute statement; however, the variable is used here for clarity's sake.

After creating the simple query to retrieve all the fields and records from the Categories table, sorted by the CategoryName field, we create a recordset of these records using the Connection's Execute method. Note that we did not need to create the Recordset object first using the Server.CreateObject method. The Execute method does this automatically for us. In addition, it opens the recordset, just as you would using the Open method. At this point, the recordset is open for business, positioned at the first record, waiting to be used.

Publishing the Recordset

Now that the recordset of all the categories is created, you can loop through it and put the data into your Web page. Add the code in Listing 11-4 to the end of your HTML page.

Listing 11-4: **Publishing the recordset with a loop**

```
<body>
<h1>Product Categories</h1>
<ul>

<%
```

```
    Do While Not rsCat.EOF
%>
    <li><% = rsCat("CategoryName") %>
<%
        rsCat.MoveNext
    Loop
%>
```

We first supply the required `<BODY>` tag, as well as a heading for the page. Use a plain `<H1>` tag to keep it simple for now. We then get ready to print a list of categories to the page. A simple way to do this is to use an unordered list, which will show each item with a bullet next to it. A `<UL>` tag is required to set up the list. The individual items will be supplied through the Do loop, which comes next.

The loop will go through all the records in the recordset. The end of the recordset is indicated with the EOF property becoming True. As long as we have a record to print, we print the `<LI>` tag, followed immediately by the category name. Note that the `<LI>` tag is outside of the ASP `<%` delimiter. The field value is printed because we used the equal sign immediately after the delimiter tag. Alternatively, you could use a Print method to show the value; however, the equal sign is less typing and does exactly the same thing.

We then use the MoveNext method to proceed to the next record, and close the loop with the Loop keyword. That's really all there is to the publishing code. The last section shows you how to clean up the page and your objects.

Cleaning Up

The last part of code you need is shown in Listing 11-5.

Listing 11-5: **Clean up code at end of page**

```
</ul>
</body>
</html>

<%
    rsCat.Close
    dcnDB.Close
%>
```

This code closes the unordered list and marks the end of the HTML page using the </BODY> and </HTML> tags. It also closes the recordset and the database connection, now that you're done publishing the page. You should make a habit of always closing all database objects before leaving the page. Each open connection stays on the server until it times out. If you can inform the server that you are done, you save a bit of processing power for other pages.

Trying It Out

When you run this page in your browser, the results should look something like Figure 11-1.

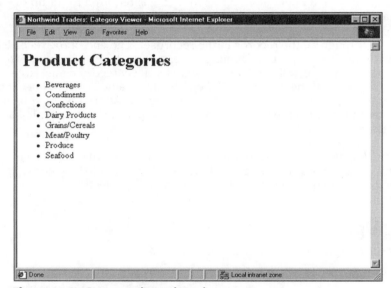

Figure 11-1: Category viewer in action

Congratulations! You just published your first database table. Of course, this is the smallest amount of code you will ever use in publishing a table. In most cases, as you see later in the chapter, you're going to need to provide a lot more functionality for the application to be of any use to your users. However, the basics of connecting and reading data will remain the same throughout all the pages you build.

Adding a Drilldown Feature

While creating simple lists of data is fine, it doesn't really help the user very much. In the following section, we add a feature to let the user get a list of the products in a category. The user will be able to click a category in the list to see a list of the products currently in the selected category. You will be making some simple changes to the file you created in the last section, as well as creating a new ASP page to view the list of products.

Modifying the Category Viewer

In order to provide a link to the product list, you need to make a minor change to the category viewer page. Listing 11-6 shows the entire page's code with the necessary changes marked.

Listing 11-6: **Changes needed for catviewer.asp**

```
<%
    Option Explicit
%>

<html>
<head>
    <title>Northwind Traders: Category Viewer</title>
</head>

<%

    Dim dcnDB                    ' As ADODB.Connection
    Dim strDatabaseLocation      ' As String
    Dim rsCat                    ' As ADODB.Recordset
    Dim strSQL                   ' As String

    strDatabaseLocation = _
        "C:\NorthwindTraders.mdb"
    Set dcnDB = Server.CreateObject("ADODB.Connection")
    dcnDB.ConnectionString = _
        "Provider=Microsoft.Jet.OLEDB.3.51;" _
        & "Persist Security Info=False;Data Source=" _
        & strDatabaseLocation
    dcnDB.Open
    strSQL = "SELECT * FROM Categories " _
        & "ORDER BY CategoryName"
    Set rsCat = dcnDB.Execute(strSQL)
%>
```

Continued

Listing 11-6 *(continued)*

```
<body>
<h1>Product Categories</h1>
<ul>

<%
    Do While Not rsCat.EOF
        Response.Write "<li><a href=""prodviewer.asp?catID=" _
            & rsCat("CategoryID") _
            & """>" _
            & rsCat("CategoryName") _
            & "</a>"
        rsCat.MoveNext
    Loop
%>

</ul>
</body>
</html>

<%
    rsCat.Close
    dcnDB.Close
%>
```

In actuality, the change is smaller than it seems. Instead of just printing an <LI> tag followed by the category name, we construct a URL following the <LI> tag. The URL destination looks like the following:

```
prodviewer.asp?catID=5
```

The number 5 is replaced by the category ID of the category being printed. The Response.Write method is used for two reasons. First, it forces the HTML to be on a single line. If the link is spread over more than one line, you occasionally see extra underlined characters near the link. The second reason is for readability in this book. The required code would stretch well beyond the width of the page.

When you run this page, your results will resemble Figure 11-2. All of the category entries are now links and are underlined and colored appropriately, based on your browser settings. In addition, when you hover over a link, you should see it in your browser's status bar (if your browser supports that feature). The category ID will be listed at the end of the URL, as per the preceding example.

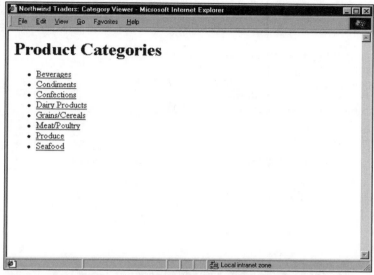

Figure 11-2: The categories are now listed with their IDs as links.

Creating the Product List Page

With the category list page ready to show the list of products, we need to build the product list page. Because it is similar to the category list, Listing 11-7 shows the code with the differences marked for reference.

Listing 11-7: **prodviewer.asp Code Listing**

```
<%
    Option Explicit

    Dim dcnDB              ' As ADODB.Connection
    Dim strDatabaseLocation  ' As String
    Dim rsProd             ' As ADODB.Recordset
    Dim strSQL             ' As String

    strDatabaseLocation = _
       "C:\NorthwindTraders.mdb"
    Set dcnDB = Server.CreateObject("ADODB.Connection")
    dcnDB.ConnectionString = _
       "Provider=Microsoft.Jet.OLEDB.3.51;" _
       & "Persist Security Info=False;Data Source=" _
       & strDatabaseLocation
```

Continued

Listing 11-7 *(continued)*

```
    dcnDB.Open
    strSQL = "SELECT * FROM Products " _
        & "WHERE CategoryID = " _
        & Request.QueryString("catID") & " " _
        & "ORDER BY ProductName"
    Set rsProd = dcnDB.Execute(strSQL)
%>
<html>
<head>
    <title>Northwind Traders: Product Viewer</title>
</head>

<body>
<h1>Products</h1>
<ul>

<%
    Do While Not rsProd.EOF
        Response.Write "<li>" & rsProd("ProductName")
        rsProd.MoveNext
    Loop
%>

</ul>
</body>
</html>

<%
    rsProd.Close
    dcnDB.Close
%>
```

Notice that the page header that includes the <HTML>, <HEAD>, and <TITLE> tags has been moved further down the page. You learn the justification for that move in the following section. Next, the name of the recordset variable changed. Instead of being named rsCat, the recordset is known as rsProd.

The first major change in Listing 11-7 is in the query used to retrieve the data. Remember that the category viewer page is sending this URL:

```
prodviewer.asp?catID=5
```

We are interested in the information following the question mark; that is, catID=5. That information indicates for which category we should retrieve products. The value following the equal sign here, 5, is available in the `Request.QueryString` object and is inserted into the query we are running against the database.

After retrieving all the products in a category, we loop through them and add each one to an unordered list, just as we did with the categories in the preceding example. The last change closes the products recordset. When you run `catviewer.asp` and click the link to Confections, for instance, you should see the page shown in Figure 11-3 in your browser.

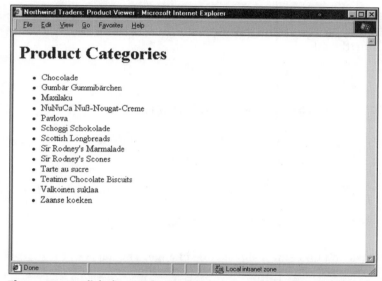

Figure 11-3: Click the Confections link and you get a list of delicious products.

As before, an unordered list of confections shows up in your browser. You can use your browser's back button to pick a new category.

This page lacks a few pieces of information:

> ✦ Without going to the previous page, we cannot identify the category in which we reside.
>
> ✦ The only way to return to the previous page is with the browser's back button.
>
> ✦ The title of the document (shown in your browser's title bar) is the same for every category we view.

The following section shows you how to remedy these problems with an extra query and a bit more HTML.

Enhancing the Product List

The first and easiest task we need to complete is to add a link to go back to the category viewer page. Make the change marked in Listing 11-8 to provide this link to your user.

Listing 11-8: **Add a Back Link to the Product List**

```
<%
    Do While Not rsProd.EOF
        Response.Write "<li>" & rsProd("ProductName")
        rsProd.MoveNext
    Loop
%>

</ul>
<a href="catviewer.asp">Return to Category List</a>
</body>
</html>

<%
    rsProd.Close
    dcnDB.Close
%>
```

The next two tasks end up being a single code change. The name of the category being viewed is required. There are two ways to do this:

✦ Use the category ID sent to prodviewer.asp to look up the category name in the database.

✦ Pass the category name to prodviewer.asp as part of the URL.

Because URLs can become quite long when dealing with ASP pages, I tend not to pass any more information than necessary in the query string. If I have a unique ID that I can use to look up other information, I only pass the ID. However, both methods are perfectly valid and are shown here.

To use the existing category ID to look up the category name, make the changes marked in Listing 11-9 to your page.

Listing 11-9: **Changes to load category name from database**

```asp
<%
    Option Explicit

    Dim dcnDB                    ' As ADODB.Connection
    Dim strDatabaseLocation      ' As String
    Dim rsProd                   ' As ADODB.Recordset
    Dim rsCat                    ' As ADODB.Recordset
    Dim strSQL                   ' As String

    strDatabaseLocation = _
        "C:\NorthwindTraders.mdb"
    Set dcnDB = Server.CreateObject("ADODB.Connection")
    dcnDB.ConnectionString = _
        "Provider=Microsoft.Jet.OLEDB.3.51;" _
        & "Persist Security Info=False;Data Source=" _
        & strDatabaseLocation
    dcnDB.Open

    strSQL = "SELECT CategoryName FROM Categories "_
        & "WHERE CategoryID = " _
        & Request.QueryString("catID")
    Set rsCat = dcnDB.Execute(strSQL)

    strSQL = "SELECT * FROM Products " _
        & "WHERE CategoryID = " _
        & Request.QueryString("catID") & " " _
        & "ORDER BY ProductName"
    Set rsProd = dcnDB.Execute(strSQL)
%>
<html>
<head>
    <title>Northwind Traders: Viewing Products
    in <% = rsCat("CategoryName") %> Category
    </title>
</head>

<body>
<h1>Products in <% = rsCat("CategoryName") %> Category</h1>
<ul>

<%
    Do While Not rsProd.EOF
        Response.Write "<li>" & rsProd("ProductName")
        rsProd.MoveNext
    Loop
%>
```

Continued

Listing 11-9 *(continued)*

```
</ul>
<a href="catviewer.asp">Return to Category List</a>
</body>
</html>

<%
    rsCat.Close
    rsProd.Close
    dcnDB.Close
%>
```

Using the first method, the changes to add the extra features are confined to this file. After declaring a new recordset variable, we retrieve the category name from the database. That category name is then added to the <TITLE> tag as well as the heading of the page. At the end of this page, we close the category recordset. The end result is shown in Figure 11-4.

Figure 11-4: The title and heading of the page now show the category. There is also a link back to the previous page.

If you choose to use the second approach and pass the category name to the product viewing page, you first have to make the changes marked in Listing 11-10 to your category viewing page.

Listing 11-10: **Changes in category viewing page**

```
<body>
<h1>Product Categories</h1>
<ul>

<%
    Do While Not rsCat.EOF
        Response.Write "<li><a href=""prodviewer.asp?catID=" _
            & rsCat("CategoryID") _
            & "&catName=" _
            & rsCat("CategoryName") _
            & """>" _
            & rsCat("CategoryName") _
            & "</a>"
        rsCat.MoveNext
    Loop
%>

</ul>
</body>
</html>
```

The changes needed to the product viewing page are marked in Listing 11-11.

Listing 11-11: **Changes in product viewing page**

```
<%
    Option Explicit

    Dim dcnDB                   ' As ADODB.Connection
    Dim strDatabaseLocation     ' As String
    Dim rsProd                  ' As ADODB.Recordset
    Dim strSQL                  ' As String

    strDatabaseLocation = _
        "C:\NorthwindTraders.mdb"
    Set dcnDB = Server.CreateObject("ADODB.Connection")
```

Continued

Listing 11-11 *(continued)*

```
    dcnDB.ConnectionString = _
        "Provider=Microsoft.Jet.OLEDB.3.51;" _
        & "Persist Security Info=False;Data Source=" _
        & strDatabaseLocation
    dcnDB.Open

    strSQL = "SELECT * FROM Products " _
        & "WHERE CategoryID = " _
        & Request.QueryString("catID") & " " _
        & "ORDER BY ProductName"
    Set rsProd = dcnDB.Execute(strSQL)
%>
<html>
<head>
    <title>Northwind Traders: Viewing Products
    in <% = Request.QueryString("catName") %> Category
    </title>
</head>

<body>
<h1>Products in <% = Request.QueryString("catName") %>
Category</h1>
<ul>

<%
    Do While Not rsProd.EOF
        Response.Write "<li>" & rsProd("ProductName")
        rsProd.MoveNext
    Loop
%>

</ul>
<a href="catviewer.asp">Return to Category List</a>
</body>
</html>

<%
    rsProd.Close
    dcnDB.Close
%>
```

If you run your pages now, you will get exactly the same results as the first method. In fact, the server even takes care of what could be a nasty problem for you. If you hover over the link for the Dairy Products category, you should see a URL that looks like the following:

```
prodviewer.asp?catID=4&catName=Dairy Products
```

If you've been on the Web for a while, you know that spaces located within URLs will cause it to fail. However, when you click this link and look at the link in the URL address bar of your browser, you see that it has been converted to the following:

```
prodviewer.asp?catID=4&catName=Dairy%20Products
```

Because the URL was enclosed in double quote characters, the Web server converted the space character to its hexadecimal equivalent for transfer over the Web. Because a space is ASCII 32, it becomes a 20 in hexadecimal notation. Hex numbers are always preceded by a percent sign when they are part of a URL. This process eliminates the problem of having spaces in the URL.

You may have also noticed that when the text was printed, the %20 was replaced by a space character. The Request.QueryString object holds the text after any hex characters are converted back to ASCII text.

Now that you have tried both ways, you can make your own choice about which method you like best. For short pieces of text, either way is fine. However, if you have a particularly long piece of text you want to transfer between pages, use the lookup method.

Adding Product Information

Let's build the final level of information that shows details about a selected product. This page will show all the information from the Products table on a page that can be accessed from the product-listing page. After making a minor change to the prodviewer.asp page, you will create a new page to show the product information. This page will be a bit longer than the other two, but is still doing the same thing: querying for data and showing it to the user.

Changing the Product Listing Page

To enable the user to click a product to get more information, we have to make a minor change to the prodviewer.asp page. The code change is marked in Listing 11-12.

Listing 11-12: Changes required for prodviewer.asp

```
<%
    Option Explicit

    Dim dcnDB                  ' As ADODB.Connection
    Dim strDatabaseLocation    ' As String
    Dim rsProd                 ' As ADODB.Recordset
    Dim rsCat                  ' As ADODB.Recordset
    Dim strSQL                 ' As String

    strDatabaseLocation = _
        "C:\NorthwindTraders.mdb"
    Set dcnDB = Server.CreateObject("ADODB.Connection")
    dcnDB.ConnectionString = _
        "Provider=Microsoft.Jet.OLEDB.3.51;" _
        & "Persist Security Info=False;Data Source=" _
        & strDatabaseLocation
    dcnDB.Open

    strSQL = "SELECT CategoryName FROM Categories "_
        & "WHERE CategoryID = " _
        & Request.QueryString("catID")
    Set rsCat = dcnDB.Execute(strSQL)

    strSQL = "SELECT * FROM Products " _
        & "WHERE CategoryID = " _
        & Request.QueryString("catID") & " " _
        & "ORDER BY ProductName"
    Set rsProd = dcnDB.Execute(strSQL)
%>
<html>
<head>
    <title>Northwind Traders: Viewing Products
    in <% = rsCat("CategoryName") %> Category
    </title>
</head>

<body>
<h1>Products in <% = rsCat("CategoryName") %> Category</h1>
<ul>

<%
    Do While Not rsProd.EOF
        Response.Write "<li>" _
            & "<a href=""prodinfo.asp?prodID=" _
```

```
                & rsProd("ProductID") _
                & """>" _
                & rsProd("ProductName") _
                & "</a>"
            rsProd.MoveNext
        Loop
%>

</ul>
<a href="catviewer.asp">Return to Category List</a>
</body>
</html>

<%
    rsCat.Close
    rsProd.Close
    dcnDB.Close
%>
```

This change should look familiar to you — we basically did the same thing for the catviewer.asp page in the preceding section. Instead of just listing the product name, we create a URL that looks like the following:

```
prodinfo.asp?prodID=5
```

The number 5 is replaced by the current product ID for the item being listed. Save this file and move on to the following section to create the prodinfo.asp page.

Creating the Product Information Page

The next step is to build a new page to show information about just one product: the product selected from the prodviewer.asp page. The ID will be passed via the prodID variable in the query string. All we have to do is to retrieve all the information about that particular product and put it on the screen. However, there is a bit of a snag in this case. In the Products table, there is a foreign key to the Suppliers table. This key provides information about the company that supplies this product to Northwind Traders. We could simply ignore this information, or we can create a query to retrieve the company name. In this example, you perform the latter operation, but the query is fairly simple to write. The code for this page is shown in Listing 11-13. The sections of interest are discussed following the listing.

Listing 11-13: **Code for prodinfo.asp**

```asp
<%
    Option Explicit

    Dim dcnDB                    ' As ADODB.Connection
    Dim strDatabaseLocation      ' As String
    Dim rsProd                   ' As ADODB.Recordset
    Dim strSQL                   ' As String

    strDatabaseLocation = _
        "C:\NorthwindTraders.mdb"
    Set dcnDB = Server.CreateObject("ADODB.Connection")
    dcnDB.ConnectionString = _
        "Provider=Microsoft.Jet.OLEDB.3.51;" _
        & "Persist Security Info=False;Data Source=" _
        & strDatabaseLocation
    dcnDB.Open

    strSQL = "SELECT Products.*, " _
        & "Suppliers.CompanyName "_
        & "FROM Suppliers " _
        & "INNER JOIN Products ON " _
        & "Suppliers.SupplierID = Products.SupplierID " _
        & "WHERE Products.ProductID = " _
        & Request.QueryString("prodID")
    Set rsProd = dcnDB.Execute(strSQL)
%>
<html>
<head>
    <title>Northwind Traders: Product Information for
    <% = rsProd("ProductName") %>
    </title>
</head>

<body>
<h1><% = rsProd("ProductName") %></h1>
<table cellpadding=5 border=1>
<tr>
    <td>Supplier:</td>
    <td><% = rsProd("CompanyName") %></td>
</tr>
<tr>
    <td>Quantity Per Unit:</td>
    <td><% = rsProd("QuantityPerUnit") %></td>
</tr>
<tr>
    <td>Unit Price:</td>
    <td><% = rsProd("UnitPrice") %></td>
</tr>
```

```
<tr>
   <td>Units In Stock:</td>
   <td><% = rsProd("UnitsInStock") %></td>
</tr>
<tr>
   <td>Units on Order:</td>
   <td><% = rsProd("UnitsOnOrder") %></td>
</tr>
<tr>
   <td>Reorder Level:</td>
   <td><% = rsProd("ReorderLevel") %></td>
</tr>
<tr>
   <td>Discontinued:</td>
   <td><%
   if rsProd("Discontinued") = True Then
      Response.Write "Yes"
   else
      Response.Write "No"
   end if
   %>
   </td>
</tr>

</table>
<p>
<%
   Response.Write "<a href=""prodviewer.asp?" _
      & "catID=" & rsProd("CategoryID") _
      & """>Return to Product Category</a>"
%>
</p>
</body>
</html>

<%
   rsProd.Close
   dcnDB.Close
%>
```

You should recognize the familiar sections of code that make a connection to the database. In this case, the query is significantly longer because we are joining the Products table to the Suppliers table in order to retrieve the supplier's company name. The end user does not understand what supplier number 12 means, but he or she will understand what the company name means.

After retrieving the product information, we create a table to display the information. The field is shown on the left, and the data is displayed on the right. The only exception to the simple code used here is for the Discontinued field. Because it is easier to show "Yes" or "No" to the user instead of True and False, we write a little piece of code here to do the translation.

The link at the bottom of the page makes the assumption that the user wishes to return to the previous page; that is, the product list for a particular category. For now, that assumption is correct.

An additional feature that you could add here provides another page to show information about the supplier. Use the model for these two pages to do the following:

✦ Provide a link from the supplier name on this page to a new page.

✦ Retrieve information about a supplier using the supplier's unique ID and show it in the new page.

✦ To return to the previous page, you need to pass along the product ID to the supplier page so that the supplier page can construct the correct URL to return.

Creating a Search Utility

While browsing works in some cases, large databases take a long time to browse and most users aren't that patient. For this reason, search screens are extremely useful for databases. In this section, you build a simple search screen that will look for products based on their name, price, discontinued status, and stock levels. If you have ever used an online catalog, you may have searched by the same criteria for products you needed.

Building the Search Form

The search form is fairly straightforward. It uses plain HTML form tags with a reference to an ASP page in the form's ACTION parameter. The code is shown in Listing 11-14.

Listing 11-14: **Search form's code**

```
<html>
<head>
   <title>Northwind Traders: Search Utility</title>
</head>

<body>
<h1>Northwind Traders Search Utility</h1>
```

```html
<form action="searchresults.asp" method="GET">
<table cellpadding=5>
<tr>
   <td>Product Name</td>
   <td><input type="Text" name="txtProductName" size="20"></td>
</tr>
<tr>
   <td>Discontinued?</td>
   <td>
      <input type="Radio" name="optDiscontinued"
         value="All" checked>Check All
      <input type="Radio" name="optDiscontinued"
         value="No">No
      <input type="Radio" name="optDiscontinued"
         value="Yes">Yes
   </td>
</tr>
<tr>
   <td>Price</td>
   <td>
      <input type="Radio" name="optPriceRange"
         value="LT">Less Than
      <input type="Radio" name="optPriceRange"
         value="EQ" checked>Equal To
      <input type="Radio" name="optPriceRange"
         value="GT">More Than $
      <input type="Text" name="txtPrice" size="20">
   </td>
</tr>
<tr>
   <td>Stock Level</td>
   <td>
      <input type="Radio" name="optStockLevel"
         value="LT">Less Than
      <input type="Radio" name="optStockLevel"
         value="EQ" checked>Equal To
      <input type="Radio" name="optStockLevel"
         value="GT">More Than
      <input type="Text" name="txtStockLevel" size="20">
   </td>
</tr>
<tr>
   <td align=center colspan=2>
   <input type="Submit" name="cmdSearch" value="Search">
   <input type="Reset" name="cmdClear" value="Clear Form">
   </td>
</tr>

</table>

</body>
</html>
```

The form resembles Figure 11-5 when viewed in a browser.

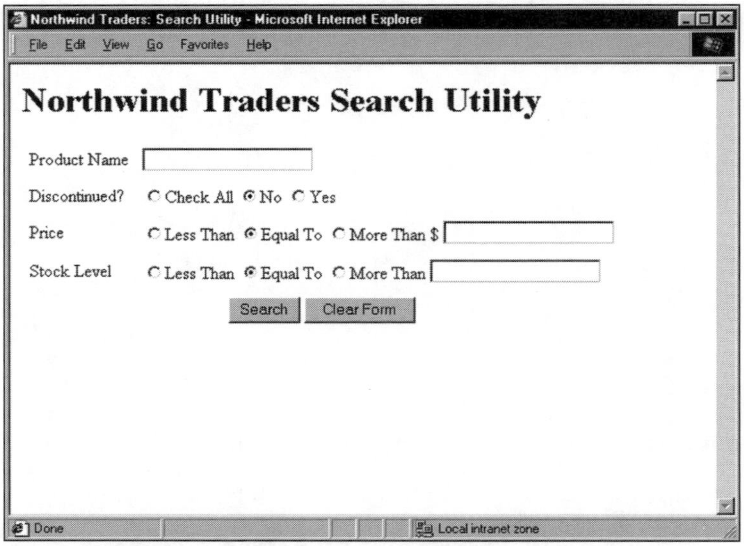

Figure 11-5: The search form as seen in Internet Explorer.

This form has quite a bit of functionality, but as the following section shows, the code required to make it work is not too difficult. The important thing to note is that the form will feed its data to `searchresults.asp`, which is the page that you will build in the next section. The data will not be passed on the command line; rather, it will be passed via the `GET` method, invisible to the user.

This form could also be a simple HTML page with an html extension; however, for consistency, it also has an ASP extension. No ASP code resides in the form, but if you were to search by category or supplier, you would need to use ASP code to build the lists for the user.

Creating the Search Results Page

Building the query is the hardest part of this page, so let's examine the code a piece at a time. The full page's code is shown at the end of this section. The first part of the code, shown in Listing 11-15, is the same as usual. Note that there is an extra declared variable named `blnAddedWhere`. You will see how this variable is used shortly.

Listing 11-15: **Start of searchresults.asp**

```
<%
    Option Explicit

    Dim dcnDB                    ' As ADODB.Connection
    Dim strDatabaseLocation      ' As String
    Dim rsProd                   ' As ADODB.Recordset
    Dim strSQL                   ' As String
    Dim blnAddedWhere            ' As Boolean

    strDatabaseLocation = _
        "C:\NorthwindTraders.mdb"
    Set dcnDB = Server.CreateObject("ADODB.Connection")
    dcnDB.ConnectionString = _
        "Provider=Microsoft.Jet.OLEDB.3.51;" _
        & "Persist Security Info=False;Data Source=" _
        & strDatabaseLocation
    dcnDB.Open
```

The next part of the code sets up the start of the query and sets the boolean flag to false. Because all of the criteria are optional on the form, we have to account for the case in which the user selected no criteria at all. In this case, the query would not need a Where clause, and we would simply bring back all the records. Depending on your situation, you may need to prevent this response. Retrieving all the records from Amazon.com's database, for instance, would cost a few days of your life.

To prevent an error, therefore, we keep track of whether we have used any criteria. We only add the word WHERE to the query after we locate criteria. Otherwise, the code finishes and creates a query without the WHERE keyword. Listing 11-16 shows this code.

Listing 11-16: **Query creation setup code**

```
    '
    ' Start with basic query
    '
    strSQL = "SELECT * FROM Products "
    blnAddedWhere = False
```

Next, we check the product name box, named txtProductName on the HTML form. The code for this process is shown in Listing 11-17.

> ## Listing 11-17: **Product name checking code**
>
> ```
> '
> ' Check product name to see if keywords
> ' need to be added to query
> '
> If Request("txtProductName") <> "" Then
>     If Not blnAddedWhere Then
>         strSQL = strSQL & " WHERE "
>         blnAddedWhere = True
>     End If
>     strSQL = strSQL & " ProductName LIKE '%" _
>         & Request("txtProductName") _
>         & "%' "
> End If
> ```

If the product name box is empty, we continue to the next piece of criteria. Otherwise, we add the WHERE keyword if it has not already been added. You may have noticed that because this is the first piece of criteria, we could make the assumption that the WHERE has not been added. However, because you may come back and make changes, leave the code in now so that you don't end up with errors later.

We then include the contents of the product name box in between percent signs. In Access and SQL Server, percent signs are wildcards and will match any characters before and after the text that was entered. This convention enables you to put in a few letters and have it match any words with those letters in it. Because many of the product names are foreign, substring searches are essential.

Listing 11-18 shows how we check the Discontinued field.

> ## Listing 11-18: **Code to check the Discontinued field**
>
> ```
> '
> ' Check Discontinued flag to see if it needs
> ' to be included.
> '
> If Request("optDiscontinued") <> "All" Then
>     If Not blnAddedWhere Then
>         strSQL = strSQL & " WHERE "
>         blnAddedWhere = True
>     Else
>         strSQL = strSQL & " AND "
>     End If
> ```

```
      strSQL = strSQL & " Discontinued = "
      If Request("optDiscontinued") = "Yes" Then
          strSQL = strSQL & "True "
      Else
          strSQL = strSQL & "False "
      End If
End If
```

Because we have the option to search for products without considering this field, we check that option first. If it is not selected, we translate the Yes and No to True and False, respectively, and add that to the query. Again, we are checking for a WHERE keyword. However, we now need to include the word AND if the WHERE is already there. This will let us build compound conditions, which is the whole point of having multiple criteria on the search page.

Next, we check is the price box. The code for this process is shown in Listing 11-19.

Listing 11-19: **Code to check the Price field**

```
'
' Check Price field to see if it needs to be
' included. If txtPrice is empty, price is
' not being used as criteria.
'
If Request("txtPrice") <> "" Then
    If Not blnAddedWhere Then
        strSQL = strSQL & " WHERE "
        blnAddedWhere = True
    Else
        strSQL = strSQL & " AND "
    End If
    strSQL = strSQL & " UnitPrice "
    If Request("optPriceRange") = "LT" Then
        strSQL = strSQL & "< "
    ElseIf Request("optPriceRange") = "EQ" Then
        strSQL = strSQL & "= "
    Else
        strSQL = strSQL & "> "
    End If
    strSQL = strSQL & CDbl(Request("txtPrice"))
End If
```

As with the keyword search criteria, we make the assumption that if the box is empty, we do not want to include it as part of the search. If it isn't blank, we have to figure out what operator we need to use: less than, equal, or greater than. By checking the value of the optPriceRange field (which is the radio button on the form), we can quickly determine the necessary operator and add the price criteria to the query.

Listing 11-20 shows the code to check the unit stock level. This code is functionally identical to the price checking code, so we list it here for completeness. If you are cutting and pasting, be sure to use the correct field name; that is, UnitsInStock and not just UnitsStock..

Listing 11-20: **Code to check Unit Stock field**

```
'
' Check Price field to see if it needs to be
' included. If txtPrice is empty, price is
' not being used as criteria.
'
If Request("txtStockLevel") <> "" Then
    If Not blnAddedWhere Then
        strSQL = strSQL & " WHERE "
        blnAddedWhere = True
    Else
        strSQL = strSQL & " AND "
    End If
    strSQL = strSQL & " UnitsInStock "
    If Request("optStockLevel") = "LT" Then
        strSQL = strSQL & "< "
    ElseIf Request("optStockLevel") = "EQ" Then
        strSQL = strSQL & "= "
    Else
        strSQL = strSQL & "> "
    End If
    strSQL = strSQL & CDbl(Request("txtStockLevel"))
End If
```

The last piece of code ends the query by adding the sort instructions to it and then executes the query, as usual. The rest of the code looks just like the prodviewer.asp page once the query has been executed. That code, as well as the rest of the page's code, is shown in Listing 11-21.

Listing 11-21: Closing out the query and displaying the results

```
    '
    ' Add sorting at end
    '
    strSQL = strSQL & " ORDER BY ProductName"
    Set rsProd = dcnDB.Execute(strSQL)
%>
<html>
<head>
    <title>Northwind Traders: Search Results</title>
</head>

<body>
<h1>Search Results</h1>
<ul>
<%
    Do While Not rsProd.EOF
        Response.Write "<li>" _
            & "<a href=""prodinfo.asp?prodID=" _
            & rsProd("ProductID") _
            & """>" _
            & rsProd("ProductName") _
            & "</a>"
        rsProd.MoveNext
    Loop
%>
</ul>

<a href="searchform.asp">Back to Search Utility</a>
</body>
</html>

<%
    rsProd.Close
    dcnDB.Close
%>
```

When you load the searchform.asp page, you can enter in none, any, or all of the criteria and watch the results show up in a list format. Clicking on an item will bring up the prodinfo.asp page for that particular product. The only other task that remains would be to link this page to a home page that enables the user to select either browse or search mode.

As promised, Listing 11-22 shows all the code for searchresults.asp.

Listing 11-22: **Complete listing for searchresults.asp**

```
<%
    Option Explicit

    Dim dcnDB                   ' As ADODB.Connection
    Dim strDatabaseLocation     ' As String
    Dim rsProd                  ' As ADODB.Recordset
    Dim strSQL                  ' As String
    Dim blnAddedWhere           ' As Boolean

    strDatabaseLocation = _
        "C:\NorthwindTraders.mdb"
    Set dcnDB = Server.CreateObject("ADODB.Connection")
    dcnDB.ConnectionString = _
        "Provider=Microsoft.Jet.OLEDB.3.51;" _
        & "Persist Security Info=False;Data Source=" _
        & strDatabaseLocation
    dcnDB.Open

    '
    ' Start with basic query
    '
    strSQL = "SELECT * FROM Products "
    blnAddedWhere = False

    '
    ' Check product name to see if keywords
    ' need to be added to query
    '
    If Request("txtProductName") <> "" Then
        If Not blnAddedWhere Then
            strSQL = strSQL & " WHERE "
            blnAddedWhere = True
        End If
        strSQL = strSQL & " ProductName LIKE '%" _
            & Request("txtProductName") _
            & "%' "
    End If

    '
    ' Check Discontinued flag to see if it needs
    ' to be included.
    '
    If Request("optDiscontinued") <> "All" Then
        If Not blnAddedWhere Then
            strSQL = strSQL & " WHERE "
            blnAddedWhere = True
        Else
            strSQL = strSQL & " AND "
        End If
        strSQL = strSQL & " Discontinued = "
```

```
        If Request("optDiscontinued") = "Yes" Then
            strSQL = strSQL & "True "
        Else
            strSQL = strSQL & "False "
        End If
    End If

'
' Check Price field to see if it needs to be
' included. If txtPrice is empty, price is
' not being used as criteria.
'
If Request("txtPrice") <> "" Then
    If Not blnAddedWhere Then
        strSQL = strSQL & " WHERE "
        blnAddedWhere = True
    Else
        strSQL = strSQL & " AND "
    End If
    strSQL = strSQL & " UnitPrice "
    If Request("optPriceRange") = "LT" Then
        strSQL = strSQL & "< "
    ElseIf Request("optPriceRange") = "EQ" Then
        strSQL = strSQL & "= "
    Else
        strSQL = strSQL & "> "
    End If
    strSQL = strSQL & CDbl(Request("txtPrice"))
End If

'
' Check Price field to see if it needs to be
' included. If txtPrice is empty, price is
' not being used as criteria.
'
If Request("txtStockLevel") <> "" Then
    If Not blnAddedWhere Then
        strSQL = strSQL & " WHERE "
        blnAddedWhere = True
    Else
        strSQL = strSQL & " AND "
    End If
    strSQL = strSQL & " UnitsInStock "
    If Request("optStockLevel") = "LT" Then
        strSQL = strSQL & "< "
    ElseIf Request("optStockLevel") = "EQ" Then
        strSQL = strSQL & "= "
    Else
        strSQL = strSQL & "> "
    End If
    strSQL = strSQL & CDbl(Request("txtStockLevel"))
End If
```

Continued

Listing 11-22 *(continued)*

```
    '
    ' Add sorting at end
    '
    strSQL = strSQL & " ORDER BY ProductName"
    Set rsProd = dcnDB.Execute(strSQL)
%>
<html>
<head>
    <title>Northwind Traders: Search Results</title>
</head>

<body>
<h1>Search Results</h1>
<ul>
<%
    Do While Not rsProd.EOF
        Response.Write "<li>" _
            & "<a href=""prodinfo.asp?prodID=" _
            & rsProd("ProductID") _
            & """>" _
            & rsProd("ProductName") _
            & "</a>"
        rsProd.MoveNext
    Loop
%>
</ul>

<a href="searchform.asp">Back to Search Utility</a>
</body>
</html>

<%
    rsProd.Close
    dcnDB.Close
%>
```

Summary

These relatively simple examples demonstrate the building blocks of publishing databases using ASP. Programming this simple application would have taken many hours of CGI programming prior to the creation of ASP. By letting you concentrate on the business functions you want to perform, ASP takes the hard work out of publishing for the Web.

✦   ✦   ✦

CHAPTER

12

◆ ◆ ◆ ◆

In This Chapter

Creating data entry forms

Validation of input data

Building multifunction pages

◆ ◆ ◆ ◆

Adding Data Entry Features

Creating a Data Entry Form

In the previous chapter, you built a data browser that had read-only access to the Northwind Traders database. While browsing data is fine for some applications, inevitably you will need to edit that data. The user may be local or remote, and may need to add, edit, or delete data. This chapter shows you how to use ASP technology to provide this key function to your applications.

We start with a simple version of the code from the last chapter. This code provides the basic drilldown capability so that a user can view details about a particular product. (We'll leave out some of the extra features for simplicity.) Listings 12-1, 12-2, and 12-3 show the code for the three files.

Listing 12-1: **Starting code for catviewer.asp**

```
<%
    Option Explicit
%>

<html>
<head>
    <title>Northwind Traders: Category
Viewer</title>
</head>

<%

    Dim dcnDB                 ' As
ADODB.Connection
    Dim strDatabaseLocation   ' As String
    Dim rsCat                 ' As
ADODB.Recordset
    Dim strSQL                ' As String

    strDatabaseLocation = _
        "C:\NorthwindTraders.mdb"
```

Continued

Listing 12-1 *(continued)*

```
    Set dcnDB = Server.CreateObject("ADODB.Connection")
    dcnDB.ConnectionString = _
        "Provider=Microsoft.Jet.OLEDB.3.51;" _
        & "Persist Security Info=False;Data Source=" _
        & strDatabaseLocation
    dcnDB.Open
    strSQL = "SELECT * FROM Categories " _
        & "ORDER BY CategoryName"
    Set rsCat = dcnDB.Execute(strSQL)
%>

<body>
<h1>Product Categories</h1>
<ul>

<%
    Do While Not rsCat.EOF
        Response.Write "<li><a href=""prodviewer.asp?catID=" _
            & rsCat("CategoryID") _
            & """>" _
            & rsCat("CategoryName") _
            & "</a>"
            rsCat.MoveNext
    Loop
%>

</ul>
</body>
</html>

<%
    rsCat.Close
    dcnDB.Close
%>
```

Listing 12-2: Starting code for prodviewer.asp

```
<%
    Option Explicit

    Dim dcnDB                    ' As ADODB.Connection
    Dim strDatabaseLocation      ' As String
    Dim rsProd                   ' As ADODB.Recordset
    Dim rsCat                    ' As ADODB.Recordset
    Dim strSQL                   ' As String
```

```
    strDatabaseLocation = _
        "C:\NorthwindTraders.mdb"
    Set dcnDB = Server.CreateObject("ADODB.Connection")
    dcnDB.ConnectionString = _
        "Provider=Microsoft.Jet.OLEDB.3.51;" _
        & "Persist Security Info=False;Data Source=" _
        & strDatabaseLocation
    dcnDB.Open

    strSQL = "SELECT CategoryName FROM Categories "_
        & "WHERE CategoryID = " _
        & Request("catID")
    Set rsCat = dcnDB.Execute(strSQL)

    strSQL = "SELECT * FROM Products " _
        & "WHERE CategoryID = " _
        & Request("catID") & " " _
        & "ORDER BY ProductName"
    Set rsProd = dcnDB.Execute(strSQL)
%>
<html>
<head>
    <title>Northwind Traders: Viewing Products
    in <% = rsCat("CategoryName") %> Category
    </title>
</head>

<body>
<h1>Products in <% = rsCat("CategoryName") %> Category</h1>
<ul>

<%
    Do While Not rsProd.EOF
        Response.Write "<li>" _
            & "<a href=""prodinfo.asp?prodID=" _
            & rsProd("ProductID") _
            & """>" _
            & rsProd("ProductName") _
            & "</a>"
        rsProd.MoveNext
    Loop
%>

</ul>
<a href="catviewer.asp">Return to Category List</a>
</body>
</html>

<%
    rsCat.Close
    rsProd.Close
    dcnDB.Close
%>
```

Listing 12-3: **Starting code for prodinfo.asp**

```asp
<%
    Option Explicit

    Dim dcnDB                    ' As ADODB.Connection
    Dim strDatabaseLocation      ' As String
    Dim rsProd                   ' As ADODB.Recordset
    Dim strSQL                   ' As String

    strDatabaseLocation = _
        "C:\NorthwindTraders.mdb"
    Set dcnDB = Server.CreateObject("ADODB.Connection")
    dcnDB.ConnectionString = _
        "Provider=Microsoft.Jet.OLEDB.3.51;" _
        & "Persist Security Info=False;Data Source=" _
        & strDatabaseLocation
    dcnDB.Open

    strSQL = "SELECT Products.*, " _
        & "Suppliers.CompanyName "_
        & "FROM Suppliers " _
        & "INNER JOIN Products ON " _
        & "Suppliers.SupplierID = Products.SupplierID " _
        & "WHERE Products.ProductID = " _
        & Request("prodID")
    Set rsProd = dcnDB.Execute(strSQL)
%>
<html>
<head>
    <title>Northwind Traders: Product Information for
    <% = rsProd("ProductName") %>
    </title>
</head>

<body>
<h1><% = rsProd("ProductName") %></h1>
<table cellpadding=5 border=1>
<tr>
    <td>Supplier:</td>
    <td><% = rsProd("CompanyName") %></td>
</tr>
<tr>
    <td>Quantity Per Unit:</td>
    <td><% = rsProd("QuantityPerUnit") %></td>
</tr>
<tr>
```

```
      <td>Unit Price:</td>
      <td><% = rsProd("UnitPrice") %></td>
</tr>
<tr>
      <td>Units In Stock:</td>
      <td><% = rsProd("UnitsInStock") %></td>
</tr>
<tr>
      <td>Units on Order:</td>
      <td><% = rsProd("UnitsOnOrder") %></td>
</tr>
<tr>
      <td>Reorder Level:</td>
      <td><% = rsProd("ReorderLevel") %></td>
</tr>
<tr>
      <td>Discontinued:</td>
      <td><%
      if rsProd("Discontinued") = True Then
          Response.Write "Yes"
      else
          Response.Write "No"
      end if
      %></td>
</tr>

</table>
<p>
<%
      Response.Write "<a href=""prodviewer.asp?" _
          & "catID=" & rsProd("CategoryID") _
          & """>Return to Product Category</a>"
%>
</p>
</body>
</html>

<%
      rsProd.Close
      dcnDB.Close
%>
```

Note   As we build new functions in this chapter, the corresponding changes in code are
marked for easy visibility.

Adding Structure to the Page

To begin building this form, we need to design the structure of how the page works. Let's consider a few things about this form:

✦ It can be used for adding a new record.

✦ It can be used for modifying an existing record.

✦ It can be used to view a record in a read-only format.

✦ It can be used to delete a record.

Each of these features will require some evaluation before showing certain parts of the form. For instance, if we are just showing data in a read-only format, we don't need to provide drop-down lists or input boxes for modifying data. If we are providing code to delete a record, we should probably ask the user to confirm the action first. While you could do all these functions in separate files, you use less of the common code (such as opening the database, retrieving data, and so forth) if you do it all in one file. For this example, we provide all the functions in a single file. As a result, we need to pass some information between the pages in order to maintain the state of what we need to do next. For starters, let's put down the information that we need to perform each of the four preceding tasks.

Adding a New Record

If we are adding a new record, the form has to be instructed that "add" is the action being performed. While we have a drop-down list that enables the user to pick a category, we can make a smarter form and automatically select a category that the user is viewing. The exception to this sequence would be if the user chooses to add a new item from the page listing all the categories. To summarize, here is the information we need:

✦ Action: Add

✦ Category ID, if available

Editing a Record

Because the record already exists, we need slightly different information than in the Add operation. We need to know that the selected action is "edit" as well as the product ID number. Because the product information page will have a link to edit the record, the product ID will be readily available. To summarize, the information we need follows:

✦ Action: Edit

✦ Product ID

Deleting a Record

Deleting a record requires the same information as the edit operation. We need to know that the selected action is "delete" as well as the product ID number. Because the product information page will have a link to delete the record, the product ID will be readily available. To summarize, here is the information we need:

✦ Action: Delete

✦ Product ID

Viewing a Record

We have already performed this action in another form, but the information follows for completeness. With the action and the product ID, we can look up the information on any product.

✦ Action: View

✦ Product ID

The last piece of information we need is whether the data being sent to the page is in "validation" mode. The page will be designed to handle both parts of data entry: accepting the data and storing the data. This design requires two different loads of the page, so we need an extra parameter to determine if the page is being loaded to enter the data or show the data.

With all of this information at our fingertips, we can add some structure to the page. The main goals are to reduce redundant code and make the code as modular as possible. These goals entail using subroutines, as discussed in a following section. We first create a subroutine called Main that determines the mode of the page. Based on this information, Main then sets various flags so that later code can evaluate them and show or hide certain pieces of code. The beginning of Sub Main is shown in Listing 12-4.

Listing 12-4: **Sub Main code**

```
<%
Option Explicit
Const Action_Add = "add"
Const Action_View = "view"
Const Action_Delete = "del"
Const Action_Edit = "edit"
Const Validate_Yes = "y"

'
' Sub Main: holds main processing loop
'
```

Continued

Listing 12-4 *(continued)*

```
Sub Main()
    Dim strAction           ' As String
    Dim blnIsValidation     ' As Boolean
    Dim lngProdID           ' As Long
    Dim lngCatID            ' As Long

    '
    ' Determine the action that was selected
    '
    strAction = Request("action")

    '
    ' Determine if we are validating a previous
    ' page's request.
    '
    blnIsValidation = _

        (Request("val") = Validate_Yes)
    '
    ' If the parameter is present, determine the
    ' product ID that was selected.
    '
    If Request("prodID") <> "" Then
        lngProdID = CLng(Request("prodID"))
    End If

    '
    ' If the parameter is present, determine the
    ' category ID that was selected.
    '
    If Request("catID") <> "" Then
        lngCatID = CLng(Request("catID"))
    End If

    Select Case strAction
    Case Action_View
        ViewRecord lngProdID
    Case Action_Add
        AddRecord lngCatID, blnIsValidation
    Case Action_Delete
        DeleteRecord lngProdID, blnIsValidation
    Case Action_Edit
        EditRecord lngProdID, blnIsValidation
    Case Else
        '
        ' If the action doesn't match up, send the
        ' control back to the category viewer.
        '
        Response.Redirect "catviewer.asp"
    End Select
```

```
End Sub
'
' After reading the entire page, code begins executing here.
'
Call Main

%>
```

To prevent any confusion, we first define some constants for the expected values of the parameters. In following sections, we take those constants and move them into a server-side include so that they can be used in all of the pages interfacing with this page.

We then start pulling the values out of the query string and storing the values in local variables. The `action` parameter is the key to how this page works. It determines the path that the page will take to execute correctly. If `action` is missing, we assume that the user found the page incorrectly and send them back to the top of the system; that is, `catviewer.asp`. That determination is made in the `Select Case` statement at the end of the subroutine.

The next parameter we check for is the validation parameter, abbreviated on the query string as `val`. We set a Boolean flag to True if the flag is equal to the constant defined at the top of the file. This setting will be important when we determine if we are accepting or saving data for a particular action. This parameter is omitted for the view action, because no validation will ever be done for a view request.

We then retrieve any of the numeric IDs that may be on the query string. We have to check for a missing string before converting it to a `Long` — an empty string would cause an error. We store both IDs in local variables and pass them to the appropriate routines in the `Select Case` statement at the end.

As we determined previously, each of the actions require certain pieces of information, and that information has been gathered through the query string parameters that we checked. Each of the routines is passed the appropriate information necessary to complete the actions. The next section of this chapter explains how to create each of the four routines used to handle the data.

Creating the ViewRecord Subroutine

The code required for this routine should look familiar. It is very similar to the code you wrote for the original `prodinfo.asp` page in the preceding chapter. However, we will be breaking it into several subroutines to make it easier to reuse code, such as the code that makes the data connection. Because we have four separate routines to handle each action, we want to reuse as much code as possible. The complete code for ViewRecord is shown in Listing 12-5. All of this code should be placed before the call to Sub Main at the end of the file.

Listing 12-5: **ViewRecord Subroutine**

```
'
' Sub ViewRecord
'
' This routine is called when the page is called
' to view a single product record.
'
Sub ViewRecord(lngProdID)
    Dim dcnDB
    Dim rsProd

    Set dcnDB = MakeConnection()
    Set rsProd = CreateRecordset(dcnDB, lngProdID, True)

    ShowPage dcnDB, rsProd, Action_View, NoCategorySelected

    rsProd.Close
    dcnDB.Close
End Sub
```

This routine looks deceptively simple; however, the functionality is in the subroutines and functions that this routine calls. The first function called by the routine is MakeConnection (shown in Listing 12-6), which makes a connection to the database.

Listing 12-6: **MakeConnection Function**

```
'
' Function MakeConnection
'
' This routine makes a data connection to the
' current database, defined in a constant at the
' top of the file.
'
Function MakeConnection()
    Dim dcnDB                    ' As ADODB.Connection

    Set dcnDB = Server.CreateObject("ADODB.Connection")
    dcnDB.ConnectionString = _
        "Provider=Microsoft.Jet.OLEDB.3.51;" _
```

```
                    & "Persist Security Info=False;" _
                    & "Data Source=" & DBLocation
            dcnDB.Open

            Set MakeConnection = dcnDB
    End Function
```

The database pathname needs to be defined as a constant at the top of the file. The exact code for that task follows, but be sure to replace the pathname with your own file name for the database.

```
    Const DBLocation = "C:\NorthwindTraders.mdb"
```

The next routine called by ViewRecord is CreateRecordset, whose code is shown in Listing 12-7.

Listing 12-7: **CreateRecordset Function**

```
'
' Function CreateRecordset
'
' This routine creates/opens a recordset to the
' products table. If the input blnIsReadOnly parameter
' is True, we retrieve strings in place of the foreign
' key values. Otherwise, we return an editable
' recordset of the Products table.
'
Function CreateRecordset(dcnDB, lngProdID, blnIsReadOnly)

    Dim rsProd                  ' As ADODB.Recordset
    Dim strSQL                  ' As String

    If blnIsReadOnly Then
If blnIsReadOnly Then
        strSQL = "SELECT Products.*, " _
            & "Suppliers.CompanyName, " _
            & "Categories.CategoryName "_
            & "FROM Suppliers " _
            & "RIGHT OUTER JOIN " _
            & "(Categories RIGHT OUTER JOIN Products ON " _
            & "Categories.CategoryID = Products.CategoryID) ON " _
            & "Suppliers.SupplierID = Products.SupplierID " _
            & "WHERE Products.ProductID = " & lngProdID
        Set rsProd = dcnDB.Execute(strSQL)
    Else
        strSQL = "SELECT * FROM Products"
```

Continued

Listing 12-7 *(continued)*

```
        If lngProdID <> NoRecordSelected Then
            strSQL = strSQL & " WHERE ProductID = " & lngProdID
        End If
        Set rsProd = Server.CreateObject("ADODB.Recordset")
        rsProd.Open strSQL, dcnDB, _
            adOpenDynamic, adLockPessimistic
    End If

    Set CreateRecordset = rsProd
End Function
```

We've worked ahead, but the first part of the code is the trickiest. This routine accepts a product ID and a flag indicating whether the recordset should be read-only. If it is read-only, the query retrieves the category and supplier names based on the unique IDs stored in the products table. Because the query has to perform two joins to get this information, this code is fairly complex. The Right Outer Join takes care of cases in which the supplier and/or the category have not been specified. While omitting the category removes the product from every category, lacking a supplier is not necessarily an error.

Tip Don't know how to create queries like this example off the top of your head? Use the query designer in Access or Visual Studio 6.0 to drag the tables and select the fields for your query. Switch to SQL mode to see the actual SQL language required and copy the text into your page.

If the recordset is not supposed to be read-only, we create an editable recordset of either a single record or the entire table. The constant `NoRecordSelected` needs to be defined at the top of the page as follows:

```
Const NoRecordSelected = -9999
```

Because the product ID is a positive number, this value indicates that we are in Add mode and have no product ID to select.

One last problem: the two constants used in the `OpenRecordset` call are not defined by default in VBScript. To get around this problem, you can include a constants file at the top of your code. The file is named `adovbs.inc`, and you may already have it on your system. If not, the file is included on the CD-ROM. Change the top of your file to look like Listing 12-8.

Listing 12-8: **Using the include file for the ADO constants**

```
<%
Option Explicit
Const Action_Add = "add"
Const Action_View = "view"
Const Action_Delete = "del"
Const Action_Edit = "edit"
Const Validate_Yes = "y"
Const DBLocation = _
    "F:\Projects\ASP Bible\Files\NorthwindTraders.mdb"
Const NoRecordSelected = -9999
Const NoCategorySelected = -9999
%>
<!--#include file="adovbs.inc" -->
<%
'
' Sub Main: holds main processing loop
'
```

The last routine called here is ShowPage, which is quite complicated and involves three of the four page actions. This routine will be covered after we discuss the other action subroutines.

Creating the AddRecord Subroutine

The next subroutine uses much of the same code as the ViewRecord subroutine, except that AddRecord needs to save the data to the database in validation mode. Examine Listing 12-9 for the details.

Listing 12-9: **AddRecord Subroutine**

```
'
' Sub AddRecord
'
' This routine is called when the page is called
' to add a new product record.
'
Sub AddRecord(lngCatID, blnIsValidation)
    Dim dcnDB
    Dim rsProd

    Set dcnDB = MakeConnection()

    If Not blnIsValidation Then
```

Continued

Listing 12-9 *(continued)*

```
      ShowPage dcnDB, rsProd, Action_Add, lngCatID
   Else
      Set rsProd = CreateRecordset(dcnDB, _
         NoRecordSelected, False)
      rsProd.AddNew
      StoreData rsProd
      rsProd.Update
      rsProd.Close
      dcnDB.Close
      Response.Redirect "catviewer.asp"
   End If
End Sub
```

After making a database connection, we check to see if the page is in validation mode. If not, we simply call ShowPage to show an empty form. If we are in validation mode, we have to open up a writeable recordset of the whole table (NoRecordSelected indicates not to pick a particular record) and add the new record. We pull the data from the form created by ShowPage (as discussed shortly), save it to the database, and send the user to the top of the catalog—the page listing all the categories. The last step is up to you, but you need to move the user to a real page; in validation mode, you haven't created any HTML for the user to view.

We use a routine called StoreData to put the data from the Request object into the database. We do this because the same code will be used for the Edit routine. The only difference: for a new record we first call the AddNew method here. The StoreData routine is shown in Listing 12-10.

Listing 12-10: **StoreData Subroutine**

```
'
' Sub StoreData
'
' This routine saves the data from the Request
' object back to the database. It assumes that
' if an AddNew is required, it has already been
' done. In addition, the Update and Close are done
' outside of the routine for consistency.
'
Sub StoreData(rsProd)

   rsProd("ProductName") = Request("txtProductName")
   rsProd("SupplierID") = Request("cboSupplier")
   rsProd("CategoryID") = Request("cboCategory")
```

```
rsProd("QuantityPerUnit") = Request("txtQuantityPerUnit")
rsProd("UnitPrice") = Request("txtUnitPrice")
rsProd("UnitsInStock") = Request("txtUnitsInStock")
rsProd("UnitsOnOrder") = Request("txtUnitsOnOrder")
rsProd("ReorderLevel") = Request("txtReorderLevel")
rsProd("Discontinued") = _
    (Request("optDiscontinued") = "Yes")

End Sub
```

You should notice that no provision has been made yet for error checking. If you were to run this page now and omit a field, you would get a `Type Mismatch` error when you attempted to save the record. Once we get the basic code done, we'll go back and add some error checking. With the modular design of the code, this addition will be easy to do later.

Creating the EditRecord Subroutine

The `EditRecord` subroutine is nearly identical to `AddRecord`, with a few minor exceptions. The code for the subroutine is shown in Listing 12-11.

Listing 12-11: **EditRecord Subroutine**

```
'
' Sub EditRecord
'
' This routine is called when the page is called
' to edit an existing product record.
'
Sub EditRecord(lngProdID, blnIsValidation)
    Dim dcnDB
    Dim rsProd

    Set dcnDB = MakeConnection()

    Set rsProd = CreateRecordset(dcnDB, _
        lngProdID, False)

    If Not blnIsValidation Then
        ShowPage dcnDB, rsProd, Action_Edit, lngCatID
    Else
        StoreData rsProd
        rsProd.Update
        rsProd.Close
        dcnDB.Close
```

Continued

Listing 12-11 *(continued)*

```
        Response.Redirect "catviewer.asp"
    End If
End Sub
```

In both edit and validation mode, we know that we will need to see the data from the database, so the `CreateRecordset` call is before the validation mode check. Other than a different input parameter and a few changes to the constants, this code is basically the same as `AddRecord`.

Creating the DeleteRecord Subroutine

The `DeleteRecord` subroutine is the exception to how these routines work. Instead of showing the form, this routine asks the user to determine if the record should really be deleted. If the user answers Yes to the question, the validation code takes care of deleting the item.

While this sequence seems simple, deleting items tends to cause problems for other tables in the database. The primary problem is that if an item is referenced by another table in the database, deleting the item will cause referential integrity problems. In the case of the products table, products are used as line items in the Orders table. If you were to delete a product, the line item for an order would be pointing to an invalid location. Most databases, if configured properly, will pop errors if you try to delete a record that is "in use." However, there are cases in which deleting items is valid. You'll have to work with your database designer to determine if and when items can be deleted from any of your tables. For now, you should avoid deleting any items that were already in the table when you started using the database. Add an item and then delete it so that you know the item is not in use.

Listing 12-12 shows the code for the `DeleteRecord` subroutine.

Listing 12-12: DeleteRecord Subroutine

```
'
' Sub DeleteRecord
'
' This routine is called when the page is called
' to delete a product record.
'
Sub DeleteRecord(lngProdID, blnIsValidation)
```

```
        Dim dcnDB
        Dim rsProd

        Set dcnDB = MakeConnection()
        If Not blnIsValidation Then
            Set rsProd = CreateRecordset(dcnDB, lngProdID, True)
%>
<html>
<head>
<title>Northwind Traders: Confirm Deletion</title>
</head>
<body>
<center>
<h2>Are you sure you wish to delete "<% = rsProd("ProductName")
%>?"</h2>
<table cellspacing=5>
<tr>
<td>
<form action="editproduct.asp" method=POST>
<input type=submit name="cmdOK" value="Yes">
<input type=hidden name="action" value="<% = Action_Delete %>">
<input type=hidden name="prodID" value="<% = lngProdID %>">
<input type=hidden name="val" value="<% = Validate_Yes %>">
</form>
</td>
<td>
<form action="catviewer.asp" method=POST>
<input type=submit name=cmdCancel value="No">
</form>
</td>
</tr>
</table>
</body>
</html>

<%
        rsProd.Close
        dcnDB.Close
    Else
        '
        ' In validation mode, delete the selected
        ' product. This code will only run if the
        ' user clicked the Yes button, since the No
        ' button goes to a different form.
        '
        dcnDB.Execute "DELETE FROM Products " _
            & "WHERE ProductID = " & Request("prodID")

        dcnDB.Close
```

Continued

Listing 12-12 *(continued)*

```
        Response.Redirect "catviewer.asp"
    End If
End Sub
```

This routine does not use the ShowPage subroutine; rather, it creates its own confirmation page and sets up two forms: one to handle a yes, and one to handle a no. This arrangement simplifies the code on the back-end and prevents the code from being called inadvertently. Also notice that instead of building a long query string, we put the parameters into hidden input fields. This practice makes the code easier to read and accomplishes the same purpose on the back-end. When the deletion is complete, the browser is sent back to the top category page.

Creating the ShowPage Subroutine

The heart of this page is the ShowPage subroutine, which handles the creation and display of data in view, add, and edit modes. This subroutine is quite long and has numerous status checks, all of which support the goal of having a single page perform all the actions. Although ShowPage may look complicated, we will deconstruct the subroutine to see its relatively basic nature.

To create the routine, follow these steps:

1. The first part of the routine, shown below, determines our mode and sets some Boolean flags accordingly. This sequence makes for easier comparisons later in the code.

```
'
' Sub ShowPage
'
' This routine constructs the form based on the current
' page mode. If view only, no input boxes are shown. If
' add, the input boxes are empty. If edit, the input boxes
' are filled appropriately.
'
Sub ShowPage(dcnDB, rsProd, strMode, lngCatID)
    Dim blnIsView      ' As Boolean
    Dim blnIsEdit      ' As Boolean
    Dim blnIsAdd       ' As Boolean
    Dim rsCat          ' As ADODB.Recordset
    Dim rsSupp         ' As ADODB.Recordset

    '
    ' Define a flag so we don't have to
```

```
' keep comparing throughout the routine.
'
blnIsView = (strMode = Action_View)
blnIsEdit = (strMode = Action_Edit)
blnIsAdd = (strMode = Action_Add)
%>
```

2. We then create the page header and show an appropriate heading on the page, which makes it easier for the user to determine what he/she is doing at the time. Note that some of this code is outside of ASP delimiter tags. Anything outside of the tags will be sent to the browser.

```
<html>
<head>
     <title>Northwind Traders:
<%
   If blnIsView Then
%>        Product Information for <% = rsProd("ProductName")
%>
<%
   ElseIf blnIsAdd Then
%>     Add New Product
<%
   ElseIf blnIsEdit Then
%>     Edit Product #
<% = rsProd("ProductID") %> _
 - <% = rsProd("ProductName") %>
<%
   End If
%>
     </title>
</head>
```

3. The next part of the code, shown below, sets up the form for data input, if necessary. Otherwise, the code simply prints the product name at the top of the page. As in preceding pages, we put all of the parameters into hidden input tags. This arrangement makes the URL shorter and makes the code easier to read (both in ASP and in the resulting HTML).

```
If blnIsView Then
%>
   <h1><% = rsProd("ProductName") %></h1>
<%
   Else
      Response.Write _
        "<form action=""editproduct.asp"" method=POST>" _
        & vbCrLf
      If blnIsAdd Then
        Response.Write "<h1>Add New Product</h1>" & vbCrLf
        Response.Write "<input type=hidden name=action " _
```

Continued

```
                  & "value=" & Action_Add & ">" & vbCrLf
        ElseIf blnIsEdit Then
            Response.Write "<h1>Edit Product</h1>" & vbCrLf
            Response.Write "<input type=hidden name=action " _
                & "value=" & Action_Edit & ">" & vbCrLf
            Response.write "<input type=hidden name=prodID " _
                & "value=""" & rsProd("ProductID") & """>" &
vbCrLf
        End If
        Response.Write "<input type=hidden name=val value=" _
            & Validate_Yes & ">" & vbCrLf
    End If
%>
```

4. The next piece of code will either show an empty box or the product name within an input box. The code used here is slightly different from the later input box code. If we are in view mode, the product name has already been shown at the top of the page, outside of the table we are creating.

```
<table cellpadding=5 border=0>
<% If Not blnIsView Then %>
<tr>
    <td>Product Name:</td>
    <td><input type="Text" name="txtProductName" size="30"
    <%
        If blnIsEdit Then
            Response.Write "value=""" _
                & rsProd("ProductName") & """"
        End If
    %>
    ></td>
</tr>
<% End If %>
```

5. The next chunk of code is somewhat more complex. As mentioned previously, the Products table has a foreign key to the Categories table. If we are viewing the product's record, the complex query created earlier will take care of providing the category name. However, if we are editing data, we need to create a list of categories. In addition, if a record has a category selected, we should reselect it when the product record is shown. Finally, we need to preselect the category in Add mode, because new records will be added by clicking a link on a particular category's page.

The following code fulfills all of these requirements. It creates a recordset of all the categories, adds each one (and a "None Selected" item), and marks one of them if it was selected previously. (This sequence should make more sense when you see the resulting HTML.) If you add the word SELECTED within an <OPTION> tag, that item will be selected in the form.

```
<tr>
    <td>Category:</td>
```

```
<td>
<% If blnIsView Then
        Response.Write rsProd("CategoryName")
    Else
      Set rsCat =dcnDB.Execute("SELECT * FROM Categories " _
          & " ORDER BY CategoryName")
        Response.Write "<select name=""cboCategory"">" _
          & vbCrLf
        Response.Write "<option value=""0"""
        If lngCatID = 0 Then Response.Write " SELECTED"
        Response.Write ">None Selected" & vbCrLf
        Do While Not rsCat.EOF
          Response.Write "<option value=""" _
            & rsCat("CategoryID") & """"
          If lngCatID = rsCat("CategoryID") Then
            Response.Write " SELECTED"
          End If
          Response.Write ">" & rsCat("CategoryName") &
vbCrLf
          rsCat.MoveNext
        Loop
        rsCat.Close
    End If
  %>
  </td>
</tr>
```

6. The next block of code performs the same operation for the supplier list. This code doesn't have to worry about preselecting an item in add mode, however.

```
<tr>
  <td>Supplier:</td>
  <td>
  <% If blnIsView Then
        Response.Write rsProd("CompanyName")
    Else
      Set rsCat = dcnDB.Execute("SELECT * FROM Suppliers " _
          & " ORDER BY CompanyName")
        Response.Write "<select name=""cboSupplier"">" _
          & vbCrLf
        Response.Write "<option value=""0"">None Selected" _
          & vbCrLf
        Do While Not rsCat.EOF
          Response.Write "<option value=""" _
            & rsCat("SupplierID") & """"
          If blnIsEdit Then
            If rsProd("SupplierID")=rsCat("SupplierID")
Then
              Response.Write " SELECTED"
            End If
          End If
```

Continued

```
                    Response.Write  ">"  & rsCat("CompanyName") _
                        & vbCrLf
                    rsCat.MoveNext
                Loop
                rsCat.Close
            End If
        %>
        </td>
    </tr>
```

7. The next piece of code is essentially duplicated for all of the remaining fields on the Product table. It determines if the page is in edit mode and, if so, shows the field data.

```
<tr>
    <td>Quantity Per Unit:</td>
    <td>
    <% If blnIsView Then
            Response.Write rsProd("QuantityPerUnit")
        Else
    %>
        <input type="Text" name="txtQuantityPerUnit" size="30"
    <%
            If blnIsEdit Then
                Response.Write "value=""" _
                    & rsProd("QuantityPerUnit") & """"
            End If
    %>
    >
    <%
        End If
    %>
    </td>
    </tr>
```

8. The code for the remaining fields is basically the same. If you are copying and pasting, be sure to check the control field name and both references to the database field.

```
<tr>
    <td>Unit Price:</td>
    <td>
    <% If blnIsView Then
            Response.Write FormatCurrency(rsProd("UnitPrice"))
        Else
    %>
        <input type="Text" name="txtUnitPrice" size="10"<%
            If blnIsEdit Then
                Response.Write "value=""" _
                    & rsProd("UnitPrice") & """"
            End If
```

```
    %>
    >
    <%
        End If
    %>
</td>
</tr>
<tr>
    <td>Units In Stock:</td>
    <td>
    <% If blnIsView Then
        Response.Write rsProd("UnitsInStock")
        Else
    %>
<input type="Text" name="txtUnitsInStock" size="10"<%
        If blnIsEdit Then
            Response.Write "value=""" _
                & rsProd("UnitsInStock") & """"
        End If
    %>
    >
    <%
        End If
    %>
</td>
</tr>
<tr>
    <td>Units on Order:</td>
    <td>
    <% If blnIsView Then
        Response.Write rsProd("UnitsOnOrder")
        Else
    %>
<input type="Text" name="txtUnitsOnOrder" size="10"<%
        If blnIsEdit Then
            Response.Write "value=""" _
                & rsProd("UnitsOnOrder") & """"
        End If
    %>
    >
    <%
        End If
    %>
</td>
</tr>
<tr>
    <td>Reorder Level:</td>
    <td>
    <% If blnIsView Then
        Response.Write rsProd("ReorderLevel")
        Else
```

Continued

```
        %>
<input type="Text" name="txtReorderLevel" size="10"<%
        If blnIsEdit Then
            Response.Write "value="""  _
                & rsProd("ReorderLevel") & """"
        End If
    %>
    >
    <%
        End If
    %>
</td>
</tr>
```

9. The following code handles the discontinued field. Because we are using radio
   buttons, we need different code to mark the correct one. We simply check the
   Discontinued field and add the word CHECKED in order to mark one of the
   radio buttons as selected.

```
<tr>
    <td>Discontinued:</td>
    <td>
    <% If blnIsView Then
        If rsProd("Discontinued") = True Then
            Response.Write "Yes"
        Else
            Response.Write "No"
        End If
    Else
    %>
    <input type="Radio" name="optDiscontinued" value="No" <%
        If blnIsEdit Then
            If rsProd("Discontinued") = False Then
                Response.Write "CHECKED"
            End If
        End If
    %>No

    <input type="Radio" name="optDiscontinued" value="Yes"<%
        If blnIsEdit Then
            If rsProd("Discontinued") = True Then
                Response.Write "CHECKED"
            End If
        End If
    %>Yes
    <%
        End If
    %>
    </td>
</tr>
```

10. The last part of the code shows (or hides) the buttons to save changes. The code also cleans up any open database references that weren't already closed.

```
<%
    If Not blnIsView Then
%>
<tr>
    <td colspan=2 align=center>
    <input type="submit" name="cmdOK" value="Save">
    <input type="reset" name="cmdClear" value="Reset Form">
    </td>
</tr>
<%
    End If
%>
</table>
<%
    If Not blnIsView then Response.Write "</form>"
%>
</body>
</html>
<%
End Sub
```

No subroutines were used within ShowPage, so you are now done with that routine. The last step before we can use this page is to add and change references within the other pages in the application.

Linking to the Other Pages

First, we need to change the prodviewer.asp page, which is used to show all the products in a category. We need to provide a link at the top of the page to add a new product into that category. Accordingly, make the changes marked in Listing 12-13 to the prodviewer.asp page.

Listing 12-13: Code to add a new product

```
<html>
<head>
    <title>Northwind Traders: Viewing Products
    in <% = rsCat("CategoryName") %> Category
    </title>
</head>

<body>
<h1>Products in <% = rsCat("CategoryName") %> Category</h1>
<%
```

Continued

Listing 12-13 *(continued)*

```
    Response.Write "<a href=""editproduct.asp?action=add" _
        & "&catID=" & Request("catID") _
        & """>Add a New Product</a><br>"
%>
<ul>
```

In addition, we need to point to a different page to view the product information. Make the change marked in Listing 12-14 to your prodviewer.asp page.

Listing 12-14: Code to use new product page

```
<ul>

<%
    Do While Not rsProd.EOF
        Response.Write "<li>" _
            & "<a href=""editproduct.asp?prodID=" _
            & rsProd("ProductID") _
            & "&action=view" _
            & """>" _
            & rsProd("ProductName") _
            & "</a>"
        rsProd.MoveNext
    Loop
%>

</ul>
<a href="catviewer.asp">Return to Category List</a>
</body>
</html>
```

The final change required to make the pages flow together is located in the editproduct.asp page. We need to provide a link to both edit and delete the current product. Make the changes marked in Listing 12-15 to editproduct.asp.

Listing 12-15: Code to provide edit and delete links

```
    </title>
</head>
<%
```

```
    If blnIsView Then
%>
    <h1><% = rsProd("ProductName") %></h1>
<%
    Response.Write "<a href=""editproduct.asp?action=edit" _
        & "&prodID=" & rsProd("ProductID") _
        & """>Edit this item</a><br>" & vbCrLf
    Response.Write "<a href=""editproduct.asp?action=del" _
        & "&prodID=" & rsProd("ProductID") _
        & """>Delete this item</a><br>" & vbCrLf
    Else
        Response.Write _
            "<form action=""editproduct.asp"" method=POST>" _
        & vbCrLf
```

That's all there is to it! You can now run your application, starting at
catviewer.asp, and add, modify, and delete records. Don't delete existing records,
which could cause errors later. If you want to test your delete code, add temporary
records first.

Because the code was broken into parts within this chapter, Listing 12-16 shows the
complete code for the editproduct.asp page.

Listing 12-16: **Code for editproduct.asp**

```
<%
Option Explicit
Const Action_Add = "add"
Const Action_View = "view"
Const Action_Delete = "del"
Const Action_Edit = "edit"
Const Validate_Yes = "y"
Const DBLocation = "C:\Inetpub\ds12005\db\nwind.mdb"
Const NoRecordSelected = -9999
Const NoCategorySelected = -9999
%>
<!--#include file="adovbs.inc" -->
<%
'
' Sub Main: holds main processing loop
'
Sub Main()
    Dim strAction        ' As String
    Dim blnIsValidation  ' As Boolean
    Dim lngProdID        ' As Long
    Dim lngCatID         ' As Long
```

Continued

Listing 12-16 *(continued)*

```
'
' Determine the action that was selected
'
strAction = Request("action")

'
' Determine if we are validating a previous
' page's request.
'
blnIsValidation = _
    (Request("val") = Validate_Yes)
' If the parameter is present, determine the
' product ID that was selected.
'
If Request("prodID") <> "" Then
    lngProdID = CLng(Request("prodID"))
End If

'
' If the parameter is present, determine the
' category ID that was selected.
'
If Request("catID") <> "" Then
    lngCatID = CLng(Request("catID"))
End If

Select Case strAction
Case Action_View
    ViewRecord lngProdID
Case Action_Add
    AddRecord lngCatID, blnIsValidation
Case Action_Delete
    DeleteRecord lngProdID, blnIsValidation
Case Action_Edit
    EditRecord lngProdID, blnIsValidation
Case Else
    '
    ' If the action doesn't match up, send the
    ' control back to the category viewer.
    '
    Response.Redirect "catviewer.asp"
    End Select
End Sub

'
' Sub AddRecord
'
```

```
' This routine is called when the page is called
' to add a new product record.
'
Sub AddRecord(lngCatID, blnIsValidation)
    Dim dcnDB
    Dim rsProd

    Set dcnDB = MakeConnection()

    If Not blnIsValidation Then
        ShowPage dcnDB, rsProd, Action_Add, lngCatID
    Else
        Set rsProd = CreateRecordset(dcnDB, _
            NoRecordSelected, False)
        rsProd.AddNew
        StoreData rsProd
        rsProd.Update
        rsProd.Close
        dcnDB.Close
        Response.Redirect "catviewer.asp"
    End If
End Sub


' Sub EditRecord
'
' This routine is called when the page is called
' to edit an existing product record.
'
Sub EditRecord(lngProdID, blnIsValidation)
    Dim dcnDB
    Dim rsProd

    Set dcnDB = MakeConnection()

    Set rsProd = CreateRecordset(dcnDB, _
        lngProdID, False)

    If Not blnIsValidation Then
        ShowPage dcnDB, rsProd, Action_Edit, rsProd("CategoryID")
    Else
        StoreData rsProd
        rsProd.Update
        rsProd.Close
        dcnDB.Close
        Response.Redirect "catviewer.asp"
    End If
End Sub


' Sub DeleteRecord
```

Continued

Listing 12-16 *(continued)*

```
'
' This routine is called when the page is called
' to delete a product record.
'
Sub DeleteRecord(lngProdID, blnIsValidation)

    Dim dcnDB
    Dim rsProd

    Set dcnDB = MakeConnection()
    If Not blnIsValidation Then
        Set rsProd = CreateRecordset(dcnDB, lngProdID, True)
%>
<html>
<head>
<title>Northwind Traders: Confirm Deletion</title>
</head>
<body>
<center>
<h2>Are you sure you wish to delete "<% = rsProd("ProductName")
%>?"</h2>
<table cellspacing=5>
<tr>
<td>
<form action="editproduct.asp" method=POST>
<input type=submit name="cmdOK" value="Yes">
<input type=hidden name="action" value="<% = Action_Delete %>">
<input type=hidden name="prodID" value="<% = lngProdID %>">
<input type=hidden name="val" value="<% = Validate_Yes %>">
</form>
</td>
<td>
<form action="catviewer.asp" method=POST>
<input type=submit name=cmdCancel value="No">
</form>
</td>
</tr>
</table>
</body>
</html>

<%
        rsProd.Close
        dcnDB.Close
    Else
        '
        ' In validation mode, delete the selected
        ' product. This code will only run if the
```

```
                    ' user clicked the Yes button, since the No
                    ' button goes to a different form.
                    '
                    dcnDB.Execute "DELETE FROM Products " _
                        & "WHERE ProductID = " & Request("prodID")

                    dcnDB.Close
                    'Response.Redirect "catviewer.asp"
            End If
    End Sub


    '
    ' Sub ViewRecord
    '
    ' This routine is called when the page is called
    ' to view a single product record.
    '
    Sub ViewRecord(lngProdID)
        Dim dcnDB
        Dim rsProd

        Set dcnDB = MakeConnection()
        Set rsProd = CreateRecordset(dcnDB, lngProdID, True)

        ShowPage dcnDB, rsProd, Action_View, NoCategorySelected

        rsProd.Close
        dcnDB.Close
    End Sub


    '
    ' Function MakeConnection
    '
    ' This routine makes a data connection to the
    ' current database, defined in a constant at the
    ' top of the file.
    '
    Function MakeConnection()
        Dim dcnDB                       ' As ADODB.Connection

        Set dcnDB = Server.CreateObject("ADODB.Connection")
        dcnDB.ConnectionString = _
            "Provider=Microsoft.Jet.OLEDB.3.51;" _
            & "Persist Security Info=False;" _
            & "Data Source=" & DBLocation
        dcnDB.Open

        Set MakeConnection = dcnDB
    End Function
    '
```

Continued

Listing 12-16 *(continued)*

```
'
' Function CreateRecordset
'
' This routine creates/opens a recordset to the
' products table. If the input blnIsReadOnly parameter
' is True, we retrieve strings in place of the foreign
' key values. Otherwise, we return an editable
' recordset of the Products table.
'
Function CreateRecordset(dcnDB, lngProdID, blnIsReadOnly)

    Dim rsProd                 ' As ADODB.Recordset
    Dim strSQL                 ' As String

    If blnIsReadOnly Then
        strSQL = "SELECT Products.*, " _
            & "Suppliers.CompanyName, " _
            & "Categories.CategoryName "_
            & "FROM Suppliers " _
            & "RIGHT OUTER JOIN " _
            & "(Categories RIGHT OUTER JOIN Products ON " _
            & "Categories.CategoryID = Products.CategoryID) ON " _
            & "Suppliers.SupplierID = Products.SupplierID " _
            & "WHERE Products.ProductID = " & lngProdID
            Set rsProd = dcnDB.Execute(strSQL)
    Else
        strSQL = "SELECT * FROM Products"
        If lngProdID <> NoRecordSelected Then
            strSQL = strSQL & " WHERE ProductID = " & lngProdID
        End If
        Set rsProd = Server.CreateObject("ADODB.Recordset")
        rsProd.Open strSQL, dcnDB, _
            adOpenDynamic, adLockPessimistic
    End If

    Set CreateRecordset = rsProd
End Function


'
' Sub StoreData
'
' This routine saves the data from the Request
' object back to the database. It assumes that
' if an AddNew is required, it has already been
' done. In addition, the Update and Close are done
' outside of the routine for consistency.
'
Sub StoreData(rsProd)
```

```
      rsProd("ProductName") = Request("txtProductName")
      rsProd("SupplierID") = Request("cboSupplier")
      rsProd("CategoryID") = Request("cboCategory")
      rsProd("QuantityPerUnit") = Request("txtQuantityPerUnit")
      rsProd("UnitPrice") = Request("txtUnitPrice")
      rsProd("UnitsInStock") = Request("txtUnitsInStock")
      rsProd("UnitsOnOrder") = Request("txtUnitsOnOrder")
      rsProd("ReorderLevel") = Request("txtReorderLevel")
      rsProd("Discontinued") = _
         (Request("optDiscontinued") = "Yes")

End Sub
'
' Sub ShowPage
'
' This routine constructs the form based on the current
' page mode. If view only, no input boxes are shown. If
' add, the input boxes are empty. If edit, the input boxes
' are filled appropriately.
'
Sub ShowPage(dcnDB, rsProd, strMode, lngCatID)
   Dim blnIsView     ' As Boolean
   Dim blnIsEdit     ' As Boolean
   Dim blnIsAdd      ' As Boolean
   Dim rsCat         ' As ADODB.Recordset
   Dim rsSupp        ' As ADODB.Recordset

   '
   ' Define a flag so we don't have to
   ' keep comparing throughout the routine.
   '
   blnIsView = (strMode = Action_View)
   blnIsEdit = (strMode = Action_Edit)
   blnIsAdd = (strMode = Action_Add)
%>
<html>
<head>
   <title>Northwind Traders:
<%
   If blnIsView Then
%>    Product Information for <% = rsProd("ProductName") %>
<%
   ElseIf blnIsAdd Then
%>    Add New Product
<%
   ElseIf blnIsEdit Then
%>    Edit Product #<% = rsProd("ProductID") %>
         - <% = rsProd("ProductName") %>
<%
```

Continued

Listing 12-16 *(continued)*

```asp
    End If
%>
    </title>
</head>
<%
    If blnIsView Then
%>
    <h1><% = rsProd("ProductName") %></h1>
<%
    Response.write "<a href=""editproduct.asp?action=edit" _
        & "&prodID=" & rsProd("ProductID") _
        & """>Edit this item</a><br>" & vbCrLf
    Response.write "<a href=""editproduct.asp?action=del" _
        & "&prodID=" & rsProd("ProductID") _
        & """>Delete this item</a><br>" & vbCrLf
    Else
        Response.Write _
            "<form action=""editproduct.asp"" method=POST>" _
            & vbCrLf
        If blnIsAdd Then
            Response.Write "<h1>Add New Product</h1>" & vbCrLf
            Response.Write "<input type=hidden name=action " _
                & "value=" & Action_Add & ">" & vbCrLf
        ElseIf blnIsEdit Then
            Response.Write "<h1>Edit Product</h1>" & vbCrLf
            Response.Write "<input type=hidden name=action " _
                & "value=" & Action_Edit & ">" & vbCrLf
            Response.write "<input type=hidden name=prodID " _
                & "value=""" & rsProd("ProductID") & """>" & vbCrLf
        End If
        Response.Write "<input type=hidden name=val value=" _
            & Validate_Yes & ">" & vbCrLf
    End If
%>
<table cellpadding=5 border=0>
<% If Not blnIsView Then %>
<tr>
    <td>Product Name:</td>
    <td><input type="Text" name="txtProductName" size="30"
    <%
        If blnIsEdit Then
            Response.Write "value=""" _
                & rsProd("ProductName") & """"
        End If
    %>
    ></td>
</tr>
<% End If %>
```

```
<tr>
    <td>Category:</td>
    <td>
    <% If blnIsView Then
          Response.Write rsProd("CategoryName")
      Else
          Set rsCat =dcnDB.Execute("SELECT * FROM Categories " _
            & " ORDER BY CategoryName")
          Response.Write _
            "<select name=""cboCategory"">" & vbCrLf
          Response.Write "<option value=""0"""
          If lngCatID = 0 Then Response.Write " SELECTED"
          Response.Write ">None Selected" & vbCrLf
          Do While Not rsCat.EOF
              Response.Write "<option value=""" _
                & rsCat("CategoryID") & """"
              If lngCatID = rsCat("CategoryID") Then
                  Response.Write " SELECTED"
              End If
              Response.Write ">" & rsCat("CategoryName") & vbCrLf
              rsCat.MoveNext
          Loop
          rsCat.Close
      End If
    %>
    </td>
</tr>
<tr>
    <td>Supplier:</td>
    <td>
    <% If blnIsView Then
          Response.Write rsProd("CompanyName")
      Else
          Set rsCat = dcnDB.Execute("SELECT * FROM Suppliers " _
            & " ORDER BY CompanyName")
          Response.Write _
            "<select name=""cboSupplier"">" & vbCrLf
          Response.Write _
            "<option value=""0"">None Selected" & vbCrLf
          Do While Not rsCat.EOF
              Response.Write "<option value=""" _
                & rsCat("SupplierID") & """"
              If blnIsEdit Then
                  If rsProd("SupplierID")=rsCat("SupplierID") Then
                      Response.Write " SELECTED"
                  End If
              End If
              Response.Write ">" & rsCat("CompanyName") & vbCrLf
              rsCat.MoveNext
          Loop
          rsCat.Close
```

Continued

Listing 12-16 *(continued)*

```
            End If
    %>
    </td>
</tr>
<tr>
    <td>Quantity Per Unit:</td>
    <td>
    <% If blnIsView Then
            Response.Write rsProd("QuantityPerUnit")
        Else
    %>
        <input type="Text" name="txtQuantityPerUnit" size="30" <%
            If blnIsEdit Then
                Response.Write "value=""" _
                    & rsProd("QuantityPerUnit") & """"
            End If
    %>
    >
    <%
        End If
    %>
    </td>
</tr>
<tr>
    <td>Unit Price:</td>
    <td>
    <% If blnIsView Then
            Response.Write FormatCurrency(rsProd("UnitPrice"))
        Else
    %>
        <input type="Text" name="txtUnitPrice" size="10"<%
            If blnIsEdit Then
                Response.Write "value=""" _
                    & rsProd("UnitPrice") & """"
            End If
    %>
    >
    <%
        End If
    %>
    </td>
</tr>
<tr>
    <td>Units In Stock:</td>
    <td>
    <% If blnIsView Then
            Response.Write rsProd("UnitsInStock")
        Else
```

```
        %>
    <input type="Text" name="txtUnitsInStock" size="10"<%
            If blnIsEdit Then
                Response.Write "value="""" _
                    & rsProd("UnitsInStock") & """"
            End If
        %>
        >
        <%
            End If
        %>
    </td>
</tr>
<tr>
    <td>Units on Order:</td>
    <td>
    <% If blnIsView Then
            Response.Write rsProd("UnitsOnOrder")
        Else
    %>
    <input type="Text" name="txtUnitsOnOrder" size="10"<%
            If blnIsEdit Then
                Response.Write "value="""" _
                    & rsProd("UnitsOnOrder") & """"
            End If
        %>
        >
        <%
            End If
        %>
    </td>
</tr>
<tr>
    <td>Reorder Level:</td>
    <td>
    <% If blnIsView Then
            Response.Write rsProd("ReorderLevel")
        Else
    %>
    <input type="Text" name="txtReorderLevel" size="10"<%
            If blnIsEdit Then
                Response.Write "value="""" _
                    & rsProd("ReorderLevel") & """"
            End If
        %>
        >
        <%
            End If
        %>
    </td>
</tr>
```

Continued

Listing 12-16 *(continued)*

```
<tr>
    <td>Discontinued:</td>
    <td>
    <% If blnIsView Then
            If rsProd("Discontinued") = True Then
                Response.Write "Yes"
            Else
                Response.Write "No"
            End If
        Else
    %>
    <input type="Radio" name="optDiscontinued" value="No" <%
        If blnIsEdit Then
            If rsProd("Discontinued") = False Then
                Response.Write "CHECKED"
            End If
        End If
    %>No

    <input type="Radio" name="optDiscontinued" value="Yes"<%
        If blnIsEdit Then
            If rsProd("Discontinued") = True Then
                Response.Write "CHECKED"
            End If
        End If
    %>Yes
    <%
        End If
    %>
    </td>
</tr>
<%
    If Not blnIsView Then
%>
<tr>
    <td colspan=2 align=center>
    <input type="submit" name="cmdOK" value="Save">
    <input type="reset" name="cmdClear" value="Reset Form">
    </td>
</tr>
<%
    End If
%>
</table>
<%
    If Not blnIsView then Response.Write "</form>"
%>
</body>
```

```
</html>
<%
End Sub

'
' After reading the entire page, code begins executing here.
'
Call Main

%>
```

Summary

ASP was designed as an easy way to publish and access a database from the Web. As you can see from these relatively simple examples, you can do a lot with ASP while avoiding extremely complex code. Make sure to familiarize yourself with the examples in this chapter — they will be the bread and butter of most of your future sites. Even though your HTML layout may be different, you can use this code to show or edit a record throughout your work.

✦   ✦   ✦

Enhancing the Data Browser

✦   ✦   ✦   ✦

In This Chapter

Create a method to page through large amounts of data

Use ADO properties for paging through data quickly

Design a security scheme for your application

Creating a Paging Mechanism

✦   ✦   ✦   ✦

In the preceding applications, the result sets have been fairly small and could fit on one page. However, other tables in the same database (Northwind Traders) are quite large and would take forever to scroll through on a single page. For this reason, this section introduces a method that you can use to let the user page through data. The pages will include all of the following features:

✦ Ability to jump to a particular page

✦ Forward/backward directional paging

✦ Multiple sort columns

✦ Use of ADO recordset properties to automate the paging calculations

This example uses the Northwind Traders Access database installed with both Microsoft Access and Microsoft Visual Studio. You can use any database and table with the techniques covered in this chapter, but we'll be focusing on the Northwind Orders table.

Creating the Basic Browser

To get started, let's create the connection and record-loading code. This page will be designed using the Sub Main method covered in Chapter 12. Because the page will be used in several different ways, this method makes the code easier to understand. Add the code in Listing 13-1 to a new file called orderbrowser.asp.

Listing 13-1: **Initial code for orderbrowser.asp**

```
<%
    Option Explicit
    Const DBLOCATION = "C:\NWind.mdb"
%>
<!--#include file="adovbs.inc" -->
<%

Function OpenDatabase()

    Dim dcnDB         ' As ADODB.Connection
    Set dcnDB = Server.CreateObject("ADODB.Connection")
    dcnDB.ConnectionString = _
        "Provider=Microsoft.Jet.OLEDB.3.51;" _
            & "Persist Security Info=False;Data Source=" _
            & DBLOCATION
    dcnDB.Open
    Set OpenDatabase = dcnDB

End Function

'----------------------------------------------------------

Function RetrieveData(dcnDB)

    Dim rsData        ' As ADODB.Recordset
    Dim strSQL        ' As String

    strSQL = "SELECT Orders.OrderID, " _
        & "Customers.CompanyName,  " _
        & "[Employees].[LastName] & ', ' & " _
        & "[Employees].[FirstName] AS Salesperson, " _
        & "Orders.OrderDate, " _
        & "Orders.RequiredDate, " _
        & "Orders.ShippedDate, " _
        & "Shippers.CompanyName AS ShipperName " _
        & "FROM Shippers " _
        & "INNER JOIN (Employees " _
        & "INNER JOIN (Customers " _
        & "INNER JOIN Orders " _
        & "ON Customers.CustomerID = Orders.CustomerID) " _
        & "ON Employees.EmployeeID = Orders.EmployeeID) " _
        & "ON Shippers.ShipperID = Orders.ShipVia" _
        & " ORDER BY Customers.CompanyName, OrderID"

    Set rsData = Server.CreateObject("ADODB.Recordset")
    rsData.CursorLocation = adUseClient
    rsData.Open strSQL, dcnDB, adOpenStatic, _
        adLockReadOnly, adCmdText
```

```
      Set RetrieveData = rsData
End Function

'-----------------------------------------------------------
Sub DisplayData(rsData)
%>
<HTML>
<HEAD>
    <TITLE>Northwind Trades - Order Browser</TITLE>
</HEAD>
<BODY BGCOLOR="#FFFFFF">
<H1>Current Orders</H1>

<TABLE BORDER=1>
<TR>
    <TH>Order ID</TH>
    <TH>Company</TH>
    <TH>Salesperson</TH>
    <TH>Order Date</TH>
    <TH>Date Required</TH>
    <TH>Date Shipped</TH>
    <TH>Shipper</TH>
</TR>
<%
    Do While Not rsData.EOF
%>
<TR>
    <TD><% = rsData("OrderID") %></TD>
    <TD><% = rsData("CompanyName") %></TD>
    <TD><% = rsData("Salesperson") %></TD>
    <TD><% = rsData("OrderDate") %></TD>
    <TD><% = rsData("RequiredDate") %></TD>
    <TD><% = rsData("ShippedDate") %></TD>
    <TD><% = rsData("ShipperName") %></TD>
</TR>
<%
      rsData.MoveNext
    Loop
%>
</TABLE>
</BODY>
</HTML>
<%
End Sub

'-----------------------------------------------------------
Sub Main()

    Dim dcnDB        ' As ADODB.Connection
```

Continued

Listing 13-1 *(continued)*

```
    Dim rsData        ' As ADODB.Recordset

    Set dcnDB = OpenDatabase()
    Set rsData = RetrieveData(dcnDB)
    DisplayData(rsData)

    rsData.Close
    dcnDB.Close

End Sub

'
' This calls the Main subroutine to get the
' page started.
'
Call Main

%>
```

With a few exceptions, this is your basic data-browsing screen. A few important things to note as we expand the page's code:

✦ The retrieval query is actually in the page and not in a stored procedure, because the query will be changed later when we add more sorting options to the page.

✦ The database name is defined in a constant at the top of the page. Be sure you point to the actual pathname of your database for this page to work.

✦ We include the adovbs.inc file at the top of the page. With the code in Listing 13-1, this file needs to be in the same directory as the ASP file. However, you can point to any valid pathname using either the file or virtual argument within the SSI directive.

You can try this page out, but it may take a little while to run. There are over 800 orders in the database, and all of the orders will be printed the first time you run the page. The orders will be sorted by company name and then by order ID. This arrangement is an arbitrary but common choice of sort keys. In a subsequent section, you'll see how to change the sorting to enable the user to pick a column for sorting.

Adding Paging Capabilities

The next step is to add the ability to page through data. We will show a much smaller number of records per page and provide the ability to go forward, backward, or jump to a particular page. The ADO Recordset object provides much of this functionality for us. In earlier versions of ADO, this work had to be done by hand. Listing 13-2 shows the revised code, which provides the following features:

✦ Records can be shown in a configurable number of records-per-page

✦ The user can jump to a particular page from a link at the top of the page

✦ The user can move forwards and backwards through the list

The new code is shown in boldface to make it easier to find.

Listing 13-2: **Revised code for orderbrowser.asp**

```
<%
    Option Explicit
    Const DBLOCATION = "C:\NWind.mdb"
    Const RECORDSPERPAGE = 40
%>
<!--#include file="adovbs.inc" -->
<%

Function OpenDatabase()

    Dim dcnDB        ' As ADODB.Connection
    Set dcnDB = Server.CreateObject("ADODB.Connection")
    dcnDB.ConnectionString = _
        "Provider=Microsoft.Jet.OLEDB.3.51;" _
          & "Persist Security Info=False;Data Source=" _
          & DBLOCATION
    dcnDB.Open
    Set OpenDatabase = dcnDB

End Function

'------------------------------------------------------------

Function RetrieveData(dcnDB)

    Dim rsData       ' As ADODB.Recordset
    Dim strSQL       ' As String
```

Continued

Listing 13-2 *(continued)*

```
    strSQL = "SELECT Orders.OrderID, " _
        & "Customers.CompanyName,  " _
        & "[Employees].[LastName] & ', ' & " _
        & "[Employees].[FirstName] AS Salesperson, " _
        & "Orders.OrderDate, " _
        & "Orders.RequiredDate, " _
        & "Orders.ShippedDate, " _
        & "Shippers.CompanyName AS ShipperName " _
        & "FROM Shippers " _
        & "INNER JOIN (Employees " _
        & "INNER JOIN (Customers " _
        & "INNER JOIN Orders " _
        & "ON Customers.CustomerID = Orders.CustomerID) " _
        & "ON Employees.EmployeeID = Orders.EmployeeID) " _
        & "ON Shippers.ShipperID = Orders.ShipVia" _
        & " ORDER BY Customers.CompanyName, OrderID"

    Set rsData = Server.CreateObject("ADODB.Recordset")
    rsData.CursorLocation = adUseClient
    rsData.Open strSQL, dcnDB, adOpenStatic, _
        adLockReadOnly, adCmdText
    Set RetrieveData = rsData
End Function

'-----------------------------------------------------------
Sub DisplayData(rsData, intPageNum)
    Dim intCount        ' As Integer

%>
<HTML>
<HEAD>
    <TITLE>Northwind Trades - Order Browser
    - Page <% = intPageNum %> of <% = rsData.PageCount
%></TITLE>
</HEAD>

<BODY BGCOLOR="#FFFFFF">
<H1>Current Orders</H1>
<%
    DisplayPageLinks rsData, intPageNum
    DisplayNavigation rsData, intPageNum
%>
<TABLE BORDER=1>
<TR>
    <TH>Order ID</TH>
    <TH>Company</TH>
    <TH>Salesperson</TH>
    <TH>Order Date</TH>
```

```
    <TH>Date Required</TH>
    <TH>Date Shipped</TH>
    <TH>Shipper</TH>
</TR>
<%
    rsData.AbsolutePage = intPageNum
    For intCount = 1 To rsData.PageSize

%>
<TR>
    <TD><% = rsData("OrderID") %></TD>
    <TD><% = rsData("CompanyName") %></TD>
    <TD><% = rsData("Salesperson") %></TD>
    <TD><% = rsData("OrderDate") %></TD>
    <TD><% = rsData("RequiredDate") %></TD>
    <TD><% = rsData("ShippedDate") %></TD>
    <TD><% = rsData("ShipperName") %></TD>
</TR>
<%
        rsData.MoveNext
        If rsData.EOF Then Exit For
    Next   ' intCount
%>
</TABLE>
<%
    DisplayNavigation rsData, intPageNum
%>
</BODY>
</HTML>
<%
End Sub


'-------------------------------------------------------------

Sub DisplayPageLinks(rsData, intPageNum)

    Dim i     ' As Integer
    Response.Write "<P>Jump to Page:"

    For i = 1 To rsData.PageCount
        If i = intPageNum Then
            Response.Write i & " "
        Else
            Response.Write "<a href=""" _
                & Request.ServerVariables("SCRIPT_NAME") _
                & "?pn=" & i _
                & """>" & i & "</a> "
        End If
    Next ' i
```

Continued

Listing 13-2 *(continued)*

```
        Response.Write "</P>"

End Sub

'-------------------------------------------------------------
Sub DisplayNavigation(rsData, intPageNum)
    Response.Write "<P>"
    If intPageNum > 1 Then
        Response.Write "<< <a href=""" _
            & Request.ServerVariables("SCRIPT_NAME") _
            & "?pn=" & intPageNum - 1 _
            & """>Previous Page</a>   "
    End If

    If intPageNum < rsData.PageCount Then
        Response.Write "<a href=""" _
            & Request.ServerVariables("SCRIPT_NAME") _
            & "?pn=" & intPageNum + 1 _
            & """>Next Page ></a> "
    End If
    Response.Write "</P>"
End Sub

'-------------------------------------------------------------
Sub Main()

    Dim dcnDB      ' As ADODB.Connection
    Dim rsData     ' As ADODB.Recordset
    Dim intPageNum ' As Integer

    Set dcnDB = OpenDatabase()
    Set rsData = RetrieveData(dcnDB)
    If Request("pn") <> "" Then
        intPageNum = CInt(Request("pn"))
    Else
        intPageNum = 1
    End If
    rsData.PageSize = RECORDSPERPAGE

    DisplayData rsData, intPageNum

    rsData.Close
    dcnDB.Close

End Sub
```

```
'
' This calls the Main subroutine to get the
' page started.
'
Call Main

%>
```

The first change is a new constant, RECORDSPERPAGE. This constant's value is somewhat arbitrary, but it specifies the maximum number of records that will be shown on a page. You want to pick a number that doesn't generate too many entries on a page, but at the same time doesn't cause the user to page through hundreds of smaller pages. For a total size of about 800 records, 40 records per page will create about 20 pages to view.

For the next change, jump down to the DisplayData subroutine. This routine now accepts a page number to show, and has a temporary counting variable declared. Before showing any rows of data, this routine navigates to the correct page in the recordset specified by the page number being passed in. The ADO Recordset object is configured later with a value for its PageSize property. This value in turn creates a new value in the PageCount property. The new loop counts to a maximum number of records, specified by the PageSize property, but exits if it runs out of records first. This arrangement takes care of the case in which you don't have an even multiple of records, as in this set of data.

Besides the page counting logic, there are also calls to display navigation on the page. The navigation is created in the DisplayPageLinks routine, which shows page numbers, and the DisplayNavigation routine, which shows a Previous and Next link. In both routines, there is logic to make sure the user can't go before the first page or after the last page. Also, the user can't click on the number of the current page.

The final change at this point is in the Sub Main routine. We will be using a query string variable to specify the desired page number. This variable, named pn, is checked in this routine and stored in the intPageNum variable. If this is the first time, we default to the first page for viewing. We also set the page size of the recordset to the constant defined at the top. This setting enables us to use the AbsolutePage property in the DisplayData routine to jump to the first record on page 15 of the data, for instance, which is significantly faster than any other method of finding a particular record.

When you run the page, your display will resemble Figure 13-1. Note the page links, the navigation links, and the customized title bar for this page.

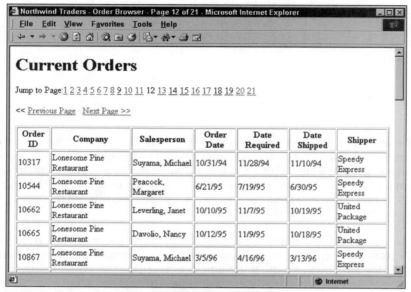

Figure 13-1: Order browser, with paging capabilities

Adding Sorting Features

In other Windows applications, you can sort data simply by clicking the column heading. In addition, clicking again on the same column heading reverses the sort. This functionality is the next feature we'll add to the browser. As marked in Listing 13-3, several changes are required to make this work.

Listing 13-3: **Code with sorting features**

```
<%
    Option Explicit
    Const DBLOCATION = "C:\NWind.mdb"
    Const RECORDSPERPAGE = 40
%>
<!--#include file="adovbs.inc" -->
<%

Function OpenDatabase()

    Dim dcnDB       ' As ADODB.Connection
    Set dcnDB = Server.CreateObject("ADODB.Connection")
    dcnDB.ConnectionString = _
```

```
            "Provider=Microsoft.Jet.OLEDB.3.51;" _
               & "Persist Security Info=False;Data Source=" _
               & DBLOCATION
         dcnDB.Open
         Set OpenDatabase = dcnDB

      End Function

      '-----------------------------------------------------------

      Function RetrieveData(dcnDB, strSortFlds, strSortOrder)

         Dim rsData      ' As ADODB.Recordset
         Dim strSQL      ' As String

         strSQL = "SELECT Orders.OrderID, " _
            & "Customers.CompanyName,  " _
            & "[Employees].[LastName] & ', ' & " _
            & "[Employees].[FirstName] AS Salesperson, " _
            & "Orders.OrderDate, " _
            & "Orders.RequiredDate, " _
            & "Orders.ShippedDate, " _
            & "Shippers.CompanyName AS ShipperName " _
            & "FROM Shippers " _
            & "INNER JOIN (Employees " _
            & "INNER JOIN (Customers " _
            & "INNER JOIN Orders " _
            & "ON Customers.CustomerID = Orders.CustomerID) " _
            & "ON Employees.EmployeeID = Orders.EmployeeID) " _
            & "ON Shippers.ShipperID = Orders.ShipVia" _
            & " ORDER BY " & strSortFlds & " " & strSortOrder

         Set rsData = Server.CreateObject("ADODB.Recordset")
         rsData.CursorLocation = adUseClient
         rsData.Open strSQL, dcnDB, adOpenStatic, _
            adLockReadOnly, adCmdText
         Set RetrieveData = rsData
      End Function

      '-----------------------------------------------------------

      Sub DisplayData(rsData, intPageNum, _
         strSortFlds, strSortOrder)

         Dim intCount         ' As Integer

      %>
      <HTML>
      <HEAD>
         <TITLE>Northwind Traders - Order Browser
```

Continued

Listing 13-3 *(continued)*

```asp
   - Page <% = intPageNum %> of <% = rsData.PageCount
%></TITLE>
</HEAD>

<BODY BGCOLOR="#FFFFFF">
<H1>Current Orders</H1>
<%
   DisplayPageLinks rsData, intPageNum, _
      strSortFlds, strSortOrder
   DisplayNavigation rsData, intPageNum, _
      strSortFlds, strSortOrder
%>
<TABLE BORDER=1>
<TR>
   <TH><% Response.Write CreateHeading(intPageNum, _
      "Order ID", "1", strSortFlds, strSortOrder) %></TH>
   <TH><% Response.Write CreateHeading(intPageNum, _
      "Company", "2", strSortFlds, strSortOrder) %></TH>
   <TH><% Response.Write CreateHeading(intPageNum, _
      "Salesperson", "3", strSortFlds, strSortOrder) %></TH>
   <TH><% Response.Write CreateHeading(intPageNum, _
      "Order Date", "4", strSortFlds, strSortOrder) %></TH>
   <TH><% Response.Write CreateHeading(intPageNum, _
      "Date Required", "5", strSortFlds, strSortOrder) %></TH>
   <TH><% Response.Write CreateHeading(intPageNum, _
      "Date Shipped", "6", strSortFlds, strSortOrder) %></TH>
   <TH><% Response.Write CreateHeading(intPageNum, _
      "Shipper", "7", strSortFlds, strSortOrder) %></TH>
</TR>
<%
   rsData.AbsolutePage = intPageNum
   For intCount = 1 To rsData.PageSize

%>
<TR>
   <TD><% = rsData("OrderID") %></TD>
   <TD><% = rsData("CompanyName") %></TD>
   <TD><% = rsData("Salesperson") %></TD>
   <TD><% = rsData("OrderDate") %></TD>
   <TD><% = rsData("RequiredDate") %></TD>
   <TD><% = rsData("ShippedDate") %></TD>
   <TD><% = rsData("ShipperName") %></TD>
</TR>
<%
    rsData.MoveNext
    If rsData.EOF Then Exit For
   Next   ' intCount
%>
```

```
</TABLE>
<%
   DisplayNavigation rsData, intPageNum, _
      strSortFlds, strSortOrder
%>
</BODY>
</HTML>
<%
End Sub

'------------------------------------------------------------
Function CreateHeading(intPageNum, strTitle, strNewSort, _
   strOldSort, strOldOrder)
   Dim strNewOrder        ' As String

   If strNewSort = strOldSort Then
      If strOldOrder = "ASC" Then
         strNewOrder = "DESC"
      Else
         strNewOrder = "ASC"
      End If
   Else
      strNewOrder = "ASC"
   End If

   CreateHeading = "<a href="""" _
      & Request.ServerVariables("SCRIPT_NAME") _
      & "?pn=" & intPageNum _
      & "&so=" & strNewSort _
      & "&sd=" & strNewOrder _
      & """>" & strTitle & "</a>"
End Function

'------------------------------------------------------------
Sub DisplayPageLinks(rsData, intPageNum, _
   strSortFlds, strSortOrder)

   Dim i     ' As Integer
   Response.Write "<P>Jump to Page:"

   For i = 1 To rsData.PageCount
      If i = intPageNum Then
         Response.Write i & " "
      Else
         Response.Write "<a href="""" _
            & Request.ServerVariables("SCRIPT_NAME") _
            & "?pn=" & i _
            & "&so=" & strSortFlds _
            & "&sd=" & strSortOrder _
```

Continued

Listing 13-3 *(continued)*

```
                & """>" & i & "</a> "
        End If
    Next ' i

    Response.Write "</P>"

End Sub

'------------------------------------------------------------
Sub DisplayNavigation(rsData, intPageNum, _
    strSortFlds, strSortOrder)

    Response.Write "<P>"
    If intPageNum > 1 Then
        Response.Write "<< <a href="""" _
            & Request.ServerVariables("SCRIPT_NAME") _
            & "?pn=" & intPageNum - 1 _
            & "&so=" & strSortFlds _
            & "&sd=" & strSortOrder _
            & """>Previous Page</a>   "
    End If

    If intPageNum < rsData.PageCount Then
        Response.Write "<a href="""" _
            & Request.ServerVariables("SCRIPT_NAME") _
            & "?pn=" & intPageNum + 1 _
            & "&so=" & strSortFlds _
            & "&sd=" & strSortOrder _
            & """>Next Page ></a> "
    End If
    Response.Write "</P>"
End Sub

'------------------------------------------------------------
Sub Main()

    Dim dcnDB          ' As ADODB.Connection
    Dim rsData         ' As ADODB.Recordset
    Dim intPageNum     ' As Integer
    Dim strSortFlds    ' As String
    Dim strSortOrder   ' As String

    If Request("so") <> "" Then
        strSortFlds = Request("so")
    Else
        strSortFlds = "1"
    End If
```

```
    If Request("sd") <> "" Then
        strSortOrder = Request("sd")
    Else
        strSortOrder = "ASC"
    End If

    If Request("pn") <> "" Then
        intPageNum = CInt(Request("pn"))
    Else
        intPageNum = 1
    End If

    Set dcnDB = OpenDatabase()
    Set rsData = RetrieveData(dcnDB, strSortFlds, _
        strSortOrder)

    rsData.PageSize = RECORDSPERPAGE

    DisplayData rsData, intPageNum, _
        strSortFlds, strSortOrder

    rsData.Close
    dcnDB.Close

End Sub

'
' This calls the Main subroutine to get the
' page started.
'
Call Main

%>
```

This feature didn't take quite as much code as the last paging feature, but this code may be more confusing. To get started, we are using two new query string variables:

✦ so — Sort Order, which specifies the column number used to sort. SQL can sort based on a column position or on the column name.

✦ sd — Sort Direction, which is either ASC (ascending) or DESC (descending).

In general, we need these variables anywhere we are constructing a link. As a result, the old routines that call the navigation constructors all have to deal with these values.

The first change is in the `RetrieveData` routine, which now uses the sort field and sort direction as the last part of the query. This arrangement is the main reason we have the query directly in the ASP. If we use a predefined query, we would have to resort the data after it is retrieved.

The next change is in the column headings, which are now links. The function is used to construct each URL. Based on the current sort order and the selected field, the link will cause the column to be sorted ascending, or if the user is clicking the same column, descending. This setting mirrors the behavior of Windows Explorer and other windows that use the `ListView` control available in Windows.

In addition, the navigation creation subroutines are passed the sort order and sort column so that they can construct the URL correctly for the next page.

> **Tip**
>
> When you run this page, you can click on a column to sort by that data. As you page through the data, the sort will remain the same, because the sort column and direction are being passed along every time.

Wrapping Up

As you can see, the ADO `Recordset` does a lot of the messy work for you in determining how many records with which you have to deal. `Recordset` has some internal performance enhancements that make it very fast to position to a particular page of data, so you don't have to do lots of `MoveNext` commands. Using that feature and some ingenuity, you can create your own paging system without too much work. This page's technology can be adapted for any type of data you are viewing. In addition, you can add on additional pages for drilldown capabilities, as we'll do in the next section of this chapter.

Creating Application Security

One of the biggest problems on the Web is that your applications are open to all sorts of attacks. Even law enforcement officials aren't immune from these attacks, as evidenced by the number of attacks on U.S. government computers every year. While your application may not be as sensitive as Department of Defense applications, your application nonetheless deserves good security.

This section will show you some simple ways to add basic security to your applications. While server-level features such as SSL and encryption are IIS-specific and beyond the scope of this book, the techniques in this section will supplement the security provided by these critical protocols. A site with only one or the other type of security is still vulnerable. Even having both doesn't guarantee perfect security; however, it will slow down most attacks on your system.

The Target: Our Order Status Application

The target application around which we'll be wrapping security is the order status application that we started in the preceding section of this chapter. First, we will add a second page to this application for showing the details of a particular order. The code for this page is shown in Listing 13-4, and the revised list page is shown in Listing 13-5. Because the changes required in Listing 13-5 are in the DisplayData subroutine, only that routine is listed here.

Listing 13-4: **vieworder.asp code**

```
<%
    Option Explicit
    Const DBLOCATION = "C:\NWind.mdb"

%>
<!--#include file="adovbs.inc" -->
<%

Function OpenDatabase()

    Dim dcnDB       ' As ADODB.Connection
    Set dcnDB = Server.CreateObject("ADODB.Connection")
    dcnDB.ConnectionString = _
        "Provider=Microsoft.Jet.OLEDB.3.51;" _
            & "Persist Security Info=False;Data Source=" _
            & DBLOCATION
    dcnDB.Open
    Set OpenDatabase = dcnDB

End Function

'------------------------------------------------------------

Function RetrieveData(dcnDB, intOrderID)

    Dim rsData      ' As ADODB.Recordset
    Dim strSQL      ' As String

    strSQL = "SELECT Orders.OrderID, " _
        & "Customers.ContactName, " _
        & "Customers.ContactTitle, " _
        & "Customers.CompanyName, " _
        & "Customers.Address, " _
        & "Customers.City, " _
        & "Customers.Region, " _
```

Continued

Listing 13-4 *(continued)*

```
            & "Customers.PostalCode, " _
            & "Customers.Country, " _
            & "[Employees].[LastName] & ', ' & " _
            & "[Employees].[FirstName] AS Salesperson, " _
            & "Orders.ShipName, " _
            & "Orders.ShipAddress, " _
            & "Orders.ShipCity, " _
            & "Orders.ShipRegion, " _
            & "Orders.ShipPostalCode, " _
            & "Orders.ShipCountry, " _
            & "Orders.OrderDate, " _
            & "Orders.RequiredDate, " _
            & "Orders.ShippedDate, " _
            & "Orders.Freight, " _
            & "Shippers.CompanyName AS ShipperName " _
            & "FROM Shippers " _
            & "INNER JOIN (Employees " _
            & "INNER JOIN (Customers " _
            & "INNER JOIN Orders " _
            & "ON Customers.CustomerID = Orders.CustomerID) " _
            & "ON Employees.EmployeeID = Orders.EmployeeID) " _
            & "ON Shippers.ShipperID = Orders.ShipVia" _
            & " WHERE Orders.OrderID = " & intOrderID

    Set rsData = Server.CreateObject("ADODB.Recordset")
    rsData.CursorLocation = adUseClient
    rsData.Open strSQL, dcnDB, adOpenStatic, _
        adLockReadOnly, adCmdText
    Set RetrieveData = rsData
End Function

'-------------------------------------------------------------
Sub DisplayData(dcnDB, rsData)
    Dim rsDetails      ' As ADODB.Recordset
    Dim strSQL         ' As String
    Dim curTotal       ' As Currency

%>

<html>
<head>
    <title>Northwind Traders -
    Order #<% = rsData("OrderID") %></title>
</head>
<body bgcolor=#FFFFFF>
<h1>Customer Order #<% = rsData("OrderID") %></h1>

<table width=500 border=1 cellpadding=3>
```

```
<tr>
    <td colspan=2 align=middle
    valign=top bgcolor=#0000CC width=250>
    <font color=#FFFFFF><b>Billing Address</b></font>
    </td>
    <td colspan=2 align=middle
    valign=top bgcolor=#0000CC width=250>
    <font color=#FFFFFF><b>Shipping Address</b></font>
    </td>
</tr>
<tr>
    <td colspan=2 valign=top align=middle>
    <% = rsData("ContactName") %>,
    <% = rsData("ContactTitle") %><br>
    <% = rsData("CompanyName") %><br>
    <% = rsData("Address") %><br>
    <% = rsData("City") %> 
    <% = rsData("Region") %> 
    <% = rsData("PostalCode") %><br>
    <% = rsData("Country") %><br>
    </td>
    <td colspan=2 valign=top align=middle>
    <% = rsData("ShipName") %><br>
    <% = rsData("ShipAddress") %><br>
    <% = rsData("ShipCity") %> 
    <% = rsData("ShipRegion") %> 
    <% = rsData("ShipPostalCode") %><br>
    <% = rsData("ShipCountry") %><br>
    </td>
</tr>

<tr>
    <td align=middle valign=top bgcolor=#0000CC width=250>
    <font color=#FFFFFF><b>Order Date</b></font>
    </td>
    <td align=middle valign=top bgcolor=#0000CC width=250>
    <font color=#FFFFFF><b>Required Date</b></font>
    </td>
    <td align=middle valign=top bgcolor=#0000CC width=250>
    <font color=#FFFFFF><b>Shipped Date</b></font>
    </td>
    <td align=middle valign=top bgcolor=#0000CC width=250>
    <font color=#FFFFFF><b>Ship Via</b></font>
    </td>
</tr>
<tr>
    <td align=middle width=125>
    <% = rsData("OrderDate") %></td>
    <td align=middle width=125>
```

Continued

Listing 13-4 *(continued)*

```
    <% = rsData("RequiredDate") %></td>
    <td align=middle width=125>
    <% = rsData("ShippedDate") %></td>
    <td align=middle width=125>
    <% = rsData("ShipperName") %></td>
</tr>
</table>

<p>

<table width=640 border=1 cellpadding=3>
<tr>
    <td align=middle valign=top bgcolor=#0000CC width=100>
    <font color=#FFFFFF><b>Quantity</b></font>
    </td>
    <td align=middle valign=top bgcolor=#0000CC width=300>
    <font color=#FFFFFF><b>Description</b></font>
    </td>
    <td align=middle valign=top bgcolor=#0000CC width=120>
    <font color=#FFFFFF><b>Unit Price</b></font>
    </td>
    <td align=middle valign=top bgcolor=#0000CC width=120>
    <font color=#FFFFFF><b>Subtotal</b></font>
    </td>
</tr>

<%
    strSQL = "SELECT [Order Details].Quantity, " _
        & " Products.ProductName, " _
        & " [Order Details].UnitPrice, " _
        & " [Order Details].Quantity * " _
        & " [Order Details].[UnitPrice] AS Subtotal " _
        & " FROM Products INNER JOIN [Order Details] " _
        & " ON Products.ProductID = [Order Details].ProductID " _
        & " WHERE [Order Details].OrderID = " _
        & rsData("OrderID") _
        & " ORDER BY Products.ProductName"

    Set rsDetails = dcnDB.Execute(strSQL)
    curTotal = 0
    Do While Not rsDetails.EOF
%>
<tr>
    <td align=middle><% = rsDetails("Quantity") %></td>
    <td><% = rsDetails("ProductName") %></td>
    <td align=right>
    <% = FormatCurrency(rsDetails("UnitPrice"), 2) %></td>
    <td align=right>
```

```
    <% = FormatCurrency(rsDetails("Subtotal"), 2) %></td>
</tr>
<%
    curTotal = curTotal + rsDetails("Subtotal")
    rsDetails.MoveNext
Loop
rsDetails.Close
%>
<tr>
    <td colspan=3 align=right><b>Product Total:</b></td>
    <td colspan align=right>
    <% = FormatCurrency(curTotal, 2) %>
    </td>
</tr>

<tr>
    <td colspan=3 align=right><b>Freight:</b></td>
    <td colspan align=right>
    <% = FormatCurrency(rsData("Freight"), 2) %>
    </td>
</tr>

<tr>
    <td colspan=3 align=right><b>Order Total:</b></td>
    <td colspan align=right>
    <% = FormatCurrency(curTotal + rsData("Freight"), 2) %>
    </td>
</tr>

</table>
</body>
</html>

<%
End Sub

'-----------------------------------------------------------
Sub Main()

    Dim dcnDB         ' As ADODB.Connection
    Dim rsData        ' As ADODB.Recordset
    Dim intOrderNum   ' As Integer

    If Request("oid") <> "" Then
        intOrderNum = CInt(Request("oid"))
    Else
        Response.Redirect "orderbrowser_unsecured.asp"
    End If
```

Continued

Listing 13-4 *(continued)*

```
    Set dcnDB = OpenDatabase()
    Set rsData = RetrieveData(dcnDB, intOrderNum)
    DisplayData dcnDB, rsData

    rsData.Close
    dcnDB.Close

End Sub

'
' This calls the Main subroutine to get the
' page started.
'
Call Main

%>
```

Listing 13-5: **Revised code for orderbrowser.asp page**

```
Sub DisplayData(rsData, intPageNum, _
    strSortFlds, strSortOrder)

    Dim intCount        ' As Integer

%>
<HTML>
<HEAD>
    <TITLE>Northwind Traders - Order Browser
    - Page <% = intPageNum %> of <% = rsData.PageCount
%></TITLE>
</HEAD>

<BODY BGCOLOR="#FFFFFF">
<H1>Current Orders</H1>
<%
    DisplayPageLinks rsData, intPageNum, strSortFlds,
strSortOrder
    DisplayNavigation rsData, intPageNum, strSortFlds,
strSortOrder
%>
<TABLE BORDER=1>
<TR>
    <TH><% Response.Write CreateHeading(intPageNum, _
        "Order ID", "1", strSortFlds, strSortOrder) %></TH>
```

```
    <TH><% Response.Write CreateHeading(intPageNum, _
        "Company", "2", strSortFlds, strSortOrder) %></TH>
    <TH><% Response.Write CreateHeading(intPageNum, _
        "Salesperson", "3", strSortFlds, strSortOrder) %></TH>
    <TH><% Response.Write CreateHeading(intPageNum, _
        "Order Date", "4", strSortFlds, strSortOrder) %></TH>
    <TH><% Response.Write CreateHeading(intPageNum, _
        "Date Required", "5", strSortFlds, strSortOrder) %></TH>
    <TH><% Response.Write CreateHeading(intPageNum, _
        "Date Shipped", "6", strSortFlds, strSortOrder) %></TH>
    <TH><% Response.Write CreateHeading(intPageNum, _
        "Shipper", "7", strSortFlds, strSortOrder) %></TH>
</TR>
<%
    rsData.AbsolutePage = intPageNum
    For intCount = 1 To rsData.PageSize

%>
<TR>
    <TD>
    <%
        Response.Write "<a href=""vieworder.asp?oid=" _
            & rsData("OrderID") _
            & """ target=_blank>" _
            & rsData("OrderID") _
            & "</a>"
    %>
    </TD>
    <TD><% = rsData("CompanyName") %></TD>
    <TD><% = rsData("Salesperson") %></TD>
    <TD><% = rsData("OrderDate") %></TD>
    <TD><% = rsData("RequiredDate") %></TD>
    <TD><% = rsData("ShippedDate") %></TD>
    <TD><% = rsData("ShipperName") %></TD>
</TR>
<%
        rsData.MoveNext
        If rsData.EOF Then Exit For
    Next    ' intCount
%>
</TABLE>
<%
    DisplayNavigation rsData, intPageNum, strSortFlds,
strSortOrder
%>
</BODY>
</HTML>
<%
End Sub
```

When you run these pages, you can click a particular order and see a display of the order details, as shown in Figure 13-2. This page has a fairly common format that you may have seen in other applications. Some extra code, which you should already be able to understand, retrieves the order details based on the order number. The rest of the data is formatted into an organized invoice format.

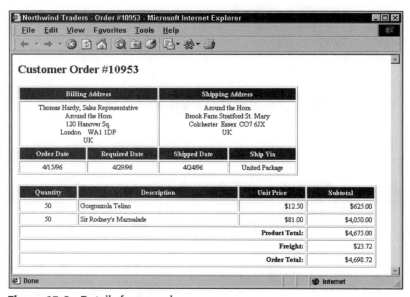

Figure 13-2: Details for an order

Once you have made sure your pages are working properly, make backups so that you can add the security pages discussed in the following sections.

Garden Gate Security

This type of security is similar to locking your garden gate door. People can't come through the gate, but they can always climb over the fence. In this type of security, a login page won't let a user pass until the proper password has been supplied. However, a user can just bookmark the page "behind the gate" and go directly to it in the future. Believe it or not, there are such sites on the Internet right now. Once you know the URLs for the pages behind the gate, you can skip right past the security at the beginning.

To build the garden gate security page, add code in Listing 13-6 into a new ASP page.

Listing 13-6: **Code for gg_login.asp**

```
<%
Option Explicit

'-------------------------------------------------------------
Sub DisplayPasswordForm(strWarning)
%>
<HTML>
<HEAD>
    <TITLE>Northwind Traders - Login</TITLE>
</HEAD>
<BODY BGCOLOR=#FFFFFF>
<h1>System Login</h1>
<p><font color=#FF0000><b><% = strWarning %></b></font></p>

<%
    Response.Write "<form action=""" _
        & Request.ServerVariables("SCRIPT_NAME") _
        & "?ac=v"" method=POST>"
%>
<table cellpadding=3>
<tr>
    <td align=right>User ID:</td>
    <td><input type="text" name="txtUserID" size="20"></td>
</tr>
<tr>
    <td align=right>Password:</td>
    <td><input type="password" name="txtPassword"
size="20"></td>
</tr>
<tr>
    <td colspan=2 align=middle>
        <input type="submit" name="cmdSubmit" value="Login">
        <input type="Reset" value="Clear">
    </td>
</tr>
</form>
</body>
</html>
<%
End Sub

'-------------------------------------------------------------

Sub ValidatePassword
    If Request("txtPassword") = "asprocks!" Then
        Response.Redirect "orderbrowser_unsecured.asp"
```

Continued

Listing 13-6 *(continued)*

```
    Else
        DisplayPasswordForm "Password was incorrect."
    End If
End Sub

'-------------------------------------------------------------

Sub Main
    If Request("ac") <> "" Then
        ValidatePassword
    Else
        DisplayPasswordForm ""
    End If
End Sub

'-------------------------------------------------------------

Call Main
%>
```

When you run this page, you'll see a display similar to Figure 13-3.

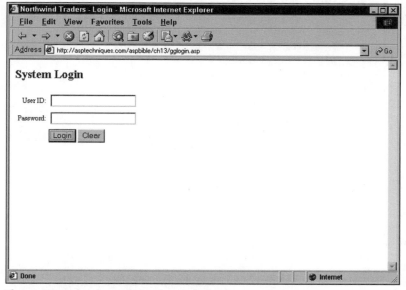

Figure 13-3: Login page as shown in browser

The trick is that the user ID doesn't matter; however, it helps fool the unsuspecting hacker into thinking that it is important. If you enter the wrong password — which is currently "asprocks!" — you'll see the window as shown in Figure 13-4.

Figure 13-4: Error message is displayed when the wrong password is entered

However, if you hurdle this security barrier successfully, you'll be greeted with the order browser page. Currently, you could simply go right to the order browser page and begin using the application. In the following section, you'll see how to show the page to only those users who have logged in recently.

Adding Session-level Security

As shown in the preceding example, if subsequent pages do not check for a valid login status, the security is nearly meaningless. This section shows you a simple way to have every page in the application check to see if the user has logged in. We'll be using the Session object to track the user's login state. By putting a temporary variable in the Session object, the variable will stay in the session as long as the session is active. However, after the session times out, the variable will disappear and the user will have to log in again.

The first change goes into the login page, which is shown in Listing 13-7.

Listing 13-7: **Modifications to login page**

```
'-----------------------------------------------------------

Sub ValidatePassword
    If Request("txtPassword") = "asprocks!" Then
        Session("LoggedIn") = Date & " " & Time
        Response.Redirect "orderbrowser_unsecured.asp"
    Else
        DisplayPasswordForm "Password was incorrect."
    End If
End Sub

'-----------------------------------------------------------
```

The remainder of the code is the same as the preceding examples. The changed code stores a value in a session variable called LoggedIn. Because we'll only be checking for empty values, the contents are irrelevant, but it makes sense to put in a value that means something in case you have to debug it later.

The next change you need to make is in the order browser's Sub Main routine, as shown in Listing 13-8.

Listing 13-8: **Changes to order browser Sub Main**

```
'-----------------------------------------------------------
Sub Main()

    Dim dcnDB          ' As ADODB.Connection
    Dim rsData         ' As ADODB.Recordset
    Dim intPageNum     ' As Integer
    Dim strSortFlds    ' As String
    Dim strSortOrder   ' As String

    If Session("LoggedIn") = "" Then
        Response.Redirect "sessionlogin.asp"
    End If

    If Request("so") <> "" Then
        strSortFlds = Request("so")
    Else
        strSortFlds = "1"
    End If
```

```
If Request("sd") <> "" Then
   strSortOrder = Request("sd")
Else
   strSortOrder = "ASC"
End If

If Request("pn") <> "" Then
   intPageNum = CInt(Request("pn"))
Else
   intPageNum = 1
End If

Set dcnDB = OpenDatabase()
Set rsData = RetrieveData(dcnDB, strSortFlds, _
   strSortOrder)

rsData.PageSize = RECORDSPERPAGE

DisplayData rsData, intPageNum, _
   strSortFlds, strSortOrder

rsData.Close
dcnDB.Close

End Sub
```

If there is no Session object variable, the user either timed out or bypassed the login page. In any event, the user is sent to the login page to try again.

The final change is in the order details page's Sub Main routine, as shown in Listing 13-9. The code has the same function here as in the browser page.

Listing 13-9: **Changes to order details page's Sub Main**

```
'-------------------------------------------------------------
Sub Main()

   Dim dcnDB        ' As ADODB.Connection
   Dim rsData       ' As ADODB.Recordset
   Dim intOrderNum  ' As Integer

   If Session("LoggedIn") = "" Then
      Response.Redirect "sessionlogin.asp"
   End If
```

Continued

Listing 13-9 *(continued)*

```
If Request("oid") <> "" Then
    intOrderNum = CInt(Request("oid"))
Else
    Response.Redirect "orderbrowser_secured.asp"
End If

Set dcnDB = OpenDatabase()
Set rsData = RetrieveData(dcnDB, intOrderNum)
DisplayData dcnDB, rsData

rsData.Close
dcnDB.Close

End Sub
```

Also remember to change your URLs if you are using different file names, as shown in these examples. For instance, the redirect in the previous listing is now pointing to `orderbrowser_secured.asp`, which has the extra security measures.

Wrapping Up

As mentioned in the beginning of this section, these types of security need to be supplemented with operating system-level security functions, such as SSL or other types of encryption. However, these techniques will still be useful to make sure that users enter your system properly and with the appropriate credentials.

You can also use the tighter security provided through Windows NT authentication, which provides you the ability to restrict your Web sites to particular NT user IDs or groups. You can also restrict the site based on an individual IP address or a range of IP addresses. Finally, you can use a product like Site Server to restrict access further to your sites. In other words, leaving a valuable site unprotected is dangerous and silly, considering the number of resources available to you.

Summary

This chapter extended the preceding chapter covering the data browser. Paging and security are in use in many different places on the Web, and both techniques help to provide more efficient and secure work on the Web. Plus, the techniques and page designs in this chapter are easily adaptable to your own applications.

✦   ✦   ✦

Advanced Database Integration

✦ ✦ ✦ ✦

In This Chapter

Learn to use parameterized queries/stored procedures to improve database access

Design a scheme for tracking user activity

Use a database to track user activity

Creating Parameterized Queries

✦ ✦ ✦ ✦

In preceding chapters, you've created different types of database queries. Some were stored in the database and others were created directly in the ASP page and then sent to the database for evaluation. For the most part, these queries were "canned"; that is, they always did the same thing. Some queries retrieved all the categories from a table, for instance. However, there were some queries that needed additional information to retrieve the correct data. The preceding chapter had a lengthy query that retrieved all the information about a particular order. In order to get the information, the query required the order ID, which was passed in from the browser page. This ID is known as a *query parameter*. This section will show you how to create queries in the database that will accept these parameters and provide the correct information back to your page. Active Data Objects has a number of properties and objects designed to make it easier to work with these types of queries, which are supported by Access, SQL Server, Oracle, and nearly every other database available for use with ASP sites.

What Are We Building?

For this example, we will take the query created in the order display page (code shown below in Listing 14-1) and create a parameterized query for it. The parameter will be the order ID value, which is supplied by the preceding page. We will also create a query for the order details SQL, which is used to populate the lower part of the invoice. Listing 14-1 shows the code before the conversion, with the code to be overhauled highlighted.

Listing 14-1: **View order page, with embedded SQL**

```
<%
   Option Explicit
   Const DBLOCATION = "C:\NWind.mdb"

%>
<!--#include file="adovbs.inc" -->
<%

Function OpenDatabase()

   Dim dcnDB        ' As ADODB.Connection
   Set dcnDB = Server.CreateObject("ADODB.Connection")
   dcnDB.ConnectionString = _
      "Provider=Microsoft.Jet.OLEDB.3.51;" _
         & "Persist Security Info=False;Data Source=" _
         & DBLOCATION
   dcnDB.Open
         Set OpenDatabase = dcnDB

End Function

'-----------------------------------------------------------

Function RetrieveData(dcnDB, intOrderID)

   Dim rsData       ' As ADODB.Recordset
   Dim strSQL       ' As String

   strSQL = "SELECT Orders.OrderID, " _
      & "Customers.ContactName, " _
      & "Customers.ContactTitle, " _
      & "Customers.CompanyName, " _
      & "Customers.Address, " _
      & "Customers.City, " _
      & "Customers.Region, " _
      & "Customers.PostalCode, " _
      & "Customers.Country, " _
      & "[Employees].[LastName] & ', ' & " _
      & "[Employees].[FirstName] AS Salesperson, " _
      & "Orders.ShipName, " _
      & "Orders.ShipAddress, " _
      & "Orders.ShipCity, " _
      & "Orders.ShipRegion, " _
      & "Orders.ShipPostalCode, " _
      & "Orders.ShipCountry, " _
      & "Orders.OrderDate, " _
      & "Orders.RequiredDate, " _
      & "Orders.ShippedDate, " _
```

```
              & "Orders.Freight, " _
              & "Shippers.CompanyName AS ShipperName " _
              & "FROM Shippers " _
              & "INNER JOIN (Employees " _
              & "INNER JOIN (Customers " _
              & "INNER JOIN Orders " _
              & "ON Customers.CustomerID = Orders.CustomerID) " _
              & "ON Employees.EmployeeID = Orders.EmployeeID) " _
              & "ON Shippers.ShipperID = Orders.ShipVia" _
              & " WHERE Orders.OrderID = " & intOrderID

      Set rsData = Server.CreateObject("ADODB.Recordset")
      rsData.CursorLocation = adUseClient
      rsData.Open strSQL, dcnDB, adOpenStatic, _
          adLockReadOnly, adCmdText
      Set RetrieveData = rsData
End Function

'-------------------------------------------------------------
Sub DisplayData(dcnDB, rsData)
    Dim rsDetails      ' As ADODB.Recordset
    Dim strSQL         ' As String
    Dim curTotal       ' As Currency

%>

<html>
<head>
   <title>Northwind Traders -
   Order #<% = rsData("OrderID") %></title>
</head>
<body bgcolor=#FFFFFF>
<h1>Customer Order #<% = rsData("OrderID") %></h1>

<table width=500 border=1 cellpadding=3>
<tr>
   <td colspan=2 align=middle
   valign=top bgcolor=#0000CC width=250>
   <font color=#FFFFFF><b>Billing Address</b></font>
   </td>
   <td colspan=2 align=middle
   valign=top bgcolor=#0000CC width=250>
   <font color=#FFFFFF><b>Shipping Address</b></font>
   </td>
</tr>
<tr>
   <td colspan=2 valign=top align=middle>
   <% = rsData("ContactName") %>,
   <% = rsData("ContactTitle") %><br>
   <% = rsData("CompanyName") %><br>
   <% = rsData("Address") %><br>
```

Continued

Listing 14-1 *(continued)*

```
    <% = rsData("City") %> 
    <% = rsData("Region") %> 
    <% = rsData("PostalCode") %><br>
    <% = rsData("Country") %><br>
    </td>
    <td colspan=2 valign=top align=middle>
    <% = rsData("ShipName") %><br>
    <% = rsData("ShipAddress") %><br>
    <% = rsData("ShipCity") %> 
    <% = rsData("ShipRegion") %> 
    <% = rsData("ShipPostalCode") %><br>
    <% = rsData("ShipCountry") %><br>
    </td>
</tr>

<tr>
    <td align=middle valign=top bgcolor=#0000CC width=250>
    <font color=#FFFFFF><b>Order Date</b></font>
    </td>
    <td align=middle valign=top bgcolor=#0000CC width=250>
    <font color=#FFFFFF><b>Required Date</b></font>
    </td>
    <td align=middle valign=top bgcolor=#0000CC width=250>
    <font color=#FFFFFF><b>Shipped Date</b></font>
    </td>
    <td align=middle valign=top bgcolor=#0000CC width=250>
    <font color=#FFFFFF><b>Ship Via</b></font>
    </td>
</tr>
<tr>
    <td align=middle width=125>
    <% = rsData("OrderDate") %></td>
    <td align=middle width=125>
    <% = rsData("RequiredDate") %></td>
    <td align=middle width=125>
    <% = rsData("ShippedDate") %></td>
    <td align=middle width=125>
    <% = rsData("ShipperName") %></td>
</tr>
</table>

<p>

<table width=640 border=1 cellpadding=3>
<tr>
    <td align=middle valign=top bgcolor=#0000CC width=100>
    <font color=#FFFFFF><b>Quantity</b></font>
    </td>
```

```
            <td align=middle valign=top bgcolor=#0000CC width=300>
            <font color=#FFFFFF><b>Description</b></font>
            </td>
            <td align=middle valign=top bgcolor=#0000CC width=120>
            <font color=#FFFFFF><b>Unit Price</b></font>
            </td>
            <td align=middle valign=top bgcolor=#0000CC width=120>
            <font color=#FFFFFF><b>Subtotal</b></font>
            </td>
</tr>

<%
    strSQL = "SELECT [Order Details].Quantity, " _
        & " Products.ProductName, " _
        & " [Order Details].UnitPrice, " _
        & " [Order Details].Quantity * " _
        & " [Order Details].[UnitPrice] AS Subtotal " _
        & " FROM Products INNER JOIN [Order Details] " _
        & " ON Products.ProductID = [Order Details].ProductID " _
        & " WHERE [Order Details].OrderID = " _
        & rsData("OrderID") _
        & " ORDER BY Products.ProductName"

    Set rsDetails = dcnDB.Execute(strSQL)
    curTotal = 0
    Do While Not rsDetails.EOF
%>
<tr>
    <td align=middle><% = rsDetails("Quantity") %></td>
    <td><% = rsDetails("ProductName") %></td>
    <td align=right>
    <% = FormatCurrency(rsDetails("UnitPrice"), 2) %></td>
    <td align=right>
    <% = FormatCurrency(rsDetails("Subtotal"), 2) %></td>
</tr>
<%
        curTotal = curTotal + rsDetails("Subtotal")
        rsDetails.MoveNext
    Loop
    rsDetails.Close
%>
<tr>
    <td colspan=3 align=right><b>Product Total:</b></td>
    <td colspan align=right>
    <% = FormatCurrency(curTotal, 2) %>
    </td>
</tr>

<tr>
    <td colspan=3 align=right><b>Freight:</b></td>
    <td colspan align=right>
```

Continued

Listing 14-1 *(continued)*

```
    <% = FormatCurrency(rsData("Freight"), 2) %>
    </td>
</tr>

<tr>
    <td colspan=3 align=right><b>Order Total:</b></td>
    <td colspan align=right>
    <% = FormatCurrency(curTotal + rsData("Freight"), 2) %>
    </td>
</tr>

</table>
</body>
</html>

<%
End Sub

'------------------------------------------------------------
Sub Main()

    Dim dcnDB          ' As ADODB.Connection
    Dim rsData         ' As ADODB.Recordset
    Dim intOrderNum    ' As Integer

    If Request("oid") <> "" Then
        intOrderNum = CInt(Request("oid"))
    Else
        Response.Redirect "orderbrowser.asp"
    End If

    Set dcnDB = OpenDatabase()
    Set rsData = RetrieveData(dcnDB, intOrderNum)
    DisplayData dcnDB, rsData

    rsData.Close
    dcnDB.Close

End Sub

'
' This calls the Main subroutine to get the
' page started.
'
Call Main

%>
```

Designing the Invoice Query

First, let's design the query used to retrieve the top part of the invoice, which includes the shipping and billing address and other general information. The instructions here are for Microsoft Access. (For other databases, refer to your documentation on how to create a stored procedure that accepts a parameter.)

1. Open the Northwind Traders database in Microsoft Access, and select the Queries tab.

2. Click the New button and select Design View from the dialog box shown in Figure 14-1.

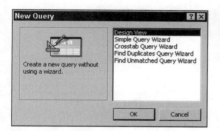

Figure 14-1: Select Design View from this dialog box.

3. Now you see the dialog box shown in Figure 14-2, which prompts you to add tables to the query. If you look at the existing SQL code, you will see that these tables are currently in use:

   - Customers

   - Employees

   - Orders

   - Shippers

   Even if you're just using a field or two from the table, the table has to be added to the query. Press the Control key and then click each of those four tables, so that all four are highlighted. Click the Add button, and then click the Close button.

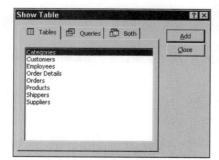

Figure 14-2: Add tables to your query through this dialog box.

4. With the tables added, your query designer window should resemble Figure 14-3. The foreign key relationships between the tables are visible as lines between fields in each of the boxes. These relationships are crucial to making this query work properly.

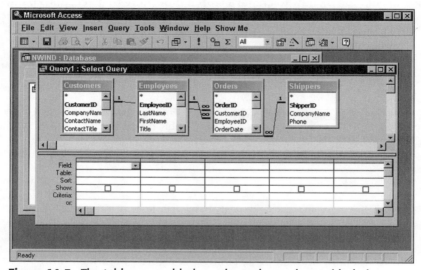

Figure 14-3: The tables you added are shown here, along with their relationships to each other.

5. Next, select the fields that you want for the query. From some of the tables, we only need a few fields. However, in other tables, we need all the fields. To get started, drag the asterisk field in the Customers table to the first column in the grid below. The asterisk field indicates that all fields should be selected. We don't really need the phone numbers, but you can always add them if desired.

6. In the Employee table, we only need the salesperson's name. However, the first and last name are stored separately. To retrieve this information, enter the following into the Field box in the second column of the grid.

```
Salesperson: [Employees].[LastName] & ", " &
[Employees].[FirstName]
```

Note The preceding code should be entered all on one line.

This will concatenate the last name and the first name with a comma between them.

7. Because the Orders table is linked to several other tables, we don't need several of the ID fields. Add these fields to the grid:

- OrderID
- OrderDate
- RequiredDate
- ShippedDate
- Freight
- ShipName
- ShipAddress
- ShipCity
- ShipRegion
- ShipPostalCode
- ShipCountry

8. Finally, drag the CompanyName field from the Shippers table into the last box. With all the items added, you should have 14 columns in your grid.

9. With all the columns selected, you can now add your parameter for selecting a particular order ID. Find the column in which OrderID is listed. In the row labeled Criteria, enter the following text:

`[lngOrderID]`

This text tells Access that we need a value for OrderID in order to run this query.

10. Click the Save button to save this query as `qryGetInvoiceInfo` or another name that is meaningful to you.

To test this query, click the exclamation point button on the toolbar. You'll be prompted for an order ID value in the dialog box shown in Figure 14-4.

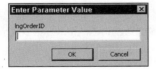

Figure 14-4: Enter the order ID you wish to retrieve

Any valid order ID can be entered here. The first order ID available is 10248, which is an order for Paul Henriot of "Vins et alcools Chevalier." If you aren't prompted for the value, make sure that you completed Step 9 from the list. Without the parameter, all orders are retrieved, which is not the desired result.

Make sure to save your query before closing the query window. Don't exit completely, however. We need to create the second query, which retrieves order details for a particular order.

Designing the Order Details Query

The second query is quite a bit shorter, so we'll skip its gory details and give you the express version for designing the query, which should be named qryGetInvoiceDetails.

1. Add the Order Details and Products tables to the query.

2. From the Order Details table, add the OrderID, UnitPrice, and Quantity fields. While there is a price field on both tables, the Order Details price represents the price at the time, including any discounts that were applied. The Products table represents the current price.

3. From the Products table, add the ProductName field.

4. Let the database calculate the Subtotal, which is the Quantity of a product multiplied by the UnitPrice. In the fifth column, enter this text in the Field row:

   ```
   Subtotal: [Order Details].[UnitPrice]*[Order
   Details].[Quantity]
   ```

 Note   The code above should be entered all on one line.

5. To specify the parameter for this order ID, enter the following code in the Criteria row for the OrderID field:

   ```
   [lngOrderID]
   ```

Save your query as qryGetInvoiceDetails, and then test it with any order number. For instance, if you test using the same order as before, you'll get the three line items from Paul Henriot's order.

Executing the Invoice Info Query

In order to use the query in the ASP page, we have to make a few changes to the code. Let's begin with the RetrieveData subroutine. The new code for this subroutine is shown in Listing 14-2.

Listing 14-2: **New code for RetrieveData subroutine**

```
'------------------------------------------------------------

Function RetrieveData(dcnDB, intOrderID)
```

```
Dim cmdQuery    ' As ADODB.Command
Dim parOrderID  ' As ADODB.Parameter
Dim rsData      ' As ADODB.Recordset

Set cmdQuery = Server.CreateObject("ADODB.Command")
Set cmdQuery.ActiveConnection = dcnDB
cmdQuery.CommandText = "qryGetInvoiceInfo"

Set parOrderID = cmdQuery.CreateParameter("lngOrderID")
parOrderID.Type = adInteger
parOrderID.Value = intOrderID
parOrderID.Direction = adParamInput
cmdQuery.Parameters.Append parOrderID

Set RetrieveData = cmdQuery.Execute()

End Function

'-------------------------------------------------------------
```

Instead of that big clumsy query, we now have nice clean lines of code. We have a new object, cmdQuery, which is used to hold the parameterized query. We supply the name of the query and the active data connection, represented by the dcnDB variable.

Next, we have to create the parameter. The name of the parameter is lngOrderID, so we send it to the CreateParameter method of the Command object. This sequence returns an object that we then populate with additional values, such as the data type, the value to use, and the direction. Finally, the parameter is appended to the Parameters collection. The query is then executed, and the results are returned to the caller.

The data type of the parameter is defined by a constant, as shown in Table 14-1.

Table 14-1
Parameter Type Values

Constant	Description
adArray	Ordered together with another type to indicate that the data is a safe-array of that type (DBTYPE_ARRAY).
adBigInt	An eight-byte signed integer (DBTYPE_I8).
adBinary	A binary value (DBTYPE_BYTES).

Continued

<table>
<tr><td colspan="2">**Table 14-1** *(continued)*</td></tr>
<tr><td>*Constant*</td><td>*Description*</td></tr>
<tr><td>adBoolean</td><td>A Boolean value (DBTYPE_BOOL).</td></tr>
<tr><td>adByRef</td><td>Ordered together with another type to indicate that the data is a pointer to data of the other type (DBTYPE_BYREF).</td></tr>
<tr><td>adBSTR</td><td>A null-terminated character string (Unicode) (DBTYPE_BSTR).</td></tr>
<tr><td>adChar</td><td>A String value (DBTYPE_STR).</td></tr>
<tr><td>adCurrency</td><td>A currency value (DBTYPE_CY). Currency is a fixed-point number with four digits to the right of the decimal point. It is stored in an eight-byte signed integer scaled by 10,000.</td></tr>
<tr><td>adDate</td><td>A Date value (DBTYPE_DATE). A date is stored as a Double, the whole part of which is the number of days since December 30, 1899, and the fractional part of which is the fraction of a day.</td></tr>
<tr><td>adDBDate</td><td>A date value (yyyymmdd) (DBTYPE_DBDATE).</td></tr>
<tr><td>adDBTime</td><td>A time value (hhmmss) (DBTYPE_DBTIME).</td></tr>
<tr><td>adDBTimeStamp</td><td>A date-time stamp (yyyymmddhhmmss plus a fraction in billionths) (DBTYPE_DBTIMESTAMP).</td></tr>
<tr><td>adDecimal</td><td>An exact numeric value with a fixed precision and scale (DBTYPE_DECIMAL).</td></tr>
<tr><td>adDouble</td><td>A double-precision floating point value (DBTYPE_R8).</td></tr>
<tr><td>adEmpty</td><td>No value was specified (DBTYPE_EMPTY).</td></tr>
<tr><td>adError</td><td>A 32-bit error code (DBTYPE_ERROR).</td></tr>
<tr><td>adGUID</td><td>A globally unique identifier (GUID) (DBTYPE_GUID).</td></tr>
<tr><td>adIDispatch</td><td>A pointer to an IDispatch interface on an OLE object (DBTYPE_IDISPATCH).</td></tr>
<tr><td>adInteger</td><td>A four-byte signed integer (DBTYPE_I4).</td></tr>
<tr><td>adIUnknown</td><td>A pointer to an IUnknown interface on an OLE object (DBTYPE_IUNKNOWN).</td></tr>
<tr><td>adLongVarBinary</td><td>A long binary value (Parameter object only).</td></tr>
<tr><td>adLongVarChar</td><td>A long String value (Parameter object only).</td></tr>
<tr><td>adLongVarWChar</td><td>A long null-terminated string value (Parameter object only).</td></tr>
</table>

Constant	Description
adNumeric	An exact numeric value with a fixed precision and scale (DBTYPE_NUMERIC).
adSingle	A single-precision floating point value (DBTYPE_R4).
adSmallInt	A two-byte signed integer (DBTYPE_I2).
adTinyInt	A one-byte signed integer (DBTYPE_I1).
adUnsignedBigInt	An eight-byte unsigned integer (DBTYPE_UI8).
adUnsignedInt	A four-byte unsigned integer (DBTYPE_UI4).
adUnsignedSmallInt	A two-byte unsigned integer (DBTYPE_UI2).
adUnsignedTinyInt	A one-byte unsigned integer (DBTYPE_UI1).
adUserDefined	A user-defined variable (DBTYPE_UDT).
adVarBinary	A binary value (Parameter object only).
adVarChar	A String value (Parameter object only).
adVariant	An Automation Variant (DBTYPE_VARIANT).
adVector	Or'd together with another type to indicate that the data is a DBVECTOR structure, as defined by OLE DB, that contains a count of elements and a pointer to data of the other type (DBTYPE_VECTOR).
adVarWChar	A null-terminated Unicode character string (Parameter object only).
adWChar	A null-terminated Unicode character string (DBTYPE_WSTR).

The direction of the parameter determines if it is input, output, or both. Table 14-2 shows the available constants, which are all defined in the ADOVBS.INC file included in this ASP page.

Table 14-2
Parameter Direction Values

Constant	Description
adParamInput	Default. Indicates an input parameter.
adParamOutput	Indicates an output parameter.
adParamInputOutput	Indicates both an input and output parameter.
adParamReturnValue	Indicates a return value.

If you remember, we didn't rename any built-in columns, other than those using formulas. For this reason, the customer CompanyName field and the shipper's CompanyName field will conflict. Access automatically prefixes the names with the table names so that there is no confusion. However, this means we have to make a few minor changes to the display logic of the DisplayData subroutine. These changes are marked in Listing 14-3.

Listing 14-3: **DisplayData subroutine changes**

```
'----------------------------------------------------------------
Sub DisplayData(dcnDB, rsData)
    Dim cmdQuery        ' As ADODB.Command
    Dim parOrderID      ' As ADODB.Parameter
    Dim rsDetails       ' As ADODB.Recordset
    Dim strSQL          ' As String
    Dim curTotal        ' As Currency

%>

<html>
<head>
    <title>Northwind Traders -
    Order #<% = rsData("OrderID") %></title>
</head>
<body bgcolor=#FFFFFF>
<h1>Customer Order #<% = rsData("OrderID") %></h1>

<table width=500 border=1 cellpadding=3>
<tr>
    <td colspan=2 align=middle valign=top bgcolor=#0000CC
width=250>
    <font color=#FFFFFF><b>Billing Address</b></font>
    </td>
    <td colspan=2 align=middle valign=top bgcolor=#0000CC
width=250>
    <font color=#FFFFFF><b>Shipping Address</b></font>
    </td>
</tr>
<tr>
    <td colspan=2 valign=top align=middle>
    <% = rsData("ContactName") %>,
    <% = rsData("ContactTitle") %><br>
    <% = rsData("Customers.CompanyName") %><br>
    <% = rsData("Address") %><br>
    <% = rsData("City") %> 
    <% = rsData("Region") %> 
```

```
        <% = rsData("PostalCode") %><br>
        <% = rsData("Country") %><br>
        </td>
        <td colspan=2 valign=top align=middle>
        <% = rsData("ShipName") %><br>
        <% = rsData("ShipAddress") %><br>
        <% = rsData("ShipCity") %> 
        <% = rsData("ShipRegion") %> 
        <% = rsData("ShipPostalCode") %><br>
        <% = rsData("ShipCountry") %><br>
        </td>
</tr>

<tr>
    <td align=middle valign=top bgcolor=#0000CC width=250>
    <font color=#FFFFFF><b>Order Date</b></font>
    </td>
    <td align=middle valign=top bgcolor=#0000CC width=250>
    <font color=#FFFFFF><b>Required Date</b></font>
    </td>
    <td align=middle valign=top bgcolor=#0000CC width=250>
    <font color=#FFFFFF><b>Shipped Date</b></font>
    </td>
    <td align=middle valign=top bgcolor=#0000CC width=250>
    <font color=#FFFFFF><b>Ship Via</b></font>
    </td>
</tr>
<tr>
    <td align=middle width=125>
    <% = rsData("OrderDate") %></td>
    <td align=middle width=125>
    <% = rsData("RequiredDate") %></td>
    <td align=middle width=125>
    <% = rsData("ShippedDate") %></td>
    <td align=middle width=125>
    <% = rsData("Shippers.CompanyName") %></td>
</tr>
</table>

' rest of code is the same, for now
```

At this point, you can run your page, select an order, and see the same results as before. Depending on your connection to your server, the display may seem a bit faster now. Now, the query doesn't have to be evaluated every time — the database has stored the query permanently and knows how best to execute it.

Executing the Invoice Details Query

The final step is to implement the invoice details query. All of the code for this query is located in the `DisplayData` subroutine, as shown in Listing 14-4. Because this code is quite similar to the previous query, the changes will be highlighted for you but not discussed.

Listing 14-4: **DisplayData subroutine with Invoice Details query**

```
'------------------------------------------------------------
Sub DisplayData(dcnDB, rsData)
    Dim cmdQuery        ' As ADODB.Command
    Dim parOrderID      ' As ADODB.Parameter
    Dim rsDetails       ' As ADODB.Recordset
    Dim strSQL          ' As String
    Dim curTotal        ' As Currency

%>

<html>
<head>
    <title>Northwind Traders -
    Order #<% = rsData("OrderID") %></title>
</head>
<body bgcolor=#FFFFFF>
<h1>Customer Order #<% = rsData("OrderID") %></h1>

<table width=500 border=1 cellpadding=3>
<tr>
    <td colspan=2 align=middle valign=top bgcolor=#0000CC
width=250>
    <font color=#FFFFFF><b>Billing Address</b></font>
    </td>
    <td colspan=2 align=middle valign=top bgcolor=#0000CC
width=250>
    <font color=#FFFFFF><b>Shipping Address</b></font>
    </td>
</tr>
<tr>
    <td colspan=2 valign=top align=middle>
    <% = rsData("ContactName") %>,
    <% = rsData("ContactTitle") %><br>
    <% = rsData("Customers.CompanyName") %><br>
    <% = rsData("Address") %><br>
    <% = rsData("City") %> 
    <% = rsData("Region") %> 
    <% = rsData("PostalCode") %><br>
```

```
        <% = rsData("Country") %><br>
        </td>
        <td colspan=2 valign=top align=middle>
        <% = rsData("ShipName") %><br>
        <% = rsData("ShipAddress") %><br>
        <% = rsData("ShipCity") %> 
        <% = rsData("ShipRegion") %> 
        <% = rsData("ShipPostalCode") %><br>
        <% = rsData("ShipCountry") %><br>
        </td>
</tr>

<tr>
    <td align=middle valign=top bgcolor=#0000CC width=250>
    <font color=#FFFFFF><b>Order Date</b></font>
    </td>
    <td align=middle valign=top bgcolor=#0000CC width=250>
    <font color=#FFFFFF><b>Required Date</b></font>
    </td>
    <td align=middle valign=top bgcolor=#0000CC width=250>
    <font color=#FFFFFF><b>Shipped Date</b></font>
    </td>
    <td align=middle valign=top bgcolor=#0000CC width=250>
    <font color=#FFFFFF><b>Ship Via</b></font>
    </td>
</tr>
<tr>
    <td align=middle width=125>
    <% = rsData("OrderDate") %></td>
    <td align=middle width=125>
    <% = rsData("RequiredDate") %></td>
    <td align=middle width=125>
    <% = rsData("ShippedDate") %></td>
    <td align=middle width=125>
    <% = rsData("Shippers.CompanyName") %></td>
</tr>
</table>

<p>

<table width=640 border=1 cellpadding=3>
<tr>
    <td align=middle valign=top bgcolor=#0000CC width=100>
    <font color=#FFFFFF><b>Quantity</b></font>
    </td>
    <td align=middle valign=top bgcolor=#0000CC width=300>
    <font color=#FFFFFF><b>Description</b></font>
    </td>
    <td align=middle valign=top bgcolor=#0000CC width=120>
    <font color=#FFFFFF><b>Unit Price</b></font>
    </td>
```

Continued

Listing 14-4 *(continued)*

```
   <td align=middle valign=top bgcolor=#0000CC width=120>
   <font color=#FFFFFF><b>Subtotal</b></font>
   </td>
</tr>

<%

   Set cmdQuery = Server.CreateObject("ADODB.Command")
   Set cmdQuery.ActiveConnection = dcnDB
   cmdQuery.CommandText = "qryGetInvoiceDetails"

   Set parOrderID = cmdQuery.CreateParameter("lngOrderID")
   parOrderID.Type = adInteger
   parOrderID.Value = rsData("OrderID")
   parOrderID.Direction = adParamInput
   cmdQuery.Parameters.Append parOrderID

   Set rsDetails = cmdQuery.Execute()

   curTotal = 0
   Do While Not rsDetails.EOF
%>
<tr>
   <td align=middle><% = rsDetails("Quantity") %></td>
   <td><% = rsDetails("ProductName") %></td>
   <td align=right>
   <% = FormatCurrency(rsDetails("UnitPrice"), 2) %></td>
   <td align=right>
   <% = FormatCurrency(rsDetails("Subtotal"), 2) %></td>
</tr>
<%

      curTotal = curTotal + rsDetails("Subtotal")
      rsDetails.MoveNext
   Loop
   rsDetails.Close
%>
<tr>
   <td colspan=3 align=right><b>Product Total:</b></td>
   <td colspan align=right>
   <% = FormatCurrency(curTotal, 2) %>
   </td>
</tr>

<tr>
   <td colspan=3 align=right><b>Freight:</b></td>
   <td colspan align=right>
   <% = FormatCurrency(rsData("Freight"), 2) %>
   </td>
</tr>
```

```
<tr>
   <td colspan=3 align=right><b>Order Total:</b></td>
   <td colspan align=right>
   <% = FormatCurrency(curTotal + rsData("Freight"), 2) %>
   </td>
</tr>

</table>
</body>
</html>

<%
End Sub

'- - - - - - - - - - - - - - - - - - - - - - - - - - - - - - - - - - - - - - - - - - - -
```

The strSQL variable isn't being used, so it could be removed. Again, to test this page, just pick an order from the previous page, and the display should look the same as before. Because the query is not overly complicated, you may not notice a speed difference. However, it does clean up your ASP code. In addition, you can change how this query operates without having to change your ASP code every time. It's also much easier to use the Access query designer than to handcode Access SQL into ASP strings.

Tracking User Activity

In print and on the Internet, advertising is the mainstay of income for many Web sites. For advertisers to be successful, they have to know their audience. If you pick up a print magazine, you will see ads that are targeted at its market. A women's magazine will have lots of ads for makeup, women's clothing stores, and so forth. You won't see power tool ads in a women's magazine, because the people who buy power tools most of the time (men) don't normally read women's magazines. How do the magazine companies know this? They do different types of market research to learn more about their audience. Some magazines send out surveys, use telephone survey people, or other methods to determine characteristics of their audience.

Mainly, magazine companies want to know more about their audience so they can get higher advertising rates. For instance, advertisers will pay more to put an ad in a magazine that targets executives in the car industry who, on average, make $75,000 or more a year and oversee purchases of $1 million and over. The advertisers know that their ad will be going to people more likely to buy their product.

One difference between print and Web advertising is that print advertisers can only guess how many people are seeing their ads. The publisher can tell the advertiser how many copies of the magazine were sold, but the publisher can't tell the advertiser how many people actually read the page of the ad. If the advertiser has a phone number for someone to call, a code or a different phone number may tell the advertiser which ad triggered the call. Overall, determining this information in print is a series of logical estimates.

The Web, on the other hand, provides a great deal more in the way of tracking ads. To begin, each time a user loads a page with an ad, the display of the ad can be counted. Each time the user clicks an ad, the click can be counted. The browser you're using provides quite a bit of information about you. For instance, as you've seen in earlier chapters, the system can easily determine from where you are browsing, whether it be America Online or through a corporate firewall. Some numeric IP addresses don't have host names, but an ISP will typically register a range of IP addresses to be used for dialup. Using this information about ranges (which is available publicly), a site can sometimes determine the general area in which you're located.

With Active Server Pages (or other similar languages), everything you do on the site can be tracked the minute you log into a site. The `Session` object in ASP automatically adds a unique cookie to the user's machine so that session state can be maintained. This cookie can be used to track your movements through the site. Cookies are not meant to make you paranoid — habits of individual users are only useful in certain situations. However, if the site administrators see a pattern of how users navigate through a site, they can use that information to make the site more efficient. For instance, let's say that a site saw lots of users hitting the home page, selecting the search page, and then selecting the same result. As a Webmaster, you should put a direct link to that result on the home page, which will reduce the number of clicks users need to get to the desired information. Without knowing how each user navigates the site, these generalizations cannot be made. You can do a similar thing using Web logs, but because many people look like they're from the same site (AOL, corporate firewalls, and so on), it's not nearly as reliable as cookie tracking.

The preceding comment about individual user habits could be construed in a negative way. However, let's look at it from the point of providing better customer service. If a store tracks my browsing through the site, it could easily determine (as you'll do in the example that follows) what I look at most often when I visit. If I've agreed to be on the store's mailing list, they could send me content that matched my interests. This personalization would make me more likely to buy what they were offering. Each user is going to have a different profile, and tracking user actions will help you determine this profile.

If you aggregate these profiles and other information that has been volunteered by the user, you can provide a more complete picture to potential advertisers. If you can show that your typical user works at a large corporation, spends 15 minutes on your site during every visit, and clicks on ads 25 percent of the time, you're going to be more likely to get more dollars for the ads you show. Providing aggregate information to advertisers in no way violates any promises you've made to users about giving out their personal information. You're not giving specific information about one user; instead, you're giving out general habits you've found by looking at everyone's actions in total. As far as the targeted advertising discussed previously, you should always give the user to "opt out" of marketing e-mail. If they have this option but have chosen to get your marketing material, the sky's the limit as to how you can use their information to target your marketing better.

This section shows you how to set up a database structure to track users' actions as they navigate through the categories and products sold by Northwind Traders. We'll be using code created in a preceding chapter to browse the Northwind catalog, and then modifying it to track user actions as they navigate the site. You'll also see how to build queries and stored procedures to support both the storage and reporting of this information to site administrators.

Determining What to Track

The hardest part of this whole topic is determining what you want to track. The primary method is to track category actions. For instance, a store might track user browsing through different product categories. If the categories are specific enough, this method can give you good information as to other, similar products that a user might buy. If a user is looking at car stereos that have multidisc changers in them, you can suggest other products in that category that might appeal to the user.

Categories can also be used for content tracking. If I saw that a user was viewing book reviews and articles about databases on the VB Techniques and ASP Techniques Web sites, it's a pretty good bet that if I sent the user an e-mail announcing a new product review for a database, they would come and read the article. This example actually combines two different categories to create a user base. For instance, I could decide that anyone had looked at more than one book review, product review, interview, or article about databases would be targeted with an e-mail about a new piece of content about databases.

You could also track by other pieces of information, such as article author or keywords in the article. An article on a financial Web site about a company like Amazon.com could be categorized in any or all of the following ways:

✦ Internet stocks

✦ Booksellers

✦ E-commerce

✦ Music stores

✦ Customer service

Based on your site, you have to determine what people will be searching for and create an appropriate category set.

As for our application, we have a classic storefront where products are categorized into fairly large groupings. For instance, we have one category called "Beverage." For a small store with few items, this category would be appropriate. However, a large store might have hundreds of beverage types: soft drink, waters, alcoholic, and so forth. The larger store would need to have subcategories of products. These subcategorizations would also give them the ability to determine that if a user liked one subcategory of wine, they might also like another subcategory of wine that has a similar flavor, for instance. For our example, we will be tracking the product categories that users view. This arrangement is enough to show how to implement the tracking, but you can always expand it for your own purposes. You'll also see how this functionality is used in the chapter that covers Active Channels, where we'll build a channel customized for a user, based on the content that they've viewed on a site like ASP Techniques.

Creating the Database Tables

For this example, we're only going to be gathering basic information about the category pages that are being viewed. However, in the chapter covering Active Channels, you'll need to tie this information with membership information in order to provide customized content. We'll sow the seeds here so that you can see how the system needs to evolve.

The first table we need is going to be called Visitors. Whenever a new user starts visiting the site, this table will be used to store certain information about that person. Right now, we'll only be storing information provided by the browser. The important part of this table is the unique ID generated by the database that we will use to track this person's movement through the site. Add these fields to the table:

VisitorID	- AutoNumber, Primary Key
VisitDate	- Date/Time
Host	- Text, 255

You can add other information, but this is enough for starters. The unique VisitorID will be stored in a temporary cookie on the user's machine. The cookie will disappear when the user leaves. In the chapter covering Active Channels, you'll see how to use both types of cookies efficiently.

The second table we need will be used to track the categories to which the visitor goes. The table should be called VisitorViews, with the following fields:

ViewID	- AutoNumber, PrimaryKey
VisitorID	- Long
CategoryID	- Long

The first field, ViewID, is a unique counter value for each record. This value is unique because we may have multiple views by the same session and category. The second field will be used to record the user's unique visitor ID, which is generated by the Visitors table. The final field records the category ID that the person decided to view. Multiple views of the same category will result in multiple records in the table. This setup is perfectly acceptable — a user may view a category, then a product, and go back to the category. As we store many page visits, the percentages of traffic will help us determine the user's interests.

Why are we using the database-generated value instead of the `SessionID` property of the `Session` object? The `SessionID` property is not guaranteed to be unique, according to the platform SDK documentation provided by Microsoft. The number can be reset if the server is rebooted. Because the `SessionID` property is not guaranteed and the database-generated ID is guaranteed to be unique, we'll use the database instead.

Lastly, we're going to track the search terms the user looked for in the database. As you'll see shortly, we are using the final version of the examples in Chapter 11 that include search functionality. In combination with the category information, this functionality can be used to provide additional information about what the user wants to see. This information is a bit harder to determine based on the keywords; however, there are ways to break up the text into manageable parts. The third table you need will be called `VisitorSearches`, and its fields are as follows:

SearchID	- AutoNumber, PrimaryKey
VisitorID	- Long
SearchTerms	- String, 255
SearchResults	- Long

The first field is a unique ID to identify this search instance. The second links it back to the particular visitor. The third holds the search terms used by the user. The fourth field records the number of search results that the user received. This field can be used to find search terms that are being used repeatedly but not finding any results. It could also be used to help make the content easier to search, especially if you're seeing obvious terms that are not getting any results.

Modifying the Code

We begin with the final version of the code from Chapter 11, which includes these five files:

```
catviewer.asp
prodviewer.asp
prodinfo.asp
searchform.asp
searchresults.asp
```

Now that you're an expert in designing ASP pages, you may want to go back and revise these pages. For purposes of clarity, however, we'll start with the same code and simply make our changes for user tracking.

General Changes

First, we will pull the common routines, such as the open database code, into a separate file that will be included into each file. There will be other functions that will be called from multiple places. The code file will be called common.asp. In some places, you'll see include files with the inc extension; however, I prefer to use the asp extension for all files with ASP code.

The code for the common.asp file is shown in Listing 14-5.

Listing 14-5: **Code for common.asp file**

```
<%
Const DBFILENAME = "C:\NWind.mdb"

'------------------------------------------------------------

Function OpenDatabase()
   Dim dcnDB        ' As ADODB.Connection
   Set dcnDB = Server.CreateObject("ADODB.Connection")
   dcnDB.ConnectionString = _
     "Provider=Microsoft.Jet.OLEDB.3.51;" _
         & "Persist Security Info=False;Data Source=" _
         & DBFILENAME
   dcnDB.Open
   Set OpenDatabase = dcnDB
End Function

'------------------------------------------------------------

%>
```

To make existing files to use the common.asp file, add a #include directive just after the Option Explicit statement. This process is shown in Listing 14-6, which is the first few lines of catviewer.asp.

Listing 14-6: **Adding the common code file to catviewer.asp**

```
<%
    Option Explicit
%>
```

```
<!--#include file="common.asp" -->
<html>
<head>
   <title>Northwind Traders: Category Viewer</title>
</head>

<%

   Dim dcnDB        ' As ADODB.Connection
   Dim rsCat        ' As ADODB.Recordset
   Dim strSQL       ' As String

   Set dcnDB = OpenDatabase()
   strSQL = "SELECT * FROM Categories " _
       & "ORDER BY CategoryName"
   Set rsCat = dcnDB.Execute(strSQL)
%>
```

You'll also see how we are now using the OpenDatabase function instead of the call to create the ADO Connection object. Make these changes throughout all the files before you continue this exercise. You don't have to change any database code in the search form, however.

Changing the Category Viewer Page

The category viewer page is presumably the first page that a user will see; however, we cannot guarantee that sequence. This page will need to create a cookie for the user with their database-generated VisitorID value. Because we'll need to use this functionality in other places, we're going to create a subroutine to do it. This subroutine will be added to the end of common.asp. The code is shown in Listing 14-7.

Listing 14-7: **CreateVisitorID subroutine in common.asp**

```
'------------------------------------------------------------

Sub CreateVisitorID(dcnDB)
    Dim rsData       ' As ADODB.Recordset
    Dim strSQL       ' As String

    If Request.Cookies("VisitorID") <> "" Then Exit Sub

    strSQL = "INSERT INTO Visitors " _
        & "(VisitDate, Host) " _
        & "VALUES (" _
        & "#" & Date & " " & Time & "#, " _
        & "'"
```

Continued

Listing 14-7 *(continued)*

```
  If Request.ServerVariables("REMOTE_HOST") <> "" Then
      strSQL = strSQL & Request.ServerVariables("REMOTE_HOST")
  Else
      strSQL = strSQL & Request.ServerVariables("REMOTE_ADDR")
  End If
  strSQL = strSQL & "')"

  Application.Lock
  dcnDB.Execute strSQL
  strSQL = "SELECT Max(VisitorID) FROM Visitors"
  Set rsData = dcnDB.Execute(strSQL)
  Response.Cookies("VisitorID") = rsData(0)
  Application.UnLock

    rsData.Close
End Sub

  '- - - - - - - - - - - - - - - - - - - - - - - - - - - - - - - - - - - - - - - - - - - - - - - -
```

Before creating a new VisitorID, the code checks to see if the browser already has one. If so, it bails out immediately. Otherwise, it constructs a SQL statement with the current date and time, as well as either the hostname or the host address of the browser viewing the site. These names and addresses are merely informational, but could be helpful if you're seeing lots of hits from the same sites.

We then use the Lock method of the Application object to prevent other pages from running while we create the cookie. Once we've inserted the row, we need to retrieve the biggest ID immediately, which was the one that we created. Using the Lock method temporarily freezes operations for everyone else while we do this. This is a very quick operation and lets us get the correct ID without having to worry about other cookies being created while we're trying to find the cookie we made. We store the cookie value into the Response object's cookies collection, which sends it to the user's browser. Because we didn't supply an expiration date, this is a temporary cookie.

To call this routine, make the change marked in Listing 14-8 to your catviewer.asp page. The entire page is not listed here, so just find the surrounding lines and add the line of code appropriately.

Listing 14-8: **Call to CreateVisitorID in catviewer.asp**

```
Dim dcnDB        ' As ADODB.Connection
Dim rsCat        ' As ADODB.Recordset
Dim strSQL       ' As String

Set dcnDB = OpenDatabase()
CreateVisitorID dcnDB

strSQL = "SELECT * FROM Categories " _
```

You have completed the necessary changes for the `catviewer.asp` page.

Changing the Product Viewing Page

This page will have two changes:

✦ A call to `CreateVisitorID`, to make sure that the user didn't bypass the first page and not receive a cookie value.

✦ A call to store the selected category ID into the table.

We'll create the second subroutine in `common.asp` first and then make the changes to `prodviewer.asp`. The new subroutine just has to write the category ID to the table. An `INSERT` statement is the quickest way to accomplish this task, as completed by the `RecordCategoryID` routine, shown in Listing 14-9.

Listing 14-9: **RecordCategoryID subroutine**

```
Sub RecordCategoryID(dcnDB, lngCatID)

    Dim strSQL       ' As String

    '
    ' Make sure that the user has a cookie created
    '
    CreateVisitorID dcnDB
    strSQL = "INSERT INTO VisitorViews " _
        & "(VisitorID, CategoryID) VALUES (" _
        & Request.Cookies("VisitorID") & ", " _
        & lngCatID & ")"
    dcnDB.Execute strSQL

End Sub
```

We have also called the `CreateVisitorID` routine from this routine. This arrangement saves us from having to put the call right into the `prodviewer.asp` page. Because we're checking and/or creating a cookie before inserting into `VisitorViews`, you may also be wondering why it's necessary to call `CreateVisitorID` from the `catviewer.asp` page. We're doing it in `catviewer.asp` because other pages, which may need the cookie, aren't going to be recording category IDs. There may also be a need to let the user login only on a single page, at which point we would only call the `CreateVisitorID` from that page. Right now, it's just a double-check in this routine.

The other change occurs in the `prodviewer.asp` page. The changed code is marked in Listing 14-10, which is just a snippet of the entire page.

Listing 14-10: **Call to RecordCategoryID**

```
Dim dcnDB              ' As ADODB.Connection
Dim rsProd             ' As ADODB.Recordset
Dim rsCat              ' As ADODB.Recordset
Dim strSQL             ' As String

Set dcnDB = OpenDatabase()

RecordCategoryID dcnDB, Request("catID")
strSQL = "SELECT CategoryName FROM Categories "_
```

At this point, you can load the category viewer, select various categories, and then go to the database to see what you've accomplished. Each time you exit your browser and restart, you'll get a new cookie. In addition, if you leave your browser and don't do anything on the site for several minutes (the number of minutes for your Session timeout; ten is the default), you'll get a new cookie. You'll also see a row in the `VisitorViews` table for each category that you viewed.

Changing the Search Results Page

The final changes we need to make are in the Search Results page (`searchresults.asp`). We need to store the search terms, as well as the number of results, into the database. We need to add a new subroutine, `RecordSearchInfo`, to the `common.asp` file. The code for this new routine is shown in Listing 14-11.

Listing 14-11: **Code for RecordSearchInfo subroutine**

```
Sub RecordSearchInfo(dcnDB, strSearch, lngResultCount)

    Dim strSQL      ' As STring

    '
```

```
' Make sure that the user has a cookie created
'
CreateVisitorID dcnDB
strSQL = "INSERT INTO VisitorSearches " _
    & "(VisitorID, SearchTerms, SearchResults) VALUES (" _
    & Request.Cookies("VisitorID") & ", '" _
    & Replace(strSearch, "'", "''") & "', " _
    & lngResultCount & ")"
dcnDB.Execute strSQL

End Sub
```

This code is fairly straightforward, except for the use of the Replace function while we're building the SQL statement. We are replacing single quotes with two single quotes because single quotes are used to delimit strings in SQL statements. If we were to have a search string that contained a single quote, it would error out. Replacing single quotes with two single quotes takes care of this problem.

The other change you need to make is to call this routine from the searchresults. asp page. The modified code is shown in a snippet from the file in Listing 14-12.

Listing 14-12: **Modifications to searchresults.asp**

```
lngRecordCount = 0
Do While Not rsProd.EOF
    Response.Write "<li>" _
        & "<a href=""prodinfo.asp?prodID=" _
        & rsProd("ProductID") _
        & """>" _
        & rsProd("ProductName") _
        & "</a>"
    rsProd.MoveNext
    lngRecordCount = lngRecordCount + 1
Loop
%>
</ul>
<a href="searchform.asp">Back to Search Utility</a>
</body>
</html>

<%
    RecordSearchInfo dcnDB, Request("txtProductName"), _
        lngRecordCount

    rsProd.Close
    dcnDB.Close
%>
```

You also need to add this variable declaration to the top of the file:

```
Dim lngRecordCount          ' As Long
```

This declaration will record the text that the user was looking for into the database. If desirable, you could expand the VisitorSearches table to include all the other criteria from the page not currently being recorded.

Wrapping Up

Now that you have all of this data, you can report on it. Based on the data you've collected, you can create the following reports:

✦ Most/least popular category

✦ Average number of categories per person

✦ Search terms by number of results returned

✦ All search terms

✦ Top three categories for each host name

These reports can either be created in Microsoft Access, Active Server Pages, Seagate Software's Crystal Reports, or any other report writer. You may also want to create a summary report that includes all of this information in a compact format. Above all, make sure to use the information and modify your site accordingly.

Summary

This chapter was designed to show you how tighter integration with your database can be used to get better and faster results. You also saw how using a database can help you improve a user's experience on your site. By tracking user activity, you can get a better feel about what users are doing on your site, how long they're staying, where they go, and so forth. All of these factors help contribute to improving the site with better navigation, more intelligent content creation, and faster performance.

✦   ✦   ✦

Integrating with Other Tools

ASP has the benefit of being able to use other components, libraries, and tools. These chapters show you how to work with Index Server, Visual Basic, and Microsoft Transaction Server.

◆   ◆   ◆   ◆

Chapter 15
Integrating with
Index Server

Chapter 16
Using Classes in
Visual Basic

Chapter 17
Using WebClasses

Chapter 18
Integrating with
Microsoft Transaction
Server

◆   ◆   ◆   ◆

Integrating with Index Server

◆ ◆ ◆ ◆

In This Chapter

Learn how Index
Server integrates
with IIS

Learn to include and
exclude directories
from indexing

Learn about the
objects involved with
Index Server

Learning Index
Server's query
language

◆ ◆ ◆ ◆

Introduction to Index Server

A few years ago, many Internet sites had a site map. This
graphical representation was designed to show the structure
of a Web site and make it easier for users to navigate. While
some sites still have these maps, most sites have become far
too large to fit on a single map.

Users still need a way to search sites, so most large Web sites
have a search feature in a prominent place. If you're like me,
you don't want to wander through pages and pages of navigation to find information. Type a few words into a box, and
voila, there's the page you wanted. Well, you may not get quite
the page you wanted, but you can always refine your search
by adding more keywords.

Internet Information Server 4.0 comes with a product known
as Index Server, which is built into the IIS structure. The
process of indexing a site is simple. First, create an index.
Next, specify the directories to index. Finally, let the index
run and then use it. The rest of this chapter shows you the
specifics of this relatively basic process. In addition, you'll
learn about the power of Index Server that lurks under its
relatively calm surface.

Configuring Index Server

Before you can perform searches on your Web server, you first
have to create at least one index. This is done using the Index
Server Manager on the machine where Internet Information
Server is running. Note that Index Server is only available for
the server edition of Internet Information Server.

To create an index, do the following:

1. Start Index Server Manager on your NT Server. By default, the icon is located in the Windows NT 4.0 Option Pack\Microsoft Index Server program group. When you start it, the interface shown in Figure 15-1 will appear. Like the IIS Manager, the Index Server console runs as a snap-in within the Microsoft Management Console.

   The right side of this window provides information about the indexes that currently exist on the machine. In this example, three indexes are maintained: ContentManagement, ExAir, and Web. The contents are not important at this point.

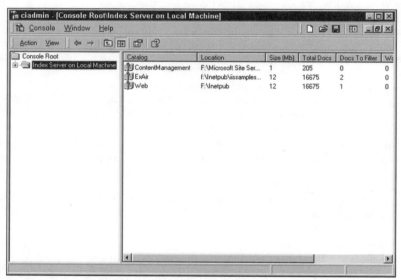

Figure 15-1: Index Server Manager console

2. To create a new catalog, right-click either the left or the right and select New ➪ Catalog. The dialog box shown in Figure 15-2 will appear.

   A catalog is the term used in Index Server to represent an index on a certain group of pages. You can put the index directory anywhere you want. For best performance, place the directory on a separate disk from your Web server. With this strategy, you won't run into a bottleneck when lots of users are hitting your Web site.

Figure 15-2: Add Catalog dialog box

3. After you specify the name and location of your index, Index Server won't start indexing immediately. First, you have to specify which Web site you wish to index. You'll get a message indicating that your new catalog will be offline until Index Server is restarted. This message is perfectly normal, so click OK to continue past the message.

4. To specify the directories to index, right-click your new catalog and select Properties from the popup menu. The dialog box shown in Figure 15-3 will appear.

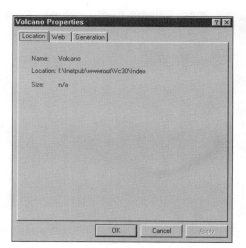

Figure 15-3: Catalog properties dialog box, Location tab

The first tab shows you what you just typed. Figure 15-4 shows the Web tab, which is where you'll specify the Web you wish to index.

The final tab (Figure 15-5) enables you to specify whether to index files with unknown extensions. You can also specify how long the "abstract," or "characterization" of a file will be. We examine characterizations closely in a following section, but basically they provide a quick look at the first specified amount of characters in a file. For now, these options can remain at their defaults.

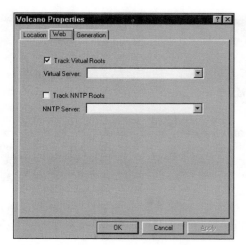

Figure 15-4: Catalog properties dialog box, Web tab

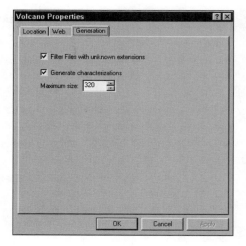

Figure 15-5: Catalog properties dialog box, Generation tab

5. Control of the indexed content is handled through the IIS Console, so you can pick a Web site that you want to have indexed by clicking the Web tab and picking a site. Select the site and then press the OK button.

6. With the catalog created, you can now pick the directories you want to include in the index. This powerful feature enables you to create several indexes that search your content in different ways. For instance, you may want to have a quick reference section that is indexed separately from the full-text version. This feature enables you to do perform this task within Index Server. To add a directory, open up the tree on the left until you can see the

catalog that you created. Open up that catalog, and then click on the Directories node. Your display will look something like Figure 15-6.

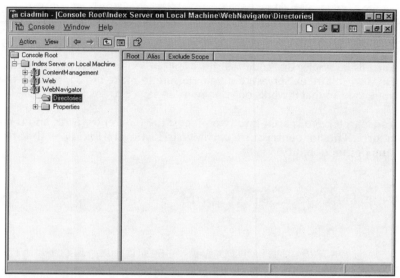

Figure 15-6: This section enables you to select directories to index.

7. To add a directory, right-click the right-hand side and select New ⇨ Directory. In the dialog box that appears, pick a directory by either pathname or UNC name here. If you have to log into the server to get the content, you can provide a user name and password that will be used to reach the content. This feature is helpful if you want to index protected content but still preserve security on the content so that only authorized users (perhaps those that paid for it) can get to the full version of the content.

You can also use this tool to exclude a subdirectory in a Web site that you don't want to index. For instance, indexing the scripts/CGI directory will not help the user. In addition, if you were keeping your index in the same location, this would be the place to exclude it from indexing. Simply specify the directory and select Exclude instead of Include on the preceding dialog box.

8. After you've included/excluded all the directories for the site, restart the Index Server service by right-clicking the left-hand side and selecting Start from the popup menu. Your server will begin looking through the indexes you've created and start indexing the content. If you see that an index is getting too large and you know there are only a few documents to be indexed, make sure that you specified a Web site to index. Otherwise, the service defaults to the default Web site, which could be quite large.

Creating a Simple Search Page

Now that your catalog has been created, you can use it to search your content. This section covers how to build a simple search page that can use a particular index and create a simple result. You'll see later how to use additional parameters and objects to create more complex searches.

Note   For this example, the code will be using an index called RootWeb, located on D:\Microsoft Index Server\RootWeb. Be sure to make the appropriate changes to your code so that it works on your own server.

The first search page is split into two pieces: the data entry form and the search results form. The data entry form is shown in Listing 15-1 and has the absolute minimum of functionality.

Listing 15-1: **Basic Query form**

```
<html>
<head>
   <title>ASP Bible: Chapter 15 - Basic Query Form</title>
</head>

<body>
<h1>Basic Query Form</h1>
<form method="POST" action="basicquery_process.asp">
Search for: <input type="text" name="txtQuery" size="20"><p>
<input type="submit" value="Search">
<input type="reset" value="Reset">

</form>
</body>
</html>
```

When you run this form, you'll see a pretty dull looking form that has a text box on it. An example of the form at runtime is shown in Figure 15-7.

The real power of searching is concentrated in the back-end page, which is separated for clarity in this example. The code for the back-end page is shown in Listing 15-2.

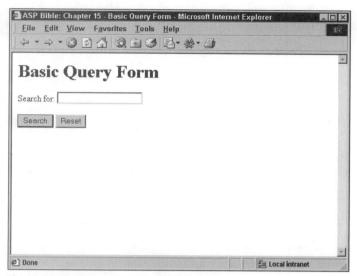

Figure 15-7: Query form in the browser

Listing 15-2: **Query Processing page**

```
<%
    Option Explicit
%>
<HTML>
<HEAD>
    <TITLE>ASP Bible: Chapter 15 - Query Results</TITLE>
</HEAD>
<BODY>
<%
    Dim objQuery        ' As ixsso.Query
    Dim rsQuery         ' As ADODB.Recordset

    Set objQuery = Server.CreateObject("ixsso.Query")
    objQuery.Query = Request("txtQuery")
    objQuery.Columns="filename,vpath,DocTitle"
    objQuery.Catalog = "D:\Microsoft Index Server\RootWeb"
    objQuery.MaxRecords = 50

    Set rsQuery = objQuery.CreateRecordset("nonsequential")
```

Continued

Listing 15-2 *(continued)*

```
%>

<h1>Search Results</h1>
<%
If rsQuery.EOF Then
%>
<font color=#FF0000>
No documents were found
that matched your query.
</font>
<%
Else
%>
<table>
<tr>
<th>Title</th>
</tr>
<%
    Do While Not rsQuery.EOF
        If rsQuery("doctitle") <> "" Then
%>
<tr>
    <td><a href="<% = rsQuery("vpath") %>">
        <% = rsQuery("doctitle") %></a>
    </td>
</tr>
<%
        End If
        rsQuery.MoveNext
    Loop
    Response.Write "</table>"

End If
%>
</body>
</html>
```

The results of running a query with the words "transaction server" are shown in Figure 15-8. Your results may vary, depending on the content of your server.

In this code, the Query object is the heart of the search engine. The object talks directly to the Index Server engine to retrieve data. As you can see from the brevity of the code, it doesn't take a lot of work to get a basic search engine up and running.

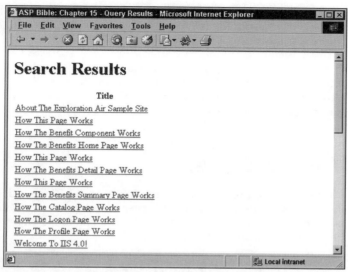

Figure 15-8: Results of a query for "transaction server"

A few key properties have to be set to get any results back: Query, Columns, and Catalog. The MaxRecords property is recommended but not required. The Query property holds the search criteria; in this case, the contents of the text box on the previous page. The Columns property holds a list of the columns to be returned from the query. The names of these columns are fixed and covered later in the chapter. The last property that must be set is the Catalog property, which specifies the directory where the index lives. In this case, we are pointing to the RootWeb folder, even though there is a Catalog.WCI folder in that folder. Index Server already knows about the Catalog.WCI folder, so you don't need to add that to the Catalog property value.

Once the Query object is populated, you create an ADO recordset from the query. This recordset is the same as recordsets created from a database and can be navigated in the same manner.

The remaining code takes care of displaying the results. After creating a table (with a single column for this example), we loop through all the records. There is a check to only show files that have titles, because Index Server is able to index other types of files (such as graphics) that won't necessarily make sense to show. In some cases, you may want to show the images, but in this case, we only want text documents.

Using the vpath and doctitle parameters, we can construct a URL to point to the document that was found. The vpath parameter is the virtual path to the file, and the `doctitle` parameter is the title of the document. For HTML documents, this is the value between the `<TITLE>` tags in the file. For other types of documents, the title will vary as to where it is stored.

With the exception of the `MaxRecords` property, this example is the absolute minimum of code required to hook up Index Server to your application. Now that you understand the basics, we can move into some of the more complex applications you can build using Index Server.

Index Server Object Model

Like everything else in this book, Index Server has an object model. This model enables you to access everything about how Index Server searches your content. This section describes the objects available to you, and you'll see these objects in use throughout the rest of this chapter in the examples.

Query Object Properties and Methods

As you've already seen, the `Query` object represents a question to the Index Server content database. You've used a few of the properties already, but this section will cover all of the available properties and methods.

AllowEnumeration Property

This property tells the Index Server engine whether it can use enumeration queries to create the query results. If your query involves recursive searches through directories, this property is used. Setting this value to True enables enumeration queries to be used, and False means that only the content index can be used.

Catalog Property

As you've seen already, the `Catalog` property points to the directory where the content index is located. This location can be either a fully qualified pathname or a UNC name. If you don't specify a name, the default catalog will be used. The default catalog name is "Web," so if you don't have that catalog on your system, you'll get a runtime error when you try to execute your query.

CiFlags Property

This property tells Index Server whether to search just a particular directory given to it in the `CiScope` property, or to search through all of the specified directory's subdirectories. You can store the following values in this property:

SHALLOW	Search only the specified directory
DEEP	Search the directory and its subdirectories

CiScope Property

This property specifies which directories to search within an index. For instance, you can provide a comma-separated list of directories so that you only search a certain part of the site instead of the whole site. You can use either forward slashes (for virtual directories) or backward slashes (for physical directories). Both this property and the `CiFlags` property are set using the `AddScopeToQuery` method of the `Utility` object, which is covered later in this section.

CodePage Property

This property enables you to specify a different code page for indexing. A code page contains all the characters for a particular language or locale. Code pages are designated by numbers such as ANSI code page 1252 for American English and OEM code page 932 for Japanese Kanji. Code pages are used for two purposes: to parse the query string and other strings such as column names, and to convert back and forth between URL sequences and query strings in the `SetQueryFromURL` and `QueryToURL` methods.

Columns Property

This property, which you've already used, enables you to pick the columns you want to get in the result set. The column names should be stored in the `Columns` property separated by commas. The available columns are shown in Table 15-1.

Table 15-1
Available Columns for Index Server Queries

Friendly Name	Property
A_HRef	Text of HTML HREF. This property name was created for Microsoft Site Server and corresponds to the Index Server property name `HtmlHRef`. Can be queried but not retrieved.
Access	Last time file was accessed.
All	Searches every property for a string. Can be queried but not retrieved.
AllocSize	Size of disk allocation for file.
Attrib	File attributes. Documented in Win32 SDK.
ClassId	Class ID of object, for example, WordPerfect, Word, and so forth.
Characterization	Characterization, or abstract, of document. Computed by Indexing Service.

Continued

Table 15-1 *(continued)*

Friendly Name	Property
Contents	Main contents of file. Can be queried but not retrieved.
Create	Time file was created.
Directory	Physical path to the file, not including the file name.
DocAppName	Name of application that created the file.
DocAuthor	Author of document.
DocByteCount	Number of bytes in a document.
DocCategory	Type of document, such as a memo, schedule, or white paper.
DocCharCount	Number of characters in document.
DocComments	Comments about document.
DocCompany	Name of the company for which the document was written.
DocCreatedTm	Time document was created.
DocEditTime	Total time spent editing document.
DocHiddenCount	Number of hidden slides in a Microsoft PowerPoint(r) document.
DocKeywords	Document keywords.
DocLastAuthor	Most recent user who edited document.
DocLastPrinted	Time document was last printed.
DocLastSavedTm	Time document was last saved.
DocLineCount	Number of lines contained in a document.
DocManager	Name of the manager of the document's author.
DocNoteCount	Number of pages with notes in a PowerPoint document.
DocPageCount	Number of pages in document.
DocParaCount	Number of paragraphs in a document.
DocPartTitles	Names of document parts. For example, in Microsoft Excel, part titles are the names of spreadsheets; in PowerPoint, slide titles; and in Word for Windows, the names of the documents in the master document.
DocPresentationTarget	Target format (35mm, printer, video, and so forth) for a presentation in PowerPoint.
DocRevNumber	Current version number of document.

Friendly Name	Property
DocSecurity	Control permissions.
DocSlideCount	Number of slides in a PowerPoint document.
DocSubject	Subject of document.
DocTemplate	Name of template for document.
DocThumbnail	Thumbnail.
DocTitle	Title of document.
DocWordCount	Number of words in document.
FileIndex	Unique ID of file.
FileName	Name of file.
HtmlHeading1	Text of HTML document in style H1. Can be queried but not retrieved.
HtmlHeading2	Text of HTML document in style H2. Can be queried but not retrieved.
HtmlHeading3	Text of HTML document in style H3. Can be queried but not retrieved.
HtmlHeading4	Text of HTML document in style H4. Can be queried but not retrieved.
HtmlHeading5	Text of HTML document in style H5. Can be queried but not retrieved.
HtmlHeading6	Text of HTML document in style H6. Can be queried but not retrieved.
HtmlHRef	Text of HTML HREF. Can be queried but not retrieved.
Img_Alt	Alternate text for <IMG> tags. Can be queried but not retrieved.
Path	Full physical path to file, including file name.
ShortFileName	Short (8.3) file name.
Size	Size of file, in bytes.
USN	Update Sequence Number (USN). NTFS file system drives only.
Write	Last time file was written.

For the fields marked as "can be queried but not retrieved," you can have Index Server search those fields (as part of a query), but you can't get the contents back as part of your result set.

Another note is that if you've done much with Microsoft Office, you should notice a lot of columns that apply directly to the suite's products. Index Server knows how to read the contents of many application-specific files. In addition, you can create your own filters to read other types of files not already supported by Index Server. Refer to the Index Server documentation for the technical details on this process, as it is beyond the scope of this book.

Dialect Property

This property value refers to the dialect of Indexing Query Language you are using. The string value "1" means dialect 1, and the value "2" means dialect 2. This property won't be of much use to you in everyday work. Refer to the documentation on Index Server for more details.

GroupBy Property

Just as you have the GROUP BY syntax in SQL, Index Server enables you to group the documents by any of the columns that you've retrieved. For instance, let's say that you want to group the documents by the name of the application that created them. The following code groups the documents by ApplicationName in ascending order:

```
objQuery.GroupBy = "DocAppName [a]"
```

You can replace the [a] with [d] to sort in descending order. In addition, if you want to group by multiple columns, you can separate the columns with plus signs (+), as follows:

```
objQuery.GroupBy = "DocAppName+Directory [d]"
```

This example will group by DocAppName and Directory together in descending order. Finally, you can create subgroups by separating the columns with commas instead of plus signs. In the following example, each different Directory value will be listed as a separate subgroup of DocAppName:

```
objQuery.GroupBy = "DocAppName,Directory [d]"
```

Again, this example sorts the values in descending order.

LocaleID Property

Like the CodePage property, this property is used to identify the language to use to perform a query on your indexes. For Web clients, browsers send a HTTP header — HTTP_ACCEPT_LANGUAGE — that specifies the locale to use in a query. This setting can be overridden with this LocaleID property. The U.S. English locale is 1033 (equivalent to the language code "en-us").

MaxRecords Property

This property, which you've already used, specifies the maximum number of records to return as a result of the query. If this property is not set, all records matching the criteria are returned in the result recordset.

Query Property

This property contains the search criteria to use for the search. The exact syntax for this property is quite complex and is covered in a following section.

QueryIncomplete Property

If this property returns True, the query was too complex to complete. This value could also mean that there was an error in the query that caused Index Server to get confused and not be able to parse it. Using parentheses and other grouping symbols can help simplify the processing of the query.

QueryTimedOut Property

If this property returns True, the query timed out before it could finish. The administrator can set the maximum search time using the Index Server Manager. If you know you're going to have many complex queries, increasing the timeout is a good idea.

SortBy Property

This property works like the GroupBy property. You can list the columns by which you want to sort and add the [a] or [d] parameter following the column to specify ascending (default) or descending sorting. Here is an example:

```
objQuery.SortBy = "DocAppName [d], DocTitle [a]"
```

This code will sort in reverse order by the name of the application, and in ascending order for the documents created by that application.

CreateRecordset Method

Using the CreateRecordset method of the Query object causes your query to be sent to the server, evaluated, and processed. This method returns an ADO Recordset that can be manipulated (but not edited) like a recordset you would return from the database. This call cannot be executed until all the Query object's parameters have been set.

DefineColumn Method

Some of the available column names have fairly long names. The DefineColumn method enables you to create aliases for those columns that you can use within your query. In cases where you have complex search criteria, creating aliases will dramatically shorten the text length of your queries. Here is an example that aliases the `DocAppName` column to the name "app":

```
objQuery.DefineColumn "app = DocAppName"
```

To create multiple aliases, each alias must be created with a separate `DefineColumn` call.

QueryToURL Method

This method creates a query string that can be used for rerunning a particular query. Index Server provides another method named `SetQueryFromURL`, which will read a URL and load the Query object with the appropriate values automatically. This method does the reverse and creates a URL with the `Query` object's parameters. Refer to the documentation for the `SetQueryFromURL` method for a list of the parameters that are used in the query string.

Reset Method

This method clears the internal state of the `Query` object and returns the object to its initial state.

SetQueryFromURL Method

This method loads the `Query` object with parameters from the input form; that is, the values in the `Request` object. These values can be either in the query string or the form. This method will look for the following properties and store them in the properties of the `Query` object, as shown in Table 15-2.

Table 15-2 Index Server Property Shortcut Names	
Shortcut Name	**Maps to Property**
ae	AllowEnumeration — values zero or one, for False and True, respectively
ct	Catalog
di	Dialect
gd	GroupBy, **descending**
gr	GroupBy, **ascending**
mh	MaxHits
qu	Query **text — used by the** Query **property**
so	Sort, **ascending**
sd	Sort, **descending**

Utility Object Methods

The Utility object provides additional features for running queries in Index Server. Some of these features will be used less often than the ones in the Query object, but they are still helpful to understand and be able to use.

To use any of these methods, you have to instantiate a Utility object using code like the following:

```
Dim objUtility  ' As IXSSO.Utility
Set objUtility = Server.CreateObject("IXSSO.Utility")
```

AddScopeToQuery Method

By default, Index Server uses the entire catalog that is specified. However, it's often helpful to only search a particular part of the catalog. For instance, Microsoft's Web site allows you to search either a product section or the entire Web for a document. This arrangement can help eliminate redundant search results. Here is the syntax for this call:

```
objUtility.AddScopeToQuery(objQuery, strPath, strDepth)
```

objUtility	The Utility object.
objQuery	Required. String. The Query object using this scope.
strPath	Required. String. The physical or virtual path of the scope to add.
strDepth	Optional. String. Case-insensitive. Whether the scope covers only the named directory ("shallow") or the named directory and all its subdirectories ("deep").

As an example, this code adds a deep scope of the techsupp directory to the existing query:

```
objUtility.AddScopeToQuery(objQuery, "/techsupp", "deep")
```

HTMLEncode Method

This method is similar to the method available in the built-in Server object. It takes HTML text and converts it so that it will display properly. For instance, this example code:

```
strReturn = objUtility.HTMLEncode("<P>This is a test.</P>")
```

strReturn, if viewed, would contain the following HTML:

```
&lt;P&gt;This is a test.&lt;/P&gt;
```

This function is helpful if you need to print HTML code on your pages.

ISOToLocale Method

This method converts a numeric language code (ISO 639) to a Win32 locale identifier. The first recognized language code found in `strLocale` is converted to a Win32 LCID. The recognized language codes include all those from the ISO 639 standard that map to Win32 language IDs and some country codes that have sublanguage codes in Win32. If a language code is recognized, but the country code is not, the language code alone is used, unless there is a better match later in the string. The syntax for this function is as follows:

```
lngLocaleID = objUtility.ISOToLocaleID(strLocale)
```

LocaleIDToISO Method

This method converts a Win32 locale identifier to a numeric language code (ISO 639). The syntax is as follows:

```
strLocaleID = objUtility.LocaleIDToISO(lngLocaleID)
```

This function is the reverse of the `ISOToLocaleID` function.

TruncatetoWhitespace Method

The `TruncateToWhitespace` method truncates a string at a whitespace character. Script writers can call this method to display short forms of the value of long properties (such as the contents of `Description` property) without truncating in the middle of a word. This function is designed to let you show the first specified number of characters of a large text field, but stop showing text at a full word and not in the middle of one. The syntax is as follows:

```
strTruncStr = objUtility.TruncateToWhitespace(strInput, lngMax)
```

This code looks at the character position specified by `lngMax` and works backwards until it finds whitespace; that is, a space or a line break.

URLEncode Method

This method is similar to `HTMLEncode`, except that it is designed for use with URLs. This method will take care of spaces that are part of the query string parameters. The resulting text can be placed in a browser URL entry field and/or clicked in a page without getting an error due to spaces. The syntax is as follows:

```
strConverted = objUtility.URLEncode("http://asptechniques.com")
```

Any spaces or other illegal characters in the URL will be converted to their numerical equivalents.

Index Server Query Language

Like Structured Query Language, Index Server's query language is quite robust. You have the ability to search in a variety of ways using any or all of the available properties. This section will show you how to use this language for your own searches.

Basic Query Rules

Searches produce a list of files that contain the word or phrase no matter where they appear in the text. This list gives the basic rules for formulating queries:

✦ Consecutive words are treated as a phrase; they must appear in the same order within a matching document.

✦ Queries are case-insensitive, so you can type your query in uppercase or lowercase.

✦ You can search for any word except for those in the exception list (for English, this list includes a, an, and, as, and other common words), which are ignored during a search.

✦ Words in the exception list are treated as placeholders in phrase and proximity queries. For example, if you searched for "Word for Windows", the results could give you "Word for Windows" and "Word and Windows", because *for* is a noise word and appears in the exception list.

✦ Punctuation marks such as the period (.), colon (:), semicolon (;), and comma (,) are ignored during a search.

✦ To use specially treated characters (such as &, |, ^, #, @, $, (, and)) in a query, enclose your query in quotation marks (").

✦ To search for a word or phrase containing quotation marks, enclose the entire phrase in quotation marks and then double the quotation marks around the word or words you want to surround with quotes. For example, "World Wide Web or ""Web""" searches for World Wide Web or "Web."

✦ You can insert any Boolean operator (such as And, Or, and Not) in your queries. You can also use the proximity operator, Near, to do additional searches.

✦ The wildcard character (*) can be used to match words with a particular prefix. For instance, if you specify Win* as the query string, any words matching Win as the beginning of the word will match.

✦ You can also query based on COM/ActiveX property values or file attribute values.

Boolean and Proximity Operators

Using Boolean and/or proximity operators can enable you to specify query criteria more accurately. The following examples show some sample queries and the results:

	Table 15-3	
	Boolean Operator Results	
To Search For	*Example*	*Results*
Both terms in a page	index and server	Pages with both the words "index" and "server"
Either term in a page	index or server	Pages with either "index" or "server"
One term and not the other	index and not server	Pages with "index" but not "server"
Pages matching a property value	@size = 100	Pages that are 100 bytes in size
Both terms in a page and close to each other	index near server	Pages with the word "index" near the word "server" in the page

You can also use symbols instead of the word operators, as shown in Table 15-4.

	Table 15-4
	Operator Equivalents
Text Keyword	*Symbol*
AND	&
OR	|
NOT	!
NEAR	~

These symbols (&, |, !, ~) and the English keywords AND, OR, NOT, and NEAR work the same way in all languages supported by Index Server.

Besides these simple queries, you can add parentheses to nest expressions within a query. The expressions in parentheses are evaluated before the rest of the query.

Use double quotes (") to indicate that a Boolean or NEAR operator keyword should be ignored in your query. For example, "green eggs and ham" will match pages with the phrase, not pages that match the Boolean expression. In addition to being an operator, the word *and* is a noise word in English.

The NEAR operator is similar to the AND operator in that NEAR returns a match if both search terms are in the same page. However, the NEAR operator differs from AND because the rank assigned by NEAR depends on the proximity of words. That is, the rank of a page with the searched-for words closer together is greater than or equal to the rank of a page where the words are farther apart. If the searched-for words are more than 50 words apart, they are not considered near enough, and the page is assigned a rank of zero.

The NOT operator can be used only after an AND operator in content queries; it can be used only to exclude pages that match a previous content restriction. For property value queries, the NOT operator can be used apart from the AND operator.

The AND operator has a higher precedence than OR. For example, the first three queries are equal, but the fourth is not:

```
a AND b OR c
c OR a AND b
c OR (a AND b)
(c OR a) AND b
```

Wildcards

Wildcard operators help you find pages containing words similar to a given word. Table 15-5 shows some examples of how to use the wildcard character.

Table 15-5 Using the Wildcard Character		
To Search For	*Example*	*Results*
Words with the same prefix	comput*	Pages with words that have the prefix "comput," such as "computer," "computing," and so forth
Words based on the same stem word	fly**	Pages with words based on the same stem as "fly," such as "flying," "flown," "flew," and so forth

Free-Text Queries

The query engine finds pages that best match the words and phrases in a free-text query. This process is done by finding pages automatically that match the meaning, not the exact wording, of the query. Boolean, proximity, and wildcard operators are ignored within a free-text query. Free-text queries are prefixed with $contents.

Property Value Queries

With property value queries, you can find files that have property values that match a given criteria. The properties over which you can query include basic file information (such as file name and file size) and ActiveX properties (including the document summary (information) stored in files created by ActiveX-aware applications).

There are two types of property queries:

✦ Relational property queries consist of an "at" character (@), a property name, a relational operator, and a property value. For example, to find all of the files larger than one million bytes, issue the query @size > 1000000.

✦ Regular expression property queries consist of a number sign (#), a property name, and a regular expression for the property value. For example, to find all of the video (.avi) files, issue the query #filename *.avi. Regular expressions will never match the special properties contents (#contents) and all (#all). Properties that are not retrievable at query time cannot be used in # queries. These properties include HTML META properties not stored in the property cache.

Property names are preceded by either the "at" (@) or number sign (#) character. Use @ for relational queries, and # for regular expression queries. If no property name is specified, @contents is assumed.

Properties available for all files include the values shown in Table 15-6.

Table 15-6 Property Names	
Property Name	**Description**
All	Matches words, phrases, and any property
Contents	Words and phrases in the file
Filename	Name of the file

Property Name	Description
Size	File size
Write	Last time the file was modified
DocTitle	Title of the document
DocSubject	Subject of the document
DocAuthor	The document's author
DocKeywords	Keywords for the document
DocComments	Comments about the document

Relational Operators

Relational operators are used in relational property queries. Table 15-7 shows the operators that are available for use.

| | Table 15-7 |
| | **Relational Operators** |

Operator	Meaning
<	Less than
>	Greater than
>=	Greater or equal
<=	Less or equal
=	Equal
!=	Not Equal

Final Notes

Some other query language features supported by Index Server are still in development at the time of this writing. For the latest information about the Index Server language, you can refer to either MSDN's Reference Library, or you can visit the author's ASP Techniques site (http://asptechniques.com) for updated articles about this powerful language. In addition, samples are installed in the following directory that provide more robust query forms than have been covered:

```
\INetPub\IISSamples\ISSamples
```

INetPub is the root of your Internet Information Server content section. By default, the Index Server samples are installed in that location.

Summary

In closing, Index Server is designed to make your Web sites easier to navigate. This feature provides a robust search engine for searching all types of content, both plain text and rich text formats. This chapter was designed to show you how to configure Index Server and how to use the content indexes created by Index Server. You also learned about the objects involved in running queries and how they interact with each other. Using these techniques will help you build more powerful Web sites without a lot of extra work.

✦   ✦   ✦

Using Classes in Visual Basic

In this Chapter

Create a data and object model of an application

Design class modules in Visual Basic

Integrate your class modules with a database

Compile, deploy, and use COM components on the Web

Introduction to VB Classes

So far, your applications have been self-contained within ASP pages. The business, data, and presentation logic have all been contained within the database and/or the ASP pages. However, if you have other applications that need the same logic, you would end up duplicating your own work by creating a separate Web application. Also, the application logic may need to run on a different machine, such as when you need to contact a credit card processor. That logic may be on one server, while the rest of the application logic resides on a separate machine.

This chapter introduces the concept of COM components. The Component Object Model is the underlying architecture that forms the foundation for higher-level software services, like those provided by OLE. OLE services span various aspects of component software, including compound documents, custom controls, interapplication scripting, data transfer, and other software interactions.

Any developer can take advantage of the structure and foundation that COM provides. This chapter will show you how to create your own COM components that can be used in both the Web and traditional client/server environments. This capability enables you to share the business logic between applications.

This chapter shows you how to design a basic object model, complete with an underlying database. You'll see how to design the classes in Visual Basic and how to create code for these classes. You'll also see how to package and deploy these objects for use on the Web. Finally, you'll learn how to use these objects in your ASP pages.

Note

In order to create the applications in this chapter, you'll need Visual Basic 6.0, Professional or Enterprise Edition. You'll also need a database, such as Access 97, SQL Server (6.5 or 7.0), or Oracle. As long as you can access the database through Visual Basic 6.0, you can use it for this chapter.

The Business Model

Let's build an object model around a simple business model: the restaurant. Eric's Pizza Parlor, introduced in a preceding chapter, has gotten very popular and is planning a major expansion. The CEO, a former developer, knows the value of a powerful infrastructure and has hired you to create the model and components to enable the business systems to work on both traditional and Web-based servers.

To keep the model simple to understand, we'll be minimizing the number of objects and properties. The point of this chapter is to create the model and the classes — not to load you down with lots of irrelevant code. This approach should make it easier to understand and replicate in your own situations.

The following entities are part of this system:

✦ Employees — Everyone who works at any Eric's Pizza Parlor location has a record here. Some of the employees are also store managers.

✦ Menu Groups — Allows menu items to be grouped by category.

✦ Menu Items — Entrees, desserts, and everything in between.

✦ Orders — An order is a group of items ordered at a particular store.

✦ Order Items — Each item that is part of a particular order.

✦ Specials — These are temporary price reductions on items in the Menu Items table.

✦ Stores — Each location of Eric's Pizza Parlor.

To keep things simple, the number of properties for each object will be limited. Feel free to expand on these properties. Tables 16-1 through 16-7 indicate the properties for each entity.

| Table 16-1 | |
| **Employee Entity Properties** | |
Property Name	*Description*
EmployeeID	Sequence number for uniqueness
LastName	
FirstName	

Property Name	Description
GetsTips	True/False flag indicating whether employee receives tips
HourlyRate	Currency value for hourly pay rate

Table 16-2
Menu Groups Entity Properties

Property Name	Description
GroupID	Sequence number for uniqueness
Description	Name of group
SortOrder	Integer to enable groups to be sorted in a non-alphabetical order; for instance, appetizers before desserts

Table 16-3
Menu Items Entity Properties

Property Name	Description
MenuItemID	Sequence number for uniqueness
Description	Name of item
GroupID	Foreign key to Menu Groups entity
Price	Currency value for price of item

Table 16-4
Order Entity Properties

Property Name	Description
OrderID	Sequence number for uniqueness
StoreID	Link to Stores entity
OrderDate	Date and time of order
EmployeeID	Employee who handled this order
IsCompleted	Yes/no value indicating whether the order has been paid and completed
TipAmount	Currency value indicating how much tip was left by customer

Table 16-5
Order Items Entity Properties

Property Name	Description
OrderItemID	Sequence number for uniqueness
MenuItemID	Link to Menu Items table
Quantity	Number of this item that was ordered

Table 16-6
Specials Entity Properties

Property Name	Description
SpecialID	Sequence number for uniqueness
MenuItemID	Link to Menu Items table
NewPrice	Currency value with temporary price
StartDate	Date/time that this price starts
EndDate	Date/time that this price ends

Table 16-7
Stores Entity Properties

Property Name	Description
StoreID	Sequence number for uniqueness
City	Location of store
State	Location of store
ManagerID	Link to Employees table indicating the manager

For this sample, there is a sample database provided on the author's Web site in Access 97 format. You can upgrade this database to Access 2000 or upsize it to SQL Server 6.5 or SQL Server 7.0 if necessary.

Creating the Classes

The next step in building this project is to create the actual classes. Visual Basic provides the Class Builder Wizard for creating classes rapidly. To use it, start a new Standard EXE project. If the Wizard is not already listed on the Tools menu, add the Class Builder Wizard by selecting it from Add-ins ⇨ Add-in Manager. For more information on using the Class Builder Wizard, refer to your documentation. After its creation by the Class Builder Wizard, the first class looks like Listing 16-1.

Listing 16-1: **Employee class code**

```
Option Explicit

'local variable(s) to hold property value(s)
Private mvarEmployeeID As Long 'local copy
Private mvarLastName As String 'local copy
Private mvarFirstName As String 'local copy
Private mvarGetsTips As Boolean 'local copy
Private mvarHourlyRate As Currency 'local copy
Public Property Let HourlyRate(ByVal vData As Currency)
'used when assigning a value to the property, on the left side
of an assignment.
'Syntax: X.HourlyRate = 5
    mvarHourlyRate = vData
End Property


Public Property Get HourlyRate() As Currency
'used when retrieving value of a property, on the right side of
an assignment.
'Syntax: Debug.Print X.HourlyRate
    HourlyRate = mvarHourlyRate
End Property


Public Property Let GetsTips(ByVal vData As Boolean)
'used when assigning a value to the property, on the left side
of an assignment.
'Syntax: X.GetsTips = 5
    mvarGetsTips = vData
End Property


Public Property Get GetsTips() As Boolean
'used when retrieving value of a property, on the right side of
an assignment.
'Syntax: Debug.Print X.GetsTips
```

Continued

Listing 16-1 *(continued)*

```
    GetsTips = mvarGetsTips
End Property


Public Property Let FirstName(ByVal vData As String)
'used when assigning a value to the property, on the left side
of an assignment.
'Syntax: X.FirstName = 5
    mvarFirstName = vData
End Property


Public Property Get FirstName() As String
'used when retrieving value of a property, on the right side of
an assignment.
'Syntax: Debug.Print X.FirstName
    FirstName = mvarFirstName
End Property


Public Property Let LastName(ByVal vData As String)
'used when assigning a value to the property, on the left side
of an assignment.
'Syntax: X.LastName = 5
    mvarLastName = vData
End Property


Public Property Get LastName() As String
'used when retrieving value of a property, on the right side of
an assignment.
'Syntax: Debug.Print X.LastName
    LastName = mvarLastName
End Property


Public Property Let EmployeeID(ByVal vData As Long)
'used when assigning a value to the property, on the left side
of an assignment.
'Syntax: X.EmployeeID = 5
    mvarEmployeeID = vData
End Property


Public Property Get EmployeeID() As Long
'used when retrieving value of a property, on the right side of
an assignment.
'Syntax: Debug.Print X.EmployeeID
    EmployeeID = mvarEmployeeID
End Property
```

Unfortunately, this code doesn't follow common standards, and a number of comments in the code aren't helpful. For this reason, this code has been modified to be more in line with the coding standards used throughout the book. The revised code is shown in Listing 16-2.

Listing 16-2: Revised version of Employee class code

```
Option Explicit

Private m_lngEmployeeID As Long
Private m_strLastName As String
Private m_strFirstName As String
Private m_blnGetsTips As Boolean
Private m_curHourlyRate As Currency

Public Property Let HourlyRate(ByVal vData As Currency)
    m_curHourlyRate = vData
End Property

Public Property Get HourlyRate() As Currency
    HourlyRate = m_curHourlyRate
End Property

Public Property Let GetsTips(ByVal vData As Boolean)
    m_blnGetsTips = vData
End Property

Public Property Get GetsTips() As Boolean
    GetsTips = m_blnGetsTips
End Property

Public Property Let FirstName(ByVal vData As String)
    m_strFirstName = vData
End Property

Public Property Get FirstName() As String
    FirstName = m_strFirstName
End Property

Public Property Let LastName(ByVal vData As String)
    m_strLastName = vData
End Property

Public Property Get LastName() As String
    LastName = m_strLastName
End Property

Public Property Let EmployeeID(ByVal vData As Long)
```

Continued

Listing 16-2 *(continued)*

```
    m_lngEmployeeID = vData
End Property

Public Property Get EmployeeID() As Long
    EmployeeID = m_lngEmployeeID
End Property
```

The first code at the top of the file defines the private storage area for the data stored in this object. The "m" prefix stands for "module", because these variables are defined at the module level. You should also note that they are private — we don't want code reading the values directly. In the listings below, some of the fields are not yet included. These fields are used for links, or foreign keys, to other tables. You'll see how to make those links work later in the chapter; for now, they have been left out.

The rest of the code consists of two types of subroutines: a `Property Get` and a `Property Let` routine. A `Property Get` is designed to return privately held data back to the caller. A `Property Let` is designed to let the caller change the data value. Each property has both a `Get` and a `Let` routine, which makes all properties currently read/write. Because the `EmployeeID` is assigned automatically, you will never need to edit that value. For this reason, the `Property Let` procedure for the `EmployeeID` value can be deleted. Because there is no way to modify the value through the class, this arrangement makes the property read-only.

The rest of the classes will follow the same pattern as the `Employee` class. The code will be evolving through this chapter, but Listings 16-3 through 16-8 show the classes that you should have at this point in the chapter.

Listing 16-3: MenuGroup Class

```
Option Explicit

Private m_lngGroupID As Long
Private m_strDescription As String
Private m_lngSortOrder As Long

Public Property Let SortOrder(ByVal vData As Long)
    m_lngSortOrder = vData
End Property

Public Property Get SortOrder() As Long
    SortOrder = m_lngSortOrder
End Property
```

```vb
Public Property Let Description(ByVal vData As String)
    m_strDescription = vData
End Property

Public Property Get Description() As String
    Description = m_strDescription
End Property

Public Property Let GroupID(ByVal vData As Long)
    m_lngGroupID = vData
End Property

Public Property Get GroupID() As Long
    GroupID = m_lngGroupID
End Property
```

Listing 16-4: **MenuItem Class**

```vb
Option Explicit

Private m_lngMenuItemID As Long
Private m_strDescription As String
Private m_curPrice As Currency

Public Property Let Price(ByVal vData As Currency)
    m_curPrice = vData
End Property

Public Property Get Price() As Currency
    Price = m_curPrice
End Property

Public Property Let Description(ByVal vData As String)
    m_strDescription = vData
End Property

Public Property Get Description() As String
    Description = m_strDescription
End Property

Public Property Let MenuItemID(ByVal vData As Long)
    m_lngMenuItemID = vData
End Property

Public Property Get MenuItemID() As Long
    MenuItemID = m_lngMenuItemID
End Property
```

Listing 16-5: **Order Class**

```
Option Explicit

Private m_lngOrderID As Long
Private m_datOrderDate As Date
Private m_blnIsCompleted As Boolean
Private m_curTipAmount As Currency

Public Property Let TipAmount(ByVal vData As Currency)
    m_curTipAmount = vData
End Property

Public Property Get TipAmount() As Currency
    TipAmount = m_curTipAmount
End Property

Public Property Let IsCompleted(ByVal vData As Boolean)
    m_blnIsCompleted = vData
End Property

Public Property Get IsCompleted() As Boolean
    IsCompleted = m_blnIsCompleted
End Property

Public Property Let OrderDate(ByVal vData As Date)
    m_datOrderDate = vData
End Property

Public Property Get OrderDate() As Date
    OrderDate = m_datOrderDate
End Property

Public Property Let OrderID(ByVal vData As Long)
    m_lngOrderID = vData
End Property

Public Property Get OrderID() As Long
    OrderID = m_lngOrderID
End Property
```

Listing 16-6: **OrderItem Class**

```
Option Explicit

Private m_lngOrderItemID As Long
Private m_lngQuantity As Long

Public Property Let Quantity(ByVal vData As Long)
    m_lngQuantity = vData
End Property
```

```
Public Property Get Quantity() As Long
   Quantity = m_lngQuantity
End Property

Public Property Let OrderItemID(ByVal vData As Long)
   m_lngOrderItemID = vData
End Property

Public Property Get OrderItemID() As Long
   OrderItemID = m_lngOrderItemID
End Property
```

Listing 16-7: **Special Class**

```
Option Explicit

Private m_lngSpecialID As Long
Private m_curNewPrice As Currency
Private m_datStartDate As Date
Private m_datEndDate As Date

Public Property Let EndDate(ByVal vData As Date)
   m_datEndDate = vData
End Property

Public Property Get EndDate() As Date
   EndDate = m_datEndDate
End Property

Public Property Let StartDate(ByVal vData As Date)
   m_datStartDate = vData
End Property

Public Property Get StartDate() As Date
   StartDate = m_datStartDate
End Property

Public Property Let NewPrice(ByVal vData As Currency)
   m_curNewPrice = vData
End Property

Public Property Get NewPrice() As Currency
   NewPrice = m_curNewPrice
End Property

Public Property Let SpecialID(ByVal vData As Long)
   m_lngSpecialID = vData
End Property

Public Property Get SpecialID() As Long
   SpecialID = m_lngSpecialID
End Property
```

Listing 16-8: **Store Class**

```
Option Explicit

Private m_lngStoreID As Long
Private m_strCity As String
Private m_strState As String

Public Property Let State(ByVal vData As String)
   m_strState = vData
End Property

Public Property Get State() As String
   State = m_strState
End Property

Public Property Let City(ByVal vData As String)
   m_strCity = vData
End Property

Public Property Get City() As String
   City = m_strCity
End Property

Public Property Let StoreID(ByVal vData As Long)
   m_lngStoreID = vData
End Property

Public Property Get StoreID() As Long
   StoreID = m_lngStoreID
End Property
```

Adding Data Access Code

Now that the basic classes are created, you can add code to access the database. The example code uses an Access 97 database and SQL statements against that database. However, you can use stored procedures and any other database that works with Visual Basic for this example.

Each object will have the following minimum abilities:

✦ Create a new instance of the object, such as a new employee

✦ Edit an existing instance

✦ Save changes to the database

Adding to the Employee Class

Let's go through the code required by looking at the Employee class. The revised version of the Employee class code, complete with all data access code, is shown in Listing 16-9. The new code is highlighted and explained following the listing.

```
Option Explicit

Private m_dcnDB As ADODB.Connection
Private m_rsData As ADODB.Recordset
Private m_blnIsNew As Boolean

Private m_lngEmployeeID As Long
Private m_strLastName As String
Private m_strFirstName As String
Private m_blnGetsTips As Boolean
Private m_curHourlyRate As Currency

Public Property Let HourlyRate(ByVal vData As Currency)
    m_curHourlyRate = vData
End Property

Public Property Get HourlyRate() As Currency
    HourlyRate = m_curHourlyRate
End Property

Public Property Let GetsTips(ByVal vData As Boolean)
    m_blnGetsTips = vData
End Property

Public Property Get GetsTips() As Boolean
    GetsTips = m_blnGetsTips
End Property

Public Property Let FirstName(ByVal vData As String)
    m_strFirstName = vData
End Property

Public Property Get FirstName() As String
    FirstName = m_strFirstName
End Property

Public Property Let LastName(ByVal vData As String)
    m_strLastName = vData
End Property
```

Continued

Listing 16-9 *(continued)*

```
Public Property Get LastName() As String
    LastName = m_strLastName
End Property

Public Property Get EmployeeID() As Long
    EmployeeID = m_lngEmployeeID
End Property

Public Sub Create(dcnDB As ADODB.Connection)
    '
    ' This method takes care of creating a new
    ' object, ready to accept new data.
    '
    Set m_dcnDB = dcnDB
    m_blnIsNew = True

End Sub

Public Sub Edit(dcnDB As ADODB.Connection, lngID As Long)

    '
    ' This method creates an object that is able
    ' to edit an existing record. The flag is set
    ' so that the save is done properly.
    '
    Set m_dcnDB = dcnDB
    Set m_rsData = _
        m_dcnDB.Execute("SELECT * FROM tblEmployees " _
        & "WHERE EmployeeID = " & lngID)
    FillObject
    m_blnIsNew = False
    m_rsData.Close

End Sub

Private Sub FillObject()
    '
    ' This method loads the data from the recordset
    ' into the private member variables.
    '
    m_lngEmployeeID = m_rsData("EmployeeID")
    m_strFirstName = m_rsData("FirstName")
    m_strLastName = m_rsData("LastName")
    m_blnGetsTips = m_rsData("GetsTips")
    m_curHourlyRate = m_rsData("HourlyRate")
    m_blnIsNew = False

End Sub

Public Sub Save()
    '
```

```
' This method puts the object's data back into
' the database. This method could use the INSERT
' statement or a stored procedure, if desired.
'
Set m_rsData = New ADODB.Recordset
If m_blnIsNew Then
    m_rsData.Open "SELECT * FROM tblEmployees", _
        m_dcnDB, _
        adOpenDynamic, _
        adLockOptimistic
    m_rsData.AddNew
Else
    m_rsData.Open "SELECT * FROM tblEmployees " _
        & "WHERE EmployeeID = " & m_lngEmployeeID, _
        m_dcnDB, _
        adOpenDynamic, _
        adLockPessimistic
End If

'
' The ID field is created automatically
' in additions and is never edited.
'
m_rsData("FirstName") = m_strFirstName
m_rsData("LastName") = m_strLastName
m_rsData("GetsTips") = m_blnGetsTips
m_rsData("HourlyRate") = m_curHourlyRate

m_rsData.Update
'
' Calling FillObject here allows the
' unique ID to be picked up in case of
' an addition
'
FillObject
m_rsData.Close

End Sub
```

The first new lines declare some module level database variables: a data connection, a recordset, and a flag indicating whether the record is a new record. Because new records are added in a slightly different way than is used to change records, the flag is used during the save.

The Create subroutine is responsible for creating a new Employee record. There's not much to it, but the important piece is that this method accepts a connection object from the "outside." The object simply uses whatever connection has already been established by the application. This arrangement saves system resources — each object doesn't have to make its own connection to the database. This method also sets the New flag for later use.

The Edit subroutine has a bit more work to do. This subroutine has to load an existing record and make it ready to be edited by the application. This routine calls a SQL statement to retrieve the selected record, which is indicated by the ID passed into the routine. Edit then calls the FillObject method to take the data from the recordset and put it into the local variables. This action essentially makes a copy of the record for editing. Note that you can also use this method for retrieving a record for view purposes. You simply don't call the Save method and the object's data will go away when you are done with it.

The FillObject method takes the data from an open recordset and populates the member variables with the appropriate data. Because any record loading data would not be a new record, the routine also clears the IsNew flag.

The final method, Save, is the longest. It first determines whether the object has been saved to the database. Depending on the answer, the recordset is created one of two ways. The data is then stored into the recordset, and the Update method saves the data to the database. In cases where a new record is being added, the unique ID (system generated) is not in the object. Because the object may be used more than once by the calling code, calling the Fill Object takes care of this problem.

To test this code, you can use the following snippet shown in Listing 16-10.

Listing 16-10: **Testing code for Employee Class**

```
Dim dcnDB As New ADODB.Connection
Dim objTest As New Employee
dcnDB.ConnectionString = "Provider=Microsoft.Jet.OLEDB.3.51;" _
    & "Persist Security Info=False;" _
    & "Data Source=D:\PizzaDB.mdb"
dcnDB.Open
objTest.Create dcnDB
objTest.FirstName = "Eric"
objTest.LastName = "Smith"
objTest.GetsTips = True
objTest.HourlyRate = 10
objTest.Save

Set objTest = Nothing
dcnDB.Close
```

This sample will create a new record in the Employees table. As long as you had the unique ID of the record you wanted to modify, you could then call the Edit method to modify this record. Also, be sure to change the database file path, or this code won't be able to make a database connection.

Adding to the Store Class

The Store class will be somewhat different from the Employee class. The reason: the Store class has a link to the Employee class through the ManagerID field. This field is used to point to an employee who manages the particular store. We'll be adding an additional feature to the Store class so that you can access information about the manager without having to do lots of extra steps to create a new employee object.

The basic data access code for the Store class is shown in Listing 16-10. This code is quite similar to the code in the Employee class.

Listing 16-10: **Store Class code, with data access enabled**

```
Option Explicit

Private m_dcnDB As ADODB.Connection
Private m_rsData As ADODB.Recordset
Private m_blnIsNew As Boolean

Private m_lngStoreID As Long
Private m_strCity As String
Private m_strState As String

Public Property Let State(ByVal vData As String)
    m_strState = vData
End Property

Public Property Get State() As String
    State = m_strState
End Property

Public Property Let City(ByVal vData As String)
    m_strCity = vData
End Property

Public Property Get City() As String
    City = m_strCity
End Property

Public Property Get StoreID() As Long
    StoreID = m_lngStoreID
End Property

Public Sub Create(dcnDB As ADODB.Connection)
    '
    ' This method takes care of creating a new
    ' object, ready to accept new data.
    '
    Set m_dcnDB = dcnDB
```

Continued

Listing 16-10 *(continued)*

```
    m_blnIsNew = True

End Sub

Public Sub Edit(dcnDB As ADODB.Connection, lngID As Long)

    '
    ' This method creates an object that is able
    ' to edit an existing record. The flag is set
    ' so that the save is done properly.
    '
    Set m_dcnDB = dcnDB
    Set m_rsData = m_dcnDB.Execute("SELECT * FROM tblStores " _
        & "WHERE StoreID = " & lngID)
    FillObject
    m_blnIsNew = False
    m_rsData.Close

End Sub

Private Sub FillObject()
    '
    ' This method loads the data from the recordset
    ' into the private member variables.
    '

    m_lngStoreID = m_rsData("StoreID")
    m_strCity = m_rsData("City")
    m_strState = m_rsData("State")
    m_blnIsNew = False

End Sub

Public Sub Save()
    '
    ' This method puts the object's data back into
    ' the database. This method could use the INSERT
    ' statement or a stored procedure, if desired.
    '
    Set m_rsData = New ADODB.Recordset
    If m_blnIsNew Then
        m_rsData.Open "SELECT * FROM tblStores", _
            m_dcnDB, _
            adOpenDynamic, _
            adLockOptimistic
        m_rsData.AddNew
    Else
        m_rsData.Open "SELECT * FROM tblStores " _
            & "WHERE StoreID = " & m_lngStoreID, _
            m_dcnDB, _
            adOpenDynamic, _
```

```
          adLockPessimistic
    End If

    '
    ' The ID field is created automatically
    ' in additions and is never edited.
    '
    m_rsData("City") = m_strCity
    m_rsData("State") = m_strState

    m_rsData.Update
    '
    ' Calling FillObject here allows the
    ' unique ID to be picked up in case of
    ' an addition
    '
    FillObject
    m_rsData.Close

End Sub
```

As mentioned previously, the ManagerID field is neither being loaded nor saved. The changes shown in Listing 16-11 allow this to happen properly.

Listing 16-11: **Revised code for Store class**

```
Option Explicit

Private m_dcnDB As ADODB.Connection
Private m_rsData As ADODB.Recordset
Private m_blnIsNew As Boolean

Private m_lngStoreID As Long
Private m_strCity As String
Private m_strState As String
Private m_lngManagerID As Long

Public Property Let State(ByVal vData As String)
    m_strState = vData
End Property

Public Property Get State() As String
    State = m_strState
End Property

Public Property Let City(ByVal vData As String)
    m_strCity = vData
End Property
```

Continued

Listing 16-11 *(continued)*

```
Public Property Get City() As String
    City = m_strCity
End Property

Public Property Get StoreID() As Long
    StoreID = m_lngStoreID
End Property

Public Property Let ManagerID(ByVal vData As Long)
    m_lngManagerID = vData
End Property

Public Property Get ManagerID() As Long
    ManagerID = m_lngManagerID
End Property

Public Property Get Manager() As Employee
    Dim objTemp As New Employee
    objTemp.Edit m_dcnDB, m_lngManagerID
    Set Manager = objTemp
End Property

Public Sub Create(dcnDB As ADODB.Connection)
    '
    ' This method takes care of creating a new
    ' object, ready to accept new data.
    '
    Set m_dcnDB = dcnDB
    m_blnIsNew = True

End Sub

Public Sub Edit(dcnDB As ADODB.Connection, lngID As Long)

    '
    ' This method creates an object that is able
    ' to edit an existing record. The flag is set
    ' so that the save is done properly.
    '
    Set m_dcnDB = dcnDB
    Set m_rsData = m_dcnDB.Execute("SELECT * FROM tblStores " _
        & "WHERE StoreID = " & lngID)
    FillObject
    m_blnIsNew = False
    m_rsData.Close

End Sub

Private Sub FillObject()
    '
    ' This method loads the data from the recordset
```

```vb
    ' into the private member variables.
    '

    m_lngStoreID = m_rsData("StoreID")
    m_strCity = m_rsData("City")
    m_strState = m_rsData("State")
    m_lngManagerID = m_rsData("ManagerID")
    m_blnIsNew = False

End Sub

Public Sub Save()
    '
    ' This method puts the object's data back into
    ' the database. This method could use the INSERT
    ' statement or a stored procedure, if desired.
    '
    Set m_rsData = New ADODB.Recordset
    If m_blnIsNew Then
        m_rsData.Open "SELECT * FROM tblStores", _
            m_dcnDB, _
            adOpenDynamic, _
            adLockOptimistic
        m_rsData.AddNew
    Else
        m_rsData.Open "SELECT * FROM tblStores " _
            & "WHERE StoreID = " & m_lngStoreID, _
            m_dcnDB, _
            adOpenDynamic, _
            adLockPessimistic
    End If

    '
    ' The ID field is created automatically
    ' in additions and is never edited.
    '
    m_rsData("City") = m_strCity
    m_rsData("State") = m_strState
    m_rsData("ManagerID") = m_lngManagerID

    m_rsData.Update
    '
    ' Calling FillObject here allows the
    ' unique ID to be picked up in case of
    ' an addition
    '
    FillObject
    m_rsData.Close

End Sub
```

The changes to the code are minor, but critical to how this code operates. The first change adds a member variable to hold the manager ID value. The next change provides a Get and Let property to retrieve and change the manager ID value, which corresponds to a valid employee ID number. The other important change was the addition of the Manager Get property. This property returns an object to the caller that represents the manager. This object is an Employee object and is loaded with the manager's information. Note that we load this object on demand and not in advance. This arrangement saves on system resources — you may not use this information regularly. If you think that you will be using this information often, you could make the temporary object a member variable and essentially "cache" the manager's information in an object within the Store class.

The other changes made to the class retrieve and store the manager ID into the appropriate field. To test this code, use the snippet shown in Listing 16-12 through 16-17.

Listing 16-12: Test code for Store class

```
Dim dcnDB As New ADODB.Connection
Dim objStore As New Store

dcnDB.ConnectionString = "Provider=Microsoft.Jet.OLEDB.3.51;" _
    & "Persist Security Info=False;" _
    & "Data Source=D:\PizzaDB.mdb"
dcnDB.Open

objStore.Edit dcnDB, 1
objStore.ManagerID = 2
objStore.Save

MsgBox "The manager of the " _
    & objStore.City & ", " & objStore.State _
    & " store is " _
    & objStore.Manager.FirstName _
    & " " & objStore.Manager.LastName _
    & "."

Set objStore = Nothing
dcnDB.Close
```

The assumption in this code is that store ID 1 was already created, and employee ID 2 has already been created. We store that employee ID into the ManagerID field, and then save the store's data. Then, we can use the code below it to print the name of the manager and the store that he or she manages. Note that we can "chain" the objects by simply accessing the Manager property. If we need to get to any other information about the manager, it's already available. In fact, you can use this object to change information about the manager, if desired. Just remember that there is only one location for permanent storage of manager information: the Employee table. Any changes you make to the `Manager` object here will be stored permanently in the Employee table, just as if you had created an `Employee` object and made the changes there.

In the other classes that we haven't coded yet, the following relationships exist and need to have object properties created for them:

- ✦ `MenuItem`—linked to `MenuItemGroup`
- ✦ `OrderItem`—linked to `MenuItem`
- ✦ `Order`—`Employee` and `Store`
- ✦ `Special`—`MenuItem`

Several relationships also involve groups of items. These relationships will involve collections and will be covered in a following section. For now, you need to add the rest of the code for the base classes that we have identified. The code, complete with all the data access code, is shown in Listings 16-13 through 16-17.

Listing 16-13: **MenuGroup Class code**

```
Option Explicit

Private m_dcnDB As ADODB.Connection
Private m_rsData As ADODB.Recordset
Private m_blnIsNew As Boolean

Private m_lngGroupID As Long
Private m_strDescription As String
Private m_lngSortOrder As Long

Public Property Let SortOrder(ByVal vData As Long)
    m_lngSortOrder = vData
End Property

Public Property Get SortOrder() As Long
    SortOrder = m_lngSortOrder
End Property

Public Property Let Description(ByVal vData As String)
    m_strDescription = vData
End Property

Public Property Get Description() As String
    Description = m_strDescription
End Property

Public Property Let GroupID(ByVal vData As Long)
```

Continued

Listing 16-13 *(continued)*

```
    m_lngGroupID = vData
End Property

Public Property Get GroupID() As Long
    GroupID = m_lngGroupID
End Property

Public Sub Create(dcnDB As ADODB.Connection)
    '
    ' This method takes care of creating a new
    ' object, ready to accept new data.
    '
    Set m_dcnDB = dcnDB
    m_blnIsNew = True

End Sub

Public Sub Edit(dcnDB As ADODB.Connection, lngID As Long)

    '
    ' This method creates an object that is able
    ' to edit an existing record. The flag is set
    ' so that the save is done properly.
    '
    Set m_dcnDB = dcnDB
    Set m_rsData = _
        m_dcnDB.Execute("SELECT * FROM tblMenuItemGroups " _
        & "WHERE GroupID = " & lngID)
    FillObject
    m_blnIsNew = False
    m_rsData.Close

End Sub

Private Sub FillObject()
    '
    ' This method loads the data from the recordset
    ' into the private member variables.
    '
    m_lngGroupID = m_rsData("GroupID")
    m_strDescription = m_rsData("Description")
    m_lngSortOrder = m_rsData("SortOrder")
    m_blnIsNew = False

End Sub

Public Sub Save()
    '
    ' This method puts the object's data back into
    ' the database. This method could use the INSERT
    ' statement or a stored procedure, if desired.
    '
```

```
        Set m_rsData = New ADODB.Recordset
        If m_blnIsNew Then
           m_rsData.Open "SELECT * FROM tblMenuItemGroups", _
               m_dcnDB, _
               adOpenDynamic, _
               adLockOptimistic
           m_rsData.AddNew
        Else
           m_rsData.Open "SELECT * FROM tblMenuItemGroups " _
               & "WHERE GroupID = " & m_lngGroupID, _
               m_dcnDB, _
               adOpenDynamic, _
               adLockPessimistic
        End If

        '
        ' The ID field is created automatically
        ' in additions and is never edited.
        '
        m_rsData("Description") = m_strDescription
        m_rsData("SortOrder") = m_lngSortOrder

        m_rsData.Update
        '
        ' Calling FillObject here allows the
        ' unique ID to be picked up in case of
        ' an addition
        '
        FillObject
        m_rsData.Close

    End Sub
```

Listing 16-14: **MenuItem Class code**

```
Option Explicit

Private m_dcnDB As ADODB.Connection
Private m_rsData As ADODB.Recordset
Private m_blnIsNew As Boolean

Private m_lngMenuItemID As Long
Private m_lngMenuGroupID As Long
Private m_strDescription As String
Private m_curPrice As Currency

Public Property Let Price(ByVal vData As Currency)
    m_curPrice = vData
End Property
```

Continued

Listing 16-14 *(continued)*

```
Public Property Get Price() As Currency
    Price = m_curPrice
End Property

Public Property Let Description(ByVal vData As String)
    m_strDescription = vData
End Property

Public Property Get Description() As String
    Description = m_strDescription
End Property

Public Property Get MenuItemID() As Long
    MenuItemID = m_lngMenuItemID
End Property

Public Property Get MenuGroupID() As Long
    MenuGroupID = m_lngMenuGroupID
End Property

Public Property Get MenuGroup() As MenuGroup
    Dim objTemp As New MenuGroup
    objTemp.Edit m_dcnDB, m_lngMenuGroupID
    Set MenuGroup = objTemp
End Property

Public Sub Create(dcnDB As ADODB.Connection)
    '
    ' This method takes care of creating a new
    ' object, ready to accept new data.
    '
    Set m_dcnDB = dcnDB
    m_blnIsNew = True

End Sub

Public Sub Edit(dcnDB As ADODB.Connection, lngID As Long)

    '
    ' This method creates an object that is able
    ' to edit an existing record. The flag is set
    ' so that the save is done properly.
    '
    Set m_dcnDB = dcnDB
    Set m_rsData = _
        m_dcnDB.Execute("SELECT * FROM tblMenuItems " _
        & "WHERE MenuItemID = " & lngID)
    FillObject
    m_blnIsNew = False
    m_rsData.Close

End Sub
```

```vb
Private Sub FillObject()
    '
    ' This method loads the data from the recordset
    ' into the private member variables.
    '

    m_lngMenuItemID = m_rsData("MenuItemID")
    m_lngMenuGroupID = m_rsData("GroupID")
    m_strDescription = m_rsData("Description")
    m_curPrice = m_rsData("Price")
    m_blnIsNew = False

End Sub

Public Sub Save()
    '
    ' This method puts the object's data back into
    ' the database. This method could use the INSERT
    ' statement or a stored procedure, if desired.
    '
    Set m_rsData = New ADODB.Recordset
    If m_blnIsNew Then
        m_rsData.Open "SELECT * FROM tblMenuItems", _
            m_dcnDB, _
            adOpenDynamic, _
            adLockOptimistic
        m_rsData.AddNew
    Else
        m_rsData.Open "SELECT * FROM tblMenuItems " _
            & "WHERE MenuItemID = " & m_lngMenuItemID, _
            m_dcnDB, _
            adOpenDynamic, _
            adLockPessimistic
    End If

    '
    ' The ID field is created automatically
    ' in additions and is never edited.
    '
    m_rsData("Description") = m_strDescription
    m_rsData("GroupID") = m_lngMenuGroupID
    m_rsData("Price") = m_curPrice

    m_rsData.Update
    '
    ' Calling FillObject here allows the
    ' unique ID to be picked up in case of
    ' an addition
    '
    FillObject
    m_rsData.Close

End Sub
```

Listing 16-15: **Order Class code**

```
Option Explicit

Private m_dcnDB As ADODB.Connection
Private m_rsData As ADODB.Recordset
Private m_blnIsNew As Boolean

Private m_lngOrderID As Long
Private m_lngStoreID As Long
Private m_lngEmployeeID As Long
Private m_datOrderDate As Date
Private m_blnIsCompleted As Boolean
Private m_curTipAmount As Currency

Public Property Let TipAmount(ByVal vData As Currency)
    m_curTipAmount = vData
End Property

Public Property Get TipAmount() As Currency
    TipAmount = m_curTipAmount
End Property

Public Property Let IsCompleted(ByVal vData As Boolean)
    m_blnIsCompleted = vData
End Property

Public Property Get IsCompleted() As Boolean
    IsCompleted = m_blnIsCompleted
End Property

Public Property Let OrderDate(ByVal vData As Date)
    m_datOrderDate = vData
End Property

Public Property Get OrderDate() As Date
    OrderDate = m_datOrderDate
End Property

Public Property Let OrderID(ByVal vData As Long)
    m_lngOrderID = vData
End Property

Public Property Get OrderID() As Long
    OrderID = m_lngOrderID
End Property

Public Property Get EmployeeID() As Long
    EmployeeID = m_lngEmployeeID
End Property

Public Property Get Employee() As Employee
    Dim objTemp As New Employee
```

```
      objTemp.Edit m_dcnDB, m_lngEmployeeID
      Set Employee = objTemp
End Property

Public Property Get StoreID() As Long
      StoreID = m_lngStoreID
End Property

Public Property Get Store() As Store
   Dim objTemp As New Store
   objTemp.Edit m_dcnDB, m_lngStoreID
   Set Store = objTemp
End Property

Public Sub Create(dcnDB As ADODB.Connection)
   '
   ' This method takes care of creating a new
   ' object, ready to accept new data.
   '
   Set m_dcnDB = dcnDB
   m_blnIsNew = True

End Sub

Public Sub Edit(dcnDB As ADODB.Connection, lngID As Long)

   '
   ' This method creates an object that is able
   ' to edit an existing record. The flag is set
   ' so that the save is done properly.
   '
   Set m_dcnDB = dcnDB
   Set m_rsData = _
      m_dcnDB.Execute("SELECT * FROM tblOrders " _
      & "WHERE OrderItemID = " & lngID)
   FillObject
   m_blnIsNew = False
   m_rsData.Close

End Sub

Private Sub FillObject()
   '
   ' This method loads the data from the recordset
   ' into the private member variables.
   '

   m_lngOrderID = m_rsData("OrderID")
   m_lngStoreID = m_rsData("StoreID")
   m_lngEmployeeID = m_rsData("EmployeeID")
   m_datOrderDate = m_rsData("OrderDate")
   m_blnIsCompleted = m_rsData("IsCompleted")
   m_curTipAmount = m_rsData("TipAmount")
```

Continued

Listing 16-15 *(continued)*

```
    m_blnIsNew = False
End Sub

Public Sub Save()
    '
    ' This method puts the object's data back into
    ' the database. This method could use the INSERT
    ' statement or a stored procedure, if desired.
    '
    Set m_rsData = New ADODB.Recordset
    If m_blnIsNew Then
        m_rsData.Open "SELECT * FROM tblOrders", _
            m_dcnDB, _
            adOpenDynamic, _
            adLockOptimistic
        m_rsData.AddNew
    Else
        m_rsData.Open "SELECT * FROM tblOrders" _
            & " WHERE OrderID = " & m_lngOrderID, _
            m_dcnDB, _
            adOpenDynamic, _
            adLockPessimistic
    End If

    '
    ' The ID field is created automatically
    ' in additions and is never edited.
    '
    m_rsData("StoreID") = m_lngStoreID
    m_rsData("EmployeeID") = m_lngEmployeeID
    m_rsData("OrderDate") = m_datOrderDate
    m_rsData("IsCompleted") = m_blnIsCompleted
    m_rsData("TipAmount") = m_curTipAmount

    m_rsData.Update
    '
    ' Calling FillObject here allows the
    ' unique ID to be picked up in case of
    ' an addition
    '
    FillObject
    m_rsData.Close

End Sub
```

Listing 16-16: **OrderItem Class code**

```
Option Explicit

Private m_dcnDB As ADODB.Connection
Private m_rsData As ADODB.Recordset
Private m_blnIsNew As Boolean

Private m_lngOrderItemID As Long
Private m_lngSpecialID As Long
Private m_lngMenuItemID As Long
Private m_lngQuantity As Long

Public Property Let Quantity(ByVal vData As Long)
    m_lngQuantity = vData
End Property

Public Property Get Quantity() As Long
    Quantity = m_lngQuantity
End Property

Public Property Let OrderItemID(ByVal vData As Long)
    m_lngOrderItemID = vData
End Property

Public Property Get OrderItemID() As Long
    OrderItemID = m_lngOrderItemID
End Property

Public Property Get MenuItemID() As Long
    MenuItemID = m_lngMenuItemID
End Property

Public Property Get MenuItem() As MenuItem
    Dim objTemp As New MenuItem
    objTemp.Edit m_dcnDB, m_lngMenuItemID
    Set MenuItem = objTemp
End Property

Public Sub Create(dcnDB As ADODB.Connection)
    '
    ' This method takes care of creating a new
    ' object, ready to accept new data.
    '
    Set m_dcnDB = dcnDB
    m_blnIsNew = True

End Sub

Public Sub Edit(dcnDB As ADODB.Connection, lngID As Long)
```

Continued

Listing 16-16 *(continued)*

```
    '
    ' This method creates an object that is able
    ' to edit an existing record. The flag is set
    ' so that the save is done properly.
    '
    Set m_dcnDB = dcnDB
    Set m_rsData = _
       m_dcnDB.Execute("SELECT * FROM tblOrderItems " _
       & "WHERE OrderItemID = " & lngID)
    FillObject
    m_blnIsNew = False
    m_rsData.Close

End Sub

Private Sub FillObject()
    '
    ' This method loads the data from the recordset
    ' into the private member variables.
    '

    m_lngOrderItemID = m_rsData("OrderItemID")
    m_lngMenuItemID = m_rsData("MenuItemID")
    m_lngQuantity = m_rsData("Quantity")
    m_blnIsNew = False

End Sub

Public Sub Save()
    '
    ' This method puts the object's data back into
    ' the database. This method could use the INSERT
    ' statement or a stored procedure, if desired.
    '
    Set m_rsData = New ADODB.Recordset
    If m_blnIsNew Then
       m_rsData.Open "SELECT * FROM tblOrderItems", _
          m_dcnDB, _
          adOpenDynamic, _
          adLockOptimistic
       m_rsData.AddNew
    Else
       m_rsData.Open "SELECT * FROM tblOrderItems" _
          & " WHERE SpecialID = " & m_lngSpecialID, _
          m_dcnDB, _
          adOpenDynamic, _
          adLockPessimistic
    End If

    '
    ' The ID field is created automatically
    ' in additions and is never edited.
    '
```

```
    m_rsData("MenuItemID") = m_lngMenuItemID
    m_rsData("Quantity") = m_lngQuantity

    m_rsData.Update
    '
    ' Calling FillObject here allows the
    ' unique ID to be picked up in case of
    ' an addition
    '
    FillObject
    m_rsData.Close

End Sub
```

Listing 16-17: **Special Class code**

```
Option Explicit

Private m_dcnDB As ADODB.Connection
Private m_rsData As ADODB.Recordset
Private m_blnIsNew As Boolean

Private m_lngSpecialID As Long
Private m_lngMenuItemID As Long
Private m_curNewPrice As Currency
Private m_datStartDate As Date
Private m_datEndDate As Date

Public Property Let EndDate(ByVal vData As Date)
    m_datEndDate = vData
End Property

Public Property Get EndDate() As Date
    EndDate = m_datEndDate
End Property

Public Property Let StartDate(ByVal vData As Date)
    m_datStartDate = vData
End Property

Public Property Get StartDate() As Date
    StartDate = m_datStartDate
End Property

Public Property Let NewPrice(ByVal vData As Currency)
    m_curNewPrice = vData
End Property

Public Property Get NewPrice() As Currency
```

Continued

Listing 16-17 *(continued)*

```
    NewPrice = m_curNewPrice
End Property

Public Property Get SpecialID() As Long
    SpecialID = m_lngSpecialID
End Property

Public Property Get MenuItemID() As Long
    MenuItemID = m_lngMenuItemID
End Property

Public Property Get MenuItem() As MenuItem
    Dim objTemp As New MenuItem
    objTemp.Edit m_dcnDB, m_lngMenuItemID
    Set MenuItem = objTemp
End Property

Public Sub Create(dcnDB As ADODB.Connection)
    '
    ' This method takes care of creating a new
    ' object, ready to accept new data.
    '
    Set m_dcnDB = dcnDB
    m_blnIsNew = True

End Sub

Public Sub Edit(dcnDB As ADODB.Connection, lngID As Long)

    '
    ' This method creates an object that is able
    ' to edit an existing record. The flag is set
    ' so that the save is done properly.
    '
    Set m_dcnDB = dcnDB
    Set m_rsData = _
        m_dcnDB.Execute("SELECT * FROM tblSpecials " _
        & "WHERE SpecialID = " & lngID)
    FillObject
    m_blnIsNew = False
    m_rsData.Close

End Sub

Private Sub FillObject()
    '
    ' This method loads the data from the recordset
    ' into the private member variables.
    '
```

```vb
      m_lngSpecialID = m_rsData("SpecialID")
      m_lngMenuItemID = m_rsData("MenuItemID")
      m_curNewPrice = m_rsData("NewPrice")
      m_datStartDate = m_rsData("StartDate")
      m_datEndDate = m_rsData("EndDate")
      m_blnIsNew = False

End Sub

Public Sub Save()
    '
    ' This method puts the object's data back into
    ' the database. This method could use the INSERT
    ' statement or a stored procedure, if desired.
    '
    Set m_rsData = New ADODB.Recordset
    If m_blnIsNew Then
       m_rsData.Open "SELECT * FROM tblSpecials", _
          m_dcnDB, _
          adOpenDynamic, _
          adLockOptimistic
       m_rsData.AddNew
    Else
       m_rsData.Open "SELECT * FROM tblSpecials " _
          & "WHERE SpecialID = " & m_lngSpecialID, _
          m_dcnDB, _
          adOpenDynamic, _
          adLockPessimistic
    End If


    '
    ' The ID field is created automatically
    ' in additions and is never edited.
    '
    m_rsData("MenuItemID") = m_lngMenuItemID
    m_rsData("NewPrice") = m_curNewPrice
    m_rsData("StartDate") = m_datStartDate
    m_rsData("EndDate") = m_datEndDate

    m_rsData.Update
    '
    ' Calling FillObject here allows the
    ' unique ID to be picked up in case of
    ' an addition
    '
    FillObject
    m_rsData.Close

End Sub
```

Compiling and Deploying the Objects

We'll be adding more to the classes in the following chapter, but you can start playing with them now. Besides the test code that you can write in Visual Basic, this section shows you how to compile these classes into an ActiveX DLL and package it for the Web.

Compiling the Component

The library must have an empty Sub Main subroutine to work properly. Right now, you may have some test code in Sub Main that creates the data connection to the PizzaDB.mdb file. That code must be removed. However, before you start panicking, remember that you will have other code that will instantiate these objects and pass the data connection object to them. You don't have to embed any data connection information in the library for it to work properly.

Your code module should look like Listing 16-18.

Listing 16-18: **Sub Main for Project**

```
Option Explicit

Sub Main()

End Sub
```

While you wouldn't want to have such code in a regular project, a DLL requires it.

Next, you need to change the type of project that you're building. Most likely, because you were testing within the same project, you have a Standard EXE project. At this point, you need to have an ActiveX DLL project. To make this change, do the following:

1. Select Project ⇨ Properties from the Visual Basic menu.

2. From the Project Type list, select ActiveX DLL.

You'll receive a message box saying that the StartMode has been changed. This message is normal and expected after the preceding actions.

Give your ActiveX DLL project a good name — you'll be using it for a little while and also deploying it. The last thing you need to do is to change each class module's Instancing property to MultiUse. This change enables your component to create multiple instances of each object. If you forget to set the `MultiUse` property, you'll get an error when you try to compile.

Finally, select Make DLL from the File menu, and VB will build your ActiveX component. Assuming the compile worked, you're ready to try out your library in a local mode before building your installation package.

Testing the Component in VB

Before we take the time and effort to deploy the component over the Web, it's a good idea to test the library within Visual Basic first. Do the following:

1. Select File ➪ Add Project from the Visual Basic menu. Add a Standard EXE project to your environment. Adding a project will add a second project within the environment. This project will enable us to test and debug the library.

2. To reference the new library, select Project ➪ References while you have the new project selected. Select the project by clicking it in the Project Explorer window. As shown in Figure 16-1, the new library will be listed as an available reference for you to add. Add your library by marking the box.

3. Because you'll also need to test using the ADO code, you should add the ADO 2.0 Library to the new project. After you've marked it, click the OK button.

4. In a code module, add the code in Listing 16-19 to test out your code. Remember to change the pathname to your database.

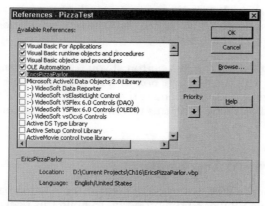

Figure 16-1: The new ActiveX component can be added as a reference

```
Option Explicit

Sub Main()

Dim dcnDB As New ADODB.Connection
Dim objEmp As New EricsPizzaParlor.Employee

dcnDB.ConnectionString = "Provider=Microsoft.Jet.OLEDB.3.51;" _
    & "Persist Security Info=False;" _
    & "Data Source=D:\PizzaDB.mdb"
dcnDB.Open

objEmp.Edit dcnDB, 3
MsgBox objEmp.FirstName & " " & objEmp.LastName
Set objEmp = Nothing

dcnDB.Close

End Sub
```

This code will make a connection to the database and then edit employee #3, which of course must reside in the database. (The sample database includes a few starter records, so if you use the sample, that record already exists.) You should also notice that the employee object was declared using the library name. Because we've referenced the library already, providing the library name is optional.

5. The last step before running this application is to right-click the test project in Project Explorer and select Set as Startup to designate this project as the project that starts. If you don't, VB will try to start the DLL, which doesn't quite make sense and won't work properly.

With all of those steps concluded, hit the Run button. If you're using the sample database, you'll be rewarded with the message box with employee #3's name. If it doesn't work or you get an error, be sure you have the correct path to the database and all references are marked correctly. With this test done, you can move to the deployment step.

Creating a Deployment Package

In order to use this library for the Web, you need to build an installation package with all of the required runtime VB files to run properly. To build this package, you'll use the VB Packaging and Deployment Wizard, which can be started by selecting it from the Start menu. Figure 16-2 shows the front page of the wizard.

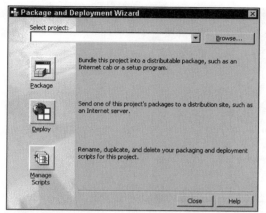

Figure 16-2: Packaging and Deployment Wizard's first page

To build your package, follow these steps through the Wizard:

1. Select your ActiveX DLL project by clicking the Browse button. Don't select the standard EXE you just used to test it. Click the Package button when you find the project.

2. If you save any files after you've created the DLL, you'll be prompted to recompile. You should recompile in this case so that the date/time stamps are correct.

3. The next step is to pick the type of package to build. Because we need to install this package on the server, the standard setup package is best for our needs. Select it and click the Next button to continue.

4. The next dialog prompts you for the location to build the setup package. Find a directory on your local machine and click the Next button to continue.

5. The Wizard will then figure out which files are required for the installation package. If you see anything missing, you can add it from the dialog shown in Figure 16-3.

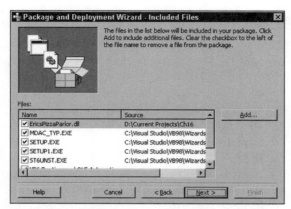

Figure 16-3: Add any dependent files on this dialog

6. The next dialog, shown in Figure 16-4, asks if you want one large CAB file or multiple, smaller files. This option allows you to build executables for floppy disk, if you're still using floppies. In our case, pick the Single CAB option and click Next to continue.

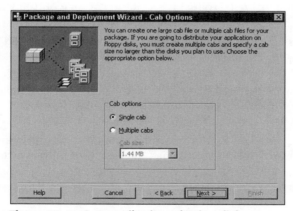

Figure 16-4: Output File size selection dialog

7. The next dialog prompts you for the title that should be shown to the user during installation. Pick an appropriate title and click the Next button.

8. The next dialog, shown in Figure 16-5, asks if you want to create any icons or program groups. Because this is a library and not an executable, you can just click the Next button to continue.

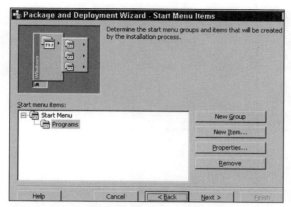

Figure 16-5: Add icons and program groups in this dialog box.

9. Figure 16-6 shows the next step in the Wizard, which enables you to specify where certain files are to be installed. You can either leave this setting as is, or use the value $(WinSysPath) to install the library to the Windows\System directory. Either way, the library will be registered and work properly, no matter where it is located. Click the Next button to continue.

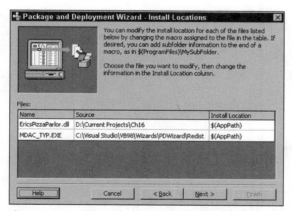

Figure 16-6: Select the target directory for these files

10. The next step (shown in Figure 16-7) is to determine whether your files should be considered shared on the system. The files required for ADO may already be on the machine and are probably used for something else, so marking them as shared won't hurt. Your library should not be marked as shared. Click Next to continue after making these changes.

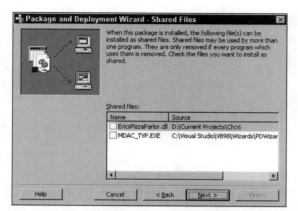

Figure 16-7: Mark files as shared or not shared from this dialog.

11. After giving your setup package a name, you're done. Click the Finish button to build the installation package.

When the wizard finishes, you will find a `SETUP.EXE`, a CAB file, and a .lst file in your destination directory. Take those files to your server and run the `SETUP.EXE` to install your library. When you've completed that step, you'll be able to test your file using an ASP page on your server.

Testing on the Web

The final test of your library is to do the same thing you did in your separate EXE — but on the Web this time. The code to test the library is shown in Listing 16-20. As long as the code has the ASP extension, you can put it in any ASP file.

Listing 16-20: **ASP Library test code**

```
<%
Dim dcnDB    ' As ADODB.Connection
Dim objEmp   ' As EricsPizzaParlor.Employee

Set dcnDB = Server.CreateObject("ADODB.Connection")
Set objEmp = Server.CreateObject("EricsPizzaParlor.Employee")

dcnDB.ConnectionString = "Provider=Microsoft.Jet.OLEDB.3.51;" _
    & "Persist Security Info=False;" _
    & "Data Source=D:\Current Projects\PizzaDB.mdb"
dcnDB.Open

objEmp.Edit dcnDB, 3
Response.Write "Employee #3's name is: " _
```

```
      & objEmp.FirstName & " " & objEmp.LastName
Set objEmp = Nothing

dcnDB.Close

End Sub
%>
```

If, as before, you see the employee's name, your library is installed correctly. You can try out the other objects with the other sample data in the database. In the next chapter, you'll learn more about objects that make it easier to work with related data.

Summary

This chapter was designed to give you an introduction in creating classes with Visual Basic for use in both VB and the Web. As you can see in even a simple example, we only had to write the code once for use in at least two different places. Plus, in a team-based development environment, this feature enables you to have one team focusing on the business objects and another team working on the interface. The interface team cannot see and doesn't need to see the code for the underlying objects, because the objects are provided via a DLL to the developers. Add these characteristics to the improved performance of running a compiled library that has already been tested, and you can see how ActiveX components can benefit your traditional and Web applications.

✦　　✦　　✦

Using WebClasses

In This Chapter

Learn about
WebClass
applications

Create a simple
WebClass
application

Use an HTML
template with your
WebClass

Combine a
WebClass with a
database

What Is a WebClass?

A WebClass is a new technology now available through Visual
Basic 6.0 to make your Web application development easier.
One of the inherent problems with Web-based applications is
the lack of reliable debugging before deployment. The latest
version of Visual InterDev, in combination with the FrontPage
server extensions, provides some debugging capabilities, but
these capabilities don't match the debugging facilities for
Visual Basic programmers. Another problem with Web-based
applications is performance. Because ASP pages have to be
evaluated each time they are loaded, there is a performance
hit for every page load. For a large server, this time can be
very costly. Internet Information Server does have some
caching capabilities, but for the most part, you have to
rerun the page each time you load the page.

With WebClasses, your compiled applications will run faster
and your code will be more reliable because you're writing
real Visual Basic code in the Visual Basic environment.
You'll also be able to debug your Web-based application — a
capability unheard of until now. No more plunking down lots
of Print statements (which you'll only have to remove later)
just to give yourself messages about why the page isn't
working in the first place. You can test your Web page
fully before it even touches your Web server.

WebClass applications also have the ability to access the ASP
objects about which you've already learned. You can access
all the built-in objects, including Request, Response, and so
forth. And just like ASP applications, you don't have to worry
about someone stealing your source code because 1) the code
is never sent across the Internet, and 2) the code is compiled
into a library and resides entirely on your server.

In order to build the examples shown in this chapter, you must meet these prerequisites:

- ✦ Visual Basic 6.0, Professional or Enterprise Edition
- ✦ Windows NT Server 4.0 with Internet Information Server 3.0 or higher, or
- ✦ Windows NT Workstation 4.0 with Peer Web Services installed, or
- ✦ Windows 95/98 with Personal Web Server installed

Internet Explorer 4.01 is installed with Visual Basic 6.0 and is recommended for use with the WebClass samples in this chapter. Output can be viewed in most Web browsers.

Building Your First WebClass

To introduce you to WebClass applications, let's build a simple program. This program will be known as the "Hello, World!" WebClass. One of the first things most programmers do when using a new tool or feature is to write a simple program to generate some sort of output, like a printed line or a message box. This example will show you how to generate some simple output to your Web browser. You'll create a new WebClass project, add a little bit of code, debug and test it, and then deploy it to your Web server.

The "Hello World" WebClass

To get started, you'll be creating a new application. Start Visual Basic, select New from the File menu, and select IIS Application from the dialog shown in Figure 17-1.

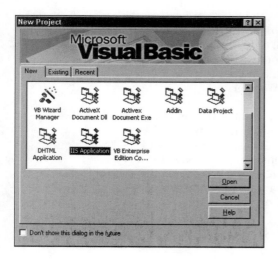

Figure 17-1: IIS Application is a new entry in the New Project dialog in Visual Basic.

After Visual Basic creates the new project, you may expect to see a class module in your project. That's not quite the case. A WebClass isn't the same as a regular class module. It has many of the same events and properties of a class, but it is designed to do much more. For this reason, you'll be saving a *designer file* (.DSR) as part of your project for each WebClass you build. Designer files are used by some of the more complex VB tools to store all the relevant data to a particular type of module, such as a WebClass. When you create your new IIS application, Visual Basic automatically adds a designer file to your project and names it WebClass1, as shown in Figure 17-2.

Figure 17-2: WebClass1 is added by default to your new IIS Application project.

The designer file saves more information than what is normally saved in a class file. In addition, even though you can instantiate this class within Visual Basic, you can't export it to a regular class module and thus can only use it in the current version of Visual Basic. In general, don't plan on using a WebClass where you would normally use a standard class module. It will work, but it's really not designed for that purpose.

To continue, double-click the WebClass1 item in the Project Explorer window. You'll see the WebClass Designer, as shown in Figure 17-3.

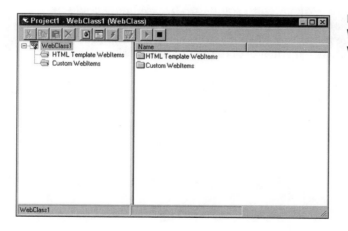

Figure 17-3: The WebClass Designer window

Figure 17-4 shows the Properties window, which displays the most relevant properties of the WebClass. You can rename the WebClass to HelloWorld or another valid name (no spaces allowed). The other property values should remain as is — you'll learn about these values in a following section.

Figure 17-4: The Properties window shows the properties for this WebClass.

Most of the work involved in building a WebClass will involve the WebClass Designer. This window shows you two categories of items:

✦ HTML Templates — an HTML document used by a WebClass. This document consists of plain text, and is edited in either Notepad or your default HTML editor. This template uses special tags that can manipulate the HTML without requiring you to write all of the HTML through code. The HTML template is not compiled into the WebClass, so you can make changes without having to rebuild the WebClass itself.

✦ Custom WebItems — a name that you define as part of the WebClass module. A WebItem can have custom events, giving you essentially a two-level hierarchy. Compared to standard VB, a WebItem could be a standard code or class module, while an event is like a procedure that is part of the module or class. Custom WebItems will be the heart of your code when you start building IIS applications.

Besides what you see in the Designer window, you can also look at the underlying code by selecting View ➪ Code. When you create a new WebClass, the code that is added is shown in Listing 17-1. Note that some of the longer lines are broken in the listing for clarity. They are intact in the project, but work the same way in either method.

Listing 17-1: **WebClass Default code**

```
Private Sub WebClass_Start()

    'Write a reply to the user
    With Response
```

```
            .Write "<HTML>"
            .Write "<body>"
            .Write "<h1><font face=""Arial"">" _
                & "WebClass1's Starting Page</font></h1>"
            .Write "<p>This response was created " _
                & "in the Start event of WebClass1.</p>"
            .Write "</body>"
            .Write "</html>"
        End With
    End Sub
```

This code, which can be altered, will be shown if you use the WebClass by itself without creating any WebItems. To see this code in action, select Run ⇨ Start. The dialog shown in Figure 17-5 will appear.

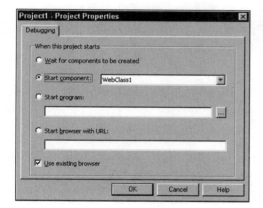

Figure 17-5: This dialog appears when you run your WebClass for the first time.

In this case, VB assumed that we want to run WebClass1, and will show its output in the browser that exists on your system. The HTML code will work with any Web browser, including non-Microsoft models.

In the Project Properties dialog, click OK to continue. At this point, Visual Basic will create a temporary virtual directory for testing these applications. Figure 17-6 shows the dialog that will appear. The directory you have defined as your temporary Windows directory (typically C:\Windows\Temp) will become a shared directory known as "Temp". This shared directory is used to allow VB to load the page in your browser. If you've already saved your files and project, VB will create a shared name for the folder in which your project resides. For this reason, you should create a new directory for each IIS application you build — it will be easier to manage the shared directories that are created.

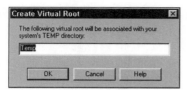

Figure 17-6: VB creates a virtual directory for testing the WebClass.

The results of this sequence are shown in Figure 17-7. The code in the WebClass_Start event procedure has been executed, and has produced some HTML output.

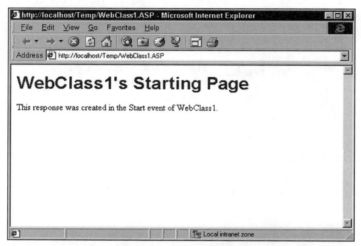

Figure 17-7: The output of your WebClass, as seen in the browser

The simple HTML code is shown in Listing 17-2.

Listing 17-2: **HTML from WebClass**

```
<HTML><body><h1><font face="Arial">WebClass1's Starting
Page</font></h1><p>This response was created in the Start event
of WebClass1.</p></body></html>
```

Why is all on one line, you might ask? Because the WebClass didn't add any line breaks to the HTML placed in the page. Even though your code is generating HTML that the browser can read in any format or layout, line breaks help *you* determine if the HTML is correct. One long line of HTML tends to hamper readability. To break up the HTML, use the vbCrLf constant within the WebClass procedure. vbCrLf adds a line break in the output HTML, which makes it much easier to read. The revised code for the WebClass_Start event procedure is shown in Listing 17-3.

Listing 17-3: **WebClass_Start code with line breaks**

```
Private Sub WebClass_Start()
    Dim sQuote As String
    sQuote = Chr(34)
    ' Write a reply to the user
    With Response
        .Write "<HTML>" & vbCrLf
        .Write "<body>" & vbCrLf
        .Write "<h1><font face=" _
            & sQuote & "Arial" & sQuote _
            & ">WebClass1's Starting Page</font></h1>" _
            & vbCrLf
        .Write "<p>This response was created " _
            & "in the Start event of WebClass1.</p>" & vbCrLf
        .Write "</body>" & vbCrLf
        .Write "</html>" & vbCrLf
    End With
End Sub
```

The resulting HTML is much easier to read with the line breaks in place, as shown in Listing 17-4.

Listing 17-4: **HTML with line breaks**

```
<HTML>
<body>
<h1><font face="Arial">WebClass1's Starting Page</font></h1>
<p>This response was created in the Start event of
WebClass1.</p>
</body>
</html>
```

If you happen to notice, the URL in the address line of your browser is referencing a file ending in .ASP. You didn't have to create the ASP page — Visual Basic did it for you. If you haven't stopped your VB program yet, look in your temporary directory using Explorer and you'll see the ASP page. However, when you stop your program, it will disappear. If you're quick, you can open up the ASP page to see what it contains. The contents are shown in Listing 17-5. As with some of the other listings, the line breaks in the listing below may not appear in the ASP file; however, the line breaks will not change how the file works.

Listing 17-5: **The contents of Project1_WebClass1.ASP**

```
<%
Server.ScriptTimeout=600
Response.Buffer=True
Response.Expires=0

If (VarType(Application("~WC~WebClassManager")) = 0) Then
    Application.Lock
    If (VarType(Application("~WC~WebClassManager")) = 0) Then
        Set Application("~WC~WebClassManager") = _
            Server.CreateObject("WebClassRuntime.WebClassManager")
    End If
    Application.UnLock
End If

Application("~WC~WebClassManager").ProcessNoStateWebClass _
    "Project1.WebClass1", _
    Server, _
    Application, _
    Session, _
    Request, _
    Response
%>
```

Visual Basic creates this Active Server page for you automatically. VB just creates an instance of your WebClass1 and executes it. When you compile and deploy your application, VB will build a copy of this file for you and put it with your compiled library. Both the ASP page and the library need to be placed on your Web server. You can't run the library by itself — it has to be started in exactly the manner shown in the ASP page. Because VB will simply overwrite your changes later, you should avoid editing the ASP page as well.

The final step in creating a WebClass application is to compile and deploy it. This step involves compiling the application into a DLL, packaging it with all of the required files needed for it to run, and then installing the package on your Web server. These tasks are discussed at the conclusion of this chapter.

Using HTML Templates

In the last example, you saw how to create a WebClass by generating HTML manually. Working with HTML requires lots of double-doublequote characters to get around VB's use of a doublequote character, as discussed in the preceding example. In addition to the tedious typing, any changes to the output format will require a recompile of the WebClass library, regardless of the scope of the change.

Finally, most larger Web sites use professional graphic designers, in addition to the coders, to create the site. Having the ability to separate the HTML from the code makes division of labor easier. This section shows you how to create a template file for use in conjunction with your WebClass. The result: Web sites that are easier to maintain.

Creating the Template

An HTML template is simply an HTML file with some special tags added. These special tags look like HTML tags, but are interpreted by your WebClass before they make it to the user's browser. Because you're writing plain HTML, you can use any text editor or HTML editor that gives you access to the actual HTML. Editors like FrontPage won't work—they make it more difficult to get to the actual HTML. I recommend and use Allaire's HomeSite 4.0 product, which doesn't get in the way of your development. You can also use Visual InterDev, but that solution is a more expensive than HomeSite.

To get started, let's create a relatively simple HTML page that has two special tags in it. The code for this page is shown in Listing 17-6.

Listing 17-6: **BasicTemplate.html code**

```
<HTML>
<HEAD>
    <TITLE><WC@Title>Title</WC@Title></TITLE>
</HEAD>
<BODY BGCOLOR="<WC@BGC>BGColor</WC@BGC>">
<H1><WC@TITLE>Title</WC@TITLE></H1>
This is a test of the HTML Template feature
in combination with WebClasses. The title and
background color of this page were substituted
through code.
</BODY>
</HTML>
```

Note that the special tags are within double quotes in the BODY tag. This arrangement is designed to isolate them from the parsing of Visual Basic. Once you've saved this file, complete the following steps:

1. If you're not already in a new IIS application (the one from the preceding section is fine to use), create a new project.

2. Open the Designer window and right-click HTML Template WebItems. From the menu that appears, select Add HTML Template.

3. From the dialog that appears, select your HTML file and click Open to let VB load it.

4. The name will be highlighted and will allow you to edit the name. Give it whatever name you wish—I normally use the same name as the template file. Hit the Enter key after you type the name.

At this point, the WebClass Designer has parsed your HTML template and added it to the WebClass. However, if you look at the right side of the Designer, the code doesn't match what you entered. This is apparently still a "feature" of Visual Basic, according to Microsoft document #Q189539. You can't put replacement tags within HTML tags, according to the Microsoft "design." This seems like an important feature, especially because you can do a similar procedure in ASP where you print a variable's value right into HTML. No workaround is provided by Microsoft other than "don't do it," but we do have an alternate method for this feature. To make the change, do the following:

1. Right-click the template in the WebClass Designer and select Edit Template.

2. Change the HTML code to look like the following:

```
<HTML>
<HEAD>
    <TITLE><WC@Title>Title</WC@Title></TITLE>
</HEAD>
<WC@BGC>BGColor</WC@BGC>
<H1><WC@TITLE>Title</WC@TITLE></H1>
This is a test of the HTML Template feature
in combination with WebClasses. The title and
background color of this page were substituted
through code.
</BODY>
</HTML>
```

3. Save the template file and close your editor.

The WebClass designer will prompt you to reload the template, which is fine. Again, notice that the display is not correct. The WebClass designer has added a BODY tag in the right pane. However, the WebClass designer didn't change the template. You can verify by editing the template again to make sure it's still working. As you can see, there are some odd design choices in this tool. However, if you can work around the bugs, it's still pretty helpful.

The next step in using the template is to write the code to handle the substitutions. VB will provide you with the tags through an event, but you have to do the work to figure out what to substitute for what. Add the code in Listing 17-7 to your WebClass. This code assumes that the name of the template is BasicTemplate. If you named your template something else, there will be an item for it in the object drop-down list in the code window.

Listing 17-7: **Substitution Code for BasicTemplate**

```
Option Explicit
Option Compare Text

Private Sub BasicTemplate_ProcessTag( _
    ByVal TagName As String, _
    TagContents As String, _
    SendTags As Boolean)

    TagName = Mid(TagName, Len(BasicTemplate.TagPrefix) + 1)
    Select Case UCase(TagName)
    Case "TITLE"
        TagContents = "The Test Worked!"
    Case "BGC"
        TagContents = "<BODY BGCOLOR=""#009900"">"
    End Select

    SendTags = False

End Sub

Private Sub WebClass_Start()
    BasicTemplate.WriteTemplate
End Sub
```

Each time the WebClass engine finds a substitution tag, it calls the `ProcessTag` event and passes the name of the tag to it. You then have to figure out what tag was sent and with what you want to replace the tag.

You should have noticed that all the tags in the page were prefixed with `WC@`. This is the default prefix for substitution tags, and is stored in the `TagPrefix` property. First, we remove the tag so we can deal with the meat of the tag. Depending on the value of the tag, whether it be `<TITLE>` or `<BGC>`, we put the replacement text in the `TagContents` parameter, which is sent back to the WebClass engine. Note that we have to send the entire `<BODY>` tag because the tags couldn't be placed within the HTML tags. The other important line of code is in the `WebClass_Start` event, which prints the template that we have added to the WebClass. In the preceding example, we had code here to print HTML we wanted to show. This present process is much easier to maintain — you can edit the HTML templates outside of Visual Basic and simply reload them.

With the basics of HTML templates covered, you're ready to move to Custom WebItems and Events.

Using Custom WebItems and Events

While the WebClass has some default events in which you can have various types of processing, those few events are too generic to respond to specific actions, such as a user clicking on a customer on a page with 100 different customers. If you didn't have another method, you'd have to have all your code in a single event, which of course would work fine. However, WebClasses provide a better approach. You can add your own custom WebItems to a WebClass. As mentioned in the introduction to this chapter, you can think of a WebItem as a set of functions or a class. Within each WebItem, you can have a number of custom events, which are the actual methods that can be performed by the WebClass. WebItems and custom events belonging to a WebClass module may be triggered from the same ASP page simply through different arguments supplied to the page. You can then use these arguments internally to produce URLs in the HTML output that the user can click, or you can call the URLs from other HTML pages you may have on your site. You'll see the syntax for these processes later in the section.

For now, you'll see how to add Custom WebItems and Custom Events to perform processing on the HTML template you just built. You'll be using a combination of Custom WebItems and Events to provide additional functionality to the user. In the process, you should start seeing how to use these features to make your own Web-based applications more modular and reliable.

First, add three Custom WebItems to your WebClass by performing the following steps:

1. Open the Designer window.

2. Right-click Custom WebItems and select Add Custom WebItem from the popup menu.

3. VB will add a new WebItem to the tree and prompt you to rename it. Add three WebItems with these names: ShowInRed, ShowInYellow, ShowInBlue.

Next, let's add some code behind the scenes. As mentioned previously, the WebClass can have variables just like any other class. In the Declarations section of the WebClass, add the following variable declaration:

```
Dim sColor As String
```

Listing 17-8 shows the code you need for the three Custom WebItems.

Listing 17-8: Custom WebItem code

```
Private Sub ShowInBlue_Respond()
    sColor = "#0000FF"
    tmpSubstitution.WriteTemplate
End Sub
```

```
Private Sub ShowInRed_Respond()
    sColor = "#FF0000"
    tmpSubstitution.WriteTemplate
End Sub

Private Sub ShowInYellow_Respond()
    sColor = "#FFFF00"
    tmpSubstitution.WriteTemplate
End Sub
```

These are each essentially event handlers for the Custom WebItems. Now you have to change the `WebClass_Start` event procedure. Because we need to give the user a few choices from which to choose, `WebClass_Start` will have to generate some HTML dynamically. You'll see why shortly. Add the code in Listing 17-9 to your WebClass.

Listing 17-9: **WebClass_Start code**

```
Private Sub WebClass_Start()
    sColor = "#FFFFFF"
    With Response
      .Write "<HTML><HEAD><TITLE>"
      .Write "Pick Your Color"
      .Write "</TITLE></HEAD>" & vbCr
      .Write "<BODY BGCOLOR=#FFFFFF>" & vbCr
      .Write "Pick the color you'd like to see:<P>" & vbCr
      .Write "<A HREF=""" _
          & URLFor(ShowInRed) _
          & """>Red</A><BR>" & vbCr
      .Write "<A HREF=""" _
          & URLFor(ShowInYellow) _
          & """>Yellow</A><BR>" & vbCr
      .Write "<A HREF=""" _
          & URLFor(ShowInBlue) _
          & """>Blue</A><BR>" & vbCr
      .Write "</HTML>"

    End With

End Sub
```

The important feature of this code is the `URLFor` function. This method generates the proper URL to access the Custom WebItems of this WebClass. The first time it is used, it generates the URL to access the `ShowInRed` Custom WebItem. The advantage of using `URLFor` is that it generates the internal ID number used by the Web server to access the method. This number is used to retrieve the location of the method within the WebClass object. This arrangement makes referencing a method faster because the WebClass doesn't have to look up a name reference. If you're generating code, always use the URLFor method for WebItems that are in your WebClass.

The last piece of code you need is a slightly modified tmpSubstitution_ProcessTag procedure. The changes are highlighted in Listing 17-10.

Listing 17-10: ProcessTag code

```
Private Sub tmpSubstitution_ProcessTag _
    (ByVal TagName As String, _
    TagContents As String, _
    SendTags As Boolean)

    TagName = Mid(TagName, _
        Len(tmpSubstitution.TagPrefix) + 1)
    Select Case UCase$(TagName)
    Case "TITLE"
        TagContents = "The Test Worked!"
    Case "BGCOLOR"
        TagContents = sColor
    End Select
    SendTags = False
End Sub
```

Instead of always using a particular color, this procedure will now use the color stored in the sColor variable. The correct color was assigned previously by the Custom WebItem triggered by the user.

Save your work and then run your project. If you look at the source, you will see the code shown in Listing 17-11.

Listing 17-11: HTML generated by WebClass_Start event procedure

```
<HTML><HEAD><TITLE>Pick Your Color</TITLE></HEAD>
<BODY BGCOLOR=#FFFFFF>
Pick the color you'd like to see:<P>
<A
HREF="HTMLTemplateTester_Substitution.ASP?WCIID=1281">Red</A><B
R>
<A
HREF="HTMLTemplateTester_Substitution.ASP?WCIID=1282">Yellow</A
><BR>
```

```
<A
HREF="HTMLTemplateTester_Substitution.ASP?WCIID=1280">Blue</A><
BR>
</HTML>
```

If you haven't saved your project yet, HTMLTemplateTester may be shown as Project1 or the current name of your project.

The WCIID reference following the question mark, the number following it, and the equal sign are known as a *parameter* in ASP lingo. With this method, one page can talk to another page. The number refers to the Custom WebItem you built. The rest of the URL is the same as before: the project name followed by the WebClass name.

If you click one of these items, you will see the same HTML template as before, except you'll now see a different background color for each item. While this may seem like a trivial example, the basic idea really expands the scope of how you can use WebClasses and HTML templates.

With the creation of Custom WebItems under your belt, creating Custom Events is just as easy. The main difference is that instead of using the default Respond event handler, you'll have a different event handler for each event you build, all under a particular WebItem. The example you'll be building simply converts the previous example to use a single WebItem and three events instead of using three different WebItems. All of the modified code will be marked so you can see the differences between the two techniques.

First of all, you need to open your Designer window and do the following: Add a Custom WebItem named ChangeColor. Then right-click ChangeColor in the list and select Add Custom Event from the popup menu. Add three Custom Events named Red, Yellow, and Blue.

You now have to add new event handlers to deal with the new events you just built. That code is shown in Listing 17-12.

Listing 17-12: **Custom Event handlers for WebClass**

```
Private Sub ChangeColor_Blue()
    sColor = "#0000FF"
    tmpSubstitution.WriteTemplate
End Sub

Private Sub ChangeColor_Red()
    sColor = "#FF0000"
```

Continued

Listing 17-12 *(continued)*

```
    tmpSubstitution.WriteTemplate
End Sub

Private Sub ChangeColor_Yellow()
    sColor = "#FFFF00"
    tmpSubstitution.WriteTemplate
End Sub
```

As you can see, these procedures use the same instructions as for the WebItems built previously, though the names of the procedures are different to take account of the new events.

The last change you need to make is in the WebClass_Start event handler. The changes are to the three calls to URLFor, as marked in Listing 17-13.

Listing 17-13: **WebClass_Start event handler**

```
Private Sub WebClass_Start()
    sColor = "#FFFFFF"
    With Response
      .Write "<HTML><HEAD><TITLE>"
      .Write "Pick Your Color"
      .Write "</TITLE></HEAD>" & vbCr
      .Write "<BODY BGCOLOR=#FFFFFF>" & vbCr
      .Write "Pick the color you'd like to see:<P>" & vbCr
      .Write "<A HREF=""" _
          & URLFor(ChangeColor, "Red") _
          & """>Red</A><BR>" & vbCr
      .Write "<A HREF=""" _
          & URLFor(ChangeColor, "Yellow") _
          & """>Yellow</A><BR>" & vbCr
      .Write "<A HREF=""" _
          & URLFor(ChangeColor, "Blue") _
          & """>Blue</A><BR>" & vbCr
      .Write "</HTML>"

    End With

End Sub
```

While the name of the WebItem (ChangeColor, in this case) is actually an object defined to Visual Basic, the name of the event has to be passed as a string in quotes. It is not defined to Visual Basic and thus has to be "protected" from Visual Basic's syntax checker. When you run your program, the string will be passed to the URLFor function, which understands how to interpret it. The end result of this code is very similar to the previous version, except in the starting page. The new HTML for the starting page is shown in Listing 17-14.

Listing 17-14: **WebClass_Start HTML using Custom Events**

```
<HTML><HEAD><TITLE>Pick Your Color</TITLE></HEAD>
<BODY BGCOLOR=#FFFFFF>
Pick the color you'd like to see:<P>
<A
HREF="HTMLTemplateTester_Substitution.ASP?WCIID=1280&WCE=Red">R
ed</A><BR>
<A
HREF="HTMLTemplateTester_Substitution.ASP?WCIID=1280&WCE=Yellow
">Yellow</A><BR>
<A
HREF="HTMLTemplateTester_Substitution.ASP?WCIID=1280&WCE=Blue">
Blue</A><BR>
</HTML>
```

Appended to the end of each URL is the name of the event to be called, prefixed with WCE (WebClass Event). This particular part of the URL is always passed as text, even in this version.

If you prefer to write this HTML page manually, you can still call the three WebItems — just in a different way. Instead of using the WCIID parameter that VB utilizes, you write the WCI parameter followed by the WebItem's name, as in this example:

```
<A
HREF="HTMLTemplateTester_Substitution.ASP?WCI=ChangeColor&WCE=R
ed">Red</A><BR>
```

This syntax enables you to create plain HTML pages that can start WebClass applications. When you use this syntax, make sure you have a default response in case parameters are omitted from the name of the ASP page. This omission may happen if plain HTML pages are referring to ASP pages that require certain information to run properly. Typically, you want a URL entered by hand to be as simple as possible. In most cases, you'll be calling the main Respond event in a class first, after which point all other URLs will be generated by the WebClass itself. You'll see more of this practice later in the chapter.

Using ADO with WebClasses

Now you're ready to start using databases with your templates. This section will show you more of the real power behind this new technology. If you've done ASP pages by hand, the following pages may convince you to abandon that method.

The main point of the Active Server Pages technology was primarily to make it easier to publish dynamic pages. These pages were typically based on database tables and queries. WebClasses are no different and even make it easier to build these types of applications. In this section, you'll build an HTML template with substitution tags. These tags will be replaced by data from a database that you access by way of ADO. You'll also be building something called a UserEvent to make it easier to show more detailed information on records in a table of data.

The database you'll be using is (no surprise here) the Northwind Traders database. By building a list of the customers in the database, you will provide the user with the ability to click a customer to see more information about his or her company. The functionality here is similar to the characteristics of your VB forms, except that the output is directed through the Web to any browser supporting a minimal set of HTML.

We'll start by creating a new IIS application. Be sure to put it in its own directory as VB will need to create a share for it. Once the project is created, you'll probably want to rename both the project and the WebClass. In the example included, the project is named `ADOWebClass`, and the WebClass is named `NWind`.

The next thing you need to do is to build an HTML template that will be used for the customer list. The only things you need to put in this page are general tags, such as `TITLE` and `BODY`. All of the customer entries will be generated dynamically with the WebClass. The HTML template should look something like Listing 17-15.

Listing 17-15: **CustomerList HTML Template**

```
<HTML>
<HEAD>

<TITLE>Northwind Traders - Customer List</TITLE>
<STYLE>
<!--
H1 {
        font-family: Arial;
        font-weight: bold;
        font-size: 16px;
        color: #800000;
}

H3 {
        font-family: Arial;
```

```
            font-size: 12px;
            color: #800000;
   }

   H4 {
            font-family: Arial;
            font-size: 10px;
            color: #000000;
   }
   -->
   </STYLE>

   </HEAD>
   <BODY bgColor=#ffffcc>
   <H1>Northwind Traders Customer List<BR>
   <H3>As Of <WC@CURRENTDATE></WC@CURRENTDATE> </H3></H1>
   <HR>
   <WC@CUSTOMERDATA></WC@CUSTOMERDATA>

   </BODY></HTML>
```

This HTML document contains cascading style sheets (CSS). The CSS feature enables you to define fonts, colors, and other text formatting features in one place in the document, instead of every time you use the text. (CSS works in the latest versions of both Netscape and Internet Explorer.) These fonts will be used to generate the data for the page. By leaving the font properties here instead of in the WebClass, you can change the format of the data without having to change the WebClass itself.

Once you've saved this template in another directory, add it to your IIS application and name it tmpCustomerList. Next, add a Custom WebItem to show the customer list, because your WebClass will probably have a wide variety of other features that will be shown first on a menu or other interface. Name the WebItem ShowCustomer. The default event for this will trigger an event that handles showing the list of customers. Create a Custom Event called ListAll as part of the ShowCustomer WebItem.

With the WebItems and Custom Events defined, you can start writing some code. We'll start with the WebClass_Start event handler. As mentioned previously, you'd probably want to have a menu from which to show the customer list, but these instructions will serve as test code so that the list of customers will come up automatically when the WebClass is started.

```
   Private Sub WebClass_Start()
      Set NextItem = ListCustomer
   End Sub
```

The simple `ListCustomer_Respond` event handler is next:

```
Private Sub ListCustomer_Respond()
   tmpCustomerList.WriteTemplate
End Sub
```

This code triggers the `CustomerList` template to load and be processed. Because we have to deal with substitution tags, the `tmpCustomerList_ProcessTags` event handler is next. Its code is shown in Listing 17-16.

Listing 17-16: **ProcessTags event handler**

```
Private Sub tmpCustomerList_ProcessTag _
   (ByVal TagName As String, _
   TagContents As String, _
   SendTags As Boolean)

   Dim sTag As String

   sTag = UCase$(Mid(TagName, _
      Len(tmpCustomerList.TagPrefix) + 1))
   Select Case sTag
      Case "CURRENTDATE"
         TagContents = Format$(Date, "mmmm d, yyyy")
      Case "CUSTOMERDATA"
         TagContents = fnGenerateCustomerList
   End Select
   SendTags = False

End Sub
```

The function procedure `fnGenerateCustomerList` reads the database and creates a table with the customers in it. This procedure is listed in Listing 17-17. Remember to use the path to your Northwind Traders database in the ADO connection.

Listing 17-17: **fnGenerateCustomerList function**

```
Private Function fnGenerateCustomerList() As String
   Dim dcnNWind As ADODB.Connection
   Dim rsCust As ADODB.Recordset
   Dim sOutput As String

   Set dcnNWind = New ADODB.Connection
```

```vb
        dcnNWind.CursorLocation = adUseClient
        dcnNWind.Open "PROVIDER=Microsoft.Jet.OLEDB.3.51;" _
            & "Data Source=C:\Visual Studio\VB98\NWind.MDB;"

        Set rsCust = New ADODB.Recordset
        rsCust.Open "SELECT * FROM Customers " _
            & "ORDER BY CompanyName", _
            dcnNWind, adOpenForwardOnly, adLockReadOnly

        If rsCust.RecordCount = 0 Then
            sOutput = _
                "<H1>No records are in the database.</H1>"
        Else
            sOutput = "<TABLE CELLPADDING=3 BORDER=1>" & vbCr _
                & "<TR><TH><H4>Customer Name</TH>" & vbCr _
                & "<TH><H4>City</TH>" & vbCr _
                & "<TH><H4>State/Region</TH>" & vbCr _
                & "<TH><H4>Country</TH>" & vbCr _
                & "</TR>" & vbCr

            Do While Not rsCust.EOF
                sOutput = sOutput & "<TR>" & vbCr _
                    & "<TD><H4>" _
                    & rsCust("CompanyName") & "</TD>" & vbCr _
                    & "<TD><H4>" _
                    & rsCust("City") & "</TD>" & vbCr _
                    & "<TD><H4>" _
                    & rsCust("Region") & "</TD>" & vbCr _
                    & "<TD><H4>" _
                    & rsCust("Country") & "</TD>" & vbCr _
                    & "</TR>" & vbCr
                rsCust.MoveNext
            Loop
            sOutput = sOutput & "</TABLE>" & vbCr
            sOutput = sOutput & "<HR><H3><I>" _
                & rsCust.RecordCount _
                & " customers listed.</I></H3>" & vbCr

        End If
        fnGenerateCustomerList = sOutput

        '
        ' Clean up objects
        '
        rsCust.Close
        Set rsCust = Nothing
        dcnNWind.Close
        Set dcnNWind = Nothing
End Function
```

After making a connection to the Northwind Traders database, a recordset is created of all the customers, sorted by company name. The `TABLE` header tags are generated next, including column headers. All of the HTML is appended to the `sOutput` string variable because it all needs to be returned to the `ProcessTags` event procedure at the end. For each retrieved record, a new table row is added. When it is generated, the HTML looks like the following for a single row:

```
<TR>
<TD><H4>Alfreds Futterkiste</TD>
<TD><H4>Berlin</TD>
<TD><H4></TD>
<TD><H4>Germany</TD>
</TR>
```

Leaving the `<H4>` tags unclosed will actually save some vertical space. The `CELLPADDING` parameter of the `<TABLE>` tag, generated by `fnGenerateCustomerList`, has already taken care of this. A summary line prints the number of records, and the database objects are closed and eliminated by Visual Basic. At this point, you can run your project and look at the results.

Now that you have the basics to combining ADO with WebClasses, you can move on to some more advanced techniques for building useful applications.

Advanced Techniques

In this section, you'll learn how to create a dynamic event associated with a WebClass. These events will enable you to respond with a different result, based on the event that is triggered. To see how this works, you're going to be modifying the example from the preceding section to enable users to click a company name to see more information about the company. In addition, you'll learn a few tricks to help simplify your code when dealing with WebClasses.

First, you need to build a new HTML template. This template will be used to show a customer's information. An example HTML template is shown in Listing 17-18.

Listing 17-18: **ViewCustomer HTML Template**

```
<HTML>
<HEAD>
<TITLE>Northwind Traders - View Customer</TITLE>
<STYLE>
<!--
H1 {
        font-family: Arial Black;
        font-size: 16px;
        color: #800000;
```

```
        }

        H3 {
                font-family: Arial;
                font-size: 12px;
                color: #800000;
        }

        H4 {
                font-family: Arial;
                font-size: 10px;
                color: #000000;
        }
        -->
</STYLE>

</HEAD>
<BODY bgColor=#ffffcc>
<H1><WC@FIELDCOMPANYNAME></WC@FIELDCOMPANYNAME></H1>
<HR>

<TABLE border=1 cellPadding=3>
<TBODY>
<TR>
<TD>
<H3>Customer ID:</H3>
</TD>
<TD>
<H3><WC@FIELDCUSTOMERID></WC@FIELDCUSTOMERID></H3>
</TD></TR>

<TR>
<TD>
<H3>Contact Name:</H3></TD>
<TD>
<H3><WC@FIELDCONTACTNAME></WC@FIELDCONTACTNAME></H3>
</TD></TR>

<TR>
<TD>
<H3>Contact Title:</H3></TD>
<TD>
<H3><WC@FIELDCONTACTTITLE></WC@FIELDCONTACTTITLE></H3>
</TD></TR>

<TR>
<TD>
<H3>Address:</H3>
</TD>
<TD>
<H3><WC@FIELDADDRESS></WC@FIELDADDRESS></H3>
</TD></TR>
```

Continued

Listing 17-18 *(continued)*

```
<TR>
<TD>
<H3>City:</H3></TD>
<TD>
<H3><WC@FIELDCITY></WC@FIELDCITY></H3>
</TD></TR>

<TR>
<TD>
<H3>Region:</H3>
</TD>
<TD>
<H3><WC@FIELDREGION></WC@FIELDREGION></H3>
</TD></TR>

<TR>
<TD>
<H3>Postal Code:</H3>
</TD>
<TD>
<H3><WC@FIELDPOSTALCODE></WC@FIELDPOSTALCODE></H3>
</TD></TR>

<TR>
<TD>
<H3>Country:</H3>
</TD>
<TD>
<H3><WC@FIELDCOUNTRY></WC@FIELDCOUNTRY></H3>
</TD></TR>

<TR>
<TD>
<H3>Phone:</H3>
</TD>
<TD>
<H3><WC@FIELDPHONE></WC@FIELDPHONE></H3>
</TD></TR>

<TR>
<TD>
<H3>Fax:</H3>
</TD>
<TD>
<H3><WC@FIELDFAX></WC@FIELDFAX></H3>
</TD></TR>
</TBODY>
</TABLE>
</BODY>
</HTML>
```

In this particular template, all of the tags to be filled with data from the database are prefixed with the word FIELD. You'll see why shortly. For now, add the template to your WebClass and name it tmpViewCustomer or another appropriate name of your choosing.

Next, add the following declarations to the general declarations section of the WebClass:

```
Dim dcnNWind As ADODB.Connection
Dim rsCust As ADODB.Recordset
```

These declarations will be used to allow event handlers to communicate with each other and to save some database activity that would be required otherwise. The next changes are to the fnGenerateCustomerList procedure and are highlighted in Listing 17-19.

Listing 17-19: **fnGenerateCustomerList changes**

```
Private Function fnGenerateCustomerList() As String
    Dim sOutput As String

    Set dcnNWind = New ADODB.Connection
    dcnNWind.CursorLocation = adUseClient
    dcnNWind.Open "PROVIDER=Microsoft.Jet.OLEDB.3.51;" _
        & "Data Source=C:\Visual Studio\VB98\NWind.MDB;"

    Set rsCust = New ADODB.Recordset
    rsCust.Open "SELECT * FROM Customers " _
        & "ORDER BY CompanyName", _
        dcnNWind, adOpenForwardOnly, adLockReadOnly

    If rsCust.RecordCount = 0 Then
        sOutput = _
            "<H1>No records are in the database.</H1>"
    Else
        sOutput = "<TABLE CELLPADDING=3 BORDER=1>" & vbCr _
            & "<TR><TH><H4>Customer Name</TH>" & vbCr _
            & "<TH><H4>City</TH>" & vbCr _
            & "<TH><H4>State/Region</TH>" & vbCr _
            & "<TH><H4>Country</TH>" & vbCr _
            & "</TR>" & vbCr

        Do While Not rsCust.EOF
            sOutput = sOutput & "<TR>" & vbCr _
                & "<TD><H4><A HREF=""" _
                & URLFor(ViewCustomer, _
                    CStr(rsCust("CustomerID"))) _
```

Continued

Listing 17-19 *(continued)*

```
                & """>" & rsCust("CompanyName") _
                & "</A></TD>" & vbCr _
                & "<TD><H4>" & rsCust("City") _
                & "</TD>" & vbCr _
                & "<TD><H4>" & rsCust("Region") _
                & "</TD>" & vbCr _
                & "<TD><H4>" & rsCust("Country") _
                & "</TD>" & vbCr _
                & "</TR>" & vbCr
        rsCust.MoveNext
    Loop
    sOutput = sOutput & "</TABLE>" & vbCr
    sOutput = sOutput & "<HR><H3><I>" _
        & rsCust.RecordCount _
        & " customers listed.</I></H3>" & vbCr

    End If
    fnGenerateCustomerList = sOutput

    '
    ' Clean up objects
    '
    rsCust.Close
    Set rsCust = Nothing
    dcnNWind.Close
    Set dcnNWind = Nothing
End Function
```

First, we remove the declarations for `dcnNWind` and `rsCust`, because they are now defined at the WebClass level. Also, instead of just printing the company name, the name is wrapped with a URL by the `URLFor` function. Omitting all of the host and directory information, this URL looks like the following when it is complete:

```
ADOWebClass_NWind.ASP?WCIID=1282&WCE=ALFKI
```

The customer ID has been appended to the URL by way of the `URLFor` method and is called a user-defined event. Obviously, we're not going to create a separate event for each possible customer ID. Instead, we will have the `ViewCustomer` WebItem respond to the `UserEvent` event handler and show the customer's information when it is requested. This task is very easy and much simpler than the same task using ordinary Active Server Pages without VB. In the ASP environment, you would have to break up the URL yourself (using the `Request` object) and then fill the page yourself. In addition, because the HTML and VBScript code are linked in ASP programming, you don't get the benefit of being able to change the template for the page without changing the code.

The next piece of code you need is shown in Listing 17-20. When a user clicks a customer name, this code will be triggered because we are providing an unknown event name (the customer ID). The customer ID will be placed in the EventName parameter to the ViewCustomer_UserEvent subroutine. It is then used in the SQL query to retrieve the correct piece of data.

Listing 17-20: **ViewCustomer_UserEvent event handler**

```
Private Sub ViewCustomer_UserEvent(ByVal EventName As String)
    Set dcnNWind = New ADODB.Connection
    dcnNWind.CursorLocation = adUseClient
    dcnNWind.Open "PROVIDER=Microsoft.Jet.OLEDB.3.51;" _
        & "Data Source=C:\Visual Studio\VB98\NWind.MDB;"

    Set rsCust = New ADODB.Recordset
    rsCust.Open "SELECT * FROM Customers " _
        & "WHERE CustomerID = '" & EventName & "'", _
        dcnNWind, adOpenForwardOnly, adLockReadOnly

    tmpViewCustomer.WriteTemplate
End Sub
```

The main purpose of this code is to find the customer record and place it in the module-level recordset. This action is done here because we don't want the ProcessTags event handler to create a new recordset for every single tag that it processes.

The next code (shown in Listing 17-21) is the ProcessTags event handler for the tmpViewCustomer template.

Listing 17-21: **tmpViewCustomer_ProcessTags event handler**

```
Private Sub tmpViewCustomer_ProcessTag _
    (ByVal TagName As String, _
    TagContents As String, _
    SendTags As Boolean)

    '
    ' At this point, we only care about tags
    ' that have the word "Field" in them.
    ' You may wish to expand this over time
    ' to handle other tags.
    '
```

Continued

Listing 17-21 *(continued)*

```
    Dim iLoc As Integer
    iLoc = InStr(TagName, "FIELD")
    If iLoc > 0 Then
        TagContents = rsCust(Mid(TagName, iLoc + 5)) & ""
    End If
    SendTags = False
End Sub
```

This handler looks for all tags beginning with the word FIELD, and substitutes the data from the field in the database whose name appears to the right of FIELD in the HTML template. This arrangement enables you to be able to change the database and the template without changing the code in the WebClass. Simply reference the field in the template — this handler will find the corresponding database field.

The last change is to the WebClass_Terminate event procedure. This change cleans up the open recordsets and connections that may have been left open by the UserEvent handler. This code is shown in Listing 17-22.

Listing 17-22: WebClass_Terminate event handler

```
Private Sub WebClass_Terminate()
    On Error Resume Next

    rsCust.Close
    Set rsCust = Nothing
    dcnNWind.Close
    Set dcnNWind = Nothing

End Sub
```

Because the WebClass has ceased execution anyway, the Resume Next error handler will skip any errors in which the recordset or connection is not open.

With these changes in place, you can run your WebClass. The customer list will now have a link for each customer that shows the customer data when you click it.

At this point, you have a model for many Web database publishing projects that you have planned (or even completed) using Active Server Pages. You can now make your code faster and more reliable by using a WebClass to consolidate all your code and building it all in Visual Basic.

Summary

As you can see from the material and examples in this chapter, WebClasses are one of the most exciting parts of this release of Visual Basic. For everyone who dreads having to write and debug Web applications built using ASPs and VBScript, this feature will save you many headaches and a lot of time. In addition, the performance and reliability increases make it worth your while to learn this new technology.

In addition to building simple pages, you can also build dynamic pages using the user-defined events. VB also provides you with the entire ASP object model to expand your developer's palette further. WebClasses are a great combination of the Visual Basic environment with the new Web programming model.

✦   ✦   ✦

Integrating with Microsoft Transaction Server

✦ ✦ ✦ ✦

In This Chapter

Learn about transactions

Learn how Microsoft Transaction Server (MTS) manages transactions

Create a simple MTS component, install it, and use it in a Web page

Create a complex MTS component that makes use of ADO and other system objects

What Is a Transaction?

✦ ✦ ✦ ✦

I n everyday life, you are constantly involved in transactions. A transaction can be a conversation you have with another person: you are exchanging messages. You might be purchasing or trading one item for another. You might be asking for another party's services. All of these examples could be considered transactions.

In computer terms, a *transaction* is a discrete unit of work performed by a computer or series of computers. Adding a record to a table could be a transaction. Viewing a table is not a transaction — no discrete task is being performed. However, the task to retrieve the data for the view could be a transaction, because the action is more defined.

To determine if a task is a transaction, you can give it the ACID test. ACID is an acronym with these four components:

✦ Atomicity — The task is either fully completed, or the whole thing is aborted. You can't have half of the task complete — it's either all or nothing.

✦ Consistency — When the task is done, the system has to be in a valid state. Any changes made during the transaction have been fully completed, and any aborted transactions have been completely reversed, or rolled back.

✦ Isolation — Isolation allows the computer to work on a single task at a time. For instance, a transaction changing a particular customer record is completed before another transaction to change the same customer record is started.

✦ Durability — Any changes made during the transaction are permanent. They don't disappear after the requestor shuts down, for instance. Durable transactions enable you to log the actions and re-create them, in case of a system failure.

Transaction processing is one of those concepts that has lots of theories and experts thinking about how best to handle it. We're not going to get into that debate in this chapter. A lot of books on the market cover transaction processing in more depth. Instead, we want to implement basic transaction processing using Microsoft Transaction Server and ASP.

What Is Microsoft Transaction Server?

Microsoft Transaction Server (MTS) is a component that you can install on Windows NT Server or Workstation. It comes with the Windows NT Option Pack, which can be downloaded free from Microsoft at the following URL (which was correct at the time of writing):

```
http://www.microsoft.com/ntserver/nts/downloads/recommended/NT4
OptPk/default.asp
```

MTS is also available through TechNet and the MSDN subscriptions. Your friendly neighborhood NT administrator probably has three or four copies — it's not hard to find.

MTS takes care of a lot of the grunt work involved in managing transactions. It takes care of creating and releasing instances of your objects. MTS handles pooling of these objects so that subsequent transactions run much faster, because they don't have to create their own objects each time. MTS takes care of reusing and recycling objects when necessary, so you don't have to worry about it in your ASP or VB applications. It also provides logging and trace features through the Transaction Server Manager console, which is a snap-in to the Microsoft Management Console (MMC).

You can install MTS on any flavor of Windows NT; however, both MTS and IIS have some administration and other features that aren't available on NT Workstation. This chapter was written using an NT Server 4.0 (Service Pack 5, at the time of writing) platform. The components were developed on a separate Windows 98 machine using Visual Basic 6.0, Service Pack 3. As usual, you have to have IIS 4.0 (or better) running to handle the ASP pages.

As you work through this chapter, you'll see how to use each of the major features of MTS involved in creating and managing your transactional components. However, we won't be hitting all the features. Several other books on the market cover MTS in much greater detail. A wealth of knowledge about MTS is also available on Usenet (Internet newsgroups), which can be accessed through Deja.com. A lot of other people probably have similar questions, so try this resource first before spending money on expensive technical support.

Creating an MTS Component

First, you're going to build a simple MTS component. Before you panic, don't worry. An MTS component is just a DLL (with a few extra properties) that lives within an MTS package. A package is just a set of components that perform related functions for your applications. You can use the Transaction Server Manager on NT to create and modify your packages with more or less components than you build in any language. For this example, we'll be using VB to build a simple component.

To get started, follow these steps:

1. Start Visual Basic and create a new ActiveX DLL project. Name the project something meaningful — this example will use the name BasicComponent for the project.

2. The project will be created with a class module in it. Name the class whatever you like — this example will use MessageObject for the class.

3. The object's sole purpose will be to produce a message back to the caller. Here's the code for the class:

```
Option Explicit

Public Function Message() As String
    Message = "This is a message from " _
        & "your friendly neighborhood " _
        & "MTS component."

End Function
```

4. At this point, you could compile the library and install it on your server. However, in order for MTS to work properly, we have to set a few extra properties on the class module itself. With the class module code window open, press F4 to open the Properties window. Change these properties:

   * Instancing: 5 — MultiUse
   * MTSTransactionMode: 1 — UsesTransactions

The first property is probably already set to the MultiUse value, so don't worry if you didn't have to change it. The second property informs MTS and NT Server that this component needs to be run using a transaction. The available values and their meanings are shown in Table 18-1.

Table 18-1
MTSTransactionMode Values

Constant Name	Value	Description
NotAnMTSObject	0	(Default) The component doesn't support Microsoft Transaction Server.
NoTransactions	1	Does not support transactions. This value indicates that the component's objects do not run within the scope of transactions. When a new object is created, its object context is created without a transaction, regardless of whether the client has a transaction.
RequiresTransaction	2	This value indicates that the component's objects must execute within the scope of a transaction. When a new object is created, its object context inherits the transaction from the context of the client. If the client does not have a transaction, MTS automatically creates a new transaction for the object.
UsesTransaction	3	This value indicates that the component's objects can execute within the scope of their client's transactions. When a new object is created, its object context inherits the transaction from the context of the client. If the client does not have a transaction, the new context is also created without one.
RequiresNewTransaction	4	This value indicates that the component's objects must execute within their own transactions. When a new object is created, MTS automatically creates a new transaction for the object, regardless of whether its client has a transaction.

Note Object context refers to the state that is associated with a particular object. This context includes server information, the creator's identity, and so forth.

You don't have to worry about any of the other class properties for now. Just save and compile your library, and then copy it to your server for registration. You can register the library by running the regsvr32 program, just as you did in preceding chapters.

To test the component in a non-transactional environment, you can create the following ASP page that will instantiate your component and execute the single function of the class:

```
<%
    Dim objTest      ' As BasicComponent.MessageObject
    Set objTest = _
       Server.CreateObject("BasicComponent.MessageObject")
    Response.Write objTest.Message
    Set objTest = Nothing
%>
```

When you run this page, you should get the message that we created in the component. This test proves that the component is running properly on the server.

The next step is to add this component to an MTS package and execute the function within a transaction. To do this, you'll need to have access to your NT server as an administrator (or someone else with rights to access the MTS console).

Follow these steps to create the package for this component:

1. In the Windows Option Pack program group on your Start menu, start the Transaction Server Explorer.

2. Use the tree on the left side of the TS Explorer to navigate down to the **Packages Installed** folder beneath your computer. When you click this folder, you will probably see a number of icons already there in the folder. These packages are installed when you install the samples included with the Option Pack.

3. Right-click the Packages Installed node on the left tree and select New ⇨ Package to create a new package.

4. In the first dialog that appears, you can select whether you want to install a prebuilt package or create an empty one. We'll be creating a new one, so select the latter option.

5. The next dialog prompts you for a name for this package. The name is for information only — you'll be instantiating components based on the component names, not the package name.

6. The final dialog asks you for the user ID under which this package will be running. There is not a single answer for this dialog. Instead, this answer depends on how your server is configured. If you have your own standalone server for testing, you could configure the package with administrator rights. Alternatively, you could create a separate user ID with almost no rights other

than the few needed for the package (this is the best approach, by the way). Either way, pick a user ID and provide the password for the user ID.

Tip   Remember to change the password here if you change the password for the user at any point in the future.

At this point, your package will be added to the right side of the TS Explorer. You can now add your DLL to the package by following these steps:

1. Open the tree on the left so that it shows the package you just created.

2. Open the package's folder so that you see the Components folder beneath the package in the tree. Right-click the folder and select New ⇨ Component.

3. In the first dialog, you can select whether you want to install new components or use components that are already registered. Because we've already registered our BasicComponent, select the latter option.

4. You'll be provided a list of all the components registered on your server. Scroll down the list to find the component (or components, if you have more than one) that you want to add to the package. Click the Finish button, and the component will be added to the window on the right.

The last step is to change the property of the component in the TS Explorer to indicate that it uses transactions. Right-click the component on the right side of the window and select Properties from the popup menu. On the second tab, labeled Transactions, check the box next to **Supports Transactions**.

With the package created and the component added, you can now modify your ASP page to use the MTS component. To make your ASP page use MTS, you have to add a single line at the top of the page:

```
<%@ TRANSACTION = Supported %>
```

When you load your page again, it may take a bit longer than before to get the result back. This delay occurs because your component has to be loaded via MTS. Once the component is loaded, however, the object stays in memory and subsequent calls are significantly faster. To make sure your component is actually running in MTS, you can use the TS Explorer to navigate to the Transaction Statistics section under your computer. As you run the component by reloading the page, you can see the statistics change. The important one to watch, in this case, is the average time for each transaction. As you run the component, it takes far less time after the first use, so the average will drop pretty rapidly. As long as you see the counters going up, you can be sure that you're using MTS.

Building an Ad Tracking System

To help you see how MTS components can be built that take advantage of many other MTS features, we're going to build a series of components that can be used to manage Web-based advertising. Before we get started, here are a few terms you need to know:

✦ Banner — a graphical advertisement that comes in a variety of shapes and sizes. Most banners are 468 pixels wide and 60 pixels high. We'll be using this standard size for the application.

✦ Impression — each time an ad is shown to a user, it is called an impression. Impressions are often priced by the thousand using a term called CPM (cost per thousand, not million). A typical ad price might be $20 CPM, which works out to two cents per impression.

✦ Clickthrough — advertisers want to know how many users clicked their ads. Each click is called a clickthrough, because you are clicking through to the destination Web site. The higher percentage of clickthroughs, the better the ad is working.

Our ad tracking system will perform the following functions:

✦ Provide the HTML to show an ad.

✦ Record the impression along with the context information, such as the page URL, the user information available through the `ServerVariables` collection, and so forth.

✦ Record a clickthrough when it occurs.

You also need to include other functions, such as reporting, but you can add those to the system as you see fit.

Design Tips for MTS

In contrast to building objects in VB, you can't rely on state being maintained in MTS. This primary difference translates to one key technique: you can't use object properties to store data. Instead, MTS objects can be thought of as providing services to the caller. One of our objects will record a clickthrough. This action is handled easily and meets the ACID test. On the contrary, an object into which you stored property values doesn't meet the ACID test because when you store one property, the value is not permanently stored anywhere and the transaction is not complete.

In this object, each method will take care of a particular action. While the ASP code will call a single function, there's no reason why you can't call multiple functions within your VB class module. You just need to make sure that the interface (the external subroutines and functions) is consistent and easy to use.

Building the Database

The database required for this mini-application has two tables. The definitions are shown in Tables 18-2 and 18-3, and the data types shown are for SQL Server 7.0. If you're not using SQL 7.0, make the appropriate adjustments for your database.

Table 18-2
tblAds Definitions

Field Name	Data Type	Default Values
AdID	int (four bytes)	identity—seed 1, initial value 1
Description	char (255)	
URL	char (255)	
Height	int (four bytes)	
Width	int (four bytes)	
Alternate Text	char (255)	
ImageURL	char (255)	

Table 18-3
tblImpressions Definitions

Field Name	Data Type	Default Values
ImpressionID	int (four bytes)	identity—seed 1, initial value 1
AdID	int (four bytes)	
ShownTime	datetime	(getdate())
PageURL	char (255)	
RemoteHost	char (80)	
BrowserType	char (160)	
IsClickthrough	bit	(0)

For testing purposes, borrow some ads from sites such as Amazon.com where banner ads are made available for free. You're not going to be using them in public, so it doesn't matter where you get them. Enter in the appropriate information about each ad in the tblAds table, and make sure you have at least three or four ads in the table before proceeding. You don't need to add any initial data to the tblImpressions table.

Creating the AdMgr Class

Next, we'll complete the `AdMgr` class module. In this section, you'll create the `Impression` method, which records the fact that an ad was shown to a user. In order to build this class, you'll need to copy a DLL from your NT Server to your development machine. The file name is `mtxas.dll`, and you can find it using NT Explorer's Find feature—the location will vary based on your system configuration. Register this DLL on your development machine, and you'll see **Microsoft Transaction Server Type Library** available in your References dialog box. Add this library to your project, as well as the ADO 2.1 library (or higher), and you're ready to go.

The declarations of the class come first, as follows:

```
Option Explicit
Implements ObjectControl

Private m_dcnDB As ADODB.Connection
Private m_objContext As ObjectContext
```

`ObjectControl` is an object referenced by the MTS Type Library, as is the `ObjectContext` object. These objects enable you to pass information to the MTS engine to indicate if the transaction completed successfully or unsuccessfully.

The next code you need goes into the `Initialize` event of the class:

```
Private Sub Class_Initialize()
   Set m_dcnDB = New ADODB.Connection
   m_dcnDB.ConnectionString = _
      "Provider=SQLOLEDB.1;uid=myuser;pwd=mypasswd;" _
      & "Persist Security Info=False;Initial Catalog=AdMgr;" _
      & "Data Source=ENTERPRISE"

End Sub
```

You should notice that we're not opening the connection here; rather, we're simply setting up the connection for later. This code will vary based on the database and options you're using. In this case, the server is named ENTERPRISE, the database is named AdMgr, and we're using SQL Server 7.0. You can modify this code for your own database configuration.

The next code is the Impression function. This function has several key features that were mentioned previously, but you'll see how they are implemented in the following code:

```
Public Function Impression(strURL As String, _
    strRemoteHost As String, _
    strUserAgent As String) As String

    Dim strSQL As String
    Dim strResult As String

    Dim rsData As ADODB.Recordset
    Dim rsImpression As ADODB.Recordset

    Dim lngAdPosition As Long

    m_dcnDB.Open
    Set m_objContext = GetObjectContext
    Randomize

    strSQL = "SELECT * FROM tblAds"
    Set rsData = New ADODB.Recordset

    rsData.Open strSQL, m_dcnDB, adOpenStatic, adLockReadOnly

    lngAdPosition = Int(Rnd() * rsData.RecordCount)
    rsData.MoveFirst
    rsData.Move lngAdPosition

    m_dcnDB.Execute "INSERT INTO tblImpressions " _
        & "(AdID, PageURL, RemoteHost, BrowserType) VALUES (" _
        & rsData("AdID") & ", '" _
        & strURL & "', '" _
        & strRemoteHost & "', '" _
        & strUserAgent & "')"
    Set rsImpression = m_dcnDB.Execute( _
        "SELECT Max(ImpressionID) FROM tblImpressions")

    strResult = "<a href=""#REPLACE#?impID=" & rsImpression(0) _
        & "&url=" & Trim(rsData("URL")) _
        & """><img src=""" & Trim(rsData("ImageURL")) _
        & """ height=" & rsData("Height") & " width=" _
        & rsData("Width") _
        & " alt=""" & Trim(rsData("AlternateText")) & """></a>"

    Impression = strResult
    rsImpression.Close
    rsData.Close
    m_objContext.SetComplete
    m_dcnDB.Close

End Function
```

After opening the database connection, we retrieve the object's context. This task will provide a link to MTS so that when the action is complete, we can signal MTS that we're done with the object.

We then retrieve all the ads from the database and put them into a recordset. Based on the size of your ad system, you may want to filter this down by section of the site, page, or other factors. Using the number of ads, we randomly pick an ad to show.

Note

The Randomize keyword causes us to have a more random result than if we hadn't used the keyword. Without the Randomize keyword, the system uses a predetermined list of random numbers and the results are the same each time you run the code.

We then record the impression in the Impressions table. We've gotten information about the current URL, the user's domain/address, and the browser type. You can retrieve other information as well; however, these are just examples.

Immediately after inserting the record, we retrieve the largest ImpressionID value for later use. Because we're within the scope of a single transaction, this should retrieve the last record that was created. If you're in an extremely busy system, you should use additional criteria to verify that you have the correct impression ID.

We then build the HTML that is going to the calling code. We do a few important things here:

1. We don't provide the URL for the page to use to handle a click. This has to be supplied by the calling code.

2. We do supply the impression ID and the destination URL. This saves a lookup later when the user does click the ad.

3. We provide a complete anchor (A tag) and the associated image tag (IMG tag) to the caller.

Because there are some limitations to this method, we'll cover some other options shortly. After that code runs, the remaining code is all clean-up code.

Before you can run this object within the MTS environment, you have to add a bit more code to the class. After setting the MTSTransactionMode to **2 — RequiresTransaction**, you'll also need to add code to handle the ObjectControl object you're implementing in your class:

```
Private Sub ObjectControl_Activate()

End Sub

Private Function ObjectControl_CanBePooled() As Boolean
    ObjectControl_CanBePooled = True
```

```
End Function

Private Sub ObjectControl_Deactivate()

End Sub
```

These methods are required for the object to work within the MTS environment. Even though two of the methods are blank, they have to be provided or you'll get an error.

Testing the Impression Code

At this point, you can compile your library and register it on your server. The ASP code you can use to test follows:

```
<%@ TRANSACTION=Required %>
<html>
<head>
<body>

<%
Dim objBanner     ' As AdMgr.BannerAd
set objBanner = Server.CreateObject("AdMgr.BannerAd")
strBanner =
    objBanner.Impression(Request.ServerVariables("URL"), _
    Request.ServerVariables("REMOTE_HOST"), _
    Request.ServerVariables("HTTP_USER_AGENT"))
strBanner = Replace(strBanner, "#REPLACE#", "ad_click.asp")
Response.Write strBanner
set objBanner = nothing
%>
</body>
</html>
```

The first important thing to note is the first line of the file. This directive indicates to the ASP engine that MTS needs to be involved with this page. After that, the code is basically the same as calling any other ActiveX DLL. You will notice that we replace the #REPLACE# placeholder with the file named ad_click.asp, which will handle the clickthrough when it occurs.

Assuming everything is hooked up properly, you'll see MTS register a transaction when you run this page. One of your ads will appear, complete with a URL to handle a clickthrough. That code is coming up next. Check your database to make sure the record was inserted successfully.

Adding the Clickthrough Code

Clicking a banner ad will run a URL similar to the following:

```
http://server.com/admgr/ad_click.asp?impID=34&url=http://www.
foo.com
```

The important items are the impression ID and the destination URL. We'll use the impression ID to update the impression record to indicate that the user clicked the ad. The destination URL will be used in a redirect to send the user to the destination site. The code for this is another public method for your AdMgr class:

```
Public Sub Clickthrough(lngImpressionID As Long)
    m_dcnDB.Open
    Set m_objContext = GetObjectContext
    m_dcnDB.Execute ( _
        "UPDATE tblImpressions " _
        & "SET IsClickThrough = 1 " _
        & "WHERE ImpressionID = " & lngImpressionID)
    m_objContext.SetComplete
    m_dcnDB.Close

End Sub
```

Nothing fancy here, but doing the code in this way saves us the effort of having a second table in the system. You can also do extra statistical analysis because you can group, count, and do grouping math on all the impressions and clickthroughs — not just one at a time.

The code that goes in the destination ASP page is as follows:

```
<%@ TRANSACTION = Required %>
<%
Dim objBanner ' As AdMgr.BannerAd
set objBanner = Server.CreateObject("AdMgr.BannerAd")
objBanner.Clickthrough Request("impID")
Response.Redirect Request("url")

%>
```

The redirection will happen fast enough that the user probably won't even see what has happened. Most of the major sites that do banner advertising have a system that performs similar actions when a click occurs. The URL for the image isn't the destination site — it's an intermediary page that allows the site to record the hit before letting you leave.

Enhancements You Can Make

Our example is a pretty rudimentary system, but there are a few enhancements that you can make immediately. For starters, the object could return the components of the HTML that it's currently generating. Instead of returning an entire image and link tag, it would return the fields from the tblAds table, as well as the impression ID for later use. The best way to do this is with a disconnected recordset and a return parameter value. Here's the revised code for the Impression method:

```
Public Function ImpressionRS(strURL As String, _
    strRemoteHost As String, _
    strUserAgent As String, _
    lngImpressionID As Long) As Variant

    Dim strSQL As String
    Dim strResult As String

    Dim rsData As ADODB.Recordset
    Dim rsImpression As ADODB.Recordset

    Dim lngAdPosition As Long

    m_dcnDB.Open
    Set m_objContext = GetObjectContext
    Randomize

    strSQL = "SELECT * FROM tblAds"
    Set rsData = New ADODB.Recordset
    rsData.CursorLocation = adUseClient
    rsData.Open strSQL, m_dcnDB, adOpenStatic, adLockReadOnly

    lngAdPosition = Int(Rnd() * rsData.RecordCount)
    rsData.MoveFirst
    rsData.Move lngAdPosition

    m_dcnDB.Execute "INSERT INTO tblImpressions " _
        & "(AdID, PageURL, RemoteHost, BrowserType) VALUES (" _
        & rsData("AdID") & ", '" _
        & strURL & "', '" _
        & strRemoteHost & "', '" _
        & strUserAgent & "')"
    Set rsImpression = m_dcnDB.Execute( _
        "SELECT Max(ImpressionID) FROM tblImpressions")
    lngImpressionID = rsImpression(0)
    rsImpression.Close

    Set rsData.ActiveConnection = Nothing
    Set ImpressionRS = rsData

    m_objContext.SetComplete
    m_dcnDB.Close

End Function
```

As you learned in the ADO chapter, the recordset (rsData in this case) has to have its CursorLocation property set to adUseClient before setting the ActiveConnection property to Nothing. The impression ID is returned in a parameter, and the return type of the function is a Variant to prevent any problems when the object returns to VBScript/ASP.

The difference at the ASP level is that the calling code has to create the ad's HTML. This is a simple task using the HTML we already created — it just has to be moved to a different location.

Summary

This chapter provided a good introduction to the basics of getting an MTS package up and running in conjunction with IIS and ASP. A number of other books cover MTS in more detail — you can read reviews of several at the ASP Techniques Web site.

✦   ✦   ✦

Building a Real-World Application

T he final chapter in the book is a start-to-finish application design and development session. The concepts introduced here are not difficult, but the chapter is designed to show you how to go from idea to finished application, all in one dose.

Creating a Discussion Forum

✦ ✦ ✦ ✦

In This Chapter

Design an object
model for a
discussion forum
application

Creating the data-
base for storing
forum data

Create the COM
components used to
retrieve and modify
forum data

Design the ASP
pages that use the
COM components

Understand how to
expand and adapt
the application for
your own use

✦ ✦ ✦ ✦

Designing a Discussion Forum

To show you how to build a full ASP application, this chapter
creates a discussion forum. Discussion forums are used
throughout the Internet on different sites to help provide a
sense of community for visitors to the site. Commercial
products provide this type of application for you; however,
you'll see that the model for the application isn't hard to
understand. The only limit is how many features you want
to add to the application. For starters, the application will
support the following features:

- ✦ Member information management and member logon

- ✦ An unlimited number of discussion groups

- ✦ An unlimited number of messages in each group

- ✦ The ability to thread messages; that is, link replies to
  a message to the original message

- ✦ Member profiles, complete with e-mail addresses and
  personal information provided by the user

- ✦ Members can subscribe and unsubscribe from groups

- ✦ The system remembers the last message read by a
  member in each group in their subscription list

The Object Model

When you get down to it, there are only four objects in
this system:

- ✦ A Member, a person who posts messages and provides
  personal information for others to see

✦ A Group, which contains Messages on a particular topic

✦ A Message, which can either be an original message or a reply to another Message

✦ A Subscription, which is a Group that a Member chooses to read

For simplicity, when a user replies to a message, it is considered a reply to the original message, even if the user is replying to a reply. This design decision keeps the model and display simple, and is in use on several popular community sites I visit regularly. There's no reason you can't adapt the system to allow replies to replies — it's simply a matter of how you display the data.

Besides these objects, we will be adding two additional objects to the system:

✦ A service object that provides lists of all types of data. Because we'll only deal with a single object at once, we don't have to build collection classes. We just need an object to generate the lists of data that we need.

✦ A service object to access the server's Registry. Information about the forum database will be stored in the Registry instead of being hard-coded in the page.

System Functions

Based on these objects, the following functions will be needed for this system:

Add and modify users

Add, modify, and delete groups

Add, modify, and delete messages

Display and modify a user's subscriptions

Display a list of all groups

Search for groups matching given keywords

Display the messages in a group

Display the replies to a message

Display a user's profile

Each of these functions will use at least one of the objects and will be contained on at least one ASP page. As you've learned in preceding chapters, it's easier to keep all the code for group modifications, for instance, in the same ASP page. This arrangement keeps all the code together and makes it easier to maintain.

With the basic design complete, the next step is to design the objects and the underlying database.

Designing the Forum Database

The next step in building the application is to create the database. As mentioned previously, there are four major entities: Group, Message, Member, and Subscription. Here are the relationships between these entities:

✦ A Message is part of a Group

✦ A Message can be related to a previous Message

✦ A Member creates the Message

✦ A Member has zero, one, or many Subscriptions to Groups

Each of these entities will map to a table in this system. The table names and the field definitions are listed in Tables 19-1 through 19-4. The data types listed here are for Access; however, it is easy enough to translate these into your favorite data-base, such as SQL Server or Oracle.

Table 19-1
tblGroups — Group Entity

Field Name	Data Type	Description
GroupID	AutoNumber	Unique ID for this Group
GroupName	Text – 80	Name of the group
Description	Text – 255	Description of the content for this group

Table 19-2
tblMembers — Member Entity

Field Name	Data Type	Description
MemberID	AutoNumber	Unique ID for this Member
UserName	Text – 20	Login name for this Member
Password	Text – 20	Password for this Member
FirstName	Text – 80	User's first name
LastName	Text – 80	User's last name
EMailAddress	Text – 255	User's e-mail address
ShowEMail	Yes/No	Indicates whether user's e-mail will be shown

Continued

Table 19-2 *(continued)*

Field Name	Data Type	Description
Age	Number – Long	User's age (optional)
Location	Text – 80	User's location (optional)
Interests	Text – 255	Personal information about the Member (optional)
HomePage	Text – 255	User's personal home page (optional)
ShowProfile	Yes/No	Indicates whether profile is made public

Table 19-3
tblMessages — Message Entity

Field Name	Data Type	Description
MessageID	AutoNumber	Unique ID for this message
GroupID	Number – Long	Links message to a Group
MemberID	Number – Long	Links message to its author
Subject	Text – 80	Subject for message
MessageDate	Date/Time	Date/time of message
MessageText	Text – 255	Text of message
IsReply	Yes/No	Indicates whether message is a reply to another message
ReplyToID	Number – Long	Links to another message that was the original message

Table 19-4
tblSubscriptions — Subscription Entity

Field Name	Data Type	Description
MemberID	Number – Long	Links subscription to Member
GroupID	Number – Long	Links subscription to Group
LastMessageID	Number – Long	Stores the last message read by the Member in the Group

Building the Object Library

With the tables out of the way, you can now build your classes to wrap these tables. We'll be using some of the same technology created in preceding chapters to build these objects. This section covers a few additions that provide extra features, but omits the massive blocks of property statements.

Creating the Group Object

The Group object represents a particular topic covered by the forum. Besides Let and Get properties for the fields in the table, you should also have an Init and Save method, both of which are shown in Listing 19-1.

Listing 19-1: **Init and Save Methods for Group Object**

```
Public Sub Init(dcnDB As Variant, Optional lngID As Long = -1)

    Set m_dcnDB = dcnDB
    m_blnIsNew = (lngID = -1)

    If Not m_blnIsNew Then
        Set m_rsData = m_dcnDB.Execute("SELECT * FROM tblGroups "
_
            & "WHERE GroupID = " & lngID)
        FillObject Me, m_rsData
        m_rsData.Close
    End If

End Sub

Public Sub Save()
    '
    ' This method puts the object's data back into
    ' the database. This method could use the INSERT
    ' statement or a stored procedure, if desired.
    '
    Dim objField As ADODB.Field

    Set m_rsData = New ADODB.Recordset
    If m_blnIsNew Then
        m_rsData.Open "SELECT * FROM tblGroups", _
            m_dcnDB, _
            adOpenDynamic, _
            adLockOptimistic
```

Continued

Listing 19-1 *(continued)*

```
        m_rsData.AddNew
    Else
        m_rsData.Open "SELECT * FROM tblGroups " _
            & "WHERE GroupID = " & m_lngGroupID, _
            m_dcnDB, _
            adOpenDynamic, _
            adLockPessimistic
    End If

    SaveObject Me, m_rsData

    m_rsData.Update
    '
    ' Calling FillObject here allows the
    ' unique ID to be picked up in case of
    ' an addition
    '
    FillObject Me, m_rsData
    m_rsData.Close

End Sub
```

The FillObject and SaveObject have been placed in a separate BAS file so that they can be shared more easily across all the classes in this library. The code for these two functions is shown in Listing 19-2.

Listing 19-2: **FillObject and SaveObject Functions**

```
Public Sub SaveObject(objInput As Object, rsInput As
ADODB.Recordset)
    Dim objField As ADODB.Field
    Dim varResult As Variant

    For Each objField In rsInput.Fields
        If objField.Attributes And adFldUpdatable Then
            varResult = CallByName(objInput, objField.Name, VbGet)
            If TypeName(varResult) <> "String" Then
                rsInput(objField.Name) = varResult
            ElseIf varResult <> "" Then
                rsInput(objField.Name) = varResult
            Else
                rsInput(objField.Name) = ""
            End If
```

```
        End If
    Next objField

End Sub

Public Sub FillObject(objInput As Object, _
    rsInput As ADODB.Recordset)

    Dim objField As ADODB.Field
    For Each objField In rsInput.Fields
        If Not IsNull(rsInput(objField.Name)) Then
            CallByName objInput, objField.Name, _
                VbLet, rsInput(objField.Name)
        End If
    Next objField

End Sub
```

These functions are designed to make it easier to load up an object with data from a database table. The premise is that for each field in the database table, there is a corresponding property. Using the CallByName function, we use the name of the field to call the corresponding property. The FillObject function is a loop that completes that function, but the SaveObject has to check for non-updatable fields, such as counters. Other than that, it's the same code in reverse.

Building the Member Object

The Member object represents a user of the forum system. It contains personal information about the user, such as profile information that can be shared or hidden from other users. The non-property code for this object is shown in Listing 19-3.

Listing 19-3: **Member Object subroutines**

```
Public Sub Init(dcnDB As Variant, _
    Optional lngID As Long = -1, _
    Optional strUserName As String = "")

    Dim strSQL As String

    Set m_dcnDB = dcnDB
```

Continued

Listing 19-3 *(continued)*

```vb
    m_blnIsNew = (lngID = -1) And (strUserName = "")

    If Not m_blnIsNew Then
        strSQL = "SELECT * FROM tblMembers "
        If lngID <> -1 Then
            strSQL = strSQL & "WHERE MemberID = " & lngID
        ElseIf strSQL <> "" Then
            strSQL = strSQL & "WHERE UserName = '" _
                & strUserName & "'"
        End If
        Set m_rsData = m_dcnDB.Execute(strSQL)
        If m_rsData.EOF Then
            Err.Raise vbObjectError + 1, "Member.Init", _
                "User ID '" & strUserName & "' does not exist."
            Exit Sub
        End If
        FillObject Me, m_rsData
        m_rsData.Close
    End If

End Sub

Public Sub Save()
    '
    ' This method puts the object's data back into
    ' the database. This method could use the INSERT
    ' statement or a stored procedure, if desired.
    '
    Dim objField As ADODB.Field

    If Not Valid() Then
        Err.Raise vbObjectError + 1, "Member.Save", _
            "Required fields were missing."
        Exit Sub
    End If

    Set m_rsData = New ADODB.Recordset
    If m_blnIsNew Then
        m_rsData.Open "SELECT * FROM tblMembers", _
            m_dcnDB, _
            adOpenDynamic, _
            adLockOptimistic
        m_rsData.AddNew
    Else
        m_rsData.Open "SELECT * FROM tblMembers " _
            & "WHERE MemberID = " & m_lngMemberID, _
            m_dcnDB, _
            adOpenDynamic, _
            adLockPessimistic
    End If
```

```
        SaveObject Me, m_rsData

        m_rsData.Update
        '
        ' Calling FillObject here allows the
        ' unique ID to be picked up in case of
        ' an addition
        '
        FillObject Me, m_rsData
        m_rsData.Close

End Sub

Private Function Valid() As Boolean

    Valid = True _
        And (m_strUserName <> "") _
        And (m_strFirstName <> "") _
        And (m_strLastName <> "") _
        And (m_strPassword <> "")

End Function
```

This object includes some basic error checking for a data save operation. It checks to make sure all of the required fields have been provided, and generates an error if the required fields have not been provided. The ASP code that you'll see shortly traps the error and handles it. The basic functions of this object are similar to the Group object in how the FillObject and SaveObject functions are used.

Creating the Message Object

The Message object has several foreign keys to other tables. To represent these keys, we will provide objects on request. The ReplyTo, Member, and Group properties will provide Message, Member, and Group objects to the caller. The code is shown in Listing 19-4.

Listing 19-4: Object properties for Message Object

```
Public Property Get ReplyTo() As Message

    If RefreshObject(m_objMember, m_lngReplyToID, "ReplyToID")
Then
        Set m_objReplyTo = New Message
        m_objReplyTo.Init m_dcnDB, m_lngReplyToID
    End If
```

Continued

Listing 19-4 *(continued)*

```
    Set ReplyTo = m_objReplyTo

End Property

Public Property Get Member() As Member

    If RefreshObject(m_objMember, m_lngMemberID, "MemberID")
Then
        Set m_objMember = New Member
        m_objMember.Init m_dcnDB, m_lngMemberID
    End If
    Set Member = m_objMember

End Property

Public Property Get Group() As Group

    If RefreshObject(m_objGroup, m_lngGroupID, "GroupID") Then
        Set m_objGroup = New Group
        m_objGroup.Init m_dcnDB, m_lngGroupID
    End If
    Set Group = m_objGroup

End Property
```

The RefreshObject method here enables us to do some basic caching of information. This function is also included in the code module that is part of the ForumObjects library, and is shown in Listing 19-5.

Listing 19-5: **RefreshObject Function**

```
Public Function RefreshObject(objInput As Object, _
    lngID As Long, strProperty As String) As Boolean

    Dim blnTest As Boolean
    blnTest = objInput Is Nothing
    If Not blnTest Then
        blnTest = blnTest Or _
            (CallByName(objInput, strProperty, VbGet) <> lngID)
    End If
    RefreshObject = blnTest

End Function
```

This object verifies that the primary key of the object hasn't changed from the object that was last instantiated and stored in the internal object variable. If the primary key changed, the object properties will re-create the object in question. This sequence saves some resources by reusing objects that are still up-to-date.

The other code in the Message object is shown in Listing 19-6 and takes care of the Init and Save methods.

Listing 19-6: **Message object code**

```
Public Sub Init(dcnDB As Variant, Optional lngID As Long = -1)

    Set m_dcnDB = dcnDB
    m_blnIsNew = (lngID = -1)

    If Not m_blnIsNew Then
        Set m_rsData = m_dcnDB.Execute("SELECT * FROM tblMessages " _
            & "WHERE MessageID = " & lngID)
        FillObject Me, m_rsData
        m_rsData.Close
    End If

End Sub

Public Sub Save()
    '
    ' This method puts the object's data back into
    ' the database. This method could use the INSERT
    ' statement or a stored procedure, if desired.
    '
    Dim objField As ADODB.Field

    Set m_rsData = New ADODB.Recordset
    If m_blnIsNew Then
        m_rsData.Open "SELECT * FROM tblMessages", _
            m_dcnDB, _
            adOpenDynamic, _
            adLockOptimistic
        m_rsData.AddNew
    Else
        m_rsData.Open "SELECT * FROM tblMessages " _
            & "WHERE MessageID = " & m_lngMessageID, _
            m_dcnDB, _
            adOpenDynamic, _
            adLockPessimistic
```

Continued

Listing 19-6 *(continued)*

```
    End If

    SaveObject Me, m_rsData

    m_rsData.Update
    '
    ' Calling FillObject here allows the
    ' unique ID to be picked up in case of
    ' an addition
    '
    FillObject Me, m_rsData
    m_rsData.Close

End Sub

Private Sub Class_Terminate()

    Set m_objGroup = Nothing
    Set m_objMember = Nothing
    Set m_objReplyTo = Nothing

End Sub
```

The Terminate event of the Class object also takes care of clearing out the cached objects that are part of the Message object. If no object has been instantiated, no harm is done by setting it to Nothing again.

Creating the Subscription Class

A Subscription is unique in this application in that it does not have an automatically generated ID assigned to it. Instead, the primary key is created by the combination of a member ID and a group ID. We also store the last message that was read in a particular group. The interesting code for this class is shown in Listing 19-7 and mimics the code you've seen already, with a few exceptions.

Listing 19-7: Subscription class code

```
Public Property Get Member() As Member

    If RefreshObject(m_objMember, m_lngMemberID, "MemberID")
Then
```

```
        Set m_objMember = New Member
        m_objMember.Init m_dcnDB, m_lngMemberID
    End If
    Set Member = m_objMember

End Property

Public Property Get LastMessage() As Message

    If RefreshObject(m_objLastMessage, m_lngLastMessageID, _
"LastMessageID") Then
        Set m_objLastMessage = New Message
        m_objLastMessage.Init m_dcnDB, m_lngLastMessageID
    End If
    Set LastMessage = m_objLastMessage

End Property

Public Property Get Group() As Group

    If RefreshObject(m_objGroup, m_lngGroupID, "GroupID") Then
        Set m_objGroup = New Group
        m_objGroup.Init m_dcnDB, m_lngGroupID
    End If
    Set Group = m_objGroup

End Property

Public Sub Init(dcnDB As Variant, _
    Optional lngMemberID As Long = -1, _
    Optional lngGroupID As Long = -1)

    Set m_dcnDB = dcnDB
    m_blnIsNew = (lngMemberID = -1)

    If Not m_blnIsNew Then
        Set m_rsData = m_dcnDB.Execute("SELECT * FROM
tblSubscriptions " _
            & "WHERE MemberID = " & lngMemberID _
            & " AND GroupID = " & lngGroupID)
        Fill
        m_rsData.Close
    End If

End Sub

Private Sub Fill()

    Dim objField As ADODB.Field
```

Continued

Listing 19-7 *(continued)*

```
        For Each objField In m_rsData.Fields
            If Not IsNull(m_rsData(objField.Name)) Then
                CallByName Me, objField.Name, VbLet, _
                    m_rsData(objField.Name)
            End If
        Next objField

End Sub

Public Sub Save()
    '
    ' This type of record will always be deleted
    ' before needing to be resaved, since it is
    ' in a cross-table.
    '
    Dim objField As ADODB.Field
    Set m_rsData = New ADODB.Recordset
    If m_blnIsNew Then
        m_rsData.Open "SELECT * FROM tblSubscriptions", _
            m_dcnDB, _
            adOpenDynamic, _
            adLockOptimistic
        m_rsData.AddNew
    Else
        m_rsData.Open "SELECT * FROM tblSubscriptions " _
            & "WHERE MemberID = " & m_lngMemberID _
            & " AND GroupID = " & m_lngGroupID, _
            m_dcnDB, _
            adOpenDynamic, _
            adLockPessimistic
    End If

    For Each objField In m_rsData.Fields
        m_rsData(objField.Name) = CallByName(Me, _
            objField.Name, VbGet)
    Next objField

    m_rsData.Update
    m_rsData.Close

End Sub

Private Sub Class_Terminate()
    Set m_objGroup = Nothing
    Set m_objLastMessage = Nothing
    Set m_objMember = Nothing
End Sub
```

In this code, the queries have to be a bit more complex to handle the differences in how the primary key is built. In addition, the Init method has to accept two arguments to create a unique subscription record or to open an existing one. We also have the same type of object-caching code you've already seen.

Generating the Library

For this example, the ActiveX DLL is named ForumObjects, and each class is included in this library. Compile the library and install it on your Web server. If you don't have VB loaded on your Web server already, you'll have to create an installation package using the Packaging and Deployment Wizard. This tool is installed with VB and takes the place of the old Setup Wizard. This tool will create a setup package for you to run on your server to use your library.

Once you start working with your library, you will probably need to recompile the library. If you've already used it within an ASP page, you'll have to stop the IIS Admin Service and close any windows that might be referencing your Web site before you can recompile the library. It's a pain to do it this way, but the alternative is rebooting, which isn't pleasant either. Once the IIS Admin service and other related services have shut down, you can recompile the library and then restart the IIS Admin service and your Web site.

Building the ASP Code

With the objects built, you can start writing the ASP code to make your application work. The basic sequence for this application is as follows:

1. Log into the system. If you don't have an account already, you can create one and then log in.

2. View the group subscriptions that you already have.

3. Pick a group to view and view the messages in the group.

4. Pick a message to read and either return to the list or reply to the message. You can view the author's profile by clicking their name.

5. You can also post a new message to any group.

6. You can also edit your profile information or change the subscriptions you have.

To make the system work, we'll have a total of eight ASP pages:

✦ `default.asp` — handles the login functions.

✦ `profile.asp` — handles creating and editing user profiles.

✦ memberinfo.asp—shows a profile selected from a message being read.

✦ groups.asp—shows all the groups to which a user has subscribed.

✦ showgroup.asp—shows the messages in a particular group.

✦ showmessage.asp—shows a particular message and provides links to any replies to the first message.

✦ message.asp—enables users to either post a new message or reply to an existing message.

✦ util.asp—shared code used in all the pages.

With these pages in mind, let's write some code.

Creating the Login Page

Let's start with the login page, default.asp. We use this name so that it loads by default when the application is loaded. The code for this page is shown in Listing 19-8 and incorporates some of the techniques you've already learned.

Listing 19-8: **Code for default.asp**

```
<!--#include file="util.asp" -->
<%
'..............................................
'
' Default.asp
'
' This page serves as the login page for the
' system. Existing users can provide a user ID
' and password, and new users can create a
' profile on a second page before logging in.
'
'..............................................

'..............................................
'
' Sub Main
'
' All processing in the page starts here.
'
'..............................................
Sub Main()

    Dim strAction    ' As String
    strAction = Request("action")
    If strAction = ACTION_VALIDATE Then
```

```
        Validate
    Else
        Display ""
    End If

End Sub

'..........................................
'
' Sub Display
'
' This subroutine displays the login form and any
' errors that might have occurred during a previous
' login attempt.
'
'..........................................
Sub Display(strError)
%>
<HTML>
<HEAD>
    <TITLE>Forum Manager - Welcome!</TITLE>
</HEAD>
<BODY BGCOLOR=#FFFFFF>
<H1>Forum Manager</H1>
<%
    If strError <> "" Then
%>
<font color=#FF0000><b><% = strError %></b></font>
<%
    End If
%>
<form action="<% = CreateValidateURL() %>" method="post">
<TABLE>
<TR>
    <TD ALIGN=right>User ID:</TD>
    <TD><input type="text"
               name="txtUserName"
               size="20"
               maxlength="20"></TD>
</TR>

<TR>
    <TD ALIGN=right>Password:</TD>
    <TD><input type="password"
               name="txtPassword"
               size="20"
               maxlength="20"></TD>
</TR>
<TR>
```

Continued

Listing 19-8 *(continued)*

```
    <TD ALIGN=center COLSPAN=2>
    <input type="submit" name="cmdOK" value="Login">
    <input type="Reset" name="cmdCancel" value="Clear">
    </TD>
</TR>
</TABLE>
</form>

<p><a href="profile.asp">Click here</a> to create
a new member profile.</p>
</BODY>
</HTML>
<%
End Sub

'..............................................
'
' Sub Validate
'
' This routine determines if the user name
' exists in the database and if so, creates a
' cookie to indicate that the user has logged
' in. The cookie is temporary and will disappear
' when the browser shuts down. If the user is not
' valid, the browser goes to the profile page
' so the user can create a new member profile.
'
'..............................................
Sub Validate()
    Dim dcnDB        ' As ADODB.Connection
    Dim objMember    ' As ForumObjects.Member

    On Error Resume Next

    Set dcnDB = OpenDB()
    Set objMember = Server.CreateObject("ForumObjects.Member")

    objMember.Init dcnDB, , Request("txtUserName")
    If Err.Number <> 0 Then
        Set objMember = Nothing
        CloseDB dcnDB
        Display Err.Description
    ElseIf objMember.Password <> Request("txtPassword") Then
        Set objMember = Nothing
        CloseDB dcnDB
        Display "Password is incorrect."
    Else
        Response.Cookies("MemberID") = objMember.MemberID
        Response.Cookies("MemberID").Expires = _
            DateAdd("m", 30, Date)
        Set objMember = Nothing
```

```
        Response.Redirect "groups.asp"
    End If

End Sub

''''''''''''''''''''''''''''''''''''''''''''''''''''''
'
' Call Sub Main to start page processing
'
''''''''''''''''''''''''''''''''''''''''''''''''''''''
Call Main
%>
```

To keep things easy to read, we use the "Sub Main" method of coding for this and all the other pages. By default, the page will be loaded with no arguments, so we make the assumption that the user is entering data for the first time. This is considered non-validation mode. After the user clicks the Login button, the page will be reloaded in validation mode, and the code in Sub Main will route the application through the Validate routine instead of the Display routine. The Display routine shows a simple HTML form, along with a link to the profile.asp page.

The interesting code is in the Validate routine. We first attempt to instantiate a Member object using the user name as an ID. If we aren't able to instantiate the object, the user doesn't exist and an appropriate error message is raised by the object. We then have to check the password against the one that was passed in the form by the user. Assuming that's correct, we create a cookie indicating that the user has logged in. This cookie will be used throughout the system to verify that the user came in the correct way initially. The cookie is good for 30 days and subsequent calls to pages within the system will work without having to re-login. A cookie is also more reliable than using a Session object or adding more information to the query string, so our example uses this method. You can use your own methods for passing data, but the simpler, the better.

We have a few common pieces of code that have been added to the util.asp page, shown in Listing 19-9.

Listing 19-9: **Common code in util.asp**

```
<%
Option Explicit
%>
<!--#include file="adovbs.inc" -->
<%
''''''''''''''''''''''''''''''''''''''''''''''''''''''
'
```

Continued

Listing 19-9 *(continued)*

```
' Application Constants
'
'...........................................
Const ACTION_VALIDATE = "v"
Const MODE_ADD = "a"
Const MODE_MODIFY = "m"
Const MODE_POST = "p"
Const MODE_REPLY = "r"


'...........................................
'
' Function OpenDB
'
' This function opens the database and returns a valid
' ADO Connection object.
'
'...........................................
Function OpenDB()

    Dim dcnDB ' As ADODB.Connection
    Set dcnDB = Server.CreateObject("ADODB.Connection")
    dcnDB.ConnectionString = _
        "Provider=Microsoft.Jet.OLEDB.3.51;" _
        & "Data Source=F:\Projects\ASP Bible\Files\Forums.mdb;"
    dcnDB.Open

    Set OpenDB = dcnDB

End Function
'...........................................
'
' Sub CloseDB
'
' This routine closes the open connection.
'
'...........................................
Sub CloseDB(dcnDB)

    dcnDB.Close

End Sub
'...........................................
'
' Function CreateValidateURL
'
' This routine creates the URL that will cause
```

```
' a page to reload in validation mode.
'
''''''''''''''''''''''''''''''''''''''''''''''''''
Function CreateValidateURL()

    Dim strTemp      ' As String
    strTemp = Request.ServerVariables("SCRIPT_NAME") _
        & "?action=" & ACTION_VALIDATE
    CreateValidateURL = LCase(strTemp)

End Function

''''''''''''''''''''''''''''''''''''''''''''''''''
'
' Sub CheckForLogin
'
' This routine verifies that the user has
' logged into the system by checking the
' cookie named "MemberID".
'
''''''''''''''''''''''''''''''''''''''''''''''''''
Sub CheckForLogin()
    If Request.Cookies("MemberID") = "" Then
        Response.Redirect "default.asp"
    End If
End Sub
%>
```

After setting Option Explicit and including the ADO constants, we have some user-defined constants that are used in query strings to indicate state. It's more reliable to put this type of information in constants so that you don't have problems comparing the values later. We also have the normal routines for opening and closing the database (which, by the way, you need to change to point to your local copy of the database). We have another routine that takes a page's name and appends the "action=v" parameters. This builds a validation URL for the page so that the page doesn't have to know its name. The server variable used here will hold that information. The final routine checks to make sure the user has logged in; if not, the page sends them to the main login page.

At this point, we have two places we can go. The first is the profile.asp page, which enables a new user to create a member profile and then log into the system. The second path is for users who have registered and logged in successfully. They are taken to the groups.asp page.

Creating the User Profile Editor

One of the lengthier pages is the User Profile editor. Much of the code is HTML, but quite a bit of logic is included, as you can see in Listing 19-10.

Listing 19-10: Code for profile.asp

```
<!--#include file="util.asp" -->
<%
'''''''''''''''''''''''''''''''''''''''''''''''''''''
'
' Profile.asp
'
' Members of the forum can have personal profiles,
' which are edited through this page. New users
' can create profiles here, and existing members
' can edit their profiles here.
'
'''''''''''''''''''''''''''''''''''''''''''''''''''''

'''''''''''''''''''''''''''''''''''''''''''''''''''''
'
' Sub Main
'
' All processing in the page starts here.
'
'''''''''''''''''''''''''''''''''''''''''''''''''''''
Sub Main()

    Dim strAction     ' As String
    Dim strMode       ' As String
    strMode = Request("mode")
    If strMode = "" Then
        strMode = MODE_ADD
    Else
        CheckForLogin
    End If

    strAction = Request("action")
    If strAction = ACTION_VALIDATE Then
        Validate strMode
    Else
        Display strMode, ""
    End If

End Sub

'''''''''''''''''''''''''''''''''''''''''''''''''''''
```

```
'
' Sub Display
'
' This subroutine displays the profile form and any
' errors that might have occurred during a previous
' save attempt.
'
'.............................................
Sub Display(strMode, strError)
    Dim strModeName        ' As String
    Dim dcnDB        ' As ADODB.Connection
    Dim objMember   ' As ForumObjects.Member
    Dim blnIsEdit       ' As Boolean

    On Error Resume Next

    Set dcnDB = OpenDB()
    Set objMember = Server.CreateObject("ForumObjects.Member")
    If strMode = MODE_ADD Then
        strModeName = "Add New"
        blnIsEdit = False
    Else
        strModeName = "Edit"
        objMember.Init dcnDB, Request("MemberID")
        blnIsEdit = True
    End If


%>
<HTML>
<HEAD>
    <TITLE>Forum Manager -
    <% = strModeName %> Member Profile</TITLE>
</HEAD>
<BODY BGCOLOR=#FFFFFF>
<H1><% = strModeName %> Member Profile</H1>
<P>Required fields are shown in red.</P>
<%
    If strError <> "" Then
%>
<font color=#FF0000><b><% = "ERROR: " & strError %></b></font>
<%
    End If
%>
<form action="<% = CreateValidateURL() %>&mode=<% = strMode %>"
        method="post">
<TABLE CELLPADDING=5 CELLSPACING=5>
<TR>
    <TD ALIGN=right><font color=#FF0000>User ID:</font></TD>
```

Continued

Listing 19-10 *(continued)*

```
    <TD>
<%
   If blnIsEdit Then
       Response.Write objMember.UserName
   Else
%>
       <input type="text"
               name="txtUserName"
               size="20"
               maxlength="20">
<%
   End If
%>
    </TD>
</TR>

<TR>
    <TD ALIGN=right><font color=#FF0000>Password:</font></TD>
    <TD><input type="password" name="txtPassword"
               value="<% = objMember.Password %>"
               size="20" maxlength="20"></TD>
</TR>

<TR>
    <TD ALIGN=right><font color=#FF0000>First Name:</font></TD>
    <TD><input type="text" name="txtFirstName"
               value="<% = objMember.FirstName %>"
               size="20" maxlength="80"></TD>
</TR>

<TR>
    <TD ALIGN=right><font color=#FF0000>Last Name:</font></TD>
    <TD><input type="text" name="txtLastName"
               value="<% = objMember.LastName %>"
               size="20" maxlength="80"></TD>
</TR>

<TR>
    <TD ALIGN=right>E-Mail Address:</TD>
    <TD><input type="text" name="txtEMailAddress"
               value="<% = objMember.EMailAddress %>"
               size="50" maxlength="80"></TD>
</TR>

<TR>
    <TD ALIGN=right>Show E-Mail Address?</TD>
    <TD><input type="checkbox"
               name="chkShowEMail"
```

```
                value="-1"
                <% If objMember.ShowEMail Then
                      Response.Write "CHECKED"
                    End If%>
    </TD>
</TR>

<TR>
    <TD ALIGN=right>Age:</TD>
    <TD><input type="text" name="txtAge"
                value="<% = objMember.Age %>"
                size="5" maxlength="3"></TD>
</TR>
<TR>
    <TD ALIGN=right>Location:</TD>
    <TD><input type="text" name="txtLocation"
                value="<% = objMember.Location %>"
                size="40" maxlength="80"></TD>
</TR>
<TR>
    <TD ALIGN=right>Interests:</TD>
    <TD>
       <textarea
          cols=40
          rows=4
          name="txtInterests"><% = objMember.Interests
%></textarea>
    </TD>
</TR>
<TR>
    <TD ALIGN=right>Home Page URL:</TD>
    <TD><input type="text" name="txtHomePage"
                value="<% = objMember.HomePage %>"
                size="40" maxlength="80"></TD>
</TR>
<TR>
    <TD ALIGN=right>Show Profile?</TD>
    <TD><input type="checkbox"
                name="chkShowProfile"
                value="-1"
                <% If objMember.ShowProfile Then
                      Response.Write "CHECKED"
                    End If
                %>
    </TD>
</TR>

<TR>
    <TD ALIGN=center COLSPAN=2>
```

Continued

Listing 19-10 *(continued)*

```
      <input type="submit" name="cmdOK" value="Save">
      <input type="Reset" name="cmdCancel" value="Reset">
      </TD>
</TR>
</TABLE>
</FORM>
</BODY>
</HTML>
<%
   Set objMember = Nothing
   CloseDB dcnDB
End Sub

'''''''''''''''''''''''''''''''''''''''''''''''''''''
'
' Sub Validate
'
' This routine either adds a new profile or
' updates an existing one. This routine also
' checks to see if a particular user ID already
' exists by instantiating a Member object with
' the selected user ID. Unless an error occurs,
' the user ID is taken. The Member object takes
' care of any other validation errors that might
' occur.
'
'''''''''''''''''''''''''''''''''''''''''''''''''''''
Sub Validate(strMode)
   Dim dcnDB        ' As ADODB.Connection
   Dim objMember    ' As ForumObjects.Member
   Dim strError     ' As String

   On Error Resume Next

   Set dcnDB = OpenDB()
   Set objMember = Server.CreateObject("ForumObjects.Member")

   If strMode = MODE_ADD Then
      objMember.Init dcnDB, , Request("txtUserName")
      If Err.number = 0 Then
         strError = "The selected user name already exists."
         Set objMember = Nothing
         Display strMode, strError
         Exit Sub
      Else
         Err.Clear
         objMember.Init dcnDB
      End If
```

```
      Else
          objMember.Init dcnDB, Request("MemberID")
      End If

      With objMember
          If strMode = MODE_ADD Then
              .UserName = Request("txtUserName")
          End If
          .Password = Request("txtPassword")
          .FirstName = Request("txtFirstName")
          .LastName = Request("txtLastName")
          .EMailAddress = Request("txtEMailAddress")
          .ShowEMail = (Request("chkShowEMail") = "-1")
          .Age = Request("txtAge")
          .Location = Request("txtLocation")
          .Interests = Request("txtInterests")
          .HomePage = Request("txtHomePage")
          .ShowProfile = (Request("chkShowProfile") = "-1")
          .Save
      End With
      If Err.Number <> 0 Then
          Set objMember = Nothing
          CloseDB dcnDB
          Display strMode, Err.Description
      Else
          If strMode = MODE_ADD Then
              Response.Redirect "default.asp"
          Else
              Response.Redirect "groups.asp"
          End If
      End If

  End Sub

  ''''''''''''''''''''''''''''''''''''''''''''''''
  '
  ' Call Sub Main to start page processing
  '
  ''''''''''''''''''''''''''''''''''''''''''''''''
  Call Main
  %>
```

Because we have four possible states, this page's Sub Main is a bit more complicated. The first two states take care of a new user, and the second two states take
care of an existing user. The main difference is that an existing user is not allowed
to edit his/her user ID. Everything else can be edited, but changing user IDs gets
pretty tricky to keep things straight. (You can modify this code to allow user IDs to
be changed.)

For adding a new user, we show the HTML form next, which has space for all the fields in the database. There are several if/then conditions to build the form, and this routine will take care of showing any errors that occur during the save process, as well.

When the user clicks the Save button, the Validate routine runs when the page reloads. This routine instantiates a Member object and, based on the current state, populates the object appropriately. All of the form's fields are put into the object, and then the Save method takes care of saving the data. The code here is basically the same for an Edit; however, the object is instantiated with the member ID so that the data can be edited.

When the save is successful, new users are sent back to the login page to finish logging in. However, existing users are sent to the page listing their current subscriptions, which is the subject of the following section.

Creating the Group Listing Page

The groups.asp page is fairly straightforward. The page is only used in one mode: viewing. The page lists all of the groups to which a user is subscribed, and provides information about the last message the user read in each group. While the code is simple and won't be listed here, the query to build it (qryGetSubscriptions) is somewhat messy. Figure 19-1 shows the query in Access, and Listing 19-11 shows its SQL code.

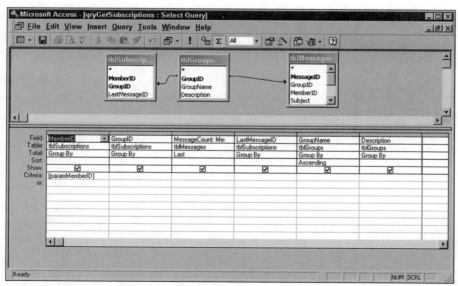

Figure 19-1: Design for qryGetSubscriptions

Listing 19-11: **SQL for qryGetSubscriptions**

```
SELECT tblSubscriptions.MemberID, tblSubscriptions.GroupID,
Last(tblMessages.MessageID) AS MessageCount,
tblSubscriptions.LastMessageID, tblGroups.GroupName,
tblGroups.Description
FROM (tblSubscriptions RIGHT JOIN tblGroups ON
tblSubscriptions.GroupID = tblGroups.GroupID) LEFT JOIN
tblMessages ON tblGroups.GroupID = tblMessages.GroupID
GROUP BY tblSubscriptions.MemberID, tblSubscriptions.GroupID,
tblSubscriptions.LastMessageID, tblGroups.GroupName,
tblGroups.Description
HAVING (((tblSubscriptions.MemberID)=[paramMemberID]))
ORDER BY tblGroups.GroupName;
```

The idea is that we join the subscriptions that a member has with the Groups table, and at the same time retrieve the biggest message ID from each table. The only catch is that if the table doesn't have any messages in it yet, you get a null back, which must be trapped in your loop code. Take a look at the file to see how this is done — it's not that tough.

The group-listing page provides links to edit a user's profile and edit a user's subscriptions, as well as links to each group. The group is shown using the showgroup.asp page.

Creating the Group Viewer

The next page, which is similar in structure to the preceding page, shows all the messages in a particular group. Like the preceding page, we use a query to retrieve the messages in a particular group. That query is done directly in the ASP page. Although the query could be done within an object, you would then have to get the data back from the object to the ASP page. You can do this in a few ways:

✦ Let the object create HTML to pass back into the page.

✦ Let the object return a recordset for the ASP page through which to loop.

✦ Do it all directly in the ASP page, as we've done.

The code for this page is quite similar to the preceding page, and is omitted here for space considerations. However, the query is shown in Figure 19-2 and listed in Listing 19-12.

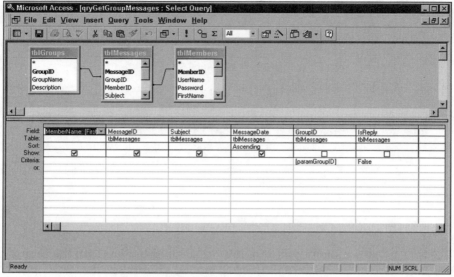

Figure 19-2: Design for qryGetGroupMessages

Listing 19-12: **SQL for qryGetGroupMessages**

```
SELECT [FirstName] & " " & [LastName] AS MemberName,
tblMessages.MessageID, tblMessages.Subject,
tblMessages.MessageDate
FROM (tblMessages INNER JOIN tblMembers ON tblMessages.MemberID
= tblMembers.MemberID) INNER JOIN tblGroups ON
tblMessages.GroupID = tblGroups.GroupID
WHERE (((tblMessages.GroupID)=[paramGroupID]) AND
((tblMessages.IsReply)=False))
ORDER BY tblMessages.MessageDate;
```

This query is easier to deal with because there are no outer joins — just inner joins to retrieve information like the author's name.

Once the user clicks a link on this page, a message will be displayed in the showmessage.asp page.

Creating the Message Viewing Page

The message-viewing page is a bit different than the preceding two pages because it has two purposes: show the selected message, and provide a list of links to the replies to the message. The code for this page is shown in Listing 19-13.

Listing 19-13: Code for showmessage.asp

```asp
<!--#include file="util.asp" -->
<%
'''''''''''''''''''''''''''''''''''''''''''''''''''''''''''
'
' ShowMessage.asp
'
' This screen shows a message and any replies
' to it on the screen.
'
'''''''''''''''''''''''''''''''''''''''''''''''''''''''''''


'''''''''''''''''''''''''''''''''''''''''''''''''''''''''''
'
' Sub Main
'
' All processing in the page starts here.
'
'''''''''''''''''''''''''''''''''''''''''''''''''''''''''''
Sub Main()

    CheckForLogin
    Display

End Sub


'''''''''''''''''''''''''''''''''''''''''''''''''''''''''''
'
' Sub Display
'
' This subroutine displays the message and provides
' links to any replies that were posted.
'
'''''''''''''''''''''''''''''''''''''''''''''''''''''''''''
Sub Display()
    Dim dcnDB       ' As ADODB.Connection
    Dim cmdQuery    ' As ADODB.Command
    Dim parID       ' As ADODB.Parameter
    Dim rsData      ' As ADODB.Recordset
```

Continued

Listing 19-13 *(continued)*

```
    Dim objMsg        ' As ForumObjects.Message
    Dim objSub        ' As ForumObjects.Subscription

    'On Error Resume Next

    Set dcnDB = OpenDB()
    Set objMsg = Server.CreateObject("ForumObjects.Message")
    objMsg.Init dcnDB, Request("MsgID")

    Set cmdQuery = Server.CreateObject("ADODB.Command")
    cmdQuery.ActiveConnection = dcnDB
    cmdQuery.CommandText = "qryGetReplies"
    set parID = server.CreateObject("ADODB.Parameter")
    Set parID = cmdQuery.CreateParameter("paramMsgID")
    parID.Type = adInteger
    parID.Direction = adParamInput
    parID.Value = Request("MsgID")
    cmdQuery.Parameters.Append parID

    Set rsData = cmdQuery.Execute
    Set objSub = _
        Server.CreateObject("ForumObjects.Subscription")
    objSub.Init dcnDB, Request("MemberID"), objMsg.GroupID
    objSub.LastMessageID = objMsg.MessageID
    objSub.Save
    Set objSub = Nothing
%>
<HTML>
<HEAD>
    <TITLE>Forum Manager - <% = objMsg.Group.GroupName %> Forum:
    Message #<% = objMsg.MessageID %></TITLE>
</HEAD>
<BODY BGCOLOR=#FFFFFF>
<H2>Message <% = objMsg.MessageID %>: <% = objMsg.Subject
%></H2>
<I>Written by
<%
    Response.Write "<a href=""memberinfo.asp?authorid=" _
        & objMsg.MemberID & """>" _
        & objMsg.Member.FirstName & " " & objMsg.Member.LastName
_
        & "</a> on " _
        & FormatDateTime(objMsg.MessageDate, vbLongDate)
%>
</I>
<hr noshade>
<blockquote>
```

```
<% = objMsg.MessageText %>
</blockquote>

<hr noshade>
Replies to this message:
<TABLE CELLPADDING=2 CELLSPACING=2 WIDTH=640>
<TR>
    <TH>Date</TH>
    <TH>Subject</TH>
    <TH>Author</TH>
</TR>
<%
    Do While Not rsData.EOF
%>
<TR>
    <TD ALIGN=center><% = rsData("MessageDate") %></TD>
    <TD>
    <%
        Response.Write "<a href=""showmessage.asp?msgid=" _
            & rsData("MessageID") & """>" _
            & rsData("Subject") & "</a>"
    %>
    </TD>
    <TD ALIGN=center><% = rsData("MemberName") %></TD>
</TR>
<%
        rsData.MoveNext
    Loop
    Response.Write "</TABLE>"
%>
<hr noshade>
[
<a href="showgroup.asp?groupID=<% = objMsg.GroupID %>">Show
Group</a> -
<a href="message.asp?groupID=<% = objMsg.GroupID %>">Post
Message</a>
<%
    If Not objMsg.IsReply Then
%>
-
<a href="message.asp?msgID=<% = objMsg.MessageID %>">Reply</a>
<%
    End If
%>
]
</BODY>
</HTML>
<%
    Set objMsg = Nothing
```

Continued

Listing 19-13 *(continued)*

```
    rsData.Close
    CloseDB dcnDB
End Sub

''''''''''''''''''''''''''''''''''''''''''''''''''''
'
' Call Sub Main to start page processing
'
''''''''''''''''''''''''''''''''''''''''''''''''''''
Call Main
%>
```

This code does several things when a message is shown. First, it retrieves the information by instantiating a Message object using the message ID that was passed in as a parameter to the page. It also uses the Member ID from the login cookie to update the user's subscription record for this group, which simply tells the subscription table that this message has been read. Finally, the message is shown along with a list of links to the replies to the message. Remember, we don't allow replies to replies for simplicity. You either reply to a thread, or you start a new thread. This arrangement makes it easier to navigate.

While you're viewing a message, you can click the author's name to see their profile information using the memberinfo.asp page. The simple code for this page is mostly HTML. The page does have a handy "Return" button, which provides a link back to the referring page. The code uses the HTTP_REFERER server variable to craft a URL around the form button on the window.

From this page, you have two choices for further action: post a new message to the group, or reply to the current message. Both of these functions are handled by the message.asp page.

Creating the Message Editor Page

Because replying to and posting a message are essentially the same action, we are using a single page for both functions. We simply maintain state information so that we can link the message to either the group or the group and the original message. The code for the page is shown in Listing 19-14.

Listing 19-14: **Code for message.asp**

```
<!--#include file="util.asp" -->
<%
''''''''''''''''''''''''''''''''''''''''''''''''''
'
' Message.asp
'
' This screen handles replies and new posts to
' groups.
'
''''''''''''''''''''''''''''''''''''''''''''''''''

''''''''''''''''''''''''''''''''''''''''''''''''''
'
' Sub Main
'
' All processing in the page starts here.
'
''''''''''''''''''''''''''''''''''''''''''''''''''
Sub Main()

    Dim strMode         ' As String
    Dim strAction       ' As String

    If Request("mode") = "" Then
        If Request("GroupID") <> "" Then
            strMode = MODE_POST
        Else
            strMode = MODE_REPLY
        End If
    Else
        strMode = Request("mode")
    End If
    strAction = Request("action")
    If strAction = ACTION_VALIDATE Then
        Validate strMode
    Else
        Display strMode, ""
    End If

End Sub

''''''''''''''''''''''''''''''''''''''''''''''''''
'
' Sub Display
'
' This subroutine displays the message form and
```

Continued

Listing 19-14 *(continued)*

```
' allows the user to enter a reply. Any errors
' are displayed at the top of the page.
'
''''''''''''''''''''''''''''''''''''''''''''''''
Sub Display(strMode, strError)
    Dim strModeName        ' As String
    Dim dcnDB        ' As ADODB.Connection
    Dim objMsg        ' As ForumObjects.Message
    Dim objGroup        ' As ForumObjects.Group
    Dim lngGroupID ' As Long
    Dim lngMsgID        ' As Long

    On Error Resume Next

    Set dcnDB = OpenDB()
    If strMode = MODE_POST Then
        strModeName = "Post New"
        Set objGroup = Server.CreateObject("ForumObjects.Group")
        objGroup.Init dcnDB, Request("GroupID")
        lngGroupID = objGroup.GroupID
        lngMsgID = 0
    Else
        strModeName = "Post Reply To"
        Set objMsg = Server.CreateObject("ForumObjects.Message")
        objMsg.Init dcnDB, Request("MsgID")
        lngGroupID = objMsg.GroupID
        lngMsgID = objMsg.MessageID

    End If
%>
<HTML>
<HEAD>
    <TITLE>Forum Manager -
    <% = strModeName %> Message</TITLE>
</HEAD>
<BODY BGCOLOR=#FFFFFF>
<H2><% = strModeName %> Message</H2>
<%
    If strError <> "" Then
%>
<font color=#FF0000><b><% = "ERROR: " & strError %></b></font>
<%
    End If
%>
<form action="<% = CreateValidateURL() %>&mode=<% = strMode %>"
        method="post">
<input type="hidden" name="GroupID" value="<% = lngGroupID %>">
<input type="hidden" name="MsgID" value="<% = lngMsgID %>">
```

```
<%
   If strMode = MODE_REPLY Then
      Response.Write "<hr noshade><blockquote>" _
         & objMsg.MessageText _
         & "</blockquote>"
   End If
%>
<hr noshade>
<table cellpadding=2 cellspacing=2 width=640>
<%
   If strMode = MODE_POST Then
%>
<TR>
   <TD ALIGN=right>Subject:</TD>
   <TD><input type="text" name="txtSubject"
            size="40" maxlength="80"></TD>
</TR>
<%
   Else
%>
<input type="hidden"
      name="txtSubject"
      value="<% = "Re: " & objMsg.Subject %>">
<%
   End If
%>
<tr>
   <td align=right>Message:</td>
   <td>
      <textarea name="txtMessageText"
               cols=60 rows=6></textarea>
   </td>
</tr>
<TR>
   <TD ALIGN=center COLSPAN=2>
   <input type="submit" name="cmdOK" value="Save">
   <input type="Reset" name="cmdCancel" value="Reset">
   </TD>
</TR>
</TABLE>
</FORM>
</BODY>
</HTML>
<%
   Set objMsg = Nothing
   Set objGroup = nothing
   CloseDB dcnDB
End Sub

''''''''''''''''''''''''''''''''''''''''''''''''''''
'
```

Continued

Listing 19-14 *(continued)*

```
' Sub Validate
'
' This routine saves the message to the database
' and handles any errors that might be shown by
' the object.
'
''''''''''''''''''''''''''''''''''''''''''''''''
Sub Validate(strMode)
    Dim dcnDB       ' As ADODB.Connection
    Dim objMsg  ' As ForumObjects.Message
    Dim objOldMsg ' As ForumObjects.Message
    Dim strError   ' As String
    Dim lngMsgID   ' As Long

    On Error Resume Next

    Set dcnDB = OpenDB()
    Set objMsg = Server.CreateObject("ForumObjects.Message")
    Set objOldMsg = Server.CreateObject("ForumObjects.Message")
    objMsg.Init dcnDB

    If strMode = MODE_REPLY Then
        objOldMsg.Init dcnDB, Request("MsgID")
    End If

    With objMsg
        If Request("GroupID") = "" Then
            .GroupID = objOldMsg.GroupID
        Else
            .GroupID = Request("GroupID")
        End If
        .MemberID = Request("MemberID")
        .Subject = Request("txtSubject")
        .MessageDate = Date & " " & Time
        .MessageText = Request("txtMessageText")
        .IsReply = (strMode = MODE_REPLY)
        If strMode = MODE_REPLY Then
            .ReplyToID = objOldMsg.MessageID
        Else
            .ReplyToID = 0
        End If
        .Save
    End With
    Set objOldMsg = Nothing
    If Err.Number <> 0 Then
        Set objMember = Nothing
        CloseDB dcnDB
        Display strMode, Err.Description
    Else
```

```
        If strMode = MODE_REPLY Then
            Response.Redirect "showmessage.asp?msgid=" _
                & Request("MsgID")
        Else
            Response.Redirect "showgroup.asp?groupid=" _
                & Request("GroupID")
        End If
    End If

End Sub

'''''''''''''''''''''''''''''''''''''''''''''''
'
' Call Sub Main to start page processing
'
'''''''''''''''''''''''''''''''''''''''''''''''
Call Main
%>
```

This routine uses the MODE_REPLY and MODE_POST constants we created previously. After loading the parameters from the preceding page, we create either a Group or Message object so that we can provide the correct information for storing the message. Both replies and posts need group information, and the group ID is not provided to us by the preceding page. We display a form, which hides the subject line if the message is a reply. By default, the subject will be whatever the existing subject was, prepended by a "Re:". This arrangement keeps messages standard and easy to find for users.

Validation is a little tricky, because we have to get all the linking values into the objects. We have to set the correct flag in the message object to indicate that it is a reply, and we also have to set the ReplyToID value so that the message is linked to the original message. Once we're all done, we either go back to the message page (for a reply) or the group page (for a post).

Summary

This framework leaves a lot of flexibility for you to use and modify. For instance, you may want to have a way to browse all the messages in a group in addition to our tree-like structure. You may want to move all the database code within the objects instead of having a little bit of the list generating code outside of the objects. However, the main point of this chapter was to put all of the techniques from the preceding chapters together into a useful application that can be easily installed and used on your Web server.

✦   ✦   ✦

Setting Up your Development Environment

Installing Personal Web Server

Personal Web Server (PWS) is designed for individual use on a single PC. While it can be used at the workgroup or LAN level, it does not have the performance or security features that are necessary for a corporate Web site open to the outside world. This section will take you through each step of the installation procedure and help you verify that your Web server is up and running on your PC.

In order to install this software, you will have to either download it from Microsoft's Web site or get it from the Windows NT Option Pack CD-ROM, which is available through the Microsoft Developer's Network. It is a free add-on, but you may have to wait a while to download the large files. Once you have the files, start the installation program called SETUP.EXE. From there, follow these steps:

1. Figure A-1 shows the first screen that will appear. The installation is started through a Web browser. Read all of the information on this screen and click the other links on the left, if you wish. When you are ready to proceed, click the Install link.

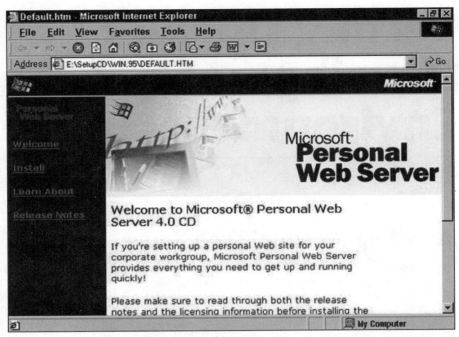

Figure A-1: The installation begins at this screen

2. The next step in the installation process is to make sure you have at least Internet Explorer 4.01 installed, because it is used by Personal Web Server for all administration tasks. Remember that when you install IE, you don't have to install the Active Desktop update, if you don't want it. Many people forget and then have trouble getting rid of the desktop update once it is installed. Figure A-2 shows the second screen in the process. If you need to install IE 4.01, click the appropriate link. Otherwise, read the license agreement and then click Install Personal Web Server to continue.

3. Once you click the link to install PWS, you should see the dialog box shown in Figure A-3. The appearance of this box is normal, because the Web browser thinks you are downloading an application from the Web. Instead, the application is being run either from CD or your hard drive, go ahead and click the Run option and then click the OK button to continue.

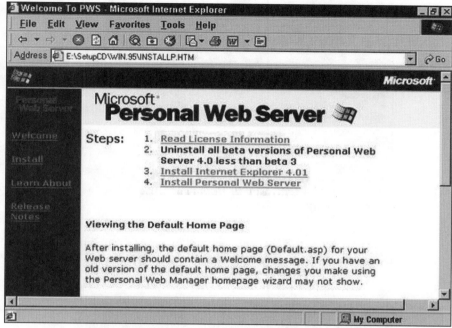

Figure A-2: Internet Explorer 4.01 is required for installation of PWS

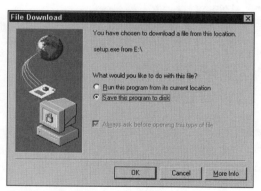

Figure A-3: You're not downloading, but IE thinks you are.

4. The next screen, shown in Figure A-4, is a warning from IE because you chose to open the file that you already have. You can go ahead and click the Yes button to continue past this screen.

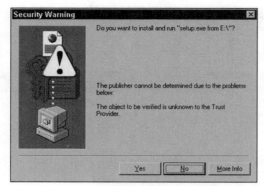

Figure A-4: A security warning from IE because you are opening a file directly

5. Now you are at the opening installation screen (shown in Figure A-5). Enjoy the lovely graphics and then click Next to continue.

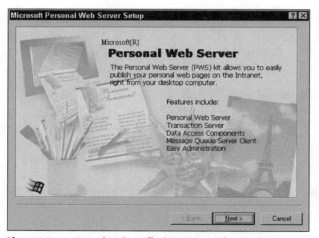

Figure A-5: Opening installation screen for PWS

6. Figure A-6 shows the license agreement to which you must agree before installation can continue. Click the Accept button to continue.

7. The next step in the process is to choose the installation type from the dialog shown in Figure A-7. For most options, always choose "Custom" so that you see exactly what is being installed on your machine.

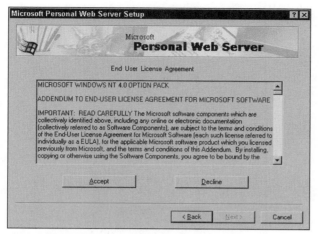

Figure A-6: License Agreement screen

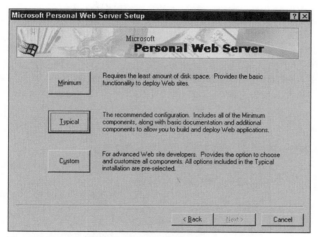

Figure A-7: Installation type dialog

8. Figure A-8 shows the component selection dialog. From here, you can select all of the installed or uninstalled components on your machine. The default configuration, which is sufficient for your needs for now, should have the following items selected:

   a. Common Program Files

   b. FrontPage 98 Server Extensions

   c. Microsoft Data Access Components 1.5

   d. Personal Web Server (PWS)

   e. Transaction Server

Click the Next button to continue installation.

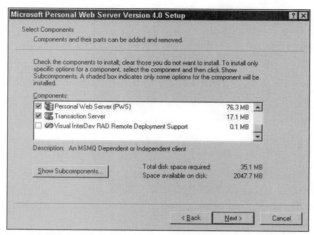

Figure A-8: Select the components to install from this dialog

9. The next step is to specify a home directory for your Web sites in the dialog shown in Figure A-9. For best results, use the provided defaults. Other applications erroneously assume that everyone keeps their Web sites in C:\INetPub, so if you deviate from that directory, these applications may have problems.

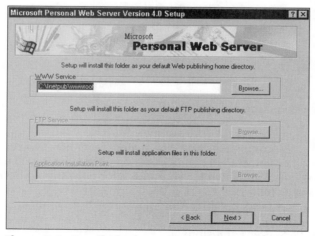

Figure A-9: Specify the home directory for your Web site here

10. Microsoft Transaction Server is next to be installed. MTS helps manage the operations of your Web site, especially when it comes to operations on databases and Web services. Define the application directory (shown in Figure A-10) with the default value or your own location. Click Next to continue.

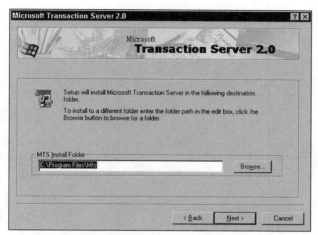

Figure A-10: Specify MTS's home directory on your machine.

11. With these steps completed, you can sit back and watch the progress meter (shown in Figure A-11) as PWS is installed on your machine. When it concludes, you can click the Finish button to continue.

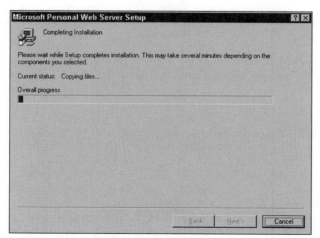

Figure A-11: Installation is proceeding normally.

12. With all good Microsoft software, an installation wouldn't be complete without at least one reboot. Let Windows reboot to finish the installation.

When your machine returns, you can check your system tray to see the icon indicating that PWS is running correctly. The icon is shown in Figure A-12, and if you float over it, the Web server's status will display for you.

Figure A-12: PWS displays an icon in the system tray when it is running.

If you double-click the icon, you will get the PWS Administration screen, shown in Figure A-13.

The easiest way to test your Web server is to request a page from it. Click the link that points to your Web server. You should be greeted with the page shown in Figure A-14.

If you really want to test the Web server and are on a LAN, have someone else connect to your machine using the same link. They should get the same page. If so, your installation is successful! If they cannot see the page and you didn't get any errors, make sure that the other person can see your machine using Windows Explorer's Network Neighborhood. If that doesn't work, contact your network administrator for more help.

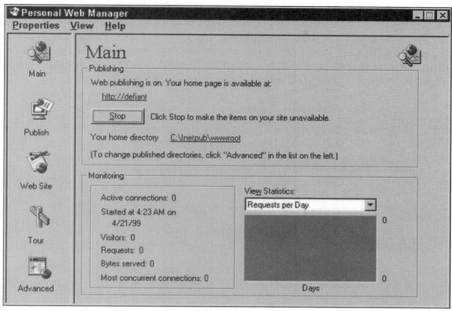

Figure A-13: PWS Administration Screen

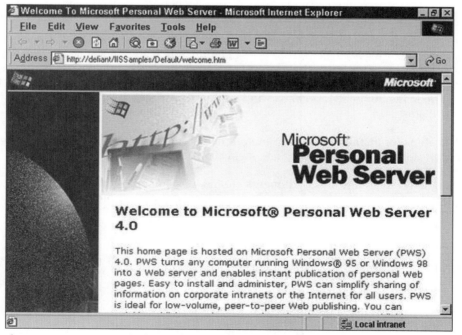

Figure A-14: Home Page for PWS (installed automatically)

To explore the features of PWS further, click the Tour icon to go through all the other features of the tool. To create your own home page for your site, click the Web Site icon and the Microsoft Agent will help you get the job done quickly. Finally, the Advanced icon will let you configure the directories used by the Web server. PWS uses shared directories to grant access to different parts of your Web server. For ASP files to work properly, you must do the following:

✦ Create a share in the Advanced tab.

✦ Edit its properties to grant Read and Script access to the directory.

After these tasks are completed, you can use ASP files in that directory.

Installing Personal Web Server for NT Workstation

Installation of PWS on NT Workstation is nearly identical to installing PWS on Windows 95/98 — they are based on the same technology. However, there are a few key differences:

✦ You must be the administrator of your machine in order to install PWS on Windows NT.

✦ IIS includes some other components not found in PWS.

To get started, use the NT Option Disk and start the setup program (if it doesn't start automatically). Like the 95/98 installation, you have to have IE 4.01 or higher installed on your machine before the installation can proceed. In addition, if you have NT 4.0 Service Pack 4 installed, you will get a warning indicating that PWS has not been tested on SP4. Go ahead and continue past that warning into the installation.

The steps for installation of PWS match the preceding section up to Step 7, so we'll pick it up there with the dialog shown in Figure A-15.

By default, the following components should be selected for the IIS installation. A few extra components are now available, so make sure they are all checked:

✦ FrontPage 98 Server Extensions

✦ Microsoft Data Access Components 1.5

✦ Microsoft Management Console

✦ Microsoft Script Debugger

✦ NT Option Pack Common Files

✦ Personal Web Server (PWS)

✦ Transaction Server

✦ Windows Scripting Host

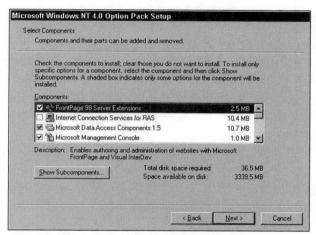

Figure A-15: Components available for IIS

When you click Next, you'll be prompted for directories for your Web documents and an installation directory for MTS. You'll also be asked about setting up a remote administrator account, as shown in Figure A-16. Because you're testing for now, you can leave this option on Local and click Next to continue. You can always reconfigure later if you need remote administration capabilities.

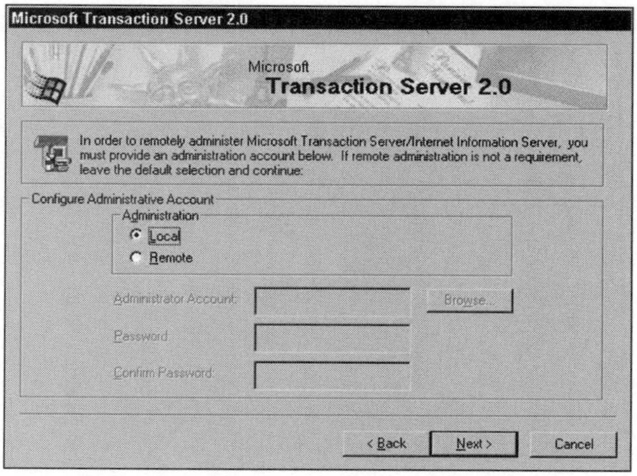

Figure A-16: IIS allows for remote administration of the server.

At this point, using the PWS is the same as the instructions given for 95/98 in the preceding section. If you can hit the test site, you're set to start working!

Summary

This appendix was designed to get you up and running with Personal Web Server. While we didn't cover all the features, you should have gotten your Web server up and running. Use the built-in wizards to help configure and build your own site — you'll be using it throughout the book to test your work.

✦   ✦   ✦

HTML Reference

<!-- -->

These tags are marked as comments in HTML. Any text displayed between these two comment tags will not be displayed in the user's browser window. However, script will still be processed even if it is nested in a comment.

Example

```
This is text that will be shown.
<BR>
The following text will NOT be shown.<BR><BR>
<!-- This is a comment which will be ignore by
the browser -->
Comments cause a browser to ignore anything
between the start and end tag.<BR>
```

Tag Parameters

None

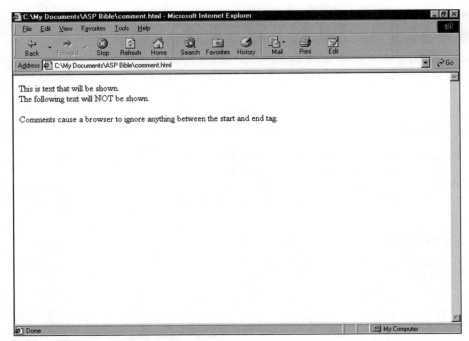

Figure B-1: Results of this code

<A></A>

The <A> tag defines either a hyperlink that allows a browser to jump to another page or frame, or it defines a bookmark that allows a browser to jump to a specific point in a page. The HREF or NAME parameter is required. Anything between the start <A> tag and the end </A> tag will be the area that must be clicked to activate the hyperlink or bookmark. This includes both text and images.

Examples

```
<A HREF="http://www.northcomp.com/">A normal hyperlink</A>

<A name="sample">A sample bookmark</A>

<A HREF="http://www.nortcomp.com/default.html#sample" >Linking
to a bookmark</A>

<A HREF="test.html" target="top">A hyperlink to a local page
test.html that will be opened in the frame named top</A>
```

Tag Parameters

Either the HREF parameter or the NAME parameter is required in the <A> tag.

HREF

The HREF parameter tells the browser the target URL of the hyperlink. Using a #
after the URL tells the browser to jump to a specific bookmark in the target URL.

NAME

The NAME parameter sets the current location as a bookmark using the indicated
Name. Bookmarks can be jumped to using the HREF parameter along with a # and
the name of the bookmark to be jumped to.

TARGET

The TARGET parameter tells the browser which frame to jump to. The possible
values for this parameter are:

✦ A frame name

✦ _blank

✦ _parent

✦ _self

✦ _top

<AREA>

The <AREA> tag marks coordinates that serve as a hotspot for a client-side
image map. This tag is used in conjunction with the <MAP> tag.

Example

```
<MAP NAME="mymap">
    <AREA SHAPE="rect"
          COORDS="0,100,200,200"
          HREF="newpage.html">
</MAP>
```

Tag Parameters

ALT

The ALT parameter displays textual information for a hotspot on an image.

COORDS

This parameter lists the coordinates for the hotspot. Depending on the value set in the SHAPE parameter, the COORDS parameter will take three or more numerical values.

For a rectangle, the values should be in this form:

```
left,top,right,bottom
```

For a circle, the values should be in the form:

```
x,y,radius
```

For a polygon, the values should be in the form:

```
x1,y1...xN,yN
```

HREF

The target URL to travel to if a hotspot is clicked.

NOHREF

If any part of the image map that is not set as a hotspot is clicked, the user will be taken to the URL specified in this parameter.

SHAPE

This parameter sets the shape of the image map. It is used with the COORDS parameter. Possible values are:

- ✦ Rect,Rectangle
- ✦ Circ,Circle
- ✦ Poly,Polygon

TARGET

This parameter sets the target frame, if any, of the hotspot.

<B></B>

The <B> tag sets any text between the start <B> tag and the end </B> tag to a boldface.

Example

```
Non bolded text<BR>
<B>The text here will appear bold</B>
```

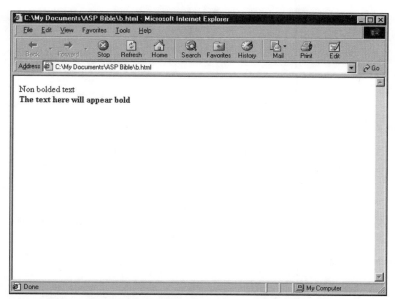

Figure B-2: Results of this code

Tag Parameters

None

<BASE>

The <BASE> tag specifies the base URL of the document. The base URL is prepended to any relative URL in the document. This tag enables you to save typing and make it easier to change directory structures without having to change the entire page.

Tag Parameters

HREF

Specifies the document's base URL.

TARGET

Specifies the target frame. Possible values for this parameter are:

+ A frame name
+ _blank
+ _parent
+ _self
+ _top

\<BASEFONT>

This tag specifies the base font and the base font attributes that will be used in the document.

Example

```
<BASEFONT COLOR="red" FACE="arial">
```

Tag Parameters

COLOR

The color of the basefont is set by this parameter.

FACE

This parameter sets the face of the basefont.

SIZE

The size parameter sets the size of the basefont. Possible values range from 1 to 7, with 7 being the largest.

\<BGSOUND>

The \<BGSOUND> tag sets the audio file that should be played while the page is being viewed.

Example

```
<BGSOUND src="test.wav" loop="infinite">
```

Tag Parameters

LOOP

The LOOP parameter takes in either a number indicating the number of times the indicated sound is to play, or INFINITE, which indicates that the sound should repeatedly be played until the page is exited or the user hits the Stop button on the browser.

SRC

The SRC parameters tell the browser where to find the sound file that is to be played. Acceptable formats vary with each browser, but the commonly accepted formats are:

✦ Basic Audio (AU) Files

✦ MIDI Definition (MID) Files

✦ Windows Audio (WAV) Files

<BIG></BIG>

The <BIG> tag will display any text between the start <BIG> tag and the end </BIG> tag in a font larger than the one currently used on the page. Note that this tag does not always provide the same functionality as the <B></B> tags.

Example

```
<BIG>The text here will be larger than</BIG> the text here.
```

Tag Parameters

None

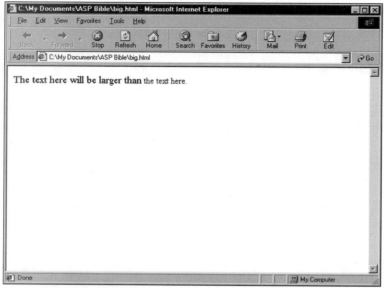

Figure B-3: Results of this code

<BLOCKQUOTE></BLOCKQUOTE>

The <BLOCKQUOTE> tag indents the text evenly between the start and end tags.

Example

```
Normal Text <BR>
<BLOCKQUOTE>The text here will be indented and set in a
blockquote <BR>
Note how the text is lined up with respect to the
borders.</BLOCKQUOTE>
```

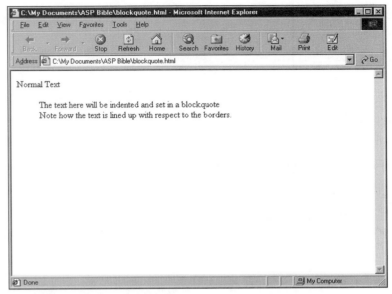

Figure B-4: Results of this code

Tag Parameters

None

<BODY></BODY>

The <BODY> tag indicates the start and end of the HTML document. The parameters in this tag are used to set various options that affect the whole document.

The main information for any page is usually contained between the beginning and ending <BODY> tags.

Example

```
<BODY>
    <B>
        Bolded Text within the body of the html document.
    </B>
</BODY>
```

Tag Parameters

ALINK

The ALINK parameter specifies the color of a hyperlink while it is being clicked.

BACKGROUND

This parameter lets the author specify an image to be displayed in the background of the HTML document. If the picture size is smaller than the size of the viewing area, the picture will be tiled.

BGCOLOR

The BGCOLOR parameter sets the background color of the HTML document.

LINK

The LINK parameter sets the color of any hyperlink that the browser has not yet seen.

TEXT

The TEXT parameter sets the color of the text in the HTML document.

VLINK

The VLINK parameter sets the color of any link that has been visited by the browser.

The <BR> tag tells the browser to add a line break to the current page.

Example

```
This text
won't be broken
up. <BR>
But this text <BR>
will be.
```

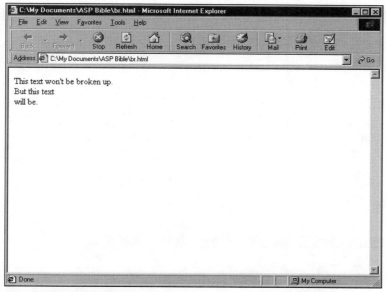

Figure B-5: Results of this code

Tag Parameters

None

<BUTTON></BUTTON>

The <BUTTON> tag places a button onto the HTML document. Any text placed between the start <BUTTON> tag and the end </BUTTON> tag will be inserted onto the button itself. This tag is usually used with a scripting language such as Javascript or VBScript.

Example

```
<BUTTON>A test button</BUTTON>
```

Tag Parameters

None

<CAPTION>

The <CAPTION> tag sets the caption for a table. It must be used in conjunction with the <TABLE> tag.

Example

```
<TABLE BORDER=1 WIDTH=300>
    <CAPTION>This is a table caption</CAPTION>
    <TR>
        <TD>
            Sample Table Data
        </TD>
    </TR>
</TABLE>
```

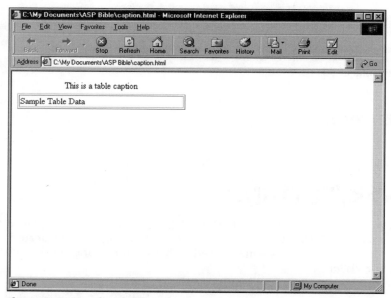

Figure B-6: Results of this code

Tag Parameters

ALIGN

The ALIGN parameter sets the alignment of the table caption. The available values for the parameter are:

✦ Bottom

✦ Center

✦ Left

✦ Right

✦ Top

VALIGN

The VALIGN parameter sets the vertical alignment of the table caption. The two available values for the parameter are:

✦ Bottom

✦ Top

<CENTER></CENTER>

The <CENTER> tag will center any text or images found between the start and the end tag. Centering of text and images will span multiple lines if necessary.

Example

```
<CENTER>This text will be set in the center of the
page.</CENTER>
```

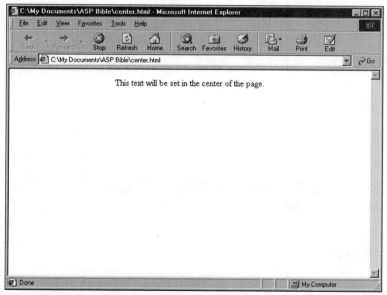

Figure B-7: Results of this code

Tag Parameters

None

<CITE>

The <CITE> tag takes any text between the start and end tag and marks it as a citation. Different browsers render citations differently, with the most common rendering having the text italicized.

Example

```
This is normal text.
<CITE> This is cited text. </CITE>
```

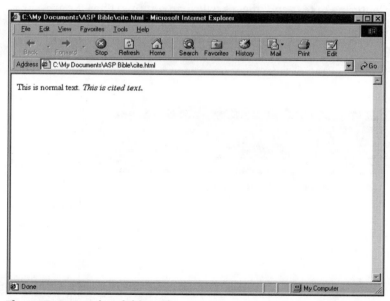

Figure B-8: Results of this code

Tag Parameters

None

<CODE>

The <CODE> tag marks any text between the start and end tag as a code snippet. Text marked as code is usually rendered in a fixed-width font, but may differ with each browser.

Example

```
This is normal text.<br><br>

<CODE>
This is a code sample:<br>
Do until rs.eof<br>
    Response.Write(rs("Name"))<br>
    Response.Write("&lt;BR&gt;")<br>
    rs.MoveNext<br>
Loop<br>
</CODE>
```

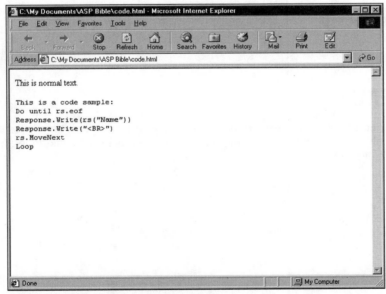

Figure B-9: Results of this code

Tag Parameters

None

<COMMENT>

This is a longer form of the <!– –> tag used for marking comments.

<DIR></DIR>

The <DIR> tag specifies a directory listing. It is used in conjunction with the <LI> tag.

Example

```
<DIR>
    <LI>One
    <LI>Two
    <LI>Three
</DIR>
```

Tag Parameters

None

<EM></EM>

The <EM> tag emphasizes any text found between the start and end tag. Different browsers emphasize text differently, but emphasized text is usually displayed in bold font or italicized font.

Example

```
Normal Text <BR>
<EM>Emphasized text.</EM>
```

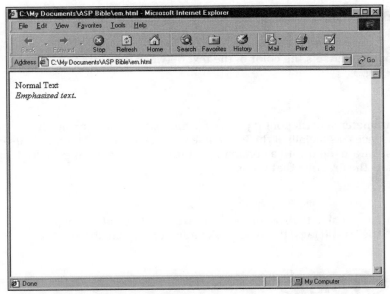

Figure B-10: Results of this code

Tag Parameters

None

<FONT></FONT>

The <FONT> tag allows formatting of any text found within the start and end tag.

Example

```
<FONT FACE="ARIAL" SIZE="2">Sample Text</FONT>
```

Tag Parameters

COLOR

The COLOR parameter sets the color of the text between the start and end <FONT> tag.

FACE

The FACE parameter sets the font typeface for the text. The font name should be enclosed in spaces, especially if the font name has a space in it. Multiple fonts can be listed — separate them with a comma. The browser will look for each font, in turn, and show the first one that it finds.

SIZE

The SIZE parameter sets the size of the font text. Possible values range from 1 to 7. Unlike the H1–H6 tags, the smaller the number, the smaller the text.

<FORM></FORM>

The <FORM> tag tells the browser that everything between the start and end <FORM> tags belongs to a form and that the information between these two tags will need to be processed.

Example

```
<FORM NAME="frmTest" ACTION="formprocess.asp" METHOD="POST">
</FORM>
```

Tag Parameters

ACTION

The ACTION parameter specifies the URL that will process the form after the form is submitted.

METHOD

The METHOD parameter specifies the way in which the form information is sent to the URL specified in the ACTION parameter. The two possible values are:

  ✦ Get — Sends the form values via the URL.
  ✦ Post — Sends the form values through the HTTP headers.

NAME

The name of the form. This name is used for programming using the form.

<FRAME></FRAME>

The <FRAME> tag indicates a frame. The <FRAME> tag must be used within the <FRAMESET> tag.

Example

```
<FRAMESET COLS="25%,75%">
    <FRAME SRC="top.html">
    <FRAME SRC="bottom.html">
</FRAMESET>
```

Tag Parameters

FRAMEBORDER

This parameter specifies whether to display a border for a specific frame. The possible values for this parameter are:

- ✦ Yes
- ✦ No
- ✦ 1
- ✦ 0

NORESIZE

This parameter prevents the frame from being resized by the user.

SCROLLING

This parameter specifies if the frame will have scroll bars. The possible values are:

- ✦ Auto
- ✦ No
- ✦ Yes

SRC

This parameter is the source URL for the frame.

<FRAMESET></FRAMESET>

This tag specifies the number and the size of both vertical and horizontal frames. The <FRAME> tag is used with the <FRAMESET> tag to set the source URL. Frames can be nested within each other to create complex layouts.

Example

```
<FRAMESET COLS="25%,75%">
    <FRAME SRC="top.html">
    <FRAME SRC="bottom.html">
</FRAMESET>
```

Tag Parameters

COLS

This parameter sets the size and number of the frames that will be split into columns. Two values can be used with this parameter. The first is a number that will specify the size of the column in pixels, while the second is a number followed by a %. This second value will set the size of the column as a percentage of the browser viewscreen.

ROWS

This parameter sets the size and number of the frames that will be split into rows. Two values can be used with this parameter. The first is a number that will specify the size of the row in pixels, while the second is a number followed by a %. This second value will set the size of the row as a percentage of the browser viewscreen.

<HEAD></HEAD>

The <HEAD> tag marks the start of the HTML document and collects information that is not normally set in the main body of the document. The <TITLE> tag is one of the tags that is found in between the two <HEAD> tags.

Example

```
<HEAD>
    <TITLE>A page Title</TITLE>
</HEAD>
```

Tag Parameters

None

<HR>

The <HR> tag displays a horizontal line across the page. The horizontal line will be displayed in pseudo 3D. The appearance of the line varies according to the browser used.

Example

```
Horizontal Rule at 20%<BR>
<HR WIDTH=20% SIZE=5><BR>
Horizontal Rule at 20 pixels<BR>
<HR WIDTH=20 SIZE=5><BR>
Horizontal Rule with no shading<BR>
<HR NOSHADE>
```

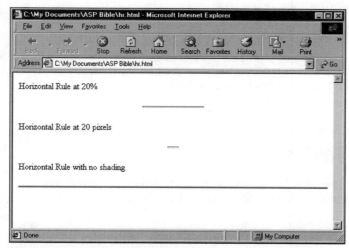

Figure B-11: Results of this code

Tag Parameters

ALIGN

Sets the horizontal alignment of the horizontal rule. Possible values for this parameter are:

- ✦ Center
- ✦ Left
- ✦ Right

COLOR

Sets the color of the horizontal rule.

NOSHADE

Removes the pseudo 3D shading from the horizontal rule.

SIZE

Sets the size of the horizontal rule in pixels.

WIDTH

Sets the width of the horizontal rule. The possible values for this parameter can either be a number or a percent. A number sets the horizontal width in pixels. A number followed by a % sets the horizontal width to a % relative to the size of the browser display.

<HTML></HTML>

This tag, which specifies the document as an HTML document, precedes the <BODY> tag and is always included in any HTML document.

Example

```
<HTML>
    <BODY>
        <P>Text</P>
    </BODY>
</HTML>
```

Tag Parameters

None

<H1> <H2> <H3> <H4> <H5> <H6>

The <H#> tags are used to specify section headings. The text displayed between a start <H#> tag and an end <H#> tag will vary in size according to the #. The text sizes are largest at <H1> and smallest at <H6>.

Example

```
<H1>A H1 Heading</H1><BR>
<H2>A H2 Heading</H2><BR>
<H3>A H3 Heading</H3><BR>
<H4>A H4 Heading</H4><BR>
<H5>A H5 Heading</H5><BR>
<H6>A H6 Heading</H6><BR>
```

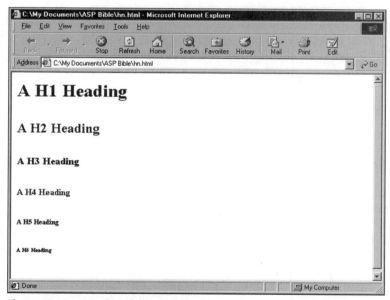

Figure B-12: Results of this code

Tag Parameters

ALIGN

Sets the horizontal alignment of the text. The possible values for this parameter are:

- ✦ Center
- ✦ Left
- ✦ Right

<I></I>

The <I> tag italicizes any text found between the start and end tag.

Example

```
Normal text.<BR>
<I>Italicized text.</I>
```

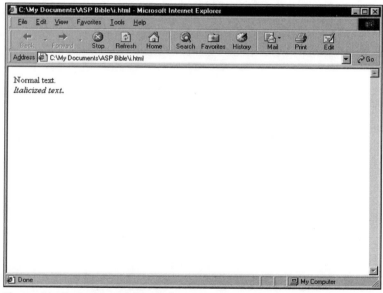

Figure B-13: Results of this code

Tag Parameters

None

<IMG>

The <IMG> tag tells the browser to include an image into the current page.

Example

```
An image lined up with <IMG SRC="sample.jpg" ALIGN="absbottom">
absbottom.
<BR><BR>
An image lined up with <IMG SRC="sample.jpg" ALIGN="absmiddle">
absmiddle.
<BR><BR>
An image lined up with <IMG SRC="sample.jpg" ALIGN="baseline">
baseline.
<BR><BR>
An image lined up with <IMG SRC="sample.jpg" ALIGN="bottom">
bottom.
<BR><BR>
An image lined up with <IMG SRC="sample.jpg" ALIGN="left">
left.
<BR><BR><BR>
An image lined up with <IMG SRC="sample.jpg" ALIGN="right">
right.
<BR><BR>
An image lined up with <IMG SRC="sample.jpg" ALIGN="middle">
middle.
<BR><BR>
An image lined up with <IMG SRC="sample.jpg" ALIGN="top"> top.
<BR><BR>
```

Tag Parameters

ALIGN

This parameter specifies the alignment for the image. The possible values for this parameter are:

- ✦ Absbottom
- ✦ Absmiddle
- ✦ Baseline
- ✦ Bottom
- ✦ Left
- ✦ Middle
- ✦ Right
- ✦ Texttop
- ✦ Top.

ALT

Sets the alternative text for the image. If the current browser is incapable of displaying the image, this text will be displayed instead. The ALT parameter should always be used with images.

BORDER

Indicates the thickness of the border around the image.

HEIGHT

Sets the height of the image. Two possible values can be set for this parameter. One is a number that sets the height of the image in pixels. The other is a % that sets the height of the image as a % of the current browser viewscreen.

ISMAP

Indicates that the current image is a server-side image map.

SRC

Sets the source URL for the image. This parameter is required.

USEMAP

Indicates that the image is an imagemap. The browser will pass coordinates to the URL when this parameter is marked.

WIDTH

Sets the width of the image. Two possible values can be set for this parameter. One is a number that sets the width of the image in pixels. The other is a % that sets the height width of the image as a % of the current browser viewscreen.

\<INPUT\>

The \<INPUT\> tag indicates that the browser should place an element that allows a form to receive input from the user. All input tags require the TYPE parameter. Depending on the value set for the parameter, a different form element will be displayed.

Tag Parameters

MAXLENGTH

The MAXLENGTH parameter indicates the maximum number of characters that can be inserted into an input of type TEXT or PASSWORD.

SIZE

The SIZE parameter indicates the size of the control.

Input Tag Types
BUTTON

The BUTTON input type places a button on the form.

Example

```
<INPUT TYPE=BUTTON  NAME="btnProceed" VALUE="OK">
```

Tag Parameters

NAME   This is the name of the form element. Any code that processes forms will use this name to refer to the element.

VALUE   This is the value of the form element.

CHECKBOX

The CHECKBOX type places a checkbox onto the form.

```
<INPUT TYPE=CHECKBOX NAME="chkOK" VALUE="1" CHECKED>
```

Tag Parameters

CHECKED   When this parameter is placed in the <INPUT> tag, the checkbox will be checked when the page loads.

NAME   This is the name of the form element. Any code that processes forms will use this name to refer to the element.

VALUE   This is the value of the form element. This value is valid only if the checkbox is checked.

HIDDEN

The HIDDEN type places a value into the form that is not seen by the user. It is usually used when information must be passed from one page to another but does not need to be seen or edited by the user.

```
<INPUT TYPE="HIDDEN" NAME="test" VALUE="OK">
```

Tag Parameters

NAME   This is the name of the form element. Any code that processes forms will use this name to refer to the element.

VALUE   This is the value of the form element.

IMAGE

The IMAGE type places an image on the form that, when clicked, will submit the form. This type is similar to the SUBMIT type except that instead of a button, the user provides an image.

```
<INPUT TYPE="IMAGE" NAME="submit" VALUE="SUBMITOK"
SRC="submit.jpg">
```

Tag Parameters

ALIGN	This specifies the alignment of the image.
NAME	This is the name of the form element. Any code that processes forms will use this name to refer to the element.
SRC	This is the source URL of the image.
VALUE	This is the value of form element.

PASSWORD

The PASSWORD type displays a text box on the form. All characters typed by the user will either be hidden or masked.

```
<INPUT TYPE="PASSWORD" NAME="password" VALUE="ok">
```

Tag Parameters

NAME	This is the name of the form element. Any code that processes forms will use this name to refer to the element.
VALUE	This sets the initial text for the password type.

RADIO

This type places one or more radio buttons on the page. All radio buttons belonging to the same group should have the same name.

```
<INPUT TYPE="RADIO" NAME="test" VALUE="Large">Large
<INPUT TYPE="RADIO" NAME="test" VALUE="SMall">Small
```

Tag Parameters

CHECKED	This parameter sets this radio button to checked.
NAME	This is the name of the form element. Any code that processes forms will use this name to refer to the element.
VALUE	This sets the value of the form element.

RESET

This type resets or clears all the form elements to the initial values.

```
<INPUT TYPE="RESET" VALUE="Reset">
```

Tag Parameters

VALUE   This sets the text displayed on the reset button.

SUBMIT

This places a button on the form that, when clicked, will submit the form.

```
<INPUT TYPE="SUBMIT" NAME="submit" VALUE="Submit">
```

Tag Parameters

NAME   This is the name of the form element. Any code that processes
              forms will use this name to refer to the element.

VALUE   This is the text displayed on the Submit button.

TEXT

The text type places a textbox onto the form.

```
<INPUT TYPE="TEXT" NAME="username">
```

Tag Parameters

NAME   This is the name of the form element. Any code that processes
              forms will use this name to refer to the element.

VALUE   This sets the initial value of the textbox.

<LI></LI>

The <LI> tag denotes a list item. It is used with both ordered and unordered lists.
The ending tag is optional.

Example

```
<UL>
    <LI>One</LI>
    <LI>Two</LI>
    <LI>Three</LI>
    <LI>Four</LI>
</UL>
```

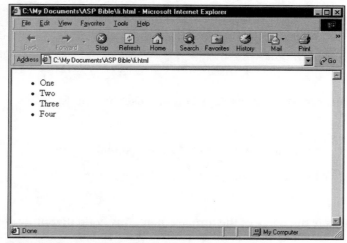

Figure B-14: Results of this code

Tag Parameters

None

<LINK>

This tag specifies a typed hyperlink between the current page and another resource. It is similar to the <HREF> tag but is not widely used.

Example

```
<LINK REL="HOME" SRC="default.html">
```

Tag Parameters

HREF

Specifies the source URL for the link.

REL

This parameter lists the relationships between current HTML document and the one specified in the HREF parameter.

REV

This parameter is similar to the REL parameter, however, instead of listing the relationships between the current HTML document and the target document, it lists the relationships between the target document and the current HTML document.

SRC

The SRC parameter specifies the target source for the link.

<MAP></MAP>

The <MAP> tag specifies a client-side image map. It is used in conjunction with the <AREA> tag.

Example

```
<MAP NAME="mymap">
    <AREA SHAPE="rect"
          COORDS="0,100,200,200"
          HREF="newpage.html">
</MAP>
```

Tag Parameters

NAME

This parameter specifies the map name.

<MENU></MENU>

The <MENU> tag specifies the start and end of a menu listing.

Example

```
<MENU>
    <LI>Listing One</LI>
    <LI>Listing Two</LI>
    <LI>Listing Three</LI>
</MENU>
```

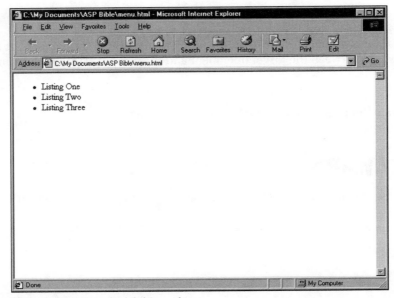

Figure B-15: Results of this code

Tag Parameters

None

<META>

The <META> tag provides information about the current HTML document to browsers and other sources such as search engines.

Examples

To have a page refresh itself in five minutes, use:

```
<META CONTENT=5 HTTP-EQUIV="REFRESH">
```

To have a page pull the user's browser to another page, use:

```
<MET CONTENT=5 HTTP-EQUIV="REFRESH"
URL="www.designreactor.com">
```

To set the keywords and description of your page for use in a search engine:

```
<META NAME="keywords" CONTENT="asp html javascript">
<META NAME="description" CONTENT="This is a sample
description">
```

The keywords are usually the values that are searched, and the description is usually displayed as the page summary on search pages such as Infoseek.

To restrict a user from caching the current page:

```
<META NAME="Pragma" CONTENT="no-cache">
```

To set a expiration date on the current page for use in a browser cache:

```
<META NAME="Expires" CONTENT="Mon, 01 Jan 2000">
```

Tag Parameters

CONTENT

The CONTENT parameter specifies certain values for the NAME and VALUE parameters. The legal values for this parameter depend on the NAME or HTTP-EQUIV parameter used.

HTTP-EQUIV

The value of this parameter is attached to the document header and its value can determine the legal values used in the CONTENT parameter.

NAME

This parameter specifies the name of the element type to be used. Either this parameter or the HTTP-EQUIV parameter must be present in a <META> tag.

URL

This parameter is used during client pulls (one page refreshing to another after a certain amount of time) and specifies the target URL.

<NOFRAMES></NOFRAMES>

This tag is used in conjunction with the <FRAMESET> tag. It is used to specify the HTML for any browser that doesn't support frames.

Example

```
<NOFRAMES>
    <BODY>
        <P>Browsers that don't support frames
            will see this text</P>
    </BODY>
</NOFRAMES>
```

Tag Parameters

None

<OL></OL>

The <OL> tag specifies the start and end of an ordered list.

Example

```
Type a Ordered List<BR>
<OL TYPE=a>
    <LI>One</LI>
    <LI>Two</LI>
</OL>
Type 1 Ordered List<BR>
<OL TYPE=1>
    <LI>One</LI>
    <LI>Two</LI>
</OL>
Type i ordered List<BR>
<OL TYPE=i>
    <LI>One</LI>
    <LI>Two</LI>
</OL>
```

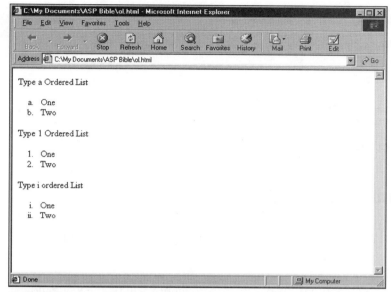

Figure B-16: Results of this code

Tag Parameters

START
This parameter sets the starting number for the ordered list.

TYPE
The value set in this parameter changes the style of the ordered listing. Possible values are:

✦ (None) — Numbers the list items

✦ a — Uses lowercase letters on the list items

✦ A — Uses uppercase letters on the list items

✦ i — Uses lowercase roman numerals on the list items

✦ I — Uses uppercase roman numerals on the list items

<OPTION></OPTION>

The <OPTION> tag inserts items into a <SELECT> drop-down box.

Example

```
<SELECT NAME="COLORS" SIZE="1">
    <OPTION VALUE="L">Large
    <OPTION VALUE="M">Medium
    <OPTION VALUE="S">Small
</SELECT>
```

Tag Parameters

SELECTED

The SELECTED parameter indicates that the current item is the default.

VALUE

If this item is selected, the value of the drop-down box will be the value indicated in this parameter.

<P></P>

The <P> tag separates individual paragraphs on the document.

Example

```
<P>a paragraph</P>
```

Tag Parameters

ALIGN

Sets the horizontal alignment for the paragraph. Possible values are:

- ◆ Center
- ◆ Left
- ◆ Right

<PRE></PRE>

This tag displays all the text in a fixed-width font and also displays all spaces and line breaks.

Example

```
The text here will not
    display exactly
as seen here.<BR>
<PRE>
The text here will
    Display exactly
As seen here.
</PRE>
```

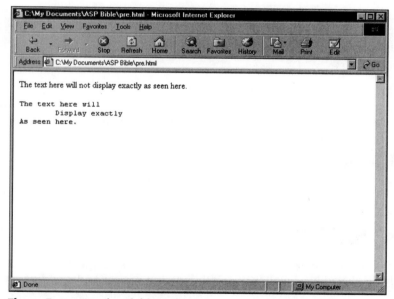

Figure B-17: Results of this code

Tag Parameters

None

<Q></Q>

The <Q> tag is used to denote text as a short quotation.

Example

```
This text is a <Q>quotation</Q>
```

Tag Parameters

None

<S></S>

All the text between the start <S> and end </S> tag is displayed with a strikethrough. This is the same as the <STRIKE> tag.

Example

```
Normal text.<BR>
<S>this text will be displayed with a strikethrough</S>
```

Tag Parameters

None

<SAMP></SAMP>

This tag sets all the text in between the start and end tag as sample text. Sample text is usually displayed in a small fixed width font, but can differ depending on the browser.

Example

```
Normal text.
<SAMP>Sample text</SAMP>
```

Tag Parameters

None

\<SCRIPT\>\</SCRIPT\>

The text between the start and end \<SCRIPT\> tag is specified as script that should be processed.

Example

```
<SCRIPT LANGUAGE="JAVASCRIPT">
</SCRIPT>
```

Tag Parameters

LANGUAGE

This parameter sets the language for the script between the start and end tags. Depending on your system, you may have other languages installed. However, the following are most common:

+ Javascript

+ Jscript

+ VBS

+ VBScript

\<SELECT\>\</SELECT\>

This tag adds a drop-down box to a form. It must be used with the \<OPTION\> tag.

Example

```
<SELECT NAME="COLORS" SIZE="1">
    <OPTION VALUE="L">Large
    <OPTION VALUE="M">Medium
    <OPTION VALUE="S">Small
</SELECT>
```

Tag Parameters

MULTIPLE

This parameter allows a user to select more than one item from the drop-down box.

NAME

This parameter specifies the name of the form element.

SIZE

This parameter indicates how many items are shown in the drop-down box.

<SMALL></SMALL>

The <SMALL> tag displays all the text between the start and end tag in a font size smaller than the current document font.

Example

```
Normal text.<BR>
<SMALL>small text</SMALL>
```

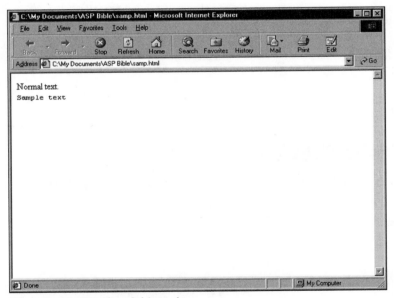

Figure B-18: Results of this code

Tag Parameters

None

<STRIKE></STRIKE>

All the text between the start <STRIKE> and end < STRIKE > tag is displayed with a strikethrough. This is the same as the <S> tag.

Example

```
<STRIKE>strikethrough</STRIKE>
```

Tag Parameters

None

<STRONG></STRONG>

This tag displays the text between the start and end tag in boldface.

Example

```
Normal text<BR>
<STRONG>strong text</STRONG>
```

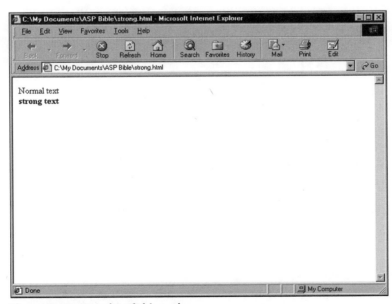

Figure B-19: Results of this code

Tag Parameters

None

The <SUB> tag displays all the text between the start and end tag as subscript.

Example

```
Normal Text. <BR>
This is <SUB>subscripted text</SUB>
```

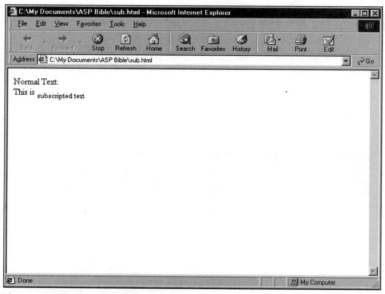

Figure B-20: Results of this code

Tag Parameters

None

The <SUP> tag displays all the text between the start and end tag as a superscript.

Example

```
Normal Text.<BR>
This is <SUP>superscripted text</SUP>
```

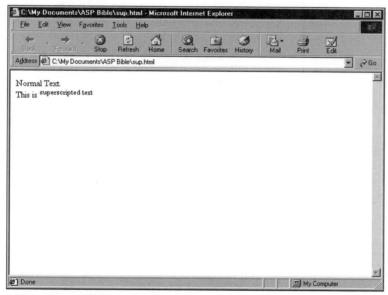

Figure B-21: Results of this code

Tag Parameters

None

<TABLE></TABLE>

The <TABLE> tag places a table onto the page. Many tags associated with the <TABLE> tag cannot be used without an associated table tag. These tags are: <CAPTION>, <TR>, <TH>, and <TD>.

Example

```
<TABLE BORDER=1>
<CAPTION>A sample table</CAPTION>
   <TR>
      <TD>
         TR one TD one
      </TD>
      <TD>
         TR one TD two
      </TD>
   </TR>
   <TR>
      <TD>
         TR two TD one
      </TD>
      <TD>
         TR two TD two
      </TD>
   </TR>
</TABLE>
<BR><BR>
<TABLE BORDER=1 CELLPADDING=5>
<CAPTION>A sample table with cellpadding set to 5</CAPTION>
   <TR>
      <TD>
         TR one TD one
      </TD>
      <TD>
         TR one TD two
      </TD>
   </TR>
   <TR>
      <TD>
         TR two TD one
      </TD>
      <TD>
         TR two TD two
      </TD>
   </TR>
</TABLE>
<BR><BR>
<TABLE BORDER=1 CELLSPACING=5>
<CAPTION>A sample table with cellspacing set to 5</CAPTION>
   <TR>
      <TD>
         TR one TD one
      </TD>
```

```
        <TD>
            TR one TD two
        </TD>
    </TR>
    <TR>
        <TD>
            TR two TD one
        </TD>
        <TD>
            TR two TD two
        </TD>
    </TR>
</TABLE>
```

Tag Parameters

ALIGN

This parameter sets the horizontal alignment of the table. The possible values are:

- ✦ Center
- ✦ Left
- ✦ Right

BORDER

This parameter sets the width of the border in pixels. If this is not set, the border around a table will be transparent. Possible values are numbers.

CELLPADDING

This parameter sets the spacing, in pixels, between the data in a cell and the border of a cell. Possible values are numbers.

CELLSPACING

This parameter sets the spacing, in pixels, between two cells. Possible values are numbers.

WIDTH

This parameter sets the width of the table. The possible values for this parameter can either be a number or a percent. A number sets the horizontal width in pixels. A number followed by a % sets the horizontal width to a % relative to the size of the browser display.

<TD></TD>

The <TD> tag is used to specify a element of a table. A table row should precede the <TD> tags.

Example

```
<TABLE>
    <TR>
        <TD>One</TD>
        <TD>Two</TD>
    </TR>
</TABLE>
```

Tag Parameters

ALIGN

Sets the horizontal alignment of the table data. The possible values can be:

- ✦ Center
- ✦ Left
- ✦ Right

BGCOLOR

This parameter sets the background color for the table element.

COLSPAN

The parameter sets the number of columns that this table element should span.

HEIGHT

This parameter sets the height of the table element.

NOWRAP

This parameter is used when the browser should not wrap text.

ROWSPAN

The parameter sets the number of rows that this table element should span.

VALIGN

This parameter sets the vertical alignment of the table element. The possible values for this parameter are:

- ✦ Baseline
- ✦ Bottom
- ✦ Center
- ✦ Top

WIDTH

This parameter sets the width of the table element.

<TEXTAREA></TEXTAREA>

The <TEXTAREA> tag places a multiline textbox on the page.

Example

```
<TEXTAREA ROWS=5 COLS=50>This is a textarea</TEXTAREA>
```

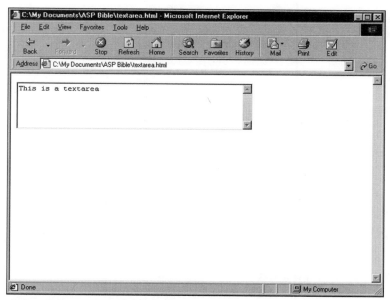

Figure B-22: Results of this code

Tag Parameters

COLS

This parameter sets the number of columns in the text area. The value should be a number.

NAME

Sets the name of the text area.

ROWS

This parameter sets the number of rows in the text area. This value should be a number.

<TH></TH>

The <TH> tag is used to set a table heading element in a table. This command is identical to the <TD>, except the text between the start <TH> tag and the end </TH> tag is boldfaced.

Example

```
<TABLE>
    <TR>
        <TH>ONE</TH>
    </TR>
</TABLE>
```

Tag Parameters

ALIGN

Sets the horizontal alignment of the table data. The possible values can be:

- ✦ Center
- ✦ Left
- ✦ Right

BGCOLOR

This parameter sets the background color for the table element.

COLSPAN

The parameter sets the number of columns that this table element should span.

HEIGHT

This parameter sets the height of the table element.

NOWRAP

This parameter is used when the browser should not wrap text.

ROWSPAN

The parameter sets the number of rows that this table element should span.

VALIGN

This parameter sets the vertical alignment of the table element. The possible values for this parameter are:

- ✦ Baseline
- ✦ Bottom
- ✦ Center
- ✦ Top

WIDTH

This parameter sets the width of the table element.

<TITLE></TITLE>

This tag sets the title of the HTML document. This tag must be used between the start <HEAD> tag and the end </HEAD> tag. The value of the title usually sets the window name of the browser.

Example

```
<HEAD>
    <TITLE>
        The title of the document
    </TITLE>
</HEAD>
```

Tag Parameters

None

<TR></TR>

The <TR> tag indicates a row in a table. The <TR> tag should precede any
<TD> tags.

Example

```
<TABLE>
    <TR>
        <TD>A table element</TD>
    </TR>
</TABLE>
```

Tag Parameters

ALIGN

This parameter sets the horizontal alignment of the table row. Possible
parameters are:

- ◆ Center
- ◆ Left
- ◆ Right

BGCOLOR

This parameter sets the background color of the table row.

VALIGN

This parameter sets the vertical alignment of the table row. The possible values are:

- ◆ Baseline
- ◆ Bottom
- ◆ Center
- ◆ Top

<TT></TT>

The <TT> tag sets any text within the start <TT> and the end </TT> tag to
teletype. Teletype font is usually rendered in a fixed width font, but can
vary between browsers.

Example

```
<TT>Teletyped Font</TT>
```

Tag Parameters

None

<U></U>

This tag underlines any text between the start <U> tag and the end </U> tag.

Example

```
Normal text. <BR>
<U>This text will be underlined</U>
```

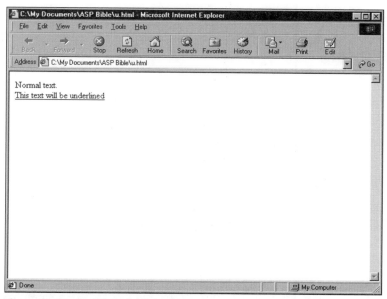

Figure B-23: Results of this code

Tag Parameters

None

<UL></UL>

This tag specifies an unordered list.

Example

```
Type a Unordered List<BR>
<UL TYPE=a>
    <LI>One</LI>
    <LI>Two</LI>
</UL>
Type 1 Unordered List<BR>
<UL TYPE=1>
    <LI>One</LI>
    <LI>Two</LI>
</UL>
Type i Unordered List<BR>
<UL TYPE=i>
    <LI>One</LI>
    <LI>Two</LI>
</UL>
```

Tag Parameters

TYPE

The value set in this parameter changes the style of the ordered listing. Possible values are:

+ 1 — Uses numbers on the list items

+ a — Uses lowercase letters on the list items

+ A — Uses uppercase letters on the list items

+ i — Uses lowercase roman numerals on the list items

+ I — Uses uppercase roman numerals on the list items

<VAR></VAR>

The <VAR> tag will set any text in between the start and end tags to a small fixed width font.

Example

```
<VAR>variable placeholder</VAR>
```

Tag Parameters

None

✦   ✦   ✦

VBScript Reference

Variant Data Type

All variables in VBScript must be of the Variant data type. This data type itself is a container that can hold any of the other data types found in Visual Basic, from integers to objects. Because it is the only datatype supported by VBScript, all built-in VBScript functions will return Variants.

Description

The Variant data type has several built-in features that aid the programmer in several ways. Initialization is taken care of for the programmer automatically: all Variants are initialized to Empty. Empty is itself a special 'subtype', as it expresses to the programmer that the Variant has not been initialized. When an Empty Variant is used in an expression, it can evaluate to 0 if it is being used as a number, or it can evaluate to a zero-length string if it is being used as a string. The Null 'subtype' is distinct as it lets the programmer know that this Variant intentionally contains no valid data. In the past, this information was difficult to convey; usually a 0 was interpreted as Null, but this is not always valid. The Variant data type eliminated this confusion by introducing the Null subtype. This subtype will often be returned when using database lookups. Table C-1 shows the data types and capacities that a Variant can hold.

Table C-1
Data Type Capacity

Subtype	Description
Empty	Variant is uninitialized
Null	Variant intentionally contains no valid data
Boolean	True or False
Byte	Integers between 0 to 255
Integer	Integers between −32,768 to 32,767
Currency	−922,337,203,685,477.5808 to 922,337,203,685,477.5807
Long	Integers between −2,147,483,648 to 2,147,483,647
Single	Single-precision, floating-point number between −3.402823E38 to −1.401298E-45 for negative values and 1.401298E-45 to 3.402823E38 for positive values
Double	Double-precision, floating-point number in the range −1.79769313486232E308 to -4.94065645841247E-324 for negative values and 4.94065645841247E-324 to 1.79769313486232E308 for positive values
Date (Time)	Number that represents a date between January 1, 100 to December 31, 9999
String	Variable-length string that can be up to approximately 2 billion characters in length
Object	An object
Array	An array of Variants
Error	An error number

Conversion and Subtype Determination

Oftentimes, it is necessary to convert between a Variant of one subtype to a Variant of another subtype. For example, a double-precision number may need to be converted into a long integer or vice versa. VBScript provides conversion functions to provide this functionality. Furthermore, when passed a reference to a Variant, the programmer has no knowledge of its contents. VBScript provides a means to determine the subtype of a variable at run time, which enables the programmer to take a variable of unknown type, and depending on its classification, perform a specific task. The determination functions provided by VBScript are: IsEmpty, IsNull, IsNumeric, IsDate, IsObject, IsError, and IsArray. If the programmer requires more specific knowledge of the subtype, the VarType function is provided. For example, if a distinction must be made between variables of subtype Integer and variables of subtype Double, the IsNumeric function cannot be used. It will return True for both variable types. Instead,

`VarType` must be used as `VarType` returns 2 for `Integer`s and 5 for `Double`s. Table C-2 shows the functions available for use with `Variant` variables.

Table C-2 Variant Subtype Functions			
Subtype	**Conversion Function**	**Determination Function**	**VarType(subtype)**
Empty	none	IsEmpty(variant)	0
Null	none	IsNull(variant)	1
Integer	CInt(variant)	IsNumeric(variant)	2
Long	CLng(variant)	IsNumeric(variant)	3
Single	CSng(variant)	IsNumeric(variant)	4
Double	CDbl(variant)	IsNumeric(variant)	5
Currency	CCur(variant)	IsNumeric(variant)	6
Date	CDate(variant)	IsDate(variant)	7
String	CStr(variant)	none	8
Object	none	IsObject(variant)	9
Error	none	IsError(variant)	10
Boolean	CBool(variant)	none	11
Byte	CByte(variant)	none	17
Array	none	IsArray(variant)	8192

Operators

Operators are used to create expressions of variables, constants, or other literals. There are operators for logical, arithmetic, and string expressions, as well as comparison of expressions.

Logical Operators

Logical operators operate on values or expressions that evaluate to True or False values.

And Operator

Performs a logical conjunction between two expressions. The syntax is as follows, and all the possible combinations are shown in Table C-3.

```
Result = Expression1 And Expression2
```

Table C-3
And Operator Results

Expression1	Expression2	Expression1 And Expression2
True	True	True
True	False	False
True	Null	Null
False	True	False
False	False	False
False	Null	False
Null	True	Null
Null	False	False
Null	Null	Null

Or Operator

Performs a logical disjunction between two expressions. The syntax is as follows, and all the possible combinations are shown in Table C-4.

```
Result = Expression1 Or Expression2
```

Table C-4
Or Operator Results

Expression1	Expression2	Expression1 Or Expression2
True	True	True
True	False	True
True	Null	True
False	True	True
False	False	False
False	Null	Null
Null	True	True
Null	False	Null
Null	Null	Null

Not Operator

Performs a logical negation on an expression. The syntax is as follows, and all the possible combinations are shown in Table C-5.

```
Result = Not Expression1
```

Table C-5
Not Operator Results

Expression1	Not Expression1
True	False
False	True
Null	Null

Xor Operator

Performs a logical exclusion between two expressions. The syntax is as follows, and all the possible combinations are shown in Table C-6.

```
Result = Expression1 Xor Expression2
```

Table C-6
Xor Operator Results

Expression1	Expression2	Expression1 Xor Expression2
True	True	False
True	False	True
True	Null	Null
False	True	True
False	False	False
False	Null	Null
Null	True	Null
Null	False	Null
Null	Null	Null

Eqv Operator

Performs a logical equivalence between two expressions. The syntax is as follows, and all the possible combinations are shown in Table C-7.

```
Result = Expression1 Eqv Expression2
```

	Table C-7	
	Eqv Operator Results	
Expression1	*Expression2*	*Expression1 And Expression2*
True	True	True
True	False	False
True	Null	Null
False	True	False
False	False	True
False	Null	Null
Null	True	Null
Null	False	Null
Null	Null	Null

Imp Operator

Performs a logical implication between two expressions. The syntax is as follows, and all the possible combinations are shown in Table C-8.

```
Result = Expression1 Imp Expression2
```

	Table C-8	
	Imp Operator Results	
Expression1	*Expression2*	*Expression1 And Expression2*
True	True	True
True	False	False
True	Null	Null
False	True	True
False	False	True
False	Null	True
Null	True	True
Null	False	Null
Null	Null	Null

Arithmetic Operators

All of the arithmetic operators available in VBScript are shown in Table C-9.

	Table C-9			
	Arithmetic Operators			
Operator	*Name*	*Description*	*Syntax*	*Null If*
+	Addition together	Adds two numbers	result = expression1+ expression2	either expression1 or expression2 are Null
-	Subtraction from another	Subtracts one number expression2	result = expression1 -	either expression1 or expression2 are Null
*	Multiplication	Multiplies two numbers	result = expression1 * expression2	either expression1 orexpression2 are Null
/	Division	Divides one number into another	result = numerator / denominator	either numerator or denominatorl are Nul
\	Integer Division	Divides one numberand returns an integer into another	result = numerator \ denominator	either numerator or denominator are Null
^	Exponentiation	Raise one number to the power of another	result = number ^ power	either number or power are Null
Mod	Modulus / Remainder	Returns the remainder of one number divided into another	result = expression1 Mod expression2	either expression1 or expression2 are Null
-	Unary Negation	Returns the additive inverse of a number	result = -expression	expression is Null

Concatenation Operators

VBScript's concatenation operators are shown in Table C-10.

	Table C-10 Concatenation Operators			
Operator	**Name**	**Description**	**Syntax**	**Null If**
&	String Concatenation	Appends one string onto the end of another	result = expression 1 & expression2	either expression 1 or expression 2 are Null
+	Addition	Appends one string onto the end of another	result = expression 1 & expression2	either expression1 or expression2 l are Nul

Comparison Operators

VBScript's comparison operators are shown in Table C-11.

	Table C-11 Comparison Operators			
Operator	**Name**	**Description**	**Syntax**	**Null If**
<	Less than	One expression evaluates to less than another expression	expression1 < expression2	either expression 1 or expression2 are Null
<=	Less than or equal to	One expression evaluates to less than or equal to another expression	expression1 <= expression2	either expression1 or expression2 are Null
>	Greater than	One expression evaluates to greater than another expression	expression1 > expression2	either expression1 or expression2 are Null
>=	Greater than or equal to than or equal	One expression evaluates to greater to another expression	expression1 >= expression2	either expression1 or expression2 are Null

Operator	Name	Description	Syntax	Null If
=	Equal to	One expression evaluates to equal to another expression	expression1 = expression2	either expression1 expression2 or are Null
<>	Not equal to	One expression evaluates to not equal to another expression	expression1 <> expression2	either expression1 expression2 or are Null
Is	Object Comparison Operator	Two object references point to the same object	object1 Is object2	either object1 or object2 are Null

Order of Operator Precedence

In general, arithmetic operators are evaluated first, followed by concatenation operators, followed by comparison operators, followed by logical operators. To evaluate an expression in an order different than specified by operator precedence, parentheses can be used.

Table C-12 shows the order of precedence in VBScript.

Table C-12
Order of Precedence

Operator	Name	Notes
^	Exponentiation	
–	Unary Negation	
*, /, \	Multiplication, Division, Subtraction	These operators have the same precedence, and are evaluated in the expression in the order in which they appear from left to right.
Mod	Modulus	
+, –	Addition or Subtraction	These operators have the same precedence, and are evaluated in the expression in the order in which they appear from left to right.
&, +	String Concatenation	These operators have the same precedence, and are evaluated in the expression in the order in which they appear from left to right.

Continued

	Table C-12 *(continued)*	
Operator	*Name*	*Notes*
=, <>, <, >, <=, >=, Is	All Comparison operators	All comparison operators have the same precedence, and are evaluated in the expression in the order in which they appear from left to right.
Not	Logical Negation	
And	Logical Conjunction	
Or	Logical Disjunction	
Xor	Logical Exclusion	
Eqv	Logical Equivalence	
Imp	Logical Implication	

Statements

This section covers the statements that are part of the VBScript language. These statements are used to perform a variety of actions in the language.

Call Statement

Transfers control to a subroutine (Sub) or function (Function)

Syntax
```
[Call] name [arguments]
```

Parameters
name   the name of the subroutine of function being called

arguments   a comma-delimited list of arguments passed into the
                subroutine or function

Notes
The keyword Call can be omitted for calls made to subroutines. When making a call that does not return a value, the argument list should not be enclosed with parentheses. For calls to functions that return values, the keyword Call must be omitted and the argument list must be enclosed in parenthesis (see the following examples).

Placing individual arguments in the argument list in parentheses passes them by value rather than by reference.

Example

```
' The following statements are equivalent.
Call DoSomething Argument1, (Argument2)
DoSomething Argument1, (Argument2)
' In the preceding example, Argument1 is passed by reference
and Argument2 is ' passed passed by value
'
' The first two calls to the Function MyFunction are equivalent
MyFunction Argument1, Argument2
Call MyFunction Argument1, Argument2
iValue = MyFunction(Argument1, Argument2)
' The last call returns a value, so the parameter list must be
enclosed in
' parenthesis
```

Const Statement

Declares a constant that can be used in place of a literal value.

Syntax

```
Const name = expression
```

Parameters

name	the name of the constant
expression	a valid expression

Notes

Multiple declarations can occur on the same line. Also, expression cannot contain VBScript or user-defined functions.

Dim Statement

Declares a variable and allocates memory for arrays.

Syntax

```
Dim name[([upperbound][,[upperbound]]...)]
```

Parameters

name	the name of the variable being declared
upperbound	optional; the upper bound of the array

Notes

When declaring a variable using Dim at the script level, the variable is assigned public scope. When Dim is used at the procedure level, the variable is declared as private. Remember that all variables are declared as Variant in VBScript.

Arrays declared using `Dim` are actually `Variant`s that contain arrays of `Variant`s. When declaring a fixed-length array, specify the `upperbound` parameter. All arrays in VBScript have a lower bound of 0. Therefore, to specify an array with *n* elements, `upperbound` should be *n*-1 (see the example below). When `upperbound` is omitted, the array is dynamic. Use the `ReDim` statement to allocate memory and the `Erase` statement to free it.

Multidimensional arrays can be declared by including multiple upperbound parameters. Each upperbound parameter must be separated by a comma. The maximum number of dimensions for an array is 60.

Example
```
' The following declares three variables are Variant
Dim Variable1
Dim Variable2, Variable3
' The following declares a Variant which contains an array of
' 11 Variants
Dim MyArray(10)
' The following declares a Variant which contains a two
' dimensional array of Variants
Dim MyTwoDimensionArray(10,10)
' The following declares a Variant which containes a dynamic
' array
Dim MyDynamicArray()
```

Do..Loop

Executes a block of statements while a condition is True or until a condition is True.

Syntax
```
Do [{While | Until} condition]
[statements]
[Exit Do]
[statements]
Loop
```
Or

```
Do
[statements]
[Exit Do]
[statements]
Loop [{While | Until} condition]
```

Parameters

statements   a series of VBScript statements and/or procedure calls to be executed

condition   a valid Boolean expression

Notes

When using the `While` keyword, the `Do...Loop` control structure will execute until condition evaluates to False. When using the `Until` keyword, the `Do...Loop` control structure will execute until `condition` evaluates to True. Note that if the condition evaluates to Null, this value is interpreted as False. Use the `Exit Do` statement to exit out of the `Do...Loop` structure immediately.

Example

```
' The following code demonstrates use of the While keyword
bContinue = True
iCount = 0
Do
    iCount = iCount + 1
    If iCount = 100 Then bContinue = False
Loop While bContinue

' The following code has the same outcome as the previous
' example, but it uses the Until keyword
bStop = True
iCount = 0
Do
    iCount = iCount + 1
    If iCount = 100 Then bStop = True
Loop Until bStop

' Exit Do can also be used to produce the same result.
iCount = 0
Do
    iCount = iCount + 1
    If iCount = 100 Then Exit Do
Loop
```

Erase Statement

Initializes the elements of a fixed-length array or frees memory of a dynamic array.

Syntax

`Erase` *array*

Parameters

`array`   the name of the variable containing the array to be erased

Notes

If `array` is a fixed-length array, each element is initialized to `Empty`. If `array` is a dynamic array, then the memory is freed, and the array cannot be access again until another call to `ReDim` has been made. Either way, all information stored in the array before the call to `Erase` is lost.

Example

```
Dim MyArray(1)
MyArray(0) = 1
MyArray(1) = "Hello World"
Erase MyArray
' After the call to Erase, MyArray(0) is Empty as is MyArray(1)

Dim MyDynamicArray()
' Other code goes here
ReDim MyDynamicArray(1)
MyDynamicArray (0) = 1
MyDynamicArray (1) = "Hello World"
Erase MyDynamicArray
' After the call to Erase, MyDynamicArray cannot be used
ReDim MyDynamicArray(10)
' Now MyDynamicArray can again be used
```

For...Next Statement

Executes a block of statements while a counter increments from start to end.

Syntax

```
For counter = start To end [Step step]
[statements]
[Exit For]
[statements]
Next
```

Parameters

counter	a variable that is to be incremented
start	the initial value of counter
end	the final value of counter
step	the amount counter is to be incremented each time Next is reached
statements	a series of VBScript statements and/or procedure calls to be executed

Notes

If step is omitted, it is assumed to be 1. If step is positive and start is greater than end, the For...Next loop is not executed. Similarly, if step is negative and start is less than end, the structure is skipped as well.

When the For...Next loop begins, counter is initialized to the value of start. Each time the Next statement is executed, counter is incremented by the value of step. If step is positive (counter is being increased), and counter is greater than the value of end, the loop ends and the line of code following the Next statement is executed. Otherwise, the line of code following the For statement is executed and the loop continues. If step is negative (counter is being decreased), and counter is less than the value of end, the loop ends and the line of code following the Next statement is executed. Otherwise, the line of code following the For statement is executed and the loop continues.

To terminate the For...Next loop before the loop is complete, use the Exit For statement.

Example

```
' This Example increments iCount from 1 to 100 while adding the
' number to the variable iSum
iSum = 0
For iCount = 1 to 100
    iSum = iSum + iCount
Next i
' This Example decrements iCount from 100 to 1 while adding the
' number to the variable iSum
iSum = 0
For iCount = 100 to 1 Step -1
    iSum = iSum + iCount
Next i
' This Example does nothing as 1 < 100
iSum = 0
For iCount = 1 to 100 Step -1
    iSum = iSum + iCount
Next
```

For Each...Next Statement

Executes a block of code while iterating through all the items in a collection or all the elements in an array.

Syntax

```
For Each element In group
[statements]
[Exit For]
[statements]
Next [element]
```

Parameters

element	a variable that will contain either an item in a collection or an element in an array
group	the collection or the array that is to be enumerated
statements	a series of VBScript statements and/or procedure calls to be executed

Notes

The For Each...Next control structure is a shorthand method of using a For...Next loop to enumerate all the items in a collection or the elements in an array. The For Each block is entered if there is at least one element in group. Once the Next statement has been reached, the loop continues as long as there are more elements in group.

Example

```
' The following loops are identical
For Each AnItem In MyCollection
   ' Do something with AnItem
Next

For iCount = 1 to MyCollection.Count
   Set AnItem = MyCollection.Item(iCount-1)
   ' Do something with AnItem
Next iCount

' This pair of loops are identical as well
For Each AnElement In MyArray
   ' Do something with AnElement
Next

For iCount = 0 to UBound(MyArray)
   Set AnElement = MyArray (iCount)
   ' Do something with AnElement
Next iCount
```

Function Statement

The Function statement is used to declare a set of statements that form the body of a function.

Syntax

```
Function name [(arglist)]
   [statements]
   [name = expression]
   [Exit Function]
   [statements]
   [name = expression]
End Function
```

Parameters

name   The name of the function. The name must be unique in the script where the function is declared.

arglist   A list of variables representing arguments that are passed to the function when it is called. Multiple variables are separated by commas. The arglist has the following syntax and parts:

```
[ByVal | ByRef] varname
```

ByVal is used to indicate that the argument is passed by value.

ByRef is used to indicate that the argument is passed by reference.

VarName is the name of the variable.

Function   Contains any group of statements to be executed within the body of the function.

Expression   Returns the value of the Function.

If...Then...Else

Executes one or more statements conditionally.

Syntax

```
If condition Then statement [Else elsestatement ]
```
Or

```
If condition Then
[statements]
[ElseIf condition-n Then
[elseifstatements]] . . .
[Else
[elsestatements]]
End If
```

Parameters

condition   a valid expression

statements   one or more VBScript statements and/or procedure calls to be executed when condition evaluates to True

elseifstatements   one or more VBScript statements and/or procedure calls to be executed when condition evaluates to False and condition-n evaluates to True

elsestatements   one or more VBScript statements and/or procedure calls to be executed when condition and condition-n evaluate to False

Notes

There are two forms of the If...Then control block: the single-line form and the multiline form. In the single-line form, all of the statements are contained in one long line of code. If the condition evaluates to True, then the statement following the Then keyword is executed. If the Else keyword is not omitted and condition evaluates to False, then the elsestatement is executed.

The multiline form is more complex and flexible, as it enables the programmer to execute blocks of code rather than just a single line. In this case, the condition is evaluated first. If it evaluates to True, the statements are executed. Once they have finished execution, the program continues with the line following the End If.

However, if condition evaluates to False, and if there exists at least one ElseIf clause, then condition-n is evaluated. If it evaluates to True, the elseifstatements code block is executed. Otherwise, any other ElseIf clauses are evaluated in the order in which they appear. Finally, if none of the condition -n expressions have evaluated to True and an Else clause exists, then the elsestatements are executed.

Example

```
' The following code uses the single line If...Then statement
If iCount = 100 Then bStop = True

' The following code uses If...ElseIf...Else...End If to
convert
' ages into titles
If iAge >= 65 Then
    sTitle = "Senior"
ElseIf iAge > 19 Then
    sTitle = "Adult"
ElseIf iAge > 12 Then
    sTitle = "Teen"
ElseIf iAge > 3 Then
    sTitle = "Child"
Else
    sTitle = "Baby"
End If
```

On Error Statement

Allows the program to trap run-time errors.

Syntax

```
On Error Resume Next
```

Notes

The On Error Resume Next statement allows the program to catch any occurrences of run-time errors without stopping execution. This statement is usually called at the beginning of a script or a procedure and as run-time errors occur in the code, they are ignored and the next sequential statement is executed. If a procedure does not implement error handling (does not use On Error Resume Next), VBScript will pop the call stack in order to find a procedure that does. If no procedures implement error handling, an error message is displayed and execution of the program stops.

VBScript run-time errors are stored in the Err object and can be accessed in code. Note that statements such as On Error Resume Next, End Function, End Sub, Exit Function, and Exit Sub reset the Err object.

Example

```
' The following code traps errors and deals with them
' accordingly.
On Error Resume Next

Call DoSomething ' This code could raise an error
If Err.Number = 6 Then ' An overflow error occurred
   Call HandleOverflowError
ElseIf Err.Number = 0 Then ' No errors occurred
   Call DoSomethingElse
Else ' An unknown error occurred
   Call HandleOtherError
End If

' Note that since DoSomething has no error handling, VBScript
' will continue to pop the call stack until it finds a
procedure
' which does use On Error Resume Next
Sub DoSomething()
   Err.Raise 6 ' Raise the overflow error
End Sub
```

Option Explicit Statement

Forces all of the variables used in VBScript to be declared explicitly.

Syntax

```
Option Explicit
```

Notes

If used, the Option Explicit statement must occur before any variables or procedures are declared. Explicitly declared variables are declared before their use in a Dim, Private, or Public statement. Implicitly declared variables are not declared before their use. The Option Explicit statement requires variables to be declared explicitly. The advantage of explicitly declaring variables is that misspelled variable names will be caught at compile-time rather than at run-time.

Example

```
Option Explicit
Dim MyVariable ' This declaration is forced by Option Explicit
```

Randomize Statement

Initializes the random number generator.

Syntax

```
Randomize [number]
```

Parameters

number   optional; any valid numeric expression

Notes

Execute this statement to initialize the random number generator. If Randomize is not used before the first call to Rnd, the seed for the random number generator is the same.

Example

```
Randomize
iValue = Int(Rnd * 10) + 1
```

ReDim Statement

Dimensions and allocates memory for dynamic arrays.

Syntax

```
ReDim [Preserve] name([upperbound][,[upperbound]])...)
```

Parameters

name   the name of the array being redimensioned

upperbound   the new upper bound of the array

Notes

Use this statement to dimension and allocate memory for dynamic arrays declared using Dim. This statement is only valid on the procedure level; it cannot be used at the script level. Use the Preserve keyword to keep the contents of the array intact during the resizing. If Preserve is omitted, all information in the array will be lost. Furthermore, when using the Preserve keyword, only the last dimension can be changed; the number of dimensions cannot be modified.

Multidimensional arrays can be declared by including multiple upperbound parameters. Each upperbound parameter must be separated by a comma. The maximum number of dimensions for an array is 60.

Example

```
' The following Example uses Dim and ReDim to allocate a
dynamic
' array
Dim MyDynamicArray()
ReDim MyDynamicArray(1,1)
MyDynamicArray(0,0) = 100
ReDim MyDynamicArray(2,2) ' All data in the array is lost
```

```
MyDynamicArray(0,0) = 100
ReDim Preserve MyDynamicArray(2,3)
' Only the last dimension can be changed when using Preserve
```

REM Statement

The Rem statement is used to mark a line in the program as explanatory remarks.

Syntax

```
REM comment
```
comment is an optional argument that contains the remarks.

Select...Case Statement

The Select...Case statement is used to execute one of several groups of statements, depending on the value of an expression.

Syntax

```
Select Case testexpression
    [Case expressionlist-n
    [statements-n]] ...
    [Case Else expressionlist-n
    [elsestatements-n]]
End Select
```

Parameters

textexpression	any numeric or string expression.
expressionlist-n	is required if the Case statement appears. It is used to delimit a list of one or more expressions.
statements-n	is one or more statements to be executed if testexpression evaluates to expressionlist-n.
elsestatements-n	is one or more statements to be executed if testexpression does not evaluate to any of the expressionlist-n.

Example

```
Dim Color, MyVar
Sub ChangeBackgound (Color)
MyVar = LCase(Color)
Select Case MyVar
    Case "red" document.bgColor = "red"
    Case "green" document.bgColor = "green"
    Case "blue" document.bgColor = "blue"
    Case Else Msgbox "pick another color"
End Select
End Sub
```

Set Statement

The Set statement is used to assign an object reference to a variable or property.

Syntax

```
Set objectvar = {[New] objectexpression | Nothing}
```

Parameters

objectvar	a requirement string expression that represents the name of the variable.
New	an optional parameter. When the New is used with Set, it creates a new instance of the class.
objectexpression	a requirement argument that contains the name of the object.
Nothing	is an option statement. It is used to discontinue association of objectvar with any specific object.

Sub Statement

The Sub statement is used to declare a set of statements that form the body of a subroutine.

Syntax

```
Sub name [(arglist)]
   [statements]
   [Exit Sub]
   [statements]
End Sub
```

Parameters

name	the name of the subroutine. The name must be unique in the script where the subroutine is declared.
arglist	a list of variables representing arguments that are passed to the Subroutine when it is called. Multiple variables are separated by commas. The arglist has the following syntax and parts:
	[ByVal | ByRef] varname
	ByVal is used to indicate that the argument is passed by value.
	ByRef is used to indicate that the argument is passed by reference.
	VarName is the name of the variable.
statements	contains any group of statements to be executed within the body of the subroutine.

While...Wend Statement

The While...Wend is a looping mechanism that executes a series of statements as long as a given condition is true.

Syntax
```
While condition
    [statements]
Wend
```

Parameters

condition   a numeric or a string expression that evaluates to true or false. The condition is checked once every iteration to see if the script should stop the loop. If the condition evaluates to True, then the statements are evaluated once more. If the condition evaluates to False, then the While loop is stopped.

Example
```
Dim iCount
iCount = 0
While iCount <= 100
    iCount = iCount + 1
    Alert iCount
Wend
```

Functions — General

This section covers the built-in functions that are part of the VBScript language. Functions return values to the caller — which is how they differ from statements.

CreateObject Function

Returns a Variant containing a reference to a newly created Automation object.

Syntax
```
CreateObject(class)
```

Parameters

Class   the AppID of the Automation object to create

Example
```
Set objExcel = CreateObject("Excel.Application")
' Returns a reference to Microsoft Excel
```

FormatCurrency Function

Returns an expression formatted as a currency value.

Syntax

```
FormatCurrency(Expression[,NumDigitsAfterDecimal
[,IncludeLeadingDigit [,UseParensForNegativeNumbers
[,GroupDigits]]]])
```

Parameters

Expression	the Expression to be formatted
NumDigitsAfterDecimal	optional parameter that indicates the number of digits to include after the decimal point in the newly formatted expression
IncludeLeadingDigit	optional parameter that indicates whether the newly formatted expression should include a leading zero for fractional values
UserParensForNegativeNumbers	optional parameter that indicates whether the newly formatted expression should use parentheses for negative values
GroupDigits	optional parameter that indicates whether the newly formatted expression is grouped using the group delimiter specified in the computer's regional settings

Notes

Whenever an optional parameter is omitted, the values for the omitted arguments are provided by the server's regional settings.

Example

```
NewExpression = FormatCurrency(25, 2)
'New Expression is assigned "$ 25.00"
```

FormatDateTime Function

Returns an expression formatted as Date and Time.

Syntax

```
FormatDateTime(Date[, NamedFormat])
```

Parameters

Date	the Date expression to be formatted.
NamedFormat	optional parameter that indicates the format of the new expression. The NameFormat can be one of the following constants shown in Table C-13.

Table C-13
FormatDateTime Constants

Constant	Value	Description
vbGeneralDate	0	Displays a date and/or time. If there is a date part, display it as a short date. If there is a time part, display it as long time. If present, both parts are displayed.
vbLongDate	1	Display a date using the long date format specified in your computer's regional settings.
vbShortDate	2	Displays a date using the short date format specified in your computer's regional settings.
vbLongTime	3	Displays a time using the long time format specified in your computer's regional settings.
VbShortTime	4	Displays a time using the short time format specified in your computer's regional settings.

Example

```
NewExpression = FormatDateTime(#January 3, 1974#, vbShortDate)
' NewExpression is assigned "1/3/74"
```

FormatNumber Function

Returns an expression that is formatted as a number.

Syntax

```
FormatNumber(Expression [,NumDigitsAfterDecimal
[,IncludeLeadingDigit [,UseParensForNegativeNumbers
[,GroupDigits]]]])
```

Parameters

Expression	the expression that is to be formatted
NumDigitsAfterDecimal	optional parameter that indicates the number of digits to include after the decimal point for the newly formatted expression
IncludeLeadingDigit	optional parameter that indicates whether the newly formatted expression should include a leading zero for a fractional value

UserParensForNegativeNumbers	optional parameter that indicates whether the newly formatted expression should use parentheses for negative values
GroupDigits	optional parameter that indicates whether numbers are grouped using the group delimiter specified in the control panel

Notes

Whenever an optional parameter is omitted, the values for the omitted arguments are provided by the server's regional settings.

Example

```
NewExpression = FormatNumber(25, 2)
'NewExpression is assigned "25.00"
```

FormatPercent Function

Returns an expression formatted as a percentage.

Syntax

```
FormatPercent(Expression[,NumDigitsAfterDecimal
[,IncludeLeadingDigit [,UseParensForNegativeNumbers
[,GroupDigits]]]])
```

Parameters

Expression	the expression that is to be formatted
NumDigitsAfterDecimal	optional parameter that indicates the number of digits to include after the decimal point for the newly formatted expression
IncludeLeadingDigit	optional parameter that indicates whether the newly formatted expression should include a leading zero for a fractional value
UserParensForNegativeNumbers	optional parameter that indicates whether the newly formatted expression should use parentheses for negative values
GroupDigits	optional parameter that indicates whether numbers are grouped using the group delimiter specified in the control panel

Notes

Whenever an optional parameter is omitted, the values for the omitted arguments are provided by the server's regional settings.

Example

```
NewExpression = FormatPercent(25, 2)
'NewExpression is assigned "25.00 %"
```

InputBox Function

Displays a prompt in a dialog box, waits for the user to input text or click a button, and returns a string containing the contents of the text box.

Syntax

```
InputBox(prompt[, title][, default][, xpos][, ypos][, helpfile,
context])
```

Parameters

prompt	required parameter that contains the message to be displayed.
title	optional string parameter that is displayed on the title bar of the dialog box.
default	optional string expression that is the default response. If omitted, the text box display is empty.
xpos	optional numeric expression that specifies the horizontal distance of the left edge of the dialog box from the left edge of the screen.
ypos	optional numeric expression that specifies the vertical distance of the top edge of the dialog box from the top edge of the screen.
helpfile	optional string expression that identifies the Help File to use to provide context-sensitive Help for the dialog box.
context	optional numeric expression that is used in conjunction with the helpfile argument. It specifies the Help context number assigned to the appropriate Help topic by the Help author.

Example

```
Dim Message, Title, Default, MyValue
Message = "Enter a value between 1 and 3"
Title = "Input Demo"
Default = "1"
MyValue = InputBox(Message, Title, Default)

'Use Helpfile and context.  The Help button is added
automatically.
MyValue = InputBox(Message, Title, , , , "Demo.Hlp", 10)
```

MsgBox Function

Displays a message in a dialog box, waits for the user to click a button, and returns an integer indicating which button the user clicked.

Syntax

    MsgBox(prompt[, buttons][, title][, helpfile, context])

Parameters

prompt	required string expression that is displayed as the message in the dialog box. The maximum length of prompt is approximately 1024 characters, depending on the width of the characters used.
buttons	optional numeric expression that is the sum of values specifying the number and type of buttons to display, the icon style to use, the identity of the default button, and the modality of the message box. If omitted, the default value for button is 0. Table C-14 shows the constants that are available for use.
title	optional string expression that is displayed on the title bar of the dialog box.
helpfile	optional string expression that identifies the Help File to use to provide context-sensitive Help for the dialog box.
context	optional numeric expression that is used in conjunction with the helpfile argument. It specifies the Help context number assigned to the appropriate Help topic by the Help author.

Table C-14
MsgBox Constants

Constant	Value	Description
vbOKOnly	0	Display OK button only.
vbOKCancel	1	Display OK and Cancel buttons.
vbAbortRetryIgnore	2	Display Abort, Retry, and Ignore buttons.
vbYesNoCancel	3	Display Yes, No, and Cancel buttons.
vbRetryCancel	4	Display Retry and Cancel buttons.
vbCritical	16	Display Critical Message icon.
vbQuestion	32	Display Warning Query icon.
vbExclamation	48	Display Warning Message icon.
vbInformation	64	Display Information Message icon.
vbDefaultButton1	0	First button is default.
vbDefaultButton2	256	Second button is default.

Constant	Value	Description
vbDefaultButton3	512	Third button is default.
vbDefaultButton4	768	Fourth button is default.
vbApplicationModal	0	Application modal; the user must respond to the message box before continuing work in the current application.
vbSystemModal	4096	System modal; all applications are suspended until the user responds to the message box.
vbMsgBoxHelpButton	16384	Adds Help button to the message box.
vbMsgBoxSetForeground	65536	Specifies the message box window as the foreground window.
vbMsgBoxRight	524288	Text is right aligned.
vbMsgBoxRtlReading	1048576	Specifies text should appear as right to left reading on Hebrew and Arabic systems.

TypeName Function

Returns a string expression that provides information about a variable.

Syntax

```
TypeName(varname)
```

Parameters

varname   required Variant containing any variable except a variable of a user-defined type

Notes

The string returned by TypeName can be any one of the following shown in Table C-15.

Table C-15	
TypeName Return Values	

String Returned	*Variable*
Object type	An object whose type is objecttype
Byte	Byte value
Integer	Integer
Long	Long integer
Single	Single-precision floating-point number
Double	Double-precision floating-point number
Currency	Currency value
Decimal	Decimal value
Date	Date value
String	String
Boolean	Boolean value
Error	An error value
Empty	Uninitialized
Null	No valid data
Object	An object
Unknown	An object whose type is unknown
Nothing	Object variable that doesn't refer to an object

Array Manipulation Functions

These functions are used to manipulate arrays and return information about them.

Array Function

Returns a Variant containing an array. The array consists of the elements found in arglist.

Syntax
```
Array(arglist)
```

Parameters

Arglist   comma-delimited list of array elements

Example
```
aValues = Array(1,2,3)
' Returns an array with three elements (1,2,3)
```

Filter Function

Returns a zero-based array containing a subset of a String array based on specified filter criteria.

Syntax
```
Filter(InputStrings, Value[, Include[, Compare]])
```

Parameters

InputStrings   required one-dimensional array of strings to be searched.

Value   required string for which to search in the InputStrings.

Include   optional Boolean value indicating whether to return substrings that include or exclude value. If Include is True, Filter returns the subset of the array that contains value as a substring. If Include is False, Filter returns the subset of the array that does not contain value as a substring.

Compare   optional numeric value indicating the kind of string comparison to use. The Compare argument can have the following values shown in Table C-16.

Table C-16
Compare Argument Options

Constant	Value	Description
vbUseCompareOption	−1	Performs a comparison using the setting of the Option Compare statement.
vbBinaryCompare	0	Performs a binary comparison.
vbTextCompare	1	Performs a textual comparison.
vbDatabaseCompare	2	This option is for Microsoft Access only. It performs a comparison based on information in your database.

Notes

If no matches of value are found within the Input Strings, the Filter function returns an array of empty values. An error occurs if Input Strings is null or is not a one-dimensional array.

Join Function

Returns a string created by joining a number of substrings contained in an array.

Syntax
```
Join(list[, delimiter])
```

Parameters

list   required one-dimensional array containing substrings to be joined.

delimiter   optional string character used to separate the substrings in the returned string. If omitted, the space character (" ") is used. If delimiter is the empty string (""), all items in the list are concatenated with no delimiters.

Example
```
VarArray = Array("a", "b", "c")
StrResult = Join(VarArray, ",")
' StrResults is assigned the string "a,b,c"
```

LBound Function

Returns a long expression that contains the smallest available subscript for the indicated dimension of an array.

Syntax
```
Lbound(arrayname[, dimension])
```

Parameters

arrayname   required array variable.

dimension   optional Variant indicating which dimension's lower bound is returned. If dimension is omitted, 1 is assumed.

Example
```
Dim A(1 to 100, 0 to 3, -3 to 4)
'Lbound(A, 1) will return 1
'Lbound(A, 2) will return 0
'Lbound(A, 3) will return -3
```

UBound Function

Returns a long expression that contains the largest available subscript for the indicated dimension of an array.

Syntax
```
UBound(arrayname[, dimension])
```

Parameters
arrayname   required array variable.

dimension   optional variant indicating which dimension's lower bound is returned. If dimension is omitted, 1 is assumed.

Example
```
Dim A(1 to 100, 0 to 3, -3 to 4)

'Ubound(A, 1) will return 100
'Ubound(A, 2) will return 3
'Ubound(A, 3) will return 4
```

String Manipulation Functions

These functions are used to manipulate strings and return information about them.

Asc Function

Returns the ANSI character code of the first letter in a string.

Syntax
```
Asc(string)
```

Parameters
string   string expression that contains at least one character.

Notes
If string evaluates to Null or Empty, then a run-time error is triggered.

Example
```
iAsc = Asc("Hello World") ' Returns the ANSI code for H
```

Chr Function

Returns a string containing the character associated with a specified ANSI character code.

Syntax

```
Chr(number)
```

Parameters

number   valid numeric expression

Notes

The value of number must evaluate to an ANSI character code (between 0 and 255). If number evaluates to Empty, it is assumed to be 0. If number evaluates to a value outside of this range or is Null, a run-time error is triggered.

Example

```
sChar = Chr(65) ' Returns "A"
```

InStr Function

Returns a Variant specifying the position of the first occurrence of one string within another.

Syntax

```
InStr([start, ]string1, string2[, compare])
```

Parameters

start   optional numeric parameter that indicates the position for the function to start the comparison. The default is 1.

string1   required string parameter that is the string on which to be searched.

string2   required string parameter that is the string for which to be searched.

compare   optional parameter that specifies the type of string comparison. It could be one of the following values, shown in Table C-17.

Table C-17
Compare Parameter Values

Constant	Value	Description
vbUseCompareOption	−1	Performs a comparison using the setting of the Option Compare statement.
vbBinaryCompare	0	Performs a binary comparison.
vbTextCompare	1	Performs a textual comparison.
vbDatabaseCompare	2	Microsoft Access only. Performs a comparison based on information in your database.

Example

```
intPosition = InStr(1, "abcdefghijk", "c")
'intPosition now is assigned a value of 3
```

InStrRev Function

Returns the position of an occurrence of one string within another, from the end of a specified string.

Syntax

```
InStrRev(string1, string2[, start[, compare]])
```

Parameters

string1	required parameter that represents the string to be searched.
string2	required parameter that represents the string for which to be searched.
start	optional numeric parameter that specifies the starting position of the search.
compare	optional parameter that specifies the type of string comparison. It could be one of the following values, shown in Table C-18.

Table C-18
Compare Parameter Values

Constant	Value	Description
vbUseCompareOption	−1	Performs a comparison using the setting of the Option Compare statement.
vbBinaryCompare	0	Performs a binary comparison.
vbTextCompare	1	Performs a textual comparison.
vbDatabaseCompare	2	Microsoft Access only. Performs a comparison based on information in your database.

Example

```
intPosition = InStrRev("abcdefghjk", "c")
'intPosition now is assigned a value of 8
```

LCase Function

Returns a string which has been converted to lowercase.

Syntax
```
LCase(string)
```

Parameters
string   contains the text to be converted to lowercase

Notes
If string is Null, LCase returns Null. If string is Empty, LCase returns a zero-length string.

Example
```
sText = LCase("Hello World")
' Returns "hello world"
```

Left Function

Returns a string containing a specified number of characters from the leftmost portion of a specified string.

Syntax
```
Left(string, number)
```

Parameters
string   contains the original text expression

number   contains the number of characters to extract from the leftmost portion of the string parameter

Notes
If number exceeds the length of string, Left returns string. If number is negative or Null, a run-time error is triggered. If string or number evaluate to Empty, a zero-length string is returned.

Example
```
sText = Left("Hello World",5) ' Returns "Hello"
```

Len Function

Returns a number representing the length of a specified string.

Syntax
```
Len(string)
```

Parameters
string   contains the text whose length is to be evaluated

Notes

If string evaluates to Empty, Len returns 0. If string evaluates to Null, a runtime error is triggered.

Example

```
sText = "Hello World"
iLength = Len(sText) ' Returns 11
```

LTrim Function

Returns a string that is a copy of a specified string without any leading spaces.

Syntax

```
LTrim(string)
```

Parameters

string   contains the text whose leading spaces are to be trimmed

Notes

LTrim does not remove carriage returns (ANSI code 13) or line feeds (ANSI code 10). If string evaluates to Null, LTrim returns Null. If string evaluates to Empty, then a zero-length string is returned.

Example

```
sText = LTrim("    Hello World") ' Returns "Hello World"
```

Mid Function

Returns a specified number of characters from a string.

Syntax

```
Mid(string, start[, length])
```

Parameters

string   contains the text of string to be extracted by the function

start   required numeric parameter that indicates the starting position of
           the extraction

length   optional numeric parameter that indicates the number of string
           characters to extract from the starting position specified

Example

```
strText = Mid("AbcdEFG", 1, 5)
'strText now is assigned "AbcdE"
```

Replace Function

Returns a string in which the specified substring has been replaced with another substring a specified number of times.

Syntax

```
Replace(expression, find, replacewith[, start[, count[,
compare]]])
```

Parameters

expression	required parameter that contains the text to replace.
find	required parameter that contains the string for which to search.
replacewith	required parameter that contains the string with which to replace find.
start	optional numeric parameter that indicates the starting position to search.
count	optional numeric parameter used in conjunction with the start parameter. The count parameter indicates the number of times to perform the replacement. If the argument is omitted, all possible substitutions are made.
compare	optional parameter that specifies the type of string comparison. It could be one of the following values, shown in Table C-19.

Table C-19
Compare Parameter Values

Constant	Value	Description
vbUseCompareOption	−1	Performs a comparison using the setting of the Option Compare statement.
vbBinaryCompare	0	Performs a binary comparison.
vbTextCompare	1	Performs a textual comparison.
vbDatabaseCompare	2	Microsoft Access only. Performs a comparison based on information in your database.

Example

```
strText = Replace("Hello World", "H", "h)
'strText now is assigned "hello World"
```

Right Function

Returns a string containing a specified number of characters from the rightmost portion of a specified string.

Syntax

```
Right(string, number)
```

Parameters

string   contains the original text to be extracted

number   optional numeric parameter that specifies the number of characters from the rightmost position to extract

Notes

If number exceeds the length of string, Right returns string. If number is negative or Null, a run-time error is triggered. If string or number evaluate to Empty, a zero-length string is returned.

Example

```
sText = Right("Hello World",5) ' Returns "World"
```

RTrim Function

Returns a string that is a copy of a specified string without trailing spaces.

Syntax

```
RTrim(string)
```

Parameters

string   contains the text whose trailing spaces are to be trimmed.

Notes

RTrim does not remove carriage returns (ANSI code 13) or line feeds (ANSI code 10). If string evaluates to Null, RTrim returns Null. If string evaluates to Empty, then a zero-length string is returned.

Example

```
sText = RTrim("Hello World    ") ' Returns "Hello World"
```

Space Function

Returns a string containing the specified number of spaces.

Syntax

```
Space(number)
```

Parameters

number   required parameter that indicates the number of spaces to return

Split Function

Returns a zero-base, one-dimensional array containing a specified number of substrings.

Syntax

```
Split(expression[, delimiter[, count[, compare]]])
```

Parameters

expression   required string parameter that contains the substrings and delimiters.

delimiter   optional string parameter that indicates the delimiter for the different substrings. If omitted, the space (" ") character is used.

count   optional numeric parameter that indicates the number of substrings to return. The default, –1, indicates that all substrings are returned.

compare   optional parameter that specifies the type of string comparison. It could be one of the following values, shown in Table C-20:

Table C-20 Compare Parameter Values		
Constant	Value	Description
vbUseCompareOption	–1	Performs a comparison using the setting of the Option Compare statement.
vbBinaryCompare	0	Performs a binary comparison.
vbTextCompare	1	Performs a textual comparison.
vbDatabaseCompare	2	Microsoft Access only. Performs a comparison based on information in your database.

StrComp Function

Returns a value indicating the result of a string comparison.

Syntax

```
StrComp(string1, string2[, compare])
```

Parameters

string1	required string parameter that can be any valid string expression.
string2	required string parameter that can be any valid string expression.
compare	optional parameter that specifies the type of string comparison. It could be one of the following values, shown in Table C-21:

Table C-21
Compare Parameter Values

Constant	Value	Description
vbBinaryCompare	0	Performs a binary comparison.
vbTextCompare	1	Performs a textual comparison.

Notes

Table C-22 lists the returned values from the function based on the comparison of string1 and string2.

Table C-22
StrComp Return Values

If	strComp returns
string1 is less than string2	−1
string1 is equal to string2	0
string1 is greater than string2	1
string1 or string2 is null	null*

String Function

Returns a repeating character string of specified length.

Syntax
```
String(number, character)
```

Parameters

number   length of the composed string

character   character code specifying the repeating character

Example
```
strText = String(5, "a")
'strText now is assigned the value of "aaaaa"
```

StrReverse Function

Returns a string in which the character order of a specified string is reversed.

Syntax
```
StrReverse(string1)
```

Parameters

string1   required parameter that contains text whose order is to be reversed

Example
```
strText = StrReverse("Hello World")
'strText now is assigned the value of "dlroW olleH"
```

Trim Function

Returns a string that is a copy of a specified string without any leading or trailing spaces.

Syntax
```
Trim(string)
```

Parameters

string   required parameter that contains text to be trimmed

Notes

Trim does not remove carriage returns (ANSI code 13) or line feeds (ANSI code 10). If string evaluates to Null, Trim returns Null. If string evaluates to Empty, then a zero-length string is returned. This function is equivalent to LTrim(RTrim(string)).

Example
```
sText = Trim("    Hello World    ") ' Returns "Hello World"
```

UCase Function

Returns a string that has been converted to uppercase.

Syntax

```
UCase(string)
```

Parameters

string   required string parameter whose value is to be converted to uppercase

Notes

If `string` is `Null`, `UCase` returns `Null`. If `string` is `Empty`, `UCase` returns a zero-length string.

Example

```
sText = UCase("Hello World") ' Returns "HELLO WORLD"
```

Date and Time Functions

These functions are used to manipulate dates and times and return information about them.

Date Function

Returns the current system date.

Syntax

```
Date()
```

Example

```
datCurrentDate = Date ' Returns current system date
```

DateAdd Function

Returns a date to which a specified time interval has been added.

Syntax

```
DateAdd(interval, number, date)
```

Parameters

interval   required string expression that is the interval of time you want to add. It can be one of the following values shown in Table C-23.

Table C-23
DateAdd Interval Options

Setting	Description
yyyy	Year
q	Quarter
m	Month
y	Day of year
d	Day
w	Weekday
ww	Week
h	Hour
n	Minute
s	Second

number	numeric expression containing the size of the time interval.
date	valid date expression to which the time interval is to be added.

Notes

If number evaluates to Empty, DateAdd returns date. If number is Null or is not a valid numeric expression, a run-time error is triggered. If date is Null, a run-time error is triggered. If date is Empty, the date is assumed to be 12:00 AM 12/30/1899.

Example
```
datToday = #12/24/77#
datNextMonth = DateAdd("m",1,datToday)  ' Returns 1/24/78
```

DateDiff Function

Returns a number representing the time interval between two dates.

Syntax
```
DateDiff(interval, date1, date2 [,firstdayofweek[,
firstweekofyear]])
```

Parameters

interval	required string expression that is the interval of time you want to add. It can be one of the following values, shown in Table C-24.
date1	valid date expression that is compared against.

date2	valid date expression that is compared with.
firstdayofweek	optional constant representing the first day of the week. The firstdayofweek argument can be one of the following values shown in Table C-25.

Table C-24
Interval Parameter Options

Setting	Description
yyyy	Year
q	Quarter
m	Month
y	Day of year
d	Day
w	Weekday
ww	Week
h	Hour
n	Minute
s	Second

Table C-25
Firstdayofweek Constants

Constant	Value	Description
vbUseSystem	0	Use the NLS API setting
vbSunday	1	Sunday (default)
vbMonday	2	Monday
vbTuesday	3	Tuesday
vbWednesday	4	Wednesday
vbThursday	5	Thursday
vbFriday	6	Friday
vbSaturday	7	Saturday

firstweekofyear   optional constant representing the first week of the
                         year. The firstweekofyear argument can be one
                         of the following values shown in Table C-26.

<table>
<tr><td colspan="3">Table C-26
Firstweekofyear Constants</td></tr>
<tr><td>*Constant*</td><td>*Value*</td><td>*Description*</td></tr>
<tr><td>vbUseSystem</td><td>0</td><td>**Use the NLS API Setting.**</td></tr>
<tr><td>vbFirstJan1</td><td>1</td><td>**Start with week in which January 1 occurs.**</td></tr>
<tr><td>vbFirstFourDays</td><td>2</td><td>**Start with the first week that has at least four days in the new year.**</td></tr>
<tr><td>vbFirstFullWeek</td><td>3</td><td>**Start with first full week of the year.**</td></tr>
</table>

Notes

If firstdayofweek is omitted, Sunday is assumed. If firstweekofyear is
omitted, the week in which January 1st occurs is assumed to be the first week. If
date1 occurs after date2, then DateDiff will return a negative number. If any
parameters are Null, or if date1 or date2 do not evaluate to a valid date, then a
runtime error will be triggered. If date1 or date2 is Empty, it is assumed to be
12:00 AM 12/30/1899.

Example

```
iDays = DateDiff("y", #12/24/77#, #11/30/77#) ' Returns -24
```

DatePart Function

Returns a number representing a particular part of a specified date.

Syntax

```
DatePart(interval, date[, firstdayofweek[, firstweekofyear]])
```

Parameters

interval   required string expression that is the interval of time you
                  want to add. It can be one of the following values shown in
                  Table C-27.

Table C-27
Interval Parameter Values

Setting	Description
yyyy	Year
q	Quarter
m	Month
y	Day of year
d	Day
w	Weekday
ww	Week
h	Hour
n	Minute
s	Second

date	required parameter that you want to evaluate.
firstdayofweek	optional constant representing the first day of the week, shown in Table C-28.

Table C-28
FirstDayOfWeek Parameter Values

Constant	Value	Description
vbUseSystem	0	Use the NLS API setting
vbSunday	1	Sunday (default)
vbMonday	2	Monday
vbTuesday	3	Tuesday
vbWednesday	4	Wednesday
vbThursday	5	Thursday
vbFriday	6	Friday
vbSaturday	7	Saturday

firstweekofyear   optional constant representing the first week of the year. The firstweekofyear argument can be one of the following values shown in Table C-29:

	Table C-29	
	Firstweekofyear Parameter Values	
Constant	*Value*	*Description*
vbUseSystem	0	Use the NLS API setting.
vbFirstJan1	1	Start with week in which January 1 occurs.
vbFirstFourDays	2	Start with the first week that has at least four days in the new year.
vbFirstFullWeek	3	Start with first full week of the year.

Notes

If firstdayofweek is omitted, Sunday is assumed. If firstweekofyear is omitted, the week during which January 1st occurs is assumed to be the first week. If interval or date is Null, or if date does not evaluate to a valid date, then a run-time error will be triggered. If date is Empty, the date is assumed to be 12:00 AM 12/30/1899.

Example

```
iDayOfYear = DatePart("y",#12/24/77#) ' Returns 358
```

DateSerial Function

Returns a Variant of subtype Date for a specified month, day, and year.

Syntax

```
DateSerial(year, month, day)
```

Parameters

    year   a valid numeric expression

    month   a valid numeric expression

    day   a valid numeric expression

Notes

The year must evaluate to a number between 100 and 9999. If month exceeds 12, it is interpreted as a combination of months and years. A value of 15 would be interpreted as 1 year 3 months. The same applies to day. If any parameter is Empty, it is interpreted as 0. If any parameter is Null or does not evaluate to a numeric expression, a run-time error is triggered.

Example
```
datDay = DateSerial(1977,12,24) ' Returns the date #12/24/1977#
```

Day Function

Returns the day of the month for a specified date.

Syntax
```
Day(date)
```

Parameters

date   a valid date expression.

Notes

If date is Null, or if date does not evaluate to a valid date, then a run-time error will be triggered. If date is Empty, the date is assumed to be 12/30/1899.

Example
```
iDay = Day(#12/24/77#) ' Returns 24
```

Hour Function

Returns the hour for a specified time.

Syntax
```
Hour(time)
```

Parameters

time   a valid time expression

Notes

If time is Null, or if time does not evaluate to a valid time, then a run-time error will be triggered. If time is Empty, the time is assumed to be 12:00 AM.

Example
```
iHour = Hour(#1:53:43 PM#) ' Returns 13
```

Minute Function

Returns the minute for a specified time.

Syntax
```
Minute(time)
```

Parameters

time   a valid time expression

Notes

If time is Null, or if time does not evaluate to a valid time, then a run-time error will be triggered. If time is Empty, the time is assumed to be 12:00 AM.

Example
```
iMinute = Minute(#1:53:43 PM#) ' Returns 53
```

Month Function

Returns the month of the year for a specified date.

Syntax
```
Month (date)
```

Parameters

date   a valid date expression

Notes

If date is Null, or if date does not evaluate to a valid date, then a run-time error will be triggered. If date is Empty, the date is assumed to be 12/30/1899.

Example
```
iMonth = Month(#12/24/77#) ' Returns 12
```

MonthName Function

Returns a string containing the name of the month for a specified date.

Syntax
```
MonthName(date[, abbreviate])
```

Parameters

date   a valid date expression that you want to evaluate

Abbreviate is an optional Boolean expression that specifies whether the month name should be abbreviated. The default is false.

Notes

If date is Null, or if date does not evaluate to a valid date, then a run-time error will be triggered. If date is Empty, the date is assumed to be 12/30/1899. If abbreviate evaluates to True, the three-letter abbreviation of the month name will be returned. If abbreviate evaluates to False or is omitted, MonthName returns the full name. If abbreviate evaluates to Null or a non-numeric expression, a run-time error will be triggered.

Example

```
sMonthName = MonthName(#12/24/77#, False) ' Returns "December"
```

Now Function

Returns the current system date and time.

Syntax

```
Now()
```

Example

```
datNow = Now ' Returns the current date and time
```

Second Function

Returns the number of seconds for a specified time.

Syntax

```
Second(time)
```

Parameters

time   a valid time expression that you want to evaluate

Notes

If time is Null, or if time does not evaluate to a valid time, then a run-time error will be triggered. If time is Empty, the time is assumed to be 12:00 AM.

Example

```
iSecond = Second(#1:53:43 PM#) ' Returns 43
```

Time Function

Returns the current system time.

Syntax

```
Time()
```

TimeSerial Function

Returns a variant containing the time for a specific hour, minutes, and seconds.

Syntax

```
TimeSerial(hour, minute, second)
```

Parameters

hour   required Variant (integer). A number between 0 (12:00 AM) and 23 (11:00 PM), inclusive.

minute   required Variant (integer). Any numeric expression.

second   required Variant (integer). Any numeric expression.

WeekDay Function

Returns a number between 1 and 7 representing the day of the week of a specified date.

Syntax

```
Weekday(date, [firstdayofweek])
```

Parameters

date   a valid date expression that you want to evaluate.

firstdayofweek   optional constant representing the first day of the week, shown in Table C-30.

Table C-30 FirstDayOfWeek Parameter Values		
Constant	**Value**	**Description**
vbUseSystem	0	Use the NLS API setting
vbSunday	1	Sunday (default)
vbMonday	2	Monday
vbTuesday	3	Tuesday
vbWednesday	4	Wednesday
vbThursday	5	Thursday
vbFriday	6	Friday
vbSaturday	7	Saturday

Notes

If firstdayofweek is omitted, Sunday is assumed. If date is Null, or if date does not evaluate to a valid date, then a run-time error will be triggered. If date is Empty, the date is assumed to be 12/30/1899.

Example
```
iWeekday = Weekday(#12/24/77#) ' Returns 7, indicating Saturday
```

WeekDayName Function

Returns a string containing the name of the weekday for a specified date.

Syntax
```
WeekdayName(date, [abbreviate], [firstdayofweek])
```

Parameters

date	required parameter that should contain a valid date expression that you want to evaluate.
abbreviate	optional parameter that indicates whether to abbreviate the week name.
firstdayofweek	optional constant representing the first day of the week, shown in Table C-31.

Table C-31
FirstDayOfWeek Parameter Values

Constant	Value	Description
vbUseSystem	0	Use the NLS API setting
vbSunday	1	Sunday (default)
vbMonday	2	Monday
vbTuesday	3	Tuesday
vbWednesday	4	Wednesday
vbThursday	5	Thursday
vbFriday	6	Friday
vbSaturday	7	Saturday

Notes

If firstdayofweek is omitted, Sunday is assumed. If date is Null, or if date does not evaluate to a valid date, then a run-time error will be triggered. If date is Empty, the date is assumed to be 12/30/1899. If abbreviate evaluates to True, the three-letter abbreviation of the weekday name will be returned. If abbreviate evaluates to False or is omitted, WeekdayName returns the full name. If abbreviate evaluates to Null or to a non-numeric expression, a run-time error will be triggered.

Example
```
sWeekdayName = WeekdayName(#12/24/77#, True) ' Returns "Sat"
```

Year Function

Returns the year for a specified date.

Syntax
```
Year(date)
```

Parameters
date   required parameter that should contain a valid date expression that you want to evaluate.

Notes
If date is Null, or if date does not evaluate to a valid date, then a run-time error will be triggered. If date is Empty, the date is assumed to be 12/30/1899.

Example
```
iYear = Year(#12/24/77#) ' Returns 1977
```

Math Functions

These functions are used to perform mathematical operations.

Abs Function

Returns the absolute value of a numeric expression.

Syntax
```
Abs(number)
```

Parameters
number   a valid numeric expression

Notes
If number evaluates to Null, Abs returns Null. If number evaluates to Empty, Abs returns 0. If number is not a valid numeric expression, a run-time error is triggered.

Example
```
iNumber = Abs(-1) ' Returns 1
```

Atn Function

Returns the arctangent of a number. The return value is expressed in radians.

Syntax

```
Atn(number)
```

Parameters

number   a valid numeric expression

Notes

The range of the function is –pi.2 <= Atn(number) <= pi/2. If number is Null, then a run-time error is triggered. If number is Empty, Atn **returns** 0. If number is not a valid numeric expression, a run-time error is triggered.

Example

```
dValue = Atn(1) ' Returns pi/4, or 45 degrees.
```

Cos Function

Returns the cosine of an angle.

Syntax

```
Cos(number)
```

Parameters

number   a valid numeric expression

Notes

Here, number represents an angle in radians. If number is Empty, Cos returns 1. If number is Null or is not a valid numeric expression, a run-time error is triggered.

Example

```
dPi = 3.1415
dValue = Cos(dPi/3) ' Returns 0.5
```

Exp Function

Returns the result of *e* raised to a numeric power.

Syntax

```
Exp(number)
```

Parameters

number   a valid numeric expression

Notes

In this context, *e* is the base of natural logarithms, or approximately 2.718282. If number is Null, then a run-time error is triggered. If number is Empty, Exp returns 1. If number is not a valid numeric expression, a run-time error is triggered.

Example
```
dValue = Exp(1) ' Returns the value of e = 2.718282
```

Fix Function

Returns the integer portion of a number.

Syntax
```
Fix(number)
```

Parameters
number   a valid numeric expression

Notes
This function does not round up to the nearest integer. Instead, it truncates all information following the decimal point. If number is Null, Fix returns Null. If number is Empty, Fix returns 0. If number is not a valid numeric expression, a run-time error is triggered. (See Int.)

Example
```
iValue1 = Fix(0.5) ' Returns 0
iValue2 = Fix(-2.5) ' Returns -2
```

Hex Function

Returns a string containing the hexadecimal (base 16) representation of a decimal number.

Syntax
```
Hex(number)
```

Parameters
number   a valid numeric expression

Notes
Any non-integral portion of number is discarded before the conversion takes place. If number is Null, Hex returns Null. If number is Empty, Hex returns 0. If number is not a valid numeric expression, a run-time error is triggered.

Example
```
sHex = Hex(10) ' Returns "A"
```

Int Function

Returns the integer portion of a number.

Syntax

```
Int (number)
```

Parameters

number   a valid numeric expression

Notes

This function does not round up to the nearest integer. Instead, it truncates all information following the decimal point. If number is Null, Int returns Null. If number is Empty, Int returns 0. If number is not a valid numeric expression, a run-time error is triggered. (See Fix.)

Example

```
iValue1 = Int(0.5) ' Returns 0
iValue2 = Int(-2.5) ' Returns -2
```

Log Function

Returns the natural logarithm of a number.

Syntax

```
Log(number)
```

Parameters

number   a valid numeric expression

Notes

The base of the natural logarithm is *e*, or approximately 2.718282. A run-time error is triggered if number is Null, Empty, or evaluates to an invalid numeric expression.

Example

```
dValue = Log(10) ' Returns the natural log of 10, or about 2.30
```

Oct Function

Returns a string containing the octal (base 8) representation of a decimal number.

Syntax

```
Oct(number)
```

Parameters

number   a valid numeric expression

Notes

Any non-integral portion of `number` is discarded before the conversion takes place. If `number` is `Null`, `Oct` returns `Null`. If `number` is `Empty`, `Oct` returns 0. If `number` is not a valid numeric expression, a run-time error is triggered.

Example

```
sOctValue = Oct(10) ' Returns 12
```

Rnd Function

Returns a randomly generated number in the range [0,1].

Syntax

```
Rnd[(number)]
```

Parameters

number   optional; a valid numeric expression

Notes

The optional parameter `number` takes on different meanings depending on its value. If `number` is negative, then it represents the seed for the random number generator. If `number` equals 0, `Rnd` returns the most recently generated random number. If `number` is positive or omitted, `Rnd` returns the next random number in the sequence.

Example

```
dValue = Fix(10 * Rnd) + 1 ' Returns a number between 1 and 10
```

Round Function

Returns a number that has been formatted to a specified number of decimal places.

Syntax

```
Round(number[,decimal_places])
```

Parameters

number   a valid numeric expression

decimal_places   optional; a valid numeric expression representing the number of decimal places

Notes

When formatting `number`, `Round` rounds to the closest decimal place. If `decimal_places` is omitted, `number` is rounded to the closest integer. If `number` is `Empty`, `Round` returns 0. If `number` is `Null` or is not a valid numeric expression, a run-time error is triggered.

Example

```
dRounded1 = Round(10.54321, 1) ' Returns 10.5
dRounded2 = Round(-10.54321) ' Returns -11
```

Sgn Function

Returns a number (0 or –1) depending on the sign of a number.

Syntax

```
Sgn(number)
```

Parameters

number   a valid numeric expression

Notes

If number is negative, Sgn returns –1. Otherwise, Sgn returns 0. If number is Empty, Sgn returns 0. If number is Null or not a valid numeric expression, a run-time error is triggered.

Example

```
iValue = Sgn(-100) ' Returns -1
```

Sin Function

Returns the sine of an angle.

Syntax

```
Sin(number)
```

Parameters

number   a valid numeric expression

Notes

Here, number represents an angle in radians. If number is Empty, Sin returns 0. If number is Null or is not a valid numeric expression, a run-time error is triggered.

Example

```
dPi = 3.1415
dValue = Sin(dPi/6) ' Returns 0.5
```

SQR Function

Returns the square root of a number.

Syntax

```
Sqr(number)
```

Parameters

number   a valid numeric expression

Notes

Here, number must be non-negative. If number is Empty, Sqr returns 0. If number is Null or not a valid numeric expression, a run-time error is triggered.

Example

```
dValue = Sqr(100) ' Returns 10
```

TAN Function

Returns the tangent of an angle.

Syntax

```
Tan(number)
```

Parameters

number   a valid numeric expression

Notes

Here, number represents an angle in radians. If number is Empty, Tan returns 0. If number is Null or not a valid numeric expression, a run-time error is triggered.

Example

```
dPi = 3.1415
dValue = Tan(dPi/4) ' Returns 1
```

Object Reference

The Request object retrieves values that the client browser passed to the server during an HTTP request. The variables are separated into five collections. If the provided variable is not found within any of the five collections, the object returns Empty. If the provided variable exists in more than one collection, then the object returns the value of the variable from the following collection precedence:

+ Query String

+ Form

+ Cookies

+ ClientCertificate

+ ServerVariables

The object is built into the ASP processing engine and does not have to be instantiated to be used.

Request Object Methods

BinaryRead Method

The BinaryRead method retrieves data sent to the server from the client as part of a POST request. This method retrieves the data from the client and stores it in a SafeArray. A SafeArray is an array that contains information about the number of dimensions and the bounds of its dimensions. The syntax is as follows:

```
variant = Request.BinaryRead(count)
```

variant	Contains an array of unsigned bytes returned by this method. This parameter will be of type VT_ARRAY | VT_UI1.

count   Before execution, specifies how many bytes to read from the client. After this method returns, count will contain the number of bytes read from the client successfully. The total number of bytes that will actually be read is less than or equal to Request.TotalBytes.

Request Object Properties

TotalBytes Property

The TotalBytes property is a read-only property that specifies the total number of bytes that was sent in the body of the request.

Request Object Collections

ClientCertificate Collection

Before you can use the ClientCertificate collection, you must configure your Web server to request client certificates. The ClientCertificate collection retrieves the certification fields (specified in the X.509 standard) from a request issued by the Web browser. If a Web browser uses the SSL3.0/PCT1 protocol (in other words, it uses a URL starting with https:// instead of http://) to connect to a server and the server requests certification, the browser sends the certification fields. The syntax is as follows:

```
Request.ClientCertificate([Key[SubField]])
```

Key   variable that specifies the name of the certification field to retrieve. A client certificate consists of the following fields shown in Table D-1.

Table D-1 Key Parameter Values	
Value	*Meaning*
Certificate *	A string containing the binary stream of the entire certificate content in ASN.1 format.
Flags *	A set of flags that provide additional client certificate information.
ceCertPresent *	A client certificate is present.
ceUnrecognizedIssuer *	The last certification in this chain is from an unknown issuer.

Value	Meaning
Issuer	A string that contains a list of subfield values containing information about the issuer of the certificate. If this value is specified without a SubField, the ClientCertificate collection returns a comma-separated list of subfields. For example, C=US, O=Verisign, and so forth.
SerialNumber	A string that contains the certification serial number as an ASCII representation of hexidecimal bytes separated by hyphens (-). For example, 04-67-F3-02.
Subject	A string that contains a list of subfield values that themselves contain information about the subject of the certificate. If this value is specified without a SubField, the ClientCertificate collection returns a comma-separated list of subfields. For example, C=US, O=Msft, and so forth.
ValidFrom	A date specifying when the certificate becomes valid. This date follows VBScript format and varies with international settings. For example, in the U.S., 9/26/96 11:59:59 PM.
ValidUntil	A date specifying when the certificate expires.

* To use these flags, you must include the client-certificate include file in your ASP page. If you are using VBScript, include cervbs.inc. If you are using JScript, include cerjavas.inc. These files are installed in the \Inetpub\ASPSamp\Samples directory.

SubField	optional parameter you can use to a retrieve an individual field in either the Subject or Issuer keys. This parameter is added to the Key parameter as a suffix. For example, IssuerO or SubjectCN. Table D-2 lists some common SubField values.

Table D-2
Common SubField Parameter Values

Value	Meaning
C	Specifies the name of the country of origin.
CN	Specifies the common name of the user. (This subfield is only used with the Subject key.)
GN	Specifies a given name.
I	Specifies a set of initials.
L	Specifies a locality.
O	Specifies the company or organization name.

Continued

Table D-2 *(continued)*	
Value	**Meaning**
OU	Specifies the name of the organizational unit.
S	Specifies a state or province.
T	Specifies the title of the person or organization.

Cookies Collection

The `Cookies` collection enables you to retrieve the values of the cookies sent in an HTTP request. The syntax is as follows:

```
Request.Cookies(cookie)[(key)|.HasKeys]
```

> `cookie` specifies the name of the cookie whose value is to be retrieved.
>
> `key` optional parameter that specifies the name of the subkey whose value is to be retrieved.
>
> `HasKeys` attribute of the cookie that indicates whether the cookie has keys.

The following example prints the value of `myCookie` in a Web page. Here is the value of the cookie named `myCookie`:

```
<%
```

Response.Write(Request.Cookies("myCookie"))

```
%>
```

Forms Collection

When the client browser passes the values entered in an HTML form that uses the POST method, the form elements and values are saved to the `Forms` collection. You can then use the `Forms` collection to retrieve values that the client browser passed to the server. The syntax is as follows:

```
Request.Form(element)[(index)|.Count]
```

> `element` specifies the name of the form element whose value is to be retrieved.
>
> `index` is used when multiple elements in the form have the same name.

The following shows a simple HTML form:

```
<FORM ACTION = "/scripts/submit.asp" Method = "post">
<P>Your first name: <INPUT NAME = "firstname" SIZE = 48>
<P>What is your favorite color: <SELECT NAME = "color">
<OPTION>Red
<OPTION>Blue
<OPTION>Black
<OPTION>White</SELECT>
<p><INPUT TYPE = SUBMIT>
</FORM>
```

The following code will demonstrate how to retrieve values from the "firstname" element and the "color" element:

```
<%
```

Response.Write Request.Form("firstname") _

 & ", your favorite color is: " _

 & Request.Form("color") & "<br>"

```
%>
```

QueryString Collection

The QueryString collection retrieves the values of the variables in the HTTP query string. The HTTP query string is specified by the values following the question mark (?). In the query string, the ampersand sign (&) is used to separate each set of variable and value. The equal sign (=) is used to assign a value to the variable. The syntax is as follows:

```
Request.QueryString(element)[(index)|.Count]
```

element   specifies the name of the form element whose value is to
            retrieved.

index   used when multiple elements in the form have the same
            name.

The following code demonstrates a simple HTTP query string:

```
MyPage.asp?variable1=value1&variable2=value2
```

Using the previous query string, the following code will retrieve the values of the two variables:

```
<%
```

Response.Write "Variable1 = " _

```
& Request.QueryString("variable1") & " " _

& "Variable 2 = " & Request.QueryString("variable2") _

& "<br>"

%>
```

ServerVariables Collection

The ServerVariables collection retrieves the values of predetermined environment variables. The syntax is as follows:

```
Request.ServerVariables(servenvar)
```

servenvar   Server Environment Variable: can be one of the strings shown in Table D-3.

Table D-3 Server Environment Variables	
String	**Description**
ALL_HTTP	All HTTP headers sent by the client.
ALL_RAW	Retrieves all headers in the raw form. The difference between ALL_RAW and ALL_HTTP is that ALL_HTTP places an HTTP_ prefix before the header name and the header name is always capitalized. In ALL_RAW, the header name and values appear as they are sent by the client.
APPL_MD_PATH	Retrieves the metabase path for the (WAM) Application for the ISAPI DLL.
APPL_PHYSICAL_PATH	Retrieves the physical path corresponding to the metabase path. IIS converts the APPL_MD_PATH to the physical (directory) path to return this value.
AUTH_PASSWORD	The value entered in the client's authentication dialog. This variable is only available if Basic authentication is used.
AUTH_TYPE	The authentication method that the server uses to validate users when they attempt to access a protected script.
AUTH_USER	Raw authenticated user name.
CERT_COOKIE	Unique ID for client certificate. Returned as a string. Can be used as a signature for the whole client certificate.

String	Description
CERT_FLAGS	bit0 is set to 1 if the client certificate is present. bit1 is set to 1 if the Certifying Authority of the client certificate is invalid (not in the list of recognized CA on the server).
CERT_ISSUER	Issuer field of the client certificate (O=MS, OU=IAS, CN=user name, C=USA).
CERT_KEYSIZE	Number of bits in Secure Sockets Layer connection key size (for example, 128).
CERT_SECRETKEYSIZE	Number of bits in server certificate private key (for example, 1024).
CERT_SERIALNUMBER	Serial number field of the client certificate.
CERT_SERVER_ISSUER	Issuer field of the server certificate.
CERT_SERVER_SUBJECT	Subject field of the server certificate.
CERT_SUBJECT	Subject field of the client certificate.
CONTENT_LENGTH	The length of the content as given by the client.
CONTENT_TYPE	The data type of the content. Used with queries that have attached information, such as the HTTP queries GET, POST, and PUT.
GATEWAY_INTERFACE	The revision of the CGI specification used by the server. The format is CGI/revision.
HTTP_<HeaderName>	The value stored in the header HeaderName. Any header other than those listed in this table must be prefixed by HTTP_ in order for the ServerVariables collection to retrieve its value. Note: The server interprets any underscore (_) characters in HeaderName as dashes in the actual header. For example, if you specify HTTP_MY_HEADER, the server searches for a header sent as MY-HEADER.
HTTPS	Returns ON if the request came in through secure channel (SSL), or returns OFF if the request is for a non-secure channel.
HTTPS_KEYSIZE	Number of bits in Secure Sockets Layer connection key size (for example, 128).
HTTPS_SECRETKEYSIZE	Number of bits in server certificate private key (for example, 1024).
HTTPS_SERVER_ISSUER	Issuer field of the server certificate.
HTTPS_SERVER_SUBJECT	Subject field of the server certificate.

Continued

Table D-3 *(continued)*

String	Description
INSTANCE_ID	The ID for the IIS instance in textual format. If the instance ID is 1, it appears as a string. You can use this variable to retrieve the ID of the Web-server instance (in the metabase) to which the request belongs.
INSTANCE_META_PATH	The metabase path for the instance of IIS that responds to the request.
LOCAL_ADDR	Returns the Server Address on which the request came in. This is important on multi-homed machines where there can be multiple IP addresses bound to a machine and you want to find out which address the request used.
LOGON_USER	The Windows NT account into which the user is logged.
PATH_INFO	Extra path information as given by the client. You can access scripts by using their virtual path and the PATH_INFO server variable. If this information comes from a URL, it is decoded by the server before it is passed to the CGI script.
PATH_TRANSLATED	A translated version of PATH_INFO that takes the path and performs any necessary virtual-to-physical mapping.
QUERY_STRING	Query information stored in the string following the question mark (?) in the HTTP request.
REMOTE_ADDR	The IP address of the remote host making the request.
REMOTE_HOST	The name of the host making the request. If the server does not have this information, it will set REMOTE_ADDR and leave this variable empty.
REMOTE_USER	Unmapped username string sent in by the User. This is the name that is sent by the user, as opposed to the ones that are modified by any authentication filter installed on the server.
REQUEST_Method	The method used to make the request. For HTTP, this is GET, HEAD, POST, and so forth.
SCRIPT_NAME	A virtual path to the script being executed. This is used for self-referencing URLs.
SERVER_NAME	The server's host name, DNS alias, or IP address as it would appear in self-referencing URLs.
SERVER_PORT	The port number to which the request was sent.
SERVER_PORT_SECURE	A string that contains either 0 or 1. If the request is being handled on the secure port, then this will be 1. Otherwise, it will be 0.

String	Description
SERVER_PROTOCOL	The name and revision of the request information protocol. The format is protocol/revision.
SERVER_SOFTWARE	The name and version of the server software that answers the request and runs the gateway. The format is name/version.
URL	Gives the base portion of the URL.

Response Object

The Response object is used to send output to the client. The object is built into the ASP processing engine and does not have to be instantiated to be used.

Response Object Methods

AddHeader Method

The AddHeader method adds an HTML header with a specified value. This method always adds a new HTTP header to the response. It will not replace an existing header of the same name. Once a header has been added, it cannot be removed. The syntax is as follows:

```
Response.AddHeader name, value
```

name   name of the header to add.

value   corresponding value to add to the header.

AppendToLog Method

The method adds a string to the end of the Web server log entry for this request. The syntax is as follows:

```
Response.AppendToLog string
```

string   text to append to the log file. Maximum length of this string is 80 characters and the string cannot contain a comma (,).

BinaryWrite Method

The method writes the given information to the current HTTP output without character-set conversion. This method is useful for writing nonstring information such as binary data required by a custom application. The syntax is as follows:

```
Response.BinaryWrite data
```

Data is output to the client.

Clear Method

The method clears the buffered HTML output. The syntax is as follows:

```
Response.Clear
```

End Method

The method stops the current ASP process and returns the current results in the buffered HTML output. The syntax is as follows:

```
Response.End
```

Flush Method

The method sends the currently buffered HTML output. The syntax is as follows:

```
Response.Flush
```

Redirect Method

The Redirect method sends a redirect message to the browser, causing it to attempt to connect to a different URL. The syntax is as follows:

```
Response.Redirect URL
```

URL   required parameter that references the URL to which the browser is redirected.

Write Method

The Write method writes the string parameter to the HTTP output. The syntax is as follows:

```
Response.Write string
```

string   string to be written to the HTTP output.

Response Object Properties

Buffer Property

The Buffer property is used to indicate whether the output is buffered before being sent to the client.

CacheControl Property

The `CacheControl` property determines whether proxy servers are able to cache the output generated by ASP.

CharSet Property

The `Charset` property appends the name of the character set (for example, `ISO-LATIN-7`) to the content-type header in the response object.

ContentType Property

The `ContentType` property specifies the HTTP content type for the response. If no `ContentType` is specified, the default is text/HTML.

Expires Property

The `Expires` property specifies the length of time before a page cached on a browser expires.

ExpiresAbsolute Property

The `ExpiresAbsolute` property specifies the date and time on which a page cached on a browser expires.

IsClientConnected Property

The `IsClientConnected` property indicates whether the client has disconnected from the server.

PICS Property

Adds the value of a PICS label to the `pics-label` field of the response header.

Status Property

The `Status` property returns the status line returned by the server.

Response Object Collections

Cookies Collection

The `Cookies` collection sets the value of a cookie. If the specified cookie does not exist, it is created. If the cookie exists, it takes the new value and the old value is discarded. The syntax is as follows:

```
Response.Cookies(cookie)[(key)] = value
```

cookie	name of the cookie whose value is changed.
key	name of the subkey within the cookie's collection whose value is changed.
value	value to be set into the cookie.

Server Object

The Server object provides access to methods and properties on the server. Most of these methods and properties serve as utility functions. The object is built into the ASP processing engine and does not have to be instantiated to be used.

Server Object Methods

CreateObject Method

The CreateObject method is used to create an instance of a specified server component. The syntax is as follows:

```
Server.CreateObject(progID)
```

| progID | specifies the type of object to create. The format for progID is [Vendor.]Component[.Version]. |

The following code demonstrates how to create an ADO Connection object:

```
<%

Dim rs

set rs = Server.CreateObject("ADODB.Connection")


%>
```

HTMLEncode Method

The HTMLEncode method applies HTML encoding to a specified string. The syntax is as follows:

```
Server.HTMLEncode(string)
```

| string | specifies the text to encode. The following code demonstrates the HTMLEncode method: |

```
<%
```

```
Dim strText

strText = Server.HTMLEncode ("The paragraph tage is <P>")

' strText now is set to:

' The paragraph tag is &lt;P&gt;

%>
```

MapPath Method

The `MapPath` method maps the specified virtual path (either the absolute path on the current server or the path relative to the current page) into a physical path. The syntax is as follows:

```
Server.MapPath(path)
```

path   specifies the relative or virtual path to map to a physical directory. If `path` starts with either a forward (/) or backward slash (\), the `MapPath` method returns a path as if `path` is a full virtual path. If `path` doesn't start with a slash, the `MapPath` method returns a path relative to the directory of the .asp file being processed.

The following example uses the server variable `PATH_INFO` to map the physical path of the current file. The following script

```
<%

Response.Write _

Server.MapPath(Request.ServerVariables("PATH_INFO"))

%>
```

produces the output

```
c:\inetpub\wwwroot\script\test.asp
```

URLEncode Method

The `URLEncode` method applies URL encoding rules, including escape characters, to the string. The syntax is as follows:

```
Server.URLEncode(URL)
```

URL   specifies the string to encode.

The following script

```
<%
```

Response.Write(Server.URLEncode("http://www.microsoft.com"))

```
%>
```

produces the output

```
http%3A%2F%2Fwww%2Emicrosoft%2Ecom
```

Server Object Properties

ScriptTimeout Property

The `ScriptTimeOut` property specifies the amount of time that a script can run before it times out. The syntax is as follows:

```
Server.ScriptTimeOut = numSeconds
```

`NumSeconds` specifies the number of seconds to set the property.

Session Object

`Session` objects are used to store information needed for a particular user session. The values stored in the `Session` objects are valid as long as the user is using the Web application. The most common usage for `Session` objects is to store user preferences that are needed throughout the Web application (for example, the `Session` object that stores the user's name, the user's ID, and the user's password). This object is built into the ASP engine and does not need to be instantiated manually.

Session Object Methods

Abandon Method

The `Abandon` method is used to destroy a `Session` object and release its resources.

Session Object Properties

CodePage Property

The `CodePage` property determines the codepage that will be used to display dynamic content.

LCID Property

An LCID specifies the locale identifier that is a standard international abbreviation that uniquely identifies one of the system-defined locales.

SessionID Property

The SessionID property returns the session identification for this user. Each session has a unique identifier that is generated by the server when the session is created. The session ID is returned as a Long data type.

Timeout Property

The Timeout property specifies the timeout period (in minutes) assigned to the Session object for this application. If the user does not refresh or request a page within the timeout period, the session ends.

Session Object Collections

Contents Collection

The Session.Contents collection contains all of the items that have been established for a session without using the <OBJECT> tag. The collection can be used to determine the value of a specific session item, or to iterate through the collection and retrieve a list of all items in the session.

The following code demonstrates the usage of the Session.Contents collection:

```
<%

Dim SessionKey

For Each SessionKey in Server.Contents

Response.Write(SessionKey) & " = " _

& Session.Contents(SessionKey) & "<BR>"

Next

%>
```

StaticObjects Collection

The StaticObjects collection contains all of the objects created with the <OBJECT> tag that have session scope. The collection can be used to determine the value of a specific property for an object, or to iterate through the collection and retrieve all properties for all objects.

The following code demonstrates the usage of the `Session.StaticObjects` collection:

```
<%

Dim objStatic

For Each objStatic in Server.StaticObjects

 Response.Write(objStatic & " = " & Session.StaticObjects(objStatic) & "<BR>"

Next

%>
```

Application Object

The `Application` object is used to store information pertaining to the Web application. The values in the Application object are valid as long as the Web application is running. The object is built into the ASP engine and does not need to be instantiated manually.

Application Object Methods

Lock Method

The `Lock` method is used to lock the `Application` object so that no other clients have access to the object. This method is most useful when trying to set, reset, or change the values stored in the `Application` object.

Unlock Method

The `Unlock` method is used to unlock the `Application` object so that other clients can have access to the object.

Application Object Collections

Contents Collection

The `Application.Contents` collection contains all of the items that have been established for a session without using the `<OBJECT>` tag. The collection can be used to determine the value of a specific application item, or to iterate through the collection and retrieve a list of all items in the application.

The following code demonstrates the usage of the `Application.Contents` collection:

```
<%

Dim ApplicationKey

For Each ApplicationKey in Application.Contents

Response.Write(ApplicationKey & " = " _

    & Application.Contents(ApplicationKey)

Next

%>
```

StaticObjects Collection

The `StaticObjects` collection contains all of the objects created with the `<OBJECT>` tag that have application scope. The collection can be used to determine the value of a specific property for an object, or to iterate through the collection and retrieve all properties for all objects.

The following code demonstrates the usage of the `Application.StaticObjects` collection:

```
<%

Dim objStatic

For Each objStatic in Application.StaticObjects

Response.Write(objStatic & " = " _

    & Application.StaticObjects(objStatic)

Next

%>
```

ADO Connection Object

Each `Connection` object represents a physical connection to a data source. After a successful connection to a data source using the `Open` method, the object acts as an interface to the data source. You can issue commands against the connected object and process the results.

Connection Object Methods

Open Method

The Open method is used to establish a physical connection to the data source specified.

```
object.Open [ConnectionString] [,UserID] [,Password]
[,OpenOptions]
```

ConnectionString	optional string parameter that contains connection information. See ConnectionString property for detailed information.
UserID	optional string parameter that contains a valid user identification that has access to the data source.
Password	optional string parameter that is used in conjunction with the UserID parameter.
OpenOptions	optional value that indicates how the connection will behave once opened.

```
<%

Sub OpenConnection()

Dim cn, strConnection


' creates an ADO Connection object

set cn = Server.CreateObject("ADODB.Connection")


' establishes the Connection string to be used

strConnection = "driver={SQL Server};server=srv;" & _

    "uid=sa;pwd=;database=pubs"


' opens the Connection object with the constructed

' connection string

cn.Open strConnection
```

```
' closes the Connection object

' and sets the reference to the object to nothing,

' which is always a good idea to relieve the computer

' of the unnecessary resources

cn.Close

set cn = nothing


End Sub

%>
```

Close Method

The Close method is used to close the connection to the data source. It is a good development habit to close the opened connection after completing all transactions. Closing the connection object releases system resources occupied by the object.

Execute Method

The Execute method is used to process prepared SQL queries, SQL statements, or stored procedures. The end results of calling the Execute method are either non-row-returning or row-returning.

```
object.Execute CommandText [,RecordsAffected] [,Options]
```

CommandText   string parameter that represents the SQL query, SQL statement, stored procedure, provider-specific text, or table name to execute. By providing the table name, the Execute method will return all records in the table.

RecordsAffected   optional numeric value that indicates the number of records that will be affected by executing the CommandText.

Options   optional long value that indicates how the provider should evaluate the CommandText argument.

EXAMPLE (for non-row-returning CommandText)
```
<% Sub ConnectionExecute()
```

```
Dim cn, strConnection, strCommand


' creates an ADO Connection object
set cn = Server.CreateObject("ADODB.Connection")


' establishes the Connection string to be used
strConnection = "driver={SQL Server};server=srv;" & _
   "uid=sa;pwd=;database=pubs"


' opens the Connection object with the constructed
' connection string
cn.Open strConnection


' establishes the Command Text to execute
strCommand = "UPDATE titles SET type = " & _
   "'self_help' WHERE type = 'psychology'"


' executes the command text using
' the connection object
cn.Execute strCommand


' closes the Connection object
' and sets the reference to the object to nothing,
' which is always good idea to relieve the computer
' of the unnecessary resources
```

```
    cn.Close

    set cn = nothing


  End Sub%>
```

EXAMPLE (for row-returning CommandText)

```
<%  Sub ConnectionExecute()

  Dim cn, strConnection, strCommand, rsResults


  ' creates an ADO Connection object

  set cn = Server.CreateObject("ADODB.Connection")


  ' creates an ADO Recordset object

  set rsResults = Server.CreateObject("ADODB.Recordset")


  ' establishes the Connection string to be used

  strConnection = "driver={SQL Server};server=srv;" & _

    "uid=sa;pwd=;database=pubs"


  ' opens the Connection object with the constructed

  ' connection string

  cn.Open strConnection


  ' establishes the Command Text to execute

  strCommand = "SELECT * FROM titles"
```

```
        ' executes the command text using

        ' the connection object

        set rsResults = cn.Execute(strCommand)


        ' closes the Recordset object

        ' and sets the reference to the object to nothing,

        ' which are always good ideas to relieve the computer

        ' of the unnecessary resources

        rsResults.Close

        set rsResults = nothing


        ' closes the Connection object

        ' and sets the reference to the object to nothing,

        ' which is always a good idea to relieve the computer

        ' of the unnecessary resources

        cn.Close

        set cn = nothing


    End Sub%>
```

BeginTrans Method

The `BeginTrans` method is used to tell the `Connection` object to begin a new set of transactions.

CommitTrans Method

The `CommitTrans` method is used to tell the `Connection` object to save any changes and to end the current transaction. It may also start a new transaction.

RollbackTrans Method

The RollbackTrans method is used to tell the Connection object to cancel any changes made during the current transaction and end the current transaction. It may also start a new transaction.

Cancel Method

For the Connection object, the Cancel method is used to terminate execution of any asynchronous Execute or Open method call.

ADO Connection Object Properties

Attribute Property

For the Connection object, the Attribute property is a read/write property that is used to indicate one or more characteristics of the object. The value contained by the Attribute property is the sum of one or more of the XactAttributeEnum values. Table D-4 lists the XactAttributeEnum values.

Table D-4 XActAttributeEnum Values	
Constant	*Description*
adXactCommitRetaining	Performs retaining commits; that is, calling CommitTrans automatically starts a new transaction. Not all providers support this value.
adXactAbortRetaining	Performs retaining aborts; that is, calling RollbackTrans automatically starts a new transaction. Not all providers support this value.

CommandTimeOut Property

The CommandTimeOut property is a read/write property. It is used to indicate the number of seconds the object will wait to execute a command before terminating the attempt and raising an error.

ConnectionString Property

The ConnectionString property is a read/write property. It is used to store information on how the connection with the data source is established. The ConnectionString property can be used to specify a data source by passing detailed connection parameters. Valid arguments for the ConnectionString property are listed in Table D-5.

Table D-5
ConnectionString Valid Arguments

Argument	Description
Provider	Specifies the name of a provider to use for the connection.
Data Source	Specifies the name of a data source for the connection; for example, a SQL Server database registered as an ODBC data source.
User ID	Specifies the user name to use when opening the connection.
Password	Specifies the password to use when opening the connection.
File Name	Specifies the name of a provider-specific file (for example, a persisted data source object) containing preset connection information.
Remote Provider	Specifies the name of a provider to use when opening a client-side connection. (Remote Data Service only.)
Remote Server	Specifies the path name of the sever to use when opening a client-side connection. (Remote Data Service only.)

ConnectionTimeOut Property

The ConnectionTimeOut property is a read/write property. It is used to indicate the number of seconds the object will wait to establish connection with the data source before terminating the attempt and generating an error.

CursorLocation Property

The CursorLocation property is a read/write property. It is used to indicate the location of the cursor engine. The CursorLocation can be adUseClient, in which case, the client-side cursors provided by the client-side cursor library is used. Or, the CursorLocation can be adUseServer, in which case, the server-side cursors are used.

DefaultDatabase Property

The DefaultDatabase property is a read/write property. It is used to map the database that is to be used by the Connection Object.

IsolationLevel Property

The IsolationLevel property is a read/write property. It is used to indicate the isolation level of the Connection object. Table D-6 lists the IsolationLevelEnum values that can be stored by the IsolationLevel property.

Table D-6
IsolationLevelEnum Values

Constant	Description
adXactUnspecified	Indicates that the provider is using a different IsolationLevel than specified, but that the level cannot be determined.
adXactChaos	Indicates that you cannot overwrite pending changes from more highly isolated transactions.
adXactBrowse	Indicates that from one transaction you can view uncommitted changes in other transactions.
adXactReadUncommitted	Same as adXactBrowse.
adXactCursorStability	Default. Indicates that from one transaction you can view changes in other transactions only after they've been committed.
adXactReadCommitted	Same as adXactCursorStability.
adXactRepeatableRead	Indicates that from one transaction you cannot see changes made in other transactions, but that requerying can bring new recordsets.
adXactIsolated	Indicates that transactions are conducted in isolation of other transactions.
adXactSerializable	Same as adXactIsolated.

Mode Property

The Model property is a read/write property. It is used to indicate the permission that is allowed by the Connection object. Table D-7 lists the ConnectModeEnum values that can be stored by the Mode property.

Table D-7
ConnectModeEnum Values

Constant	Description
adModeUnknown	Default. Indicates that the permissions have not yet been set or cannot be determined.
adModeRead	Indicates read-only permissions.
adModeWrite	Indicates write-only permissions.

Continued

Table D-7 *(continued)*	
Constant	*Description*
adModeReadWrite	Indicates read/write permissions.
adModeShareDenyRead	Prevents others from opening connection with read permissions.
adModeShareDenyWrite	Prevents others from opening connection with write permissions.
adModeShareExclusive	Prevents others from opening connection.
adModeShareDenyNone	Prevents others from opening connection with any permissions.

Provider Property

The Provider property is a read/write property. It is used to store information about the provider of the Connection object.

State Property

The State property is a read-only property. It is used indicate whether the Connection object is opened or closed. The value stored in the State property for the Connection object can either be adStateClosed, for a closed Connection object, or adStateOpen, for an open Connection object.

Version Property

The Version property is a read-only property. It is a string property that stores the ADO version number.

ADO Connection Object Collections

Errors Collection

The Errors collection contains Error objects generated by the provider regarding a single execution through the Connection object. During a single operation, the provider can generate one or more errors. When an error is encountered, it is placed into an Error object and the Error object is added to the Errors collection. If another operation encounters more errors, the Errors collection is cleared before adding new Error objects into the collection.

+ The `Clear` method of the `Errors` collection deletes all `Error` objects from the collection.

+ The `Item` method of the `Errors` collection returns an indexed `Error` object in the collection.

+ The `Count` property of the `Errors` collection indicates the number of `Error` objects that are contained in the collection.

ADO Recordset Object

Each `Recordset` object represents a set of records that is the result of executing a SQL statement, a store procedure, a `Command` object, or simply a table. After a recordset is opened and depending on the type of the cursor and the type of the locking specified, all data manipulation can be executed through the `Recordset` object.

ADO Recordset Object Methods

AddNew Method

The `AddNew` method is used to create a new record for an updatable `Recordset` object. The syntax is as follows:

```
object.AddNew [FieldList, ValueList]
```

FieldList   either a string indicating the field to update or an array of strings mapping to fields to update.

ValueList   used in conjunction with the `FieldList` parameter. If the `FieldList` is an array of field names, then the `ValueList` must be an equal-sized array of field values. Additionally, the order of field values in `ValueList` must match the order of field names in `FieldList`.

```
<% Sub RecordsetAddNew()

Dim cn, strConnection, strCommand, rsResults


' creates an ADO Connection object

set cn = Server.CreateObject("ADODB.Connection")
```

```
' creates an ADO Recordset object

set rsResults = Server.CreateObject("ADODB.Recordset")


' establishes the Connection string to be used

strConnection = "driver={SQL Server};server=srv;" & _

  "uid=sa;pwd=;database=pubs"


' opens the Connection object with the constructed

' connection string

cn.Open strConnection


' establishes the Command Text to execute

strCommand = "employee"


' executes the Command Text using

' the connection object

rsResults.open strCommand, cn, , , adCmdTable


rsResults.AddNew

rsResults("employeeid") = <employee_id>

rsResults("fname") = <first_name>

rsResults("lname") = <last_name>

rsResults.Update
```

```
' closes the Recordset object

' and sets the reference to the object to nothing,

' which are always good ideas to relieve the computer

' of the unnecessary resources

rsResults.Close

set rsResults = nothing


' closes the Connection object

' and sets the reference to the object to nothing,

' which are always good ideas to relieve the computer

' of the unnecessary resources

cn.Close

set cn = nothing


End Sub%>
```

Cancel Method

For a `Recordset` object, the `Cancel` method is used to cancel the execution of a pending asynchronous `Execute` method.

CancelBatch Method

For a `Recordset` object, the `CancelBatch` method is used to cancel the execution of a batch update. If the `Recordset` object is in immediate update mode and the `CancelBatch` method is called without providing the `AffectNum` parameter, an error will be generated.

```
object.CancelBatch [AffectRecords]
```

AffectRecords   optional parameter that represents an `AffectEnum` value. Table D-8 lists all `AffectEnum` values with brief descriptions.

Table D-8 AffectEnum Values	
Constant	**Description**
adAffectCurrent	Cancel pending updates only for the current record.
adAffectGroup	Cancel pending updates for records that satisfy the current Filter property setting. You must set the Filter property to one of the valid predefined constants in order to use this option.
adAffectAll	Default. Cancel pending updates for all the records in the Recordset object, including any hidden by the current Filter property setting.

CancelUpdate Method

The CancelUpdate method is used to cancel any updates made to the current record or to cancel the addition of a new record before the execution of the Update method is applied.

Clone Method

The Clone method is used to create a copy of the supplied recordset. The result of the Clone method is a recordset. The syntax is as follows:

```
set rstDuplicate = object.Clone([LockType])
```

rstDuplicate	the duplicated recordset.
Object	the recordset to be duplicated.
LockType	optional parameter that is used to indicate the permission of the duplicated recordset. The LockType parameter can be one of the two LockTypeEnum values listed in Table D-9.

Table D-9 LockType Values	
Constant	**Description**
adLockUnspecified	The clone is created with the same lock type as the original object (default value).
adLockReadOnly	The clone is created as read-only.

Delete Method

The `Delete` method is used to delete the current record in the recordset or to delete a group of records.

```
object.Delete [AffectRecords]
```

`AffectRecords` is an optional parameter that represents an `AffectEnum` value. The following table lists all the `AffectEnum` values with brief descriptions.

Table D-10 **AffectEnum Values**	
Constant	*Description*
adAffectCurrent	Cancel pending updates only for the current record.
adAffectGroup	Cancel pending updates for records that satisfy the current `Filter` property setting. You must set the `Filter` property to one of the valid predefined constants in order to use this option.
adAffectAll	Default. Cancel pending updates for all the records in the `Recordset` object, including any hidden by the current Filter property setting.

Move Method

The `Move` method is used to move the cursor of the `Recordset` object to a specified record. The syntax is as follows:

```
object.Move NumRecords [,Start]
```

NumRecords	signed long parameter specifying the number of positions that the cursor should move.
Start	optional string or variant parameter that represents a bookmark. One of the `BookmarkEnum` values shown in Table D-11 can be used in the `Start` parameter.

Table D-11 **Start Parameter Values**	
Constant	*Description*
adBookmarkCurrent	Default. Start at the current record.
adBookmarkFirst	Start at the first record.
adBookmarkLast	Start at the last record.

MoveFirst Method

The `MoveFirst` method is used to move the cursor to the first record in an opened `Recordset` object.

MoveLast Method

The `MoveLast` method is used to move the cursor to the last record in an opened `Recordset` object.

MoveNext Method

The `MoveNext` method is used to move the cursor to the next record in an opened `Recordet` object. If the `MoveNext` method is called while the cursor is pointing to the end of the `Recordset` object, then an error is generated.

MovePrevious Method

The `MovePrevious` method is used to move the cursor to the previous record in an opened `Recordset` object. If the `MovePrevious` method is called while the cursor is pointing to the beginning of the `Recordset` object, then an error is generated.

NextRecordset Method

The `NextRecordset` method is used to clear the current `Recordset` object and to retrieve the next recordset by executing a series of commands. This method is used only if you are executing a command that returns multiple recordsets or if you are executing a stored procedure that returns multiple recordsets. After executing the command or the stored procedure specified, the `Recordset` object returns the first recordset in the command or stored procedures. You must issue the `NextRecord` call to access the other recordsets. The syntax is as follows:

```
Set recordset2 = object.NextRecordset([RecordsAffected])
```

`RecordsAffected` is an optional variable to which the provider will return the number of records that the current operation affected.

Open Method

The `Open` method is used to open a cursor that represents records from a table, or result-records from executing a query. The syntax is as follows:

```
object.Open [Source] [,ActiveConnection] [,CursorType]
[,LockType] [,Options]
```

Source   optional string parameter that evaluates to a SQL statement, table name, name of a valid `Command` object, or stored procedure.

ActiveConnection   optional parameter that can be a string parameter, in which case, the parameter must contain ConnectionString (see ADODB.Connection object) properties. Or, the ActiveConnection can be a variant that references an opened ADO Connection object.

CursorType   optional parameter that specifies the type of cursor to open. CursorType can be one of the values shown in Table D-12.

Table D-12
CursorTypeEnum Values

Constant	Description
adOpenForwardOnly	Default. Opens a forward-only-type cursor.
adOpenKeyset	Opens a keyset-type cursor.
adOpenDynamic	Opens a dynamic-type cursor.
adOpenStatic	Opens a static-type cursor.

LockType   optional parameter that specifies the type of locking that should be applied to the recordset. LockType can be one of the LockTypeEnum values shown in Table D-13.

Table D-13
LockTypeEnum Values

Constant	Description
adLockReadOnly	Default. Read-only—you cannot alter the data.
adLockPessimistic	Pessimistic locking, record by record—the provider does what is necessary to ensure successful editing of the records, usually by locking records at the data source immediately upon editing.
adLockOptimistic	Optimistic locking, record by record—the provider uses optimistic locking, locking records only when you call the Update method.
adLockBatchOptimistic	Optimistic batch updates—required for batch update mode as opposed to immediate update mode.

Options   optional long parameter that tells the provider how to evaluate the `Source` parameter if the `Source` parameter represents things other than a `Command` object. The values can be one of the constants shown in Table D-14.

Constant	Description
	Table D-14 **Open Method Options**
adCmdText	Indicates that the provider should evaluate `Source` as a textual definition of a command.
adCmdTable	Indicates that the provider should evaluate `Source` as a table name.
adCmdStoredProc	Indicates that the provider should evaluate `Source` as a stored procedure.
adCmdUnknown	Indicates that the type of command in the `Source` argument is not known.

Requery Method

The `Requery` method is used to refresh the records returned by the `Recordset` object. The method does so by re-executing the query upon which the `Recordset` object is based.

Resync Method

The `Resync` method is used to resynchronize the records in the current `Recordset` object. By calling this method on a forward-only or a read-only `Recordset` object, the changes in the underlying database will be refreshed into the `Recordset` object. Calling the `Resync` method also cancels all pending batch updates.

Supports Method

The `Supports` method is used to determine if the `Recordset` object supports a certain type of functionality. The method returns a `Boolean` expression indicating whether the `Recordset` object supports the indicated function. The syntax is as follows:

```
set varBoolean = object.Supports(CursorOptions)
```

CursorOptions   one of the following `CursorOptionEnums`:

Table D-15
CursorOptionEnum Values

Constant	Description
adAddNew	You can use the AddNew method to add new records.
adApproxPosition	You can read and set the AbsolutePosition and AbsolutePage properties.
adBookmark	You can use the Bookmark property to access specific records.
adDelete	You can use the Delete method to delete records.
adHoldRecords	You can retrieve more records or change the next retrieve position without committing all pending changes.
adMovePrevious	You can use the MoveFirst and MovePrevious methods, and Move or GetRows methods to move the current record position backward without requiring bookmarks.
adResync	You can update the cursor with the data visible in the underlying database, using the Resync method.
adUpdate	You can use the Update method to modify existing data.
adUpdateBatch	You can use batch updating (UpdateBatch and CancelBatch methods) to transmit changes to the provider in groups.

Update Method

The Update method is used to save any changes that you have made to the current record in the Recordset object. The syntax is as follows:

```
object.Update [FieldList] [, ValueList]
```

FieldList   either a string indicating the field to update or an array of strings mapping to fields to update.

ValueList   used in conjunction with the FieldList parameter. If the FieldList is an array of field names, then the ValueList must be an equal-sized array of field values. Additionally, the order of field values in ValueList must match the order of field names in FieldList.

UpdateBatch Method

The UpdateBatch method is used to save all changes that you have made to the records in the Recordset object.

```
object.UpdateBatch [AffectedRecords]
```

AffectedRecords is an optional parameter that specifies which records to save. It is one of the following AffectEnum values:

Table D-16
AffectEnum Values

Constant	Description
adAffectCurrent	Cancel pending updates only for the current record.
adAffectGroup	Cancel pending updates for records that satisfy the current Filter property setting. You must set the Filter property to one of the valid predefined constants in order to use this option.
adAffectAll	Default. Cancel pending updates for all the records in the Recordset object, including any hidden by the current Filter property setting.

ADO Recordset Object Properties

AbsolutePage Property

The AbsolutePage property specifies in which page the current record resides. It sets or returns a long value from 1 to the number of pages in the Recordset object.

AbsolutePosition Property

The AbsolutePosition property specifies the ordinal position of the current record in the Recordset.

ActiveConnection Property

The ActiveConnection property specifies which Connection object to which the Recordset object is connected.

BOF Property

The BOF property indicates whether the current cursor is pointing at the beginning of the Recordset object.

EOF Property

The EOF property indicates whether the current cursor is pointing at the end of the Recordset object.

BookMark Property

The BookMark property returns a bookmark that identifies the current record in the Recordset object. It can also set the current record in the Recordset object to the record identified by a valid bookmark.

CacheSize Property

The CacheSize property returns the number of records that are cached locally in memory.

CursorLocation Property

The CursorLocation property returns or sets the location of the cursor engine. The value of the CursorLocation property can be one of the following constants.

Table D-17 CursorLocation Values	
Constant	**Description**
adUseClient	Uses client-side cursors supplied by a local cursor library. Local cursor engines will often allow many features that driver-supplied cursors may not, so using this setting may provide an advantage with respect to features that will be enabled. For backward-compatibility, the synonym adUseClientBatch is also supported.
adUseServer	Default. Uses data provider or driver-supplied cursors. These cursors are sometimes very flexible and allow for some additional sensitivity to reflecting changes that others make to the actual data source. However, some features of the Microsoft Client Cursor Provider (such as disassociated recordsets) cannot be simulated with server-side cursors and these features will then become unavailable with this setting.

Cursortype Property

The CursorType property indicates the type of cursor that is opened. The value of the CursorType property can be one of the following constants.

Table D-18
CursorType Values

Constant	Description
adOpenForwardOnly	Default. Forward-only cursor. Identical to a static cursor except that you can only scroll forward through records. This improves performance in situations when you only need to make a single pass through a recordset.
adOpenKeyset	Keyset cursor. Like a dynamic cursor, except that you can't see records that other users add, although records that other users delete are inaccessible from your recordset. Data changes by other users are still visible.
adOpenDynamic	Dynamic cursor. Additions, changes, and deletions by other users are visible, and all types of movement through the recordset are allowed, except for bookmarks if the provider doesn't support them.
adOpenStatic	Static cursor. A static copy of a set of records that you can use to find data or generate reports. Additions, changes, or deletions by other users are not visible.

EditMode Property

The EditMode property indicates the editing status of the current record. The value of the EditMode property can be one of the following EditModeEnum values.

Table D-19
EditModeEnum Values

Constant	Description
adEditNone	Indicates that no editing operation is in progress.
adEditInProgress	Indicates that data in the current record has been modified but not yet saved.
adEditAdd	Indicates that the AddNew method has been invoked, and the current record in the copy buffer is a new record that hasn't been saved in the database.

Filter Property

The Filter property is used to indicate the filter for the data in the Recordset object. The Filter property sets or returns a string containing the filtered field and the filter value.

LockType property

The LockType property is used to indicate the editing permission on the Recordset object. Setting the LockType property before opening the Recordset object will specify the type of locking to apply the Recordset object.

The LockType property sets or returns one of the following LockTypeEnum values:

Table D-20 LockTypeEnum Values	
Constant	**Description**
adLockReadOnly	Default. Read-only—you cannot alter the data.
adLockPessimistic	Pessimistic locking, record by record—the provider does what is necessary to ensure successful editing of the records, usually by locking records at the data source immediately upon editing.
adLockOptimistic	Optimistic locking, record by record—the provider uses optimistic locking, locking records only when you call the Update method.
adLockBatchOptimistic	Optimistic batch updates—required for batch update mode as opposed to immediate update mode.

MarshalOptions Property

The MarshalOptions property is only applied to a client-side Recordset object. It is used to indicate which record to marshal back to the server from the client.

The property sets or returns one of the following constants:

Table D-21 MarshalOptions Values	
Constant	*Description*
adMarshalAll	Default. Indicates that all rows are returned to the server.
adMarshalModifiedOnly	Indicates that only modified rows are returned to the server.

MaxRecords Property

The MaxRecords property sets or returns the number of maximum records the query should return to the Recordset object. The default is zero, which indicates no limit.

PageCount Property

The PageCount property indicates how many pages of the data the Recordset object contains.

PageSize Property

The PageSize property indicates how many records are in each page in the Recordset object.

RecordCount Property

The RecordCount property indicates how many records are in the Recordset object.

Sometimes the Recordset object does not know the number of records that are contained in the object. In that case, the object will return a value of –1 when the RecordCount property is being accessed. Using the MoveLast method will cause the whole recordset to be read, at which point the RecordCount property should be correct.

Sort Property

The Sort property specifies on which fields the Recordset object is sorted, and how each field is sorted (ascending or descending). If multiple fields are being sorted on, then the Sort property returns a string with commas separating each field name. The records are not physically sorted, but are accessed in the sorted order.

Source Property

The Source property indicates the source of the data in the Recordset object (command object, SQL statement, table name, or stored procedures).

State Property

For a Recordset object executing an asynchronous method, the State property describes the current state of the object.

The State property can be one of the following constants:

	Table D-22 State Values
Constant	**Description**
adStateClosed	Default. Indicates that the object is closed.
adStateOpen	Indicates that the object is open.

Status Property

The Status property of the Recordset object indicates the status of the current record in regards to bulk operations, such as a batch updated.

The property returns one or more of the following RecordStatusEnum values:

	Table D-23 RecordStatusEnum Values
Constant	**Description**
adRecOK	The record was successfully updated.
adRecNew	The record is new.
adRecModified	The record was modified.
adRecDeleted	The record was deleted.
adRecUnmodified	The record was not modified.
adRecInvalid	The record was not saved because its bookmark is invalid.
adRecMultipleChanges	The record was not saved because it would have affected multiple records.

Continued

Table D-23 *(continued)*	
Constant	**Description**
adRecPendingChanges	The record was not saved because it refers to a pending insert.
adRecCanceled	The record was not saved because the operation was canceled.
adRecCantRelease	The new record was not saved because of existing record locks.
adRecConcurrencyViolation	The record was not saved because optimistic concurrency was in use.
adRecIntegrityViolation	The record was not saved because the user violated integrity constraints.
adRecMaxChangesExceeded	The record was not saved because there were too many pending changes.
adRecObjectOpen	The record was not saved because of a conflict with an open storage object.
adRecOutOfMemory	The record was not saved because the computer has run out of memory.
adRecPermissionDenied	The record was not saved because the user has insufficient permissions.
adRecSchemaViolation	The record was not saved because it violates the structure of the underlying database.
adRecDBDeleted	The record has already been deleted from the data source.

ADO Recordset Object Collections

Fields Collection

The Fields collection contains Field objects. Each Field object corresponds to a column in the Recordset object.

Append Method

The Append method of the Fields collection appends a Field object to the collection. The syntax is as follows:

```
object.Append Name, Type [,DefinedSize] [,Attrib]
```

Name   indicates the name of the field to append.

Type	indicates the data type of the new field.
DefinedSize	optional parameter that indicates the size of the field.
Attrib	optional parameter that specifies the attribute of the new field.

Delete Method

The Delete method of the Fields collection deletes a Field object in the collection. The syntax is as follows:

```
object.Delete Field
```

Field   a variant designating the Field object to delete.

Refresh Method

The Refresh method of the Fields collection refreshes all Field objects in the collection.

Count Property

The Count property of the Fields collection indicates the number of Field objects that are contained in the collection.

ADO Command Object

Command objects are used to hold definitions of database actions, such as stored procedures or queries that you are going to execute. You can use a Command object to return records into a Recordset object, run a query with or without parameters, or read and change the structure of a database.

ADO Command Object Methods

Cancel Method

The Cancel method cancels execution of a pending execution of the Command object.

CreateParameter Method

The CreateParameter method creates a new parameter object with the specified properties within the Command object. The syntax is as follows:

```
object.CreateParamter [Name] [, Type] [, Direction] [,Size]
[,Value]
```

Name   optional String parameter specifying the name of the parameter object.

Type	optional type Long parameter specifying the data type of the parameter.
Direction	optional type Long parameter specifying the type of parameter.
Size	optional type Long parameter specifying the maximum length or byte size of the value of the parameter.
Value	optional Variant parameter specifying the value of the parameter.

```
<% Sub CommandCreateParameter()


    Dim cnn1 As ADODB.Connection

    Dim cmdByRoyalty As ADODB.Command

    Dim prmByRoyalty As ADODB.Parameter

    Dim rstByRoyalty As ADODB.Recordset

    Dim rstAuthors As ADODB.Recordset

    Dim intRoyalty As Integer

    Dim strAuthorID As String

    Dim strCnn As String


    ' Open connection.

    Set cnn1 = New ADODB.Connection

    strCnn = "driver={SQL Server};server=srv;" & _

      "uid=sa;pwd=;database=pubs"

    cnn1.Open strCnn

    cnn1.CursorLocation = adUseClient
```

```
' Open command object with one parameter.
Set cmdByRoyalty = New ADODB.Command
cmdByRoyalty.CommandText = "byroyalty"
cmdByRoyalty.CommandType = adCmdStoredProc


' Get parameter value and append parameter.
intRoyalty = Trim(InputBox("Enter royalty:"))
Set prmByRoyalty = _
   cmdByRoyalty.CreateParameter("percentage", _
   adInteger, adParamInput)
cmdByRoyalty.Parameters.Append prmByRoyalty
prmByRoyalty.Value = intRoyalty


' Create recordset by executing the command.
Set cmdByRoyalty.ActiveConnection = cnn1
Set rstByRoyalty = cmdByRoyalty.Execute


' Open the Authors table to get author names
Set rstAuthors = New ADODB.Recordset
rstAuthors.Open "authors", cnn1, , , adCmdTable


' Print current data in the recordset, adding
' author names from Authors table.
```

```
Debug.Print "Authors with " _

    & intRoyalty & " percent royalty"

Do While Not rstByRoyalty.EOF

  strAuthorID = rstByRoyalty!au_id

  Debug.Print "  " & rstByRoyalty!au_id & ", ";

  rstAuthors.Filter = "au_id = '" & strAuthorID & "'"

  Debug.Print rstAuthors!au_fname & " " _

    & rstAuthors!au_lname

  rstByRoyalty.MoveNext

Loop


rstByRoyalty.Close

rstAuthors.Close

cnn1.Close


End Sub %>
```

Execute Method

The `Execute` method is used to execute the query, SQL Statement, or stored procedure specified by the `CommandText` property. The syntax is as follows:

```
object.Execute [RecordsAffected] [, Parameter] [, Option]
```

`RecordsAffected`	optional type `Long` parameter that specifies the number of records that will be affected by executing the `Command` object.
`Parameter`	optional type `Variant` array, which contains parameter values to be used with SQL statements.
`Option`	optional type `Long` value that tells the provider how to evaluate the `CommandText` property of the object. `Option` can be one of the following values:

<table>
<tr><td colspan="2" align="center">Table D-24
Options Values</td></tr>
<tr><td>Constant</td><td>Description</td></tr>
<tr><td>adCmdText</td><td>Indicates that the provider should evaluate CommandText as a textual definition of a command, such as an SQL statement.</td></tr>
<tr><td>adCmdTable</td><td>Indicates that the provider should evaluate CommandText as a table name.</td></tr>
<tr><td>adCmdStoredProc</td><td>Indicates that the provider should evaluate CommandText as a stored procedure.</td></tr>
<tr><td>adCmdUnknown</td><td>Indicates that the type of command in CommandText is not known.</td></tr>
</table>

```
<%  Sub CommandExecute()


  ' assuming that rsResults is a valid Recordset object

  ' and that cmdFetch is a valid Command object

  set rsResults = cmdFetch.Execute


  ' rsResults now contains the result set of executing

  ' the command object


  End Sub %>
```

ADO Command Object Properties

ActiveConnection Property
The ActiveConnection property sets or returns the connection string or the name of the Connection object to which the Command object belongs.

CommandText Property
The CommandText property sets or returns a type string value, which contains a SQL statement, a table name, or a stored procedure call.

CommandTimeout Property

The CommandTimeout property indicates how long the object would wait while executing the command before canceling the execution and generating an error.

CommandType Property

The CommandType property specifies the type of Command object. The property sets or returns one of the following CommandTypeEnum values:

Table D-25 **CommandTypeEnum Values**	
Constant	*Description*
adCmdText	Evaluates CommandText as a textual definition of a command.
adCmdTable	Evaluates CommandText as a table name.
adCmdStoredProc	Evaluates CommandText as a stored procedure.
adCmdUnknown	Default. The type of command in the CommandText property is not known.

Name Property

The Name property indicates the name of the Command object.

Prepared Property

The Prepared property sets or returns a Boolean value that indicates whether to save a compiled version of a command before execution.

State Property

The State property describes the current state of the object. It sets or returns one of the following constants:

Table D-26 **State Property Values**	
Constants	*Description*
adStateClosed	Default. Indicates that the object is closed.
adStateOpen	Indicates that the object is open.

ADO Command Object Collections

Parameters Collection

The Parameters collection contains all parameter objects of the Command object.

Append Method

The Append method of the Parameters collection appends a parameter object into the collection. The syntax is as follows:

```
object.Append ParameterObject
```

ParameterObject   Parameter object to be appended to the collection.

Delete Method

The Delete method of the Parameters collection deletes a parameter object from the collection. The syntax is as follows:

```
object.Delete Index
```

Index   a type String value that represents the name of the object or the ordinal position of the object to be deleted.

Refresh Method

The Refresh method of the Parameters collection refreshes the entire collection. For the Parameters collection, executing the Refresh method will cause the Command object to retrieve provider-side parameter information for the stored procedure or parameterized query specified in the Command object.

Count Property

The Count property of the Parameters collection indicates the number of parameter objects that are contained in the collection.

ADO Error Object

An Error object contains descriptive information regarding errors that occurred during a single operation of any of the ADO objects.

ADO Error Object Properties

Description Property

The Description property contains a type string value that describes the nature of the error that occurred.

HelpContext Property

The HelpContext property contains a type long value that indicates the Context ID mapping to a topic in a Microsoft Windows Help file.

HelpFile Property

The HelpFile property contains a type string value that evaluates to a fully resolved path to the help file.

NativeError Property

The NativeError property contains a type long value that indicates error-code associated with the provider.

Number Property

The Number property contains a type long value that uniquely identifies the Error object.

Source Property

The Source property contains a type string value that represents the name of the object or the name of the application that caused the error.

SQLstate Property

The SQLState property contains a five-character type string value that indicates the state of the Error object.

ADO Field Object

A Field object represents a column of data with a common data type.

ADO Field Object Methods

AppendChunk Method

The AppendChunk method is used to append a large text or binary data to the Field object. The syntax is as follows:

```
object.AppendChunk Data
```

Data   type Variant data that is to be appended to the Field object.

GetChunk Method

The GetChunk method is used to retrieve all or a portion of the data in the Field object. The syntax is as follows:

```
object.GetChunk(Size)
```

Size   a type Long variable that specifies the byte-size or number of
characters to retrieve from the Field object.

ADO Field Object Properties

Actualsize Property

The ActualSize property returns the length of the Field object's value.

Attributes Property

The Attributes property indicates the characteristics of the Field object. The property is read-only and it can be one or the sum of the following FieldAttributeEnum values:

<table>
<tr><td colspan="2" align="center">Table D-27
FieldAttributeEnum Values</td></tr>
<tr><td>*Constant*</td><td>*Description*</td></tr>
<tr><td>adFldMayDefer</td><td>Indicates that the field is deferred, that is, the field values are not retrieved from the data source with the whole record, but only when you explicitly access them.</td></tr>
<tr><td>adFldUpdatable</td><td>Indicates that you can write to the field.</td></tr>
<tr><td>adFldUnknownUpdatable</td><td>Indicates that the provider cannot determine if you can write to the field.</td></tr>
<tr><td>adFldFixed</td><td>Indicates that the field contains fixed-length data.</td></tr>
<tr><td>adFldIsNullable</td><td>Indicates that the field accepts Null values.</td></tr>
<tr><td>adFldMayBeNull</td><td>Indicates that you can read Null values from the field.</td></tr>
<tr><td>adFldLong</td><td>Indicates that the field is a long binary field. Also indicates that you can use the AppendChunk and GetChunk methods.</td></tr>
<tr><td>adFldRowID</td><td>Indicates that the field contains some kind of record ID (record number, unique identifier, and so forth).</td></tr>
<tr><td>adFldRowVersion</td><td>Indicates that the field contains some kind of time or date stamp used to track updates.</td></tr>
<tr><td>adFldCacheDeferred</td><td>Indicates that the provider caches field values and that subsequent reads are done from the cache.</td></tr>
</table>

DefinedSize Property

The `DefinedSize` property returns the defined size of the `Field` object.

Name Property

The `Name` property returns the name of the `Field` object.

NumericScale Property

The `NumericScale` property indicates the scale of numeric value in the `Field` object. This property is usually used to determine the number of decimal places to use with numeric `Field` object.

OriginalValue Property

The `OriginalValue` property is used to indicate the original value of the `Field` object before any changes were made.

Precision Property

The `Precision` property is used to determine the degree of precision for a numeric `Field` object.

Type Property

The `Type` property is used to determine the data type of the `Field` object. The property returns one of the following `DataTypeEnum` values:

Table D-28 DataTypeEnum Values	
Constant	**Description**
adArray	Ordered together with another type to indicate that the data is a safe-array of that type (DBTYPE_ARRAY).
adBigInt	An eight-byte signed integer (DBTYPE_I8).
adBinary	A binary value (DBTYPE_BYTES).
adBoolean	A Boolean value (DBTYPE_BOOL).
adByRef	Ordered together with another type to indicate that the data is a pointer to data of the other type (DBTYPE_BYREF).
adBSTR	A null-terminated character string (Unicode) (DBTYPE_BSTR).
adChar	A String value (DBTYPE_STR).
adCurrency	A currency value (DBTYPE_CY). Currency is a fixed-point number with four digits to the right of the decimal point. It is stored in an eight-byte signed integer scaled by 10,000.

Constant	Description
adDate	A Date value (DBTYPE_DATE). A date is stored as a Double, the whole part of which is the number of days since December 30, 1899, and the fractional part of which is the fraction of a day.
adDBDate	A date value (yyyymmdd) (DBTYPE_DBDATE).
adDBTime	A time value (hhmmss) (DBTYPE_DBTIME).
adDBTimeStamp	A date-time stamp (yyyymmddhhmmss plus a fraction in billionths) (DBTYPE_DBTIMESTAMP).
adDecimal	An exact numeric value with a fixed precision and scale (DBTYPE_DECIMAL).
adDouble	A double-precision floating point value (DBTYPE_R8).
adEmpty	No value was specified (DBTYPE_EMPTY).
adError	A 32-bit error code (DBTYPE_ERROR).
adGUID	A globally unique identifier (GUID) (DBTYPE_GUID).
adIDispatch	A pointer to an IDispatch interface on an OLE object (DBTYPE_IDISPATCH).
adInteger	A four-byte signed integer (DBTYPE_I4).
adIUnknown	A pointer to an IUnknown interface on an OLE object (DBTYPE_IUNKNOWN).
adLongVarBinary	A long binary value (Parameter object only).
adLongVarChar	A long String value (Parameter object only).
adLongVarWChar	A long null-terminated string value (Parameter object only).
adNumeric	An exact numeric value with a fixed precision and scale (DBTYPE_NUMERIC).
adSingle	A single-precision floating point value (DBTYPE_R4).
adSmallInt	A two-byte signed integer (DBTYPE_I2).
adTinyInt	A one-byte signed integer (DBTYPE_I1).
adUnsignedBigInt	An eight-byte unsigned integer (DBTYPE_UI8).
adUnsignedInt	A four-byte unsigned integer (DBTYPE_UI4).
adUnsignedSmallInt	A two-byte unsigned integer (DBTYPE_UI2).
adUnsignedTinyInt	A one-byte unsigned integer (DBTYPE_UI1).
adUserDefined	A user-defined variable (DBTYPE_UDT).

Continued

Constant	Description
adVarBinary	A binary value (Parameter object only).
adVarChar	A String value (Parameter object only).
adVariant	An Automation Variant (DBTYPE_VARIANT).
adVector	Or'd together with another type to indicate that the data is a DBVECTOR structure, as defined by OLE DB, that contains a count of elements and a pointer to data of the other type (DBTYPE_VECTOR).
adVarWChar	A null-terminated Unicode character string (Parameter object only).
adWChar	A null-terminated Unicode character string (DBTYPE_WSTR).

Table D-28 *(continued)*

UnderlyingValue Property

The UnderlyingValue property is used to return the Field object's current value in the database.

Value Property

The Value property is used to set or return the Field object's value.

ADO Parameter Object

A Parameter object represents a parameter or argument associated with a Command object based on a parameterized query or stored procedure.

ADO Parameter Object Methods

AppendChunk Method

The AppendChunk method is used to append a large text or binary data to the Parameter object. The syntax is as follows:

```
object.AppendChunk Data
```

Data   a type Variant value that represents the data to be appended to the Parameter object.

ADO Parameter Object Properties

Attributes Property

The Attributes property describes the characteristics of the Parameter objects. The values of the Attributes property can be one or the sum of the following ParameterAttributesEnum values:

Table D-29
ParameterAttributesEnum Values

Constant	Description
adParamSigned	Default. Indicates that the parameter accepts signed values.
adParamNullable	Indicates that the parameter accepts Null values.
adParamLong	Indicates that the parameter accepts long binary data.

Direction Property

The Direction property is used to indicate whether the Parameter object is an input parameter, an output parameter, or both, or if the parameter is the return value from a stored procedure. The Direction property sets or returns one of the following ParameterDirectionEnums:

Table D-30
ParameterDirectionEnum Values

Constant	Description
adParamInput	Default. Indicates an input parameter.
adParamOutput	Indicates an output parameter.
adParamInputOutput	Indicates both an input and output parameter.
adParamReturnValue	Indicates a return value.

Name Property

The Name property refers to the name of the Parameter object.

NumericScale Property

The NumericScale property is used to set or to return a byte value, indicating the number of decimal places to which numeric values will be resolved.

Precision Property

The Precision property is used to set or to return a byte value, indicating the maximum total number of digits used to represent values. This property is read/write.

Size Property

The Size property is used to set or to return a long value that indicates the maximum size in bytes or characters of the value in a Parameter object.

Type Property

The Type property is used to indicate the data type of value of the Parameter object. The Type property maps to one of the DataTypeEnum values.

Value Property

The Value property indicates the assigned value of the Parameter object. This property can be used to set or retrieve the value of the Parameter object.

Ad Rotator Object

The Ad Rotator object automates the rotation of advertisement images on a Web page. Each time a user loads or refreshes the page, the object display a new advertisement based on the information specified in the Rotator Schedule File.

Ad Rotator Object Methods

GetAdvertisement Method

The object uses the GetAdvertisement method to get the specifications for the next scheduled advertisement from the data file and to format that information into HTML.

Ad Rotator Object Properties

Border Property

The Border property specifies the size of the border around the advertisement.

Clickable Property

The `Clickable` property indicates whether the advertisement is clickable.

TargetFrame Property

The `TargetFrame` property specifies the name of the frame in which to display the advertisement.

Rotator Schedule File

The Rotator Schedule file contains information that the `Ad Rotator` component uses to manage and display the various advertisement images. This file must be available on a Web server virtual path. In it, you can specify the details for the advertisements, such as the size of the advertisement space, the image files to use, and the percentage of time that each file should be displayed.

The Rotator Schedule file has two sections. The first section sets parameters that apply to all advertisement images in the rotation schedule. The second section specifies file and location information for each individual advertisement and the percentage of display time that each advertisement should receive. A line containing only an asterisk (*) separates the two sections.

The first section has four global parameters, each consisting of a keyword and a value. All are optional. If you do not specify values for the global parameters, the `Ad Rotator` uses default values. In this case, the first line of the file must contain only an asterisk (*). The syntax for the file is as follows:

```
[REDIRECT URL]
[WIDTH numWidth]
[HEIGHT numHeight]
[BORDER numBorder]
*
adURL
adHomePageURL
Text
impressions
```

URL
: specifies the path to the dynamic-link library (.dll) or application (.asp) file that implements redirection. This path can be specified either fully (`http://MyServer/MyDir/redirect.asp`) or relative to the virtual directory (`/MyDir/redirect.asp`).

numWidth
: specifies the width of the advertisement on the page, in pixels. The default is 440 pixels.

numHeight
: specifies the height of the advertisement on the page, in pixels. The default is 60 pixels.

numBorder	specifies the thickness of the hyperlink border around the advertisement, in pixels. The default is a one-pixel border. Set this parameter to 0 for no border.
adURL	location of the advertisement image file.
adHomePageURL	location of the advertiser's home page. If the advertiser does not have a home page, put a hyphen (-) on this line to indicate that there is no link for this ad.
Text	alternate text that is displayed if the browser does not support graphics, or has its graphics capabilities turned off.
impressions	number between 0 and 4,294,967,295 that indicates the relative weight of the advertisement.

For example, if a Rotator Schedule file contains three ads with impressions set to 2, 3, and 5, the first advertisement is displayed 20 percent of the time, the second 30 percent of the time, and the third 50 percent of the time.

The following script demonstrates how you can use a Rotator Schedule file to display a variety of advertisements and how to include a redirection file.

```
REDIRECT /scripts/adredir.asp
WIDTH 440
HEIGHT 60
BORDER 1
*
http://kabaweb/ads/homepage/chlogolg.gif
http://www.bytecomp.com/
Check out the ByteComp Technology Center
20
http://kabaweb/ads/homepage/gamichlg.gif
-
Sponsored by Flyteworks
20
http://kabaweb/ads/homepage/ismodemlg.gif
http:// www.proelectron.com/
28.8 internal PC modem, only $99
80
http://kabaweb/ads/homepage/spranklg.gif
http://www.clocktower.com/
The #1 Sports site on the net
10
```

Redirection File

The Redirection file is a file that you create. It includes script to parse the query string sent by the Ad Rotator object and redirect the user to the URL associated with the advertisement that the users can click.

You can also include script in the Redirection file to count the number of users that have clicked a particular advertisement, and save this information to a file on the server.

The following example redirects the user to the advertiser's home page.

```
<% Response.Redirect(Request.QueryString("url")) %>
```

Dictionary Object

The Dictionary object is used to store pairings of data keys and items. This object is often useful when used as an associative array. Items, which can be any form of data, are stored in the array. Each item is associated with a unique key. The key is used to retrieve an individual item and is usually an integer or a string, but can be anything except an array.

Dictionary Object Methods

Add Method

The Add method is used to add a key and item pair to the Dictionary object. If the key exists in the object already, then the method will generate an error. Thus, before using the Add method, the developer should use the Exists method to check to see if the key is referenced in the object already. The syntax is as follows:

```
object.Add key, item
```

> key   required parameter that indicates the key of the item to be added.
>
> item   required parameter that is associated with the key.

Exists Method

The Exists method is used to check to see if a provided key is referenced in the object already. The method returns a True Boolean value if the key is referenced already; otherwise, the method returns a False Boolean value. The syntax is as follows:

```
object.Exists key
```

> key   required string parameter that specifies the name of the key to check for existence.

Items Method

The Items method is used to return an array containing all items in the Dictionary object. Here is an example of using the Items method:

```
<% Function DicDemo

    Dim a, d, i, s    'Create some variables

    Set d = CreateObject("Scripting.Dictionary")

    d.Add "a", "Athens"   'Add some keys and items

    d.Add "b", "Belgrade"

    d.Add "c", "Cairo"

    a = d.Items       'Get the items

    For i = 0 To d.Count -1 'Iterate the array

      s = s & a(i) & "<BR>" 'Create return string

    Next

    DicDemo = s

  End Function %>
```

Keys Method

The Keys method is used to return an array containing all keys in the Dictionary object. Here is an example of how to use the Keys method:

```
<% Function DicDemo

   Dim a, d, i     'Create some variables

   Set d = CreateObject("Scripting.Dictionary")

   d.Add "a", "Athens"   'Add some keys and items.

   d.Add "b", "Belgrade"

   d.Add "c", "Cairo"

   a = d.Keys      'Get the keys

   For i = 0 To d.Count -1 'Iterate the array
```

     s = s & a(i) & "<BR>" 'Return results

  Next

  DicDemo = s

  End Function %>

Remove Method

The Remove method is used to remove a key and item pairing from the Dictionary object. The syntax is as follows:

```
object.Remove key
```

    key   required string parameter that specifies the name of the key to delete.

RemoveAll Method

The RemoveAll method is used to remove all key-item pairings from the Dictionary object.

Dictionary Object Properties

CompareMode Property

The CompareMode property is used to set and to return the comparison mode for comparing string keys in the Dictionary object. The property can be one of the following constants:

Table D-31		
CompareMode Options		
Constant	**Value**	**Description**
vbBinaryCompare	0	Perform a binary comparison.
vbTextCompare	1	Perform a textual comparison.

Count Property

The Count property is a read-only property that returns the number of items in the Dictionary object.

Item Property

The Item property is used to set or to return an Item for a specified Key in the Dictionary object. The syntax is as follows:

```
object.Item(key)
```

> key   the Key associated with the Item in the Dictionary object.

Key Property

The Key property is used to set a key in the Dictionary object. The syntax is as follows:

```
object.Key(key) = newKey
```

> Key   required string parameter that specifies the Key to be changed.
>
> NewKey   required string parameter that specifies the new name of the Key.

FileSystemObject Object

The FileSystemObject is an object used to provide access to the computer's file system.

FileSystemObject Object Methods

BuildPath Method

The BuildPath method inserts an additional path separator (only if necessary) between the existing path and the name. The syntax is as follows:

```
object.BuildPath(Path, Name)
```

> Path   required string parameter that specifies the existing path to which Name is appended. Path can be absolute or relative and need not specify an existing folder.
>
> Name   required string parameter that specifies the Name to append to the Path parameter.

CopyFile Method

The CopyFile method copies one or more files from the source location to the destination location. The syntax is as follows:

```
object.CopyFile Source, Destination [, OverWrite]
```

Source
: required string parameter that specifies the file(s) to copy to the destination location. Wild card characters can be used to include one or more files to copy.

Destination
: required string parameter that specifies the destination file(s). Wild card characters are not allowed in this parameter.

OverWrite
: optional Boolean value that indicates if any existing file(s) can be overwritten with the new file(s).

CopyFolder Method

The CopyFolder method copies one or more folders from the source location to the destination location. The syntax is as follows:

```
object.CopyFolder Source, Destination [, OverWrite]
```

Source
: required string parameter that specifies the folder(s) to copy to the destination location. Wild card characters can be used to include one or more folders to copy.

Destination
: a required string parameter that specifies the destination folder(s). Wild card characters are not allowed in this parameter.

OverWrite
: an optional Boolean value that indicates if any existing folder(s) can be overwritten with the new folder(s).

CreateFolder Method

The CreateFolder method is used to create a folder as specified in the FolderPath parameter. The syntax is as follows:

```
object.CreateFolder FolderPath
```

FolderPath
: required string parameter that specifies the location and the name of the new folder to create.

CreateTextFile Method

The CreateTextFile method is used to create a specified file name and to return a TextStream object that can be used to read from or write to the new file. The syntax is as follows:

```
object.CreateTextFile FileName [, OverWrite] [,Unicode]
```

FileName
: required string parameter that specifies the location and the name of the file to create.

OverWrite
: optional Boolean parameter that indicates whether to overwrite an existing file.

Unicode   optional `Boolean` parameter that indicates whether the new file created is an Unicode file (true) or an ASCII file (false). If the parameter is omitted, then an ASCII file is assumed.

DeleteFile Method

The `DeleteFile` method is used to delete the file specified in the parameter. The syntax is as follows:

```
object.DeleteFile FileSpec [, Force]
```

FileSpec   required string parameter that specifies the location and the name of the file to delete.

Force   optional `Boolean` parameter. If the value of `Force` is true, then even if the specified file has read-only attribute, it will still be deleted.

DeleteFolder Method

The `DeleteFolder` method is used to delete the folder specified in the parameter. The syntax is as follows:

```
object.DeleteFolder FolderSpec [, Force]
```

FolderSpec   required string parameter that specifies the location and the name of the folder to delete.

Force   optional `Boolean` parameter. If the value of `Force` is true, then even if the specified folder has read-only attribute, it will still be deleted.

DriveExists Method

The `DriveExists` method is used to indicate whether the specified drive exists. The syntax is as follows:

```
object.DriveExists DriveSpec
```

DriveSpec   required string parameter that indicates the drive letter or a complete path specification.

FileExists Method

The `FileExists` method is used to indicate whether the specified file exists. The syntax is as follows:

```
object.FileExists FileSpec
```

FileSpec   required string parameter that specifies the location and the name of the folder to check for existence.

FolderExists Method

The FolderExists method is used to indicate whether the specified folder exists. The syntax is as follows:

```
object.FolderExists FolderSpec
```

FolderSpec   required string parameter that specifies the location and the name of the folder to check for existence.

GetAbsolutePathName Method

The GetAbsolutePathName method is used to return a complete and unambiguous path from a provided path specification. The syntax is as follows:

```
object.GetAbsolutePathName PathSpec
```

PathSpec   required string parameter that indicates the path specification to change to a complete and unambiguous path.

Assuming the current directory is c:\mydocuments\reports, the following table illustrates the behavior of the GetAbsolutePathName method.

Table D-32
GetAbsolutePathName Results

PathSpec	Returned Path
c:\	c:\mydocuments\reports
c:..	c:\mydocuments
c:\\\	c:\
c:*.*\may97	c:\mydocuments\reports*.*\may97
region1	c:\mydocuments\reports\region1
c:\..\..\mydocuments	c:\mydocuments

GetBaseName Method

The `GetBaseName` method is used to return a string containing the base name of the file (less any file extension) or folder in a provided path specification. The syntax is as follows:

```
object.GetBaseName Path
```

    `Path`   required string parameter that indicates the path specification for the file or the folder whose base name is to be returned.

GetDrive Method

The `GetDrive` method is used to return a `Drive` object from the drive specified by the parameter. The syntax is as follows:

```
object.GetDrive DriveSpec
```

    `DriveSpec`   required string parameter that can be a drive letter, a drive letter with a colon appended, a drive letter with a colon and path separator appended, or any network share specification.

GetDriveName Method

The `GetDriveName` method is used to return a string containing the name of the drive for a specified path. The syntax is as follows:

```
object.GetDriveName Path
```

    `Path`   required string parameter that specifies the path specification for the component whose drive name is to be returned.

GetExtensionName Method

The `GetExtensionName` method is used to return a string containing the extension name for the last component in a path. The syntax is as follows:

```
object.GetExtensionName Path
```

    `Path`   required string parameter that specifies the path specification for the component whose extension name is to be returned.

GetFile Method

The GetFile method is used to return a File object corresponding to the file specified by the parameter. The syntax is as follows:

    object.GetFile FileSpec

    FileSpec   required string parameter that specifies the location and the name of the file to return.

GetFileName Method

The GetFileName method is used to return the last file name or folder of a specified path that is not part of the drive specification. The syntax is as follows:

    object.GetFileName PathSpec

    PathSpec   required string parameter that specifies the path (absolute or relative) to a specific file.

GetFolder Method

The GetFolder method is used to return a Folder object corresponding to the folder specified by the parameter. The syntax is as follows:

    object.GetFolder FolderSpec

    FolderSpec   required string parameter that specifies the path (absolute or relative) to a specific folder.

GetParentFolderName Method

The GetParentFolderName method is used to return a string containing the name of the parent folder of the last file or folder in a specified path. The syntax is as follows:

    object.GetParentFolderName Path

Path is a required string parameter that specifies the file or the folder whose parent folder name is to be returned.

GetSpecialFolder Method

The GetSpecialFolder method is used to retrieve the special folder specified. The syntax is as follows:

    object.GetSpecialFolder FolderSpec

    FolderSpec   required string parameter that indicates the name of the special folder to return. The parameter can be any of the following constants.

<table>
<tr><td colspan="3" align="center">Table D-33
FolderSpec Values</td></tr>
<tr><td>*Constant*</td><td>*Value*</td><td>*Description*</td></tr>
</table>

Constant	Value	Description
WindowsFolder	0	The Windows folder contains files installed by the Windows operating system.
SystemFolder	1	The System folder contains libraries, fonts, and device drivers.
TemporaryFolder	2	The Temp folder is used to store temporary files. Its path is found in the TMP environment variable.

GetTempName Method

The GetTempName method is used to return a randomly generated temporary file or folder name that is useful for performing operations that require a temporary file or folder.

MoveFile Method

The MoveFile method is used to move one or more files from the source location to the destination location. The syntax is as follows:

```
object.MoveFile Source, Destination
```

Source required string parameter that specifies the location and the name of the file(s) to move. This parameter can contain wild card characters to include multiple files to move.

Destination required string parameter that specifies the location and the name of the new file. Wild card characters are not permitted in this parameter.

MoveFolder Method

The MoveFolder method is used to move one or more folders from the source location to the destination location. The syntax is as follows:

```
object.MoveFolder Source, Destination
```

Source required string parameter that specifies the location and the name of the folder(s) to move. This parameter can contain wild card characters to include multiple folders to move.

Destination required string parameter that specifies the location and the name of the new folder(s). Wild card characters are not permitted in this parameter.

OpenTextFile Method

The `OpenTextFile` method is used to open a specified file and to return a `TextStream` object that can be used to read from, write to, or append to the file. The syntax is as follows:

```
object.OpenTextFile FileName [, IOMode] [,Create] [,Format]
```

FileName   required string parameter that indicates the file to open.

IOMode   optional parameter that indicates the permission to file. The parameter can be one of the following constants:

Table D-34
IOMode Constant Values

Constant	Value	Description
ForReading	1	Open a file for reading only. You can't write to this file.
ForWriting	2	Open a file for writing. If a file with the same name exists, its previous contents are overwritten.
ForAppending	8	Open a file and write to the end of the file.

`Create` is an optional `Boolean` parameter. If the parameter is true, then if the file specified by `FileName` does not exist, the method will create a new file.

`Format` is an optional parameter used to indicate the format of the opened file. If omitted, the file is opened as ASCII. The parameter can be one of the following constants:

Table D-35
Format Constant Values

Constant	Value	Description
TristateUseDefault	−2	Opens the file using the system default.
TristateTrue	−1	Opens the file as Unicode.
TristateFalse	0	Opens the file as ASCII.

FileSystemObject Object Properties

Drives Property

The Drives property returns a Drives collection consisting of all Drive objects available on the local machine.

FileSystemObject Drive Object

The Drive object represents a disk or network drive. In addition, any third-party tools that map drives on your machine can be read with this object.

Drive Object Properties

AvailableSpace Property

The AvailableSpace property is used to return the amount of space available to a user on the specified drive or network share.

DriveLetter Property

The DriveLetter property is a read-only property that is used to return the drive letter of a physical local drive or a network share.

DriveType Property

The DriveType property is a read-only property that indicates the type of the specified drive. The following table shows the mapping of the types.

Table D-36	
DriveType Values	
Value	*Description*
0	Unknown
1	Removable
2	Fixed
3	Network
4	CD-ROM
5	RAM Disk

FileSystem Property

The `FileSystem` property returns the type of file system in use for the specified drive.

FreeSpace Property

The `FreeSpace` property is a read-only property that returns the amount of free space available to a user on the specified drive or network share.

IsReady Property

The `IsReady` property is used to indicate the status of the specified drive. The property returns true if the specified drive is ready; if it is not, the property returns false. For removable-media drives and CD-ROM drives, `IsReady` returns true only when the appropriate media is inserted and ready for access.

Path Property

The `Path` property returns the path for the specified drive.

RootFolder Property

The `RootFolder` property is a read-only property that returns a `Folder` object representing the root folder of a specified drive.

SerialNumber Property

The `SerialNumber` property returns the decimal serial number used to identify a disk volume uniquely.

ShareName Property

The `ShareName` property returns the network share name for a specified drive.

Totalsize Property

The `TotalSize` property returns the total space, in bytes, of a drive or network share.

Volumename Property

The `VolumeName` property is used to set or to return the volume name of the specified drive.

FileSystemObject Folder Object

A Folder object represents a directory that is part of a Drive.

Folder Object Methods

Copy Method

The Copy method is used to copy the folder referenced by the Folder object to the destination specified in the parameter. The syntax is as follows:

```
object.Copy Destination [, OverWrite]
```

Destination   a required string parameter that specifies the location where the folder will be copied.

OverWrite   an optional Boolean parameter that indicates whether the existing folder will be overwritten.

Delete Method

The Delete method is used to delete the folder referenced by the Folder object.

Move Method

The Move method is used to move the folder referenced by the Folder object to the destination specified in the parameter. The syntax is as follows:

```
object.Move Destination
```

Destination   required string parameter that specifies the location to move the folder. Wild card characters are not allowed in this parameter.

CreateTextFile Method

The CreateTextFile method is used to create a specified file in the folder referenced by the Folder object and to return a TextStream object that can be used to read from or write to the new file. The syntax is as follows:

```
object.CreateTextFile FileName [, OverWrite] [,Unicode]
```

FileName   required string parameter that specifies the location and the name of the file to create.

OverWrite   optional Boolean parameter that indicates whether to overwrite an existing file.

Unicode   optional `Boolean` parameter that indicates whether the new file
created is a Unicode file (true) or an ASCII file (false). If the
parameter is omitted, then an ASCII file is assumed.

Folder Object Properties

Attributes Property

The `Attributes` property is used to set or to return the attributes of the folder
reference by the `Folder` object. The property is read/write or read-only, depending
on the attribute. The `Attributes` property can have any of the following values:

Table D-37 Folder Attribute Values		
Constant	**Value**	**Description**
Normal	0	Normal file. No attributes are set.
ReadOnly	1	Read-only file. Attribute is read/write.
Hidden	2	Hidden file. Attribute is read/write.
System	4	System file. Attribute is read/write.
Volume	8	Disk drive volume label. Attribute is read-only.
Directory	16	Folder or directory. Attribute is read-only.
Archive	32	File has changed since last backup. Attribute is read/write.
Alias	64	Link or shortcut. Attribute is read-only.
Compressed	128	Compressed file. Attribute is read-only.

DateCreated Property

The `DateCreate` property is a read-only property that returns the date and time
that the folder referenced by the `Folder` object was created.

DateLastAccessed Property

The `DateLastAccessed` property is a read-only property that returns the date and
time that the folder referenced by the `Folder` object was last accessed.

DateLastModified Property

The `DateLastModified` property is a read-only property that returns the date and
time that the folder referenced by the `Folder` object was last modified.

Drive Property

The `Drive` property is a read-only property that returns the drive letter of the drive on which the folder referenced by the `Folder` object resides.

Files Property

The `Files` property returns a `Files` collection consisting of all `File` objects contained in the folder referenced by the `Folder` object, including those with hidden and system file attributes set. The following example produces a list of files, given a valid directory pathname.

```
<% Function ShowFileList(folderspec)

    Dim fso, f, f1, fc, s

    Set fso = CreateObject("Scripting.FileSystemObject")

    Set f = fso.GetFolder(folderspec)

    Set fc = f.Files

    For Each f1 in fc

      s = s & f1.name

      s = s & "<BR>"

    Next

    ShowFileList = s

  End Function %>
```

IsRootFolder Property

The `IsRootFolder` property returns true if the specified folder is the root folder. Otherwise, the property returns false.

Name Property

The `Name` property sets or returns the name of the specified folder.

Parentfolder Property

The `ParentFolder` property returns a `Folder` object referencing the parent of the specified folder.

Path Property

The `Path` property returns the path for the folder referenced by the `Folder` object.

ShortName Property

The ShortName property returns the short name of the folder referenced by the Folder object. The ShortName is in the 8.3 naming convention.

ShortPath Property

The ShortPath property returns the short path to the folder referenced by the Folder object. The ShortPath property is in the 8.3 file naming convention.

Size Property

The Size property returns the size, in bytes, of all files and subfolders contained in the folder referenced by the Folder object.

SubFolders Property

The SubFolders property returns a Folders collection consisting of all folders contained in the folder referenced by the Folder object. The Folders collection includes those folders with Hidden and System file attributes set.

FileSystemObject File Object

File Object Methods

Copy Method

The Copy method is used to copy the file referenced by the File object to the destination specified in the parameter. The syntax is as follows:

```
object.Copy Destination [, OverWrite]
```

Destination	required string parameter that specifies the location where the file will be copied.
OverWrite	optional Boolean parameter that indicates whether the existing file will be overwritten.

Delete Method

The Delete method is used to delete the file referenced by the File object.

Move Method

The Move method is used to move the file referenced by the File object to the destination specified in the parameter. The syntax is as follows:

```
object.Move Destination
```

Destination   required string parameter that specifies the location to move the file. Wild card characters are not allowed in this parameter.

OpenAsTextStream Method

The `OpenAsTextStream` method is used to open the specified file referenced by the `File` object and to return a `TextStream` object that can be used to read from, write to, or append to the file. The syntax is as follows:

```
object.OpenAsTextStream [IOMode] [, Format]
```

IOMode   optional parameter that indicates the permission to file. The parameter can be one of the following constants:

Table D-38
IOMode Option Values

Constant	Value	Description
ForReading	1	Open a file for reading only. You can't write to this file.
ForWriting	2	Open a file for writing. If a file with the same name exists, its previous contents are overwritten.
ForAppending	8	Open a file and write to the end of the file.

Format   optional parameter used to indicate the format of the opened file. If omitted, the file is opened as ASCII. The parameter can be one of the following constants:

Table D-39
Format Option Values

Constant	Value	Description
TristateUseDefault	−2	Opens the file using the system default.
TristateTrue	−1	Opens the file as Unicode.
TristateFalse	0	Opens the file as ASCII.

File Object Properties

Attributes Property

The Attributes property is used to set or to return the attributes of the file reference by the File object. The property is read/write or read-only, depending on the attribute. The Attributes property can have any of the following values:

Constant	Value	Description
Normal	0	Normal file. No attributes are set.
ReadOnly	1	Read-only file. Attribute is read/write.
Hidden	2	Hidden file. Attribute is read/write.
System	4	System file. Attribute is read/write.
Volume	8	Disk drive volume label. Attribute is read-only.
Directory	16	Folder or directory. Attribute is read-only.
Archive	32	File has changed since last backup. Attribute is read/write.
Alias	64	Link or shortcut. Attribute is read-only.
Compressed	128	Compressed file. Attribute is read-only.

DateCreated Property

The DateCreated property is a read-only property that returns the date and time that the file referenced by the File object was created.

DateLastAccessed Property

The DateLastAccessed property is a read-only property that returns the date and time that the file referenced by the File object was last accessed.

DateLastModified Property

The DateLastModified property is a read-only property that returns the date and time that the file referenced by the File object was last modified.

Drive Property

The Drive property is a read-only property that returns the drive letter of the drive on which the file referenced by the File object resides.

Name Property

The Name property sets or returns the name of the specified file.

ParentFolder Property

The `ParentFolder` property returns a Folder object referencing the parent of the specified file.

Path Property

The `Path` property returns the path for the file referenced by the `File` object.

ShortName Property

The `ShortName` property returns the short name of the file referenced by the `File` object. The `ShortName` is in the 8.3 naming convention.

ShortPath Property

The `ShortPath` property returns the short path to the file referenced by the `File` object. The `ShortPath` property is in the 8.3 file naming convention.

Size Property

The `Size` property returns the size, in bytes, of the specified file.

Type Property

The `Type` property returns information about the type of the specified file. For example, for files ending in .TXT, "Text Document" is returned.

FileSystemObject TextStream Object

A `TextStream` represents a connection to a text file. Multiple `TextStream` objects can be created from the same `FileSystemObject`.

TextStream Object Methods

Close Method

The `Close` method closes an opened `TextStream` file.

```
object.Close
```

Read Method

The `Read` method reads a specified number of characters from the `TextStream` file and returns the resulting string.

```
object.Read NumberOfCharacters
```

    `NumberOfCharacters`   required long integer that indicates the number of characters to read from the `TextStream` file.

ReadAll Method

The `ReadAll` method reads the entire `TextStream` file and returns the resulting string.

```
object.ReadAll
```

ReadLine Method

The `ReadLine` method reads an entire line (up to, but not including, the newline character) from a `TextStream` file and returns the resulting string.

```
object.ReadLine
```

Skip Method

The `Skip` method skips a specified number of characters when reading a `TextStream` file.

```
object.Skip NumberOfCharacters
```

    `NumberOfCharacters`   required long integer that indicates the number of characters to skip when reading from the `TextStream` file.

SkipLine Method

The `SkipLine` method skips the next line when reading a `TextStream` file.

```
object.SkipLine
```

Write Method

The `Write` method writes the specified string to the `TextStream` file.

```
object.Write Text
```

    `Text`   required string parameter that is to be written to the `TextStream` file.

WriteLine Method

The `WriteLine` method writes a specified string and newline character to a `TextStream` file.

```
object.WriteLine [Text]
```

    `Text`   optional string parameter that is to be written to the `TextStream` file.

WriteBlankLines Method

The `WriteBlankLines` method writes a specified number of newline characters to the `TextStream` file.

```
object.WriteBlankLines NumberOfBlankLines
```

    `NumberOfBlankLines`   required numeric value indicating the number of newline characters to write to the `TextStream` file.

Object Properties

AtEndOfLine Property

The `AtEndOfLine` property is a read-only property that returns true if the file pointer immediately precedes the end-of-line marker in the `TextStream` file. Otherwise, the property returns False.

AtEndOfStream Property

The `AtEndOfStream` property returns true if the file pointer is at the end of the `TextStream` file. Otherwise, the property returns false.

Column Property

The `Column` property is a read-only property that returns the column number of the current character position in the `TextStream` file.

Line Property

The `Line` property is a read-only property that returns the current line number in the `TextStream` file.

✦   ✦   ✦

What's New in ASP 3.0

This appendix identifies the methods, properties, and events that are new to ASP 3.0, which is being introduced with IIS 5.0 in Windows 2000. As this information may change between the time this book was written and the release of Windows 2000, be sure to check the ASP Techniques Web site (http://www.asptechniques.com) for the latest updates to this appendix and rest of the book.

Application Object

Table E-1 shows the features of the Application object and shows which methods are new under ASP 3.0.

Table E-1 **Application Object Features**		
Feature	*ASP 2.0*	*ASP 3.0*
Contents **Collection**	X	X
Contents.Remove **method**		X
Contents.RemoveAll **method**		X
Lock **Method**	X	X
OnStart **Event**	X	X
OnEnd **Event**	X	X
StaticObjects **Collection**	X	X
Unlock **Method**	X	X

Contents.Remove Method

This method removes a specified item from the `Contents` collection of the `Application` object. The usage is similar to other collection methods:

```
Application.Contents.Remove("Mode")
```

This code will remove the item named "Mode" from the `Contents` collection.

Contents.RemoveAll Method

This method removes all items that had been added to the `Contents` collection. The syntax is as follows:

```
Application.Contents.RemoveAll
```

ASPError Object

`ASPError` is a brand-new object in ASP 3.0. It is designed to make it easier to create custom error pages that appear when server errors (#500) occur. When IIS encounters an error when either compiling or running an .asp file, it will generate a 500;100 custom error. By default, all Web sites and applications will transfer processing of a 500;100 custom error to the file `500-100.asp`, which is installed by default to the Help\iisHelp\common directory under your Windows directory. After a 500;100 custom error is generated, IIS will also create an instance of the `ASPError` object that describes the error condition. The `ASPError` object is returned from the `Server.GetLastError` method. The file `500-100.asp` uses the properties of this object to display a page describing the error condition. You can develop additional error processing by either modifying `500-100.asp` or by creating a new ASP file for processing errors.

The code in Listing E-1 shows how you can use this object in a page.

Listing E-1: **Using the ASPError object**

```
<%
Option Explicit
Dim e      ' As ASPError
Set e = Server.GetLastError()
%>
<TABLE>
<TR>
   <TD>ASP Code</TD>
   <TD><%= e.ASPCode %></TD>
```

```
</TR>

<TR>
   <TD>Number</TD>
   <TD><%= e.Number %></TD>
</TR>

<TR>
   <TD>Source</TD>
   <TD><% = e.Source %></TD>
</TR>
<TR>
   <TD>FileName</TD>
   <TD> <%= e.FileName %></TD>
</TR>

<TR>
   <TD>LineNumber</TD>
   <TD> <%= e.LineNumber %></TD>
</TR>

<TR>
   <TD>Description</TD>
   <TD> <%= e.Description %></TD>
</TR>

<TR>
   <TD>ASP Description</TD>
   <TD> <%= e.ASPDescription %></TD>
</TR>

</TABLE>
```

ASPCode Property

This property returns the error number generated by IIS. Typically, this number will be 500, which indicates a server error.

ASPDescription Property

This property returns a more complete description of the error that occurred (if available) so you can provide more information to your users.

Description Property

This property has a short description of the error. It is typically a short message that you might see in a Visual Basic error message. The `ASPDescription` property will sometimes hold a more complete description of the error.

FileName Property

This property holds the name of the file that was being processed when the error occurred.

LineNumber Property

This property holds the line number within the file where the error occurred. Remember that the actual error may not actually be on this line, especially if it is a case in which preceding bad code (such as missing tags or quotes) causes errors later.

Number Property

This property holds the error number that occurred. This property will also have any COM error numbers.

Source Property

This property returns a string indicating why the error occurred, whether it was an ASP error, a scripting error, or an error from a component.

ObjectContext Object

At the time of printing, the `ObjectContext` object had no changes or new features identified in Microsoft's documentation.

Request Object

At the time of printing, the `Request` object had no changes or new features identified in Microsoft's documentation.

Response Object

At the time of printing, the Response object had no changes or new features identified in Microsoft's documentation.

Server Object

The Server object has several new methods that make it easier to break your ASP application into multiple pages. The new methods are shown in Table E-2.

Table E-2 **Server Object Features**		
Feature	*ASP 2.0*	*ASP 3.0*
ScriptTimeout Property	X	X
CreateObject Method	X	X
Execute Method		X
GetLastError		X
HTMLEncode	X	X
MapPath	X	X
Transfer		X
URLEncode	X	X

Execute Method

This method gives you a way to call another ASP page without loading the page and using server-side includes to add it to your page. It's similar to the way you might call a subroutine or function—you execute the page, the code runs, and control returns to the caller.

The best part of this feature is that it enables you to break your application into multiple files that can each be used as subroutines. For instance, instead of having one large include or ASP file with all of your code in it, you can put each subroutine in a separate file. The benefit of this approach is that you are only loading the code that you need. If you are going to view data, you don't have to have all the code to add, edit, or delete records.

Here's an example of how this approach could work. This code shows a subroutine in a page. However, there are no Sub or Function tags in the code.

```
<%
Response.Write "Subroutine is being called now."
%>
```

This code shows another file executing the first file, which we'll call filef2.asp.

```
<%
Response.Write "Here's some text from the first file."
Response.Write "Here comes the text from the Executed file."
Server.Execute "filef2.asp"
Response.Write "And here's some more text from the first file."
%>
```

This is similar to using a server-side include, as follows:

```
<%
Response.Write "Here's some text from the first file."
Response.Write "Here comes the text from the Executed file."
%>
<!--#include file="filef2.asp" -->
<%
Response.Write "And here's some more text from the first file."
%>
```

However, server-side includes cannot be conditional or dynamically generated. Because it can take a variable argument, the Execute method enables you to bypass this limitation. For instance, look at this code:

```
<%
If blnFlag = True Then
    Server.Execute "file1.asp"
Else
    Server.Execute "file2.asp"
End If
%>
```

If you've done anything with server-side includes and run into their limitations, you're going to love this feature.

GetLastError Method

This method is used in conjunction with the ASPError object. It returns the last error that occurred. Refer to the preceding ASPError object section for more information on this method.

Transfer Method

The Transfer method is used to pass control to a second ASP page. You can do this with the Response.Redirect method; however, you have to pass all the data yourself. You have to get all the data from the Request object to the second page through query string or Session variables. Any variables or objects that have been assigned a value in the current page, during the current session, or within the current application-state will be maintained. In addition, all of the current contents for the request collections will be available to the .asp file receiving the transfer.

Session Object

Table E-3 shows the features of the Session object and shows which methods are new under ASP 3.0.

Table E-3 Session Object Features		
Feature	*ASP 2.0*	*ASP 3.0*
Abandon **Method**	X	X
CodePage **Property**	X	X
Contents **Collection**	X	X
Contents.Remove **Method**		X
Contents.RemoveAll **Method**		X
LCID **Property**	X	X
OnEnd **Event**	X	X
OnStart Event	X	X
SessionID **Property**	X	X
StaticObjects **Collection**	X	X
Timeout **Property**	X	X
Value **Property**	X	X

Contents.Remove Method

This method removes a specified item from the Contents collection of the Session object. The usage is similar to other collection methods:

```
Session.Contents.Remove("Mode")
```

This code will remove the item named "Mode" from the Contents collection.

Contents.RemoveAll Method

This method removes all items that had been added to the Contents collection. The syntax is as follows:

```
Session.Contents.RemoveAll
```

✦   ✦   ✦

Index

SYMBOLS

! (exclamation point), 384
! (not equal), 387
(number sign), 386
#config directive, 98-103
#echo directive, 103-105
#exec directive, 105-106
#flastmod directive, 106-107
#fsize directive, 107-109
#include directives, 109-110, 356
% (percent sign), 150
& (ampersand), 384
( ) (parentheses), 42
* (asterisk), 41
    field, 340
, (comma), 57, 128
/ (forward slash), 41
: (colon), 57
@ (at sign), 386
\ (backslash), 41, 151
^ (caret), 42
_ (underscore), 51
    Select/Case structure, 58-59
-(minus sign), 40
| (pipe symbol), 384
~ (tilde), 384
' ' (single quotes), 222, 361
" " (double quotes), 38, 150, 247, 385
+ (plus sign), 40
< (less than), 44, 387
< > (not equal to), 44
</BODY> tag, 236
<H4> tag, 454
<HEAD> tag, 240
<HTML> tag, 240
</HTML> tag, 236
<LI> tag, 238
<TITLE> tag, 240
<= (less than or equal to), 44, 387
= (equal sign), 44, 235, 387
    delimiter characters, 151
> greater than), 44, 387
>= (greater than or equal to), 44, 387

A

A_HRef column, 375
Abs function, 73
AbsolutePage property, 311
Access column, 375
ACID (Atomicity, Consistency, Isolation,
    Durability) test, 463-464, 469
Active Data Objects. See ADO
Active Server Pages. See ASP
ActiveConnecton parameter, 224
ad tracking system
    AdMgr class, creating, 471-474
    building, 469-477
    Clickthrough code, adding, 475
    databases, building, 470-471
    design tips, 469-470
    enhancing, 476-477
    Impression code, testing, 474
adArray constant, 343
adBigInt constant, 227, 343
adBinary constant, 343
adBoolean constant, 227, 343
adBSTR constant, 344
adByRef constant, 344
adChar constant, 227, 344
adCurrency constant, 227, 344
Add New Catalog dialog box, 367
Add Project command (File menu), 425
adDate constant, 227, 344
adDBDate constant, 344
adDBTime constant, 344
adDBTimeStamp constant, 344
adDecimal constant, 344
Add-in Manager command (Add-ins menu), 393
Add-ins menu commands, Add-in Manager, 393
addition, 40
adDouble constant, 227, 344
AddRecord subroutine
    code, 275-276
    creating, 275-277
AddScopeToQuery method, 381
adEmpty constant, 344
adError constant, 344

adGUID constant, 344
AdID field, 470
adIDispatch constant, 344
adInteger constant, 227, 344
adIUnknown constant, 344
adLockBatchOptimistic constant, 220
adLockOptimistic constant, 220
adLockPessimistic constant, 220
adLockReadOnly constant, 220
adLongVarBinary constant, 344
adLongVarChar constant, 344
adLongVarWChar constant, 344
AdMgr class
    creating, 471-474
    declarations code, 471
    Initialize event code, 471
adNumeric constant, 344
ADO (Active Data Objects), 209
    constants, code for include file, 274-275
    objects, 211-212
    records, code to add, 222
    WebClasses, 450-454
adOpenDynamic constant, 219
adOpenForwardOnly constant, 219
adOpenKeyset constant, 219
adOpenStatic constant, 219
ADOVBS.INC file, 345
adParamInput constant, 227, 345
adParamInputOutput constant, 227, 345
adParamOutput constant, 227, 345
adParamReturnValue constant, 227, 345
adSingle constant, 227, 345
adSmallInt constant, 227, 345
adTinyInt constant, 227, 345
adUnsignedBigInt constant, 345
adUnsignedInt constant, 345
adUnsignedSmallInt constant, 345
adUnsignedTinyInt constant, 345
adUserDefined constant, 345
adVarBinary constant, 345
adVarChar constant, 227, 345
adVariant constant, 345
adVarWChar constant, 345
adVector constant, 345
advertising at Web sites, 351-353
adWChar constant, 345
ae shortcut name, 380
Age field, 484
ALIGN parameter

HR tag, 15
TABLE tag, 21
TD tag, 23
TH tag, 22
TR tag, 21
ALINK parameter, BODY tag, 4
All column, 375
All property, 386
ALL_HTTP variable, 104, 141, 144-146
AllHTTPDump.asp code, 144-145
AllocSize column, 375
AllowEnumeration property, 374
Alternate Text field, 470
American Standard Code for Information
    Interchange. *See* ASCII
ampersand (&), 384
anchor tag, 25-26
AND operator, 384-385
And operator, 45
API (Application Programming Interface), 209
Application event, 186
    creating, 193-194
Application object, 183
    Application events, 186
    code to add information, 184
    Contents collection, 184-185
    Lock method, 186, 358
    StaticObjects collection, 185-186
    Unlock method, 186
Application Programming Interface (API), 209
applications, security, 318-332
arctangent function, 73
arrayname parameter (LBound and UBound
    functions), 39
arrays, 32-33
    functions, 36-39
Asc function, 71
ASCII (American Standard Code for Information
    Interchange), 71
ASP (Active Server Page)
    code, building, 495-519
    constants files, 97
    group listing page, creating, 508-509
    group viewer page, creating, 509-510
    Library test code, 430-431
    Login page, creating, 495-501
    message editor page, creating, 514-519
    message-viewing page, creating, 511-514
    modular code, 109-111

sequence, 495-496
Techniques Web site, 387
User Profile editor, creating, 502-508
asterisk (*), 41
field, 340
at sign (@), 386
Atn functgion, 73
Atomicity (ACID test), 463
Attrib column, 375
AUTH_PASSWORD variable, 104, 141
AUTH_TYPE variable, 104, 141
AUTH_USER variable, 104, 141
author information, memberinfo.asp page, 514

B

B tag, 12
back slash (\), 41,151
BACKGROUND parameter
    BODY tag, 4
    TABLE tag, 21
    TD tag, 23
    TH tag, 22
    TR tag, 21
Base Conversion function, 72
basicform.html file code, 115-116
basicform_process.asp code, 116-117
basicqs.html code, 134
basicqs_process.asp code, 134
BasicTemplate.htlm code, 441
BasicTemplate, substitution code, 443
BGCOLOR parameter
    BODY tag, 4
    TABLE tag, 21
    TD tag, 23
    TH tag, 22
    TR tag, 21
blank actions, performing, 58
blnAddedWhere variable, 254
BLOCKQUOTE tag, 8
BODY tag, 235
    parameters 4
Boolean
    expressions, 44
    operators, 384-385
BORDER parameter, TABLE tag, 21
BR tag, 13, 56
browsers. *See also* data browsers
    application security, 318-322
    cookies, 162

creating, 303-306
garden gate security, 326-329
Internet Explorer 4 and 5, configuring, 162
Netscape 4.6l, configuring, 162
Recordset, 318
redirecting, 153
session-level security, 329-332
sorting features, 312-318
Web browsers, data, viewing, 231
BrowserType field, 470
Buffer property, 153
buffering output, 153-154
built-in objects, 89-93
business models, 392
    employee entity properties, 390-391
    menu groups entity properties, 391
    menu items entity properties, 391
    order entity properties, 391
buttons
    code for viewing which one pressed, 117-118
    Login, 499
    radio, 119-121
    Submit, 114, 116, 137
    Test Connection, 216

C

CacheControl property, 154
caching output, 154-155
caret (^), 42
Cascading Style Sheets (CSS), 6, 451
Case Else keyword, 57-58
case sensitivity, TYPE parameter, 20
Catalog command (New menu), 366
Catalog properties dialog box, 367-368
Catalog property, 373, 374
category names, code to load from databases,
    243-244
category viewer page
    changing, 357-359
    code, 245
    modifying, 237-239
catviewer.asp code, 237-238, 263-264, 356-357
    CreateVisitorID subroutine, 359-360
CBool function, 67
    test code, 68
CByte function, 68
CCur function, 68
CDate function, test code, 69
CDbl function, 70

CD-ROMs, Northwind Traders database, 231
CELLPADDING parameter, TABLE tag, 21
CELLSPACING parameter, TABLE tag, 21
CENTER tag, 12
chaining objects, 410
Character to Number function, 71
Characterization column, 375
check boxes, 121-127
Chr function, 54, 71
CiFlags property, 374
CiScope property, 375
City property, 392
Class Builder Wizard, 393
Class object, Terminate event, 492
classes
    AdMgr, creating, 471-474
    Employee, adding to, 404-404
    Employee, code, 393-394, 395-396
    MenuGroup, code, 396-397
    MenuItem, code, 397
    Order, code, 398
    OrderItem, code, 398-399
    Special, code, 399
    Store, adding to, 405-423
    Store, code, 400
    Subscription, code, 492-494
    Subscription, creating, 492-495
    Visual Basic, 389
ClassID column, 375
Clear method, 153, 154
Clickthrough code, 475
CLng function, 70
CLnt function, 70
Close method, 216
closing connections, 216
cmdQuery object, 343
Code command (View menu), 436
CODE tag
    comparing with PRE tag, 10-11
    source code, 10
code
    #include directive file samples, 110
    AddRecord subroutine, 275-276
    AdMgr class declarations, 471
    AdMgr class, Initialize event code, 471
    AllHTTPDump.asp, 144-145
    Application event template, 193
    Application object, adding information, 184
    ASP (Active Server Pages), building, 495-519

ASP (Active Server Pages), sequence, 495-496
ASP (Active Server Pages) modular, 109-111
ASP Library test, 430-431
back-end for cookies, 175-182
BasicErrorHandler.asp code, 201
basicform.html, 115-116
basicform_process.asp, 116-117
basicqs.html, 134
basicqs_process.asp, 134
BasicTemplate.htlm, 441
BasicTemplate, substitution, 443
buttons pressed viewing, 117-118
category viewing pages, 245
catviewer.asp, 237-238, 263-264, 356-357, 359-360
CBool function, 67-68
CDate function, 69
Clickthrough, 475
CODE tag, 10
common.asp, 356, 357-358
connection for SQL server 6.5 database, 213
connections, 212-213
contents, retrieving, 184
cookies, creating or updating, 16-167
CreateCookie, 163-165
CreateRecordset function, 273-274
CreateVisitorID subroutinep, 357-358, 359-360
Custom WebItem, 444-445
CustomerList HTML template, 450-451
data access, 400-423
Data Link, 216
database connection, 231
database error handling, 228
default.asp, 496-499
DeleteRecord subroutine, 278-280
Dictionary object, testing, 90
Discontinued field check, 256-257
DisplayData subroutine, 346-347
drives, obtaining information on, 91
editproduct.asp, 289-301
EditRecord subroutine, 277-278
Employee class, 393-394, 395-396, 401-403, 404
EnhancedErrorHandler.asp code, 203-204
envdump.asp, 143
error handling, adding, 229
ErrorSource.asp code, 202, 205
FileDateTime function, 106-107
FileSize function, 108-109

Filter function test, 80
fnGenerateCustomerList changes 457-458
fnGenerateCustomerList function, 452-453
FunctionLibrary.asp for virtual paths, 111
general changes, 356-357
gg_longin.asp, 327-328
GIF extension files, counting, 92
gryGetShipper query, 225-226
hidden input fields, 133
HTML fromWebClass, 438
HTML heading tags, 5
HTML tables, 23-24
HTML with line breaks, 439
Impression function, 472
Impression method, 476
Impression, testing, 474
include file for ADO constants, 274-275
information, retrieving, 187
Init method, 485-486
invoice details queries, executing, 348-351
kilobypes, printing size, 107
links, editing and deleting, 288-289
lists within lists, 17
loading category names from databases,
    243-244
login pages, modifying, 330
MakeConnection function, 272-273
Member Object subroutines, 487-489
MenuGroup class, 396-397, 411-413
MenuItem class, 397, 413-415
Message object, 491-492
Message object, object properties, 489-490
message.asp, 515-519
modifying, 35-362
ObjectControl object, 473-474
OL tag, 17-18
order browser Sub Main, changing, 330-331
Order class, 398, 416-418
order details page Sub Main, 331-332
orderbrowser.asp, 304-306, 324-325
orderbrowser.asp, revised, 307-311
OrderItem class, 398-399, 419-421
PATH_INFO variable, 146-147
pizza delivery form, 127-128
pizzaaform.html, 122-123
PizzaDeliveryForm, 168-169
PizzaDeliveryForm, completed, 175-181
PizzaDeliveryForm, new, 170-174
pizzaform.html with select list, 128-129

pizzaform_process.asp, 124-125
pizzaform2_process.asp, 130-132
PRE tag, 8-9
Price field check, 257
ProcessTag, 446
ProcessTags event handler, 452
prodinfo.asp, 250-251, 266-267
product list, adding back links, 242
product name checking, 256
product pages, 288
product viewing pages, 245-246
products, adding, 287-288
prodviewer.asp, 239-240, 248-249, 264-265
profile.asp, 502-507
Project1_WebClass1.asp, 440
publishing recordsets with loops, 234-235
qryGetGroupMessages 510
qryGetSubscriptions, 509
queries, closing and displaying results, 259
queries, setup, 255
query forms, 370
query processing, 371-372
radio buttons, creating, 119-120
RecordCategoryID subroutine, 359-360
records, adding via ADO (Active Data
    Objects), 222
records, editing, 221
RecordSearchInfo subroutine, 360-362
Recordset object, opening, 218
RecordSet, creating, 223-224
recordsets, creating from databases, 233-234
recordsets to loop, 220
RefreshObject function, 490
RemoveCookie.asp, 167
RetrieveData subroutine, 342-343
Save method, 485-486
SaveObject function, 486-487
search forms, 252-253
searchresults.asp, 255, 260-262
Session event template, 194
showmessage.asp, 511-514
ShowPage subroutine, 280-287
SingleForm.asp, 135-136
sorting features, 312-317
Special class, 399, 421-423
SQL server connection, 233
Stock field check, 258
Store class, 400

Continued

code *(continued)*
    Store class, data access enabled, 405-407
    Store class, revised, 407-409
    Store class, testing, 410
    StoreData subroutine, 276-277
    StructuredForm.asp, 138-140
    sub main, 269-271
    Subscription class, 492-494
    systems values, checking, 188
    time/date formatting, 99
    tmpViewCustomer_ProcessTags event
        handler, 459-460
    util.asp, 499-501
    view order page with embedded SQL
        (Structured Query Language), 334-338
    ViewCustomer HTML template, 454-456
ViewCustomer_UserEvent event handler, 459
    vieworder.asp, 319-324
    ViewRecord subroutine, 272
    WebClass_Start event handler, 448
    WebClass_Start event procedure, 446-447
    WebClass_Start HTML, 449
    WebClass_Start, 439, 445
    WebClass_Terminate event handler, 460
    WebClasses custom event handlers, 447-448
CodePage property, 189, 375
collections
    Contents, 184-185, 187-188
    Request.ServerVariables, 204
    ServerVariables, 140
    StaticObjects, 185-186, 188
colon (:), 57
COLOR parameter
    FONT tag, 11
    HR tag, 15
COLS parameter, TABLE tag, 21
COLSPAN parameter
    TD tag, 23
    TH tag, 22
Columns property, 373, 375-378
columns
    A_HRef, 375
    Access, 375
    All, 375
    AllocSize, 375
    Attrib, 375
    Characterization, 375
    ClassID, 375
    Contents, 376

    Create, 376
    Directory, 376
    DocAppName, 376
    DocAuthor, 376
    DocByteCount, 376
    DocCategory, 376
    DocCharCount, 376
    DocComments, 376
    DocCompany, 376
    DocCreatedTm, 376
    DocEditTime, 376
    DocHiddenCount, 376
    DocKeywords, 376
    DocLastAuthor, 376
    DocLastPrinted, 376
    DocLineCount, 376
    DocManager, 376
    DocNoteCount, 376
    DocPageCount, 376
    DocParaCount, 376
    DocPartTitles, 376
    DocPresentationTarget, 376
    DocRevNumber, 376
    DocSecurity, 377
    DocSlideCount, 377
    DocSubject, 377
    DocTemplate, 377
    DocThumbnail, 377
    DocTitle, 377
    DocWordCount, 377
    FileIndex, 377
    FileName, 377
    HtmlHeading1, 377
    HtmlHeading2, 377
    HtmlHeading3, 377
    HtmlHeading4, 377
    HtmlHeading5, 377
    HtmlHeading6, 377
    HtmlHRef, 377
    Img_Alt, 377
    for Index Server queries, 375-377
    Path, 377
    ShortFileName, 377
    Size, 377
    USN, 377
    Write, 377
COM (Component Object Model), 389
    business models, 390-392
    classses, creating, 393-400

objects, compiling and deploying, 424-431
comma (,), 57, 128
Command object, 225-227
    records, copying, 223-224
    RecordSet, code to create, 223-224
commands, SSI (server-side includes), 97
CommandText parameter, 224
common.asp code, 356
    CreateVisitorID subroutine, 357-358
companies, demographic information, 161
comparison operators, 44
compiling components, 424-425
Component command (New menu), 468
Component Object Model. *See* COM
components
    compiling, 424-425
    non-transactional environment, testing, 467
    testing in Visual Basic, 425-426
conditional expressions, 49
configuring
    Index Server, 365-369
    Internet Explorer 4 and 5, 162
    Netscape 4.6l, 162
connection code for SQL server 6.5 database,
    213
Connection object
    connections, closing, 216
    connections, making, 212-213
    Data Link files, 214-216
connections
    closing, 216
    code, 212-213
    making, 212-213
    managing, 156-157
ConnectionString property, 213
Consistency (ACID test), 463
Const keyword, 30
constants, 29-30
    adArray, 343
    adBigInt, 227, 343
    adBinary, 343
    adBoolean, 227, 343
    adBSTR, 344
    adByRef, 344
    adChar, 227, 344
    adCurrency, 227, 344
    adDate, 227, 344
    adDBDate, 344
    adDBTime, 344

adDBTimeStamp, 344
adDecimal, 344
adDouble, 227, 344
adEmpty, 344
adError, 344
adGUID, 344
adIDispatch, 344
adInteger, 227
adInteger, 344
adIUnknown, 344
adLockBatchOptimistic, 220
adLockOptimistic, 220
adLockPessimistic, 220
adLockReadOnly, 220
adLongVarBinary, 344
adLongVarChar, 344
adLongVarWChar, 344
adNumeric, 344
adOpenDynamic, 219
adOpenForwardOnly, 219
adOpenKeyset, 219
adOpenStatic, 219
adParamInput, 227, 345
adParamInputOutput, 227, 345
adParamOutput, 227, 345
adParamReturnValue, 227, 345
adSingle, 227, 345
adSmallInt, 227, 345
adTinyInt, 227, 345
adUnsignedBigInt, 345
adUnsignedInt, 345
adUnsignedSmallInt, 345
adUnsignedTinyInt, 345
adUserDefined, 345
adVarBinary, 345
adVarChar, 227, 345
adVariant, 345
adVarWChar, 345
adVector, 345
adWChar, 345
data type, 227
direction, 227
files, 97
NotAnMTSObject, 466
NoTransactions, 466
RECORDSPERPAGE, 311
RequiresNewTransaction, 466
RequiresTransaction, 466
UsesTransaction, 466

content of Web sites
   rating, 156
   types, changing, 155-156
CONTENT_LENGTH variable, 104,
CONTENT_TYPE variable, 104, 141
Contents collection, 184-185, 187-188
Contents column, 376
Contents property, 386
ContentType property, 155
continuation characters, 51
conversion functions, 40
converting logical expressions, 60
cookies
   back-end code, 175-182
   browsers, 162
   CreateCookie.asp code, 163-165
   creating or updating code, 166-167
   creating, 163-166, 499
   demographic information, 161
   DoubleClick, 160
   forms, creating, 168-170
   forms, testing, 181
   introduction, 159-162
   modifying, 166-168
   Motley Fool's, 160
   preferences, tracking, 168-182
   privacy concerns, 161
   RemoveCookie.asp code, 167
   removing, 166-168
   Session object, 352
   Size, 170-171
   Toppings, 171-175
copying records, 223-224
Cos function, 73
cosine function, 73
Create column, 376
Create subroutine, 403
CreateCookie.asp code, 163-165
CreateObject method, 190
CreateParameter method, 226, 343
CreateRecordset
   function, code, 273-274
   method, 379
CreateVisitorID subroutine
   catviewer.asp, 359-360
   common.asp, 357-358
CSng function, 70
CSS (Cascading Style Sheets), 6, 451
CStr function, 70

ct shortcut name, 380
CursorType parameters, 219
Custom Events, 444-449
Custom.WebItem, 444-449
   code, 444-445
CustomerList HTML template code, 450-451

D
DAO (Data Access Objects), 209
data access adding, 400-423
data browsers
   recordsets, publishing, 234-235
   application security, 318-332
   browsers, creating, 303-306
   category viewer, 237-239
   cleaning up, 235-236
   databases, paging through, 307-312
   garden gate security, 326-329
   product information, adding, 247-252
   product list pages, 239-241
   product lists, 242-247
   Recordset, 318
   search utilities, 252-262
   session-level security, 329-332
   sorting features, 312-318
   starting, 231-233
   table data, retrieving, 233-234
   testing, 236
data conversion functions, 67-72
data entry forms
   AddRecord subroutine, creating, 275-277
   creating, 263-301
   DeleteRecord subroutine, creating, 278-280
   EditRecord subroutine, creating, 277-278
   linking to pages, 287-301
   ShowPage subroutine, creating, 280-287
   structure, adding, 267-271
   ViewRecord subroutine, 271-275
Data Link
   code, 216
   Connection dialog box, 214
   files, 214-216
   Provider dialog box, 215
Data Source parameter, 213
data types
   constants, 227
   Double, 70
   Integer, 70
   Single, 70

VBScript, 31-40
data
    accessing through interfaces, 210
    formatting functions, 77-79
    viewing on Web browsers, 231
database queries
    building, 333-338
    code, modifying, 355-362
    invoice details queries, code to execute, 348-351
    invoice info, designing, 342-343
    invoice queries, 339-342
    order details, designing, 342
    tables, creating, 354-355
    user activity, tracking, 351-362
    Visitors table, 354
    VisitorSearches table, 355
    VisitorViews table, 354-355
databases
    building, 470-471
    code to load category names, 243-244
    connection code, 231
    designing, 482-484
    error handling code, 228
    paging through, 307-312
    sorting features, 312-318
    table data, retrieving, 233-234
    tables, creating, 354-355
Date function, 86
date/time, #flast mod directive, 106
DATE_GMT variable, 104, 141
DATE_LOCAL variable, 104, 141
DateAdd function, 87
DateDiff function, 87
DatePart function, 88
dates
    creating with VBScript code, 100-103
    expiration, 154-155
DateSerial function, 88
DateValue function, 88
Day function, 88
decision structures, 48-64
declarations, AdMgr class code, 471
declaring
    objects, 195
    variables, 31
default prefixes, WC@, 443
default.asp code, 496-499
DefineColumn method, 379-380

DeleteRecord subroutine code, 278-280
deleting records, 268-269
delimiter characters
    = (equal sign), 151
    HTML (HyperText Markup Language), 151-152
demographic information from cookies, 161
deployment packages, creating, 426-430
Description
    field, 470, 483
    property, 391
design tips for MTS (Microsoft Transaction Server), 469-470
designer file (.DSR), 435
di shortcut name, 380
Dialect property, 378
dialog boxes
    Add New Catalog, 367
    Catalog properties, 367 368
    Data Link Connection, 214, 215
    Data Link Provider, 215
    Project Properties, 437
Dictionary object, code testing, 90
Dim
    keyword, 31, 32
    statement, 32
dimension parameter (LBound and UBound functions, 39
direction constants, 227
direction values, parameters, 345
directives
    #config, 98-103
    #echo, 103-105
    #exec, 105-106
    #flastmod, 106-107
    #fsize, 107-109
    #include, 109-110, 356
    SSI (server-side includes), 98-109
Directory
    column, 376
    command (New menu), 369
Discontinued field, code to check, 256-257
discussion forums
    ASP code, building, 495-519
    creating, 481-482
    databases, designing, 483-484
    libraries, generating, 495
    object library, building, 485-495

Continued

discussion forums *(continued)*
   object model, 481-482
      Subscription class, creating, 492-495
      system functions, 482
DisplayData subroutine, 311
   code, 346-347
DisplayNavigation routine, 311
DisplayPageLinks routine, 311
division, 41
DLLs, packages, adding to, 468
Do keyword, 61
Do While keywords, 63
Do/Loop structure
   exiting, 63
   logical expressions, converting, 60
   loops, exiting, 61-62
   nesting, 62-63
   operators, reversing, 59-61
   structures unsupported, 64
DocAppName column, 376
DocAuthor
   column, 376
   property, 387
DocByteCount column, 376
DocCategory column, 376
DocCharCount column, 376
DocComments
   column, 376
   property, 387
DocCompany column, 376
DocCreatedTm column, 376
DocEditTime column, 376
DocHiddenCount column, 376
DocKeywords
   column, 376
   property, 387
DocLastAuthor column, 376
DocLastPrinted column, 376
DocLastSavedTm column, 376
DocLineCount column, 376
DocManager column, 376
DocNoteCount column, 376
DocPageCount column, 376
DocParaCount column, 376
DocPartTitles column, 376
DocPresentationTarget column, 376
DocRevNumber column, 376
DocSecurity column, 377
DocSlideCount column, 377

DocSubject
   column, 377
   property, 387
DocTemplate column, 377
DocThumbnail column, 377
DocTitle
   column, 377
   property, 387
doctitle parameter, 373-374
DOCUMENT_NAME variable, 104, 141
DOCUMENT_URI variable, 104, 141
documents
   CSS (Cascading Style Sheets), 451
   HTML (HyperText Markup Language)
      structure, 3-4
DocWordCount column, 377
DoEvents keyword, 64
Double data type, 70
double quotes (" "), 38, 150, 247, 385
DoubleClick cookie, 160
Drive object, 91
drivers, providers, 210
Drives object, 91
drives, code to get information on, 91
drop-down lists (select lists), 127-133
.DSR file, 435
Durability (ACID test), 464

E
Edit
   menu commands, Preferences, 162
   method, 404
   subroutine, 404
editing
   records in recordsets, 221-222
   records, 268
editproduct.asp code, 289-301
EditRecord subroutine code, 277-278
Elself keyword, 53
EMailAddress field, 483
Employee class
   adding to, 401-404
   code, 393-394, 401-403
   code, revised, 395-396
   code, to test, 404
employee entity properties, 390-391
EmployeeID property, 390, 391
End If statement, 50
End method, 157

EndDate property, 392
end-of-file (EOF), 220-221
envdump.asp code, 143
 variables, HTTP (HyperText
        Transfer Protocol), 104-105, 141-142
EOF (end-of-file), 220-221
    property, 235
equal sign (=), 235, 387
    delimiter characters, 151
equal to (=), 44
Eqv operator, 47
Erase statement, syntax, 38
Err object, 90
error handling, 198-200
    BasicErrorHandler.asp code, 201
    code to add, 229
    code to test databases, 228
    EnhancedErrorHandler.asp code,
        203-204
    ErrorSource.asp code, 202, 205
    log files, 205
    On Error Resume Next, 197
    Resume Next, 460
error messages, 198-201
Error object, 228
Errors collection, 228-230
event procedures, ProcessTags, 454
events
    Application, 186
    Custom Events, 440-449
    Initialize, code, 471
    OnEnd, 189
    OnStart, 189
    ProcessTag, 443
    Respond, 449
    Session object, 189
    Terminate, 492
    WebClass_Start, 443
exclamation point (!), 384
Execute method, 190-191, 217, 224
exiting
    Do/Loop structure, 63
    loops, 61-62
Exp function, 74
expiration dates, 154-155
Expires property, 164
exponentiation operator, 42
expressions
    Boolean, 44

    conditional, 49
    grouping, 42-44

F
FACE parameter, FONT tag, 11
False keyword, 30
Field object
    queries, executing, 217-218
    records, adding to tables, 222-223
    Recordset, code to open, 218
    recordsets, editing records, 221-222
    recordsets, navigating, 220-221
    recordsets, opening, 218-220
FIELD tags, 460
fields
    * (asterisk), 340
    AdID, 470
    Age, 484
    Alternate Text, 470
    BrowserType, 470
    Description, 470, 483
    Discontinued, code to check, 256-257
    EMailAddress, 483
    FirstName, 483
    GroupID, 483, 484
    GroupName, 483
    Height, 470
    hidden input, code 133
    HomePage, 484
    ImageURL, 470
    ImpressionID, 470
    Interests, 484
    IsClickthrough, 470
    IsReply, 484
    LastMessageID, 484
    LastName, 483
    Location, 484
    MemberID, 483, 484
    MessageDate, 484
    MessageID, 484
    MessageText, 484
    optPriceRange, 258
    PageURL, 470
    Password, 483
    Price, code to check, 257
    RemoteHost, 470
    ReplyToID, 484
    ShowEMail, 483

                                    Continued

fields (continued)
  ShownTime, 470
  ShowProfile, 484
  Subject, 484
  Unit Stock, code to check, 258
  URL, 470
  UserName, 483
  Width, 470
File
  menu commands, Add Project, 425
  object, 91
FileDateTime function, code, 106-107
FileIndex column, 377
FileName column, 377
Filename property, 386
Files object, 91
files
  #include directive samples code, 110
  ADOVBS, 345
  AllHTTPDump.asp code, 144-145
  basicform.html, code, 115-116
  basicform_process.asp code, 116-117
  basicqs.html code, 134
  basicqs_process.asp code, 134
  BasicTemplate.htlm code, 441
  catviewer.asp code, 237-238, 263-264, 356-357
  catviewer.asp code, CreateVisitorID
    subroutine, 359-360
  common.asp code, 356
  common.asp code, CreateVisitorID
    subroutine, 357-358
  constants, 97
  contents, transferring, 109
  Data Link, 214-216
  default.asp code, 496-499
  .DSR, 435
  editproduct.asp code, 289-301
  EnhancedErrorHandler.asp code, 203-204
  envdump.asp code, 143
  ErrorSource.asp code, 202, 205
  FunctionLibrary.asp code for virtual paths,
    111
  gg_longin.asp code, 327-328
  GIF extension, counting, 92
  global.asa, 192-196
  log, 205
  message.asp code, 515-519
  Motley Fool's cookie, 160

  orderbrowser.asp code, 304-306, 324-325
  orderbrowser.asp code, revised, 307-311
  pizzaaform2_process.asp code, 130-132
  pizzaform.html, 122-123
  pizzaform.html with select list, 128-129
  pizzaform_process.asp code, 124-125
  prodinfo.asp code, 250-251, 266-267
  prodviewer.asp code, 239-240, 248-249,
    264-265,
  profile.asp code, 502-507
  Project1_WebClass1.asp code, 440
  searchform.asp, 259
  searchresults.asp code, 255, 260-262
  searchresults.asp, code to modify, 361
  showmessage.asp code, 511-514
  SingleForm.asp code, 135-136
  StructuredForm.asp code, 138-140
  URLs (Uniform Resource Locators),
    changing, 332
  util.asp code, 499-501
  vieworder.asp code, 319-324
FileSize function, code, 108-109
FileSystem object, 90-93
FileSystemObject, 91
FillObject
Function, code, 486-487
  method, 404
Filter function, 81
  code for testing, 80
FirstName field, 483
Fix function, 71
flags, IsNew, 404
Flush method, 153, 154
fnGenerateCustomerList
  code changes 457-458
  function code, 452-453
Folder object, 91
Folders object, 91
FONT tag, parameters, 11
For Each/Next
  keyword, 64
  statement, 185
For/Next, 53
  loops, exiting, 55
  nested loops, 55-56
  Step keyword, 54-55
FormatCurrency function, 77-78
FormatDateTime function, 78-79
FormatNumber function, 79

FormatPercent function, 79
formatting tags, 12
    tables, 20-25
formatting
    data functions, 77-79
    text, 5-12
    time/date codes, 99
forms
    check boxes, 121-127
    creating, 168-170
    data entry, adding structure, 267-271
    data entry, creating, 263-301
    data entry, creating AddRecord subroutine,
        275-277
    data entry, creating DeleteRecord
        subroutine, 278-280
    data entry, creating EditRecord subroutine,
        277-278
    data entry, creating ShowPage subroutine,
        280-287
    data entry, linking to pages, 287-301
    data entry, ViewRecord subroutine, 271-275
    hidden input fields, code 133
    information, 114-133
    pizza delivery code, 127-128
    queries, code, 370
    radio buttons, 119-121
    search boxes, creating, 114-119
    search, 252-254
    select lists, 127-133
    testing, 181
forward slash (/), 41
forward-only recordset, 219
free-text queries, 386
FunctionLibrary.asp, code for virtual paths, 111
functions
    Abs, 73
    arctangent, 73
    arrays, 36-39
    Asc, 71
    Atn, 73
    Base Conversion, 72
    CBool, 67-68
    CByte, 68
    CCur, 68
    CDate, test code, 69
    CDbl, 70
    Character to Number, 71
    Chr, 54, 71

CLng, 70
CLnt, 70
conversion, 40
Cos, 73
cosine, 73
CreateRecordset, code, 273-274
CSng, 70
CStr, 70
data conversion, 67-72
data formatting, 77-79
Date, 86
DateAdd, 87
DateDiff, 87
DatePart, 88
DateSerial, 88
DateValue, 88
Day, 88
Exp, 74
FileDateTime, code, 106-107
FileSize, code, 108-109
FillObject, code, 486-487
Filter, 80-81
Fix, 71
fnGenerateCustomerList code, 452-453
FormatCurrency, 77-78
FormatDateTime, 78-79
FormatNumber, 79
FormatPercent, 79
Hour, 88
Impression code, 472
InStr, 81
InStrRev, 81-82
Int, 71
Integer Conversion, 72
IsArray, 33
IsDate, 33
IsEmpty, 34
IsNull, 34
IsNumeric, 34
Join, 82
LBound, 38-39
LCase, 83
Left, 83
Len, 83
Log, 74
loopvar, 54
LTrim, 83
MakeConnection, code, 272-273

Continued

funtions *(continued)*
   mathematical, 72-76
   Mid, 83
   Minute, 88
   Month, 89
   MonthName, 89
   Now, 89
   RefreshObject, code, 490
   Replace, 84
   Rnd, 74-75
   Round, 75
   RTrim, 84
   SaveObject, code, 486-487
   Second, 89
   Sgn, 76
   Sin, 76
   Space, 85
   Split, 85, 132
   Sqr, 76
   String, 86
   StrReverse, 85-86
   system, 482
   Tan, 76
   Trim, 86
   type conversion, 67-70
   UBound, 38-39
   UCase, 86
   URLFor, 445-446, 458
   variable-checking, 33-36
   VarType, return values, 35-36
   Weekday, 89
   WeekdayName, 89
   Year, 89

G

garden gate security, 326-329
GATEWAY_INTERFACE variable, 104, 141
gd shortcut name, 380
Generation tab (Catalog properties
      dialog box), 368
Get property, 410
GetLastError method, 191
GetsTips property, 391
gg_longin.asp code, 327-328
GIF, files, code to count, 92
global.asa, 192-196
   Application event code, 193-194
   objects, declaring, 195
   Session event code, 194

GoSub/Return keyword, 64
GoTo keyword, 64
gr shortcut name, 380
greater than (>), 44, 387
greater than or equal to (>=), 44, 387
group listing page, creating, 508-509
Group object, 482
   creating, 485-487
group viewer page, creating, 509-510
GroupBy property, 378
GroupID
   field, 483, 484
   property, 391
grouping expressions, 42-44
GroupName field, 483
gryGetShipper query code, 225-226

H

H1 tag, 235
HEAD tag, 4
headings tags, 6-7
   source code, 5
Height field, 470
HEIGHT parameter, TABLE tag, 21
Hello World WebClass, 434-440
hidden input code, 133
HomePage field, 484
Hour function, 88
HourlyRate property, 391
HR tag, 13
   code, 14
parameters, 15
HTML (HyperText Markup Language)
   </BODY> tag, 235
   </HTML> tag, 236
   <H4> tag, 454
   <HEAD> tag, 240
   <HTML> tag, 240
   <LI> tag, 238
   <TITLE> tag, 240
   anchor tag, 25-26
   BLOCKQUOTE tag, 8
   BODY tab, 235
   BODY tag, parameters 4
   BR tag, 13, 56
   breaking up, 438-439
   CENTER tag, 12
   code for lists within lists, 17
   code from WebClass, 438

CODE tag, 10-11
CODE tag, source code, 10
code with line breaks, 439
CSS (Cascading Style Sheets), 451
delimiter characters, 151-152
FIELD tags, 460
FONT tag, parameters, 11
formatting tags, 12
H1 tag, 235
HEAD tag4,
heading tags, 5-7
heading tags, source code, 5
HR tag, 13
HR tag, code, 14
HR tag, parameters, 15
HTML tag,
image tag, 26
learning resources, 26-27
LI tag, 235
list tags, 15-20
OBJECT tab, 195
OL tag, 17-20
OL tag, source code, 17-18
ordered lists, 17-20
page structure, 3-4
pages, creating, 441
PARAGRAPH tag, 13
positioning tags, 12-15
PRE tag, source code, 8-9
START tag, 18
START tag, code for ordered lists, 19
substitution tags, 443
TABLE tag, 20-21, 454
tables, code, 23-24
tags, 4, 5
TD tag, 22-23
templates, 440-443
templates with substitution tags, 450
text formatting, 5-12
TH tag, parametes, 22
TITLE tag, 4
TR tag, parameters, 21
TYPE tag, 18
TYPE tag, code for ordered lists, 19
UL tag, 15-17, 235
WebClass_Start event procedure code,
    446-447
HTMLEncode method, 191, 381
HtmlHeading1 column, 377

HtmlHeading2 column, 377
HtmlHeading3 column, 377
HtmlHeading4 column, 377
HtmlHeading5 column, 377
HtmlHeading6 column, 377
HtmlHRef column, 377
HTTP (HyperText Transfer Protocol)
    cookies, 159-162
environment variables, 104-105, 141-142
HyperText Markup Language. See HTML

I
I tag, 12
Ids, query parameters, 333
If keyword, 49
If/Then/Else structure
    conditional expressions, 49
    continuation characters, 51
    Elself keyword, 53
    End If statement, 50
    nested, 51-52
    readability, 51
    syntax, 49
image tag, 26
ImageURL field, 470
Img_Alt column, 377
Imp operator, 47
implicit type conversion, 48
Impression
    function, code, 472
    method, code, 476
    testing, 474
ImpressionID field, 470
include file, code for ADO constants, 274-275
Index Server
    ASP Techniques Web site, 387
    Boolean operators, 384-385
    columns for queries, 375-377
    configuring, 365-369
    Index Server Manager, 365
    indexes, creating, 366-369
    object model, 374-382
    properties, 386-387
    property shortcut names, 380
    proximity operators, 384-385
    queries, free-text, 386
    queries, property value, 386-387
    query language, 383-388

Continued

Index Server *(continued)*
    Query object, properties and methods, 374-380
      relational operators, 387
      search pages, creating, 370-374
      Utility object methods, 381-382
      wildcards, 385
indexes, creating, 366-369
information
    code to retrieve, 187
    retrieving code, 184
    sources, Request object, 113-114
Init method code, 485-486
Initialize event code, 471
Initializing variables, 32
INSERT statement, 359
InStr function, 81
InStrRev function, 81-82
Int function, 71
Integer Conversion function, 72
Integer data type, 70
Interests field, 484
Internet Explorer 4 and 5, configuring, 162
Internet Information Server 4.0, Index Server, 365
Internet. *See also* Web pages; Web sites
    WWW (World Wide Web), testing libraries, 430-431
invoice details queries, code to execute, 348-351
invoice info query, designing, 342-343
invoices, queries, 339-342
IsArray function, 33
IsClickthrough field, 470
IsClientConnected property, 157
IsCompleted property, 391
IsDate function, 33
IsEmpty function, 34
IsNew flag, 404
IsNull function, 34
IsNumeric function, 34
IsObject function, 35
Isolation (ACID test), 463
ISOToLocale method, 382
IsReply field, 48

J-K

Join function, 82
keywords
    Case Else, 57-58
    Const, 30
    Dim, 31, 32
    Do, 61
    Doevents, 64
    DoWhile, 63
    ElseIf, 53
    False, 30
    For Each/Next, 64
    GoSub/Return, 64
    GoTo, 64
    If, 49
    Loop, 61, 62, 235
    Next, 56
    Not, 60
    Null, 30
    On Error GoTo, 64
    Preserve, 36
    Randomize, 473
    Step, 54-55
    True, 30
    Until, 59, 50, 62
    WHERE, 255
    While, 60, 62
    With/End With, 64
kilobytes, printing size, 107

L

languages, query (Index Server), 383-388
LAST_MODIFIED variable, 104, 141
LastMessageID field, 484
LastName field, 483
LBound function, 38
    parameters, 39
LCase function, 83
LCID property, 189
learning resources, HTML (HyperText Markup Languge), 26-27
Left function, 83
Len function, 83
less than (<), 44, 387
less than or equal to (<=), 44, 387
Let property, 410
LI tag, 235
libraries
    components, compiling, 424-425
    components, testing, 425-426
    deployment packages, creating, 426-430
    generating, 495
    Microsoft Transaction Server Type Library, 471
    objects, 485-495

testing on WWW (World Wide Web), 430-431
type, referencing, 195-196
LINK parameter, BODY tag, 4
links, code to edit and delete, 288-289
list tags, 15-20
lists
    code for lists within lists, 17
    ordered, 17-20
    ordered, START tag code, 19
    ordered, TYPE tag code, 19
    product, 242-237
    UL tag, 15-17
lngOrderID parameter, 343
LocaleID property, 378
LocaleIDToISO method, 382
Location field, 484
Location tab (Catalog properties dialog box),
        367
    Lock method, 186, 358
LockType parameters, 220
log files, 205
Log function, 74
logical expressions, converting, 60
logical operators, 48. *See also* operators
    And, 45
    Eqv, 47
    Imp, 47
    implicit type conversion
    Not, 44-45
    Or, 46
    Xor, 46
Login
    button, 499
    page, creating, 496-501
login pages, code to modify, 330
Long data type, 70
Loop keyword, 61, 62, 235
looping structures, 48-63
    unsupported, 64
loops
    code to publish recordsets with, 234-235
    exiting, 61-62
    For/Next, exiting, 55
    nested, 55-56
loopvar function, 54
LTrim function, 83

M
MakeConnection function, code, 272-273
Manager property, chaining objects, 410

ManagerGet property, 410
ManagerID property, 392
MapPath method, 191-192
mathematical functions, 72-76
mathematical operations
    addition, 40
    comparison operators, 44
    division, 41
    exponentiation operator, 42
    grouping expressions, 42-44
    modulus/remainder function, 41-42
    multiplication, 41
    subtraction, 40
MaxRecords property, 373, 379
Member object, 481
building, 487-489
    subroutines, code, 487-489
MemberID field, 483, 484
memberinfo.asp page, author information, 514
menu groups entity properties, 391
menu items entity properties, 391
MenuGroup class, code, 396-397, 411-413
MenuItem class,code, 397, 413-415
MenuItemID property, 392
message editor page, creating, 514-519
Message object, 482
    code, 491-492
    creating, 489-492
    object properties, code, 489-490
message.asp code, 515-519
MessageDate field, 484
MessageID field, 484
messages
    error, 198-201
    validating, 519
MessageText field, 484
message-viewing page, creating, 511-514
methods
    AddScopeToQuery, 381
    clear, 153, 154
    Close, 216
    CreateObject, 190
    CreateParameter, 226, 343
    CreateRecordset, 379
    DefineColumn, 379-380
    Edit, 404
    End, 157
    Execute, 190-191, 217, 218, 223
    FillObject, 404

Continued

methods *(continued)*
   Flush, 153, 154
   GetLastError, 191
   HTMLEncode, 191, 381
   Init, code, 485-486
   ISOToLocale, 382
   LocaleIDToISO, 382
   Lock, 186, 358
   MapPath, 191-192
   MoveNext, 235
   Query object, 379-380
   QueryToURL, 380
   Redirect, 154
   Remove, 185, 188
   RemoveAll, 185, 188
   RequestServerVariables, 105
   Reset, 380
   Response.Redirect, 153
   Response.Write, 150-151, 238
   Save, 404
   Save, code, 485-486
   Server.CreateObject, 233
   SetQueryFromURL, 380
   Transfer, 192
   TruncatetoWhitespace, 382
   Unlock, 186
   URLEncode, 192, 382
   Utility object, 381-382
mh shortcut name, 380
Microsoft Management Console (MMC), 464
Microsoft Transaction Server Type Library, 471
Microsoft Transaction Server. *See* MTS
Microsoft Universal Data Access strategy,
     209-212
   ODBC (Open Database Connectivity), 210-211
   OLE DB, 210
   RDS (Remove Data Service), 211
Mid function, 83
minus sign (-), 40
Minute function, 88
MMC (Microsoft Management Console), 464
models, business, 392
   employee entity properties, 390-391
   menu groups entity properties, 391
   menu items entity properties, 391
   order entity properties, 391
modifying cookies, 166-168
modular ASP (Active Server Pages), 109-111
modulus/remainder function, 41-42
Month function, 89

MonthName function, 89
Motley Fool's cookie file, 160
MoveNext method, 235
MTS (Microsoft Transaction Server), 463-464
   ad tracking systems, 469-477
   AdMgr class, creating, 471-474
   components, creating, 465-468
   databases, building, 470-471
   design tips, 469-470
   packages, creating, 467-468
MTSTransactionMode values, 466
multiplication, 41

N

NamedFormat parameter values, 78-79
navigating recordsets, 220-221
NEAR operator, 384-385
nested If/Then/Else structure, 51-52
nested loops, 55-56
nesting Do/Loop structure, 62-63
New menu commands
   Catalog, 366
   Component, 468
   Directory, 369
   Package, 467
NewPrice property, 392
Next keyword, 56
NorthwindTraders database (CD-ROM), 231
NOSHADE parameter, HR tag, 15
not equal (!), 387
not equal to (< >), 44
Not keyword, 60
NOT operator, 384-385
Not operator, 44-45
NotAnMTSObject constant, 466
NoTransactions constant, 466
Now function, 89
Null keyword, 30
number sign (#), 386

O

object library
   building, 485-495
   generating, 495
   Group object, creating, 485-487
   Index Server, 374-382
   Member object, building, 487-489
   Messsage object, creating, 489-492
   Subscription class, creating, 492-495
OBJECT tag, 195

ObjectControl object code, 473-474
objects
    Active Data Objects. *See* ADO
    Application. *See* Application object
    built-in, 89-93
    chaining, 410
    cmdQuery, 343
    Command. *See* Command object
    compiling and deploying, 424-431
    Connection. *See* Connection object
    declaring, 195
    Dictionary, 90
    Drive, 91
    Drives, 91
    Err, 90
    Field. *See* Field object
    File, 91
    Files, 91
    FileSystem, 90-93
    FileSystemObject, 91
    Folder, 91
    Folders, 91
    Group, 482
    Group, building, 485-487
    Member, 481
    Member, building, 487-489
    Message, 482
    Message, code, 491-492
    Message, creating, 489-492
    Parameter. *See* Parameter object
    Recordset. *See* Recorset object
    Request. *See* Request object
    Response. *See* Response object
    Server. *See* Server object
    Session. *See* Session object
    Subscription, 482
    TextStream, 91
    Utility object, methods, 381-382
ODBC (Open Database Connectivity), 209,
        210-211
OL tag, 17-20
    source code, 17-18
OLAP (Online Analytical Processing), 210
OLE DB, 210
On Error GoTo keyword, 64
On Error Resume Next, 197
OnEnd event, 189
    Online Analytical Processing
        (OLAP), 210
OnStart event, 189

Open Database Connectivity (ODBC), 209
operators. *See also* logical operators
    AND, 384-385
    Boolean, 384-385
    comparison, 44
    equivalents, 384-385
    logical, 44-48
    NEAR, 384-385
    NOT, 44, 384-385
    OR, 384-385
    proximity, 384-385
    relational, 387
    reversing, 59-61
Option Explicit, 232
    statement, #include directive, 356
optPriceRange field, 258
OR operator, 384-385
Or operator, 46
order browser Sub Main, code to change,
        330-331
Order class, code, 398, 416-418
order details
    page Sub Main code, 331-332
    query, designing, 342
order entity properties, 391
order items entity properties, 392
order specials entity properties, 392
order status applications, security, 319-326
orderbrowser.asp code, 304-306, 324-325
    revised, 307-311
OrderDate property, 391
ordered lists, 17-20
    START tag code, 19
    TYPE tag code, 19
OrderID property, 391
OrderItem class, code, 398-399, 419-421
OrderItemID property, 392
output
    = (equal sign), delimiter characters, 151
    browsers, redirecting, 153
    buffering, 153-154
    caching, 154-155
    content, rating, 156
    content types, changing, 155-156
    creating, 150-152
    delimiter characters, HTML (HyperText
        Markup Language), 151-152
    expiration dates, 154-155
    managing, 153-156
    Response.Write method, 150-151

P

Package command (New menu), 467
packages
    deployment, creating,426–430
    DLL, adding, 468
Packaging and Deployment Wizard, 426–427
pages. *See* Web pages
PageURL field, 470
paging through databases, 307-312
PARAGRAPH tag, 13
Parameter object, 223-227
    queries, running with parameters, 224-227
parameters
    ActiveConnection,224
    ALIGN (HR tag), 15
    ALIGN (TABLE tag), 21
    ALIGN (TD tag), 23
    ALIGN (TH tag), 22
    ALIGN (TR tag), 21
    ALINK (BODY tag), 4
    arrayname (LBound and
        UBound functions), 39
    BACKGROUND (BODY tag), 4
    BACKGROUND (TABLE tag), 21
    BACKGROUND (TD tag), 23
    BACKGROUND (TH tag), 22
    BACKGROUND (TR tag), 21
    BGCOLOR (BODY tag), 4
    BGCOLOR (TABLE tag), 21
    BGCOLOR (TD tag), 23
    BGCOLOR (TH tag), 22
    BGCOLOR (TR tag), 21
    BODY tag, 4
    BORDER (TABLE tag), 21
    CELLPADDING (TABLE tag), 21
    CELLSPACING (TABLE tag), 21
    COLOR (FONT tag), 11
    COLOR (HR tag), 15
    COLS (TABLE tag), 21
    COLSPAN (TD tag), 23
    COLSPAN (TH tag), 22
    commandText, 224
    CursorType, 219
    Data Source, 213
    dimension (LBound and
        UBound functions), 39
    direction values, 345
    doctitle, 373-374
    FACE (FONT tag), 11

FONT tag, 11
HEIGHT (TABLE tag), 21
LBound function, 39
LINK (BODY tag), 4
lngOrderID, 343
LockType, 220
NamedFormat values, 78-79
NOSHADE (HR tag), 15
Preserve, 37
queries, 333
queries, running with, 224-227
ReDim statement, 37
Rnd function, 75
ROWSPAN (TD tag), 23
ROWSPAN (TH tag), 22
SIZE (FONT tag), 11
SIZE (HR tag), 15
START values, 20
strLocation, 204
Subscripts, 37
TagContents, 443
TD tag, 23
TEXT (BODY tag), 4
TH tag, 22
TR tag, 21
TYPE values, 20
type values, 343-345
VALIGN (TD tag), 23
VALIGN (TH tag), 22
Varname, 37
VLINK (BODY tag), 4
vpath, 373-374
WIDTH (HR tag), 15
WIDTH (TABLE tag), 21
WIDTH (TD tag), 23
WIDTH (TH tag), 22
parentheses ( ), 42
Password field, 483
passwords, changing, 468
Path column, 377
PATH_INFO variable, 104, 142
    code, 146-147
PATH_TRANSLATED variable, 104, 142
percent sign (%), 150
PICS (Platform for Internet Content
        Selection), 156
pipe symbol (|), 384
pizza delivery form code, 127-128
PizzaDeliveryForm.asp code, 168-169

completed code, 175-181
new code, 170-174
pizzaform.html file code, 122-123
pizzaform.html with select list, code, 128-129
pizzaform_process.asp, code, 124-125
pizzaform2_process.asp, code, 130-132
Platform for Internet Content
            Selection (PICS), 156
plus sign (+), 40
pn variable, 311
positioning tags, 12-15
PRE tag
    comparing with CODE tag, 10-11
    source code, 8-9
Preferences command (Edit menu), 162
preferences, tracking with cookies, 168-182
prefixes, WC@, 443
Preserve
    keyword, 36
    parameter, 37
Price field, code to check, 257
Price property, 391
privacy, cookies, 161
procedures, stored, 218
ProcessTag
    code, 446
    event, 443
    event handler code, 452
    event procedure, 454
prodinfo.asp code, 250-251, 266-267
product information, Web pages, adding to,
            247-252
product list page, creating, 239-241
product list, code to add back links, 242
product listing page, changing, 247-249
product lists, 242-247
product names, checking code, 256
product pages, code, 288
product viewing page
    changing, 359-360
    code, 245-246
products, code to add, 287-288
prodviewer.asp, code, 239-240, 248-249, 264-265
profile.asp code, 502-507
Project Explorer window, 435
Project menu commands, References, 425
Project Properties dialog box, 437
Project1_WebClass1.asp code, 440
properties

AbsolutePage, 311
ae shortcut name, 380
All, 386
AllowEnumeration, 374
Buffer, 153
CacheControl, 154
Catalog, 373, 374
CiFlags, 374
CiScope, 375
City, 392
CodePage, 189, 375
Columns, 373, 375-
ConnectionString, 213
Contents, 386
ContentType, 155
ct shortcut name, 380
Description, 391
di shortcut name, 380
Dialect, 378
DocAuthor, 387
DocComments, 387
DocKeywords, 387
DocSubject, 387
DocTitle, 387
employee entities, 390-391
EmployeeID, 390, 391
EndDate, 392
Expires, 164
Filename, 386
gd shortcut name, 380
Get, 410
GetsTips, 391
gr shortcut name, 380
GroupBy, 378
GroupID, 391
HourlyRate, 391
Index Server shortcut names, 380
IsClientConnected, 157
IsCompleted, 391
LCID, 189
Let, 410
LocaleID, 378
Manager, chaining objects, 410
ManagerGet, 410
ManagerID, 392
MaxRecords, 373, 379
menu groups entities, 391
menu items entities, 391

Continued

properties *(continued)*
MenuItemID, 392
mh shortcut name, 380
NewPrice, 392
order entities, 391, 392
order specials entities, 392
OrderDate, 391
OrderID, 391
OrderItemID, 392
Price, 391
Provider, 213
qu shortcut name, 380
Quantity, 392
Query object, 374-379
Query, 373, 379
QueryIncomplete, 379
QueryTimeOut, 379
read/write, 398
Response.Buffer, 154
ScriptTimeOut, 190
sd shortcut name, 380
Session object, 189
SessionID, 189, 355
Size, 387
so shortcut name, 380
SortBy, 379
SortOrder, 391
SpecialID, 392
StartDate, 392
State, 392
StoreID, 391, 392
stores entities, 392
TipAmount, 391
Write, 387
Property Get routine, 398
Property Let routine, 398
property value queries, 386-387
Provider property, 213
providers, 210
proximity operators, 384-385
publishing recordsets, 234-235

Q
qryGetGroupMessages code, 510
qryGetSubscriptions code, 509
qu shortcut name, 380
Quantity property, 392
queries
    building, 333-338
    code, closing and displaying results, 259
    code, modifying, 355-362
    database tables, creating, 354-355
    executing, 217-218
    forms, code, 370
    free-text, 386
    gryGetShipper code, 225-226
    Index server columns, 375-377
    invoice, 339-342
    invoice details, code to execute, 348-351
    invoice info, designing, 342-343
    order details, designing, 342
    parameters, 333
    processing pages code, 371-372
    property value, 386-387
    Query object, 372
    rules for formulating, 383
    running with parameters, 224-227
    setup code, 255
    tables, adding, 33
    user activity, tracking, 351-362
    Visitors table, 354
    VisitorSearches table, 355
    VisitorViews table, 354-355
query language (Index Server), 383-388
Query object
    methods, 379-380
    properties, 374-379
    search engines, 372
Query property, 373, 379
query string variables
    sd (Sort Direction), 317
    so (Sort Order), 317
query strings, 133-140
QUERY_STRING variable, 104, 142
QUERY_STRING_UNESCAPED variable, 105, 142
QueryIncomplete property, 379
QueryTimeOut property, 379
QueryToURL method, 380
quotes
    double (" "), 38, 150, 247, 385
    single (' '), 222, 361

R
RACi (Recreational Solftware Advisory Council
        on the Internet) Web site, 156
radio buttons, 119-121
    code to create, 119-120
Randomize
    keyword, 473
    statement, 74-75

RDO (Remote Data Objects), 209
RDS (Remote Data Service), 211
read/write properties, 398
readability, If/Then/Else structure, 51
RecordCategoryID subroutine code, 359-360
records
    adding, 268
    code, adding with ADO (Active Data
        Objects), 222
    code, editing, 221
    copying, 223-224
    deleting, 268-269
    editing, 268
    viewing, 269-271
RecordSearchInfo subroutine code, 360-362
Recordset object, 318
    code, creating, 223-224
    code, opening, 218
    queries, executing, 217-218
    records, adding to tables, 222-223
    Recordset, code to open, 218
    recordsets, editing records, 221-222
    recordsets, navigating, 220-221
    recordsets, opening, 218-220
recordsets
    code, creatomg from databases, 233-234
    code, looping, 220
    code, publishing with loops, 234-235
    forward-only, 219
    navigating, 220-221
    opening, 218-220
    publishing, 234-235
    records, editing, 221-222
RECORDSPERPAGE constant, 311
Recreational Solftware Advisory Council on the
        Internet (RACi) Web site, 156
ReDim statement, 36, 38
    parameters, 37
    syntax, 37
Redirect method, 154
redirecting browsers, 153
References command (Project menu), 425
RefreshObject function, code, 490
relational operators, 387
Remote Data Objects (RDO), 209
Remote Data Service (RDS), 211
REMOTE_ADDR variable, 105, 142
REMOTE_HOST variable, 105, 142
REMOTE_USER variable, 105, 142
RemoteHost field, 470

Remove method, 185, 188
RemoveAll method, 185, 188
RemoveCookie.asp code, 167
removing cookies, 166-168
Replace function, 84
ReplyToID field, 484
Request object
    form information, 114-133
    information sources, 113-114
    query strings, 133-140
    server variables, 140-147
    ServerVariables collection, 140
    variables, server, 140-147
Request.ServerVariables
    collection, 204
    method, 105
REQUEST_METHOD variable, 105, 142
RequiresNewTransaction constant, 466
RequiresTransaction constant, 466
Reset method, 380
Respond event, 449
Response object
    connections, managing, 156-157
    output, creating, 150-152
    output, managing, 153-156
Response.Buffer property. 154
Response.Redirect method, 153
Response.Write method, 150-151, 238
Resume Next error handler, 460
RetrieveData subroutine code, 342-343
retrieving table data, 233-234
reversing operators, 59-61
Rnd function, 74
    parameters, 75
Round function, 75
routines
    Create subroutine, 403
    CreateVisitorID subroutine code in
        catviewer.asp, 359-360
    CreateVisitorID subroutine code in
        common.asp, 357-358
    DisplayData subroutine, 311
    DisplayData subroutine, code, 346-347
    DisplayNavigation, 311
    DisplayPageLinks, 311
    Edit subroutine, 404
    Member object subroutines, code, 487-489
    Property Get, 398
    Property Let, 398

Continued

routines *(continued)*
  RecordCategoryID subroutine code,
    359-360
  RecordSearchInfo subroutine code,
    360-362
  RetrieveData subroutine code, 342-343
  ShowPage, 276
  StoreDate, 276
  Sub Main, 311, 331
  Validate, 499, 508
  ViewRecord subroutine, creating, 271-275
ROWSPAN parameter
  TD tag, 23
  TH tag, 22
RTrim function, 84
Run menu commands, Start, 437

S

S tag, 12
Save method, 404
    code, 485-486
SaveObject function, code, 486-487
sColor variable, 446
SCRIPT_NAME variable, 105, 142
ScriptTimeOut property, 190
sd (Sort Direction) query string variable, 317
sd shortcut name, 380
search box creating, 114-119
search engines, Query object, 372
search forms, 252-254
search code, 252-253
search pages, creating, 370-374
search results pages
    changing, 360-362
    creating, 254-262
search utilities
    creating, 252-262
    search forms, 252-254
    search results pages, 254-262
searchform.asp. 259
searchresults.asp code, 255, 260-262
    code to modify, 361
Second function, 89
security
    #exec directive, 105
    applications, 318-322
    garden gate, 326-329
    order status applications, 319-326
    passwords, changing, 468

session-level, 329-332
select lists, 127-133
Select/Case structure, 56
    _ (underscore), 58-59
    blank actions, performing, 58
    Case Else keyword, 57-58
Server object, 189
    CreateObject method, 190
    Execute method, 190-191
    GetLastError method, 191
    HTMLEncode method, 191
    MapPath method, 191-192
    ScriptTimeOut property, 190
    Transfer method, 192
    URLEncode method, 192
Server.CeateObject method, 233
SERVER_NAME variable, 105, 142
SERVER_PORT variable, 105, 142
SERVER_PORT_SECURE variable, 105, 142
SERVER_PROTOCOL variable, 105, 142
SERVER_SOFTWARE variable, 105, 142
servers. *See also* Index Server
    SQL connection code, 233
    variables, 140-147
server-side includes (SSI)
    commands, 97
    directives, 98-109
ServerVariables collection, 140
Session event, creating, 194
Session object
    code to retrieve information, 187
    Contents collection, 187-188
    cookies, 352
    properties, 189
    session control, 188-189
    session events, 189
    session-level security, 329-332
    StaticObjects collection, 188
    syntax, 186
    systems values, code to check, 188
SessionID property, 189, 355
session-level security, 329-332
sessions, controlling, 188-189
SetQueryFromURL method, 380
Sgn function, 76
ShortFileName column, 377
ShowEMail field, 483
showmessage.asp code, 511-514
ShownTime field, 470

ShowPage routine, 276
  code, 280-287
    creating, 280-287
ShowProfile field, 484
Sin function, 76
Single data type, 70
single quotes (' '), 222, 361
SingleForm.asp code, 135-136
sites, Web. *See* Web sites
Size
  column, 377
  cookie, 170-171
  property, 387
SIZE parameter
  FONT tag, 11
  HR tag, 15
slashes
  back (\), 41, 151
  forward (/), 41
so (Sort Order) query string variable, 317
so shortcut name, 380
Sort Direction (sd)) query string variable, 317
Sort Order (so) query string variable, 317
SortBy property, 379
sorting features, code, 312-317
SortOrder property, 391
source
  CODE tag, 10
  HTML heading tags, 5
  OL tag, 17-18
  PRE tag, 8-9
Space function, 85
Special class code, 399, 421-423
SpecialID property, 392
Split function, 85, 132
SQL (Structured Query Language)
  qryGetGroupMessages code, 510
  qryGetSubscriptions code, 509
  server connection code, 233
  server 6.5 database, connection code, 213
Sqr function, 76
SSI (server-side includes)
  commands, 97
  directives, 98-109
Start command (Run menu), 437
START parameter, values, 20
START tag, 18
  code for ordered lists, 19
StartDate property, 392

State property, 392
state, 159
statements
  Dim, 32
  End If, 50
  Erase, 38
  INSERT, 359
  Option Explicit, 356
  Randomize, 74-75
  ReDim, 36, 37-38
  UPDATE, 222
StaticObjects collection, 185-186, 188
Step keyword, 54-55
Store class
  adding to, 405-423
  code, 400
  code, data access enabled, 405-407
  code, revised, 407-409
  code, testing, 410
stored procedures, 218
StoreData routine, 276
  code, 276-277
StoreID property, 391, 392
stores entity properties, 392
String function, 86
strings, query, 133-140
strLocation parameter, 204
StrReverse function, 85-86
Structured Query Language. *See* SQL
StructuredForm.asp code, 138-140
structures
  decision, 48-64
  Do/Loop, 59-63
  For/Next. 53-56
  If/Then/Else, 49-53
  looping, 48-64
  Select/Caase, 56-59
  While/Wend, 63
sub main code, 269-271
Sub Main routine, 311, 331
  components, compiling, 424
Subject field, 484
Submit button, 114, 116
  results of pressing, 137
subDisplayData, 311
Subscription class
  code, 492-494
  creating, 492-495
Subscription object, 482

Subscripts parameter, 37
substitution tags, 443
    templates, 450
subtraction, 40
symbols
    addition, 40
    division, 41
    exponentiation operator, 42
    grouping expressions, 43
    multiplication, 41
    subtraction, 40
syntax
    Erase statement, 38
    If/Then/Else structure, 49
    ReDim statement, 37
    Session object, 186
systems
    functions, 482
    values, code to check, 188

T

TABLE tag, 20-21, 454
tables
    code, 23-24
    creating, 354-355
    data, retrieving, 233-234
    formatting tags, 20-25
    queries, adding to, 339
    records, adding, 222-223
    Visitors, 354
    VisitorSearches, 355
    VisitorViews, 354-355
tabs
    Generation (Catalog properties
        dialog box), 368
    Location (Catalog properties
        dialog box), 367
    Web (Catalog properties dialog box), 368
TagContents parameter, 443
tags
    HTML (HyperText Markup Language). See
        indivudal listings under HTML
    substitution, 443,
    table formatting, 20-25
Tan function, 76
tblAds definitions, 470
tblGroups-group entity, 483

tblImpressions definitions, 470
tblMembers-member entity, 483-484
tblMessages-message entity, 484
tblSubscriptions-subscription entity, 484
TD tag, 22
    parameters, 23
templates
    creating, 441-443
    HTML (HyperText Markup Language),
        440-443
Terminate event, 492
test CBool function, 68, 69
Test Connection button, 216
testing
    components in non-transactional
        environment, 467
    Employee class code, 404
    forms, 181
    Store class code, 410
TEXT parameter, BODY tag, 4
text
    formatting, 5-1
    manipulation functions, 80-86
textStream object, 91
TH tag, parameters, 22
tilde (~), 384
time/date formatting codes, 99
TipAmount property, 391
TITLE tag, 4
tmpViewCustomer_ProcessTags event handler
        code, 459-460
Toppings cookie, 171-175
TR tag, parameters, 21
tracking
    ads, 469-477
    users choices at Web sites, 353-354
transactions, 463
Transfer method, 192
Trim function, 86
True keyword, 30
TruncatetoWhitespace method, 382
TS (Transaction Server) Explorer, 467-468
type conversion functions, 67-70
type libraries, referencing, 195-196
TYPE parameter, values, 20
TYPE tag, 18
    code for ordered lists, 19

U

U tag, 12
UBound function, 38
    parameters, 39
UCase function, 86
UL tag, 15-17, 235
underscore (_), 51
    Select/Case structure, 58-59
    Unit Stock field, code to check, 258
Unlock method, 186
unordered lists, UL tag, 15-17
unsupported looping structures, 64
Until keyword, 59, 60, 62
UPDATE statement, 222
URL
    field, 470
    variable, 105, 142
URLEncode method, 192, 382
URLFor function, 445-446, 458
URLs (Uniform Resource Locators)
    " " (double quotes), 247
    changing, 332
    constructing, 373-374
User Profile editor, creating, 502-508
UserName field, 483
users
    activities, tracking, 351-362
    constant, 466
USN column, 377
util.asp code, 499-501
utilities, searches, creating, 252-262
Utility object, methods, 381-382

V

Validate routine, 499,
validating messages, 519
VALIGN parameter
    TD tag, 23
    TH tag, 22
variables
    ALL_HTTP, 104, 141, 144-146
    AUTH_PASSWORD, 104, 141
    AUTH_TYPE, 104, 141
    AUTH_USER, 104, 141
    blnAddedWhere, 254
    checking functions, 33-36
    CONTENT_LENGTH, 104, 141
    creating, 31-32

DATE_GMT, 104. 141
DATE_LOCAL, 104, 141
delcaring, 31
DOCUMENT_NAME, 104, 141
DOCUMENT_URI, 104, 141
GATEWAY_INTERFACE, 104, 141
HTTP (HyperText Transfer Protocol)
    environment, 104-105, 141-142
initializing, 32
IsArray function, 33
IsDate function, 33
IsEmpty function, 34
IsNull function, 34
IsNumeric function, 34
IsObject function, 35
LAST_MODIFIED, 104, 141
PATH_INFO, 104, 142
PATH_INFO, code, 146-147
PATH_TRANSLATED, 104, 142
pn, 311
QUERY_STRING, 104, 142
QUERY_STRING_UNESCAPED, 105, 142
REMOTE_ADDR, 105, 142
REMOTE_HOST, 105, 142
REMOTE_USER, 105, 142
REQUEST_METHOD, 105,
sColor, 446
SCRIPT_NAME, 105, 142
sd (Sort Direction), 317
server, 140-147
SERVER_NAME, 105, 142
SERVER_PORT, 105, 142
SERVER_PORT_SECURE, 105, 142
SERVER_PROTOCOL, 105, 142
SERVER_SOFTWARE, 105, 142
so (Sort Order), 317
URL, 105, 142
VarType function, return values, 35-36
VBScript, 31-40
Varname parameter, 37
VarType function, return values, 35-36
VB. *See* Visual Basic
VBScript. *See also* Visual Basic
    built-in objects, 89-93
    constants, 29-20
    data conversion functions, 67-72
    data formatting functions, 77-79

Continued

VBScript *(continued)*
    data types, 31-40
    dates, code to create, 100-103
    decision structures, 48-64
    error handling, 197-205
    error messages, 198-201
    logical operators, 44-48
    looping structures, 48-64
    mathematical functions, 72-76
    mathematical operations, 40-44
    objects, built-in, 89-93
    text manipulation functions, 80-86
    variables, 31-40
View menu commands, Code, 436
view order page with embedded SQL
        (Structured Query Language), code,
        334-338
ViewCustomer HTML template code, 454-456
ViewCustomer_UserEvent event handler code,
        459
viewing records, 269-271
vieworder.asp code, 319-324
ViewRecord subroutine
    creating, 271-275
    code, 272
Visitors table, 354
VisitorSearches table, 355
VisitorViews table, 354-355
Visual Basic. *See also* VBScript
    deployment packages, creating, 426-430
    Class Builder Wizard, 393
    classes, creating, 393-400
    COM (Component Object Model), 389
    components, testing, 425-426
    data access code, 400-423
    objects, compiling and deploying, 424-431
    Packaging and Deployment Wizard, 426-427
VLINK parameter, BODY tag, 4
vpath parameter, 373-374

W–Y

WC@ (default prefix), 443
WCE (WebClassEvent), 449
Web browsers, data, viewing, 231
Web pages. *See also* Web sites
    building, 231-233
    category viewer, 357-359
    category viewer, modifying 237-239
    category viewing, 245

cleaning up, 235-236
code to clean up, 235
group listing, creating, 508-509
group viewer, creating, 509-510
HTML (HyperText Markup Language)
    structure, 3-4, 441
indexes, creating, 366-360
linking, 287-301
login, 330
Login, creating, 496-501
memberinfo, author information, 514
message editor, creating, 514-519
message-viewing, creating, 511-514
Option Explicity, 232
order details Sub Main, 331-332
product, 288
product information, adding, 247-252
product list page, creating, 239-241
product listing, 247-249
product lists, 242-247
product viewing, 245-246, 359-
recordsets, publishing, 234-235
search pages, creating, 370-374
search results, 254-262
search results, changing, 360-362
table data, retrieving, 233-234
View order with embedded SQL (Structured
    Query Language), 334-338
Web sites. *See also* Web pages
    advertising, 351-353
    ASP Techniques, 387
    RACi (Recreational Solftware Advisory
        Council on the Internet), 156
    users choices, tracking, 353-354
Web tab (Catalog properties dialog box), 368
WebClass Designer, 435, 436
WebClass_Start code, 439, 445
WebClass_Start event, 443
    handler code, 448
    event procedure code, 446-447
WebClass_Start HTML, 449
WebClass_Terminate event handler code, 460
WebClasses
    ADO (Active Date Objects), 450-454
    advanced techniques, 454-460
    building, 434-440
    custom event handlers code, 447-448
    Custom Events, 444-449
    Custom WebItems, 444-449

Hello World, 434-440
　　HTML templates, 440-443
　　WCE (WebClassEvent), 449
WebClassEvent (WCE), 449
WebItems (Custom), 444-449
Weekday function, 89
WeekdayName function, 89
WHERE keyword, 255
While keyword, 60, 62
While/Wend structure, 63
Width field, 470
WIDTH parameter
　　HR tag, 15
　　TABLE tag, 21
　　TD tag, 23
　　TH tag, 22

wildcards, 385
windows
　　Project Explorer, 435
　　WebClass Designer, 435
With/End With keyword, 64
wizards
　　Class Builder Wizard, 393
　　Packaging and Deployment Wizard, 426-427
Write column, 377
Write property, 387
WWW (World Wide Web), libraries, testing,
　　430-431
Xor operator, 46
Year function, 89

my2cents.idgbooks.com

Register This Book — And Win!

Visit **http://my2cents.idgbooks.com** to register this book and we'll automatically enter you in our fantastic monthly prize giveaway. It's also your opportunity to give us feedback: let us know what you thought of this book and how you would like to see other topics covered.

Discover IDG Books Online!

The IDG Books Online Web site is your online resource for tackling technology — at home and at the office. Frequently updated, the IDG Books Online Web site features exclusive software, insider information, online books, and live events!

10 Productive & Career-Enhancing Things You Can Do at www.idgbooks.com

- Nab source code for your own programming projects.
- Download software.
- Read Web exclusives: special articles and book excerpts by IDG Books Worldwide authors.
- Take advantage of resources to help you advance your career as a Novell or Microsoft professional.
- Buy IDG Books Worldwide titles or find a convenient bookstore that carries them.
- Register your book and win a prize.
- Chat live online with authors.
- Sign up for regular e-mail updates about our latest books.
- Suggest a book you'd like to read or write.
- Give us your 2¢ about our books and about our Web site.

You say you're not on the Web yet? It's easy to get started with IDG Books' *Discover the Internet,* available at local retailers everywhere.